THE WAR
DIARIES

THE WAR DIARIES

An Anthology of
Daily Wartime Diary Entries
Throughout History

EDITED BY
Irene and Alan Taylor

CANONGATE
Edinburgh · New York · Melbourne

First published in Great Britain in 2004 by
Canongate Books Ltd., Edinburgh, Scotland

For details of copyright permissions, see pages 665–668.

Printed in the United States of America

FIRST AMERICAN PAPERBACK EDITION

ISBN-10: 1-84195-826-3
ISBN-13: 978-1-84195-826-2

Book designed by Paddy Cramsie at etal-design.com

Canongate
841 Broadway
New York, NY 10003

Distributed by Publishers Group West

www.groveatlantic.com

06 07 08 09 10   10 9 8 7 6 5 4 3 2 1

Contents

Introduction

WAR blights everything it touches, laying waste to whatever happens to fall into its path. It is pervasive in its destructiveness, indiscriminate in its cruelty, random in its brutality. When a country goes to war every one of its citizens is enlisted, whether they take an active part in it or not. It is always there, insidious, polluting, inextinguishable, degrading. Not all wars are inevitable but there comes a point when the momentum to go to war has gathered such force and speed that it seems unstoppable. It is as if there is an invisible power propelling us forward into a fathomless pit. The sand runs ever faster through the hour-glass. The wind gets up and the temperature drops. Moods swing. Voices lower. Clouds gather though the skies are cloudless. The future is put on hold. Soon options, like rations, run out.

'I don't quite know in what year I first knew for certain that the present war was coming,' wrote George Orwell in the autumn of 1940, a year after the start of the Second World War. 'After 1936, of course, the thing was obvious to anyone except an idiot. For several years the coming war was a nightmare to me, and at times I even made speeches and wrote pamphlets against it. But the night before the Russo–German pact was announced [on 22 August, 1939] I dreamed that the war had started.'

For some, war is a galvanising phenomenon. It is as if until the moment of declaration they had only been half alive. With such an obvious and real threat to their existence, they suddenly realise how precious and fragile life is. This is the irony of war, the harbinger of death. No longer can we take life for granted. Indeed, nothing may be taken for granted. War sweeps away the old verities and undermines received wisdom. Society is turned upside down. War and peace; peace and war. Like oil and water, they are incompatible. 'Why did millions of people kill one another,' asked Tolstoy in a postscript to his epic novel, 'when it had been known since the world began that it is physically and morally bad to do so? Because it was such an inevitable necessity that in doing it men fulfilled the elemental zoological law which bees fulfil when they kill one another in autumn, and which causes male animals to destroy one another. One can give no other reply to that terrible question.'

If Tolstoy could give no coherent reason why human beings wage war it would be presumptuous of us even to try. Thankfully, that is not the *raison d'être* of this book. Rather it is an attempt to describe how war infiltrates every aspect of life, embracing those who 'marched away' and those who remained at home, those in positions of high command who never fired a shot in earnest and those who chose to be 'conscientious objectors'. Their witness is borne through their published diaries, almost 200 of which are represented in the pages that follow, a record that is at once immediate and impressionistic.

Wars have always been a tremendous growth period for diaries. This should come as no surprise since it is human instinct to record extraordinary experience. In wartime, that experience is shared by the whole population but everyone reacts individually to it. For some, it is so disturbing it drives them demented or to suicide. Others seem to be able to sail through it almost carefree.

Nowhere is this better illustrated than in war diaries, the keeping of which can be traced back several centuries. Sailors in particular, used to keeping ships' logs, often kept personal records. In the seventeenth century, during the English Civil War, many diaries were kept by combatants on both sides of the divide, desperately trying to justify their actions in the eyes of God. The same sense of guilt is evident in many of the diaries produced during the American War of Independence. Many of these diaries amounted to little more than bald statements of fact but others delved deeper, giving not only details of a day but articulating feelings and fears and opinions.

Throughout history the keeping of journals has sometimes been banned by military authorities worried lest they should fall into enemy hands. More often than not, however, soldiers tended to pay lip service to such orders, even during World War I when diaries were forbidden. By then, though, the nature of war diaries had begun to change significantly. From the Crimean War, for example, there emerged diaries by doctors and nurses cataloguing the horrors they saw. It was during the Crimean War, too, that Sir William Russell, the first war correspondent, kept a journal, a practice he continued at the Battle of Bull Run in the American Civil War and later in the Zulu War.

Why did diary keeping become so common in the nineteenth

century? One factor surely was the publication in the early decades of that century of two of the most popular and enduring diarists, namely Samuel Pepys and John Evelyn, who were near contemporaries, friends and prominent figures in seventeenth-century London. Their diaries record whatever took their fancy, from the mundane to the momentous. Nothing, it seems, was unworthy of memorial. But neither did they shrink from describing the great events of their day, such as the execution of Charles I, the Great Fire of London and the Plague. War was never far off and it is interesting to compare how both diarists reacted to it. Here, for example, are their entries for 11 June, 1667, a humiliating day in English history, in the midst of a prolonged war with Holland.

'To London,' writes Evelyn, who at the time had been appointed to prepare a report on the condition of St Paul's Cathedral, 'alarmed by the Dutch, who were fallen on our fleet at Chatham by a most audacious enterprise. They entered the very river with part of their fleet, and did us not only disgrace but incredible mischief in burning several of our best men-of-war lying at anchor and moored there – and all this through our unaccountable negligence in failing to set out our fleet in time. Fearing lest the enemy might adventure up the Thames even to London – which they might have done with ease, and fired all the vessels in the river too – this alarm caused me to send away my best goods, plate, etc, from my house to another place. The alarm was so great that it put both county and city in panic, fear, and consternation such as I hope I shall never see more. Everyone was flying, none knew why or whither. Now were land forces dispatched, with the Duke of Albemarle, Prince Rupert, and the Duke of York, to hinder the Dutch coming to Chatham. They fortified Upnor Castle, and laid chains and booms. But the resolute enemy broke through all, set fire to our ships, and retreated in spite, stopping up the Thames, with the rest of their fleet lying before the mouth of it.'

Pepys, like Evelyn, never saw action. He was, however, first secretary to the Admiralty, a key role in a country whose national security depended heavily on the strength of its navy. His account of 11 June is therefore that of an insider with much personally to lose:

'Up, and more letters still from Sir W. Coventry about more fireships, and so Sir W. Batten and I to the office, where Bruncker come to us, who is just now going to Chatham upon a desire of Commissioner Pett's, who is in a very fearful stink for fear of the Dutch, and desires help from God and the King and kingdom's sake. So Bruncker goes down and Sir J. Minnes also, from Gravesend. This morning Pett writes us that Sheerness is lost last night, after two or three hours' dispute. The enemy hath possessed himself of that place, which is very sad, and puts us in great fear of Chatham. Sir W. Batten and I go down by the water to Deptford, and there Sir W. Pen and we did consider of several matters relating to the dispatch of the fire-ships, and so W. Batten and I home again. To business hiring some fire-ships and receiving every hour almost letters from Sir W. Coventry calling for more fire-ships, and an order from Council to enable us to take any man's ships; and Sir W. Coventry in his letter to us says he do not doubt but at this time under an invasion, as he owns it to be, the King may by law take any man's goods. At this business late, and then home, where a great deal of serious talk with my wife about the sad state we are in, and especially from the beating up of drums this night for the trainbands upon pain of death to appear in arms tomorrow morning with bullet and powder, and money to supply themselves with victuals for a fortnight.'

Pepys' initial concern when he learned a day later that the Dutch had actually broken the chain across the Medway and taken the *Royal Charles* was to preserve his personal savings. His second thought, as his biographer, Claire Tomalin notes, was that the Navy Board would be held responsible for the débâcle and that he would be made a scapegoat, with execution a real possibility. Luckily for him, the Dutch withdrew.

What Pepys gives, says Tomalin, is a 'backstage' view of war. 'There is confusion, jealousy, backbiting and greed; blame is laid, loyalties are divided; there is rejoicing – sometimes premature – as well as panic and despondency. The sound of guns is heard in the distance several times, and more immediate turmoil is produced by rioting, unpaid soldiers and the weeping of wives of pressed men. His job throughout was to supply and maintain the fighting force.'

For Pepys, then, war was witnessed at a remove, his sentiments those of an educated, cultured man who had no desire, or necessity, to place himself in danger. War in the seventeenth century, as it was until the twentieth century, was largely waged by those who had little alternative but to join up. Conscription – the forced recruitment of men into the military – has long been established as a means of supplying troops, whether by statute or force. Conscripts though were often unwilling soldiers and some countries preferred to rely on recruitment. Britain, for example, did not maintain a large conscript army in the years leading up to World War I. The poster featuring the face and pointed finger of Lord Kitchener with the words 'Your country needs you' remains one of the most potent images of that conflict. So successful was the recruitment campaign that Britain did not need to introduce conscription until 1916, by when many millions were already dead.

World War I has been described by Ronald Blythe, author of *Each Returning Day: The Pleasure of Diaries* as 'the most diarised event in history'. Over fifty diaries for the years 1914–18 are listed in William Matthews' *Annotated Bibliography of British Diaries*, which first appeared in 1945, and many more have come to light since. Almost every aspect of the war is represented. In August 1914, Beatrice Webb reports that there is no enthusiasm about the war. It is, she writes, 'a passionless war, a terrible nightmare sweeping over all classes, no one able to realise how the disaster came about'. Arnold Bennett's reaction is to stockpile petrol while W.N.P. Barbellion feels physically sick at the thought of the carnage to come.

None of them has any chance of seeing action. They will sit out the war at home. That is not the case with Private Horace Bruckshaw, who rushed to join up, driven by patriotism and eager to leave behind his humdrum life. In his Gallipoli diary, Bruckshaw relates with deadpan humour the reality of war. He goes out hunting for snipers as if they are wild boar. A comrade is wounded in the chest. 'It made us a wee bit nervous as he was sitting next to me,' he writes. A day later we learn that nearly all the officers have been killed by snipers. It pours with rain but he sleeps soundly nonetheless. A shell drops just after they have completed their ablutions. Shrapnel is served up for breakfast. He helps make a new road and bury a dead officer. What is remarkable about Bruckshaw's record is its laconic good humour and lack of self-pity. The facts are left to speak for themselves. A conservative estimate puts the number of dead at Gallipoli at over a quarter of a million, of whom 26,000 were British. Bruckshaw survived only to be killed two years later at the Battle of Gavrelle. His body was never found.

It is a familiar story. In diary after diary, the misery of the 'war to end all wars' is graphically depicted, in contrast to the life the soldiers have left behind. But what is also remarkable is the way hope gives way to despair. In 1914, wrote the historian Lyn Macdonald, 'the spirit and the attitude of the men who were actually doing the fighting was strikingly different from the attitudes of the civilians and those who were flocking to the colours at home and around the Empire. Their war, their blooding and their disillusionment was yet to come. Brooke, Grenfell, Owen, Sassoon, Hodgson, made no secret of their idealism (and how soon it changed with the experience of war!) and it is difficult for succeeding generations to identify with their extraordinary view of war as a purification, their strange resignation to dying, their passive embracement of fate, their unquestioning acceptance. The questioning and the bitterness were born later, in the stultifying horrors of trench warfare.'

There is no better illustration of how that bitterness developed than Siegfried Sassoon's diary. When war broke out, Sassoon enjoyed the empty life of an English country gentleman, hunting in particular. He joined up in 1914 and saw no action until 1916. In France, in December 1915, he writes as if he is still back in rural England. His pony tries to jump a ditch and fails. He sees a heron 'which sailed slowly across the misty flats of ploughed land'. Robert Graves gives him some of his poems to read. 'I am happy, happy,' he writes on 17 December. 'I've escaped and found peace unbelievable in this extraordinary existence I thought I should loathe. The actual life is mechanical; and my dreams are mine, more lonely than ever. We're safe for another year of war, too, so next summer ought to do something for me. Anything but a "cushy" wound. That would be an awful disaster. I must endure, or else die.'

But it is not long before Sassoon's humour turns sour. In the summer of 1916 at the Battle of the Somme, at which every infantry regiment in the British army fought, Sassoon kept a daily, at times hour-by-hour, record. By end of the opening day of the battle – 1 July – the British had lost 57,470 officers and men – 19,240 of them killed, 2,152 missing, the rest wounded. The British army had never suffered losses like it. But it was not alone. Over the course of the 142-day battle, it is estimated there were also 650,000 German casualties.

'Since 6.30 there has been hell let loose,' wrote Sassoon. 'I could see one man moving his left arm up and down as he lay on his side: his head was a crimson patch.'

As the months pass, he becomes almost anaesthetised to the horror. Where once there was respect now there is cynicism. Near the end of the war, on 16 June, 1918, all innocence lost, Sassoon wrote: '"What's the weight of *your* pig?" asked a witty Colonial. Coming up a communication-trench, he squeezed himself against the chalky side of the trench to make room for two men who were coming down; they were carrying a dead body slung on a pole. This is how the Canadians take their corpses away from the front-line. They tie the hands together at the wrists; feet ditto. Then sling the body on a pole. What splendid common-sense! And how jolly the War is! But I wished they'd put a sandbag over his face.'

Sassoon's diary, unlike his poems, appeared long after World War I was finished but some diarists, such as Sarah Macnaughtan, published their diaries while the war was ongoing. Of independent means and unmarried, Macnaughtan had some training as a nurse and during the Boer War went to South Africa as a volunteer with the Red Cross. When World War I broke out, she joined Mrs St Clair Stobart's Red Cross women's unit as head orderly. When the unit was ordered to evacuate Antwerp, besieged by the Germans on their advance to France, she stayed on to continue her work independently.

Macnaughtan had to deal with the fallout of war. She makes soup and tea ceaselessly for frozen troops, treating Allied and German casualties as necessary. Helping her in the kitchen are ladies who have never peeled a spud in their lives. George V pays a visit and she remarks, 'God bless him! He always does the right thing.' On 12 December, 1914, she writes: 'Such a nice boy died to-night. We brought him to the hospital from the station, and learned that he had lain for eight days wounded and untended. Strangely enough he was naked, and had only a blanket over him on the stretcher. I do not know why he was alive ... No one knew who he was. He had a woman's portrait tattooed on his breast.' Macnaughtan herself died in 1916, a year after the publication of A Woman's Diary of the War.

But while the war rumbled on in Europe, its reverberations could be felt all over the globe. In England, in particular, with only the Channel as a buffer, news from abroad was awaited with trepidation. On 27 April, 1915, Lady Cynthia Asquith learns of the death of Rupert Brooke, who had died four days earlier, not on the battlefield but of septicaemia en route to the Dardanelles. 'It does stab one to think of his beautiful poet's face with the cornfield head,' she writes. 'I am told he was absolutely convinced he would be killed in this war and he wrote lovely poems bidding farewell to things he loved – the "touch of fur" was one I thought original. It is rather sad it that it should have been an illness.'

Meanwhile Virginia Woolf tries to maintain some semblance of normality – attending a concert, writing a novel, doing odd jobs – only to find herself repelled by London crowds and the faces of people on the tube. 'Really,' she writes, 'raw red beef and silver herrings give me more pleasure to look upon.' Another home-front perspective comes from Mrs Henry Dudeney, a bestselling novelist of the day. Based in Lewes in Sussex on the south coast, she veers between depression ('No good attempting to keep a diary. War news awful, the whole of life grim') and dealing with domestic traumas and trivia ('At lunch, I was so tired and when poor Ernest asked me to sew a button on his breeks I flew into a rage').

These differing perspectives are a reminder that war affects us all in varying ways depending upon our situation. What is universal, however, is the sense that this is an event which cannot be ignored. For good or ill, it is transformative, whether a war is just or unjust, justified or unjustified. But it is worth bearing in mind the words of A.J.P. Taylor: 'Bismarck fought "necessary" wars and killed thousands, the idealists of the twentieth century fight "just" wars and kill millions.'

War in the twentieth century certainly became industrial in its capacity to kill human beings, largely through technological 'advances'. 'The First World War,' wrote Phillip Knightley in *The First Casualty*, 'was like no other war before or since. It began with the promise of splendour, honour and glory. It ended as a genocidal conflict on an unparalleled scale, a meaningless act of slaughter that continued until a state of exhaustion set in because no one knew how to stop it.' According to H.G. Wells, it would be 'the last war'.

It was one of his more ludicrous predictions. There was never any prospect that war in the twentieth century would become redundant. When one war ended another sprang up. It was like trying to put out bush fires. And when nations weren't fighting one another they were at war with themselves. In Spain, in 1936, Nationalists faced Republicans, in a bloody conflict in which approximately 300,000 died. George Orwell was one of the fortunate ones. Fighting on the Republican side, he was wounded by a stray bullet and invalided out. 'The pain,' he wrote, 'was diabolical, making me swear and then try not to swear, because every time I breathed too hard the blood bubbled out of my mouth.'

By then, though, a much bigger and even more brutal war was looming. Whether Hitler actually set out to cause the Second World War as part of an evil master plan or blundered into it partly by accident with more than a little help from his incompetent and ignorant cohorts has much exercised historians. But what is beyond doubt is that long before Austria was annexed to the Nazi Reich in March 1938 or Germany marched into Czech Sudetenland in the autumn of the same year, war was unavoidable whatever the most optimistic appeasers believed.

As early as 1933, Victor Klemperer, a Dresden Jew who had fought for Germany during World War I, recognised the danger of Hitler. On 30 March, two months after Hitler became Chancellor, and a month after the burning of the Reichstag, he writes: 'Mood as before a pogrom in the depths of the Middle Ages or in deepest Czarist Russia . . . The dominant feeling . . . is that this reign of terror can hardly last long, but that its fall will bury us. Fantastic Middle Ages: "We" – threatened Jewry. In fact I feel shame more than fear, shame for Germany. I have always imagined: The twentieth century and Mitteleuropa were different from the fourteenth century and Romania. Mistake – Dember [a friend] describes the effects on business: Stock Exchange, setbacks for Christian industry – and then "we" would pay for all of it with our blood. Frau Dember related the case of the ill-treatment of a Communist prisoner which leaked out: torture with castor oil, beatings, fear – attempted suicide . . . Our parting (after abundant good food) was like a leave-taking at the front. Yesterday a wretched statement in the *Dresdner Neueste Nachrichten* – "on our own account". They are 92.5 per cent founded on Aryan capital, Herr Wollf, owner of the remaining 7.5 per cent has resigned as chief editor, one Jewish editor has been given leave of absence . . . , the other ten are Aryans. Terrible! – In a toy shop a children's ball with the Swastika.'

But you did not need to be a Jew in Germany to sense the coming catastrophe. When finally war was declared there was a clamour of foreboding. 'Even as when someone dies,' wrote Harold Nicolson, a Member of Parliament, 'one is amazed that the poplars should still be standing quite unaware of one's own disaster, so when I walked down to the lake to bathe, I could scarcely believe that the swans were being sincere in their indifference to the Second German War.' 'It's the gnats and flies that settles on non-combatants,' noted Virginia Woolf. 'This war has begun in cold blood. One merely feels that the killing machine has to be set in action.' Edward Robb Ellis, a journalist and an inveterate diarist, wrote: 'I realise I am but one of millions of worried Americans living our daily lives amidst a rumbling, as though of an oncoming earthquake.'

The Second World War surely eclipsed its predecessor in the number of diaries it produced. The diarists came from every walk of life, every nation involved in the war, and every theatre of war. Many were written by soldiers, sailors and airmen, by generals, despots and pacificists. Count Ciano, Mussolini's son-in-law, kept a diary, as did Goebbels, Hitler's right-hand man, and Field Marshal Lord Alanbrooke and John Colville, both of whom had Churchill's ear. Among the writers who kept diaries during the war were Jean-Paul Sartre, Evelyn Waugh, Naomi Mitchison and Norman Lewis. William L. Shirer, an American journalist, described what life was like in Berlin, as did Marie 'Missie' Vassiltchikov, a White Russian *émigrée*, who managed to maintain an idyllic lifestyle until as late as 1941.

Everyone's war was unique. James Lees-Milne worried about the devastation to country houses. Walter Musto, a sixty-year-old eccentric civil servant was interrupted by air-raid sirens while sunbathing nude in his garden. Iris Origo, in Tuscany, housed evacuated children and hid escaped POWs. Joan Wyndham, meanwhile, fell for a diminutive Yugoslav painter who insisted on making love to the accompaniment of Beethoven's C Minor Quartet, and Joyce Grenfell and Noël Coward entertained the troops.

'This is the war of the unknown warriors,' said Winston Churchill in 1940, contrasting World War II with World War I. 'The whole of the warring nations are engaged, not only soldiers, but the entire population, men, women and children. The fronts are everywhere. The trenches are dug in the towns and streets. Every village is fortified. Every road is barred. The front lines run through the factories. The workmen are soldiers with different weapons but the same courage.'

On the continent of Europe, of course, Hitler's killing machine was working round the clock in an insane attempt to wipe out Jews. There are countless diaries by victims and survivors of the Holocaust, some even written in concentration camps, others chronicles of life in the ghetto. They are a record of what it is like to live through hell, the scale of the tragedy hard to comprehend. Yet through many of these diaries, burdened as they are with despair, hope persists. The oppressed wanted in their hearts to believe the best of their tormentors. They couldn't have been more misguided. 'The Germans want to drain the marrow from our bones,' wrote Avraham Tory, a survivor of the Kovno Ghetto in Lithuania, on 8 April, 1943, 'they want to use us until the last moment of our lives, when they will takes us to the Ninth Fort, or to a forest, to exterminate us.'

There is no more poignant diary, and none more famous, than that of Anne Frank. 'How can we explain the continuing influence of her diaries on both Jewish and non-Jewish readers alike?' asked Elie Wiesel. 'Is it the age of the author that so affects us? Her innocence perhaps? Other young people, her contemporaries, have described what they saw and experienced in the ghettoes of Poland and Czechoslovakia. Hers is the only account to have captured and conquered the hearts and imagination of the wider public.'

Frank's age – she started her diary on 12 June 1942, her thirteenth birthday, and died while imprisoned at Bergen-Belsen, three months short of her sixteenth birthday – and her innocence are undoubtedly part of the diary's appeal, but a large part of it must also be because of the peculiarity of the situation in which she and her family found themselves. Fearful of arrest and deportation to a concentration camp, the Franks – Anne and her sister Margot, her mother, Edith, and her father, Otto, went into hiding on 6 July 1942 and remained there until they were betrayed and discovered by Nazi collaborators on 4 August 1944. Only Otto Frank survived the war.

Anne's diary, addressed to an imaginary friend called Kitty, was found by a friend of the family after they were arrested and returned to Otto Frank after the war. For a while he could not bear to read it but when he did he was overcome. 'What I'm reading in her book is so indescribably exciting,' he wrote to members of his family, 'and I read on and on. I cannot explain it to you! I've not finished reading it yet, and I want to read it right through before I make some excerpts or translations for you. She writes about her growing up with incredible self-criticism. Even if it hadn't been written by her, it would have interested me. What a great pity that this life had to go . . . We are all changed, only the core of our being remains.'

The diary was first published in Holland in 1947 with the title, *Het Achterhuis*, a literal translation of which is 'The Back House'. It was immediately hailed as a classic but foreign publishers were slow to pick it up. After initial reluctance, it appeared in Germany in 1950 but sales were slow. English and American publishers were even more reluctant and it was rejected by many of them. In England it was published in May 1952 by Vallentine Mitchell, a small Jewish publisher, and a month later in the United States. There was considerable controversy over the title. Among the suggestions were *Beauty Out of the Night, Families in Hiding, Behind the Hidden Door, The Hidden Annexe* and *The Secret Annexe*, which was the title of a novel Anne hoped to write using her diaries as source material. 'The title alone,' she wrote, 'would make people think it was a detective story.' Ultimately, it was agreed to call it *Anne Frank: The Diary of a Young Girl*. By 1971, sales in paperback in English alone had reached a million.

For Elie Wiesel, himself a survivor of Auschwitz and Buchenwald and a winner of the Nobel Peace Prize, Frank's diary was not so much a book as 'a wound'. Whether it was one that could ever heal he did not say. What is not in doubt is that more than fifty years since it was first published this very special document still has the capacity to speak directly to us and render us speechless at the knowledge of what human beings are capable of doing to one another. Frank's diary was her testimony to future generations, her way of bearing witness. 'I look upon our life in hiding as an interesting adventure, full of danger and romance, and every privation as an amusing addition to my diary,' she wrote on 3 May, 1944. She would rather give herself up than surrender her diary. When, on Easter Sunday 1944, police almost discovered the inhabitants of the secret annexe, they became even more paranoid and one of them – 'the most terrified member of the group' – suggested she burn it. But that was unconscionable. 'Oh, not my diary; if my diary goes, I go too!'

Anne Frank was one victim among millions in a war that contaminated every continent and almost every country. WWII ought to have been the war that ended all wars but there was little likelihood of that. 'The danger,' wrote the poet and painter Keith Vaughan in his diary in September 1945, 'is that it will be only too easy to slip back into taking everything for granted, and everything we have learned in these years will be forgotten. It will be so easy to go on again just as if nothing had happened.' How prophetic Vaughan's words proved to be. The second half of the twentieth century may not have been as bloody as the first but there were still wars aplenty, still too many instances of man's inhumanity to man. Korea. Vietnam. Nigeria. Bosnia. The Middle East. The Falklands. India and Pakistan. Chechnya. Iraq. Haiti. The list goes on and on and we seem to learn nothing from the experience other than to acknowledge that when it comes to killing one another human beings have an appetite for it like no other species. War, it seems, like the poor, will always be with us.

This anthology includes extracts from around 200 diarists published in English, dating from the seventeenth century to the present day. Many of the wars which happened during that period are included, though not all are. A short account of each war mentioned is given at the end of the book together with biographical details of the diarists. Inevitably, given their scale, there are more entries devoted to the First and Second World Wars than any other. Entries are arranged day by day throughout the year, which sometimes means that the strict chronology is disrupted and for which we beg the reader's indulgence. Original spellings and idiosyncratic syntax have been retained though we have undertaken some silent editing for the sake of clarity. Our aim was not to attempt comprehensiveness. Rather, we hoped to provide a portrait of war drawn from as many points of view and from as many perspectives as possible. War is tragic, but not exclusively so. The gloom is relieved with humour, comradeship and moments of epic grandeur. There is courage and cowardice, fear and loathing, love and hatred, selfishness and generosity. War is full of such contradictions. As Anne Frank, the doyenne of war diarists, said, 'We still love life, we haven't yet forgotten the voice of nature, and we keep hoping, hoping for . . . everything.'

Acknowledgements

Books do not come out of the ether; they are the product of centuries of accumulated thought, anthologies such as this more than most. Our first debt, therefore, is to the diarists who kept faith with their diaries no matter what they had to face. We found many of the diaries in, or through, Edinburgh's Central Library and the National Library of Scotland, both of whose staff were unfailingly helpful. We are also grateful to Leslie Clark, Alastair Reid, Penelope Jardine, Dame Muriel Spark, Trevor Royle and Diana Crook for offering suggestions and finding diaries which we would not otherwise have laid our hands on. At Canongate, Jamie Byng remained patient in the face of much provocation. It is a pleasure to work with him, as it has been with Pru Rowlandson in publicity, Jim Hutcheson, doyen of design, and Helen Bleck, our eagle-eyed editor. As ever, however, the buck stops with those named on the title page.

JANUARY

What did you do in the Great War, daddy?

Recruiting placard, 1914–18

1 January

1826 [Abbotsford]

A year has passed – another has commenced. These solemn divisions of time influence our feelings as they recur. Yet there is nothing in it; for every day in the year closes a twelvemonth as well as the 31st December.

The latter is only a solemn pause, as when a guide, showing a wild and mountainous road, calls on a party to pause and look back at the scenes they have just passed. To me this new year opens sadly. There are these troublesome pecuniary difficulties,[1] which however, I think, this week should end. There is the absence of all my children, Anne excepted, from our little family festival. There is, besides, that ugly report of the 15th Hussars going to India. Walter[2] I suppose, will have some step in view, and will go, and I fear Jane [his wife] will not dissuade him.

Sir Walter Scott

1916 [Lewes, England]

At midday, horrid shock. Letter from Lock Hospital,[3] saying Bessie G [former servant] going to have a baby. I must 'remove' her. Poor Bessie, the 150 soldiers at the Grammar School[4] were her undoing.

Mrs Henry Dudeney

1940 [Yorkshire]

I look out of the window into the fog and gloom of a New Year's morning. So much as I can see of the garden gleams fully of congealed

---

[1] Scott had debts of £130,000 following the collapse of the printer and the publisher of his books.

[2] His elder son who rose to the rank of Lieutenant Colonel in the Hussars.

[3] Women suffering from VD were forced, due to a late nineteenth-century Act of Parliament, to remain in 'lock' hospitals until they were cured.

[4] Soldiers were billeted in the Grammar School situated next door to the author's house.

snow. No sound of bird nor any sign save a confusion of claw prints about the terraces of the rockery where yesterday the birds were fed. A bitter cold and still silence prevails without having the rumourless indifference to life of a maiming cartwheel, unpersonal as the earthquake in Turkey, as relentless as warring man's inhumanity to man these troubled days.

A very different story is this from my entry of a year ago when first I started this diary; nor could one then see the calamities upon us. Sitting by the comfortable fireside of my cosy room this night it is not easy to realize the horrors of present-day political and military events, or the truth of the fantastic stories of the organized mutilation of thousands of Jews by sterilization, of the urination by their guards into the mouths of prisoners in concentration camps, of awful floggings and suicides by compulsion and all the rest of the sadistic stuff going on behind the scenes in the name of war for political domination. In the twentieth century, in spite of the better distribution of wealth, spreading education, improved social amenities, general material advancement and wider culture, we are back to the bestially crude indignities and violences of the Dark Ages.

Walter Musto

1940 [Silesia]
Olga Pückler,[1] Tatiana[2] and I spent the New Year quietly at Schloss Friedland. We lit the Christmas tree and tried to read the future by dropping melted wax and lead into a bowl of water. We expect Mamma and Georgie [her brother] to appear any minute from Lithuania. They have announced their arrival repeatedly. At midnight all the village bells began to ring. We hung out of the windows listening – the first New Year of this new World War.

Marie 'Missie' Vassiltchikov

1940 [Wiltshire]
As midnight struck, Ralph [her husband] and I went out into the garden to see if we could hear the bells from the village church. But only total silence met our ears, and 1940 crept its way in, in a dense cold mist. We gathered up the prophecies for the New year,

---

[1] Olga and her husband were hosts to the Vassiltchikovs and had loaned them money.
[2] Her sister who later became Princess Metternich.

made that afternoon with Faith and Nicko Henderson and R. sealed them and put them away in an envelope. How wrong will they be? Then he brought us tiny glasses of neat whiskey to drink to the future.

Frances Partridge

1941 [USA]

I really must try to keep this journal more regularly. It will be invaluable to me if I do. Because this year is going to be one of the decisive periods of the twentieth century – and even the doings and thoughts of the most remote and obscure people will reflect the image of events.

That's a hell of a paragraph to start with. Why are we all so pompous on New Year's Day. Come off it – you're not Hitler or Churchill. Nobody called on you to make a statement. As a matter of fact what did you actually do?

Christopher Isherwood

2 January

1777 [Allentown, New Jersey]

This morning we were called up at 2 o'clock under a pretended alarm that we were to be attacked by the enemy but by daylight we were ordered to march for Trenton, and when we reached Crosswicks found that the brigade had gone. We reached Trenton about 11 o'clock and found all the troops from our different posts in Jersey, collected there under Gen. Washington himself; and the regular troops were already properly disposed to receive the enemy, whose main body was then within a few miles and determined to dispossess us.

Trenton stands upon the River Delaware, with a creek called the Assanpink passing through the town across which there is a bridge.

The enemy came down on the upper side of the creek, through the town, and a number of our troops were posted with Riflemen and artillery to oppose their approach.

The main body of our army was drawn up on a plain below, or on the lower side of the Assanpink, near the bridge, and the main force of our Artillery was posted on the banks and high ground along the creek in front of them.

Gen. Mercers brigade was posted about 2 miles up the creek, and the troops under Gen. Cadwalader were stationed in a field on the right about a mile from the town, on the main road, to prevent the enemy from flanking. We had five pieces of Artillery with our division about 20 more in the field, near, and at the town. Our numbers were about five thousand and the enemy's about seven Thousand.

The attack began about 2 o'clock and a heavy fire upon both sides, chiefly from the artillery continued until dark.

At this time the enemy were left in possession of the upper part of the town, but we kept possession of the bridge, altho' the enemy attempted several times to carry it but were repulsed each time with great slaughter.

After sunset this afternoon the enemy came down in a very heavy column to force the bridge. The fire was very heavy and the Light troops were ordered to fly to the support of that important post, and as we drew near, I stepped out of the front to order my men to close up; at this time Martinas Sipple was about 10 steps behind the man next in front of him; I at once drew my sword and threatened to cut his head off if he did not keep close, he then sprang forward and returned to the front. The enemy were soon defeated and retired and the American army also retired to the woods, where they encamped and built up fires.

I then had the roll called to see if any of our men were missing and Martinas was not to be found, but Lieut. Mark McCall informed me, that immediately on my returning to the head of the column, after making him close up, he fled out of the field.[1]

We lost but few men; the enemy considerably more. It is thought Gen. Washington did not intend to hold the upper part of the town.

Thomas Rodney

1781 [Pennsylvanian Line, New Jersey]
Yesterday being the last time we (the officers of the regiment), expected to be together, as the arrangements was to take place this day, we had an elegant Regimental Dinner and entertainment, at which all the Field and other officers were present, with a few from the German Regiment, who had arrived with the men of their regiment that belong to the Pennsylvanian Line. We spent the day very pleasantly

---

[1] The author later noted: 'In justice to Martinas I must add that he afterwards joined the Delaware Regiment under Col. David Hall and became a brave and faithful soldier.'

and the evening 'till about ten o'clock as cheerfully as we could wish, when we were disturbed by the huzzas of the soldiers upon the Right Division, answered by those on the Left. I went on the Parade and found numbers of small groups whispering and busily running up and down the Line. In a short time a gun was fired upon the Right and answered by one on the right of the Second Brigade, and a skyrocket was thrown, and accompanied by a general huzza throughout the Line, and the soldiers running out with their arms, accoutrements and knapsacks. I immediately found it was a mutiny, and that the guns and skyrocket were the signals. The officers in general exerted themselves to keep the men quiet, and keep them from turning out. We each applied himself to his own company, endeavoured to keep them in their huts and lay by their arms, which they would do while we were present, but the moment we left one hut to go to another, they would be out again. Their excuse was they thought it was an alarm and the enemy coming.

Next they began to move in crowds to the Parade. Lieut. White of our regiments, in endeavouring to stop one of these crowds, was shot through the thigh, and Capt. Samuel Tolbert in opposing another party was shot through the body, of which he is very ill. They continued huzzaing and firing in a riotous manner, so that it soon became dangerous for an officer to oppose them by force. We then left them to go their own way.

This day Col. Stewart and Richard Bulter joined Gen. Wayne in hopes they could turn them when they grew cooler, being much agitated with liquor, when they went off, it being New Years day they had drawn half a pint per man. The men have continued going off in small parties all day. About one o'clock one hundred head of cattle came in from the Eastward, which they drove off to their main body, which lay in a wood near Vealtown, leaving a few behind for use of the officers.

When we came to draw provisions and State stores this day, we found that near half of the men of our regiment had remained.

The men went off very civilly last night to what might have been expected from such a mob. They did not attempt to plunder our officers' huts or insult them in the least, except those who were obstinate in opposing them. They did not attempt to take with them any part of the State stores, which appears to me a little extraordinary, for men when they get but little want more.

The militia are called out, they are to assemble at Chatham, in order to oppose the enemy if they come out, or the mutineers if they attempt going to them.

Eno Reeves

1916 [Russian Front]

Our doctors went to visit an invalid soldier in a remote corner of the village and to their horror found lodged in one small hut no fewer than 17 soldiers. There was no room even to move, they said, and the air was so foul and thick one could have cut it with a knife. The soldiers pointed out that they preferred to be huddled together and warm under a roof to being frozen outside under a tree. We knew that accommodation was very scarce; we knew, too, that there were refugees who at night would crowd twenty or thirty into one dug-out. The District Commandant was approached, but seemed powerless to help. 'It is only for a time,' he repeated, 'only while the soldiers are in reserve. In a few days' time, they will be back with their regiments and there will be room enough and to spare.' Some of the poor peasants' huts were in a disgraceful condition; hygiene was totally lacking; pigs and hens, taken under cover for the winter, lived with the family and spread dirt and discomfort on every side. Rightly or wrongly, these terribly unhealthy conditions are being accepted as inevitable in wartime. No one can, or dare, raise a finger to change them.

Florence Farmborough

1973 [New York]

I am so anguished and angered by the American bombing of North Vietnam that I've written letters of protest to President Nixon and our New York Senators.

It's possible that some time in the future someone may ask what I did to try to stop such horrors, and I want to be able to say that I lifted my voice against them. In fact, I'm urging all my friends to write similar letters. If millions of Americans were to do this, and if a tally were kept in the basement of the White House, perhaps Nixon might get our message.

In my letter to Senator Jack Javits I said that for the first time in my life I am ashamed to be an American.

Edward Robb Ellis

3 January

1915 [London]

It is strange how old traditions, so long buried as one thinks, suddenly crop up again. At Hyde Park Gate we used to set apart Sunday morning for cleaning the table silver. Here I find myself keeping Sunday morning for odd jobs – typewriting it was today – and tidying the room – and doing accounts which are very complicated this week. I have three little bags of coppers, which each owe the other something. We went to a concert at the Queen's Hall, in the afternoon. Considering that my ears have been pure of music for some weeks, I think patriotism is a base emotion. By this I mean that they played a National Anthem and a hymn, and all I could feel was the entire absence of emotion in myself and everyone else. If the British spoke openly about WCs and copulation, then they might be stirred by universal emotions. As it is, an appeal to feel together is hopelessly muddled by intervening greatcoats and fur coats. I begin to loathe my kind, principally from looking at their faces in the tube. Really, raw red beef and silver herrings give me more pleasure to look upon. But then I was kept standing forty minutes at Charing Cross Station, and so got home late, and missed Duncan [Grant][1] who came here. Moreover, London on a Sunday night now, with all its electric globes half muffled in blue paint, is the most dismal of places. There are long mud coloured streets, and just enough daylight and insufficient electric light to see the naked sky, which is inexpressibly cold and flat.

Virginia Woolf

1966 [The White House]

Lyndon slept little. In the morning he said he had thought just as long as he could about Vietnam, and then he thought about the Budget for awhile. Sometimes I think the greatest bravery of all is simply to get up in the morning and go about your business.

Lady Bird Johnson

1967 [Vietnam]

The villages we passed through were really poverty-stricken. People go to the bathroom in the streets, and the kids run alongside the convoy

---

[1] A painter and member of the Bloomsbury Group, was a friend of VW. Though homosexual, he was the lover of her sister Vanessa.

begging for food. They held up two fingers for victory and a thumb for good luck; at least that's what we thought. When they banged their fists against their open hands, that meant their mother or sister was available for two bucks.

David Parks

4 January

1855 [Crimea]

Snow deep. How the men are to get wood for cooking is to me a puzzler; and yet, I believe, no steps have been taken to supply them with any. One week of this weather will bring the Army to a standstill, and then what is to be done, God only knows. Heavy fall of snow.

Lieut. General Sir Charles Ash Windham

1940 [Wiltshire]

Tea nowadays is an extremely snug meal, with hot buttered toast and the shutters drawn, and my beautiful jardinière (which I have painted white and filled with cacti, cyclamen and hyacinths) adding to the greenhouse effect. Three huge pots of arum lilies stand in the corner on a tin tray. After tea today I set to work to wash their leaves, which looked dusty, with an old sock and water in a child's pail. I felt like a zoo keeper washing his elephants' ears. I get intense pleasure from the richness and intensity of my awareness of our circumscribed private world, contrasted with the bleakness and horror of the public one.

War rumours brought us by Paul Cross, who came to lunch: how the Germans have a new kind of bomb no bigger than an orange, which can be stowed in millions in their bombing planes. How the ARP [Air Raid Precautions] authorities were expecting 70,000 deaths in the first raid on London and had enough papier mâché coffins ready.

Frances Partridge

1942 [Leningrad]

It seems to me that unless the blockade is broken within the next ten days the city cannot hold out . . . Leningrad has had all it can take from this war – the Germans should get back as good as they have given in full measure. USSR is being called the Saviour of Mankind, and indeed it is so.

I am proud to possess a Soviet passport. It is a modest document, olive-green in colour, nevertheless to me it gives out a sort of radiance.

But if people knew *how* Leningrad is suffering! And we still have a long winter ahead of us. The frosts are grim. Today is warmer, but then there is a snowstorm instead. Outside the city I'm sure there is a blizzard.

One cannot listen unmoved to the people of this dark, hungry, frozen city rejoicing in the frosts because the Germans are dying from the same cold at the Front. 'Serves them right!' people repeat. This from lips blue with cold as they stand inside the covered gateways during the shelling. The Leningrad blockade is usually called the 'Fire Ring' . . . No, an ice ring would be more appropriate.

Vera Inber

5 January

1915 [England]

We worked as usual: as usual it rained. After lunch we took the air in the Old Deer Park, and marked by a line of straw how high the river had been; and how a great tree had fallen across the towing path, crushing the railing beneath it. Three bodies were seen yesterday swiftly coursing downstream at Teddington. Does the weather prompt suicide? *The Times* has a queer article upon a railway smash, in which it says that the war has taught us a proper sense of proportion with respect to human life. I have always thought we prized it absurdly high; but I never thought *The Times* would say so.

Virginia Woolf

1940 [Berlin]

So far as politics and the war are concerned, everything is quiet as the grave. But Roosevelt has spoken to the House of Representatives. Covert but very malicious jibes against our regime and the Reich. He says he still hopes to keep America out of the war. That sounds anything but hopeful.

The Russians are making absolutely no progress in Finland. The Red Army really does seem to be of very little military worth.

In London there is great outrage about our radio broadcasts in English. Our announcer has been given the nickname 'Lord Haw-Haw'.

He is causing talk, and that is already half the battle. The aim in London is to create an equivalent figure for the German service. This would be the best thing that could happen. We should make mincemeat of him.

Josef Goebbels

1941 [Dresden]

Yesterday to the Reichenbachs to have tea, 'real' tea. Reichsstrasse 7 (first floor), it had no doubt constituted a single grand apartment; now half a dozen Jewish families live there. Cooking stoves in the corridor. The Reichenbachs have two rooms, one as parlor, one as *kitchen*-parlor. Oil paintings, original engravings, bronzes, valuable furniture, the man was a lawyer with a good position, now lives in poverty as an official (foreign adviser) of the Jewish Community. Was in a concentration camp, his wife was also imprisoned. A couch in each room, they sleep separately. Next door one can hear a man's voice praying loudly in Hebrew. It goes on all day, he's a devout old man. 'If it consoles him . . .' – Reichenbach told us the latest news, which is a catastrophe for us: From January 1 a new Jewish tax: 15 percent of income. That means my 400 shrink to 340M. I again and again resolve not to worry about money. We are coming to the bitter end – but not just for the Jews.

Cold again with lots of snow.

Victor Klemperer

1967 [The White House]

Now is indeed 'the Valley of the Black Pig'. A miasma of trouble hangs over everything. If I had to draw a graph of when it began, or when it at least seeped through me, I would say about December 10. All during December there was the constant grind with the budget. Once Charlie Schultze of the Bureau of the Budget, looking very intently at Lyndon, said, 'You will go down in history as the man who kept this nation together fighting a limited war.' He and Lyndon were talking about the difficulty of doing that. The temperament of our people seems to be, "you must get excited, get passionate, fight it, get it over with, or we must pull out.' It is unbearably hard to fight a limited war.

There are the big troubles of Vietnam, and the growing threat of inflation, and a whole flock of little troubles like gnats.

Lady Bird Johnson

6 January

1777 [Virginia]

News that Washington has taken 760 Hessian prisoners at Trenton in the Jerseys. Hope it is a lie.

Nicholas Cresswell

1853 [Caucasus]

A stupid parade. Everyone drinks – especially my brother – and it's very unpleasant for me. War is such an unjust and evil thing that those who wage it try to stifle the voice of conscience within them. Am I doing right? Oh God, teach me and forgive me if I'm doing wrong.

Leo Tolstoy

1942 [Jersey]

RAF dropped leaflets early this morning. We found one in our garden near the bee-hive! They were all written in French. They were not addressed specially to Channel Islanders. German officers were searching the countryside for them but our eyes are sharper than theirs! It is nice to think that our British friends were close to us today. We are not forgotten after all!

Nan Le Ruez

1943 [Berlin]

Yesterday Eva[1] spent all day in bed, only got up of necessity towards seven o'clock to make our main meal. Today, although snow is lying and she is only half recovered, she has gone into town and to the dentist. I am worried whether it will do her any good, my conscience is suffering because her getting up and going out – which she has not done since midday on Saturday – takes much of the burden off my shoulders. I myself am extremely handicapped if I do the shopping. In a bakery I was refused bread, even though the ban *only* refers to wheat products – obviously because of the salesgirl's fear and stupidity, not because of malice – but it was nevertheless painful for me. I was completely unable to come by any matches; once Reichenbach

---

[1] Eva Klemperer, née Schlemmer, a Protestant, whom the Jewish Klemperer had married, much against the wishes of both their families, in 1906.

gave me a dozen loose as a present, once Frau Eisenmann gave me a box. Here I gave an onion in return. On the other hand I was very touched when, in a shop on Blumenstrasse, I found Krone, the same sales assistant who had been my friend at Plauen station by Dölzschen. A theatrical figure, young face, hair brushed stiffly upwards, slim, he greeted me with a handshake (a deed, a profession not without risk) and immediately let me have a pound of minced fish and meat with real fishtails. It remains to be seen whether today's trip did Eva's nerves good or makes them worse again. I always reproach myself for not showing her enough sympathy. Things are wretched for both of us – but so much worse for the people in the camp, which is a *solamen miserrimum*[1] however. My hands, my feet too, are covered in small cuts because of the frost; exhaustion makes me fall asleep without fail for ten to thirty minutes every morning and afternoon. Certainly I am already reading aloud in the very early morning; but then I am also asleep by eleven o'clock at the latest.

Victor Klemperer

7 January

1855 [Crimea]
Walked with Earle to Headquarters, and suggested to Wetherall the propriety of having three or four thousand snow-boots made out of blankets.

Lieut. General Sir Charles Ash Windham

1871 [Paris]
The sufferings of Paris during the siege? A joke for two months. In the third month the joke went sour. Now nobody finds it funny any more, and we are moving fast towards starvation or, for the moment at least, towards an epidemic of gastritis. Half a pound of horsemeat, including the bones, which is two people's ration for three days, is lunch for an ordinary appetite. The prices of edible chickens or pies put them out of reach. Failing meat, you cannot fall back on vegetables; a little turnip costs eight sous and you have to pay seven francs for a pound of onions. Nobody talks about butter any more, and

---

[1] Cold comfort.

every other sort of fat except candle-fat and axle-grease has disappeared too. As for the two staple items of the diet of the poorer
classes – potatoes and cheese – cheese is just a memory, and you have
to have friends in high places to obtain potatoes at twenty francs a
bushel. The greater part of Paris is living on coffee, wine, and bread.

The Brothers Goncourt

1916 [Essex]

The village gossips are much exercised over the Government's exhor-
tations to practise economy, addressed to a village where no one has
ever done anything else and where there is no increase of money
received, since no one has war-work, and appeals to invest money in
war-funds, where no one has any reserve either to give or invest.
They have an instance in point, if extravagance is sinful (as the
Government says) why did Mr Asquith not check it in the case of
his daughter's marriage. If the national funds are in such need as the
Government says, why doesn't Mr Asquith sacrifice a tenth of his
large income and other members of the Government likewise, to the
national need?

Andrew Clark

1918 [Limerick]

Bells tolling from Limerick Cathedral; much nicer than sirens from
Bryant & May's factory.[1]

Siegfried Sassoon

1940 [Germany]

The Poles arrived yesterday at the hotel, and Mutti says already she
can tell it's an improvement on the Bavarian 'sluts' who took the
opportunity to leave her in the lurch for 'war work'. I'm only waiting
for Hilde [her maid] to go . . . so many domestics are keener to serve
their country than their employers. I don't know that I would qualify
for slave labour, though. Mutti has been told she need not feed hers
beyond the necessity of health. They are not used to a high standard
of living. She said she understood, but of course intends to treat them
well – and she saves money by not having to give them wages.

Elisabeth von Stahlenberg

[1] Famous makers of matches.

1940 [Berlin]
Film: *Ben Hur.* Old Jewish hokum. But well made.

Josef Goebbels

8 January

1940 [Berlin]
Did a mike interview with General Ernst Udet tonight, but Göring[1] his boss, censored four scripts so badly that it wasn't even interesting. I spent most of the day coaching the general on his English, which is none too good. Udet, a likeable fellow, is something of a phenomenon. A professional pilot, who only a few years ago was so broke he toured America as a stunt flyer, performing often in a full-dress suit and a top hat, he is now responsible for the designing and production of Germany's war planes. Though he never had any business experience, he has proved a genius at his job. Next to Göring and General Milch, he is given credit in inner circles here for building up the German air force to what it is today. I could not help thinking tonight that a man like Udet would never be entrusted with such a job in America. He would be considered 'lacking in experience'. Also, businessmen, if they knew of his somewhat Bohemian life, would hesitate to trust him with responsibility. And yet in this crazy Nazi system he has done a phenomenal job. Amusing: last night Udet put on a little party at his home, with three generals, napkins slung over their shoulders, presiding over his very considerable bar. There were pretty girls and a great deal of cutting up. Yet these are the men who have made the Luftwaffe the most terrible instrument of its kind in the world.

William L. Shirer

1900 [Moscow]
I'm reading about war in the Philippines and Transvaal, and am seized with horror and revulsion. Why? The wars of Frederick and Napoleon were honest wars and therefore not without a certain grandeur. This was so even with the Crimean War. But the wars of the Americans

---

[1] Reichsmarschall Hermann Göring, Commander-in-Chief of the Luftwaffe, and from 1939–45, Hitler's chosen successor.

and the British in the midst of a world where even schoolchildren condemn war are terrible.

Leo Tolstoy

1941 [Dungannon, Ireland]

The men bring tins of food, loaves and packets of margarine into the billets and leave the floor, the table, the fire-buckets full of stale food and empty tins all night. Two of the biggest gorgers are Jim Newman and Nick Carter, who were railing against the Irish the other day. Another is a suburban toff called Fred Forrester. Until I came, he was the only man in the intake with any experience of life at all, and he passes for a highly sophisticated individual. He is podgy and talks with an awful North London voice which sounds to the Cockneys like the peak of refinement. Conversation has apparently produced on the others the impression that he hobnobs with the big names, sleeps nightly with showgirls and has plumbed the depths of cosmopolitan vice. In fact, I fancy that he has been twice to the Windmill[1] and buys his reading matter in Charing Cross Road.

Rayner Heppenstall

9 January

1942 [on board the *Otranto*]

During my guard I had political arguments with a foreman of stevedores and my fellow guard, a Welsh R.A.F. electrician. I slept in the saloon, spreading my hammock over a number of hard chairs.

Yes, the prospect is gloomy. Our space between decks is unnaturally overcrowded and the ceiling is very low. A large cage rails off one of the holds which is covered above by a tarpaulin. The whole scene resembles very closely the living quarters in the *Victory*.

This is the first time I have known real discomfort without any escape which money or influence or friends can provide. There is nothing to be done but to accept the situation and I really feel quite cheerful, considerably more so than most of my companions.

We had lunch at 12.00 hours. It was edible, if not particularly

---

[1] London Theatre, famous for its girlie revues and its boast that, during wartime, 'We never close'.

appetising: a tasteless soup drunk out of our mess tins, boiled beef with potatoes and multi-coloured, bullet-like peas, and sago pudding.

I have found two observers who, more lucky than most of us, have a cabin on an upper deck with a wash basin. They have agreed to let me shave there, which is as well since below there are only twelve basins for about four hundred of us.

It is interesting to note how often one hears it said, here and everywhere, that Russia has turned the scales in this war and has saved us. It is also noticeable what a trend there seems to be towards the Left, coupled with an almost universal faith in Winston. We were blamed for cold-shouldering Russia before. How short the public memory is!

John Colville

10 January

1940 [London]

The glass dome of Paddington Station looked beautiful out of our hotel bedroom in the transparent morning light. Icy cold. London seemed full of pathetic couples having last flings together, their possibly dull and ill-assorted lives suddenly sharpened by a stab of acute anguish.

Dined with Clive, Raymond and Eddy[1] at the Ivy. Eddy spotty and tired. Raymond arrived saying, 'I'm in a *frightful* temper, *madly* irritable' and was quite the reverse. We ate oysters and little bleeding plovers.

Frances Partridge

11 January

1777 [Virginia]

Very cold weather for three days. Almost stupid for want of employment.

Nicholas Cresswell

1916 [Lewes, England]

Went to tea with the Doyles, and one of those good Christian old maids got up and *literally* danced on the hearthrug. 'Aren't you glad

---

[1] Bell, Mortimer, Sackville-West.

the Kaiser's going to kick the bucket? There's no mistake; it's cancer of the throat!'[1]

Mrs Henry Dudeney

1940 [Berlin]

Cold. Fifteen degrees below zero centigrade outside my window. Half the population freezing in their homes and offices and workshops because there's no coal. Pitiful to see in the streets yesterday people carrying a sack of coal home in a baby-carriage or on their shoulders. I'm surprised the Nazis are letting the situation become so serious. Everyone is grumbling. Nothing like continual cold to lower morale. Learned today from a traveller back from Prague that producers of butter, flour, and other things in Slovakia and Bohemia are marking their goods destined for Germany as 'Made in Russia'. This on orders from Berlin, the idea being to show the German people how much 'help' is already coming from the Soviets.

William L. Shirer

1941 [Scotland]

Go by train to Glasgow. They are all alive and vivid, and I feel that the M. of I. [Ministry of Information] can leave Scotland to look after itself. The clean sense of the Scottish makes me feel sick at heart with the muddly timidity of the English. Even Alan Hodge[2] who comes from Liverpool, catches the atmosphere. 'Are Scottish people really nicer and more alive than English people, or is it only a first impression?' He is very bright in the head, that boy.

Harold Nicolson

1967 [Bolivia]

Day of the *boro*.[3] We took the flies' larvae out of Marcos, Carlos, Pombo, Antonio, Moro and Joaquín.

Ernesto 'Che' Guevara

1967 [Vietnam]

Seen very little action so far. Captured a couple of VC [Vietcong]. They were children, not more than fifteen or sixteen years old, short

---

[1] Kaiser Wilhelm, German emperor, 1888–1918. Died 1941.
[2] Assistant Private Secretary to the Minister of Information.
[3] Fly which leaves its larvae in its bite.

and skinny. If this is what we're fighting, I wonder why the war is taking so long.

We destroyed some huts today that we suspected belong to the VC. The flame trucks pulled up and shot a stream of napalm for about fifty yards and the huts went up in flame. It's really strange, this war. For two days you search and destroy. On the next day pull up next to a town and dig in. Then the people come out and sell you the stuff Charlie has stolen from us. We are receiving snipe fire. Got to go.

David Parks

1991 [Bahrain]
We got our anthrax shots a few days back. This is for any biological weapons, specifically anthrax, that Saddam might use against us. I don't know how much good it will do. I've heard that doctors are saying the shots need to be administered about six months in advance and that once administered they only work against one strain of the virus, when there are millions out there that will kill you. Oh, well. Maybe it's just to make us feel better anyway. Sometimes I think almost everything they do is just to make us feel better.

The shots were actually pretty painful as far as shots go. They poked a big long needle into your hip just above the ass and injected the fluid in. You could feel it going in, thick and hot, and the area stayed tender for a day or two. They say we have to get a new anthrax shot every two months, which is not something I'll be looking forward to.

Sean T. Couglin

12 January

1918 [Limerick]
Peace of mind; freedom from all care; the jollity of health and good companions. What more can one ask for? But it is a drugged peace, that *will* not think, dares not think. I am home again in the ranks of youth – the company of death. The barrack-clock strikes eleven on a frosty night, 'Another night; another day.'

Siegfried Sassoon

1940 [London]
The barrage balloons, which are much in evidence again, gleam frost-
ily in the upper air. But it is comfortable this night sitting by the
glowing fire as I conceive plans for my small land loom, the construction of which I want to begin as soon as possible. It's good to occupy
myself during these weeks of war and political dissension with interests so remote from events. The knitting I had undertaken is too monotonous for my taste, but I wouldn't myself refuse a task that others had
so willingly agreed to share for the common cause, yet 70 stitches per
row for the khaki woollen scarf I am making seems interminable. It is
devastating to reflect that some 14,000 stitches are required for the
whole job, representing – at my rate of progress – about 34 hours of
continuous work. However, I must persevere.

Walter Musto

1941 [London]
Reading Gide – the best antidote possible to the triumphant commonplace of an English Sunday. Not even the Blitzkrieg has been able to
break the spell which the Sabbath casts over the land. One could not
fail by just putting one's head out of the window and smelling and
looking and listening for two minutes to recognize that this is Sunday.
In my mind's eye I can see the weary wastes of the Cromwell Road
beneath a sullen sky where a few depressed pedestrians straggle as though
lost in an endless desert. One's soul shrinks from the spectacle.

Charles Ritchie

13 January

1942 [Wiltshire]
Up to London for the night, with suitcases full of eggs for our friends.

Frances Partridge

1943 [Amsterdam]
Dearest Kitty,[1]
We have a new pastime, namely filling packets with powdered gravy.
The gravy is one of Gies & Co.'s products. Mr Kugler hasn't been able

[1] An imaginary friend to whom she wrote her diary.

to find anyone else to fill the packets, and besides, it's cheaper if we do the job. It's the kind of work they do in prisons. It's incredibly boring and makes us dizzy and giggly.

Terrible things are happening outside. At any time of night and day, poor helpless people are being dragged out of their homes. They're allowed to take only a rucksack and a little cash with them, and even then, they're robbed of these possessions on the way. Families are torn apart; men, women and children are separated. Children come home from school to find their parents have disappeared. Women return from shopping to find their houses sealed, their families gone. The Christians in Holland are also living in fear because their sons are being sent to Germany. Everyone is scared. Every night hundreds of planes pass over Holland on their way to German cities, to sow their bombs on German soil. Every hour hundreds, or maybe even thousands, of people are being killed in Russia and Africa. No one can keep out of the conflict, the entire world is at war, and even though the Allies are doing better, the end is nowhere in sight.

As for us, we're quite fortunate. Luckier than millions of people. It's quiet and safe here, and we're using our money to buy food. We're so selfish that we talk about 'after the war' and look forward to new clothes and shoes, when actually we should be saving every penny to help others when the war is over, to salvage what we can.

Anne Frank

1945 [Bergen-Belsen]

Yesterday marked our first year here. It has been a terrible year, far from home, from the children, without news from them, a year of disappointment. The transport to Palestine, the peace that did not come, a year of hunger, cold, hounding, persecution and humiliation. Fortunately, though, apart from a few bouts of dysentery, we have not been seriously ill.

The food is getting worse and worse. At midday, swede soup, every day without a single potato. The 'extra' food is distributed centrally now. Every day there are genuine punch-ups over a ticket. From time to time there is no bread at all here – from time to time (tonight, for example) we are not allowed to use the toilet. Those who have diarrhoea must go outdoors. We have procured some buckets for ourselves, discarded jam buckets.

This morning, my neighbour had to resort to them.

This morning his bunkmate discovered to his horror that his shoes were full. The other had soiled himself twice during the night.

We are living amid the lice. For months I have not been able to change into clean underwear, nor had a shower. Naturally there is also no heating here, we suffer terribly from the cold in the huts, which are draughty and where the door is never shut.

Deaths, deaths, deaths.

For how long?

The persecution of the Jews continues. Nevertheless we are a year nearer to peace than on 13 January 1944.

Abel J. Herzberg

14 January

1777 [Virginia]
News that Washington has entirely routed our Army and the few that had escaped had been obliged to take refuge on board the ships. This must certainly be a lie.

Nicholas Cresswell

1915 [Furnes, Belgium]
Some people enjoy this war. I think it is far the worst time, except one, I ever spent. Perhaps I have seen more suffering than most people. A doctor sees a hospital, and a nurse sees a ward of sick and wounded, but I see them by the hundred passing before me in an endless train all day. I can make none of them really better. I feed them, and they pass on.

Sarah Macnaughtan

1942 [Kovno Ghetto, Lithuania]
An order to bring all dogs and cats to the small synagogue on Veliuonos Street, where they were shot.

Avraham Tory

1967 [Vietnam]
I'll never forget last night. Christiensen and I were on the outer perimeter pulling guard duty. It was about eleven o'clock and I was copping a nod outside a fox-hole. Suddenly Christiensen jumped out of the

hole and onto me, scaring me shitless. At the same time I felt something run over my leg and go off into the bushes. 'Man,' Christiensen said, 'Charlies [the Vietcong] out there!' We let go with everything we had, hand grenades, machine gun, side weapons, you name it. Anything out there had to be dead.

I called Sgt. Paubar on the phone. He just said, 'Sorry about that. Keep your eyes open. Nobody can move around in the dark – you're on your own.' It was a long time until dawn. When it finally came, we went out for a body count and found just a lot of singed grass. The other guys gave us a hard time, laughing like hell. It's going to be hard to live that one down. I looked at our ammo and we'd used seven grenades and 150 rounds on nothing.

David Parks

15 January

1940 [Berlin]
A new government decree: no baths excepting on Saturdays and Sundays. This is quite a blow, as one gets amazingly dirty in a big town and it was one of the few ways to be warm.

Marie 'Missie' Vassiltchikov

1941 [Hampshire]
We have had a shock. In the devastating German raid on London on 29 December all our books, bound and unbound – seven thousand volumes – were destroyed. At first I was downcast, but Sidney [her husband] was more philosophical: he reckoned that our present income from books was only £200 to £300 a year and would dwindle year by year, and that had to be cut by 9s in the pound taxation – also it might lead to the surtax on surplus income. When in the six o'clock B.B.C. news we are told that five million books had been swept away, I was consoled by the feeling that 'we are all in it', and had no reason to feel specially injured.

Beatrice Webb

1943 [Barrow, England]
A group of naughty little boys crept in [to the canteen] and started playing with the table-tennis gear. I went to chase them off, and collided

with two little girls about twelve and fourteen. I said, "allo, my dears, what do you want?'and got a very evasive answer. I noticed they were very bold-looking little things. It appears that they have haunted the canteen all week, and when Mrs. Diss came, I said, 'o you know, I've never before seen girls or women hanging round the canteen' and she answered, 'No, but we have not had Scotties or Australians before. We were warned of the queer attractions they – and the Americans too – have for young girls.' She had talked firmly and kindly to the two girls, and asked, 'Whatever would your mother think if she knew?' She had got a pert but pitiful reply. 'Oh, *she* wouldn't say anything – but Dad would thrash me.' However, it appeared Dad was in the Middle East. The other said her mum was working, and she could not get in the house till seven o'clock when she came in.

When I told Mary, she said that, at Fulwood Barracks in Preston, it was really shocking to see such young girls 'seeking trouble'. We have seen little of it openly in Barrow, and it set me thinking again of the 'new world'. I wonder if the ones with such beautiful ideas, who blah so much about what will happen after the war, even dimly realise the stupendous tasks and problems awaiting them, the cosmic swing of change, the end of all things as we know them, I read in the paper of American school-teachers' problems with unruly adolescents who have never been disciplined.

Nella Last

16 January

1855 [Crimea]

A very cold day, with a heavy and keen north wind. Two men of the 20th frozen to death on returning from the trenches this morning. One man of the 21st, whom I got carried with my kitchen, will lose his fingers from frost in spite of all our care.

Lieut. General Sir Charles Ash Windham

1917 [Essex, England]

One indirect result of the war has been an enormous increase in cigarette smoking, both among ladies and lads. This began before the war but the example of officers and men, who are continually smoking cigarettes, has given it a great impulse. You never meet now a farm lad in the road, especially on a Sunday, who is not smoking a cigarette. Like Amy in Tennyson's 'Locksley Hall' I make no pretence to be myself 'exempt'. Since my man (Charles Henry Ward) was called up I have had to do all the out-door work. In these months I have smoked in each week more cigarettes than I used to do in any whole year before the war.

Andrew Clark

1967 [Vietnam]
The South Viet people call the Negro soldiers 'souls' . . . When the girls call you 'soul one' they are calling you a good lover.

David Parks

17 January

1855 [Crimea]
Cold and snow the same as yesterday, but the sun warm. Rode to Headquarters and saw General Aires, who gave me another letter to Commissary-General Filder about the divisional transport ponies. Went to Balaclava and presented it when Filder told me that he had no ponies, owing to the ship they had given him for them having been filled with the sick. These latter could not be disembarked, and, therefore, his horses could not be embarked.

Thus the Division will have to go without fuel, and everything will have to be fetched by the men.

I hope to God I may never be attached to so helpless an Army again; once in a man's life is quite enough to have to do with such a set of incapables. I have not seen the papers yet, but understand the attacks on Lord Raglan are most severe. It is now, however, too late.

Lieut. General Sir Charles Ash Windham

1940 [Berlin]
These days one must weigh every word as carefully as gold on the scales.

Josef Goebbels

1940 [Rome]

Mussolini, in his present seesawing of feelings, is somewhat hostile to the Germans today. He says, 'They should allow themselves to be guided by me if they do not want to make numerous unpardonable *faux pas*. In politics it is undeniable that I am more intelligent than Hitler.' I must say that until now the Chancellor of the Reich doesn't appear to share this opinion.

Count Ciano

1941 [Dungannon, Ireland]

Observations on the sex-life of the military. Despite the continual talk of 'crumpet' or 'grumble and grunt' and the occasional furtive copulations against a wall, the men's real outlet is in horseplay among themselves, one man hitting and wrestling with another, knocking his cap off, picking his pockets and so on. This homosexual horse-play is rather unedifying, but I suppose one must always be loving somebody.

Rayner Heppenstall

1991 [Ramallah]

9.30 a.m. I was in a deep sleep when the telephone rang. Someone was trying to wake me up to tell me what I did not want to hear. The ringing would not stop. I left my bed and walked to the telephone and picked it up. It was Mark Taylor, Penny's [his wife] colleague at the university. 'I'm phoning to let you know the war has started,' he said. It was 2.30 a.m.

Raja Shehadeh

1991 [Bahrain]

With all our seemingly phenomenal success, I can't figure out what the hell Saddam Hussein is trying to do. He keeps talking big, even now, but he is getting his ass kicked. He hasn't attacked Israel, has only put up a haphazard resistance to the . . . attacks, and Baghdad wasn't even blacked out until half an hour into the air assault. I thought for sure once he knew we were going in he would launch everything he had at all our defensive and supporting positions and at Israel, to drag them into this, if it took everything he had to do it. But he hasn't done anything. I kept picturing a scenario when he would saturate pre-planned targets with a Soviet-style barrage of weapons and missiles, setting us back a bit and killing as many of us as possible, to set America and Americans back a step wondering if all this was worth it. But it just hasn't happened. What the hell is he waiting for?

Sean T. Couglin

18 January

1871 [Paris]
At three o'clock I was going through the gate at the Étoile when I saw some troops marching past and stopped to look. The monument to our victories, lit by a ray of sunshine, the distant cannonade, the immense march-past, with the bayonets of the troops in the rear flashing beneath the obelisk, all this was something theatrical, lyrical, epic in nature. It was a grandiose, soul-stirring sight, that army marching towards the guns booming in the distance, an army with, in its midst, grey-bearded civilians who were fathers, beardless youngsters who were sons, and in its open ranks women carrying their husband's or their lover's rifle slung across their backs. And it is impossible to convey the picturesque touch brought to the war by this citizen multitude escorted by cabs, unpainted omnibuses, and removal vans converted into army provision wagons.

The Brothers Goncourt

1940 [Wiltshire, England]
In writing a diary all the most important things get left out. Only the decorations get mentioned and the shape of the building is taken for granted. Far the greatest pleasure I have almost every day of my life is simply being with R., or, when I'm not with him, from remembering everything to tell him afterwards. In some ways the outer bleakness created by the war has intensified this very great happiness.

Frances Partridge

1940 [Amsterdam]
Ed[1] and I are here for a few days to discuss our European coverage,

---

[1] Ed Murrow, American broadcaster.

or at least that's our excuse. Actually, intoxicated by the lights at night and the fine food and the change of atmosphere, we have been cutting up like a couple of youngsters suddenly escaped from a stern old aunt or a reform school. Last night in sheer joy, as we were coming home from an enormous dinner with a fresh snow drifting down like confetti, we stopped under a bright street-light and fought a mighty snow-ball battle. I lost my glasses and my hat and we limped back to the hotel exhausted but happy. This morning we have been ice-skating with Mary Marvin Breckinridge, who has forsaken the soft and dull life of American society to represent us here. The Dutch still lead the good life. The food they consume as to both quantity and quality (oysters, fowl, meats, vegetables, oranges, bananas, coffee – the things the warring peoples never see) is fantastic. They dine and dance and go to church and skate on canals and tend their business. And they are blind – oh, so blind – to the dangers that confront them. Ed and I have tried to do a little missionary work but to no avail, I fear. The Dutch, like everyone else, want it both ways. They want peace and the comfortable life. But they won't make the sacrifices or even the hard decisions which might ensure their way of life in the long run. The Queen, they say, stubbornly refuses to allow staff talks with the Allies or even with the Belgians. In the meantime, as I could observe when I crossed the border, the Germans pile up their forces and supplies to the Dutch frontier.

William L. Shirer

1945 [Auschwitz, camp hospital]

During the night of the evacuation the camp kitchens continued to function, and on the following morning the last distribution of soup took place in the hospital. The central-heating plant had been abandoned; in the huts a little heat still lingered on, but hour by hour the temperature dropped and it was evident that we would soon suffer from the cold. Outside it must have been at least 5°F below zero; most of the patients had only a shirt and some them not even that.

Nobody knew what our fate would be. Some SS men had remained, some of the guard towers were still occupied.

About midday an SS officer made a tour of the huts. He appointed a chief in each of them, selecting from among the remaining non-Jews, and ordered a list of the patients to be made at once, divided into Jews and non-Jews. The matter seemed clear. No one was surprised that the Germans preserved their national love of classification until the very end, nor did any Jew seriously expect to live until the following day.

It was soon night but the electric light remained on. We saw with tranquil fear that an armed SS man stood at the corner of the hut. There were no clocks but it must have been about 11p.m. when all the lights went out, even those of the reflectors on the guard towers. One could see the search beams in the distance. A cluster of intense lights burst out in the sky, remaining immobile. One could hear the roar of the aeroplanes.

Then the bombardment began. It was nothing new: I climbed down to the ground, put my bare feet into my shoes and waited.

It seemed far away, perhaps over Auschwitz.

But then there was an explosion near by, and before one could think, a second and a third one, loud enough to burst one's ear-drums. Windows were breaking, the hut shook, the spoon that I had fixed in the wall fell down.

Then it seemed all over. Cagnolati, a young peasant from the Vosges, had apparently never experienced a raid. He leapt out naked from his bed and was concealed in a corner, screaming. After a few minutes it was obvious that the camp had been struck. Two huts were burning fiercely, another two had been pulverised, but they were all empty. Dozens of patients arrived, naked and wretched, from a hut threatened by fire: they asked for shelter but it was impossible to take them in. They insisted, begging and threatening in many languages. We had to barricade the door. They dragged themselves elsewhere, lit up by the flames, barefoot in the melting snow. Many trailed behind them streaming bandages. There seemed no danger to our hut, so long as the wind did not change.

The Germans were no longer there. The towers were empty.

Primo Levi

1968 [The White House]
[At the Woman Doers' Luncheon of the Year]
As Lyndon turned to leave Miss Eartha Kitt[1] who had been seated at a table close to the podium, rose in his path and said, 'Mr. President, what do you do about delinquent parents – those who have to work and are too busy to look after their children?' Lyndon told her, 'We

---

[1] Black actress and singer.

have just passed a Social Security Bill that allots millions of dollars for day-care centers.' She moved, I think, a step more in front of him. 'But what are we going to do?' she said. 'That's something for you women to discuss here,' Lyndon replied; then turned and walked briskly out.

Miss Kitt sat down, stubbed out a cigarette, tossing her long hair, and from then on I watched her, expecting something – I didn't know what. Apparently she did not eat, nor did she applaud any of the speakers. She smoldered and smoked. The last speaker was Katherine Peden, of the eleven members of the Advisory Commission on Civil Disorders.

When she finished I asked the guests for their observations and discussions, and Judge Caroline Simon, who had been on my right, was the first up. There were several more. I noticed Miss Kitt's hand go up and I knew I must, in turn, get to her. I did not know what to expect – only I sensed that she had come to say something and that it would not be good. When some speaker finished I nodded to her. She arose and began to talk, swiftly and passionately, beginning with an angry accusation that welfare checks were so small – just four dollars. 'What can you get for four dollars?' And then, oddly, an attack on high taxes. 'The young people are angry. Their parents are angry, because they are being so highly taxed.' Mounting to a crescendo, she came to her real destination – to denounce the war in Vietnam. 'Boys I know across the nation feel it doesn't pay to be a good guy. They figure with a record they don't have to go off to Vietnam.' Then, advancing a step toward me and looking with intense directness at me (she is a good actress), she said, 'We send the best of this country off to be shot and maimed. They rebel in the streets. They take pot and they will get high. They don't want to go to school, because they are going to be snatched off from their mothers to be shot in Vietnam.'

I am glad to say that I looked back just as directly, stare for stare. She continued, pointing her finger at me, the papers later reported. She said: 'You are a mother too, although you have daughters and not sons. I am a mother and I know the feeling of having a baby come out of my guts. I have a baby and then you send him off to war. No wonder the kids rebel and take pot. And, Mrs. Johnson, in case you don't understand the lingo that's marijuana!'

What do you feel in a situation like this? First, a wave of mounting disbelief. Can this be true? Is this a nightmare? Then a sort of surge of adrenalin into the blood, knowing that you are going to answer, that you've *got* to answer, that you *want* to answer, and at the same time somewhere in the back of your mind a voice that says, 'Be calm, be dignified.' Somewhere along the way – I think between the words 'gut'and 'pot' – I had the sense that maybe she was undoing her point. Miss Kitt stopped for breath to a stunned silence in the room and for a second I waited to see whether it was a comma or a period. Then Mrs. Hughes of New Jersey rose to her feet and said, 'I feel morally obligated. May I speak in defense of the war? My first husband,' she said, 'was killed in World War II, and I have eight sons. One of them is now in the Air Force. None of them wants to go to Vietnam. All will go. They and their friends. I think anybody who takes pot because there is a war on is a kook. These young people are still juniors. They have to be regulated. I hope we adults are still in control.' The room thundered with applause.

One paper said that I was pale and that my voice trembled slightly as I replied to Miss Kitt. I think that is correct. I did not have tears in my eyes, as another paper reported. 'Because there is a war on,' I said, 'and I pray that there will be a just and honest peace – that still doesn't give us a free ticket not to try to work for better things – against crime in the streets, and for better education and better health for our people. I cannot identify as much as I should. I have not lived the background that you have, nor can I speak as passionately or as well, but we must keep our eyes and our hearts and our energies fixed on constructive areas and try to do something that will make this a happier, better-educated land.'

Once more there was thunderous applause. I felt that I must not let the meeting end there. I had seen the pencils racing across the pads of the press ladies – several more had come in as the program started – and I didn't want the occasion to seem like a riot. Several hands went up. There were three or four more observations. One came from a Negro woman who said there was a double standard of justice and that we would not be done with juvenile delinquency until that was changed. She meant that if a Negro kills a Negro the crime is not pursued as diligently and with the full force of the law as when a white person is concerned. I believe there is truth in that.

Lady Bird Johnson

1991 [Ramallah]
For the second night, the persistent ringing of the telephone woke me up. But I already knew that the war is on. What is it this time?

Penny got up to answer it. She came back and said in the unnaturally calm voice people use in emergencies, 'Rita says they're
bombing Jerusalem. We had better seal ourselves in.'

I wondered if it might not already be too late – Jerusalem is only
a few miles away. Penny went to use the toilet and I waited outside. I
needed to use it too. When she came out she said, 'I saw flashes in the
sky, try and be quick.' Then it must be too late, I thought, looking out
at the night from the toilet's open window. The air must already be
contaminated.

Nevertheless, I closed all the inside doors and threw blankets down
to seal the gaps between the doors and the ground. Then I went into
our famous room and taped the door up behind us.

Raja Shehadeh

19 January

1918 [Limerick]
How many miles to Craiglockhart?[1] Hell seems nearer.

Siegfried Sassoon

1945 [Auschwitz, camp hospital]
The Frenchmen [fellow inmates] agreed. We got up at dawn, we three.
I felt ill and hopeless, I was cold and afraid.

The other patients looked at us with respectful curiosity: did we not
know that patients were not allowed to leave Ka-Be [infectious diseases
unit]?[2] And if the Germans had not all left? But they said nothing,
they were glad that someone was prepared to make the test.

The Frenchman had no idea of the topography of the Lager [camp],
but Charles was courageous and robust, while Arthur was shrewd, with
the practical common sense of the peasant. We went out into the wind
of a freezing day of fog, poorly wrapped up in blankets.

What we saw resembled nothing that I had ever seen or heard
described.

The Lager, hardly dead, had already begun to decompose. No more
water, or electricity, broken windows, doors slamming to in the wind,

[1] Military hospital in Edinburgh, where both Sassoon and Wilfred Owen convalesced.
[2] Levi had scarlet fever. The camp had been evacuated on the approach of the liberating Allied forces, only the sick had been left behind.

loose iron-sheets from the roofs screeching, ashes from the fire drifting high, afar. The work of the bombs had been completed by the work of man: ragged, decrepit, skeleton-like patients at all able to move dragged themselves everywhere on the frozen soil, like an invasion of worms. They had ransacked all the empty huts in search of food and wood; they had violated with senseless fury the grotesquely adorned rooms of the hated *Blockältester* [block superintendents], forbidden to the ordinary *Häftlinge* [prisoners] until the previous day; no longer in control of their own bowels, they had fouled everywhere, polluting the precious snow, the only source of water remaining in the whole camp.

Primo Levi

1991 [Ramallah]

9.00.a.m. Went to sleep at eleven last night and slept through the dreaded two-thirty watershed. At five, I woke up and heard a summary of the news. There was nothing new. At seven-thirty we got up and put on the radio but didn't notice anything unusual. Only later did we hear an official-sounding announcement in Hebrew. Even with my poor Hebrew, I could tell it had to do with the missiles, but I was not quite sure whether they were telling people to leave or go into their sealed rooms.

Then Penny despaired of my ability to comprehend Hebrew and turned to the morning Israeli English-language broadcast. There we heard that we should be in our sealed rooms with our masks on.

'The Missiles have hit Israel,' they said.

On our side, we are jubilant that Tel Aviv was hit, not once but twice. The full extent of the damage is unknown, even though two hours have passed since the missiles fell. Why jubilation? Because they have destroyed thousands of our homes in the occupied Territories and have pounded our refugee camps in Lebanon for years. Maybe this will make them realise what it means to lose one's home.

Raja Shehadeh

20 January

1940 [London]

We listen to Winston Churchill on the wireless after dinner. He is a little too rhetorical, and I do not think that his speech will really have gone with the masses. He is too belligerent for this pacifist age, and although once anger comes to steel our sloppiness, his voice will be welcome to them, at the moment it reminds them of heroism which they do not really feel.

Harold Nicolson

1941 [England]

Today we have hauled and hugged and staggered with sacks of coal through continuous rain, the dirt and wet working miserably into one's skin. It was too wretched even to offer the simple excitement of physical exercise. There is nothing exhilarating in breaking one's nails on wet sacks which are too heavy to lift and feeling the black slush working its way up the inside of your sleeves. The only consolation was to know one shared it with others of the same opinion.

Keith Vaughan

1941 [Dresden]

A couple of weeks ago at the Jewish tea downstairs with the Katzes and Kreidles, Leipziger, an elderly medical officer and insurance doctor, garrulously and somewhat boastfully and conceitedly monopolized the conversation; recently Frau Voss comes back enchanted from one of her bridge parties: The medical officer has read so interestingly from a book about the doctor, it is his own life. So now all the Jews who have been thrown out are writing their autobiography, and I am one of twenty thousand . . . And yet: The book will be good, and it helps *me* pass the time. But then the old doubt also revived again, whether it would not have been better for me to learn English. Now on the one hand the new reduction in our money is in the offing, on the other the block on American visas has been lifted and it will soon be the turn of our quota number, and Sussman [a friend in Vienna] has passed on my documents by airmail to Georg [his nephew in America]. Wait and see . . .

Victor Klemperer

1945 [Auschwitz, camp hospital]

The dawn came and it was my turn to light the stove. Besides a general feeling of weakness, the aching of my joints reminded me all the time that my scarlet fever was far from over. The thought of having to plunge into the freezing air to find a light in the other huts made me shudder with disgust. I remembered my flints: I sprinkled a piece of paper with spirits, and patiently scraped a small pile of black dust on top of it and then scraped the flint more vigorously with my knife. And finally, after a few sparks, the small pile caught fire and the small bluish flame of alcohol rose from the paper.

The camp was silent. Other starving spectres like ourselves wandered around searching, unshaven with hollow eyes, greyish skeleton bones in rags. Shaky on their legs, they entered and left the empty huts carrying the most varied of objects: axes, buckets, ladles, nails; anything might be of use, and those looking furthest ahead were already thinking of profitable commerce with the Poles of the surrounding countryside.

In the kitchen we found two of them squabbling over the last handfuls of putrid potatoes. They had seized each other by the rags, and were fighting with curiously slow and uncertain movements, cursing in Yiddish between their frozen lips.

In the courtyard of the storehouse there were two large piles of cabbages and turnips (those large, insipid turnips, the basis of our diet). They were so frozen that they could only be separated with a pickaxe. Charles and I took turns, using all our energy at each stroke, and we carried out about 100 pounds. There was still more: Charles discovered a packet of salt and ('*Une fameuse trouvaille*') a can of water of perhaps twelve gallons, frozen in a block.

For the past three days the Wehrmacht in flight passed by in waves. Armoured cars, Tiger tanks camouflaged in white, Germans on horseback, Germans on bicycles, Germans on foot, armed and unarmed. During the night, long before the tanks came into sight, one could hear the grinding of their tracks.

It seemed as if it would never end.

Primo Levi

1991 [Ramallah]

1.00 p.m. 'To the inhabitants of Ramallah,' the soldier bellowed, 'it is permitted to move around between 9.00 a.m. and midday.'

Funny way of putting it, I thought, or has the curfew become the natural state and moving around a privilege which the army bestows when it wishes on 'the inhabitants of Ramallah'. The hostages?

Raja Shehadeh

21 January

1917 [Hertfordshire]

Instead of going to church, a party conducted by Lord Desborough went over to see the German prisoners. There are about a hundred of them in the park and they work in the woods. I was not allowed to talk German to them. The specimens I saw were of the meek-and-mild type, not at all 'blond beasts'. They had rather ignominious identification marks in the form of a blue disc patched somewhere onto their backs: it looked as though its purpose was to afford a bull's eye to the marksman if they attempted to escape.

Lady Cynthia Asquith

1945 [Auschwitz, camp hospital]

Instead it ended. On the dawn of the 21st we saw the plain deserted and lifeless, white as far as the eye could see, lying under the flight of crows, deathly sad. I would almost have preferred to see something moving again.

We had to inaugurate the cabbages and turnips. While I went in search for wood and Charles collected the snow for water, Arthur mobilised the patients who could sit up to help with the peeling. Towarowski, Sertelet, Alcalai and Schenck answered the call.

The news that a soup was being cooked spread rapidly through the crowd of the semi-living; a throng of starved faces gathered at the door. Charles, with ladle uplifted, made a short, vigorous speech, which although in French needed no translation. The majority dispersed but one came forward. He was a Parisian, a high-class tailor (he said), suffering from tuberculosis. In exchange for two pints of soup he offered to make us clothes from the many blankets still to be found around the camp.

Maxine showed himself to be really able. The following day Charles and I were in possession of a jacket, trousers and gloves of rough fabric of striking colours.

In the evening, after the first soup, distributed with enthusiasm and devoured with greed, the great silence from the plain was broken. From our bunks, too tired to be really worried, we listened to the bangs of mysterious artillery groups apparently hidden on all the points of the horizon, and to the whistle of shells over our heads.

Primo Levi

1991 [Kuwait]

There is no time or place for thinking or writing since duties are many. News comes from the radio or from those returning from their homes to join regiments. One says they have destroyed Baghdad and demolished it and another says there is no water, electricity or telephone lines. Some of them turn the world black in your eyes. Others come to pacify you saying nothing has happened there – they have only bombed the military installations. Others say they have bombed the civilian buildings. You don't know who to believe and who is lying. All news are hallucinations. They are all lying. The truth is lost.

Anonymous Iraqi soldier

1991 [Ramallah]

6.30 p.m. Wars are a time when those in power attempt to prove more decisively than at other times that all is in their hands, that they control earth, sea and sky. And you, the puny individual, count for nothing.

Every time I sit here to write I feel that I am proving them wrong. By insisting on my world and articulating it here, I am holding on to my own and proving that their claim is empty despite all their sound and fury.

Raja Shehadeh

22 January

1940 [Berlin]

The Führer has set his mind on a great war against England. As soon as the weather is good. England must be chased out of Europe, and France destroyed as a great power. Then Germany will have hegemony and Europe will have peace. This is our great, eternal goal. Afterwards, the Führer will remain in office for a few years, carry through social reforms and his building projects, and then retire. Then let the others try their hands. He intends to act only as a benevolent spirit hovering over the political world. And write down everything that is in the thick of now. A bible of National Socialism, so to speak.

Josef Goebbels

1945 [Auschwitz, camp hospital]
If it is courageous to face a grave danger with a light heart, Charles and I were courageous this morning. We extended our explorations to the SS camp, immediately outside the electric wire-fence.

The camp guards must have left in a great hurry. On the tables we found plates half-full of a by-now frozen soup which we devoured with an intense pleasure, mugs full of beer, transformed into yellow-ish ice, a chessboard with an unfinished game. In the dormitories, piles of valuable things.

We loaded ourselves with a bottle of vodka, various medicines, news-papers and magazines and four first-rate eiderdowns, one of which is today in my house in Turin. Cheerful and irresponsible, we carried the fruits of our expedition back to the dormitory, leaving them in Arthur's care. Only later did we learn what happened perhaps only half an hour later.

Some SS men, perhaps dispersed, but still armed, penetrated into the abandoned camp. They found that eighteen Frenchmen had settled into the dining-hall of the SS-Waffe. They killed them all methodically, with a shot in the nape of the neck, lining up their twisted bodies in the snow on the road; then they left. The eighteen corpses remained exposed until the arrival of the Russians; nobody had the strength to bury them.

Primo Levi

1967 [Bolivia]
We shot two turkeys; an animal was caught in the trap, but it bit off one of its legs and got away.

Ernesto 'Che' Guevara

1991 [Ramallah]
8.00 a.m. Day six. Only six days have passed!

Raja Shehadeh

23 January

1665 [London]
Up, and with Sir W. Batten and Sir W. Penn, to Whitehall and there did our usual business. And here I met the great newes confirmed by the Duke's own relation, by a letter from Captain Allen — first, of our own loss of two ships, the Phœnix and Nonesuch, in the Bay of Gibraltar —

then, of his and his seven ships with him, in the bay of Cales, or there-abouts, fight with the 34 Duch Smyrna fleet, sinking the *King Salamon*, a ship worth 150,000L some say and another, and taking of three merchant ships. Two of our ships were disabled by the Duch unfortunately falling against their will against them. The Duch men-of-war did little service. The Spaniards on shore at Cales did stand laughing at the Duch to see them run away and fly to the shore, 34 or thereabouts, against 8 Englishmen at most. I do purpose to get the whole relation, if I live, of Captain Allen himself.

Thence to Jervas's, my mind, God forgive me, running too much after sa fille, but elle not being within I away by coach to the Change, and thence home to dinner and finding Mrs. Bagwell waiting at the office after dinner, away elle and I to a cabaret where elle and I have été before. So to my office a little and to Jervas's again, thinking avoir rencontré Jane, mais elle n'etait pas dedans. So I back again to my office, where I did with great content faire a vow to mind my business, and laisser aller les femmes for a month and am with all my heart glad to find myself able to come to so good a resolution, that thereby I may follow my business, which, and my honour, thereby lies a-bleeding. So home to supper and to bed.

Samuel Pepys

1944 [London]

At 10.30 Stuart [Preston, American on military duty] met me at Paddington Station. While waiting for him I watch a woman passen-ger have a row with an officious woman ticket collector at the barrier. The first threw the other's ticket puncher to the ground. The second threw the first's handbag to the ground, took off her own coat, and flew at her opponent. They punched and scratched and finally became interlocked, each grasping the other's hair which came away in hand-fuls. I felt quite sick and intervened. Then they both hit me. I roared for help, and two policemen dragged the combatants apart. The other passengers, mostly soldiers, merely looked on.

James Lees-Milne

1945 [Auschwitz, camp hospital]

Our potatoes were finished. For days past the rumour had circulated through all the huts that an enormous trench of potatoes lay some-where outside the barbed wire, not far from the camp.

Some unknown pioneer must have carried out patient explorations, or someone else knew the spot with precision. In fact, by the morning of the 23rd a section of the barbed wire had been beaten down and a double file of wretches went in and out through the opening.

Charles and I left, into the wind of the leaden plain. We were beyond the broken barrier.

'*Dis donc, Primo, on est dehors!*'

It was exactly like that; for the first time since the day of my arrest I found myself free, without armed guards, without wire fence between myself and home.

Perhaps 400 yards from the camp lay the potatoes – a treasure. Two extremely long ditches, full of potatoes and covered by alternate layers of soil and straw to protect them from the cold. Nobody would die of hunger any more.

Primo Levi

24 January

1916 [Essex]

1 p.m. Miss Eliza Vaughan called. She is on the staff of the VAD [Voluntary Aid Detachment] hospital, Braintree: Some of the patients are Scots or at least of Scots Regiments. Miss Vaughan told us a hospital story, of a man who was brought in unconscious. When he came to himself he found himself in bandages, head and foot. She explained that he had a vinegar head-swathe because of his fever; a mustard-plaster on his chest because of his lungs; and salt bags on his feet because of frost-bite. 'Then, Miss, I think you ought to bring some pepper, and I'll be the complete cruet.'

Andrew Clark

1940 [Lille, France]

This evening dined with Pagézy[1] at the Huîtrière in Lille in order to attend a gala performance of the film *The Lion has Wings*. Pagézy was in good form telling us about his efforts to learn English with a gramophone while he shaves. The gramophone says 'Why will you not dance

---

[1] General B.H.G. Pagézy, commander of the Lille region.

with Helen? Because it is dangerous. And why is it dangerous? Because Helen will smoke cigarettes and I am wearing a cellulose collar!!!'

Field Marshal Lord Alanbrooke

1942 [Jersey]

Things are depressing all the time. Almost every night, the *Evening Post* reports sudden deaths. It is very strange – lack of proper nourishment must be the cause. Then there are lots of 'foreign' workmen in the island, brought by the Germans. These are half-starved, and half-clothed, and reported to have strange and dangerous diseases. However, we have all had a ration of a quarter pound of chocolate each this week. It was wonderful – chocolate!

Nan Le Ruez

1943 [London]

Breakfasting at Brooks's I sat with Lord Spencer who told me with disgust that during a seven-day absence from London 'they' took away the contemporary gates from Spencer House for scrap. Attended High Mass at the little Sardinian chapel in Warwick Street. It is far and away my favourite worshipping place in London. The candlelight flickered across the silver hearts which line the walls of the presbytery while the transalpine chants made me long for Italy and for peace and good-will among nations.

James Lees-Milne

1945 [Auschwitz, camp hospital]

Liberty. The breach in the barbed wire gave us a concrete image of it. To anyone who stopped to think, it signified no more Germans, no more selections, no work, no blows, no roll-calls, and perhaps, later, the return.

But we had to make an effort to convince ourselves of it, and no one had time to enjoy the thought. All around lay destruction and death.

The pile of corpses in front of our window had by now overflowed out of the ditch. Despite the potatoes everyone was weak; not a patient in the camp improved, while many fell ill with pneumonia and diarrhoea; those who were unable to move themselves, or lacked the energy to do so, lay lethargic in their bunks, benumbed by cold, and nobody realised when they died.

Primo Levi

1991 [Saudi Arabia]

The war coverage continues constantly. It's on the TV outside the offices when we go to work. It's on the radio when we eat and in the tent when we sleep. It's in the papers and magazines from home. News of the war completely inundates our lives.

And where did CNN get that theme music? It sounds like a warm-up for the Olympics or something, like NBC's sombre theme for the 1988 games. It highlights the fact that all the coverage makes this seem like some kind of sporting events, a fact which almost everybody is remarking upon.

Sean T. Couglin

25 January

1944 [Algiers]

The ENSA [Entertainments National Service Association] Lieutenant had spots on his neck, not his own teeth and no personality. He seemed, like all ENSA personnel, to exude inefficiency and a dampness. The welfare officer shook us rather. She looked so exactly right for what I've always thought a Madame of a brothel should look like that I could hardly credit her. The rouge, a strong carmine, the lipstick put on with a hit or miss technique and the rusty black dress and coat were all in the picture. But she spoke good English and drove with Viola[1] and me to the hostel which is at Point Pescade, about five miles out to the left. I asked the matron if the house was flats, for the stairs seemed to be outside the front door, but she said, but no, it is '*une maison particulaire*' which was an understatement. After very good coffee with bread and a sort of guava jelly we left and went for a walk. The hills rise up at once from the coast road and we went up a little lane with high walled villas on either side. Through a paling gate we saw a tree covered in lemons, della Robbia, and lovely against the pale blue sky. Geraniums seem to like the thin red soil and they grew in great hedges, deep scarlet, cyclamen pink and white. Almond trees are *out*. As we climbed we picked wild iris, wild marigold (tiny and yellow), a bean flower, white with a feathery mimosa-y leaf, bee orchid, a little yellow furled flower that a French

[1] Viola Tunnard, her pianist.

gardener told us was vinaigrette, a sort of giant stitchwort growing over a hedge like a great vine. We walked for two hours. Then baths. This was a major operation. Two Arabs carried baths and we ran the cold tap till the temperature suited our toes. Viola and I shared the water. Delicious supper. The ENSA chairs were uncompromisingly hard so I blew up my air cushion for Viola's use and sat on my baby pillow myself.

On our walk we saw an Arab wearing a hairnet.

Joyce Grenfell

1945 [Auschwitz, camp hospital]

It was Sómogyi's turn. He was a Hungarian chemist, about fifty years old, thin, tall and taciturn . . . he suffered from typhus and scarlet fever. He had not spoken for about five days; that day he opened his mouth and said in a firm voice:

'I have a ration of bread under the sack. Divide it among you three. I shall not be eating any more.'

We could not find anything to say, but for the time being we did not touch the bread. Half his face had swollen. As long as he retained consciousness he remained closed in a harsh silence.

But in the evening and for the whole of the night and for two days without interruption the silence was broken by his delirium. Following a last interminable dream of acceptance and slavery he began to murmur: 'Jawohl' [yes, sir], at every collapsing of his wretched frame, thousands of times, enough to make one want to suffocate him, at least to make him change the word.

I never understood so clearly as at that moment how laborious is the death of a man.

Primo Levi

1968 [The White House]

The city is in a state of tension that has been mounting since Monday, when North Korea seized the *Pueblo*. Sometime in the morning the news came to me that Lyndon had called up the Reservists, Air Force and Navy – about fourteen thousand of them – for active duty, a partial answer to the North Koreans seizing our ship.

Liz[1] came over, looking as if the sky had fallen. Secretary John Gardner's

---

[1] Liz Carpenter, Lady Bird Johnson's staff director and press secretary.

resignation had been announced and the Viet Cong were attacking at Khe Sanh in what looked like a major offensive. We were badly outnumbered there. What a day! Of course, I had already had five days to absorb my sadness at Gardner's resignation.

When we finished with letters and invitations and answers to questions, I went over to the EOB [Executive Office Building] for two fast, hard games of bowling. They do help. Back upstairs, I put on a gold lamé dress and fared forth to the first big dinner of 1968 – the party honouring the Vice President, the Speaker, and the Chief Justice, with, I hope, a brave front – though with a sinking heart – on as inauspicious an evening as could possibly be.

I went into the Yellow Room to meet the honoured guests, Hubert and Muriel [Humphrey], the Speaker and Miss Harriet, and the Chief Justice and Mrs. Warren. I always think of this as a sort of family party and how easy it is to forget that the Chief Justice is a member of the other political party! This dinner has a very different mood from one honouring a Chief of State.

I found myself talking too fast and too much, an attempt to combat the gloom that the troubles of the day brought down. When the Honour Guard came in – this is the first time I can remember that it has not been led by Chuck – I missed him and imagined that it moved less skilfully with something less than the usual ballet precision. We followed them downstairs, I walking with my husband this time, with the Speaker and Miss Harriet using the elevator, but joining us at the foot of the stairs. We marched in and just as we reached the door an unprecedented thing happened. The room burst into spontaneous applause. Never before that I can remember has this happened either for us or for any other President.

As the 190 guests came down the receiving line, I sensed something of what may be the feeling of the whole country. One pressed my hand. Another murmured, 'We are praying for you.' Others, I think, tried to convey sympathy and understanding with a look. I do not believe their solicitude had any particular reference to Lyndon and Lady Bird Johnson. I think it simply meant: 'You are the President, and we know it is tough and we are in it with you.'

Lady Bird Johnson

26 January

1871 [Paris]

The shells are coming closer. New batteries seem to be opening fire. Shells are exploding every few minutes along the railway line, and people cross our boulevard on their hands and feet.

The Brothers Goncourt

1915 [Essex]

8.10 a.m. I made bold to send a letter to this effect to the Rt. Hon. the Lord Kitchener:

My Lord,

Soldiers' letters often speak of the difficulty and loss experienced in taking messages and supplies from the second to the front-line trench, across the exposed interval.

I make bold to suggest a simple contrivance which seems capable of minimising these.

Let there be in each trench an ordinary salmon-rod reel, with the ordinary length of line. Let the message be enclosed in a waterproof satchel . . . fastened securely to the two lines at their ends. By winding and unwinding the reel in the trenches, the case could be drawn backwards and forwards across the zone of fire . . .

Andrew Clark

1940 [Wiltshire]

I tried to analyse why it pleases me to find time slipping by so fast and uneventfully. Is it because every day got through brings one nearer the end of this hateful old war? I deliberately set myself to cultivate tastes like reading and music, which seem – at present anyhow – inviolable. As far as the war is concerned, I have entered into a phase of shying away like a horse from the news in *The Times*, and trying just to get the gist of the headlines without reading it properly. So much of it rouses a reaction of impotent fury or despair. We have missed listening to the wireless news several evenings.

Frances Partridge

1942 [Leningrad]

For the first time I cried from grief and fury: inadvertently I overturned the saucepan of porridge on the stove. I.[lya] D.[avidovitch, her husband] nevertheless swallowed a few spoonfuls, mixed with the ashes.

Vera Inber

1945 [Auschwitz, camp hospital]

We lay in a world of death and phantoms. The last trace of civilisation had vanished around and inside us. The work of bestial degradation, begun by the victorious Germans, had been carried to its conclusion by the Germans in defeat.

It is man who kills, man who creates or suffers injustice; it is no longer man who, having lost all restraint, shares his bed with a corpse. Whoever waits for his neighbour to die in order to take his piece of bread is, albeit guiltless, further from the model of the thinking man than the most primitive pygmy or the most vicious sadist.

Part of our existence lies in the feelings of those near to us. This is why the experience of someone who has lived for days during which man was merely a thing in the eyes of man is non-human. We three were for the most part immune from it, and we owe each other mutual gratitude. This is why my friendship with Charles will prove lasting.

But thousands of feet above us, in the gaps in the grey clouds, the complicated miracles of aerial duels begin. Above us, bare, helpless and unarmed, men of our time sought reciprocal deaths with the most refined of instruments. A movement of the finger could cause the destruction of the entire camp, could annihilate thousands of men; while the sum total of all our efforts and exertions would not be sufficient to prolong by one minute the life of even one of us.

The saraband stopped at night and the room was once again filled with Sómogyi's monologue.

In full darkness I found myself suddenly awake. '*L'pau' vieux*' was silent; he had finished. With the last gasp of life, he had thrown himself to the ground: I heard the thud of his knees, of his hips, of his shoulders, of his head.

'*La mort l'a chassé de son lit*,' Arthur defined it.

We certainly could not carry him out during the night. There was nothing for it but to go back to sleep again.

Primo Levi

1991 [Ramallah]

Every Friday evening there is an Arabic film on Israeli television. By the evening yesterday, I was bored enough to want a diversion, even in the form of an Egyptian soap opera.

The hero had just had his first contact with the evil seductress when the film was interrupted and the word ALERT was flashed up on the screen. I was proud to be the first to know this time and made sure Penny heard the news from me. Then began the scramble which always puts us in such a state of high anxiety. Every time it is the same question: Will it be gas this time?

I opened my box and took out the mask. Penny sat on the bed and held the lame rubbery thing with the round muzzle and wondered aloud whether or not we should wear them. Somehow it seemed ridiculous. To be sitting on one's bed, breathing through a huge filter and whining like a pig.

Raja Shehadeh

27 January

1941 [Wales/England]
A wild day travelling. All trains fantastically late and crowded. When the train came in at Cardiff, there were Firsts opposite where I was and we all scrambled away from them, one man saying: Bloody Firsts. Shouldn't be no bloody firsts. A long and cold wait at Bath; only a very few buns. Cups of tea, but nothing much else. Later in a train with two Canadians, one very fed up with the rain, wanting to go home, saying why did anyone want to come to this country? He'd had pneumonia with the weather. We tried to persuade him that it could be nice in Spring. In a corner a London woman coming back from Devon, saying she couldn't live anywhere except in London: It's my home, see? The Canadian said he'd been to London, there wasn't anything like as much damage as there seemed to be from the Canadian papers. The woman and another man sprang to London's defence, saying You ought to see the Docks. They wouldn't bomb the West End, not likely! Come over regular as buses they did, something wicked. The Canadian had a burst boil on his hand; I suggested he should tie it with the bandage out of his first aid case, but a young airman reproved us, saying that could only be used in an emergency.

Naomi Mitchison

1942 [London]

Nancy[1] at luncheon: 'I said to myself, "in the bloodiest war in all history it's no good being squeamish over one wounded moorhen." So I shut my eyes and twisted its neck.' Spot had mauled it.

James Lees-Milne

1945 [Auschwitz, camp hospital]

Dawn. On the floor, the shameful wreck of skin and bones, the Sómogyi thing.

There are more urgent tasks: we cannot wash ourselves, so that we dare not touch him until we have cooked and eaten. And besides: '. . . *rien de dégoûtant que les débordements*,' said Charles justly; the latrine had to be emptied. The living are more demanding; the dead can wait. We began to work as on every day.

The Russians arrived while Charles and I were carrying Sómogyi a little distance outside. He was very light. We overturned the stretcher on the grey snow.

Charles took off his beret. I regretted not having a beret.

Primo Levi

28 January

1938 [Spain]

This morning we worked like mad in the ward. We did all the dressings and then washed as many as we had time for and did the beds of the ones who could not move. The spine is worse, and I am afraid he will die tonight, but maybe not. He spends his time moaning and saying he is going to die which is very trying.

Priscilla Scott-Ellis

1940 [Wiltshire]

'Is it raining?' we asked Edie [their maid] this morning, when she called us. 'Why no, I don't think so, but the trees are all covered with icicles.' A sharp frost on top of the rain had encased every twig in ice as thick as a man's thumb – a fabulous sight. Each leaf and each blade of grass had its glass envelope and the plants in the rockery were solid coral.

[1] Nancy Mitford, novelist and one of the famous Mitford girls.

The sound of the ghostly glass trees swaying and clanking in the wind was enough to freeze the blood.

Towards evening boughs began to break from the laden trees and fall crashing to the ground. I felt I knew what it was like to be in an air-raid. Crash – Crrack – BUMP. And then a terrible sound like a giant's fart; and all the time the wind rose, and whirled those poor icy skeleton trees until they cracked again. It was awful to think of our poor old friends out there, the beech, the aspen, the ilex, and wonder which would be struck next. R. and I sat over the library fire, and while I tried to read he was finishing his review for the *New Statesman*. Then I got out my typewriter and typed what he had written. We were sitting thus, R. writing, I typing, at quarter to twelve when all the lights went out. We groped about in the kitchen, found some candles and took them to bed with us, where we lay for some time listening to that fearful, unceasing, shattering, Crrrash, BOOMP, Crrack.

'I believe this is Hitler's secret weapon,' said R. 'If it is, I surrender at once. I can't stand it.'

Frances Partridge

1943 [Leningrad]
The liquidation of the 6th German Army at Stalingrad is practically over.

Vera Inber

1943 [Kent]
On Monday – to meet someone who just takes you as you are – charming! – no fuss! We just walked on and on through the rain, down the muddy cow-smelling lane. The elms swayed and speared the misty wetness with their scarecrow fingers. We linked arms, walking tightly and neatly together. It was comfort and pleasure to walk in that tidy rhythm and to talk loudly and gaily about the blitz days.

I heard stories thrilling and gruesome about Portsmouth in those fires. My new friend said, 'I was in Civvy Street then. One morning I had just climbed over a huge pile of rubble (to get across to a shop, you see) when just behind me a terrible explosion took place. I was thrown on to my face and stunned, but when I came to I was only bruised. It was a time bomb, just across the street from me. Then there was the time when I came back from work and found the road near the aerodrome lined with fire engines. Three hundred and sixty five I counted. Three hundred and sixty five! Can you imagine it? I began to get the wind up. I hared home and had my tea, when, just as I'd put the last cup to my lips there was a terrible bang and tea went all over the floor. I ran to the front door and saw the sky all red, right across. It was just like a long sausage of lit-up sky.

'That night thousands of people were killed. One landmine did for two thousand in some shelters. But do you think the Government would tell the people beforehand that there was going to be a large scale raid? Not on your life! They knew about it, as was proved by all those fire engines down from London and God knows where. But they don't dare tell the people about the damage at Portsmouth. Talk about the people going out into the hills at night! Can you blame them? Hundreds of thousands went to the hillside nearby, then a landmine came down and blows most of them skyhigh. Can you beat it?'

We walked on, cosily talking of these horrors. It was so warming. We railed against the war and the blood spilt out. The rain came down thicker.

'Do you think there's any shelter here?' the soldier said.

'There might be a cattle byre or whatever you call it. Let's go on a little further and look.'

But there was nothing, so we sat on a fence under some trees and told each other our ages and what we could remember as small children. A car passed, a bicycle, and then another bicycle. Why can't we do this with strangers more often? Why can't we just talk and amuse each other a little without any necessity for intricate or lasting understanding? Why can't we just go for walks in the rain and come back pleased?

Denton Welch

1967 [Vietnam]

We have been damn busy the last two days. Fired off two missions against the VC [Vietcong], but nearly killed a squad of our own men when a mortar round landed forty metres from them. Their FO called for help, and in the next few minutes they were in more trouble from their own support than they were with the enemy. Somebody just goofed.

David Parks

29 January

1941 [London]

Talking to Christine [her cousin] and others I realise that by no means the whole population are engaged in the 'war effort' as one tended to think from the papers. Nor even wanting to. Quite a bit of normal life, quarrels and intrigue going on. Michael [cousin's husband] stationed in Ireland leading a childish kind of life, with no intellectual interests and a lot of drinking – nothing else to do.

Elizabeth [Pakenham] says that one of the refugee dons arrested and now released from the Isle of Man has kept a diary, showing exactly how all the internees quarrelled with one another, and the various grades; the Jews took it for granted that others were Jews too; and this don may or mayn't be but he took a copy of Homer with him and read it whenever possible – even so, one ringleted old boy came up and said: What a lovely Talmud! Quite a bit of anti-Semite feeling here, mostly against the middle-class refugees, partly from the south coast. None against the working-class ones from Coventry etc.

Naomi Mitchison

1944 [Tuscany]

The bombing of central Italy is increasing. Within the last three days Orvieto, Orte, Terni, Arezzo, Foiano, Siena, Poggibonsi, Potedera, Pontassieve, have all again been bombed. Yesterday a train, carrying Allied prisoners and civilians evacuated from Rome, was hit on the bridge of Alerona near Chiusi. The arches of the bridge were also hit, and some of the carriages plunged into the river: there were over four hundred dead and wounded. Such incidents, however horrible, are part of war. But the almost total destruction of a little town like Arezzo, including the districts furthest away from the railway – and of country churches, like the convento dell'Osservanze outside Siena – these, and the machine-gunning of the civilian population, cannot easily be explained. It is diffi-cult to believe that public opinion in England, if fully informed, would approve of all this.

Iris Origo

1945 [London]
Never read the diaries or impressions of men who have written in the fear of death, for their records cannot be honest.

James Lees-Milne

30 January

1871 [Paris]
In a newspaper giving the news of the capitulation, I read the news of King William's enthronement as Emperor of Germany at Versailles, in the Hall of Mirrors, under the nose of the stone Louis XIV in the courtyard outside. That really marks the end of the greatness of France.

The Brothers Goncourt

1915 [Moscow]
Preparations for my departure are well under way. I am breathlessly impatient to be off, but there is much to be done and the Unit itself is not yet fully organised. My nurse's dresses, aprons and veils have been made already, and I have bought a flannel-lined, black leather jacket. An accessory to this jacket is a thick sheepskin waistcoat, for winter wear, whose Russian name, *dushegreychka*, means 'soul warmer'. I hear our Unit will be stationed for a time on the Russo–Austrian Front in the Carpathian Mountains and that we will have to ride horseback, as direct communication can be established there only by riding; so high boots and black leather breeches have been added to my wardrobe.

At the moment of my departure, Anna Ivanovna, my Russian 'mother', bade me kneel before her. Taking from her pocket a little chain, she fastened it round my neck. Then she blessed me, kissed me three times, 'In the name of the Father, of the Son and of the Holy Spirit', and wished me 'God speed'. I, too, was a soldier, going to war, for thus did all Russian mothers to their soldier sons. The little chain, with a small icon and cross attached to it, has already been blessed by a priest.

Florence Farmborough

1941 [Germany]

Invited by the Görings to the Leipziger Platz. Hugo [her husband] could not get over the collection of paintings. Looted from everywhere he said afterwards. He is rather shocked. The Reich Marshal boasted that he had thirty-one Dürer sketches from Poland. 'But I pay for them. Don't listen to the rumours. I always pay.'

Elisabeth von Stahlenberg

1942 [Kovno Ghetto, Lithuania]

A Lithuanian policeman shot and killed the physician Dr. Zerah Gerber on a Ghetto street. The reason: the doctor did not remove his hat in the presence of the police, as required.

Avraham Tory

1943 [Tuscany]

The first refugee children have arrived. They were due yesterday evening at seven – after a twelve hours' journey from Genoa – but it was not until nine p.m. that at last the car drew up and seven very small sleepy bundles were lifted out. The eldest is six, the others four and five – all girls except one, a solemn little Sardinian called Dante Porcu. We carry them down into the play-room of the nursery-school (where the stove is burning, and supper waiting) and they stand blinking in the bright light, like small bewildered owls. White, pasty faces – several with boils and sores – and thin little sticks of arms and legs.

The Genoese district nurse who has brought them tells me that they have been chosen from families whose houses have been totally destroyed, and who, for the last two months, have been living in an underground tunnel beneath the city, without light or sufficient water, and in bitter cold. Their fathers are mostly dock-labourers; two of them have been killed.

The children eat their warm soup, still too bewildered fully to realize where they are – and then, as they gradually thaw and wake up, the first wail goes up 'Mamma, Mamma, I want my Mamma!' We hastily produce the toys which we have prepared for just this moment; the little girls clutch their dolls, Dante winds up his motor, and for a few minutes tears are averted. Then we take them upstairs and tuck them up in their warm beds. Homesickness sets in again – and two of them, poor babies, cry themselves to sleep.

Iris Origo

1944 [Amsterdam]
Dearest Kitty,
I have an intense need to be alone. Father has noticed I'm not my usual self, but I can't tell him what's bothering me. All I want to do is scream 'Let me be, leave me alone!' Who knows, perhaps the day will come when I'm left alone more than I'd like!

Anne Frank

31 January

1900 [Hampshire]
The last six months, and especially the last days at Plymouth, have been darkened by the nightmare of war. The horrible consciousness that we have, at the best, shown ourselves to be unscrupulous in methods, vulgar in manners and inefficient to the last degree, is an unpleasant background to all one's personal life – this thought is always present when one wakes in the night and returns to it every hour of the day. The Boers are, man for man, our superiors in dignity, devotion and capacity – yes, *in capacity*. That is the hardest of these admissions. It may be that conflict was inevitable. I incline to think it was. But that it should come about through muddy intrigues and capitalist pressure and that we should have shown ourselves incapable both in statesmanship and in generalship is humiliating.

I wonder whether we could take a beating and benefit by it. This would be the *real* test of the heart and brain of the English race; much more so than eventual success in a long and costly conflict. If we ultimately win, we shall forget the lessons. We shall say once again, 'We muddled through all right!'

Beatrice Webb

1939 [Irish Sea]
Today is a great day – a wonderful day. At dawn, even before darkness lifted, we could smell that wonderful smell of land, earth, long before we could see it. In the early dawn we slipped quietly into Loch Foyle. Immediately went alongside a British tanker where we filled our near-empty oil tanks brimming. Ireland looks beautiful. Guess any solid earth looks beautiful at a moment like this. We sailed twenty miles up Loch Foyle and at dusk tied up in Londonderry. Everyone busy buying fresh

cream, live chickens for packages of cigarettes. I headed ashore for the first time in Ireland – went along with Yearsley, and we wandered around in the blackout and rain, finally finding a chip shop where we had a feed of chips. Returned early – drew two pound casual.

Frank Curry, Royal Canadian Navy

1943 [Leningrad]

A story about the Party Secretary of the Public Library, last winter.

F. and another library worker went to a flat, where, according to their information, a little girl was said to be left.

In the flat it was dead and cold. It had the dreadful look of a flat of last year. F. and her companion were about to leave when all of a sudden it seemed to them that they could hear a faint sound of breathing.

'Someone is alive here,' said F., and approached the bed which was covered with rags. 'I'll hold the torch and you have a look,' F. said to her companion.

'No,' he replied. 'It's better if I hold it and you have a look.' Both of them were afraid.

But F. braved it. She threw back the tangled ice-cold blanket. An old man and an old woman were lying in the bed – both dead. In between them a pair of bright eyes shone from the pillow. It was their grandchild, a little girl of three or four years old.

F. took her home. She was covered with bed sores and lice. When she was washed she said:

'Give some porridge.'

She was fed and taken to hospital where everything possible was done for her but she died seventeen days later. Not even her name was fully established – Mashenka, or perhaps Ninotchka. In her diary, F. Calls her 'Ninochka-Mashenka.'

Vera Inber

FEBRUARY

Life meanwhile – real life, with its essential interests of health and sickness, toil and rest, and its intellectual interests in thought, science, poetry, music, love, friendship, hatred and passions – went on as usual, independently of and apart from political friendship or enmity with Napoleon Bonaparte . . .

Leo Tolstoy, *War and Peace*

1 February

1915 [London]

We went up to London – L.[eonard, her husband] to the London Library, I to Day's.[1] I walked with him across the Green Park. In St James Street there was a terrific explosion; people came running out of Clubs; stopped still and gazed about them. But there was no Zeppelin or aeroplane – only, I suppose, a very large tyre burst. But it is really an instinct with me, and most people, I suppose, to turn any sudden noise, or dark object in the sky, into an explosion or a German aeroplane. And it always seems utterly impossible that one should be hurt.

Virginia Woolf

1940 [France]

An excellent express of Julien Green's in *Le Figaro*, to denote the week that preceded the war: 'a catastrophe in *slow motion*'.

Jean-Paul Sartre

1942 [London]

It is only lately, as the world plays Götterdämmerung, that I have been lonely; it is a new and distressing emotion and I realise that it will perhaps be my future fate. Only a few years ago I was handsome, lustful, a favourite at Court, a protégé of Mr Chamberlain's, a millionaire, happy at the Foreign Office; now I am none of these things. So I will now go to bed and finish *Doctor Thorne*, which I am enjoying for the second time. I am still a tremendous Trollopian, whatever else I no longer am.

'Chips' Channon

1944 [Algiers]

We went to Hospital No.95. Incredible place, ex-boys' school, miles and miles of it, vaulted, monastic, cool in summer and cold right now. 2500 there. Far grimmer than 94. How lucky the boys were at Taplow

[1] Day's Library, a popular circulating library, mainly fiction, for fashionable women.

– air, light, space, newness and even gaiety. In the first ward (we did orthopaedics yesterday) there were two of the illest men I have ever seen, I think. Just skulls but with living wide, very clear eyes. It was a huge ward and difficult to know where to put the piano. We put it in the centre in the end which meant that I had to keep spinning round as I sang. I tried a monologue, but it was no good in there – too big, too decentralised. While I was walking around talking before we began I said to the illest of the two very ill ones that I hoped he'd excuse my back when I had to turn it on him and he said he would if I'd excuse him for not being shaved. Oh, gosh. [He died two days later.]

Joyce Grenfell

1991 [The Gulf]

The day was technically a rest day. I took the opportunity to sort out my kit in my flip-flops, my feet not having seen daylight for some time. Mid-morning we lined up for our second Anthrax jab and, horror of horrors, a Bubonic Plague jab. Bubonic Plague is one of the most infectious diseases known to man and, although it can now be cured, it must be treated within 12 hours of the first symptoms or it is invariably fatal. While Plague was on the menu of biological weapons, its use by the Iraqis was considered unlikely. The real risk was to unprotected Europeans entering enemy trenches and dugouts where troops had been living for months in what was assessed to be very unsanitary conditions. Bubonic Plague being endemic to the region, the risk of infection was considered very high. With little chance of meeting the 12-hour treatment deadline, the jab was a sensible precaution. Once again they were deep-muscle and hurt like hell. Again some of the troops were pole-axed for about 48 hours with flu-like symptoms and again, fortunately, I was fine.

Andrew Gillespie

1991 [Kuwait]

I haven't found enough time to write so much, so much passes away. The wounds of war pass, years of our lives pass, the lives of young people have gone for no return.

Iraq attacked Al-Khafg (Saudi Land): and the fighting is still going on. They are bombing our sites using planes and machine guns. There is no peace or liveliness in the world. I am dead. We were born dead.

Anonymous Iraqi soldier

2 February

1916 [Essex]

8.45 a.m. morning's post brought me a letter from my daughter, Mildred, 30:1:1916 – '. . . Miss Beattie in her duties as a censor in Danish at the War Office has discovered two spies. A St Andrews lady travelling to Newcastle was suspicious about a man in her carriage. Wired to York giving the name of the carriage – heard nothing till 6 months later she got a cheque for £100 from the War Office "for information received".'

Andrew Clark

1940 [London]

The snow remains, slightly pocked, but the road is clear. I forgot to make extracts from the papers, which boom, echoing, emptily, the BBC. Hitler's speech – Churchill's – a ship sunk – no survivors – a raft capsized – men rowing for ten or twelve or thirty hours. How little one can explode now, as perhaps one would have done, had it been a single death. But the Black Out is far more murderous than the war. Prices rise by twopence then threepence. So the screw tightens gradually; and I can't even imagine London in peace – the lit nights, the buses roaring past Tavistock Square, the telephone ringing, and I scooping together with the utmost difficulty one night or afternoon alone. Only the fire sets me dreaming – of all the things I mean to write: the break in our lives from London to country is a far more complete one than any change of house. Odd how often I think with what is love I suppose of the City: of the walk to the Tower: that is my England; I mean, if a bomb destroyed one of those little alleys with the brass bound curtains and the river smell and the old women reading I should feel – well, what the patriots feel.

Virginia Woolf

1991 [Ramallah]

9.15 a.m. I opened the window after I took my shower. The sky was a soft blue, cloudless, and the sun was sparkling on the droplets of water caught in the leaves of the olive trees. I heard the army announcing, 'Mamnoo et Tajawul hatta ishar akler' (It is forbidden to leave the house until further notice).

Raja Shehadeh

3 February

1940 [England]

There is snow everywhere. The little paths cut through it are strewn with ashes. All very ugly and sad. On my table is a bowl of *Iris reticulata*. Those gay and fragile flowers remind me of the life that existed before 3rd September [the day war was declared]. It is as if some apoplectic dimly remembered the days before he had his stroke.

Harold Nicolson

1943 [Germany]

Such a shock today.[1] I was listening to the radio – when the programme was broken into, for a special announcment. There was a roll of drums, which made my heart feel quite cold. Then they played the second movement of Beethoven's Fifth Symphony (one of the few things I recognise!) and then it was announced *We have been overcome*. I couldn't believe it. Hugo held me and said it was a terrible set-back, but it was only one battle lost in so many victories. We can't be expected to have it all our own way all the time.

But it is such an *important* victory. Hitler knows. There are to be four days of national mourning – cinemas are to be closed.

Elisabeth von Stahlenberg

1944 [Algiers]

One of the very ill men in the first ward we did [a show] on Monday died that night. I wish I could tell his family how he smiled and even sang with us the day before he died. Tuesday was the hardest day we've done so far because of the tents. The courtyards of [Hospital No.] 95 have enormous dark brown marquees in them holding about sixty beds. They are narrow, ill-lit and their acoustic properties are exactly nil. However, the need for entertainment in these surroundings was obvious, and it turned out that no one ever does sing in the tents, so we said we'd go. I tried standing in the middle, walking up and down, standing at one end. It was equally bad wherever we went, but even so the programme was welcomed and we got them singing FF [fortissimo] for ages. Such nice sisters in both tents. One, Barr, with a face like a friendly balloon, egg-shaped, had been torpedoed

---

[1] German forces had capitulated at Stalingrad.

coming out – I think they both had, now I come to think about it. The very matter of fact account the pretty little Scots sister gave of it over our tea and egg sandwiches was the more sensational because of its understatement.

'We held hands in the water,' she said, and 'Oh, it *does* feel funny when a depth-charge goes off and you're floating about near by.'

Joyce Grenfell

4 February

1915 [England]

A wealthy maltster called to tell me all he knew about spies and suspects. He said there was nothing of the sort, and all he could speak of were one or two people afflicted with 'cussedness' – people who would argue that the English were no good and that the Germans must win, etc. He saw this cussedness in various forms all over the country. I agreed. But he said that it was all due to the abolition of flogging. He brought ingenious old arguments in support of flogging. The chief was that if you fined or imprisoned a man you punished his wife and children. Whereas if you flogged him you punished him and the thing was over at once. He got quite excited on this subject, and could scarcely leave. A quiet, nervous man – public school, etc.

Arnold Bennett

1938 [Spain]

Yesterday a poor man was looking for his brother who died here three months ago. As they are unnamed, he had to disinter a hundred and twenty three-month-old corpses. In the end he never found his brother. Horrid, sordid, part of the war.

Priscilla Scott-Ellis

1942 [Rome]

Göring is leaving Rome. We had dinner at the Excelsior Hotel, and during dinner Göring talked only about the jewels he possesses. In fact, he had some beautiful rings on his fingers. He explained that he bought them for a relatively small sum in Holland after all jewels were confiscated in Germany. I am told that he plays with his gems like a little boy with his marbles. During the trip he was nervous, so his aides brought him a small cup filled with diamonds. He placed them on the table and counted them, lined them up, mixed them together, and was happy again. One of his top officers said yesterday evening: 'He has two loves – beautiful objects and making war.' Both are expensive hobbies. He wore a great sable coat to the station, something between what automobile drivers wore in 1906 and what a high-flying prostitute wears to the opera. If any of us tried something like that we would be stoned in the streets. He, on the contrary, is not only accepted in Germany but perhaps even loved for it. That is because he has a dash of humanity.

Count Ciano

1944 [on board USS *Montpelier*, in the Pacific]
Some of the men must be coming 'Asiatic', they have holes drilled into their ears and put a ring through it. It didn't last long as they put a stop to it.

James J. Fahey, Seaman First Class

1991 [Kuwait]
I was listening to news from Iran's broadcasting station. Earlier I was listening to news from the Voice of America and the BBC. I listened although I know the news wasn't true because both countries belong to those against us in this ongoing war. They know we are listening to them so they try to undermine our morale. But how absurd . . .

I wish I could drink the blood of those infidels. My hatred increased since they bombed civilians and buildings where my family is living nearby.

Because I know nothing of my family my grudge against them is bigger. I wish they would start their ground war, whatever the consequences might be. Anyway, I am waiting for this hour to happen every day. Whether I like it or not it is bound to happen so we'll see . . . God supports the oppressed.

Anonymous Iraqi soldier

5 February

1916 [France]
A memorable day. Brilliant sunlight and sailing white clouds all the morning. About 12.30 a German aeroplane came over and our anti-

aircraft guns let off about two hundred shells – little puffs of white hanging aloft, dispersing slowly while the big hawk forged ahead and then turned and went back, superb and insolent. After lunch rode across to the Citadel under the same blue weather, startling the hares and partridges across the fallows and wheatlands, to find our batteries busily booming away at the Huns who had been playing hell with the trenches occupied by R.W.F. [Royal Welch Fusiliers]. Got there at 4.30, and had some trouble getting up to C. Company and the front line, as the communication-trenches were very much knocked about. Found Greaves, Stansfield, Orme,[1] and Wadd all serene, and no one hurt, though they had been peppered with trench-mortars etc from 8.30 to 3.30, I left them at 7.45, when all the stars were out and the young moon on her back, and an owl flitting across the trenches. Through the dusk came the loud rattle of Hun machine-gun fire on the left; the sky roared unheeding of the war-lines, and the trenches ankle-deep in wet clay, and men grimly peering from under their round steel caps. The mare brought me home straight as a die across the four miles of plough and mud – gloom all around and stars, stars, overhead, and hanging low above the hills – the rockets going up behind, along the line – brief lights soon burnt out – the stars wheeling changeless and untroubled, life and deathless beauty, always the same contrast. So I still see the war as a looker-on; catching a glimpse of the grim places, and then ride back to village lights and evening talk with old Cotterill and the interpreter. But my time will come – never doubt it.

Siegfried Sassoon

1941 [Tuscany]

The following anecdote told by Gide in his *Journal* is rather comforting. In World War I, a German officer in occupied France was shopping when a woman came in with a baby in her arms. It seemed to have no hands but only two stumps. The officer jumped to the conclusion that they had been cut off, and rushed out of the shop crying out in despair: 'Then it is true, it is true that we have cut off children's hands.' As a matter of fact the baby was born like that.

Bernard Berenson

---

[1] E.L. Greaves, N. Stansfield, E.O. Orme became the characters Barton, Mansfield and Ormond in Sassoon's *Memoirs of an Infantry Officer*.

1944 [Naples]

There have been newspaper accounts of urban buses seen careering away into the remote fastness of the Apennines, there to be reduced in comfort to their component parts. Trams, left where they had come to a standstill when the departing Germans wrecked the generating station, have been spirited away in the night. A railway engine, stranded in open country owing to the looting of rails and sleepers, was driven off when these rails and sleepers were quite incredibly relaid, to a place more discreetly located for its demolition.

No feat, according to the newspapers, and to public rumour, both of which dwell with great delight on such flamboyant acts of piracy, is too outrageous for this new breed of robber. In the region of Agropoli small ships left unguarded have been lifted out of the water and mysteriously transported away, and portions of their superstructures have later been discovered miles inland, hidden in orchards as if they had been carried there and left high and dry by some tidal wave. In revenge, said the newspaper reporting this case, a party of fishermen raided an isolated castle in the area and went off with tapestries which they used to repair their sails.

Nothing has been too large or too small – from telegraph poles to phials of penicillin – to escape the Neapolitan kleptomania. A week or two ago an orchestra playing at the San Carlo to an audience largely clothed in Allied hospital blankets, returned from a five-minute interval to find all its instruments missing. A theoretically priceless collection of Roman cameos was abstracted from the museum and replaced by modern imitations, the thief only learning – so the reports go – when he came to dispose of his booty that the originals themselves were counterfeit. Now the statues are disappearing from the public squares, and one cemetery has lost most of its tombstones. Even the manhole covers have been found to have marketable value, so that suddenly these too have all gone, and everywhere there are holes in the road.

Norman Lewis

1944 [Algiers]

Harold [Macmillan] is a revelation to me. At home I would, having only *looked* at him, have said he was worthy and dull; without humour and heavy. Can it be the Algerian air or was I always wrong? He turns out to be a character of charm, understanding, wit, kindliness and an endearing small-boy type. Last night he told us about an official morning call he went to pay on de Gaulle. As it was no distance to the de Gaulle villa Harold, in his old grey flannel suit, walked down the hill. When he entered the gates a fanfare of soprano French bugles blew at him. Rather surprised, he look around to see who it was for and then realised it honoured him. He was interesting about de Gaulle. Says the reason Winston and F.D.R. [Franklin D. Roosevelt] don't like him is that he is very nearly the same calibre as themselves and they resent it. Undoubtedly a really big man, H. says. He is sensitive and devout (very) and completely soaked in the tragedy of France. He cannot forget for an instant. Unlike Giraud[1] who is the lightweight type and can be gay as a butterfly at dinners and fêtes while his wife and daughters languish in German hands. He says de Gaulle is very like a Highlander – single-minded, melancholy, sentimental, slow to move but powerful; with a deep fire and strong wit. I'd like to meet him, I must say.

Joyce Grenfell

1944 [Florence]

A good deal of firing during the night. Generally it is merely the younger Fascists letting off pistols for fun (but occasionally hitting someone) – but last night a militiaman, who was leaning on the embankment of the Arno looking at the river, received two revolver bullets in his neck from a man passing by on a bicycle. The oddest story circulating in Florence is that a meeting took place in the Grand Hotel a few days ago between the German military and civil authorities to discuss, in cold blood, whether or not the city (when the time comes to retreat) shall be sacked. The Consul and other civilian officials were said to be against the looting, the soldiers in favour. The ultimate decision is not known, but it is certain that, at the present rate, there won't be much left to be sacked, as all that is left in the shops is systematically being taken off to Germany.[2] Ugolini, for instance, told me that in the last few days ninety-six thousand lire worth of woollen goods has been removed from his shop – and as

---

[1] General Henri Giraud, a five-star general whom the Americans were backing (unsuccessfully) to take over as leader of the Free French in North Africa, from the two-star de Gaulle.

[2] The Florentines had actually hidden large quantities of goods which reappeared in the shops when the Allies arrived in the city.

he spoke a large lorry was going down Via Tornabuoni, collecting goods from each shop in turn. Some of these goods are, theoretically, paid for – with enormous quantities of paper money, specially printed in the Vienna Mint, of which every German soldier carries great rolls in his belt.

Iris Origo

6 February

1941 [Lewes, England]
Jean Massey came in with a good story. Count Ciano,[1] who married Mussolini's daughter Edda, came to Mussolini in great distress saying: 'Edda's in bed with peritonitis'. Mussolini: 'Those damned Greeks are everywhere.'

Mrs Henry Dudeney

1941 [Holland]
Today I wasn't in the best of moods. A little disappointed in myself. I went to visit Miep who didn't go to school because she wasn't well. A friend of theirs has been arrested. We're all supposed to register, we can't postpone it any longer, and I guess we'll get a 'J' stamped on our papers. Anyway. Whatever happens, happens. I don't want to think about it too much. Letter from Guus,[2] dated December. He's so happy there, he's turning into a real American. Only he misses us, of course, but he says he thinks the country is even more beautiful and wonderful than our own lovely little country. Then it must be pretty special! He describes all sorts of domestic appliances, butter, tinned goods, advertisements, the bright lights, etc. and we meanwhile sitting here in the dark, simply drooling over his descriptions of the good life over there . . .

Edith Velmans

[1] Count Galezzo Ciano, an Italian diarist and politician in charge of fascist propaganda before becoming foreign minister, a post he held from 1936 until 1943 when he was tried and executed on charges of betraying his father-in-law, Mussolini, whom he planned to poison.
[2] Her brother, who had been a sickly child, had got a year's deferment of his military service to go to work in his father's timber company in America.

7 February

1917 [England]
At home again – for the last time before I go back to the unmitigated hell of 'the spring offensive'.

Siegfried Sassoon

1942 [Lewes, England]
Mrs Jervis said there was a perfect *famine* in elastic and that I had better go to Mitchell's – the only shop that had any – early on Monday. Newspaper says that the Japanese are now scattering plague germs and dropping infected rats. Talk about Hell! We are living in it!

Mrs Henry Dudeney

1991 [The Gulf]
Brigadier Christopher Hammerbeck talked to all the Officers of the Regiment. He spoke of the likelihood of war, about what to expect and the importance of preparing ourselves mentally for what might lie ahead. I particularly remember he laid great emphasis on writing a last letter home, to be held safely and sent to our loved ones should we be killed. There and then I determined that I would do no such thing. I could not imagine myself able to put on paper any words that would adequately express my feelings to Annie and the children. Besides there appeared a degree of defeatism in the gesture and in times of real desperation the knowledge that I had left such a letter might just be enough to make me give up.

Andrew Gillespie

8 February

1864 [Virginia]
I am a soldier, or at least that is what I was drafted for in the 6th USCI; have been in the service since Aug., last. I could not afford to get a substitute, or I would not be here now and my poor wife at home almost starving. When I was at home I could make a living for her and my two little ones; but now that I am a soldier they must do the best they can or starve. It almost tempts me to desert

and run a chance of getting shot, when I read her letters, hoping that I would come to her relief. But what am I to do? It is a shame the way they treat us; our officers tell me now that we are not soldiers; that if we were we would get the same pay as the white men; that the government just called us to dig and drudge, that we are to get but $7.00 pr month. Really I thought I was a soldier, and it made me feel somewhat proud to think that I had a right to fight for Uncle Sam. When I was at Chelton Hill I felt very patriotic; but my wife's letters have brought my patriotism down to the freezing point, and I don't think it will ever rise again; and it is the case all through the regiment. Men having families at home, and they looking to them for support, and they not being able to send them one penny.

Anon, 6th United States Colored Infantry

1942 [Buckinghamshire]

After dinner I took up my knitting – 'the true sock' Clementine[1] calls it, which on St Milne's Day, instead of liquefying, will unravel if there is to be a good harvest. Cecil[2] had hiccoughs he laughed so much. Eddy[3] took up his knitting, an endless khaki scarf. We were sitting side by side on a pair of upright Chinese Chippendale chairs before the fire, Eddy wearing his blue cloak with silver buckles, and his red velvet waistcoat with the Sackville coachman's gold livery buttons. I suppose we were an odd spectacle. Still, I wish Helen[4] would not call us the two old bombed houses.

James Lees-Milne

1945 [Bergen-Belsen]

I had hung my coat in a cupboard. Someone has stolen the buttons.

Abel J. Herzberg

1991 [Saudi Arabia]

One funny thing that goes on all the time over here is how much

---

[1] Clementine Beit, nee Mitford, was a cousin of the Mitford sisters, and was married to Sir Alred Beit, art collector and sometime Conservative MP.
[2] Cecil Beaton, famous photographer and diarist.
[3] Hon. Edward Sackville-West, novelist, critic and musician.
[4] Wife of Sir John Dashwood, whose house in Buckinghamshire, West Wycombe Park, was the wartime HQ for the National Trust.

everybody tries to live up to images they have of what it must have been like in Vietnam.

Troops are constantly getting chewed out by the Staff NCOs and NCOs for walking around with bandanas on their heads, like Bunny in *Platoon*, and it seems that every outfit or unit I run into has some-body in it with a nickname like Swede or Animal Mother. Everybody, troops and officers, loves to look the look, walk the walk, and talk the talk of their heroes in 'the Nam'. Which is where this all comes from. We listen to the same music, write the same shit on our helmets, and talk the same shit that we've heard on the TV, radio, and on the movies for the past fifteen years.

Sean T. Couglin

1991 [Kuwait]

Everybody is waiting. Everybody goes on leave. I can count the ones who return on my fingers. Some go without leave and never come back, and everybody is waiting. I've heard nothing about my family and they've heard nothing about me for exactly 30 days since I joined my regiment. Both the news broadcasts and those who come back from leave say that our home district, Al-Amyria, is being showered with bombs and rockets because it is near strategic targets.

Anonymous Iraqi soldier

9 February

1940 [Italy]

In general, the man who is readily disposed to sacrifice himself is one who does not know how else to give meaning to his life.

Cesare Pavese

1941 [POW camp, Germany]

Last night's rumour of thousands of parcels was apparently true – except that they were all for Obermassfeld. But however disappointing it may be for us, I'm extremely glad this hospital is at last getting them, as they have had a rotten time. Wounds were taking twice as long to heal because the patients hadn't the food to build up on. Hunger must have cost hundreds of lives. However, tho' no food parcels, we hear there are 21 smoke ones – and smoke is half the battle. It is extraordinary, looking round the room during meals the number of backs which are now rounded. Anybody sitting with a straight back looks enormous. I suppose due to hard benches and stools. How odd it will seem to sit in an armchair again.

Captain John Mansel

1991 [Ramallah]
Father's words have been coming back to mind: 'What power do you have? Where will your moral arguments take you?'

Nowhere. We're into the fourth week of almost continuous curfew. Yet who has spoken? And who can stop them?

The military today called the municipal and village councils and ordered them to begin recruiting groups of 150 men for every district of their towns and villages to handle emerging situations. They asked them to designate an area of land in every town and village for mass graves. Then they told them they must have bulldozers ready to carry out the digging.

The 'mass graves' are now the talk of the town.

Raja Shehadeh

10 February

1943 [Tuscany]
The second batch of children has now arrived: six little girls from Turin. They are older than the Genoa children – eight to ten-year-olds – and much more self-possessed; but they show more clearly the effects of what they have been through. One of them, Nella, is suffering from a mild form of 'St. Vitus' dance'; another, Liberata, has sudden fainting-fits. All are very nervy and easily become hysterical. But all – the 'big girls' from Turin and the 'little ones' from Genoa – are quite astonishingly well-behaved. We have had, of course, to struggle with their hair (some of them had had their heads shaved), but otherwise their 'habits' contrast most favourably with what I have heard of the little evacuees in English villages – and their manners are charming. All of them have had their homes destroyed by air-raids – and most of them have parents working in the Turin factories, and fully realize that they will be bombed again. At post time they hurry up to the *fattoria* – and if for three days one of them has no letter, they go about with white, pitiful faces. Each child has at

once had a medical examination and is now under the district nurse's daily care – the older ones go to the school next door, the little ones do some nursery-school lessons with their own teacher. I have written long letters to each of their mothers, and we have taken a photograph of them to send home. Perhaps later on, their mothers will be able to come to see them.[1]

Iris Origo

1944 [London]
Bertie van Thal[2] is getting more and more like Tenniel's Dormouse. Showed me his War diary, pretending that it is modelled on *Ego* [Agate's diaries]. Here is the enchanting beginning:

May 1, 1941. The season has opened brilliantly with the death of old Lady Tweedle . . .

James Agate

1991 [The Gulf]
A parcel was waiting for me when I arrived back at the Battlegroup. It was marked 'British Embassy Riyadh' and was from Ginnie Sincock, the wife of the Defence Attaché. It contained a couple of films, a book, some tea bags, some tapes (Paul Simon and Elkie Brooks) and, best of all, some fresh dates from her garden. That evening [Lance Bombardier] Witt collected me and took me back to A2 to watch the family video sent out from Münster. The video had been made by Captain Peter Doyle, our families officer, and its arrival had been awaited with great expectation. For me the journey to A2 was a three-hour round trip while some from the fun batteries had walked miles in the dark for the viewing. As we sat expectantly in the darkened tent most must have thought, as I did, that perhaps we were seeing our loved ones for the last time. As we peered intently to catch sight of a wife or a child there was a succession of giggling women, some refusing to say anything, some with a garbled message or worse, and some with their hands over their faces saying 'I don't want to be filmed.' There was a brief clip with John, my son, but only a brief glimpse of Annie and my daughter Kate at the back of the crowd. I will never forget the awful, almost overpowering feeling

---

[1] They did, and this led to other brothers and sisters being sent out to join them.
[2] Herbert van Thal, editor of Agate's diaries.

of disappointment that descended in that tent when finally the video ended. Many sat around in depressed silence, others just walked off into the darkness.

Andrew Gillespie

11 February

1939 [Atlantic]
Still (I repeat still) smooth as smooth. Grand warm sun came out and poured down on us all this long day. If you were trying to convince anyone back home that winter in the north Atlantic was not exactly a picnic, you would have a tough time today. Seems more like a summer cruise in the Caribbean. But we are not complaining a bit . . .

Frank Curry, Royal Canadian Navy

1940 [Dresden]
Everywhere there are prison sentences for listening to enemy broadcasts. Reason: The nation must be protected from the subversive poison of lies. In the *Freiheitskampf* they are now threatening the death sentence for listening illegally.

Victor Klemperer

12 February

1864 [Wisconsin]
Tonight I volunteered for duty with the 26th Regiment Wis. Infantry Volunteers for 3 years or duration of the war.

Pvt Frederick C. Buerstatte, 26th Regiment, Wisconsin Volunteers

1939 [Atlantic]
Does not take it long to change. This morning it is rather rough and much, much, colder. Guess we have moved out of the Gulf Stream and are now getting closer to the dear shores of Newfoundland. Feeling in an awful mood, and thought I would go raving mad on the 2400–0400 watch. Staggered through it somehow.

Frank Curry, Royal Canadian Navy

1940 [Berlin]
Frau [. . .]¹ visits me this afternoon. We see the American Disney film *Snow White*, a magnificent artistic achievement. A fairy tale for grown-ups, thought out into the last detail and made with a great love of humanity and nature. An artistic delight!

Josef Goebbels

13 February

1966 [The White House]
Tonight Lyndon talked about his trip to Hawaii. He'd been greatly impressed with [General William] Westmoreland, actually rather impressed with Ky.² He talked about some of 'our side' of the story of what happens in Vietnam which, for some reason, never seems to get in print. For instance, how our expert medical service, plus the boon of helicopters, makes it possible to get to a wounded man within an hour, and get him into a hospital in not longer than three hours, which so greatly reduces fatalities among the wounded.

He talked about the SEATO Treaty, which had been passed by the Senate in February 1955, 82 to 1; Langer was the one against it. Incidentally, Johnson and Kennedy did not vote. Lyndon was in Mayo Clinic having a kidney stone operation and Senator Kennedy was absent with his serious back trouble. 'Now,' Lyndon said, 'we are trying to carry out the contracts they made.' We were discussing the debate in the country, on the Vietnam policy, as opened up by the debate in the Senate. At lunch, Lafayette Park had been full of picketers. The White House was picketed 166 times last year. Lyndon said, 'This thing is assuming dangerous proportions, dividing the country and giving our enemies the wrong idea of the will of this country to fight.'

One looks at the bombing pause in retrospect – those thirty-seven days when we were hopefully setting the stage for peace or for getting together at the conference table – running all over the world, asking everybody to join in peace efforts. Was it a good idea or not? As of today, one doubts it, but I still believe that it's a

¹ Unnamed female friend.
² Nguyen Coa Ky, an official of the Vietnamese Government.

national proof of going the last mile, being willing to make every effort.

Lady Bird Johnson

1991 [The Gulf]

With the mail came a small brown 'Jiffy' bag with German postage stamps. It was from Herr Peter Arnotl, the historian at the Hanoverian Regiment that had fought alongside The Rocket Troop[1] at the Battle of The Nations in 1813. To wish us luck in whatever was to come, Peter had sent a small flat piece of pine wood. It had been cut especially from a tree at Taucha, outside the city of Leipzig, the scene of The Rocket Troop's great battle.

By early evening the temperature had changed from oppressive heat to bitter cold. After the routine evening Orders Group I made my way over to the 432 [a tank]. The crew had built a Trivial Pursuit board, having brought only the cards with them from Germany. After three successful games in a row, I was banned from playing. I whiled away the rest of the evening sitting on the engine decks watching the flashes to our north and the flickering glow to our east which, I surmised, were the Kuwait oil wells burning.

Andrew Gillespie

14 February

1941 [POW camp, Germany]

How sick and tired I am of the nightly visitors' excited entry with 'What's the news?' As if we knew any. To make matters worse I heard somebody in the room talking defeatism – 'if we lose' and 'when we lose'. Slaving in salt mines in Silesia, etc. Hell, one tries to think of home, etc., to keep cheerful if possible, but it would drive one permanently mental if one had to contend with defeatism. Actually, I think half of us, if not the majority, are slowly going mental – tho' *we* think we're sane.

Captain John Mansel

---

[1] Gillespie commanded O Battery of the 2nd Field Regiment Royal Artillery, who were known as The Rocket Troop.

1991 [Kuwait]
Today my pen dried. The ink no longer exists, likewise, my family if
God is not merciful to them. The shelter which was bombed in Amyria
is near our home. I doubt that my family was not at home during the
bombing. Yesterday didn't sleep. Not a wink of sleep. My rage intensified so much that it blinded me. So I couldn't wake up tidy from my
nap.

I swore by God to take revenge for my family – the most horrible
kind of revenge. If I survive I will make all the attackers meat for the
vultures. By God, I swear that my mind will never find rest until I have
revenge for the blood that was shed. May the West die! May the cowards
who are with them die too. Allah, Allah! My God, I rely on you. I
beg you to be kind to them. God is the Most Merciful of those who
show mercy.

Anonymous Iraqi soldier

15 February

1944 [Tuscany]
Yesterday the Abbey of Monte Cassino, fourteen centuries old, was
destroyed by Allied bombs – to the accompaniment of a flood of
radio propaganda from both sides. The Allies state that they refrained
from damaging the Abbey until the Germans began to use it as an
armed fortress; the Germans deny it. The Abbot states that German
soldiers came out of the ruins; the Germans, that the Abbot, some
of the monks, and many refugee women and children from the
town below, were still there. Most of the precious library has been
saved.

Iris Origo

16 February

1940 [near Coventry]
Up today at 11.30 and it was cold but not freezing. Florence and Jack
went out to deliver packets of seeds – my duty as Secretary of the
Women's Institute – all around this district. Every kind of small house
and cottage had to be visited and the wonderfully comprehensive packet

of Sutton's seeds delivered. They are only 2s. 6d. – a special price – though containing every ordinary vegetable seed, perfectly packed and labelled.

The news of the Finns is not good. They are worn out with this giant remorseless power of Russia against them. Who can help them? The Swedes have decided not to help by sending soldiers to fight, though volunteers are already there. It is so difficult to get to them, though we have sent aeroplanes, medical supplies, ambulances, clothes and money, and still they cry in their agony: 'If help does not come soon . . .'

Clara Milburn

1944 [London]
News has come of the bombing of the Monte Cassino monastery. This is comparable with the German shelling of Rheims cathedral in the last war. No war-mindedness can possibly justify it.

James Lees-Milne

17 February

1824 [Missolonghi, Greece]
Upon February 15th – (I write on the 17th of the same month) I had a strong shock of a Convulsive description but whether Epileptic Paralytic – or Apoplectic is not yet decided by the two medical men who attend me – or whether it be of some other nature (if such there be) it was very painful and had it lasted a moment longer must have extinguished my mortality – if I can judge by sensations – I was speechless with the features much distorted – but *not* foaming at the mouth – they say – and my struggles so violent that several persons – two of whom – Mr Parry the Engineer – and my Servant Tita the Chasseur are very strong men – could not hold me – it lasted about ten minutes – and came on immediately after drinking a tumbler of Cider mixed with cold water in Col Stanhope's apartments. – This is the first attack that I have had of this kind to the best of my belief. I never heard that any of my family were liable to the same – though my mother was subject to *hysterical* affections. Yesterday (the 16th) Leeches were applied to my temples. I had previously recovered a good deal – but with some feverish and variable symptoms; – I bled profusely – and as they went too near the temporal Artery – there

was some difficulty in stopping the blood – even with the Lunar Caustic – this however after some hours was accomplished about eleven o'clock at night – and this day (the 17th) though weakly I feel tolerably convalescent. –

With regard to the presumed cause of this attack – as far as I know there might be several – the state of the place and of the weather permits little exercise at present; – I have been violently agitated with more than one passion recently – and a good deal occupied politically as well as privately – and amidst conflicting parties – politics – and (as far as regards public matters) circumstances; – I have also been in an anxious state with regard to things which may be only interesting to my own private feelings – and perhaps not uniformly so temperate as I may generally affirm that I was wont to be – how far any or all of these may have acted on the mind or body of One who had already undergone many previous changes of place and passion during a life of thirty-six years I cannot tell – nor – but I am interrupted by the arrival of a report from a party returned from reconnoitring a Turkish Brig of War just stranded on the Coast – and which is to be attacked the moment we can get some guns to bear upon her. – I shall hear what Parry says about it – here he comes.

Lord Byron

1991 [The Gulf]

Another maintenance day, warm and sunny, but still very windy, so sand was everywhere. The news was that, although they had deployed, the British guys had not fired. No reason was given. All very puzzling! Rumour control had it that the area of deployment had not been fully cleared. Of what? By whom? The Intelligence brief could add nothing further. The Americans had cut over twenty 100-metre breaches in the sand walls in the 'neutral' area as part of their preliminary operations, but had suffered a disastrous 'blue on blue' in the dark. First reports indicated that an Apache helicopter had destroyed two vehicles, killing some of the crew. Just before the enemy Orders Groups we received word that fresh rations had arrived at Al Echelon and so promptly despatched a foraging party. Earlier, the driving rain had given way to drizzle. With less wind noise I attempted to make a tape recording to Annie and the children, to dispatch with the Paymaster. Just as I finished, disaster struck. I dropped the machine in the sand. Two hours of solid cleaning failed to get rid of the scratching and grinding from the mechanism.

The wing Orders Group did nothing to enlighten anyone as to what was happening. We were once again living for the hourly World Service news broadcasts. Spirits went up and down with each broadcast and it was becoming a real strain. Orders over, I made my way back to the crew. The fresh rations had been a bit of a lottery but welcome none the less; beef-burgers and some bread but mostly pork chops and sausages. The optimists chirped that they were clearing the larders at Al Jubayl in order to feed Moslem prisoners, while the more pragmatic Mancunian wits retorted that it was simply our last meal of pork before we were captured.

Andrew Gillespie

18 February

1940 [London]
A. P. Herbert [barrister and writer] on the radio last night made timely, if somewhat scathing, reference to the growing tendency of Whitehall to what in glib official language might be described as verbal circumlocution, i.e., simple statements wrapt up in high-falutin language that not only confuses and irritates plain folk but often defeats its object, wastes paper as well as words, and stamps the author as a verbal snob. If Nelson's immortal signal had been written by one of our fat word-breeders in Whitehall, Herbert said, it would probably have read, 'England anticipates that with regard to the current emergency, personnel will duly implement their obligations in accordance with the functions allocated to their respective age groups.'[1] Mr Churchill had shown, he added, that it was unnecessary to speak of big things in 'long woolly words'.

Walter Musto

1940 [France]
Civilian's view. Madame X says to my mother: 'They shouldn't allow them any leave really, because they'll only go back with lower morale.'

Jean-Paul Sartre

[1] At the Battle of Trafalgar, Nelson said: 'England expects every man will do his duty.'

19 February

1836 [The Alamo]

We are all in high spirits, though we are rather short of provisions for men who have appetites that could digest anything but oppression; but no matter, we have a prospect of soon getting our bellies full of fighting.

Davy Crockett

1938 [Spain]

A hard day's work at the hospital. We never stopped all day. Ten operations: 6 stomach wounds, 3 heads, one arm amputation and one man who was wounded in the lungs who died on the stretcher before they could operate on him. We had just got back from a hasty lunch of fried potatoes and foul tinned meat and found him on a stretcher obviously dying. Consuelo sent for the priest to give him the Last Sacrament and we could do nothing at all, just sat around miserably watching him die. He was unconscious and as pale as a sheet. We looked through this pockets to see if there was any address of his family to write to, but only found one pathetic crumpled letter from his fiancée saying that, after all the difficulties there had been with his family, when he came back from the war they would let them marry and how happy they would be. It was pathetic reading it with him dying at our feet. As there was no address we couldn't even write to tell her what had happened to him. The worst was that there was a hurry to start operating on another, the *capitan*, who is a brute, got angry and told them to take him away to the mortuary for the dead and the man was still living. Suppose he came to life to find himself just thrown anyhow amongst the dead corpses or burned alive. It must happen to lots of them.

Priscilla Scott-Ellis

20 February

1918 [London]

We now ask nearly everyone whom we ask to dinner to bring some food. On Saturday I finished off the proofs of *The Pretty Lady*. I can now see things that I have left out of that novel. Nevertheless the story well held me as I read it again – a good test.

Arnold Bennett

1940 [France]

Klein's wife, a nurse at the Strasbourg hospital, which has been moved a few kilometres back from the front, goes down with a sudden attack of appendicitis. But there's only one surgeon in this mixed hospital, where they treat both civilians and soldiers – and his situation is somewhat odd. Disabled and declared unfit for service, he's not been called up, though very young, he has been requisitioned. This makes him very gloomy, moreover: if he was an MO, he'd get army pay; as a civilian, he operates all day long for the army – and for nothing. For every operation he has to request authorisation from the military command. He examines Mme Klein and decides on an urgent emergency operation. But the authorisation takes 48 hours to come through and Mme Klein dies on the operating table.

Jean-Paul Sartre

1941 [Dresden]

The next blow to be expected is the confiscation of the typewriter. There is one way of safeguarding it. It would have to be lent to me by an Aryan owner. There is Frau Voss' curious friend Frau Paul. Her second marriage was a very happy one to a Jewish businessman, she is now having a very unpleasant divorce trial with her third husband, an Aryan teacher. She would very much like to help me; she is *afraid* because of the trial. Everyone is afraid of arousing the least suspicion of being friendly to Jews, the fear seems to grow all the time.

Victor Klemperer

1943 [Germany]

Eva Braun telephoned and asked me to have lunch with her in the Osteria. She was more het-up than I've ever seen her – about the ban on cosmetic production! And permanent wave apparatus! I couldn't care less about the last – I'm growing my hair again, I've decided I'd like to be able to put it up – but I wouldn't be able to *exist* without lipstick. She says she is going to speak to 'Adolf' about it. 'I've never interfered with anything before, but this time I'm going to have my say.'

Elisabeth von Stahlenberg

1966 [The White House]

Lyndon talked about Vietnam – in fact, this is about two thirds of what we talk about these days. He talked about the individual feelings of every mother who has a son in Vietnam, and in comparison, about his feelings. He said, 'There's not a mother in the world who cares more about it than I do, because I have two hundred thousand of them over there – and they think I am in charge, and if I am not, God help them – who the Hell is!'

Lady Bird Johnson

21 February

1940 [Rome]

The Duce[1] intends to satisfy the Germans, and at the Palazzo Venezia there is a meeting with Riccardi[2] and Giannini.[3] Both of them are insistent on the need to refuse goods which we ourselves lack, such as hemp, copper, and other raw materials. But the Duce decides to give 3,500 tons of copper anyway, from the amount which he is preparing to extort from the homes of the Italians. He thinks that this requisition will amount to 20,000 tons, but perhaps this estimate is too high. Nevertheless, the requisition will not be well received, and worse still if it becomes known that a part of the copper will have to be handed over to the hated Germans. I insist with the Duce that he should not requisition sacred objects in churches. He refused. 'The churches do not need copper but faith, and there is very little faith left now. Catholicism is wrong in demanding too much credulity on the part of modern man.'

Count Ciano

1943 [Lewes, England]

We are all very anxious about Winston Churchill who has inflammation of the lungs. Also the American forces have fallen back in Tunisia and had to be 'stiffened' by our Guards! That perhaps will 'larn' them not to brag so much.

Mrs Henry Dudeney

[1] The title chosen by Benito Mussolini, meaning 'leader'.
[2] Raffaello Riccardi, Minister of Currency and Exchange.
[3] Amedeo Giannini, ambassador, senator and General Director of the Ministry of Foreign Affairs.

1944 [London]
Dining with the [Viscount] Moores in Ladbroke Grove, Garrett
Moore said, 'Look at Jim's nose!' and indeed I felt it burning red
from the sudden heat after the intense cold outside. Emerald [Cunard]
said that a certain Duke – she would not disclose which – remarked
about his wife, whom E. had been praising, 'Yes, but you don't have
to sleep with her.' 'Now, dear,' E. remarked, 'isn't that what you call
caddish?' There was only one answer. Joan [Moore] said that recently
a visiting Polish general sat next to a handsome English general who
spoke in a deep voice about strategy. Suddenly the English general
took out a powder puff, then a lipstick. It was the Duchess of
Marlborough.

James Lees-Milne

22 February

1836 [The Alamo]
The Mexicans, about sixteen hundred strong, with their president, Santa
Anna at their head, aided by Generals Almonte, Cos, Sesma, and
Castrillon, are within two leagues of Bexar.

Davy Crockett

1943 [London]
Cecil [Beaton] dined with me. I was rather alarmed having him alone.
For one so sophisticated he is shy. And his polished courtesy makes
me shy at first. He is very observant, misses nothing, the speck of potato
on one's chin, the veins in one's nose, the unplucked hair sprouting
from the ear. Yet how sensitive and understanding he is! After ten
minutes I succumb to his charm, and am at ease. For there is nothing
one cannot say to him. At least I think there is nothing. Talking of
the Kents whom he knows well, he said the Duke refused to take the
war more seriously than a tiresome interruption of his life, and was
never moved with compassion for the R.A.F. This irritated Cecil. So
did the Duke's pernicketiness and perpetual grumbling. But he had
innate good taste, without knowledge of the arts. We talked till 11.20
and went our several ways. I drank too much this evening. Pompey
[his dog] was sick on my bed during the night.

James Lees-Milne

23 February

1836 [The Alamo]

Early this morning the enemy came in sight, marching in regular order and displaying their strength to the greatest advantage in order to strike us with terror. But that was no go. We held a short council of war, and, finding that we should be completely surrounded and overwhelmed by numbers if we remained in the town, we concluded to withdraw to the fortress of Alamo and defend it to the last extremity.

We accordingly filed off in good order, having some days before placed all the surplus provisions, arms, and ammunition in the fortress. We have had a large national flag made; it is composed of thirteen stripes, red and white alternately, on a blue ground with a large white star of five points in the center, and between the points the letters T-E-X-A-S.

As soon as all our little band, about one hundred and fifty in number, had entered and secured the fortress in the best possible manner, we set about raising our flag on the battlements. The enemy marched into Bexar and took possession of the town, a blood-red flag flying at their head, to indicate that we need not expect quarter if we should fall into their clutches.

In the afternoon a messenger was sent from the enemy to Colonel Travis, demanding an unconditional and absolute surrender of the garrison, threatening to put every man to the sword in case of refusal. The only answer he received was a cannon shot; so the messenger left us with a flea in his ear, and the Mexicans commenced firing grenades at us, but without doing any mischief.

At night Colonel Travis sent an express to Colonel Fanning at Goliad, about three or four days' march from this place, to let him know that we are besieged. The old pirate volunteered to go on this expedition and accordingly left the fort after nightfall.

Davy Crockett

1967 [Bolivia]

At dawn yesterday, I overheard Marcos telling a comrade to fuck off and during the day he said it to another man. I must speak with him.

Ernesto 'Che' Guevara

24 February

1916 [the Russian Front]

This morning our little Jewish dressmaker brought my new grey cotton dress. I noticed that she was agitated and enquired why. It seemed that, last evening, three Cossacks had come to the house, seeking, they declared, a lodging for the night. She told them that all the rooms were occupied, but they forced themselves into the room where she and her husband were sitting and began looking round as though in search of something important. Suddenly one of them pulled an object out of a cupboard and, shouting fiercely at her husband, demanded an explanation as to the presence there of a revolver. (Weapons of every description are strictly forbidden among the town inhabitants.) The Jew and his wife began to protest loudly, disowning the revolver. 'We have never had a revolver in our lives,' the woman said tearfully. I believed her implicitly and realised it was all a plot on the part of the Cossacks. They had thundered out a demand for ten roubles, or, as an alternative, an immediate journey to the house of the Town Commandant! The Jews were fully aware that if the latter happened the resulting punishment would, at least, mean a severe flogging; at worst, death! So the ten roubles were scraped together and handed over to the Cossacks who, as they left, commented in loud, scandalised voices on the treachery of the heathen Jewish race. Such tales of injustice are commonplace in this part of the world; it would seem the very name 'Jew' is, to Russian soldiers, a word of scorn.

Florence Farmborough

1917 [France]

'The necessary supply of heroes must be maintained at all costs.' (Sir Edward Carson[1] at Dublin.)

Siegfried Sassoon

1942 [Hampshire]

Confronted with a domestic dilemma. The heroic Annie suffering from influenza and her gall-bladder is affected – Jean in bed with a similar attack. Mrs Grant maintains her egotistic aloofness and I am at once ignorant of all domestic service and somewhat unsafe in the use of

---

[1] Irish barrister and politician, and from 1917, First Lord of the Admiralty and a member of the War Cabinet.

my hands and feet through old age. If only I had been brought up to know how to cook and clean. Rosy [her sister] can do it, but I can't and I am too feeble to learn; nor could any of my older sisters. Music and painting, languages and literature, the four rules of arithmetic and a smattering of mathematics and philosophy were imparted to us by resident governesses, and visiting minor Canons of the nearby Cathedral town. But we were not even taught to mend our clothes, leave alone to make them. Today, even the daughters of noblemen and wealthy businessmen are taught and practise Domestic arts – cooking, cleaning, the use of electric, gas and Aga stoves, washing and mending the clothes – because of the difficulty of getting servants or because they no longer can afford them.

Beatrice Webb

25 February

1855 [London]
We saw 26 of the sick and wounded of the Coldstreams . . . There were some sad cases; one man who had lost his right arm at Inkermann [the Crimea], was also at the Alma, and looked deadly pale – one or two others had lost their arms, others had been shot in the shoulder and legs, – several, in the hip joint . . . A private, Lanesbury, with a patch over his eye, and his face tied up, had had his head traversed by a bullet, penetrating through the eye, which was gone, – through the nose, and coming out at the neck! He looked dreadfully pale, but was recovering well. There were 2 other very touching and distressing cases, 2 poor boys, I cannot say how touched and impressed I have been by the sight of these noble brave, and so sadly wounded men and how anxious I feel to be of use to them, and to try and get some employment for those who are maimed for life. Those who are discharged will receive very small pensions but not sufficient to live upon.

Queen Victoria

1941 [Berlin]
Magnificent box-office returns for our cinema industry. Fifty-six million in profit last year. This year it is looking even better. And all the films originated by me have notched up record audiences.

Josef Goebbels

1941 [Wiltshire]
The limp, frozen-up leaves of the winter honeysuckle, seen out of the dining-room window, appear all too symbolical of the state of human beings after two and a half years of war.

Frances Partridge

1942 [Holland]
It is now half-past seven in the morning; I have clipped my toenails, drunk a mug of genuine Van Houten's cocoa, and had some bread and honey, all with what you might call abandon. I opened the Bible at random, but it gave me no answers this morning. Just as well, because there were no questions, just enormous faith and gratitude that life should be so beautiful, and that makes this a historic moment, that and not the fact that we are on our way to the Gestapo this morning.

Etty Hillesum

26 February

1940 [Bisley, England]
On Thursday the Brigadier appeared in our tent where we were stripping the Bren and told Messer-Bennetts that we were to spend the day with him on Saturday. He picked us up at 12.30 and, driving all over the road, took us to a depraved villa of stockbroker's Tudor. I asked if he had built it himself. 'Built it? It's four or five hundred years old.' That was a bad start. He turns slate-grey instead of red when he is angry. Inside the villa there was evidence that the nucleus of the house had been an old cottage. Mrs Morford was pretty and bright. She seems to me to lead a peculiar life with the Brigadier. She told us with great relish how, the night before, she had had to get up several times to look after a sick child. Each time the Brigadier laid a booby trap against her return by putting his boots on the top of the door. He shouts, 'Woman, get the cigarettes!' and she trots off cheerfully. Most of the Brigadier's family reminiscences dealt with floggings he administered or with grave accidents resulting from various dangerous forms of holiday-making. After luncheon, we went for a walk in fine weather and fine country round Sutton Place. He said that he missed his hockey in wartime. Golf was not the same thing; nor rackets (at which his wife excelled). 'One has to play team games as long as one

possibly can. Last war I was centre-half for my company. It was worth £100 a minute. You get hold of your men that way. I had hold of my men. If a man was brought up before me for a crime, I used to say, "Will you have a court-martial or take if from me?" They always took it from me. I bent 'em over and gave 'em ten, as tight as I could. My company had the best record for crime in the regiment.'

Evelyn Waugh

1941 [England]

I walk back under the cold stars with some shells bursting around them. I am rather fussed about this diary. It is not intimate enough to give a personal picture. The really important things that I know I cannot record. And this gives a picture of someone on the edge of things who is so certain that he knows what is really happening that he does not dare to say. The day-to-day impressions of a greengrocer in Streatham would really be more interesting. I must try henceforward to be more intimate and more illuminating. It is half that I feel that if I survive, this diary will be for me a record from which I can fill in remembered details. And half that I find some relief in putting down on paper the momentary spurts and gushes of this cataract of history.

Harold Nicolson

1941 [England]

Yesterday in the ladies lavatory at the Sussex Grill at Brighton I heard: She's a simpering little thing. I don't like her. But then he never did care for big women. He has wonderful white teeth. He always had. It's fun having the boys . . . If he don't look out he'll be court-martialled. They were powdering and painting, these common little tarts, while I sat, behind a thin door, p—ing as quietly as I could. Then at Fuller's. A fat, smart woman. In red hunting cap, pearls, check shirt, consuming rich cakes. Her shabby dependant also stuffing. They ate and ate. Something scented, shoddy, parasitic about them. Where does the money come to feed these fat white slugs. Brighton a love corner for slugs. The powdered, the pampered, the mildly improper. We cycled. Irritated as usual by the blasphemy of Peacehaven. No walks for ever so long. People daily. And rather a churn in my mind. And some blank spaces. Food becomes an obsession. I grudge giving away a spice bun. Curious – age, or the war? Never mind. Adventure. Make solid. But shall I ever write again one of those sentences that gives me intense pleasure?

There is no echo in Rodmell – only waste air. No life; and so they cling to us. This is my conclusion. We pay the penalty for our rung in society by infernal boredom.

Virginia Woolf

1967 [Bolivia]

We continued walking, trying to reach the Grande river. We made it and we were able to follow it for a little more than one kilometre, but we had to climb again because the river flowed past a cliff. Benjamin fell behind because of difficulties with his rucksack and physical exhaustion; when he did come up to us, I gave him orders to carry on and he did so. He walked about 50 metres but he lost the trail up. As he was looking for it along a ledge, and as I was ordering Urbano to tell him the way he made a sudden movement and fell into the water. He did not know how to swim. The current was very strong and swept him away while he was still touching bottom; we rushed to his help and, we were taking our things off, he disappeared in a whirlpool. Rolando swam out there and tried to dive, but the current swept him far away. After five minutes, we gave up all hope for Benjamin. He was a weak boy and very unfit, although he had tremendous willpower; the test was stronger than him; his physical qualities did not match his will, and we have now had our baptism of death on the banks of the Grande river in a most absurd manner.

Ernesto 'Che' Guevara

27 February

1836 [The Alamo]

The cannonade began early this morning, and ten bombs were thrown into the fort, but fortunately exploded without doing any mischief. So far it has been a sort of tempest in a teapot, not unlike a pitched battle in the Hall of Congress.

Davy Crockett

1942 [London]

Invitation from Churchill to be Lord High Commissioner [to the General Assembly of the Church of Scotland]. I saw that there was a letter from his office but I didn't open it; took it up to Muriel [his wife] in bed with the others. Next time I went up she told me there was something to refuse 'from that cur'.

Lord Reith

1942 [Holland]

How rash to assert that man shapes his own destiny. All he can do is determine his inner responses. You cannot know another's inner life from his circumstances. To know that you must know his dreams, his relationships, his moods, his sickness, and his death.

Very early on Wednesday morning a large group of us were crowded into the Gestapo hall, and at that moment the circumstances of all our lives were the same. All of us occupied the same space, the men behind the desk no less than those about to be questioned. What distinguished each one of us was only our inner attitudes. I noticed a young man with a sullen expression, who paced up and down looking driven and harassed and making no attempt to hide his irritation. He kept looking for pretexts to shout at the helpless Jews: 'Take your hands out of your pockets' and so on. I thought him more pitiable than those he shouted at, and those he shouted at I thought pitiable for being afraid of him. When it was my turn to stand in front of his desk, he bawled at me, 'What the hell's so funny?' I wanted to say, 'Nothing's funny here except you,' but refrained. 'You're still smirking,' he bawled again. And I, in all innocence, 'I didn't mean to, it's my usual expression,' and he, 'Don't give me that, get the hell out of here,' his face saying, 'I'll deal with you later.' And that was presumably meant to scare me to death, but the device was too transparent.

I am not easily frightened. Not because I am brave, but because I know that I am dealing with human beings and that I must try as hard as I can to understand everything that anyone ever does. And that was the real import of this morning, not that a disgruntled young Gestapo officer yelled at me, but that I felt no indignation, rather a real compassion, and would have liked to ask, 'Did you have a very unhappy childhood, has your girl-friend let you down?' Yes, he looked harassed and driven, sullen and weak. I should have liked to start treating him there and then, for I know that pitiful young men like that are dangerous as soon as they are let loose on mankind. But all the blame must be put on the system that uses such people. What needs eradicating is the evil in man, not man himself.

Something else about this morning: the perception, very strongly borne in, that despite all the suffering and injustice I cannot hate others.

All the appalling things that happen are no mysterious threats from afar, but arise from fellow beings very close to us. That makes these happenings more familiar, then, and not so frightening. The terrifying thing is that systems grow too big for men and hold them in a satanic grip, the builders no less than the victims of the system, much as large edifices and spires, created by men's hands, tower high above us, dominate us, yet may collapse over our heads and bury us.

Etty Hillesum

1943 [Amsterdam]
Dearest Kitty,
Guess what's happened to us now? The owner of the building sold it without informing Mr Kugler and Mr Kleiman.[1] One morning the new landlord arrived with an architect to look the place over. Thank goodness Mr Kleiman was in the office. He showed the gentlemen all there was to see, with the exception of the Secret Annexe. He claimed he'd left the key at home and the new owner asked no further questions. If only he doesn't come back demanding to see the Annexe. In that case, we'll be in big trouble!

Father emptied a card file for Margot and me and filled it with index cards that are blank on one side. This is to become our reading file, in which Margot and I are supposed to note down the books we've read, the author and the date. I've learned two new words: 'brothel' and 'coquette'. I've bought a separate exercise-book for new words.

Anne Frank

1944 [London]
Read the papers in Brooks's and walked to the London Library in my corduroy trousers and an old golfing jacket. Joined the volunteers for two exhausting hours in salvaging damaged books from the new wing which sustained a direct hit on Wednesday night. They think about 20,000 books are lost. It is a tragic sight. Theology (which one can best do without) practically wiped out, and biography (which one can't) partially. The books lying torn and coverless, scattered under debris and in a pitiable state, enough to make one weep. The dust overwhelming. I looked like a snowman by the end.

James Lees-Milne

[1] Colleagues of her father, who helped Anne's family.

28 February

1836 [The Alamo]

Santa Anna appears determined to verify his threat and convert the blooming paradise into a howling wilderness. For just one fair crack at that rascal even at a hundred yards distance I would bargain to break my Betsey and never pull a trigger again. My name's not Crockett if I wouldn't get glory enough to appease my stomach for the rest of my life.

Davy Crockett

1942 [Kovno Ghetto, Lithuania]

Today is the deadline for handing over all the books in the Ghetto, without exception, as ordered by the representative of the Rosenberg organization, Dr. Benker.[1]

Avraham Tory

1991 [Ramallah]

The war is over as of seven this morning.

I must admit I am unrepentant. Yes, I did relish Saddam's military bravado. Yes, I felt a thrill seeing the Scuds zooming overhead and landing on the enemy's cities. There is no point in moralizing or pretending. I did. I did. At the same time I do not believe I am one who prefers war to non-violence. I would like to believe that justice can be achieved using other means. But I tried and saw that we were getting nowhere. Justice seemed to be reserved for the powerful . . . We were at rock bottom.

Now we are back there again. Perhaps this is why I don't feel so depressed by Saddam's defeat. The relationship had a short life and put down no roots. But as long as it lasted it gave me a taste of hope. It put up a mirror to reflect the depth of my defeat. It proved to me how vulnerable the enemy was.

Raja Shehadeh

1991 [Saudi Arabia]

Well, as of 0800 this morning the war is over. President Bush called for a cease-fire at 0800 unless Iraqi forces continue to resist.

---

[1] Many books were saved, particularly by the young people of the ghetto, despite the threat of the death penalty.

This war has been unbelievable, and I called it wrong every single step of the way, thinking the Iraqis would put up a fight. It has turned into a total rout. The last battle was fought yesterday, 'a classic tank battle in driving rain', with our side destroying 200 tanks.

Sean T. Couglin

29 February

1836 [The Alamo]

I had a little sport this morning before breakfast. The enemy had planted a piece of ordnance within gunshot of the fort during the night, and the first thing in the morning they commenced a brisk cannonade point-blank against the spot where I was snoring.

I turned out pretty smart and mounted the rampart. The gun was charged again, a fellow stepped forth to touch her off, but before he could apply the match I let him have it and he keeled over.

A second stepped up, snatched the match from the hand of the dying man, but Thimblerig, who had followed me, handed me his rifle, and the next instant the Mexican was stretched on the earth beside the first.

A third came up to the cannon, my companion handed me another gun, and I fixed him off in a like manner. A fourth, then a fifth, seized the match, who both met with the same fate, and then the whole party gave it up as a bad job and hurried off to the camp, leaving the cannon ready charged where they had planted it. I came down, took my bitters,[1] and went to breakfast.

Davy Crockett

[1] An alcoholic drink flavoured with bitter herbs.

MARCH

In our heart of hearts believing
    Victory crowns the just,
    And that braggarts must
    Surely bite the dust,
Press we to the field ungrieving,
In our heart of hearts believing
    Victory crowns the just.
        Thomas Hardy, 'Men Who March Away'

1 March

1836 [The Alamo]

The enemy's forces have been increasing in numbers daily, notwithstanding they have already lost about three hundred men in the several assaults they have made upon us.

Davy Crockett

1917 [France]

Sunny and breezy. Wrote to Helen, Mother, Eleanor and Ellis. Indoors all morning doing nothing. Mostly a quiet morning. Out with Berrington round the march towards 244 who were doing their 1st shoot. Enemy planes over. 2 rounds across 244 [Battery] position on to Doullens Road. Great deal of anti-aircraft shells singing by. Sat down on hill above 244 and watched German lines. At Beaurains ghastly trees and ruins about Achicourt church tower. A bullet passes. General (Poole) who was all for 'Fire, fire, fire! Loose her off! Deliver the goods! Annoy the Hun.' With artillery shelling heavy from about 5 a.m. I only dressed because I thought it would be better to have my clothes on. In any case I had to be up at 6 to go to Achicourt. A very misty still morning: could see nothing from bedroom except the trees and the stone dog – our artillery really made most of the noise, and I being just wakened and also inexperienced mistook it.

Edward Thomas

1940 [Germany]

I had a long talk with Heinrich Himmler at a Braun House reception – he told me about Teutonic types. He said I fitted into the 'Falian' mould. He says there are six pure types, and they must be kept unadulterated, that moral and racial life go hand in hand as the basis of a strong society.

I asked him what he thought about illegitimate births, and he said he was speaking unofficially, but he believed it was the duty of every German to produce a pure child, and that it is the sublime task of all German women of good blood to become pregnant – particularly from soldiers going to war, since they may die for Germany.

I though of Heidi, and said I knew a girl who had deliberately conceived from a chosen SS donor, and had had her baby adopted. Himmler said this was the greatest gift she could give to the future, and essential. 'You have only to look at the Polish pigs that are coming here to work on the land to see the degradation of the inferior genetic strain.'

Elisabeth von Stahlenberg

1941 [Dresden]
In the morning the milkmaid refused to come up. She is no longer allowed to deliver to Jews' Houses.

Victor Klemperer

1943 [Barrow, England]
My husband has to do different work now – less 'large' work, and nearly all blitz repairs that take him into people's houses. He comes in *horrified* sometimes – really shocked – to tell of people with no coal, no sugar till they went downtown for their rations, meat for only two days a week, bread and jam for tea, women *ill* with standing for hours in queues. He stands and gazes on my gaily embroidered cloth, spread 'extravagantly with all *kinds* of food' – and never sees it's only cheese on toast, vegetable salads etc!

Nella Last

1967 [Vietnam]
I think I'm getting a little too casual about death. This morning we were out on patrol with an ARVN [Army of the Republic of Vietnam] until when we spotted a guy about forty years old. He was sitting inside the tree line. The ARVN sergeant suspected he was a VC [Vietcong] and he tried to question him, but the guy tried to get away. The ARVN just gunned him down with his carbine; I don't even remember he told him to halt.

A carbine is a pretty accurate weapon. In the next few seconds the guy's guts were spilling into the mud. His legs were torn off. It was so awful I couldn't react. These ARVNs are really crazy, and they don't think much of human life. Well, they've been fighting a long time. When, after a few minutes I find myself eating a can of C rations, I begin to wonder about myself. But I finished it.

David Parks

2 March

1917 [France]

Up at 5.30 and went out to Achicourt Chateau to see 141's gun into its forward position. A misty frosty morning, luckily and no plane could observe. Afternoon to Faubourg Ranville, its whistling deserted ruined streets, deserted roadway, pavement with single files of men. Cellars as dugouts, trenches behind and across the road. Dead dry calf in stable. Rubble, rubbish, filth and old plush chair. Perfect view of No Man's Land winding level at foot of Hun slope, and Beaurains above to one side and woods just behind crest on other side (M.B.110). With Horton and Lushington to see 3 O.P.s there: – Letters from Helen, Mother, Eleanor and J. Freeman.

Edward Thomas

1940 [Palestine]

Probably because I had sat up all night on a hard seat being serenaded by the Australian soldiers singing 'Waltzing Matilda' and 'We're the boys from way down under' I found Palestine in the dawn rather disappointing – it was flat and less colourful than I expected. I ate breakfast on the train and reached Rehovoth at eleven. I climbed out on to sand, hardly daring to believe I was going to see Dan [her husband, serving in the Yeomanry].

I saw him a long way down the train looking up at the carriages. Tall, bronzed by the sun, wearing khaki shorts and tunic, marvellously good-looking . . . I stood and watched him, spellbound. I thought my heart would burst . . . Heaven is being together.

Countess of Ranfurly

3 March

1917 [France]

No post [it was his birthday]. Morning dull spent in office. But afternoon with Colonel to Achicourt to see O.P.s and then to new battery positions. A chilly day not good for observing. Court of Inquiry on a man burnt with petrol – Lushington presiding and afterwards I went back with him to 244's new billet and saw my new quarters to be. Wrote to Mother and Helen.

Edward Thomas

1940 [Germany]

I don't think my clothing coupons are going to be sufficient. We only get 150 [marks], and you have to give forty for a brassière. It seems excessive – my summer coat (being made now) is taking thirty-five. Frau Smital is going to put me in touch with a family who will be happy to sell theirs, or to exchange them for my cast-offs.

Elisabeth von Stahlenberg

1943 [London]

An air-raid this evening in retaliation for our having bombed Berlin. The guns made a terrible noise. Miss Paterson [National Trust colleague] and I crouched together, she knitting furiously, I reading with grim concentration. We were both so horribly frightened that we drank glasses of neat whisky.

James Lees-Milne

1944 [Naples]

A story has come to light of yet another almost incredible scheme dreamed up by A-Force – operating in enemy-occupied territory – which has ended in typical catastrophe. It seems likely that the germ of this macabre idea originated as a result of a circular sent to all units at about Christmas, worded in part as follows: From reports that have been received it is apparent that prostitution in occupied Italy, and Naples in particular has reached a pitch greater than has ever been witnessed in Italy before. So much is this so that it has led to a suggestion that the encouragement of prostitution is part of a formulated plan arranged by pro-Axis elements, primarily to spread venereal disease among Allied troops.

A-Force mulling over this, would have known that the incidence of VD in German-occupied areas is very low indeed. This is partly because it is a criminal offence under Italian law, punishable by one year in prison, to communicate syphilis to a second person, and partly because the Germans have maintained the strictest of medical supervision over brothels. Thus, for one reason or another, the German-occupied North is virtually free of streptococci and gonococci which to all intents and purposes were reintroduced into Italy with the arrival of the American troops. A-Force's plan was to arrange for the spread of these infections, which have reached epidemic levels in the South, across the lines of the uninfected North, and thus diminish the fighting efficiency of the German Army, while turning their backs on all such considerations as the suffering likely to be endured by the civilian population, and the many babies doomed to be born blind.

By the first week of January, a number of attractive young Neapolitian prostitutes had been rounded up, and of these twenty were selected, who, while showing no outward sign of infection, were believed by the medical men called in to co-operate with the A-Force scheme to be suffering from an exceptionally virulent and virtually ineradicable form of syphilis.

They were removed to a guarded villa in the Vomero, pampered in every way, given all the army white bread and spaghetti they could eat, taken on a day-trip to Capri – although of necessity denied any form of medical attention, apart from regular inspections to see that no unsightly chancres had developed. The news was then broken to them what was expected of them, and the trouble began. However many inducements were offered, they were naturally terrified at the idea of crossing the lines in the care of A-Force agents. Payment was to be made in the form of gold coins to be carried in the rectum, as well as original lira notes; but handsome as it was, the girls knew only too well how harsh was the economic climate of the North by comparison with Naples, and how hard and how risky it would be to make a living once the original bonuses were spent. One girl recruited from a staff of twelve resident prostitutes employed by the Albergo Vittoria Sorrento, taken over as a rest hotel for American personnel, was accustomed to receive 1000 lire a night. In Rome she would be lucky to earn 100 lire, and could not be convinced that her condition would long escape discovery by the German doctors.

But the main obstacle to the enterprise appears to have been an emotional one. All these girls had pimps from whom they could not bear to be parted. Some of these pimps were big enough in the scale of their professions, too, to be able to buy favours, and they were beginning to make trouble through AMGOT.[1] Finally, like so many wild A-Force schemes, the thing was dropped, and the girls were then simply turned loose on the streets of Naples. The situation now is that as many hospital beds in the Naples area are occupied by sufferers from the pox as from wounds and all the other sicknesses put together.

Norman Lewis

[1] Allied Military Government of Occupied Territory.

1991 [Saudi Arabia]

Lots of speculation about when we will be leaving. Could be two weeks to six months. I hope it will be sooner rather than later. I talked to my father today over the phone and told him about my disappointment of not having been involved in any type of real combat, or even under fire. As usual he was much more practical about the whole thing and managed to put it in a little better perspective. 'That,' he said, 'is stupid thinking. You should be glad you weren't involved and didn't have to see or suffer through that. All it takes is one stray bullet, and there are a lot worse things than can happen to you than dying.'

Sean T. Couglin

4 March

1836 [The Alamo]

Shells have been falling into the fort like hail during the day, but without effect. About dusk in the evening, we observed a man running toward the fort, pursued by about half a dozen Mexican cavalry. The bee hunter immediately knew him to be the old pirate who had gone to Goliad, and calling to the two hunters, he sallied out of the fort to the relief of the old man, who was hard pressed. I followed close after.

Before we reached the spot the Mexicans were close on the heels of the old man, who stopped suddenly, turned short upon his pursuers, discharged his rifle, and one of the enemy fell from his horse. The chase was renewed, but finding that he would be overtaken and cut to pieces, he now turned again and, to the amazement of the enemy, became the assailant in his turn. He clubbed his gun and dashed among them like a wounded tiger, and they fled like sparrows.

By this time we reached the spot and in the ardour of the moment followed some distance before we saw that our retreat to the fort was cut off by another detachment of cavalry. Nothing was to be done but to fight our way through. We were all of the same mind. 'Go ahead!' cried I, and they shouted, 'Go ahead, Colonel!'

We dashed among them, and a bloody conflict ensued. They were about twenty in number, and they stood their ground. After the fight had continued about five minutes, a detachment was seen issuing from the fort to our relief; and the Mexicans scampered off, leaving eight of their comrades upon the field.

But we did not escape unscathed, for both the pirate and the bee hunter were mortally wounded, and I received a sabre cut across the forehead. The old man died, without speaking, as soon as we entered the fort.

Davy Crockett

1917 [France]

Cold but bright, clear and breezy. Nothing to do all morning but trace a map and its contours. Colonel and I went down to 244 before lunch to see the shell holes of last night and this morning. Hun planes over. More shells came in the afternoon. The fire is warm but the room cold. Tea with Lushington and Thorburn. Shelling at 5.30 – I don't like it. I wonder where I shall be hit as in bed I wonder if it is better to be on the window or outer side of the room or on the chimney or inner side, whether better to be upstairs where you may fall or on the ground floor where you may be worse crushed. Birthday parcels from home.

Edward Thomas

1941 [England]

At Wallington. Crocuses out everywhere, a few wallflowers budding, snowdrops just at their best. Couples of hares sitting about in the winter wheat and gazing at one another. Now and again in this war, at intervals of months, you get your nose above water for a few moments and notice that the earth is still going round the sun.

George Orwell

1943 [Amsterdam]

Gandhi[1] is eating again.

Anne Frank

5 March

1836 [The Alamo]

Pop, pop, pop! Bom, bom, bom! throughout the day. No time for memorandums now. Go ahead! Liberty and independence forever!

Davy Crockett

---

[1] Gandhi was on hunger strike for Indian independence.

1917 [France]

Out early to see a raid by VI Corps, but snow hid most but singing of Field Shells and snuffling of 6". – Ronville's desolate streets. To 244's orchard which has had numerous 4.2 shells over, meant for the road. Wrote to Helen, Mervyn and Bronwen. Afternoon indoors paying etc. After tea to 244 to dine, not very happy with Lushington, Horton and Smith. They have the wind up because of the shells (which may have been meant for the road behind). Letters from Helen, Bronwen, and de la Mare[1]. A beautiful clear moonlit night after a beautiful high blue day with combed white clouds.

Edward Thomas

1945 [Bergen-Belsen]

Sleepless nights, filled, filled with the central problem: life or death, and when will it end? Filled, filled with the central national problems, the place of Judaism in the world. Religion, the concept of God. Constantly reaching back to the One eternal god – its meaning and how mankind deludes itself with having vanquished God. Will we manage with materialism? We cannot ignore what has happened, but what really matters is that we should stay alive! I have so much to say still.

The dying continues. One thing: the pessimists were right. Pessimists, optimists, they say nothing about the war. They all talk about themselves. For lack of facts, no one has insights. At most *Ahnung* [premonition] of the relative strengths. And I knew that Germany was powerful.

Everything is getting less, forty grams of butter a week instead of sixty. Half a piece of sausage, et cetera.

Starving, starving. Starving.

Abel J. Herzberg

1992 [Sarajevo]

Oh, god! Things are heating up in Sarajevo. On Sunday (1 March) a small group of armed civilians (as they say on TV) killed a Serbian wedding guest and wounded the priest. On 2 March (Monday) the whole city was full of barricades. There were '1,000' barricades. We didn't even have bread. At 18.00 people got fed up and went out into the streets. The procession set out from the cathedral. It went past the parliament building and made its way through the entire city. Several people were

---

[1] Walter de la Mare, poet.

wounded at the Marshal Tito army barracks. People sang and cried 'Bosnia, Bosnia', 'Sarajevo, Sarajevo', 'We'll live together' and 'Come and join us'. Zdravko Grebo[1] said on the radio that history was in the making.

Zlata Filipovic

6 *March*

1915 [Essex]

Joseph Nicholls who is reported killed had been for some time in the Northamptonshire Regiment. Mrs Nicholls, of Little Leighs, cannot read. On receiving a letter from the War Office, she knew something was wrong and took it to Little Leighs Rectory. It was the official tidings of the death.

Andrew Clark

1916 [France]

Coming back to the war I find the country as I left it, under white-ness, snow; and this lovely vesture is like a sheet hung in a dark room; I see against it all the bright images which my ten days at home have brought me. The faces of my friends, smiling welcome, fire lit rooms with books and noble paintings on the walls, the beauty of London streets by night with their mazes of red and orange lamps, passing and meeting, or burning steadily away into the vistas of streets like dark waterways between the mystery of lofty buildings. Woods and fields in Sussex, in clear sunlight of early March, and the scarlet-coated hunts-man galloping his jaunty little grey nag, cheering his hounds to a find or casting them across the wet ploughs, and the violinist leading the orchestra from height to height of noble rapture, lost in the splendour of his task, an austere Apollo in a black coat.

Siegfried Sassoon

1917 [France]

Bright and clear early and all day and warm at 1. Walked over to 244's position with Colonel and then up to 234 beyond Dainville station,

---

[1] President of the Soros Foundation in Sarajevo and editor-in-chief of ZID, the independent radio station.

and listened to larks and watched aeroplane fights. 2 planes down, one in flames, a Hun. Sometimes 10 of our planes together very high. Shells into Arras in afternoon.

Edward Thomas

1940 [California]

A month since I last wrote in this book– and where are we? A little nearer the advertised blitzkrieg outbreak, and perhaps the entry of the US into the war. The Russians still haven't got Viipuri, the Turks haven't attacked Odessa, the President hasn't declared himself for a third term.

Christopher Isherwood

1941 [London]

I was talking to a chauffeur today about the bombings. 'What aston-ishes me,' he said, 'is the way those old houses fall down so easy. You take that big house on the corner of Berkeley Square – used to belong to Lord T. My mother used to work there when I was a lad. It always seemed such a fine well-built old house and now it's just a pile of rubble. I would have thought they would have stood up better – some of those big houses.' Although his tone was practical I thought I could catch an undernote of dismay queerly mixed with relief. That great gloomy house may have hung on in his memory since childhood. It must have seemed as permanent as a natural feature of the landscape and clothed in dim prestige. Now brutally it vanishes. This sudden destruction of the accustomed must shake people out of the grooves of their lives. This overnight disappearance of the brick and mortar framework of existence must send a shock deep into the imagination. These high explosions and incendiaries are like the falling stars and blazing comets – noted of old as foretelling great changes in the affairs of man.

Charles Ritchie

1942 [Poland]

8.40 a.m. Posen. Our destination 100 km from here – by the map in the corridor. We seem well North. There are horse cabs in the station yard and a 1914–18 War Memorial. Two [Nazi] Party officers are strolling about on the platform looking very smart in their immaculate brown uniforms. Am rather amused to see a girl get into a waiting train near ours and pick up the Menu Card in the Dining Car. I can't think what it could have had on it bar Klippfisch and Sauerkraut. Also shaken to see some cold coffee thrown out of a window of that same train. I would have given anything for it. Crumbs from the rich man's table. We move out of Posen. 12 Noon – Wreschen. We learn here that we haven't a hope of getting to our destination today. About another 200 miles to go. We are travelling very slowly and apparently 2 sides of a triangle. No more food – no more smokes. All stations have been taken over by the Reichsbahn. Is this country Our War Aim? Blimey! Miles upon miles of sweet F.A. except mud and more mud.

Captain John Mansel

1943 [Germany]
The big speech by Goebbels reached a new pinnacle of filthy demagoguery directed against the upper classes. Here is an example of the effect on imbeciles. The wife of Minister Thomsen steps out of the subway. A man in uniform, heavy with braid – she thinks it was a police officer – storms up to her, snatches an ordinary, much-worn kid glove out of her hand, and bellows: 'Haven't you heard that Goebbels has forbidden the wearing of kid gloves!' A peroxide blonde passing by chimed in: 'Quite right!' Incidentally, Goebbels had not said anything against kid gloves; he said that in such times as these one couldn't handle them with kid gloves. But the stirring up of animosities and hatreds is getting worse, and what makes it still worse is that it originates in 'high places'.

Ulrich Von Hassell

7 *March*

1917 [France]
A cold raw dull day with nothing to do except walk round to 244 to get a pair of socks. The wind made a noise in the house and trees and a dozen black crumpled sycamore leaves dance round and round on terrace. Wrote to Pearce and Irene. Rather cold and depressed and solitary.

Edward Thomas

1965 [The White House]

In talking about the Vietnam situation, Lyndon summed it up quite simply, 'I can't get out. I can't finish it with what I have got. So what the Hell can I do?'

Lady Bird Johnson

1967 [Vietnam]

Went looking for action today and got it. But once we made contact the tracks couldn't go in. So we dismantled in front of the wood line, then the CO ordered the sweep. I was tense and pouring with sweat. Our squad was positioned in a house . . . inside the wooded area. The rest of the company moved on to rejoin the trucks and cut off possible escape. Lt. Wyeth gave us observation posts inside the house. And we waited. I was starting to plot our firing range when Wyeth spotted the first VC [Vietcong] and opened up with his M-16. He kept hollering, 'Get them! Get them bastards! Keep firing.' I hit the floor and called back the company as Charlie returned our fire. He wasn't too accurate, thank God. Most of his stuff went over our heads. The company trucks came blasting through in about three minutes and Charlie took off, but not until we had killed about two. While we were making a body count Sgt. Young kicked a VC's body to see if he was really dead. He had to be. Bullets had punctured him from head to toe. Young asked for my knife. I gave it to him and watched him cut off the VC's finger and remove a gold ring. I walked away real quick. I didn't wait for my knife because I was too sick.

David Parks

8 March

1917 [France]

Snow blizzard – fine snow and fierce wind – to Achicourt O.P. But suddenly a blue sky and soft white cloud through the last of the snow – with Colonel and Berrington. Returned to hear that the Group has to leave this billet. I liked the walk. Indoors afternoon fitting together aeroplane trench photographs. Letters from Helen, Eleanor, Oscar and Frost (saying he had got an American publisher for my verses). A still quiet night up to 11 with just one round fired to show we have not left Arras. Up till 1 for a despatch from Corps.

Edward Thomas

1942 [Baltimore]
The following is from the leading editorial in this morning's [Baltimore] *Sun* –

> The *Sun* is attempting to print every bit of material information about the war, in its military and its civil aspects, that can be printed with safety. At the same time, every attention is paid not only to the censorship rules, but to the responsibilities in wartime which every newspaper and every citizen must bear in guarding against disclosure of information to the enemy. Out of regard for these responsibilities, the *Sunpapers* have voluntarily imposed upon themselves a code of censorship more rigid than the one required or requested by the Federal Government.

In other words, To hell with the news! No matter how onerous the censorship imposed by the wizards at Washington, the *Sunpapers* will accept it and go it one better.

H.L. Mencken

9 March

1917 [France]
Snow and very cold indoors doing nothing but look at a sandbag O.P. My last day at the Group. Weir of 2/1 Lowland takes my place. I return to 244 – Lushington, Horton and Rubin. I am fed up with sitting on my arse doing nothing that anybody couldn't do better. Wrote to de la Mare, Frost[1] and Eleanor.

Edward Thomas

1942 [London]
The sun was shining and the air almost balmy as I walked through Belgravia. For the first time this year I inhaled that familiar scent of London, which ought to be so full of promise and happy days. But alas, now it augurs despair, inevitable misery, and destruction. For the spring is a season one has come to dread. Yet the birds in the Green Park were singing oblivious of the future; and in spite of my awareness of it I found my feet skimming over the grass.

[1] Robert Frost, American poet.

I once firmly believed in the permanency of human relationships. I suppose I read about their impermanency in books, but could not bring myself to acknowledge it. Now I know it to be a fact, just as every physical creation is transitory. The realization ought doubtless to strengthen my divine love, but I do not think it does.

James Lees-Milne

1943 [Hampshire]

I was awake when at 2 a.m. there sounded the loudest alarm we have had – from Bramshott I think – followed by gun-fire, which shook the door. I looked behind the curtain, there were searchlights and the shining of flickering lights in the skies over to the South-East. Presently there appeared eight brilliant stars from which dropped endless streams of incendiary bombs over one particular spot which remained stationary . . . The raid lasted for two hours, concentrated on the camps and munitions works on the way from the south coast to Woking and London. That made me feel slightly ashamed of myself. It had interested me, and in the spirit of exhilaration I forgot that it might mean hundreds of dead and wounded, while we, being a mile or two off the target, might be exempt from the danger of being involved. With my continuous discomfort – or even pain – it is a queer distraction from physical pain and mental depression!

Beatrice Webb

10 March

1917 [France]

Up at 5.15 for a raid, but nothing doing. A misty mild morning clearing slightly to a white sky. 10 rounds gunfire C–B. Snowdrops at foot of pear-trees by Decanville Railway, R.F.C. Wireless man reading 'Hiawatha'. 3 shoots of 10 rounds gunfire suddenly at N.F. Targets unobserved. Men mending a caved-in dugout in the dark. Parcel from Janet Hooten.

Edward Thomas

1943 [Hampshire]

This morning's papers report that three enemy bombers were brought down and the crew of two killed, with one wounded pilot who became a prisoner of war. What *did* happen, bringing an interesting souvenir to the Webb household, was the fall of a German balloon [a parachute] and the acquisition of enough white silk to furnish all the household with silk night-gowns. The balloon – with its yards of silk and its long cords of white rope, at the end of which were the empty containers of the flares – I had noticed in the sky. Unless the government claims them we shall keep them as a record of the second great war.

Beatrice Webb

11 *March*

1917 [France]
Out at 8.30 to Ronville O.P. and studied the ground from Beaurains N. Larks singing over No Man's Land – trench mortars. We were bombarding their front line: they were shooting at Arras. R.A.F. Officer with me who was quite concerned till he spotted a certain familiar Hun sentry in front line. A clear, cloudy day, mild and breezy. 8th shell carrying into Arras. Later Ronville heavily shelled and we retired to dugout. At 6.15 all quiet and heard blackbirds chinking. Scene peaceful, desolate like Dunwich moors except sprinkling of white chalk on the rough brown ground. Lines broken and linesmen out from 2.30 to 7 p.m. A little rain in the night . . .

Edward Thomas

12 *March*

1917 [France]
A beautiful moist clear limpid early morning till the Raid at 7 and the retaliation on Ronville at 7.30 – 8.45 with 77cm. 25 to the minute. Then back through 6 ins. of chalk mud in trenches along battered Ronville Street. Rooks in tall trees on N. side of Arras – they and their nests and the trees black against the soft clouded sky. W. wind and mild but no rain yet (11 a.m.). Letters, mess accounts, maps. Afternoon at maps and with Horton at battery. Evening of partridges calling and pipsqueaks coming over behind.

Edward Thomas

1944 [Rome]

Hear the broadcast of the Pope's Benediction of the faithful in Piazza San Pietro – a crowd chiefly composed of the homeless and starving refugees who have now flocked into the city. It was a short address, without any political flavour: an admission of the Pope's inability to stop or mitigate the horrors of war even within his own city, a final appeal to the rulers on both sides – and, to the congregation before him, a repetition of the well-known words of Christian consolation: 'Come unto me, all ye that are weary and heavy-laden.' Perhaps never, in all the history of suffering humanity, have these words been spoken to so great an assembly of the homeless, the penniless and the bereft. And when, the address ended, the Pope paused a moment before the Benediction, from thousands of throats came a cry of supplication, unforgettable by anyone who heard it – a cry which sounded like an echo of all the suffering that is torturing the world: 'give us peace; oh, give us peace'.

Iris Origo

13 March

1917 [France]

Blackbird trying to sing early in dull marsh. A dull cold day. One N.F. shoot at nightfall. I was in position all day. Letters from Eleanor, Mother and Ellis; wrote to Bronwen, Mother and Eleanor.

Edward Thomas

1940 [near Coventry]

We are all sad today to think of Finland having to give in to a godless nation like the Russians. It is a real calamity! An armistice now waits on a cruel 'peace' treaty. For the moment one feels a real setback, for we learn that the allies could have gone with 50,000 men and equipment if Finland had called for men, *and if Norway and Sweden had co-operated* against these brutal Russians.

Clara Milburn

1941 [Linz]

To the meeting in the evening. Between huge crowds. The cheering never stops. Meeting overflowing. Fantastic atmosphere. I speak on the war situation. Each sentence is punctuated by storms of applause. I am on good form. Then the Gauleiter makes a short speech. And now, completely unexpected so far as the meeting is concerned, the Führer arrives. The storm of applause is quite indescribable. The Führer is lively and buoyant. He speaks for thirty minutes with the greatest élan. Total confidence in victory. The crowd goes wild.

Drive between endless crowds. At the hotel. Then I stand with the Führer on the balcony of his hotel room, and we look out over his home town. He loves this city very much, and this is understandable. He intends to establish a new centre of culture here. As a counterweight to Vienna, which will have to be gradually phased out of the picture. He does not like Vienna, basically for political reasons. I tell him a few things that I know about Vienna, aspects downright hostile to the Reich, which annoy him greatly. But Linz is his darling. I give him an account of my impressions, which he is very pleased with. A wonderful evening with the Führer. He expounds his views on the situation to me: everything is going well, both militarily and diplomatically. We can be very satisfied.

Josef Goebbels

1941 [Wiltshire]
Two sirens tonight, quantities of aeroplanes, a rattle of gunfire. And I was horrified to realize that we were sitting over our nice warm fire, listening quite calmly to this sound – which was after all the noise of human beings trying to kill other human beings.

Frances Partridge

1966 [The White House]
One thing about our life, you never can tell who you'll find in Lyndon's bedroom. I walked in this morning for coffee – Lyndon had made a surprise visit the night before to the Gridiron Dinner – and who should be sitting there but Richard Nixon! He had come down for the dinner. He was looking relaxed and affable and well-tailored. Lyndon was stretched out in his pajamas, drinking tea, and they were apparently enjoying their visit.

Mostly they talked about the international situation, especially Vietnam, where Mr. Nixon is generally in strong support of Lyndon. He said that opponents say we are risking World War III in Vietnam, that we are risking war with China in Vietnam, but that is not so, we are avoiding a big war. He said that the Chinese are cautious, and the Communists are cautious. If we are going to have any discussion with China, it should come now, rather than later, three or four years from now.

Mr. Nixon looked prosperous, vital, at home in the world, and it sounded as if Pat [his wife] were enjoying life too. I told him I hoped she would come to the Senate Ladies' Luncheon some time. On leaving, he said, 'Mr. President, you know this is campaign year and I'll be getting out, speaking up for the Republicans. They'll need all the voices they can get. But there won't be anything personal about you in what I say about the Democratic Administration.'

Lady Bird Johnson

14 March

1917 [France]

Ronville O.P. Looking out towards No Man's Land what I thought first was a piece of burnt paper or something turned out to be a bat shaken at last by shells from one of the last sheds in Ronville. A dull cold morning, with some shelling of Arras and St Sauveur and just 3 for us. Talking to Birt and Randall about Gloucestershire and Wiltshire, particularly Painswick and Marlborough. A still evening – blackbirds singing far-off – a spatter of our machine guns – the spit of one enemy bullet – a little rain – no wind – only far-off artillery.

Edward Thomas

1858 [Kaiserbagh]

The scene of the plunder was indescribable. The soldiers had broken up several of the store-rooms, and pitched the contents into the court, which was lumbered with cases, with embroidered clothes, gold and silver brocade, silver vessels, arms, banners, drums, shawls, scarves, musical instruments, mirrors, pictures, books, accounts, medicine bottles, gorgeous standards, shields, spears, and a heap of things, the enumeration of which would make this sheet of paper like a catalogue of a broker's sale. Through these march the men, wild with excitement, 'drunk with plunder'. I had often heard the phrase but never saw the thing itself before. They smashed to pieces the fowling pieces and pistols to get at the gold mountings and the stones set in the stocks.

They burned in a fire, which they made in the centre of the court, brocades and embroidered shawls for the sake of the gold and silver. China, glass, and jade they dashed to pieces in pure wantonness; pictures they ripped up, or tossed on the flames; furniture shared the same fate.

William Howard Russell

1941 [Dresden]

For a long time I feared a large fine because of the failure to black out on February 15. When nothing happened, I thought I had not been charged. This morning summons of a *prison sentence* of eight days, and to present myself at police headquarters within two weeks. I am dreadfully afraid of it, and my heart is very, very heavy at leaving Eva [his wife] alone. But I must force myself to be calm, simply for her sake.

By comparison my stored-up little notes seem futile.

I now fetch our milk from Chemnitzer Platz. It is forbidden to deliver anything to Jews' Houses, our shop was far away, and the shops nearby are not taking any new customers. I have old friends at Chemnitzer Platz. That is where Eva must now go.

The Jewish world today. A lady who was downstairs visiting the Kreidls conveys greetings from my niece Käte Sussmann (in Switzerland). Käte was in a tuberculosis sanatorium there, is now employed there (as dressmaker) – Cohn, an honest man, who often collects donations for the Jewish Community and to whom I have been unable to give anything recently, brought me (with anxious secretiveness – he could be punished for it) two pairs of socks. The Community board refused my request for a reduction of the enormously high tax (279M); there were no grounds for a reduction, I should sell my house to alleviate my situation. These people have no time for a baptized Jew. Especially when, as I do, he gives one third of this tax to the Confessing Church.

It was Frau Voss's birthday on March 11. She spent half the night in the kitchen and made four cakes; homemade cakes are de rigueur for her on such occasions. Petit bourgeois proper thing to do. Later ten ladies came for tea. We had to be there too.

It's less the lack of space, dirt, bad food, etc. of these days that I dread than the anticipated complete lack of activity and emptiness of those 192 hours.

Victor Klemperer

1944 [Naples]

Today another horrible example of what can happen to the poor when the army decides on a counter-offensive on the black market. A boy of about ten was brought into the 92nd General Hospital by his distracted mother. He'd had three fingers chopped off. These she handed over, wrapped in newspaper, with the request that they be sewn on again. Somebody had told her that only the British were capable of this kind of surgery. The story was that this little boy was one of a juvenile gang that specialized in jumping on the backs of lorries when held up in traffic and snatching anything pilferable. We heard that they had been dealt with by having a man with a bayonet hidden under a tarpaulin in the back of every supply-lorry. As soon as a boy grabbed the tailboard to haul himself in, the waiting soldier chopped down at his hands. God knows how many children have lost their fingers in this way.

Norman Lewis

15 March

1943 [London]

After breakfast I carried out what I had resolved. That is to say I took Pompey's basket, hid it away, burned his two bones, his cotton reel, his blanket and cushion in the incinerator in the yard. I threw his chain as far as I could into the river. I got a taxi, and told the driver to take me to the vet. I held the little dog on my knees without looking at him, without thank God, seeing his eyes. I told the vet to destroy him, and walked out, and away. All this I did without a qualm, for his cough was getting worse, and his fits persisted. For five or ten minutes I felt almost jubilant. Had I not done the right thing? Would someone ever do the same service for me? In walking rapidly along the embankment I felt, at first with surprise, then shame, the tears coursing down my cheeks. By the time I reached the door I felt nothing but unmitigated grief. I had been no better than a murderer.

James Lees-Milne

1944 [Naples]

A bad raid last night with heavy civilian casualties, as usual, in the densely populated port areas. I was sent this morning to investigate the reports of panic, and frantic crowds running through the streets crying,

'Give us peace' and 'Out with the soldiers.' In Santa Lucia, home territory of the Neapolitan ballad, I saw a heart-rending scene. A number of tiny children had been dug out of the ruins of a bombed building and lay side by side in the street. Where presentable, their faces were uncovered, and in some cases brand-new dolls had been thrust into their arms to accompany them to the other world. Professional mourners, hired by the locality to reinforce the grief of the stricken families, were running up and down the street, tearing at their clothing and screaming horribly. One man climbed into the rubble and was calling into a hole where he believed his little boy was trapped under hundreds of tons of masonry, begging him not to die before he could be dug out. 'Hang on, son. Only a few minutes longer now. We'll have you out of there in a minute. Please don't die.' The Germans murder only the poor in these indiscriminate raids, just as we did.

Norman Lewis

16 March

1941 [Surrey]
Paying a visit to my old father who, for all his years, is still active and in good fettle, I found him grumbling because he couldn't get a job. I had to break it gently to him that even in wartime it was most unlikely that a man of 84 would secure paid employment. I advised him to cultivate his garden, and if that didn't give him occupation enough, to take on a small allotment as well.

Walter Musto

1944 [Monte Cassino]
Flew spare. Saw two ships collide and explode. Chet Angell, V.E. Miller & Wise. My buddies all dead. Flew back to field. Sick. 13 good men dead. Can't stand it much more. Guess I'm a sissy.

Technical Sergeant Harry Schloss, 17th Bomb Group, 34th Bomb Squadron, USAAF

1945 [Bergen-Belsen]
Every day now transports of thousands of people are arriving from concentration camps. Men and women, including Dutch people, acquaintances, friends.

Twenty to twenty-five per cent are dead, sometimes more. On the way to our latrines there is a field full of corpses and more corpses. It is a gruesome sight. And no one knows about it or will believe it. It makes us profoundly dejected and pessimistic. The corpses are being thrown into lime now. The crematorium can no longer cope with the volume. The mortality rate in our camp is declining slightly. Except that we have had the first case of spotted fever.

T. [his wife] also has fever again, day after day. I am worn out and can hardly move. Almost the entire day I lie on the bed (if one can call it such). The filth is increasing. We are sick of it. For weeks I have been unable to make my bed.

Abel J. Herzberg

1967 [Bolivia]
We decided to eat the horse, as our swellings are alarming.

Ernesto 'Che' Guevara

17 March

1944 [Carradale, Scotland]
I can't think of anything except something horrible I have had to do, getting the warble fly maggots out of the cattle, oh god it was filthy. The chap came to license Timo [the bull], said he'd pass him but he wasn't very good, he thought I'd best sell him locally, gave me a lot of good advice, then said he had warble flies and pressed an awful maggot out of his back, I was nearly sick. Duncan [a neighbour] says not to worry too much, they all have them, but give them a dressing of sheep dip. He was very lousy too. I got in the two Ayrshires, we rubbed the dip into their backs, neither had any lice, but Linda had two warble maggots, I pressed them out, I couldn't make Joan [her friend] do it. They pop out, it is a real nightmare. I couldn't bear one to touch me, nor could Joan. I tried to do Timo but he kicked like a sledgehammer. I expect all the Galloways have it. Oh dear, it is one of the many things I didn't know about . . .

Naomi Mitchison

1968 [Texas]
The four of us drove in to St Barnabas – Lynda and Chuck, Lyndon [daughter, son-in-law and husband, the President] and I, for the 11

o'clock service. Chuck will be leaving very soon [for Vietnam]. On the way in, Lyndon said something I will remember for its perception. We were talking about the rising tide of isolationism in this country, and I was saying how strong it was becoming in me – not thought, just pure emotion, fed by the actions of such countries as Sweden hosting a 'trial' of the United States as 'a war criminal' and France manipulating the gold market. I made a hothead statement about when we got the Vietnam war finally settled I didn't want to have another thing to do with any foreign country. Lyndon looked at me very calmly and said, 'That's like saying James David's children have smallpox, and I'm not going to do anything about it.' James and his children live about a block from us. If they had the smallpox, my first thought would be, I've got to be sure they've got the best doctor and care. And my next thought would be for our *own* safety. Or, maybe those thoughts would be reversed. At any rate, we couldn't separate ourselves from them, no matter how much we wished it.

Lady Bird Johnson

18 March

1941 [Berlin]
Get rid of a mass of degenerate art. This rubbish continues to appear on the market.

Josef Goebbels

1941 [POW camp, Germany]
The whole place seemed particularly cheerless this morning. When Appell [roll call] was sounded and the passages and stairs became filled with the mob going to parade, the scene struck me as being for all the world like a plague of rats and the only item missing a Pied Piper. The moat level passages are after all, in the dark, very like enormous sewers.

The talk in the room this morning started off with a discussion as to the way in which POWs are now and will be after the war regarded at home. Peter Tunstall told us how in his aerodrome before he was captured, if any one was known to have been captured, they all said 'Oh well, he's all right for the rest of the war.' A popular opinion is that one will be greeted by 'You lucky devil having been a prisoner of war, you missed it all.'

Captain John Mansel

19 March

1916 [France]
This morning came the evil news from the trenches – first that 'Tracker' Richardson had died of wounds after being knocked over by a shell last night in front of the trenches; this was bad. But they came afterwards and told that my little Tommy[1] had been hit by a stray bullet and died last night. When last I saw him, two nights ago, he had his notebook in his hand, reading my last poem. And I said good night to him, in the moonlit trenches. Had I but known! – the old, human-weak cry. Now he comes back to me in memories, like an angel, with the light in his yellow hair, and I think of him at Cambridge last August when we lived together four weeks in Pembroke College in rooms where the previous occupant's name, Paradise, was written above the door.

Siegfried Sassoon

20 March

1941 [London]
A lot of bombs at Greenwich, one of them while I was talking to E.[ileen, his wife] over the phone. A sudden pause in the conversation and a tinkling sound:
I: 'What's that?'
E: 'Only the windows falling in.'

George Orwell

1944 [Naples]
Oh, God, the sights I've seen today. We haven't *touched* the war till today. Bed after bed filled with mutilated men, heads, faces, bodies. It's the most inhuman, ghastly, bloody, hellish thing in the world. I couldn't think or

[1] Lieutenant David Thomas, Sassoon referred to him in his poems, 'A Subaltern', 'The Last Meeting' and 'A Letter Home'.

work or even feel in the end. It was quite numbing. The first ward (it was at 65) was a huge surgical full of casts, pulleys, and very sick men. All the time we were playing there were sisters doing dressings, patients feeding from tubes, orderlies bringing people in from the theatres and newly arrived from the line. About half the room was too ill to listen or care; the others lay and took it in with their eyes. It was no fun to see the suffering going on in there. I struggled to get a clear mind and do the job and eventually I think I did. But it was an experience I don't often wish to witness. By far the illest people I've seen as yet. The nurses are at it every minute and seem so calm and encouraging. I take my hat off to them. It's a terrific job and they are going it beautifully here.

There is a head and face surgery team at this hospital which means they get the full burden of all such cases. We did three shows, three of the most extraordinary I ever hope to do. A blinded Scotch boy called Dan – still dazed by his wounds and in a sort of awful gaiety. Their tenderness to each other is heartbreaking. In two wards patients were out of the minds and struggling, and in both cases there was a fellow patient, now convalescent, holding the sick man down gently and patiently, watching him all the time. And a bad case who was also shell shocked had a friend to see him and he just sat and held his hand in silence. The warmth of human contact and the restoring confidence of a friend must help at a time like this. I *must* forget all this or I shan't be any good but in another way I must remember it for the effort I, as an individual, must make to see that there are never any more wars. If the striking miners and factory workers could be in one of those wards for an hour and see those boys they'd never strike again.

Joyce Grenfell

21 March

1858 [Lucknow]
Napier[1] is engaged in drawing up of report on the altercations and defences of Lucknow, of a *grandiose* and very elevated character. It is

[1] Field Marshal Robert Cornelis Napier, 1st Baron. He fought at the Siege of Lucknow during the Indian Mutiny, and later served in China and Abyssinia, finally becoming Commander-in-Chief in India, then Governor of Gibraltar.

imperial in conception; but where is the money to come from? We had, for a wonder, divine service in the Mess-tent to-day, at which there was limited attendance. Sir Colin Campbell is of the Scottish Church; but he might have listened without harm to an eloquent but illogical sermon from the Rev. Mr. McKay, wherein that excellent divine sought to prove that England would not share the fate common to all the empires of the world hitherto, because she was Christian and carried the Ark of the Covenant, whereas they had been heathen – *non constat domine!* Our tent was surrounded with Hindus and Mohammedans. They were our subjects, and part of our State. The Christianity of a Roman Emperor would not save his empire; and as 'Saramaria fell unwept without a crime', so might we fall unwept with many crimes, of which our people know nothing, in spite of our being Christian, with a Protestant constitution and an Empire of all the religions in the world. I believe that we permit things to be done in India which we would not permit to be done in Europe, or could not hope to effect without public reprobation, and that our Christian character in Europe, our Christian zeal in Exeter hall, will not atone for usurpation and annexation in Hindustan, or for violence and fraud in Upper India.

William Howard Russell

1940 [France]
On the way home collected my new dentures, they are real 'soldiers' dentures' to look at, and a good mouthful.

Field Marshal Lord Alanbrooke

22 March

1940 [London]
From all sides come disgusting accounts of the German terror in Poland: young men shot in hundreds, girls sterilised and conscripted for the soldiers' brothels, old people sent to hard labour in concentration camps or driven from their houses to die of exposure. At the same time the Germans continue their attacks on neutral ships, firing torpedoes without warning and leaving the crews to their fate. I suppose there is a natural strain of brutality in the German character and as great an insensitivity to human suffering as there is a sensi-

tivity to beauty. Certainly the Nazi doctrine has sublimated all that is most despicable in human nature, and it is difficult to see how this pernicious philosophy can be eradicated from the minds of the rising generation in Germany. However I still refuse to believe they are wholly abominable, and I think we ought sometimes to try and see ourselves reflected in their eyes: pharisaical, oblivious of the acts of aggression in our own history, rich and anxious to keep those riches for ourselves. Undoubtedly we are, as a nation, irritatingly self-righteous.

John Colville

1940 [Berlin]

It is Good Friday today, but I had to work my head off just the same. Typed for nine hours without stopping.[1] When he sees me on the verge of collapse, my Boss, Herr E., produces schnapps, a kind of brandy; it picks me up a bit but tastes horrible. He and his wife squabble all the time. When I see and hear them, I am dead against husband and wife working together. I dislike him cordially and am tempted to give him a shove when he leans far out of the window to get a breath of air after one of their rows. Katia Kleinmichel feels the same. I see a lot of her now, as she works on our shift, and often, when the couple get too much for me, we take turns at the typewriter. We have moved into another building at the Charlottenstrasse. It makes our bosses more independent of Goebbels' constant nagging. Before, when our offices were closer, the Herr Minister would summon them every hour or so. Now he can only get excited over the phone.

I came home dead beat.

Marie 'Missie' Vassiltchikov

1941 [Berlin]

Thomas Mann[2] has appealed to the German people. Senile windbag! In London they have started using the phrase 'Huns' again. So things must be bad for England.

Josef Goebbels

---

[1] She worked for the D.D. (Drahtloser Dienst – The Wireless Service which was Germany's version of the B.B.C.).

[2] Thomas Mann, German novelist.

23 March

1938 [Spain]

We were both shattered today. While I was washing, Conchita had to aid a stomach-washing which she said almost made her vomit. My unpleasant experience was very funny. The over-sexed head wound suddenly threw off his bedclothes, let out a wild shout and produced his penis, then he left it to its own devices and proceeded to spray fountains in all directions. I rushed for the pot and chased after the fountain, but it was so damned elusive that I finally had to grab the damn thing and hang on. I thought he would never stop. How any nurse can look at a man, let alone touch him, I don't know, after all the unattractive things one has to do with them.

Priscilla Scott-Ellis

1941 [POW camp, Germany]

We had the most wonderful surprise this evening. Eric had collected some spare biscuits and the cook made us 2 roly-poly cakes. They looked as if they had come out of Gunter's.[1] Cocoa powder on the top looked like chocolate icing. Some sultanas had been included. At home one would probably have given it to the dog, but it tasted marvellous. The bits of biscuit looked like nuts. A bit of sugar on the top and the answer was no lemon.

The strafe is lessening again – the window boards are to come down tomorrow morning. We have a feeling we are going from here.

Captain John Mansel

1943 [USA]

It seems we are advancing in Tunisia. At least the British 8th Army is attacking and we are advancing without opposition. The Russian front seems to be at a standstill. I read all Churchill's speech on the postwar world – *very* British. Very imperialist ('We mean to hold our own', etc), very down to earth (written in 'Pounds, Shillings and Pence', 'no rosy promises', 'no fairy tales'), but so completely honest. One cannot help but admire the man's integrity.

Anne Morrow Lindbergh

---

[1] Famous tea-rooms in London.

24 March

1915 [London]

It is fortunate I am ill[1] in one way for I need not make my mind up about this war. I am not interested in it – this filth and lunacy. I have not yet made up my mind about myself. I am so steeped in myself – in my moods, vapours, idiosyncrasies, so self-sodden, that I am unable to stand clear of the data, to marshal and classify the multitude of facts and thence draw the deduction what manner of man I am. I should like to know – if only as a matter of curiosity. So what in God's name am I? I fool, of course, to start with – but the rest of the diagnosis?

They tell me that if the Germans won it would put back the clock of civilisation for a century. But what is a meagre 100 years? Consider the date of the first Egyptian dynasty! We are now only in AD 1915 – surely we could afford to chuck away a century or two? Why not evacuate the whole globe and give the ball to the Boches to play with – just as an experiment to see what they can make of it. After all there is no desperate hurry. Have we a train to catch? Before I could be serious enough to fight, I should want God first to dictate to me his programme of the future of mankind.

W.N.P. Barbellion

1940 [Berlin]

Easter Sunday, grey and cold, but the rain held off. I cancelled my engagements with some German friends for lunch and tea. Couldn't face a German today, though they are no friends of Hitler. Wanted to be alone. Got up about noon and listened to a broadcast from Vienna. The Philharmonic, and a nice little thing from Haydn.

In the afternoon, a stroll. Surely the Germans must be the ugliest-looking people in Europe, individually. Not a decent-looking woman in the whole [Under den] Linden. Their awful clothes probably contribute to one's impression. Comparatively few soldiers in the streets. Few leaves granted? Meaning? Offensive soon?

I was surprised to notice how shabby the Kaiser's Palace at the end of the Linden is. The plaster falling off all over the place. Very dilapidated. The stone railing of the balcony on which Wilhelm II

---

[1] He suffered from an incurable and progressive paralysis.

made his famous appearance in 1914 to announce to the delirious mob at the feet the coming of war appeared to be falling to pieces. Well, they were not delirious before Hitler's balcony when this war started.

I tried to read in the face of the thousands what was in their minds this Easter day. But their faces looked blank. Obviously they do not like the war, but they will do what they're told. Die, for instance.

William L. Shirer

1941 [Berlin]

In the USA, the Rabbis are praying for Roosevelt. He has earned it. The USA is returning escaped German prisoners-of-war to Canada. Scum!

Josef Goebbels

1941 [London]

Letter from the WAAF's at last. They order me to report immediately to Victory House for my medical and end, 'Yours sincerely, Commander in charge of WAAF recruiting. PS. Do not come when your period is in progress.'

Joan Wyndham

1944 [London]

Stuart [Preston] told me what he considers the worst thing ever said of anyone: John Betjeman's[1] description of Charles Fry[2] as 'a phallus with a business sense.'

After dinner the sirens went. The guns sounded very distant, so borrowing Stuart's American steel helmet I decided to walk home from Tyburnia. While in Hyde Park and before I reached the Serpentine, the guns beside me opened up cruelly. I put on the steel helmet and cowered under a tree, with the trunk between me and the tarmac road. As there was no building to shelter in I decided it was safer to stay under the tree branches, which might break the fall of shrapnel raining down like hailstones. I heard it crackling through the leaves and thudding in the grass. On the road it struck sparks as it fell. The noise of the Hyde Park guns was deafening and the rocket

[1] John Betjeman, poet, writer and broadcaster. He was appointed Poet Laureate in 1972.
[2] Of B.T. Batsford, publishers.

shells were specially frightening. One gun close to me blew out the tails of my overcoat with blast at every shot.

James Lees-Milne

1992 [Sarajevo]

There's no more trouble in Sarajevo. But there is in other parts of B-H [Bosnia-Herzegovina]: Bosanki Brod, Derventa, Modrica. Terrible reports and pictures coming in from all over. Mummy and Daddy won't let me watch TV when the news is on, but you can't hide all the bad things that are happening from us children. People are worried and sad again. The blue helmets (actually they're blue berets) have arrived in Sarajevo. We're safer now. And the 'kids' [a popular term for politicians] have retreated from the scene.

Zlata Filipovic

25 March

2003 [Baghdad]
10.05a.m. (Day 6)

One mighty explosion at 12 midnight exactly. The raid lasted for ten minutes, then nothing. We had and are still having horrible weather. Very strong winds – hope we don't get up a sandstorm.

In the oh-the-irony-of-it-all section of my life I can add the unbelievable bad luck that when I wanted to watch a movie, because I got sick of all the news, the only movie I had which I have not seen a hundred times is *The American President*. No joke. A friend gave me that video months ago and I never watched it. I did last night. The American 'presidential palace' looks quite good. But Michael Douglas is a sad ass president.

Salam Pax

26 March

1941 [Egypt]

Into the office this morning came an example of the deformity the tongue of Shakespeare and Milton may be twisted into . . . paragraph two of a circular on ammunition returns:

A direction that promptitude in the rendering of a particular return is not given without a substantial underlying reason, and Units should realise that, bearing in mind that all returns should automatically arrive on due date without any necessity for emphasis, any special reference to the necessity for promptitude calls for the utmost vigilance in preventing delay.

Erik de Mauny

1944 [Naples]

The streets of Naples are full of people hawking personal possessions of all kinds: pieces of jewellery, old books, pictures, clothing, etc. Many of them are members of the middle class, and the approach is made in a shamefaced and surreptitious way. One and all, they are in a state of desperate need.

Today at the top of the Via Roma near the Piazza Dante I was stopped by a pleasant-faced old lady, who had nothing for sale but who implored me to go with her to her house in a side-street nearby. She had something to show me, and was so insistent that I followed her to a typical *basso* in a side-street, where she lived. The single, windowless room was lit by a minute electric bulb over the usual shrine, and I saw a thin girl standing in a corner. The reason for the appeal now became clear. This, said the women, was her child, aged thirteen, and she wished to prostitute her. Many soldiers, it seems, will pay for sexual activity less than full intercourse, and she had a revolting scale of fees for these services. For example, the girl would strip and display her pubescent organs for twenty lire.

I told the woman that I would report her to the police, and she pretended to weep, but it was an empty threat, and she knew it. Nothing can be done. There are no police to deal with the thousands of squalid little crimes like this committed every day in the city.

On my way back I was stopped and drawn into a corner by a priest, white-lipped and smiling. He opened a bag full of umbrella handles, candlesticks and small ornaments of all kinds carved out of the bones of the saints, i.e. from bones filched from one of the catacombs. He, too, had to live.

Norman Lewis

27 March

1940 [Rome]

At luncheon Teleki[1] asks me abruptly, 'Do you know how to play bridge?' 'Why?' 'For the day when we are together in the Dachau concentration camp.' This is the real state of mind of this man.

Count Ciano

1941 [Dresden]

I should have reported for my sentence today. I went there (to Police Headquarters), but I was told, my petition was 'being considered', it had been 'passed on with a positive recommendation', the decision lay with a department head, I should wait and see what happens. At the police station they are very courteous, but since in the end some senior Party members make the decision and my name is Victor Israel . . .

Victor Klemperer

28 March

1942 [Rome]

In Venice we have had the first popular demonstrations occasioned by the bread shortage. Many people who had used all their ration stamps before they became due are protesting because the bakers refuse to sell. The Duce was resentful and sad; he gave orders that the crowd be scattered by using leather scabbards.

Count Ciano

1967 [Bolivia]

The radio is still full of news of the guerrillas. We are surrounded by 2,000 men within a radius of 120 kilometres, and the circle is closing in, backed by napalm raids.

Ernesto 'Che' Guevara

---

[1] Count Pal Teleki, former Hungarian Prime Minister.

29 March

1944 [Amsterdam]

Dearest Kitty,

Mr Bolkestein, the Cabinet Minister, speaking on the Dutch broadcast from London, said that after the war a collection would be made of diaries and letters dealing with the war. Of course, everyone pounced on my diary. Just imagine how interesting it would be if I were to publish a novel about the Secret Annexe. The title alone would make people think it was a detective story.

Anne Frank

30 March

1916 [France]

Bullets are deft and flick your life out with a quick smack. Shells rend and bury, and vibrate and scatter, hurling fragments and lumps and jagged splinters at you; they lift you off your legs and leave you huddled and bleeding and torn and scorched with a blast straight from the pit. Heaven is furious with the smoke and flare and portent of shells, but bullets are a swarm of whizzing hornets, mad, winged and relentless, undeviating in their malicious onset.

Siegfried Sassoon

1940 [Rome]

Mussolini is irritated for the nth time at Catholicism, which is to blame for 'having made Italy universal, hence preventing it from becoming national. When a country is universal it belongs to everybody but itself.'

Count Ciano

1942 [Middle East]

Stacy, the pilot who has been flying the Duke of Gloucester around, told me he had to go and identify the crew of an aircraft that burnt out at Heliopolis this morning. He said a well-cooked body is not too bad to look at – it's quite unrecognisable; it's when it's partially cooked, as these were, that you feel weak.

Cecil Beaton

1992 [Sarajevo]

Hey, Diary! You know what I think? Since Anne Frank called her diary Kitty, maybe I could give you a name too. What about:

ASFALTINA

PIDZAMETA

SAFIKA

HIKMETA

SEVALA

MIMMY

or something else???

I'm thinking, thinking . . .

I've decided! I'm going to call you

MIMMY

All right, then, let's start.

Dear Mimmy,

It's almost half-term. We're all studying for our tests. Tomorrow we're supposed to go to a classical music concert at the Skenderija hall. Our teacher says we shouldn't go because there will be 10,000 people, pardon me, children there, and somebody might take us as hostages or plant a bomb in the concert hall. Mummy says I shouldn't go. So I won't.

Hey! You know who won the Yugovision Song Contest?! EXTRA NENA!!!???

Zlata Filipovic

2003 [Baghdad]

No good news anywhere. No light at the end of the tunnel – and the American advance doesn't look that reassuring. If we had a mood barometer in the house it would read TO HELL WITH SADDAM AND MAY HE QUICKLY BE JOINED BY BUSH. No one feels like they should welcome the American army. The American government is getting as many curses as the Iraqi.

Salam Pax

31 March

1918 [France]

I read *War and Peace* of an evening; a grand and consoling book – a huge vista of life and suffering humankind which makes the present troubles easier to endure, and the loneliness of death a little thing.

Siegfried Sassoon

1941 [London]

Called up for WAAF [Women's Auxiliary Air Force] – I go in a week, 7th April. All of a sudden I feel dreadfully depressed. Rowena and I went to the Galeries Lafayette and bought tarty underwear.

Joan Wyndham

1942 [Baltimore]

On March 29, Palm Sunday, there were 22 inches of snow in Baltimore. The *Sun* of yesterday, of course, had to mention the storm, but it did not give the snowfall – something that every reader was speculating about. I complained at the office today that this was an absurd excess of compliance with the war-time order against giving weather information that could be of use to the public enemy. I argued that if there were actually any rule against giving snowfalls or rainfalls it ought to be resisted as senseless. So far as I could make out, no such rule has been issued: the omission of the snowfall was a mere effort to bend backward.

H.L. Mencken

APRIL

All a poet can do today is warn.

Wilfred Owen

1 April

1942 [Monte Estoril]
The wife of the Director of British Studies at the University of Coimbra, a Scotswoman, former elementary school teacher, gives parties to Portuguese students, and attempts to teach them folk-dancing. A scene of ineffable imbecility; Singapore lost, but Sir Roger de Coverley danced in Coimbra.

Malcolm Muggeridge

2 April

1940 [London]
Dine with Kenneth Clark.[1] Willie Maugham,[2] Mrs Winston Churchill and Leslie Howard[3] are there. We have an agreeable dinner and talk mostly about films. Leslie Howard is doing a big propaganda film and is very keen about it. We discuss the position of those English people who have remained in the United States. The film-stars claim that they have been asked to remain since they are more useful in Hollywood, but we all regret bitterly that people like Aldous Huxley, Auden and Isherwood should have absented themselves. They want me to write a *Spectator* article attacking them. That is all very well but it would lose me the friendship of three people whom I much admire. I come back with Leslie Howard and he continues to talk excitedly about his new film. He seems to enter into such things with the zest of a schoolboy, and that is part of his charm.

Harold Nicolson

---

[1] Director of the Film Division of the Ministry of Information. Later Lord Clark of *Civilisation* fame.
[2] Novelist.
[3] Film star, later shot down and killed in 1943.

1942 [Paris]
One of the maids in the hotel has had her head shaved. Lili [an old school friend] says it is because she slept with a German, the French women do this to girls who 'collaborate'. Poor girl – why shouldn't she go out with a German soldier – they are much better looking than the French. I think the Frenchy had better get used to the idea we're here to stay.

Elisabeth von Stahlenberg

1982 [London]
Today the Argentinean Navy were sent to the Falkland Islands, thousands of troops appear to have landed and overwhelmed the British garrison of seventy marines and a population of 1,800. The Government's defence policy has been completely shown up – not that I would favour sending the British forces in, because it's a colony we grabbed years ago from somebody and we have no right to it; neither has Argentina, though it is closer to South America. Some 1,800 British settlers do not constitute a domestic population whose views can be taken seriously, or rather whose views can be allowed to lead us into war. But of course the real interest there is the oil. There is oil around the islands, and Caroline [his wife] pointed out that we should have done a deal years ago. Take the oil, divide it into two – say Argentina can have half the oil and overall theoretical sovereignty. While we would retain the administration and the population would be given shares in our oil. But that isn't the way these things actually work.

Tony Benn

1982 [Kent]
I was due to go down to Plymouth this morning. But when I looked in at Dean's Yard to collect correspondence for signing in the train the whole room seemed to know that the Falkland Islands had been invaded. Delighted to cancel, I made my way over to the Chamber; but somewhat apprehensive as Atkins[1] was due to make a statement at 11a.m.

No point in hanging about. I got back to Sandling at six o'clock. 'We've lost the Falklands,' I told Jane [his wife]. 'It's all over. We're a Third World country, no good for anything.'

She is used to my suddenly taking the *apocalyptic* view. Didn't say

[1] Humphrey Atkins, MP for Spelthorn.

much. I ate some brown toast and crab apple jelly and, it being such
a lovely evening, went for a meander down the valley. I am so depressed
by what I heard today – the shuffling and fudging, the overpowering
impression of timidity and incompetence. Can it have felt like this in
the Thirties, from time to time, on those fine weekends when the
dictators, Hitler and Musso, decided to help themselves to something
– Durazzo, Memel, Prague – and all we could do was wring our hands
and talk about 'bad faith'? I have a terrible feeling that this is a step
change, down, for England. Humiliation for sure, and not impossible,
military defeat. An apparition that must have been stalking us, since
we were so dreadfully weakened at Passchendaele I suppose, for the
last sixty-five years.

Alan Clark

2003 [Baghdad]
Non-stop bombing. At the moment the US/UK are not winning any
battle to 'win the heart and mind' of this individual. No matter which
way this will go, my life will end up more difficult.

You see the news anchors on BBC, Jazeera and Arabiya so often
you start dreaming of them – even noticing when they get a haircut
and in one case on al-Jazeera, a bad dye-job.

Salam Pax

3 April

1982 [London]
My fifty-seventh birthday.

The Falklands Islands is the big news.

The House was in the grip of jingoism. John Silkin and John Nott
made very poor speeches, Nott trying to turn it into a party attack,
which didn't go down very well. I came away full of gloom because
it is obvious that a huge fleet of forty or so warships will set sail for
the Falklands, arrive three weeks later, probably be attacked by the
Argentineans, and then there will be a major battle. The Falklanders
are in effect hostages, and I don't think the US will support us, since
the last thing they want is a big British fleet in the South Atlantic
overturning the Argentinean dictatorship. And that's what will happen,
because General Galtieri, the Argentinean President who attacked the

islands to divert attention from the fall in living standards in Argentina, could himself be deposed. The Americans don't want that, since the whole of Latin America would be set ablaze. Very difficult.

Tony Benn

4 *April*

1916 [France]

What's all this rancour about? Is it my liver? Anyhow I am living in a sort of morose hunger for the next time I can get over the wire and look for the Germans with a bludgeon. Major Stockwell wants a prisoner, and I am going to try and get one for him, but it isn't for that I am going out. I want to smash someone's skull; I want to have a scrap and get out of the war for a bit or for ever. Sitting in a trench waiting for a rifle-grenade isn't fighting: war is clambering out of the top trench at 3 o'clock in the morning with a lot of rum-drugged soldiers who don't know where they're going – half of them to be blasted with machine-guns at point-blank range – trying to get over the wire which our artillery have failed to destroy. I can't get my own back for Hamo[1] and Tommy[2] that way. While I am really angry with the enemy, as I am lately, I must work it off, as these things don't last long with me as a rule. If I get shot it will be rotten for some people at home, but I am bound to get it in the neck some-time, so why not make a creditable show, and let people see that poets can fight as well as anybody else? And death is the best adventure of all – better than living idleness and sinking into the groove again and trying to be happy. Life is precious to us all now; too precious to keep long. 'And sweeter for the fading of those eyes The World seen once for all.'[3]

Siegfried Sassoon

1916 [London]

The state of my own and other people's mind surprises me. We are becoming callous to the horrors of the war. At first it was a continuous

---

[1] His younger brother, killed at Gallipoli, November 1915.
[2] Lieutenant David Thomas, see note for 19 March, 1916.
[3] From Herbert Trench's poem 'Come let us make love deathless'. For 'sweeter' read 'nobler'.

waking nightmare. But within a few months of it one ceases to feel about it. Today one goes on with one's researches, enjoys one's comforts and pleasures and even reads the daily war news with mild interest, exactly as if slaughter and devastation, on a colossal scale, were part of the expected routine of life. This callousness to the horrors of war explains the way in which the wealthy governing class have tolerated the horrors of peace due to the existing social order. Is there no depth of misery and degradation, endured by other persons, which will not be accepted as normal and inevitable?

Beatrice Webb

1940 [Berlin]
Every day we get the verbatim monitored record of all B.B.C. News and other foreign broadcasts. Labelled *streng geheim* [top secret], the colour of the paper depends on the degree of 'secrecy', pink being the most secret of them all. It makes interesting reading. Nobody in Germany is supposed to know what the rest of the world is up to except what appears in the daily papers and that is not much. Our D.D. is one of the exceptions. This afternoon our Foreign Ministry colleague came in for lunch looking haggard – he had forgotten one of these volumes in a restaurant. This is a most serious offence and visions of the death penalty – by axe (the latest invention of our rulers) – chills his mind. He has raced off to his Ministry to 'confess'.

Marie 'Missie' Vassiltchikov

1941 [Berlin]
Magda's father [his father-in-law] is dying. I scarcely know him and his passing will be no loss.

Josef Goebbels

5 April

1940 [Rome]
Last night I saw the German film about the conquest of Poland. I had previously refused to attend, but if I had again been absent last night, it would have looked too strange. It is a good film if the Germans

wish merely to portray brute force, but it is awful for propaganda purposes. The audience, composed in part of pro-German officials and in part of self-appointed pro-German pimps, did not go beyond the limits of mere courtesy in its applause.

Count Ciano

6 April

1942 [Monte Estoril]

I went yesterday to a bull fight, accompanied by a middle-aged Russian woman Madame Sazanov, émigrée twice removed, from Russia and then from France, and her son Dmitry. He came up to me and said rather apologetically: 'Je suis plein d'enthousiasme, monsieur.' It was true, the poor soul was full of enthusiasm. Later, he repeated the same remark. It appeared to be the sole content of his being – this sense of being 'plein d'enthousiasme'. The bull fight was exciting for ten minutes or so, and then rather boring. It was very like the war – all the worst features of bull fighting, deception, vanity, cruelty, etc., but no kill; same bull, it seemed, used again and again.

Malcolm Muggeridge

7 April

1855 [Crimea]

I have received this night an order to prepare for an attack to-morrow, and everything is ordered to be in readiness. For aught I know, it may please God to prevent my seeing either wife or children again in this world; and, therefore, I am writing with serious feelings, and with no levity. Yet I wish to record my feelings; and I do say that the imbecility of the conduct of the Allies, arising from I know not what beyond pure stupidity, surpasses human comprehension.

Lieut. General Sir Charles Ash Windham

1916 [Essex, England]

4 p.m. Dr R. P. Smallwood called: very tired and with much less in the way of notes than usual: Officers, back from the front say that the

label 'reported missing: believed killed' covers a good many cases of men shunning duty from cowardice, or inflicting wounds on themselves in hope of being sent to hospital.

Andrew Clark

1917 [France]

I don't suppose anyone would believe me if I said I was absolutely happy and contented. Of course this is written after a good meal of coffee and eggs. But the fact remains that if I had the choice between England to-morrow and the battle, I would choose the battle without hesitation. Why on earth is one such a fool as to be pleased at the prospect? I can't understand it. Last year I thought it was because I had never been through it before. But my feeling of quiet elation and absolute confidence now is something even stronger than last summer's passionate longing for death and glory.

Siegfried Sassoon

1942 [Worcestershire]

Talked with Mama in her bedroom this morning. She is full of complaints as usual. Papa has let the large cottage for only £2 although it is fully furnished; there are endless parties of people in the house; the garden boy is leaving, and the gardener, who is only forty-three, may be called up; and Gertrude is to be married in a fortnight. She is the only servant in the house now, and Colonel Riley, who is billeted on them, has to be waited upon, hand and foot. Mama is very distressed because Gertrude is due to have the curse the very day of her wedding, which could not be arranged otherwise because her young man has to take his leave when he is given it. Mama says the curse will come precisely at 11.55 a.m. that day, that it always comes regular as clockwork with strong healthy girls, a thing I never knew before and can scarcely credit.

James Lees-Milne

1965 [Baltimore]

[After President Johnson's speech on Vietnam to the Johns Hopkins University] I had the high, thrilling feeling that we have taken the initiative. We are beginning to really explain to the world about Vietnam, about what we can do, about the promise of this epoch in history – that we are on the move against the negation of war and communism. It was exciting. I felt as if the stalemate had had a fire-cracker put under it.

Lady Bird Johnson

2003 [Baghdad]
11.30 a.m. (Day 19)

The Americans called it 'a show of force' and NOT the anticipated invasion of Baghdad. Well, it was definitely a great show for anyone watching it from a high orbit. Added to the constant whooshes of missiles going over our heads and the following explosions, another sandstorm decided to make our life even more difficult than it already is. I mean your – ahem – boogers come out red, because of all the sand you inhale. Closing the windows is madness. It is safer to open the windows when the explosions start.

Since the day the airport was seized we have no electricity and water is not reliable. At times if you have a tap that is higher than 50 cm you won't get water from it. We turn on the generator for four hours during the day and four at night, mainly to watch the news. Today my father wanted to turn on the generator at eight in the morning, because of the news of an attack on the centre of Baghdad. We sat for two hours watching the same images until Kuwait TV showed footage taken from Fox News of American soldiers in Al-Sijood Palace. Totally dumb-struck. Right after that we saw al-Sahaf denying once again what we have just seen minutes ago. He kept insisting that there are no American troops in Baghdad and for some reason kept insisting that al-Jazeera has become 'a tool of American media'. Idiot. Jazeera has been obvi-ously very critical of the American 'invasion' (they insist on calling it that) and what does the super-smart Information Minister do? Ostracize them some more.

Salam Pax

8 April

1917 [France]
A bright warm Easter day but Achicourt shelled at 2.15 so that we all retired to cellar. I had to go over to battery at 3 for a practice barrage, skirting the danger zone, but we were twice interrupted. A 5.9 fell 2 yards from me as I stood by the f/C post. One burst down the back

of the office and a piece of dust scratched my neck. No firing from 2–4. Rubin left for a course.

> The light of the new moon and every star
> And no more singing for the bird[1]

Edward Thomas

1941 [London]

Have just read *The Battle of Britain*, the M.O.I.'s [Ministry of Information] best bestseller. (There was so great a run on it that copies were unprocurable for some days.) It is said to have been compiled by Francis Beeding[2], the writer of thrillers. I suppose it is not as bad as it might be, but seeing that it is being translated into many languages and will undoubtedly be read all over the world – it is the first official account, at any rate in English, of the first great air battle in history – it is a pity that they did not have the sense to avoid the propagandist note altogether. The pamphlet is full of 'heroic', 'glorious exploits' etc., and the Germans are spoken of more or less slightingly. Why couldn't they simply give a cold accurate account of the facts, which, after all, are favourable enough? For the sake of the bit of cheer-up that this pamphlet will accomplish in England, they throw away the chance of producing something that would be accepted all over the world as a standard authority and used to counteract German lies.

But what chiefly impresses me when reading *The Battle of Britain* and looking up the corresponding dates in this diary, is the way in which 'epic' events never seem very important at the time. Actually I have a number of vivid memories of the day the Germans broke through and fired the docks (I think it must have been the 7th September), but mostly trivial things. First of all, riding down in the bus to have tea with [Cyril] Connolly, and two women in front of me insisting that shell-bursts in the sky were parachutes, till I had a hard job of it not to chip in and correct them. Then sheltering in a doorway in Piccadilly from falling shrapnel, just as one might shelter from a cloud-burst. Then a long line of German planes filing across the sky, and some very young R.A.F. and naval officers running out of one of the hotels and passing a pair of field glasses from hand to hand. Then

---

[1] The last entry in Thomas's diary: he was killed a few hours later.

[2] Pseudonym of two men, Hilary St George Saunders and John Palmer.

sitting in Connolly's top-floor flat and watching the enormous fires beyond St Paul's, and the great plume of smoke from an oil drum somewhere down the river, and Hugh Slater[1] sitting in the window and saying, 'It's just like Madrid – quite nostalgic.' The only person suitably impressed was Connolly, who took us up to the roof and, after gazing for some time at the fires, said 'It's the end of capitalism. It's a judgement on us.' I didn't feel this to be so, but was chiefly struck by the size and beauty of the flames. That night I was woken up by the explosions and actually went out into the street to see if the fires were still alight – as a matter of fact it was almost as bright as day, even in the N.W. Quarter – but still didn't feel as though any important historical event were happening. Afterwards, when the attempt to conquer England by air bombardment had evidently been abandoned, I said to Fyvel,[2] 'That was Trafalgar. Now there's Austerlitz,' but I hadn't seen this analogy at the time.

The *News Chronicle* very defeatist again, making a great outcry about the abandonment of Bengazi, with the implication that we ought to have gone for Tripoli while the going was good instead of withdrawing troops to use in Greece. And these are exactly the people who would have raised the loudest squeal if we had gone on with the conquest of the Italian empire and left the Greeks in the soup.

George Orwell

1942 [Monte Estoril, Portugal]

A half-caste woman is singing in the garden in the sun. A human being has only to sing spontaneously for hope to take possession of my heart, but not of any victory or defeat in this or any other war; hope of the outcome of life for me and all who ever have or ever will live, delight in life because of this life.

Malcolm Muggeridge

1942 [Rome]

Somebody was talking about illiteracy in certain Italian regions, when Mussolini said: 'Even if this were true, what is the difference? In the fourteenth century Italy was populated by nothing but illiterates, and

---

[1] Hugh (Humphrey) Slater, writer, painter, Communist, organiser of Home Guard training, friend of Orwell.

[2] T.R. (Tosco) Fyvel, broadcaster, writer, journalist, friend of Orwell.

this did not prevent the flowering of Dante Alighieri. Today, when everybody knows how to read and write, we have instead the poet [Corrado] Govoni, who, while not exactly insignificant, is certainly something less than Dante.'

Count Ciano

1943 [Kovno Ghetto, Lithuania]

We have received information from various sources about the shocking scenes of the massacre at Ponar. The engineer who drove the train carrying scores of Jews to the slaughter relates with anguish the details of the executions. The train with seventy or eighty locked and sealed boxcars was brought to Ponar. Waiting for it there was a large contingent of the auxiliary units of the Lithuanian police. The Lithuanian policemen wore black uniforms, and were supervised by Germans of the Gestapo. A Gestapo reinforcement from Kovno was also brought in.

In a field nearby, a barrel of vodka had been put at the disposal of the policemen; they helped themselves to their favorite drink throughout. The drink helped them to carry out their assignment.

The train stopped. The Jews were taken out of it in small groups of twenty to eighty people and ordered to march forward. They were surrounded by German and Lithuanian policemen, beasts of prey in human disguise, ready for action. The policemen would then open fire, turning their rifles and machine guns on the stunned victims. The air quickly became thick with fire and smoke. Under the hail of bullets, the victims started running about in distress. They fell down, individuals and groups, in the field.

When the anguished cries of the victims, running in all directions under the rain of bullets, reached the ears of those who were still in the sealed boxcars, they were seized with panic and the terror of death. Through the apertures in the boxcars' walls – so the engineer continues – one could see the tense faces of throngs of frightened people. They saw annihilation lying ahead – the end. Those first to get down from the cars were at a loss to know in which direction they should go, but were mowed down by a hail of bullets. The others, following behind them, made desperate attempts to flee. In one car, the intended victims succeeded in making a hole in the wall, jumped out, and started running in all directions. Some of them got away. These were the ones about whom [SS Master Sergeant] Schtitz warned Lipzer[1] that should they arrive in the Kovno Ghetto they must be handed over to the Gestapo.

The fields of Ponar became the scene of a spectacle of horror. A deep and wide pit was dug into which the fallen victims were thrown like so many corpses. The fields of Ponar were strewn with the bodies of thousands of martyrs. In the thick of the deluge of gunfire, several Jews rose up and defended themselves with stones which they picked up from the ground. They also pounced with sticks on the murderers. They even tried to snatch weapons from the hands of some of them. The Jews succeeded in beating to death some of the Lithuanian 'hired' killers. In the ensuing pandemonium, the Lithuanian policemen fired at each other and also at the Germans of the Gestapo.

The horrible scenes keep coming alive before the eyes of the engineer; the field swarming with people running in all directions, searching for shelter; the dead and the wounded being thrown into the pit. One image inscribed itself on his memory with particular force; a blond Jewish girl, seventeen or eighteen, who fell down into a puddle of blood right next to the engine. She was lying there, her face turned skyward.

News of the horror has already reached many in the city. Even the Germans describe the killing as a heinous murder. We keep hearing terrible details from the workers at the railway workshops, and from workers in other workplaces who heard them from witnesses of the slaughter. We hear, and we refuse to believe, even though we know that the victims were thousands of Jews from the Vilna district.

Avraham Tory

9 April

1940 [California]
German troops landing in Denmark and Norway. All day long, the radio and the special editions were full of sinking ships, occupied towns, air raids, scares, rumours and lies. Felt too depressed to write the new scene for *Rage in Heaven*. Appropriately enough, it plays in a death-house cell.

---

[1] Benno Lipzer, a Jew who worked with the Gestapo in order to help other Jews, but who was eventually murdered by the Germans.

Vernon[1] [his companion] left, this morning, for New York to visit his mother. Berthold also left for New York, two days ago. He has been asked to produce a play, called Thumbs – a thriller starring Oscar Homalka.

I'm about to sign a contract which will tie me to Metro for a year. It's a long prospect of drudgery with the Chopin film as a beginning.

Saw Gerald[2] in the evening. We talked about the enlargement of consciousness. Three stages: first, you see something – some single object – as it really is, 'in its own right'; then you see that the object is part of a plan – its position in time and space is inevitable – it isn't there by accident; then in the highest state of illumination, you see beyond objects altogether – you trace, as it were, the line which connects them all with a single focal point, the absolute reality.

Experience of the first stage is quite common to artists and other observant people. I have often had it myself. It may be achieved, for example, by an accident of light, or a disturbance of the normal laws of perspective. The door of Chris's[3] bedroom is set at an angle to the wall, and this gives it – at moments when you happen to notice it – a most disturbing air of being, somehow, 'outside the picture frame'. Gerald told me how, the other day, he was looking into the bowl of the toilet: a green light fell on the porcelain, through the leaves outside the window, and it appeared to him 'as it really was'. 'Nothing else mattered to me at that moment. I could have gone on looking at it for ever.'

Christopher Isherwood

1942 [London]

At tea-time went to Mayfair hotel to see demonstration of 'Liberty cut' sponsored by Min of Health, as an anti-typhus measure. New line of country for me; place crowded with hairdressers, representatives of the Press (mostly hard-working women plainly dressed), and fashionable ladies in mink coats looking as if they'd never heard of the war. Several leading hairdressers talked on importance of shorter hair for women in present crisis. Demonstration of 'Liberty cut' on different girls followed, including a showing of the 'cut' itself. The number of

---

[1] Vernon Old (not his real name), American painter, boyfriend of Isherwood until Feb. 1941. Later married and had a son.
[2] Gerald Heard (1885–1971) Irish writer, broadcaster, religious teacher, a disciple of Swami Prabhavananda.
[3] Chris Wood (d 1976) rich, extravagant companion of Gerald Heard.

men present interested me; it showed how much money there is to be
made out of women's hair.

Vera Brittain

1976 [The Philippines, on the set of *Apocalypse Now*]
Several hundred South Vietnamese people were recruited from a
refugee camp near Manila to play North Vietnamese in the film.
As I passed their rest area today they were rehearsing a little play
while they waited for the next shot. They speak no English but one
young man called out 'Stand by' and everyone got quiet and ready.
Then he clapped two sticks together and called 'Action' and the
play began in Vietnamese. Later I noticed the group leader called
lunch the same way. He said 'Stand by' and they all assembled; he
clapped his sticks and called 'Action' and they walked to lunch in
a neat line.

Eleanor Coppola

1982 [Kent, during the Falklands War]
As I said on the walks to Jane: 'It's even a fudge; two to one a disaster and The Lady[1] resigning from the despatch box; three to one a
naval victory and the bunting round Nelson column.'

Alan Clark

10 April

1940 [England]
Norway and Denmark invaded. Oslo bombed. The compositors reach
for their two inch sans-serif.

Keith Vaughan

1942 [Lisbon]
An American journalist has written an article pointing out that Japan
suffers earthquakes every thirty years, and that one is now due. Thus
will the sinking of the American fleet in Pearl Harbor be easily avenged,
and America's enemy easily be defeated.

Malcolm Muggeridge

[1] The Prime Minister, Margaret Thatcher.

2003 [Baghdad]

3.00p.m. (Day 22)

After having a house full of people for a while it feels pretty empty now. Most of the family has decided to go back to their houses. We had an amazing couple of days.

4 April: The Americans in the airport.

7 April: They move into Baghdad.

9 April: Troops are in Firdaws Square ('firdaws' means 'heaven') with no Iraqi military Presence in the streets whatsoever. They just disappered – puff! – into thin air. The Big Disappearing Act. Army shoes and uniforms are thrown about in every street; army cars abandoned in the middle of the road. An act of the Almighty made every army member disappear at exactly the same time, fairy-tale-like: '. . . and the golden carriage was turned back to a pumpkin at the stroke of twelve.'

Around 6 p.m. yesterday we turned on the electricity generator to check the news. Lo-and-behold! Holy cow in the sky! What do we see? Iraqis trying to pull down the Saddam statue in Al-firdaws Square. That the American troops are so deep in the city was not as surprising as the bunch of people trying to pull that thing down. By now any relatives and friends have told us that they saw a lot of American soldiers in the city, even before the 9th of April. Not only the presidential palaces, but also in many residential districts. The news does not tell you everything. They quickly mentioned the Saddam Bridge, not saying that this was right beside the University of Baghdad and a stone's throw from the main presidential complex.

Salam Pax

11 April

1941 [Gloucester]

My first pay parade. Got ten bob and tried to look suitably grateful. Still very cold, but apple blossom is flowering between the huts.

We're getting to be seasoned warriors now, our discipline is terrific. You should have seen the suicidal precision with which we marched, three abreast, straight into a stone wall the other day because we hadn't heard the 'left wheel'!

It's been pouring with rain and the parade-ground is covered with deep pools, which we try to skirt when on the march. 'Go through it, you slackahs!' yells our Sergeant. 'A little watah won't hurt you!'

The food gets better and better. This morning for breakfast we had stewed figs and baked beans on toast with *real* coffee!

In the afternoon we had some free time, so Samantha washed out her knickers and put them on the line outside the hut. When she came back after tea there was a note pinned in their place saying 'These drawers are now the property of Aircraftman Jenkins. If you wish to reclaim them please report to hut nine at eight o'clock.' Poor Samantha is very upset as they were her best knickers.

Joan Wyndham

1945 [in transit from Bergen-Belsen camp in Germany]

The night is hell. We are sitting on our bench, folded double, rolled up, with pain in every muscle, and get in each other's way; aggression – bad as it is already – is mounting. The wagons are packed out. In our coach, which has seating for forty-eight people, sixty-two must live and sleep. Last night they gave us butter, one pound per four persons for four days. It is a lot, relatively, and we are not dissatisfied. The promised sausage – for which we are longing – has not arrived yet.

The night dragged by. First we experienced a heavy bombardment at Bergen station. Then suddenly a jerk and our journey had begun. Supposedly to Theresienstadt and Switzerland. The train crept forward. The sky was filled with bombardments and combat. It thundered and cracked. The night was cold and dark. I was constantly quarrelling with the women facing me because of our feet. We were unable to sleep. From time to time someone would doze off and after a few minutes wake up with a sigh. That was the second night. How many more will there be?

It is deathly quiet in Germany. We see nothing but soldiers and SS. It is dismal in Germany. Everyone expects the end any day now, the political catastrophe.

Abel J. Herzberg

1982 [London]

Papers at 8 o'c. Jock [newsvendor] said to me 'Will you be going to entertain the troops in the Falklands campaign?' There have been quite a few remarks like this lately.

Kenneth Williams

12 April

1941 [Berlin]

Himmler[1] has banned the sale of contraceptive devices. This is very important at the moment. Let people make provision for children. On the other hand, child benefits will do more to increase our population than bureaucratic edicts.

Josef Goebbels

1942 [Barrow, England]

Often, I think how much later people marry. When I was a girl, it was considered very odd not to be married at twenty-one or twenty-two, and my mother said seventeen or eighteen was the age most girls thought of marriage when she was young. Gran spoke of ploughmen with two and three children by the time they were twenty-one. I wonder if the war is going to cause a swing to earlier marriages. Looking around among friends' and acquaintances' boys and girls – sons of twenty-five to thirty with still no thoughts of marriage, and girls who are going off to the Services and saying, 'Oh, we will wait till after the war to get married.' If the country wants babies, I feel this conscription of women will be a backward step, for it is taking the best, most formative years from a girl's life, and giving her a taste of freedom from home drudgery that many crave for. Will they settle later to homes and children?

It's not very profitable to sit and think nowadays. So many problems, and they seem all to have such twists to them – *nothing* is straightforward.

Nella Last

1944 [Tuscany]

To-day I have received a visit from two other Englishmen, whom I found sitting in deck-chairs in my garden! I suggest that we should move up to a more secluded spot in the woods and there we have an agreeable conversation. Both educated men, who have now been prisoners in Italy for nearly three years, they speak of recent events ('from a worm's eye view', as they say themselves) with great moderation and good sense. They are only too well aware of the change in feeling here

---

[1] Heinrich Himmler, Head of the SS 1940–45, and Germany's Minister of the Interior 1943–45.

in the last few months – caused partly by the indiscriminate bombing, but even more by the Allies' dilatoriness. 'Do you realize,' they say, 'that for the last fifty miles everyone whom we have asked for help has sent us to you? Hadn't you better be careful?' They are, however, unable to suggest what form such carefulness should take – and as we are sitting talking, at the edge of a pine wood over the brow of the hill, I become aware that someone is standing behind us – a ragged, unshaven figure, watching us in silence. I hastily get up, my mind full of the tales of Fascist spies, and go towards him – only to observe, to my intense relief, that he is wearing Antonio's [her husband] tennis shoes! He is one of Bert's friends – and with great relief I take back the news to the other POWs, who have meanwhile moved off into a thicket. 'What a life you do lead!' – they remark, and we part with mutual expressions of good will.

Iris Origo

13 April

1942 [Monte Estoril, Portugal]
I have now moved away from Lisbon and its streets to Estoril, and sit looking at the sea. In the evenings I sit with Madame Sazanov and her son Dimitry, and she tells me about her adventures escaping from Russia after the Revolution, about literary personages in Paris, about Russian literature. It means talking in French and soon makes me tired. She is shabby, spirited, rather forlorn; her son sickly, pathetic, rather sweet-natured. They will push along together, he dreaming of being an aviator, she hoping for little, and in that praiseworthy. This evening she arranged chessmen on the table to illustrate the Russian Front, the queen Leningrad, and king Moscow, the other pieces smaller places. After lunch she came up to my room with 'des petites choses qui peuvent vous intéresser'. The petites choses turned out to be a collection of British and Free French propaganda. These two are exiles, hopeless, rather weary; they cling to the idea of England; there, perhaps, clinging to nothing.

Malcolm Muggeridge

1945 [England]
It was announced at midnight that yesterday afternoon President Roosevelt died at Warm Springs, Georgia, from a cerebral haemorrhage.

Thought all day of my talk with him at the White House in December 1937 &, despite the altercations over bombing, felt I had lost a personal friend. Above all I was stunned with dismay, wondering what would happen to the future organisation. Sent a cable to Eleanor Roosevelt. Seems an ironic end – like Lincoln's – when the victory he worked for is almost here & both armies are approaching Berlin.

Vera Brittain

1945 [England]

It's no fun, waiting for the war to end. A year ago, these days would have seemed like the anteroom to Paradise! Now, each day brings more confusions, more anxieties – and no relief. It's pretty bad on a Bomber Station here at home; on the Western Front, or in Italy, or the Far East, it must be almost unbearable.

Henry Treece

1945 [Carradale, Scotland]

Angus met me at 8.30 at the workshop saying bad news, I said what is it, he said Roosevelt's dead and told me the details. We talked of the possible implications, he asked what sort of man Truman[1] was, and so on. We then talked about sowing but the weather is bad still and the ground, cold and damp, would clog the seeder. I was wondering if this would mean another war and felt deeply depressed. Fred was depressed too, on his way down to work on the ditches. I came back, thought I'd see what everyone said. Rita Grant . . . Isn't it awful. He looked so ill when I saw him last – in the pictures, after Yalta, quite worn out. Rita Flynn . . . Yes, Joan told me he's dead. He must had had too much work. Humphrey . . . God!, this is frightful. Then after a few noises, a pity it wasn't Dewey[2] last time. I say why, I think it's a kind of fate. Jean Semple . . . Isn't it sad. Such a good man and he never saw the end of his labours. A nice way for him but awful shock for his people.

Then Margaret Cole . . . This is rather a blow . . . What the bloody hell will happen to the treaties . . . Then, after a little silence and a few remarks between us about Truman and the general situation: They (Americans) won't be able to do anything about it . . . why couldn't it have been Churchill! Me: Quite! Just what I was thinking. I'm not

[1] Harry S. Truman, Roosevelt's vice-president. President of the United States 1945–52.
[2] Thomas Edmund Dewey, Republican nominee for president in 1944 and 1948.

sure, even, why couldn't it have been Stalin! We went on to consider that both Churchill and Stalin were older than Roosevelt, and what a situation it would be if they both died before the peace, leaving Hitler and Mussolini alive. I said it shows God isn't on our side. Margaret said I don't think I can stand for a joke of those dimensions.

Naomi Mitchison

14 April

1917 [France]

I have seen the most ghastly sights since we came up here. The dead bodies lying about the trenches and in the open are beyond description – especially after the rain. (A lot of the Germans killed by our bombardment last week are awful.) Our shelling of the line – and subsequent bombing etc – has left a number of mangled Germans – they will haunt me till I die. And everywhere one sees the British Tommy in various states of dismemberment – most of them are shot through the head – so not so fearful as the shell-twisted Germans. Written at 9.30 sitting in the Hindenburg underground tunnel on Sunday night, fully expecting to get killed on Monday morning.

Siegfried Sassoon

1943 [England]

I made a potato and leek soup for supper – then went fire watching. It was a beautiful evening. On the bridge I saw a girl warden (rather plain) being kissed by a Doughboy (a hidey-ho, a sweet and lo, a come and go boy). Lucky pigs I thought.

Barbara Pym

1945 [England]

Everybody on the Station has had to fill in a form stating where he will live after the war, what job he intends to do, what training he would like to have, to prepare him for that job, while in the Services.

I really haven't a clue. I wrote 'Not known,' 'Nil,' etc, to nearly all my questions. I don't want to be taught anything. I'm not even sure I want to do anything ever again! For four years the R.A.F. has taught me to do a certain job in a certain way, and I don't feel now that I have the interest or energy left to start anything new.

In fact, in some ways I rather dread the war ending. I can quite understand how shaken a regular man must feel at leaving to go into the big bad outside world, and fend for himself.

Henry Treece

15 April

1941 [London]
Last night went to the pub to listen to the 9 o'clock news, and arriving there a few minutes late, asked the landlady what the news had been. 'Oh, we never turn it on. Nobody listens to it, you see. And they've got the piano playing in the other bar, and they won't turn it off just for the news.' This at a moment when there is a most deadly threat to the Suez canal. Cf. during the worst moment of the Dunkirk campaign, when the barmaid would not have turned on the news unless I had asked her . . . Cf. also the time in 1936 when the Germans reoccupied the Rhineland. I was in Barnsley at the time. I went into a pub just after the news had come through and remarked at random, 'The German army has crossed the Rhine.' With a vague air of remembering something, someone murmured, 'Parley-voo.' No more response than that . . . So also at every moment of crisis from 1931 onwards. You have all the time the sensation of kicking against an impenetrable wall of stupidity. But of course at times their stupidity has stood them in good stead. Any European nation situated as we are would have been squealing for peace long ago.

George Orwell

1982 [London]
Chris Mullin[1] rang to tell me the *Daily Star* had a heading 'Whose Side Are They On?' with pictures of the ten of us opposed to the Task Force [heading for the Falkland Islands], implying our treachery. It is bound to happen; you couldn't expect otherwise at this early stage of jingoistic fervour.

Tony Benn

---

[1] Chris Mullin, newly-appointed editor of the *Tribune*, later MP.

16 April

1915 [Reigate]

Beb[1] told me they really think they are going to the front on Thursday. It is very difficult to believe that history will interfere in one's private life to such an extent. Beb going to the front seems too melodramatic to be true. It is a thing I cannot at all imagine in anticipation until it has happened. I don't know what I shall feel like. He is excited and very keen. They have had definite orders, but of course they may be revoked.

Lady Cynthia Asquith

1942 [Monte Estoril]

Lunched with Rita Windsor and others from the Embassy, including Press Attaché, at English Club, piece of land forever England, leather chairs, subdued light, florid men reading newspapers, etc., etc. Inevitably discussed war. Rita said we were fighting for a chance to go on living as we were accustomed to, though as a matter of fact there was no possibility of our doing so in any case. It was, I said, like fighting a duel over a woman who was in fact dead and buried. But suppose, little man called Bush said, you won and had to sleep with the corpse. I agreed that that was the most appalling prospect of all.

Malcolm Muggeridge

17 April

1918 [Lewes, England]

No good attempting to keep a diary. War news awful, the whole of life grim.

Mrs Henry Dudeney

1940 [London]

Halifax was most amusing about his interview yesterday with Dr Marie Stopes,[2] who came to the Foreign Office, and said that she had had

---

[1] Herbert Asquith, her husband. Son of Herbert Asquith, Prime Minister 1908–15, head of Coalition Government May 1915 to Dec 1916.

[2] Dr Marie Stopes, scientist who devoted herself to birth control and family planning.

affairs with over 100 Germans and then with at least 100 Americans, so she knew men better than most women. She was prepared, she told Lord Halifax, to accept Cabinet Office and would he pass on her request to the Prime Minister?

'Chips' Channon

1941 [Surrey]

Last night London had its fiercest blitz of the war. With transport badly organized, by train I could travel no nearer the office than Clapham Junction and thence by tram only so far as Wandsworth Road station. For the rest the two-mile walk in bright spring sunshine would have been enjoyable but for the havoc caused by enemy bombing, which everywhere was a gruesome reminder of the horrors of war in this bitter struggle for mastery. For almost two miles a continuous line of hosepipes, fire brigades and ambulances, the scores of tired firemen attested to the intensity of the attack and its effects. So spent were the firemen, I found some asleep in doorways and corners amidst the ruins of burnt-out buildings. Pitifully the chattels of many a home lay exposed naked in doorless niches, or were still clinging to some blasted wall, for the curious to gape at. What could be rescued of the furniture was huddled together on the pavement. Perched on top of one pile a canary in its cage was singing lustily. Arriving two hours late I found that every window in front of the office had been blown out and even the heavy window frame shattered by the blast from a nearby bomb. Radiators had cracked and flooded some of the rooms. Equipment, files and papers covered in debris. Office routine was suspended while the staff cleared up the mess. Not until the following day did we resume normal duties; even so the draughty discomfort drove most of the women staff to the basement shelter to work.

Walter Musto

1941 [London]

There was not much sleep to be had last night. London, particularly the West End, was bombed continuously until four o'clock this morning, when day began to break. And a good many of the bombs were very large ones. Most of the guests in the hotel made themselves comfortable in the lobby, playing cards or talking. I had gone to my room, and at half-past two was trying to pass the time by finishing up *War and Peace*, when Herschel[1] rang me up and invited me down to his room on the first floor. There we sat talking about everything, while our conversation was punctuated by tremendous explosions in every direction, many of which made the structure of the whole hotel tremble. What seemed peculiar about this bombardment was the fact that at hardly any minute was there any absence of enemy machines droning overhead. Large fires lighted the horizon in our quarter, and although we gained the impression that the West End was taking a terrible beating, now I have a notion that all of London was suffering. This was easily the worst attack that London has sustained at night. The only one I can think of which would compare with it was the daylight attack on Dockland which initiated the Battle of London.

I could not help but think this is a very queer life. During the height of the blitz Herschel and I spent about an hour discussing Hugo's *Les Misérables* and Thomas Wolfe's books. He knew Thomas Wolfe and told me quite a lot about him. Also, after we had finished this, Herschel began bringing out some beautiful pieces of porcelain which he had there, and we talked about Chinese art. All this time I had a sickening feeling that hundreds of people were being murdered in a most savage way almost within a stone's throw and there was nothing to do about it.

General Raymond E. Lee

1941 [Berlin]
Purchase a few glorious van Dycks from Holland.

Josef Goebbels

1944 [Tuscany]
Spent the morning trying to alter the date of birth on the identity card of a young deserter who turned up this morning and firmly requested this service – with the same confidence with which others have asked for a clean shirt or some food. It is much more difficult to do than one would think, even though the type of my machine is fortunately of the same size as that used in his document, the difficulty being to put the new figure precisely in line with the others.

[1] Herschel V. Johnson, chargé d'affaires and second in command at the American Embassy in London.

And clumsiness is lent to one's fingers by the thought that the boy's life may hang on it being done well.

Iris Origo

1945 [London]

I took my son with me to the House of Commons where I picked up two tickets for the Service at St Paul's in memory of President Roosevelt. Then we drove through the crowded traffic and parked our car in Amen Court. The great church was not full, though there were many people in the nave where we sat, surrounded by peers, MPs, soldiers and notabilities. The Lord Mayor stood at the steps of the Cathedral to meet the sovereigns and he held the Sword of State high and erect. We saw the Royal Procession form, and then slowly advance up the aisle. We were very near. The King was in Naval uniform, the Queen in black. Immediately behind them were the King of Norway, escorting the Queen of Holland. The Norwegian King was tall and slender and stately. Next came George of Greece and Peter of Yugoslavia, both in uniform, Olaf of Norway, the Princess Royal looking as cross as ever; the Duchess of Kent, a dream, was with Lord Harewood. Four Kings and Queens made an impressive array, and the service then began. Winant[1] read from Revelation. The Star Spangled Banner was sung like a negro spiritual, and the words of the Anthem were magnificent. The service lasted three-quarters of an hour, and then the Royal Procession defiled past us again, and left the Cathedral as the bells slowly tolled. The Last Post and Reveille were sounded, and then Winant, dark and romantically handsome, escorted Winston, who was in tears, to the door. After that, everyone in England walked to the exits. Paul[2] and I slipped out, and turning back towards St Paul's we saw Winston standing bare-headed, framed between two columns of the portico, and he was sobbing as the shaft of sunlight fell on his face and the cameras clicked. We hurried sadly home to lunch in the nursery.

'Chips' Channon

[1] John Winant, American Ambassador.
[2] Paul Channon, his son, who later became an MP.

18 April

1915 [Reigate]

When I got out of bed I found my neck and chest were covered with a rash. A little man exactly like Dr Dose in Happy Families [card game] came to see me and, to my horror and amusement, said he thought it must be German measles (Hun pox). It was comic bathos to have German measles just now, but I gnashed my teeth in rage. It seemed too cruel if I shouldn't be able to be with Beb [her husband] at Portsmouth for these last few days. I can't count how many people I kissed on Friday! Beb went off [en route to the front] about 10.30.

Lady Cynthia Asquith

1917 [France]

A quiet day in bed in the tend of D. Ward. A pouring wet, raw day outside. Ten officers in the tent, including a charming little R.F.C. [Royal Flying Corps] boy called D.T. Leyshon (late of the Second Welsh). Been in France since January 1915 and is now only eighteen and a half! A gunner major opposite me has been gassed. He is only about twenty-six, and carries on the usual discussions common among such gatherings of officers who don't know one another's failings. 'Seniority' – 'Decorations' – 'Wound-stripes' etc. These discussions are always an airing of personal grievances. The man who has received a decoration never complains of the unfairness of the system. The man who *has* got one listens, and knows damn well how much it is worth to him. The conscientious professional soldier is the dullest man on earth.

Siegfried Sassoon

1940 [London]

Started my first figure from life with Henry Moore. The model smelt awful. She has red hair. Today the Germans captured Trondheim.

Joan Wyndham

1940 [USA]

There has been a dreadful air raid of London 'in retaliation', the Germans say. Oh, why gloss over brutality with an excuse. War is just war. It is the falseness of everything that drives me crazy now. The false self-righteousness of the Germans, the false hopefulness and 'morale' of the lying headlines here.

Anne Morrow Lindbergh

1945 [Wiltshire]

Lying on the lawn this afternoon in weather more appropriate to July than April, I could neither read nor think – only wonder. I wonder, for instance, why our present situation seems more like the last years of peace than the earlier part of the war. We haven't had a single rocket or bomb on England for two weeks. The attempts made to encourage bitter hatred are common to this fag-end of the war and the last weeks of peace. Perhaps we should pull ourselves together and shake off this uneasy waiting state and try and accommodate ourselves to the new order of things. R. says we are like returned prisoners-of-war – we need rehabilitation. The pressure has let off, the prison bars are being raised, but we don't know how to get used to freedom. Dick Rendel[1], who was here a short while ago, was telling us about our prisoners, returning in their thousands from German camps. Their state is really pitiable. They get home and find their wives look older, or have fatter legs or a lover, or they don't care for them as much as they thought they did. Going to bed together isn't a success, and the wife has got so used to running the house and family single-handed that she doesn't want his interference. He feels guilt at ever having been a prisoner (a very 'loaded' word after all), resentment against the country and the system that ever let him in for such an experience – and the net result is that he sits silent by the fireside groping for some sort of orientation. His wife tries to drag him out to parties 'to cheer him up'. He feels miserable, has forgotten how to behave, is even rude. And so on. Dick is now in charge of a rehabilitation centre at Hatfield House. He plans to put on a naked show from the Windmill Theatre there.

Frances Partridge

[1] Colonel Dick Rendel, Partridge's brother-in-law and nephew of Lytton Strachey.

19 April

1915 [Essex]

Owing to alleged existence of a German spy in British officer's clothing and in a car, in this district, order that no officer shall be out at night in a car unless on duty and with the password of the day. Personally, I don't see what good this will do. Highly inconvenient for officers. One officer, coming through Chelmsford, got stopped on his way to this district. He did not know of order, and had no password. He telephoned for help. A despatch cyclist was sent from Great Bentley to give him the password. This cyclist, although on General Hoare's orders, was not allowed to go through Colchester, and in the end the officer had to get home by train.

Arnold Bennett

1917 [France]

On 20 April 1916 I left the trenches in front of Mametz and went for those four divine, sunlit weeks at the Fourth Army School, half-way between Amiens and Abbeville. This year I am being set free from even more hellish places, and before me lies a vision of green fields sloping to a vale full of white orchards – mazes of cherry-blossom where tiny rills tell their little tales, while the 'shy thrush at mid-May flutes from wet orchards flushed with the triumphing dawn'. And beyond it all a deep blue landscape chequered.

Siegfried Sassoon

1940 [Berlin]

Hitler's fifty-first birthday tomorrow, and the people have been asked to fly their flags. Said Dr. Goebbels in a broadcast tonight: 'The German people have found in the Führer the incarnation of their strength and the most brilliant exponent of their national aims.' When I passed the Chancellery tonight, I noticed some seventy-five people outside for a glimpse of the leader. In other years on the eve of his birthday, there were ten thousand.

William L. Shirer

1941 [London]

Had a few drinks, then went to the Savoy. Pretty bad blitz, but not so bad as Wednesday. A couple of bombs fell very near during dinner.

Orchestra went on playing, no one stopped eating or talking. Blitz continued. Carroll Gibbons played the piano, I sang, so did Judy Campbell and a couple of drunken Scots Canadians. On the whole, a strange and very amusing evening. People's behaviour absolutely magnificent. Much better than gallant. Wish the whole of America could really see and understand it. Thankful to God I came back. Would not have missed this experience for anything.

Noël Coward

1943 [Hampshire]

The most amazing fact is that the history of mankind is happening as I write these words. Tonight when we were listening to the wireless the B.B.C. Broadcast and the electric fire suddenly ceased. Sidney and Mrs Grant and Annie [domestic staff] all asserted that it was accidental. But presently (as I write these words) the B.B.C. ceased its activity and my cup of tea went cold – so did Sidney's glass of sherry. Annie came to tell me that two British air-machines had passed low over our house and they had suddenly disappeared. At the same time I felt that I must go to the water closet and I had an action which seemed to clear away all unnecessary excreta, and I couldn't for the next few hours get my feet warm and comfortable. But suddenly I ceased to exist. So did Annie and Jean and Mrs Grant and Sidney. So we are all having a painless death as I had longed for. For if my reasoning is right we shall all disappear, including the *Germans themselves from the territory which they have conquered.* There will be no Jews, no conquered peoples, no refugees. The garden will disappear and all our furniture, the earth and the sun and the moon. God wills the destruction of all living things, man, woman and child. We shall not be frozen or hurt. We should merely – not exist (never even have existed). It all seems incredible and therefore is worth noting. Even Churchill and Roosevelt, states and kingdoms, would disappear! No one would fear, it will be sudden and complete, so no one need worry, and we can go on as long as we are conscious that we do not exist. It is as ridiculous as it is terrifying. Annie as she left me said she would bring me my breakfast, and even offered to stay with me during the night so that I should not be lonely. So I kissed her and said good-night. I thought it kinder not to tell Sidney and Mrs Grant. We shall none of us suffer pain and discomfort; it will be sudden, complete, as the wireless set in its broadcast, and the fire and the electric light, the chairs and the cushions, and the kitchen, the dining-room, the study and the sitting-room. What an amazing happening, well worth recording in my diary, but that also will suddenly disappear even if I went on with this endless writing. As I turn out the light and heat up my tea kettle and hot water bottle, so my stomach may no longer pain me, I feel that this is *inconceivable – and therefore that it will not happen.*[1]

Beatrice Webb

20 April

1915 [Russian Front]
The priest gave us what little help he could: supplying us with fresh water, carrying off receptacles of blood-stained clothes and bandages. In and out among the wounded he walked; placing more straw under one man's head, raising a leg into a more comfortable position, holding, now and then, a cup of water to thirsty lips. His lips were compressed, his face drawn, but only once did I notice that he was affected by the sights around him. A soldier was lying in a corner, breathing heavily, but otherwise quiet. It was his turn now; I went and knelt down on the straw at his side. His left leg and side were saturated with blood. I began to rip up the trouser-leg, clotted blood and filth flowing over my gloved hands. He turned dull, uncomprehending eyes towards me and I went on ripping up the cloth up to the waist. I pushed the clothes back and saw a pulp, a mere mass of smashed body from the ribs downwards; the stomach and abdomen were completely crushed and his left leg was hanging to the pulped body by only a few shreds of flesh. I heard a stifled groan at my side and, glancing round, I saw the priest with his hand across his eyes turn and walk heavily across the room towards the door. The soldier's dull eyes were still looking at me and his lips moved, but no words came. What it cost me to turn away without aiding him, I cannot describe, but we could not waste time and material on hopeless cases, and there were so many others . . . waiting . . . waiting . . .

Florence Farmborough

[1] She died on 30 April, 1943.

1941 [Tuscany]
Enemy number one is the Machine, in whatever form.

Bernard Berenson

1967 [Vietnam]
While we were waiting for the choppers to take us out, Hickman
spotted a Charlie grenade on the ground. He went over to it. 'Better
leave that damn thing alone!' I hollered at him. He picked it up anyway
and *wham!* the thing went off, and suddenly he was lying on the ground.
When he tried to get up he screamed, 'My hand! My god, my hand's
gone!' We ran over and applied a tourniquet to try and stop the bleeding until a medic arrived. He started to cry and begged us to find his
hand. 'Oh God, I can't go home this way. I just can't.' We made out
we were looking. But we all knew we wouldn't find it. It had been
blown to bits. Why the damn fool picked that grenade up I'll never
know. Well, he's homeward bound now, and all the guys from my truck
are in my tent, drunk as hell. And now I'm going to join them.

David Parks

21 April

1915 [Buxton]
Sometimes I can hardly believe I am I. I feel as if I were writing a
novel about someone else, & not myself at all, so mighty are the things
happening just now. If, that summer just after I came out & things
seemed as though they would always be stagnant & dull, someone had
said to me 'Before three years are over you will not only have fallen
deeply in love with someone, but that very person will be fighting on
the battlefields of France in the greatest war ever known to man. And
your anguish of anxiety on his account will be greater than anything
you have dreamed possible', I should not have believed it could really
ever happen. To-night – not only when I heard from Roland but before
– I have been full of a queer excitement – almost exultation. There
has been no apparent reason for it, so I very much wonder why.

Apparently the hill we have taken near Ypres is a real advantage to
us, but our losses are reported to be heavy. That means terrible long
casualty lists within the next few days.

Vera Brittain

1940 [Germany]
Michael [her son] back and fit [from Hitler Youth Camp]. He looks brown and keeps showing me how to click my heels – a very useful accomplishment!

Elisabeth von Stahlenberg

22 April

1915 [Ypres]
Left at 6.30 p.m. for reserve trenches and reached our reserve dugouts via St Julien. Just rat holes! One hell of accommodation! Got to the trenches as a fatigue party with stake and sandbags, and thought they were reserve trenches, they were so rotten. No trenches at all in parts, just isolated mounds. Found Germans' feet sticking up through the ground. The Gurkhas had actually used human bodies instead of sandbags.

Right beside the stream where we were working were the bodies of two dead, since November last, one face downwards in full marching order, with his kit on his back. He died game! Stench something awful and dead all around. Water rats had made a home of their decomposed bodies.

Sergeant S. V. Britten, 13th Battalion,
The Royal Highlanders of Canada

1916 [Russian Front]
Sister Anna and I strolled off into the countryside in the afternoon and to our delight we came across quite a number of trees already in flower. Under a wild cherry tree, the long branches of which were flecked with white-pink blossom, we sat and looked around at the bright sunlit scene. A swarm of May beetles made an unexpected appearance buzzing around our heads. Far away, we heard a sporadic burst of rifle fire. Firing became fiercer during the night.

Florence Farmborough

1941 [Berlin]
Now we have lost a football match to Switzerland. No incidents, unfortunately. I forbid such risky matches in future.

Josef Goebbels

1942 [London]

Malcolm[1] has been lunching today with Winston. He said that the latter has no illusions at all about the decline in his popularity. 'I am like a bomber pilot,' he said. 'I go out night after night, and I know that one night I shall not return.' Malcolm is in fact rather appalled by the slump in Winston's popularity. A year ago he would have put his stock at 108, and today, in his opinion, it is as low as 65. He admits that a success will enable it to recover. But the old enthusiasm is dead for ever. How foul is public life and popular ingratitude!

Harold Nicolson

1944 [Maqil, the Middle East]

Brigadier Clark told us about a Londoner in his unit who asked if he could have a word with him concerning a cable he'd just had from home. It read: 'Son born both doing well love Mary.' The Brigadier said how splendid, and the private said it wasn't, because he hadn't been home for two years. 'Oh,' invented the Brigadier wildly, 'perhaps the cable has been a long time coming?' The man wasn't to be comforted and went away very low. Sometime later he came rushing back with a letter in his hand: 'I've got a letter from my wife, sir, and it's all right, it's not her it's my mother. She's a widow. Must have been playing around with some man.' He was fully comforted and indeed delighted. So was the Brigadier.

Joyce Grenfell

23 April

1915 [Ypres]

Terrible day, no food or water, dead & dying all around.

Sergeant S. V. Britten, 13th Battalion, The Royal Highlanders of Canada

1915 [written 22–23 April in Marseilles]

Just before dinner I got a wire from Eddie[2] saying 'there is bad news of Rupert [Brooke] – he is ill with blood-poisoning on French hospital

[1] Malcolm MacDonald, former Minister of Health in Churchill's Government, later UK High Commissioner in Canada.
[2] Sir Edward 'Eddie' Marsh, Assistant Private Secretary to Prime Minister Asquith, 1915–16, art connoisseur and close friend of Rupert Brooke.

ship. Condition grave. I am hoping & will wire you directly I hear more.'
I felt frozen with terror at first & then − I don't know why − a cause-
less reaction of relief − & sort of wave of trust that Life wld. recognize
Rupert's preciousness − that Fate itself wld. recoil before so cruel a plat-
itude as his death wld. be. I sent off 2 wires to Eddie & Bongie [her
husband Maurice] − then dressed & came down to dinner. It was like
having to take part in a play till 11 − & not really very difficult . . .

. . . [after dinner] the telephone bell rang . . . I stood in Lady Scott's
room waiting & with a half sense that it might be for me. [Sir Matthew]
Nathan came out with a very grave face & said gently 'It's bad news
I'm afraid' − I asked − is he *dead*? He said 'yes.'

I went back next evening − after a nightmare day of trying to live
outwardly decently . . .

Bongie that angel was up & waiting whitely about the house for
me. I lay down & he came up to see me. He said nothing but his love
& his dumb, solid, minding, strong presence comforted me a little. I
think it is the best selfish sorrow I have ever had − it was not only for
me I minded but for the world − that this perfect thing should be no
more − this being without compare. It was like Spring being dead −
or music − or flowers − like seeing some marvellous vase shattered
before one's eyes. And I wanted so much more of him for myself.
Never to be able to dip into his mind − never to be able to look into
his eyes again.

I went alone to St Paul's at 12. It rained all day. After tea I saw Eddie
− quite broken poor darling. It is the first thing that has given me
control − the feeling that he was feeling it *for* me − it somehow seemed
to lighten the weight and & dull the edge.

Violet Bonham Carter

1945 [Carradale, Scotland]
In the late afternoon I dashed back and drove my car-load over to
Campbeltown where we duly had our blood transfusion taken.
Obviously the organisers were having difficulties as half the people
who said they were going to come didn't while others came who
weren't expected. The only unpleasant thing was horrible cups of sweet
tea that we were made to have . . .

My fellow blood transfusers talking about prison camps. That really
seems to have got under the skin of even Carradale. I keep on saying
that when some of us talked about concentration camps three years

before the war the people who talk about them now wouldn't listen. One just can't imagine the quality of the hell it must be in Berlin. I suppose Hitler and Goering will either get themselves killed or commit suicide. I hope they won't be martyrs anyhow!

Naomi Mitchison

24 April

1940 [London]
Italy is moving still further from war. Mussolini is reported to have said, 'Germany is trying to drag me into the war by the hair, but luckily I am bald.'

John Colville

1941 [Berlin]
News of Churchill. He is said to be in very depressed state, spending the entire day smoking and drinking. This is the kind of enemy we need.

I initiate a campaign against the widespread saying that 'The English are more stubborn than we are.' This must be eradicated.

New figures for box-office receipts. Another 30 million in profits. We are awash with money. Every film is a box-office hit.

A few shortages in Berlin, particularly tobacco and beer. I arrange for them to be alleviated. The public must be kept happy at the moment.

Josef Goebbels

25 April

1915 [Gallipoli]
At last, boats came alongside and we unload the boxes into them, and I go ashore with the first batch, and there I meet 86th and 87th Supply Officers, who landed two hours earlier. My servant meets me and asked where shall I sleep. What a question! What does he expect me to answer – 'Room 44, first floor'? I say, 'Oh, shove my kit down there,' pointing to some lying figures on the sand. Five minutes after he comes up, and with a scared voice says, 'Them is all stiff corpses, sir; you can't sleep there.' I reply, 'Oh, damn it; go and sit down on my kit till I come

back.' I start to work to get the stores higher up the cliff. Oh! the sand. It is devilish heavy going, walking up and down with my feet sinking in almost ankle-deep. It is quite dark now, and I stumble at frequent intervals over the dead. Parties are removing them, not for burial, but higher up the beach out of the way of the working parties. I run into the Brigade quartermaster-sergeant and ask him 'How's the Brigadier?' He replies, 'Killed, sir.' I can't speak for a moment. 'And the Brigade Major?' 'Killed also, sir.'

Major John Gillam, DSO

1941 [London]

C., of my section of the Home Guard, a poulterer by trade but at present dealing in meat of all kinds, yesterday bought 20 zebras which are being sold off by the Zoo. Only for dog meat, presumably, not human consumption. It seems rather a waste . . . There are said to be still 2,000 race-horses in England, each of which will be eating 10–15 lb. of grain a day, i.e. these brutes are devouring *every day* the equivalent of the bread ration of a division of troops.

George Orwell

1941 [Berlin]

At home, complete essay against 'the stubborn English'. It will cause a furore. But it has to be said. We Germans are always far too fair-minded towards our enemies.

Josef Goebbels

1944 [London]

Came home at 7 to find that a bomb had fallen near by and my water tank had in consequence burst. All my best books are saturated which makes me very unhappy. I spent a melancholy evening mopping up. There was an inch of water in the big room.

James Lees-Milne

26 April

1915 [London]

I feel a peculiar appetite for buying clothes just now. So far from not wanting them in wartime, I think they are the one thing to distract one, and I long for lovely ones. Went to Miss North's where I tried on resurrected Paisley coat, réchauffé black evening dress, made fashionable, tully and sticky-out. The clothes have undergone enormous change since the war and have become practically early Victorian with real full skirts. I thought war would produce reactions to womanliness.

Lady Cynthia Asquith

1943 [en route for the Tunisian front]
Why do so many of our regular army officers – colonels up – have faces like monkey wrenches; all beaten together, pulpy, expressionless? The faces of street-car conductors, train brakemen, barkeepers, ex-pugs. Not really unpleasant or dishonest or even stupid faces. But they look as if they had spent their lives bawling other people out in a chronic condition of acute constipation. On the other hand, the enlisted men and second lieutenants are often so good-looking, and alive and polite, with just a little American whimsy rippling beneath the surface. They seem to take things in with a surprisingly mature urbanity. They are sure of themselves the way some of the colonels are not, and so can afford to be gracious.

George Biddle

1982 [Somerset]
South Georgia retaken from the Argentines, island discovered by Captain Cook, wholly British, to which Argentina has not the smallest claim. Newspaper headline: *Junta breaks the news gently*, evoking Max Beerbohm cartoon.

Anthony Powell

27 April

1915 [London]
So very sorry to hear Rupert Brooke has died in Dardanelles of poisoning or sunstroke.[1] I have only met him once or twice, never got to know him, but always looked forward to doing so some day, and it does stab one to think of his beautiful young poet's face with the cornfield head. He had the most lovely *regard* I have ever seen I think. Poor

[1] He died of septicaemia aboard a French hospital ship on its way to the Dardanelles.

Eddie [Marsh] will be broken-hearted – I think he was his favourite protégé. I am told he was absolutely convinced he would be killed in this war and he wrote lovely poems bidding farewell to things he loved – the 'touch of fur' was one I thought original. It is rather sad that it should have been an illness.

Lady Cynthia Asquith

1942 [Monte Estoril, Portugal]
Where there is life, however strange its manifestations, however tortuous the form it takes, there is the gleam, the glisten, the glow. Only death is dull.

Malcolm Muggeridge

1943 [en route for Tunisia from Trinidad]
We left Trinidad this morning at dawn. The sun was hidden in banks of cumulus clouds, rising up on the northeast trades behind the coco palms. My thirteen fellow-passengers are bound for Akra, Oran, Iran, India, two for Algiers, three for China, Recife, the Bahrain Islands, Baghdad, Natal, and Palestine. There is global poetry to this war. We have on board a Polish general and a Polish army chaplain, a French naval captain, a Brazilian from Rio Grande do Norte. He speaks no English and his little French could not have gotten him far in Cleveland, Detroit, and Los Angeles. He has the harassed, ruffled, muddied expression characteristic of the camel, or of a cow disturbed in the rumination of her cud. But when I spoke to him in Portuguese his face lit up with a 'through-shine' glow of confidence and affection.

George Biddle

28 April

1940 [Berlin]
The virtual disappearance of many indispensables since the start of the war has had a comical aftermath at my office; for some time now our bosses had been complaining about the inexplicable consumption of unaccountable quantities of W.C. paper. At first they concluded that the staff must be suffering from some new form of mass diarrhoea, but as weeks passed and the toll did not diminish, it finally dawned on them that everyone was simply tearing off ten times more than he (or

she) needed and smuggling it home. A new regulation has now been issued: all staff members must betake themselves to a Central Distribution Point, where they are solemnly issued with the amount judged sufficient for their daily needs!

Marie 'Missie' Vassiltchikov

1940 [Wiltshire]

Hester[1] is staying here. A conversation between her and R. about what we are fighting for. 'Because a Nazi regime, concentration camps, etc. are worse than death,' says Hester. 'Yes, but worse than whose death?' says R. 'Your young men friends? If not, suicide is the correct answer.'

Frances Partridge

1941 [Cairo]

I slept tormented by sandflies after a torpid day. Bonner Fellers [American Attaché] fetched me for lunch. He said, 'We reckon this is one of your worst emergencies – the whole Mediterranean is threatened. America must declare war soon.' Then he talked about the German 88-millimetre gun which he says is excellent. He grumbled because the US War Department and our War Office turned the gun down before the war as it has only a small shield to protect the crew and both thought it would prove too costly in men. As it outranges most other weapons and is very mobile, Bonner thinks this was a grave mistake. 'Anyway,' he said, 'the Germans now have it in the Desert where it is deadly.' The Germans also have a very good Fifth Column.

The Desert war continues. We have bombed Barce. This evening I took Whitaker [her husband's valet] and his friend McCall to a movie – we saw *Congo Maisie*, 'a tropical love tangle with allure and alligators'. I got home in time to hear Mr Churchill's broadcast. He made a long and very honest statement.

Countess of Ranfurly

1943 [England]

Amy [her housekeeper] came late & tearful to announce that her sister Lily's husband was killed in N. Africa on April 6th and the news came by letter to the War Office yesterday. Her fellow-workers at the factory collected about £10 for her so that she could have a few days away

---

[1] Hester Chapman, novelist.

from work. She asked if I would draft a letter of thanks for her which I did. She & the young man only had about 3 weeks together all told after they were married – & never a home of their own at all. Such is war for the 'little people' whom the politicians indifferently sacrifice to satisfy their own swollen egos.

Vera Brittain

1969 [Vietnam]
Life at BMB [brigade main base] was fairly slow. The days usually revolved around meal times and the opening of the club in the evening . . . I ate my evening meal at the officers' club where I could enjoy a steak or hamburger in one of the four air-conditioned buildings in the camp. Popular US beers, fine wines and the best of brand name spirits flowed freely. The walls were lined with slot machines and several card games of various stakes were ongoing. A band played several nights a week. Movies, usually less than a week old, were shown when no live entertainment was available.

Here waitresses were young attractive Vietnamese who definitely know how to wear the fashionable miniskirt. They were attractive and friendly yet hesitant . . . I doubt if there was a story or line they had not heard.

Michael Lee Lanning

1982 [London]
An exhausting day. I got another 400 letters today, making 2,500 this week. Overwhelmingly supportive[1] – I suppose coming primarily from middle-class people. Some white feathers and vulgar abuse. The mail is the biggest I've ever had.

Tony Benn

29 April

1945 [London]
The *Sunday Express* announced Germany's unconditional surrender to all three allies. This headline is mischievous and misleading as it is not true, although it probably will be in the next day or two. Mussolini

---

[1] Tony Benn was against sending a Task Force to the Falkland Islands.

has been tried and executed. It is hardly believable that after all these dreadful years it is really nearly the end.

It is strange to be back at the Savoy, having been here so much in 1941, when our world was so black. These supremely melodramatic days are somehow anticlimactic and confusing. Report of the deaths of Hitler and Goering. Mussolini shot yesterday and hung upside down in the street and spat at. The Italians are a lovable race.

Noël Coward

1969 [Vietnam]
My first night ambush was uneventful – yet exciting and scary. Your mind races with anticipation – when you sit in the dark waiting for your fellow human being to appear so you can kill or be killed. I was filled with a dread that the enemy might not appear, and an even more powerful dread that he would . . .

Soldiers were close together in two- and three-man positions and scheduled watches. We slept within arm's reach of each other so we could change guard with the minimum noise and movement. The heavy flak jackets served as passable pillows. Ammo magazines and hand grenades were stacked by each man.

There was no talking, eating or smoking. When we had to urinate, we crawled a few feet from our position and did it on our knees. This way we limited our exposure to the skyline and also prevented noisy splashing. Those who snored were awakened. If a man repeated the noise, he had to sleep wearing a gas mask.

Michael Lee Lanning

1982 [London]
Argentina invaded the Falkland Islands – big, boring drama, the press love it and we are sending an army.

Ossie Clark

30 April

1942 [London]
I sent Lord Esher a cutting from *The Times* of today quoting a Wilhelmstrasse statement that they will make a point of bombing English country houses, those haunts of bloated plutocrats and aristocrats, especially the

famous 'Tudor' ones. I think the Germans have now plumbed the depths of human degradation by a positive intention to destroy monuments of art.

James Lees-Milne

1942 [POW camp, Java]

Today is Princess Juliana's [of the Netherlands] birthday and the D[utch] are observing the day as a Sunday, each dressed as neatly as possible and wearing the Orange emblem.

Today D officers came to see me re electric lighting – our needs [Australian POWs] to be used as a lever to enable them to send a purchasing commission down town. Yet the Dutch commander tells me that we are a separate camp and must deal separately with N [Japanese] and particularly will not supply me with brooms, cleaning materials etc. I saw van Lingham [POW Commandant] in presence of this officer and was not offered a chair. D commander was put very smartly in his place by me and gave with the blow, saying that he would do his best for us with the Ns and we could try ourselves as well. I do not entirely trust this man.

I then wrote a formal letter thanking him for previous efforts on our behalf (negligible), stating our desire for full co-operation, and to that end requesting representation on all executive bodies common in interest to the two camps and including rations – supply and cooking etc.; electric light; water supply; camp sanitation. Also medical (particularly supplies), clothes and personal requirements. A reply was requested in writing. This is a step to stop this business of the D having all control of stores and rations and according us 'charity'.

Weary Dunlop

MAY

Though Waterloo was won upon the playing fields of Eton,
The next war will be photographed, and lost, by Cecil Beaton.

Noël Coward

1 May

1915 [Gallipoli]

This afternoon I have a bathe off 'W' Beach. Crowds are bathing. What a difference to this time last week! Only a week ago we landed, and now 'W' Beach is like a seaside resort as far as the bathing is concerned. I felt in holiday mood, and with that delightful refreshed feeling that one has after a dip, I strolled along the sand up to the depot for a cup of tea. But the screams of a shell overhead from Achi, which fell in the water beyond the bathers, brought my holiday mood to an abrupt end.

Major John Gillam, DSO

1940 [Lewes, England]

Mr Clarke said his uncle was born in 1808 and clearly remembered the coach coming through the village after Waterloo and all the passengers standing up and waving and shouting '*Boney's taken.*' If only a Southdown 'bus could rush down the High Street now with everybody yelling '*Hitler's Murdered.*'

Mrs Henry Dudeney

1941 [New York]

I've received my draft classification: 3-A. This means I'm safe from active service awhile – provided the US doesn't plunge into war. I guess having a wife and a hernia helped me. I'm pessimistic about the future. It seems Roosevelt is doing all he can to drag us into the war.

Edward Robb Ellis

1944 [Tuscany]

Yesterday an uncomfortable little episode. Two German soldiers turned up in the farm, one in plain clothes and one in uniform. They immediately inquired whether there were any Fascists here; and then asked to see Antonio [her husband], told him that they were deserters, and asked for food, money and plain clothes for the one in uniform. Antonio, feeling something fishy about them, firmly

179

refused, whereupon they professed great astonishment. 'But,' they cried, 'haven't we come to the right place? Aren't you the gentleman who speaks German and English – and his wife too – and who have helped thirty-three British prisoners to escape? Didn't you give civilian clothes to two Austrian deserters? Why won't you help us, too?' Antonio firmly denied it all. And now they became threatening: 'You'll live to regret it – the Cassino line can't hold – and you'll see what will happen to you afterwards!' But in the end they went off, grumbling. Later on we discovered that they came here with the two so-called Austrian deserters, who have been wandering about the country for some time, and presumably got this information from them – that they lunched to-day at one of the farms, called and asked questions at the clinic and workmen's club (where they forced the men playing bowls to buy them some socks) and eventually asked the farmer, in whose house they had lunched, for arms, saying: 'Two hundred Germans are at the Castelluccio, and we must defend ourselves!' The farmer fortunately said he had none, and they went off. We still have no idea whether they were spies or genuine deserters.

Iris Origo

1945 [Wiltshire]

11p.m. Have just switched on the late news and heard a portentous voice say: HITLER IS DEAD. I went up to bed before R. and heard his voice and Saxon's[1] from the music-room below. 'What were you talking about?' I asked when he appeared. 'Horses for the Guineas,' he said. 'Trust Saxon never to mention anything of such immediate interest as the end of Hitler.'

Frances Partridge

1945 [England]

This morning's papers contained horrible photographs of Mussolini and his young mistress hanging upside down from the top of a garage in a Milan Square.

Churchill in House said he would announce end of war when it came. But at 10.30 Mrs Burdett rang me to say programme had been interrupted to announce death of Hitler & appointment of Admiral

[1] Saxon Sydney-Turner (1880–1962), a member of the not-so-secret society, The Apostles. He joined the Treasury after university and remained there until he retired, never marrying.

Doenitz as his successor. Heard this at midnight. Three world-figures gone in 3 weeks is too much to take in.[1]

Vera Brittain

2 May

1861 [Macon]
From Savannah to Macon, 191 miles, the road passes through level country only partially cleared. There were but few negroes but invisible at work, nor did the land appear rich, but I was told the rail was laid along the most barren part of the country. Among the passengers to whom I was introduced was the Bishop of Georgia, the Rev. Mr. Elliott, a man of exceeding fine presence, of great stature and handsome face, with a manner easy and grateful, but we got on the unfortunate subject of slavery, and I rather revolted at hearing a Christian prelate advocating the institution on scriptural grounds. The miserable sophists who expose themselves to the contempt of the world by their paltry thesicles on the divine origin and uses of slavery, are infinitely more contemptible than the wretched bigots who published themes long ago on the propriety of burning witches, or on the necessity for the officers of the Inquisition.

William Howard Russell

1942 [London]
After inspecting our mill at Burnham Staithe I walked to Burnham Market. No food at the Hoste Arms, but at the Nelson I got beer, sausage rolls and hot meat rolls. There were evacuees toping at the bar and recounting their bomb experiences in London. 'The wife said to me, she said, did you ever? Me and my kiddies,' etc. Slightly drunk on a pint of bitter, after my walk, I joined in the conversation and found myself recounting my experiences (they were non-existent) of the Germans and their atrocities. 'Would you believe it,' I said, 'they cut out the heart and began . . . ?' 'Well, I never,' they said in a chorus of delight. Cockneys are good-hearted people. These particularly deplored warfare against women and children. Yes, I said, and put in a plea against the deliberate bombing of our cathedrals and churches, to test their reaction. Reaction: 'One in a hundred may care for such old-fashioned

---

[1] President Roosevelt had died in April.

places. They are all right to see now and then. It's flesh and blood what matters. For myself, the whole lot can go. Hear! Hear!' All most good-natured and honestly meant. Philistines!

James Lees-Milne

1943 [Amsterdam]

Dearest Kitty,

The Attitude of the Annexe Residents Towards the War

Mr van Daan. In the opinion of us all, this revered gentleman has great insight into politics. Nevertheless, he predicts we'll have to stay here until the end of '43. That's a very long time, and yet it's possible to hold out until then. But who can assure us that this war, which has caused nothing but pain and sorrow, will then be over? And that nothing will have happened to us and our helpers long before that time? No one! That's why each and every day is filled with tension. Expectation and hope generate tension, as does fear – for example, when we hear a noise inside or outside the house, when the guns go off or when we read new 'proclamations' in the paper, since we're afraid our helpers might be forced to go into hiding themselves sometime. We don't know how many people are actually in hiding; of course, the number is relatively small compared with the general population, but later on we'll no doubt be astonished at how many good people in Holland were willing to take Jews and Christians, with or without money, into their homes. There're also an unbelievable number of people with false identity papers.

Mrs van Daan. When this beautiful damsel (by her own account) heard that it was getting easier these days to obtain false IDs, she immediately proposed that we each have one made. As if there were nothing to it, as if Father and Mr van Daan were made of money.

Pim [van Daan, Mrs van Daan's son] is a big optimist, but he always has his reason.

Mr Dussel makes up everything as he goes along, and anyone wishing to contradict His Majesty had better think twice. In Albert Dussel's home his word is law, but that doesn't suit Anne Frank in the least.

What the other members of the Annexe family think about the war doesn't matter. When it comes to politics, these four are the only ones who count. Actually, only two of them do, but Madame van Daan and Dussel include themselves as well.

Anne Frank

1945 [Carradale, Scotland]
One feels Hitler's death is just rather pointless now. He should have died some time ago. I wonder how many people comfort themselves with thinking he's frizzling.

Naomi Mitchison

1945 [London]
There is still much uncertainty about Hitler. Some think that he is not dead at all but has gone underground. Others think that he has had a stroke and died a week ago. Others say that he and Goebbels committed suicide. It will be many months, if ever, before we learn the truth.

Harold Nicolson

1945 [Nottinghamshire]
They've announced on Hamburg radio that Hitler is dead! Berlin has surrendered to the Russians.

As soon as we came off watch we all piled into cars and set out for the nearest pub, with Oscar, Pandora and I crammed into Dizzy's car.

When we had drunk so many toasts that we could hardly stand, someone took over the piano and we sang till closing time. The whole pub turned out to shout goodbye. The ride home was a nightmare – we went tearing through the night, whooping and singing, with screeching brakes and screaming horns. Then three times round the WAAF Mess, howling like wolves – according to custom – and when we reached the RAF Mess we found it practically ablaze.

Some types had got hold of 'Fodo', the stuff they use to clear fog, and had lit it all over the bars. They were dancing round it, wearing huge negro masks from the Xmas pantomime, and waving broomsticks – a fantastic sight!

We spotted Gussy and Vlady sitting entwined in the dark of the Ladies' Room with a bottle of vodka between them listening to the Warsaw Concerto – all very romantic. Dizzy put on the most hideous mask he could find and jumped on them from behind – terrible screams!

Then the rest of the drunken horde rushed in, somebody got the piano and we did all sorts of crazy dances. Dizzy is a wizard dancer, he leaps all over the floor like a cat. At midnight we all went over to the WAAF Mess for sausages and tea in the kitchen.

Joan Wyndham

1969 [Vietnam]

Greg Morrison of the then-popular television series Mission Impossible few into Elvira by helicopter. He was very friendly and shook everyone's hand while saying that he was proud of us. His visit seems more significant today as I look back and realise that I never saw another movie or TV personality at a field location during the rest of my tour.

Michael Lee Lanning

3 May

1915 [Essex]

In this morning's paper the sinking of the *Recruit* was noted. Serving in this ship was Ernest Cloughton, son of Fred Cloughton, shepherd on Lyons Hall farm. This afternoon his father received a telegram (official) informing him his son was among the drowned.

Andrew Clark

1915 [Gallipoli]

Today an enterprising Greek landed in a small sailing vessel with a cargo of oranges, chocolate, and cigarettes, and in a very short time was quite sold out. We shall be having a Pierrot troupe on the beach next.

Major John Gillam, DSO

1941 [London]

We drove down to the East End and had a look at Stepney, West Ham, and the London docks. We were shown incident after incident where the destruction was terrific.

At West Ham, we were taken around by a Scots Presbyterian chaplain who had at one time been a coal miner. After he was called to the ministry he took up his work in the church alongside the docks. The church has now been destroyed. He led us around from one huge crater to another, each surrounded by blocks of shattered and crumbling dwellings.

The chaplain said there was a growing vindictiveness and hate in his parishioners and people of the district which he deplored. He called it 'falling from grace'. Well, in my opinion, they have plenty of reason for falling from grace insofar as the Germans are concerned.

I asked him whether he knew of any subversive activities amongst the workers of this part of town, which was the most fertile field for them before the war. He said the few they had had either been run out, or had changed their opinions after they had been bombed a few times.

It does not make one proud of the Victorian era to see this great area of sordid dwellings, where life had nothing whatever to make it pleasant or attractive for so many people. But it is an inspiring thing to think that on this dung heap there grow such fine flowers of courage, endurance and patriotism. Battered and wounded, gasping and bleeding, the riverside workers, who had been exploited for years by British capital and British politics, are still [resolute]. They are cheerful, dogged, and determined to win! If they had only had the farsighted, skillful and courageous leadership for the past twenty years to which they are so richly entitled.

General Raymond E. Lee

1941 [Berlin]
A book on Churchill reports that he drinks too much and wears pink silk underwear. He dictates messages in the bath or in his underpants; a startling image which the Führer finds hugely amusing.

Josef Goebbels

1944 [Amsterdam]
Dearest Kitty,
I've often been down in the dumps, but never desperate. I look upon our life in hiding as an interesting adventure, full of danger and romance, and every privation as an amusing addition to my diary.

Anne Frank

1945 [London]
Never was there such a day of news as yesterday. Surrender of the whole German Army in Italy – one million men. Fall of Berlin. Death of Hitler & Goebbels – & yet what is so odd is that one feels no wild excitement, no exhilaration or kick – no desire to throw one's hat into the air – only the sense of having reached a long foregone conclusion – at last. One never, even in the blackest hour, had any doubt of the end.

Violet Bonham Carter

4 May

1939 [London]

Drafted telegram to Hambro[1] giving assurance that we should hang on to Northern Norway. To Foreign Office at 5.30. Found 20 boxes [of documents]! Got through as much as I could. Home by 8. Dined and worked. Planning conquest of Iceland for next week. Shall probably be too late! Saw several broods of ducklings.

Sir Alexander Cadogan

1942 [Holland]

We're all wearing our stars. I can't stop laughing – I can't help it. It's such a hoot, this star business. You hear the most ridiculous stories, and the jokes are making the rounds faster than the rumours. The people wearing stars are greeted warmly by strangers, people take their hats off to you in the street, make all sorts of comments like 'Keep your chin up' – it's wonderful. Today apparently even a German soldier greeted Father. I had sewn mine on my scarf, you are not supposed to, but I'll just wait until someone says something about it. Everybody was incredibly nice at the Distribution Office. Someone said to me, 'Why don't you take that silly thing off! Throw it away.' It really is a hoot.

Edith Velmans

1945 [London]

I am dreading the victory celebrations and have no sort of heart for them. I am feeling absolutely rotten and utterly soured of everything even religion if an essential is loving one's neighbour and feeling kindly to them – for I hate and loathe them. It seems to me that anyone who has decency, unselfishness, kindliness, public spirit and such like is a fool. He is put on. It is the opposite sort of qualities which bring success and contentment. Everything is upside down. The undesirable are subsidized from birth to grave at our expense: they are given everything and nothing is expected of them. We who pay for it all are pushed about, insulted and soon will be driven out of existence.

Lord Reith

[1] Sir Charles Hambro, who worked in the Special Operations Executive.

1945 [England]
During these long years of war the one o'clock news has so often
brought disappointment or dread, that we have learned to brace
ourselves for almost any kind of shock. Yesterday, we were caught off
guard, and could hardly grasp what had happened when we learned
of the utter and complete collapse of Germany.

Cecil Beaton

5 May

1692 [London]
The Reports of an Invasion now so hott, alarmed the City, Court and
people exceedingly, nothing but securing and Imprisoning suspected
persons; sending downe forces to the sea side, hastening out the Fleet, and
an universal consternation what would be the event of all this expectation.

John Evelyn

1916 [Scotland]
We had a lecture on behaviour – i.e., Not to go into pubs; this could
be done in France, where officers and men were not sharply distinguished; we were not to go about with tarts, nor get drunk. We could,
however, do all these things if few would get into mufti – the usual
assumption that all civilians somehow fall short of gentility.

Arthur Graeme West

1940 [Kent]
I read Dylan Thomas's *Portrait of the Artist as a Young Dog*. I am slightly
disgusted by all the urine and copulation which occurs. I have a feeling
that these people do not believe that they can write powerfully unless
they drag in the latrines. And yet it is quite clear that this young Thomas
is a writer of great merit.

The lovely day sinks to sunset among the flowering trees. The Italian
news is bad. It seems incredible to us that Italy should really come in.
If she does, it must mean that Mussolini is convinced of our early
defeat. That is what fills me with such depression. Not Italy an enemy,
but Italy convinced as an intelligent and most admirably informed
nation that Germany is going to win this war.

Harold Nicolson

1969 [Vietnam]

We spent most of the day walking back to Binh Chank, a larger base
with its own mess hall. The small village just outside the case provided
what the troops had been without for a long time in the paddies –
women.

I had no problem with the men's visits to the local bordellos. After
all, if the men were there to fight for the country, they should be able
to enjoy part of it. My only instructions were that they should go in
groups for their safety and see Doc Bass for prophylactics, which were
considered a medical item. The men face dangers enough without
adding the risk of venereal disease.

One of my soldiers was convinced he was in love with one of the
ladies. He felt his ardour was returned until he ran out of money and
learned differently.

Michael Lee Lanning

1976 [The Philippines, on the set of *Apocalypse Now*]

We got to the set about 10.30. It was like a real war going on. The
shoot had started, so we had to watch from a distance. About eight
helicopters circled and landed in smoke flares, ground rocket fire and
water hits. Lines of GIs off-loaded and ran up the beach, crouching,
firing and advancing. Between takes we got a boat to take us close to
where the main camera was. We waded ashore with our gear and got
up the beach, near enough to get some good shots of Bob Duvall in
his cavalry hat, taking the beach. He looked terrific, he knew it, and
was real up and radiating energy. Everyone could feel it. There was a
photographer from *Newsweek* who kept taking my picture every time
I looked through my camera. I had that feeling of being merchandised:
'Wife of FFC [Francis Ford Coppola] making movies too.' I wanted to
just pick up my stuff and walk out of there; I reminded myself that I
am asking all the people on the production not to walk away when
I am shooting them.

Eleanor Coppola

1982 [Kent]

Now nearly four weeks into the Falklands 'Crisis', and for the last
three of them I have been almost ceaselessly occupied. *Every single day*
I have done at least one TV or radio broadcast, sometimes as many
as three. On two of the Sundays a Citron Pallas has been sent down

plus a 'backup' car!) to take me up to studio and back again, for the direct, grand, bit of Brian Walden's *Weekend World* – itself the grandest of all the current affairs programmes. Hailed as man-of-the-week in the *Daily Express.*

Alan Clark

6 May

1861 [St Louis]

I am packing up for New York, my object being to get out of the secession fever which now agitates the city and state. There are 27 boxes of books.

Many friends urge my return to the army. But I have no heart for engaging in a civil war. I cannot think of it. If fighting could preserve the Union (or restore it) I might consider what I could do to take part – but when did fighting make friends? To my vision – and I note it with a feeling of dread – the great American Republic is broken up. What is to come out of it can hardly be imagined just now.

Ethan Allen Hitchcock

1864 [Battle of the Wilderness, America]

Did a good deal of marching. Made one reconnaissance through thick wood. Scared the rebs but did not hurt them. Were then marched back to the rear and lay there in the woods till 4 o'clock; then the rebs made a charge on our lines in front of us [manned by General Hancock's II Corps]. The first line withstood the charge a short time and then broke and came rushing back over our breastworks, saying for us to run but we had no notion of that; so we gave them a few rounds and then rushed forward to the front line of our works which our men had deserted and drove the Rebs back clean and clear. Without doubt our brigade saved the day at that point. Through the goodness of God I was spared for which I feel thankful.

Pvt Bingham Findley Junkin, 100th Pennsylvania Volunteer Infantry

1915 [Gallipoli]

Tommies play on mouth-organs and sing Tommy's tunes. At Lemnos, Tommy was marching round the decks of the transports singing 'Who's Your Lady Friend?' A few days after he goes through one of the most sanguinary fights of the war; a week after he is on the beach with a mouth-organ making a horrible execution of 'A little Grey Home in the West.' A unique creation, the British Tommy. If he ever does think of death or getting wounded, he always thinks it will be his pal and not he who will get hit, and goes on with his mouth-organ, washing his shirt, or writing to his latest girl at the last town he was billeted in. Those with the girls are the cheeriest.

Major John Gillam, DSO

1944 [London]

Lunched with Eddy,[1] who was in spanking form. He spied across the room a young officer, tanned darkest brown and wearing a kilt. He was sitting opposite me. Eddy made me change places before I realized his intention. Having reseated himself he said, 'You had better put your spectacles on.' I said, 'That's a bit late in the day in view of your extraordinary behaviour.'

James Lees-Milne

1945 [Barrow, England]

Last week I would not go to see the Belsen horror-camp pictures. I felt the ones in the paper quite dreadful enough. They were shown again tonight, as 'requested' by someone. I looked in such pity, marvelling how human beings could have clung so to life: the poor survivors must have had both a good constitution and a great will to live. What kept them alive so long before they dropped as pitiful skeletons? Did their minds go first, I wonder, their reasoning, leaving nothing but the shell to perish slowly, like a house left unattended? Did their pitiful cries and prayers rise into the night to a God who seemed as deaf and pitiless as their cruel jailers?

I've a deep aversion to interference, having suffered from it all my life till recent years. I've always said, 'Let every country govern itself, according to its own ways of thought and living. Let them develop their own way and not have standards forced upon them, standards so often governed by commercial or political considerations, rather than their own good. Let them reach out in friendly neighbourliness, rather than "by order" or treaties or pacts.' Now I see it would not do. Germany had that creed, developed to a degree of isolationism. People knew

---

[1] Edward Sackville-West, fifth Baron Sackville, a novelist and man-of-letters.

about concentration camps, but nothing could seemingly be done about it. This horror is not just one of war. No power can be left so alone that, behind a veil of secrecy, *anything* can happen.

Nella Last

1982 [London]

Conversations in the pub become unpleasantly heated. Someone is bragging about how the Argentinian army has no experience of fighting anyone except its own civilian population, when I have to point out that the British Navy does not even have this experience.

I can't really make up my mind about the Falklands dispute. Galtieri has always struck me as a decent, reasonably sound sort of person, but I don't care for some of his friends – Tony Benn and Ken Livingston in particular.

Mrs Thatcher should use this as a golden opportunity to blow up the huge grain silos in Northern Argentina, containing all the wheat intended for Russia. In fact I was urging her to do this long before the Argentinians invaded. But nowadays she listens only to Ferdinand Mount[1] and Jimmy Savile.[2] I might as well babble of green fields.

Auberon Waugh

7 May

1944 [Naples]

A shameful example of the perfidiousness and injustice of this war we conduct behind the scenes. The General has not been able to get over the episode of the two rival bands fighting a battle over the right to pillage one of our trains, nor has he been mollified by the news of the capture of the bandit Lupo. One man is not enough. He wants mass arrests, and yesterday all the Italian chiefs of police were called before him and threatened with every kind of sanction including charges of sabotage if they failed to produce immediate results. The police chiefs are said to have replied that their forces were grossly under-manned, and their hands tied by excessive scruples shown by the Allies in the matter of repression. Only if given a free hand to solve this

---

[1] Adviser to the Prime Minister, Mrs Margaret Thatcher.
[2] Disc jockey and presenter of television show, *Jim'll Fix It*.

problem in their own way could results be guaranteed. Thus today I took part as an observer in one of the new-style operations: a raid on a bandit hideout carried out by a mixed force of Carabinieri and Pubblica Sicurezza, under orders to get results at all costs.

This time the combined force numbered about 50 men, but included the same Carabinieri as at Frattamaggiore and the same hyena-faced Pubblica Sicurezza Commissario, with his pin-striped suit, red-devil hand-grenades and squeaking shoes. The fields we moved into in a wide then gradually tightening circle were as before, fenced in by their enormous vines, with little grey cubes of houses, and occasional straw-shelters where the peasants kept their tools and took a nap in the shade in the worst of the noonday sun. In one of these four armed men were discovered. They immediately surrendered, were hand-cuffed, chained together and led away. But now a problem presented itself. Only four prisoners had been taken, and a man could be charged with banditry only if he was a member of a criminal association of not less than five persons. As it was the four captured men, who by legal defi-nition were not bandits, could have applied for bail, with the near-certainty of getting it. In this country there are fifty lawyers to every one policeman, and the lawyers expect to win. But a bandit gets no bail and faces a sentence of from five to thirty years.

The solution in this case was to go straight to the nearest village to the house of a man who happened to have a criminal record and arrest him. He became the essential fifth bandit. His resignation was aston-ishing. He kissed his family goodbye, allowed himself to be chained up without protest and was led off. Solitary confinement in the iron womb of Poggio Reale awaited him. Then a long, slow wasting away of body and mind on the island of Procida, of which little but blood-chilling legends are known. When, if ever, he returned to his village he would find his children gone and his wife grown old. How much better it would have been, how much more humane, simply to have shot all five 'while attempting to escape'.

Norman Lewis

1945 [England]

They had no wireless in the cottage where I had supper, so I didn't hear the nine o'clock News. Walking back to camp afterwards, the first sign of anything unusual that I noticed was a string of small triangu-lar flags being hoisted up across the road by some workmen. The flags appeared quite suddenly out of the leaf-laden boughs of a chestnut, crossed a patch of sago-coloured sky, and disappeared into the dark foliage of another tree. They looked surprised to be there. They were not new flags. They had flapped for a jubilee and a coronation and numerous local festivals, and now they seemed to be getting a little tired of it all. They were faded and grubby and washed-out looking. They hung languidly in the bluish evening air. The workmen tapped away at the trees and thrust ladders up into the ripe foliage, bringing down showers of leaves and a snow of pink and white blossom. Further on there was a cottage with two new Union Jacks thrust out from the window-sill. They hung down stiffly to attention. Against the mellow sun-bleached texture of the stone their strident colours looked ridiculous, and because they were there on purpose to disturb the quiet and familiar contours they gave a feeling of uneasiness. From there onwards all the little cottages were sprouting flags.

Keith Vaughan

1976 [The Philippines, on the set of *Apocalypse Now*]
12.15 am. – There is a discussion going on behind me between the stunt man and a military advisor. The next scene includes the shooting of a Viet Cong prisoner in the side of the head. The question is, how should he fall? A bottle of blood and a tube are rigged to his back, so it's best if he falls backwards to cover it. The military advisor says if he got shot at that close range with a .45 pistol, it would blow his head off and it wouldn't make any difference which way he fell.

Eleanor Coppola

8 May

1915 [London]
Papers full of *Lusitania*. They think 1,500 have been drowned, among them Sir Hugh Lane. It shows vividly how one's standards have altered – in fact, how out of drawing everything is. Very nearly as big as the *Titanic*, which loomed so large in one's life for months, and this is merely an incident, so full has one 'supped of horrors'. It will however, arouse great rage, and one wonders how America will take it.

Lady Cynthia Asquith

1944 [Amsterdam]

Dearest Kitty,

Have I ever told you anything about our family? I don't think I have, so let me begin. Father was born in Frankfurt am Main to very wealthy parents: Michael Frank owned a bank and became a millionaire, and Alice Stern's parents were prominent and well-to-do. Michael Frank didn't start out rich; he was a self-made man. In his youth Father led the life of a rich man's son. Parties every week, balls, banquets, beautiful girls, waltzing, dinners, a huge house, etc. After Grandpa died, most of the money was lost, and after the Great War and inflation there was nothing left at all. Until the war there were still quite a few rich relatives. So Father was extremely well-bred, and he had to laugh yesterday because for the first time in his fifty-five years, he scraped out the frying pan at the table.

Mother's family wasn't as wealthy, but still fairly well-off, and we've listened open-mouthed to stories of private balls, dinners and engagement parties with 250 guests.

We're far from rich now, but I've pinned all my hopes on after the war. I can assure you, I'm not so set on a bourgeois life as Mother and Margot. I'd like to spend a year in Paris and London learning the languages and studying art history. Compare that with Margot, who wants to nurse newborn babies in Palestine. I still have visions of gorgeous dresses and fascinating people. As I've told you many times before, I want to see the world and do all kinds of exciting things, and a little money won't hurt!

Anne Frank

1945 [London]

[VE Day] Later that evening we decided to brave the West End. Mummy and Sid [her mother's companion], who both remembered scenes of rape and wild debauchery from World War 1, put on the most unseductive clothes they could find, with heavy man-proof trousers – everything in fact bar a couple of chastity belts.

There was wild excitement in Trafalgar Square, half London seemed to be floodlit – so much unexpected light was quite unreal. There were people dancing like crazy, jumping in the fountains and climbing lampposts, and a dull red glow in the sky from bonfires which reminded us of the Blitz.

Most of the pubs seemed to be running out of booze, so I took them both to the York Minster where red wine was flowing in torrents. We sat at the little round corner table, the same table where I first got drunk with Rupert – it seems like a hundred years ago. A French sailor kissed Mummy and changed hats with her, taking her little brown velvet cap and giving her his with a pom-pom on top. Very embarrassed, she hastily rearranged her hair, pulling it over her ears. She never could stand people seeing her ears, although they are perfectly nice ones.

Sid got squiffy on one pernod – it reminds her of absinthe and her art student days in Paris.

We were all fairly unsteady by the time we left Soho and headed for Piccadilly, fighting our way slowly through the crowds towards Whitehall, where we had heard Churchill was appearing. Everyone was singing the old songs, 'Roll Out the Barrel', 'Bless 'em All', and 'Tipperary', and dancing in circles. At one point I got whirled away into the dance by a group of Polish airmen and I thought I was lost for ever, but managed to keep one eye on the beacon of Sid's bright red hair. As I fought my way back, one of my shoes came off and had to be abandoned.

We linked arms and slowly made our way towards Whitehall – when we got there we were packed like sardines. Everybody was singing 'Why Are We Waiting?' and 'We Want Winnie' – a few people fainted but suddenly all the floodlights came on, sirens wailed and there he was on the balcony making the V sign, just like on *Pathé* Gazette.

He made a wonderful speech but I don't remember very much of it except for the bit where he said, 'Were we downhearted?' and we all yelled, 'No!' Then we sang 'Land of Hope and Glory' and I think we all cried – I certainly did. It was one of the most exciting moments of my life.

Limped home with my stockings in ribbons, the whole sky ringed with searchlights.

Joan Wyndham

1945 [Surrey]

It is 7 a.m. I have just hoisted the Union Jack over Shieling [his house] and decorated the front with a string of bunting. The rising sun peeps over the tree tops, shedding a golden light over the village. A thrush perched on a nearby sycamore fills the air with his triumphant song. So I look around my little house standing in its pleasant garden and in a mood of chastened contemplation regard the much that has been spared to me through the war years. In a surge of gratitude for this great dawning of peace over the earth I offer my thanks to God.

For this is VE Day, announcing as complete the formal surrender of the enemy on all European fronts. The day for which so many like my splendid nephew Clifford and many more died, and without whom London itself might have joined Carthage. It is a miraculous culmination to D Day for the success of which we then put our trust in Providence and the valiant efforts of our crusading legions.

I have the impression from a newsreel picture that our Prime Minister [Winston Churchill] looks very tired. It is no small wonder. At 70 years of age to be still carrying with vigour the masterly direction of the Nation's affairs in the greatest and most terrific events of its long history is nothing short of superhuman. As the managing director of the biggest firm in the world his services are beyond price. God bless and preserve him for a few quiet years of repose when at last his task is done. In the annals of the human race, no man so richly deserved immortality.

It is late evening. The King has spoken and, after a last stand to in reverent toast of my neighbour's guests, I sit quietly to reflect on the day's happenings. And so we slip with the ease of well-conditioned gearing into normal running and the daily routines, secure from enemy disturbance and at night safe in our beds. Our private lives are once more our own. Yes, tomorrow I shall be glad to get back to the chores.

Walter Musto

1945 [London]

We had lunch at the Café [Royal] at 12.45. It wasn't very full or decorated, nor did the people look special in any way. But when we got out there was quite a crowd. The children had wanted to go to the Zoo but Piccadilly Circ[us] seemed better, so we wandered along slowly, looking on. A number of other people were doing the same thing, in fact almost everyone was tired and wanting to look rather than do. They were sitting when possible, lots of them on the steps of St Martin's. Most people were wearing bright coloured clothes, lots of them red white and blue in some form (I was wearing my kilt and a blouse, much too hot, as I found). Most women had lipstick and a kind of put on smile but all the very young looked very tired when they stopped actually smiling.

Of course there were Americans and young ATS [Auxiliary Territorial Service] girls making whoopee, and indeed I have seldom seem so many ATS so much drunk on so little! A lot of hats were worn, and occasionally someone had put on one which looked really chic, though most were rather silly; hardly any but the elderly had real hats. The sellers didn't nearly get rid of all their flags and badges and things, but I thought other street sellers were doing a good trade. I bought a comb for Val. There were huge queues for ice cream so we never got any.

Naomi Mitchison

9 May

1915 [Essex]
The resentment of farm-labourers at being badgered to enlist is shown by the fact that every recruiting poster from the Rectory to Lyons Hall has been torn down; torn into shreds; and cast away.

Andrew Clark

1918 [France]
X's story of Lord Kitchener in South African war. He imported fifteen well-known harlots from London to Pretoria and some other town. They were paid to give away officers who gave them military information. When will someone write the true life of Lord Kitchener, Britain's syphilitic hero?

Siegfried Sassoon

1918 [Gloucestershire]
I motored over to the hospital with Sister Orde in a blue funk, feeling the mixed sensations of a 'new boy', a night traveller, and an actress on her first night. There is a sort of supper meal at eight, but I didn't have any – I washed up the things and stood about. Lights are put out in the ward at nine o'clock, and occasionally one walks round the dim lantern-lit room. It is rather creepy – surrounded by all those huddled forms sleeping aloud. The porridge is put on early and has to be stirred all through the night, and one has to stoke the furnace. When there is nothing to do we sit quite comfortably in the little sitting room talking, reading, or writing. The queer anomalous meals are great fun

in the setting and the eating: at about twelve one has what I suppose represents lunch (something is left in the larder in the nature of eggs, sardines, and so on, and one drinks what one likes, such as Horlicks, tea, cocoa, or coffee) and at four one has a delicious meal of porridge, and so on – the porridge is far the best I have ever tasted.

The pet and the interest of A Ward now is poor little Harris, who has got his leg off right high up. A few days ago he had to have a lot more taken off his stump and he has nearly died of haemorrhage ever since. He is much better now, but still a very bad colour. He is such a darling – so brave and always smiling. It's still very painful – pray God I never have to see that stump naked!

My first night was eventful. At about eleven there came a knock at the door. In burst Nurse Ewing, who is alone in B Ward (where they are supposed not to have bad cases). She was white as paper and told us one of her men (obviously a case of bad shell shock) was quite unmanageably walking in his sleep – thinking he was at the Front, poor fellow – hurling missiles about in the delusion that they were bombs and labouring under the impression that his companions were Germans. He was 'hollering' like anything and Nurse Ewing said she couldn't be left alone with him. Away went Nurse Orde with her, leaving me quite alone in that snoring ward. I was in terror lest Harris should have a haemorrhage or something, but after a time they – to my intense relief – returned.

Lady Cynthia Asquith

1942 [London]

Over a cup of tea in Brooks's I opened the *New Statesman* and began an article by Raymond Mortimer on the Royal Academy exhibition. I read that there was one gallery devoted entirely to pictures by Wilson Steer and Sickert, that there was a Vanessa Bell of the Queen and princesses, someone else of the Prime Minister and a Moynihan of Eddy Sackville-West. I was so excited that I did not even finish the article or my tea, and rushed to the Academy before it shut, bought a catalogue and went the rounds. Nowhere could I find any of the sixty or so pictures by the most eminent contemporary artists mentioned by Raymond. The beast had, by way of skit, written a mock review of all those artists' works which he would have liked to see exhibited. I was furious with him.

James Lees-Milne

10 May

1940 [London]

Rode at Richmond in summer heat. As I dismounted the groom told
me that Holland and Belgium had been invaded.

John Colville

1940 [near Coventry]

The most eventful day of the war! This morning Holland and Belgium
were both invaded by Germany, and very soon afterwards they both
appealed to the allies for help. The reply was given in the affirmative
half an hour later, and now Holland and Belgium are our allies. Now
we know where we stand.

We were up in good time and, on hearing the news via the postman
and Kate, we had the wireless on at 8 a.m. All day at intervals we have
been listening in – at 10.30 a.m., at 12, at 1 p.m., 4.15 p.m., 6 p.m.
And lastly at 9 p.m. Air raids over Brussels and many other Dutch and
Belgian towns, as well as towns in France. Nancy – of loved memory
to us – has been raided and 16 civilians killed. There was a raid in
south-east England and incendiary bombs were dropped at Canterbury.
The last news spoke of the dash over the Belgian frontier of our mechanized forces after the call for help – an historic moment.

Mr Chamberlain[1] has resigned the Premiership and Mr Churchill
takes his place. The former spoke before the 9 o'clock news, rather
sadly, but putting his country's wish before himself, as one knew he
would – a truly great man!

Clara Milburn

1940 [Oxfordshire]

Today Germany invaded Holland and Belgium. It may be a good thing
to put down how one felt before one forgets it. Of course the first
feeling was the usual horror and disgust and the impossibility of finding
words to describe this latest *Schweinerei* by the Germans. Then came
the realisation that the war was coming a lot nearer to us – air bases
in Holland and Belgium would make air-raids on England a certainty.
People one met were either gloomy (Mr Beauclerk, the electrician,
and Mr Cobb, the wireless shop), slightly hysterical (Miss Bloomer) or

[1] Neville Chamberlain, Prime Minister May 1937 until May 1940.

just plainly calm like Steele. I think I was rather frightened, but hope I didn't show it, and anyway one still has the 'it couldn't happen to us' feeling. Then there is the very real, but impotent feeling of sympathy for these poor wretches who are the latest victims. In the news the Dutch and Belgian Ministers spoke and the Dutch minister sent a greeting to his wife and children and grandchildren. Then it was the most difficult thing to control oneself, and I know that if I had been alone I couldn't have done. Later came the news of Mr Chamberlain's resignation and his speech, in that voice which brings back so many memories mostly of crisis. But even if he has failed, and we can't be sure yet that he has, there is no more courageous man in the government or indeed anywhere, I'm sure of that. But Winston Churchill will be better for this war – as Hilary [her sister] said, he is such an old beast! The Germans loathe and fear him and I believe he can do it.

It was odd to remember that this day used to be a great anniversary for me. Seven years ago, on May 10th 1933, I first went out with Henry [an ex-boyfriend]. Imagine a lovely summer evening at the Trout with the wisteria out and the soft murmuring of the water. And my heart so full of everything. And now, emotion recollected in tranquillity . . . dust and ashes, dry bones. Or are they not so dry as all that? I don't suppose I shall ever know.

Barbara Pym

1940 [Germany]
The grocer said that with the collapse of Denmark and Holland our butter shortage will be over!

Elisabeth von Stahlenberg

1942 [Jersey]
Tonight, we all listened to Mr Churchill's speech – it was one of the most encouraging he has made and we felt cheered and began to hope that the war and this Occupation might end this year. There were 16 of us in the breakfast-room listening-in. I wonder what the Germans would have said if they had seen us, smiling at our Prime Minister's remarks!

Nan Le Ruez

1982 [London]
One thing I record with regret and sadness. A woman from Portsmouth rang me up in great distress and started to abuse me. It transpired that

her husband had gone down in HMS *Sheffield*, and she felt, as she was bound to, that his death had been in a good cause, and therefore she hated me for having opposed the war. I tried to tell her how sorry I was, but she rang off.

Tony Benn

11 May

1915 [Gallipoli]
Getting our full share of casualties. Poor Capt. Andrews killed by a sniper just after dinner. We have lost our best friend. We have only about five officers left. We are to be relieved today sometime. Left the trenches after dark and made our way back to some open ground about a mile and a half back. We had to doss down in the open. To make things worse it started raining.

Pvt Horace Bruckshaw, Royal Marine Light Infantry

1940 [London]
It was a particularly idyllic early evening. Cyril Connolly paid a visit. London was looking defiantly beautiful, its parks with their blue vistas of Watteauesque trees – so different from the trees that grow in the country – and its gardens behind the railing a mass of lilac and blossoming trees. As Cyril was about to leave, we stood at the front door enjoying the opalescent evening light. The sun made the barrage balloons very bright gold, and the Gothic towers of the Victoria and Albert Museum at the end of the road and the peach blossom trees in the Emlyn Williams's garden opposite were seen in an apricot haze. We remarked on the paradox of the scene. Nothing here was indicative of the turmoil in the world today, a turmoil created by one gangster. We could feel the peace and repose of the evening so forcibly that it was almost tangible, or something that one could eat.

I dined with Loelia Westminster.[1] After six months she had thrown aside the dust covers and re-opened her drawing-room. To celebrate this great event she gave a party. We all felt the dinner to be so excellent that we wanted to keep the menu in an album, as an archaeological

---

[1] Loelia, Duchess of Westminster.

specimen showing that this was the meal that we, in England, were fortunate enough to enjoy even after six months of war effort. Perhaps it would be the last of its sort. Anyhow, while we could, we would be as gay as possible. We went out to night clubs and danced all night. When we came back to our beds Germany had invaded Holland, Belgium and Luxembourg. Hell had broken loose.

Cecil Beaton

1945 [England]
Paul – the German interpreter – came into the office this afternoon. 'What part does Hitler play now in their lives [i.e. German prisoners-of-war]? What is the attitude over the reports of his death?' I asked him. 'All I can say is that some of the young ones cried when it was announced.'

Keith Vaughan

12 May

1916 [Scotland]
My feeling of impotent horror, as of a creature caught by a proprietor of some travelling circus and forced with formal brutality to go through meaningless tricks, was immensely sharpened by a charcoal drawing of C's called 'We want More Men!' showing Death with the English staff cap on and a ragged tunic, standing with a jagged sickle among a pile of bleeding, writhing bodies and smoking corpses – a huge gaunt figure that haunted me horribly.

Arthur Graeme West

1941 [Berlin]
This afternoon I went to try on hats. Now that clothes are rationed and hats are not, they have come into their own. They provide a sartorial diversion and we are slowly accumulating them. At least they change one's appearance a bit.

Marie 'Missie' Vassiltchikov

1944 [London]
Feeling utterly disgusted – debates about civil aviation and education; empire conferences; parties of all sorts; and I am nothing and nowhere.

It makes me seethe with indignation at the bloody and dastardly treatment I have had and still have. To hell and torture with Churchill and all the lousy swine of politicians and civil servants.

Lord Reith

13 May

1915 [Gallipoli]
Enjoyed a good, long night's sleep for we were very tired. Our artillery has been bombarding since yesterday afternoon. We dug a hole in the ground first thing and put a waterproof sheet in it, which we filled with water. Stripping ourselves we then enjoyed a much needed bath. Soon after we had completed our rough and ready toilet a big shell dropped right in amongst us knocking out seven or eight. Pollard and Madden were two victims out of our section. Duckworth, the man who did such good work in the landing was blown to atoms. It gave us a terrible shaking up. We got shelled all the afternoon so were obliged to remain in the trenches. It went quieter towards evening however. The Turks very rarely fire the big guns after dark, thank goodness, so that we can get a bit of peace at night.

Pvt Horace Bruckshaw, Royal Marine Light Infantry

1915 [Gallipoli]
For the benefit of those who have been so fortunate as to never have heard a shell burst in anger, a slight description of it may prove interesting. The first thing one hears is a noise like the rending of linen, or perhaps the rush of steam describes it better. This gets louder and louder, and then, as the projectile nears the end of its journey, one hears a whine, half whistle, half scream, and then the explosion. If it is very near there is an acrid smell in the air. One's feelings are difficult to describe. You duck your head instinctively – you feel absolutely helpless, wondering where the thing will burst, and as you hear the explosion a quick wave of feeling sweeps over you as you murmur, 'Thank Heaven, not this time!'

Major John Gillam, DSO

1916 [Scotland]

The C.O. today ordered all the spittoons to be removed from the canteen because of the look they gave the place; the canteen-man had paid eighteen shillings for them.

Arthur Graeme West

1940 [Lewes, England]

Princess Juliana of Holland after making the heroic utterance: 'After 500 years, people should realise that the House of Orange never deserts' is now in England with her infants and her German husband! Also Queen Wilhelmina.[1] I go down the High Street, foaming at the mouth, and saying 'How about Queen Boadicea?' and am told (with perfect truth) by some persons like Dr Wells that times have changed since Queen Boadicea's time. Also I want to know why, when we are already rationed and when in the end decision of victory may rest on whether we are starved or not, are 2,000 Dutch refugees allowed to come here?

Mrs Henry Dudeney

1940 [Wiltshire]

Everyone makes jokes about the likelihood of German parachutists landing in our Wiltshire fields dressed as nuns or clergymen – a good farcical subject on which to let off steam. This afternoon I was alone in the kitchen when the doorbell rang, and there on the step stood three tall bearded men who addressed me in strong German accents, and wore something between clergyman's and military dress! Aha! I thought, the parachutists already. But when they asked for Mrs. Nichols[2] I realised that it was some of the Brüderhof, a community of Christian Pacifists of all nations who live the simple life near Swindon. Curiosity was too much for me, so I asked them to have some tea. Two were very unattractive redheads with scarlet mouths above their beards. It was the maddest of Mad Hatter tea parties, consisting of me and these three Jesus Christs, all looking at me sweetly and speaking in gentle voices. I told them we were pacifists. 'Are you persecuted much?' they asked, rather taking the wind out

---

[1] Queen Wilhelmina did put her Dutch fleet and her diamond and gold reserves at the disposal of the British for the war effort.

[2] Lady Phyllis Nichols, who had stayed with the Partridges at the outbreak of war.

of my sails. I felt as if Jesus Christ had mistaken me for John the Baptist.

Frances Partridge

1940 [Rome]

Mussolini began to talk as follows: 'Some months ago I said that the Allies had lost the victory. Today I tell you that they have lost the war. We Italians are already sufficiently dishonoured. Any delay is inconceivable. We have no time to lose. Within a month I shall declare war. I shall attack France and England in the air and on the sea. I am no longer thinking of taking up arms against Yugoslavia because it would be a humiliating replacement.' Today, for the first time, I did not answer. Unfortunately, I can do nothing now to hold the Duce back. He has decided to act, and act he will. He believes in German success and in the swiftness of that success. Only a new turn in military events can induce him to alter his decision, but for the time being things are going so badly for the Allies that there is no hope.

Count Ciano

1940 [London]

After Jo had gone I looked at my flushed face in the glass and tidied my hair, thinking what an awful tart I am. There was a terrible love-bite on my cheek, so I got a pin and made a few scratches across it, and told Mummy a cat had scratched me, but I don't think she believed me. Later we listened to a very stirring speech by Churchill about 'blood, toil, sweat and tears'.

Joan Wyndham

1941 [Berlin]

Appalling news comes in this evening. [Rudolf] Hess,[1] against the Führer's orders, has taken off in a plane and has been missing since Saturday. We must presume him dead. His adjutants, who were the only ones aware of his intentions, have been arrested on the Führer's orders. The Führer's statement gives delusions as the reason for his action, some madness to do with illusionary peace-feelers. The entire affair is

[1] Rudolf Hess, Hitler's deputy, parachuted from a crashing plane, landing in a field near Glasgow. He was found by a local ploughman who took him to his house and offered him a cup of tea. Hess was reported to have replied that he never drank tea late at night.

thoroughly confused at the moment. We are forced to issue the statement immediately. A hard, almost unbearable blow. At the moment it is impossible to see where the affair will end.

I receive a telephone call from the Berghof [Hitler's chalet at Berchtesgaden]. The Führer is quite shattered. What a sight for the world's eyes: the Führer's deputy a mentally disturbed man. Dreadful and unthinkable. Now we shall have to grit our teeth.

Josef Goebbels

1941 [Carradale, Scotland]
The milkman says that Hess [Hitler's deputy] has come down in Glasgow with a sprained ankle by parachute! He says it was in the midnight news . . .

And after all it was! We all yelled with surprise when it really was true, and what a lovely story, the hay fork and the cup of tea and everything. Wonder what they'll do with him and how useful he can be made.

Naomi Mitchison

1941 [London]
Strangely enough, the Allies have had their first real break. It happened Saturday night, but no one was allowed to know of it until about midnight last night when the news of Hess's sudden flight to Scotland was announced at 10 Downing Street. It is something which could only have occurred in an E. Phillips Oppenheim novel, or in this present scatter-brained, lunatic world. He is the third man in the Nazi hierarchy, who steals a Messerschmitt 110 and flies from southern Germany, with a stop at Munich for refuelling, across the North Sea to Scotland, where he comes down at the end of his gasoline, with a parachute, and is captured by a farmer. The Germans have already made a radio broadcast, which was very silly, for they say that he is insane and has committed suicide. He behaved very queerly for an insane man, for his plan to escape must have been very carefully arranged, and he brought with him a series of photographs of himself at different ages so that it would be certain he could be identified as Hess. It takes more than an insane man to fly from southern Germany to Scotland, too! And he was not too insane to make a speech to the Nazi Party on April 23 and to take part in the May 1 ceremonies only two weeks ago.

It leads to a great many interesting speculations: first, that there is a definite breach in the Nazi Party; second, that it will have a profound effect on German public opinion; and third, what information, if he will talk, will be at the disposal of the British. He might as well tell them everything for certainly his life is forfeit now unless the British win.

To sum the whole affair up, it seems to me that no matter what his mission may be, or his attitude, there is no assumption on which his flight is not going to be discouraging and injurious to the Germans. Nevertheless, there is a danger, that in the United States, where they are so prone to grasp straws, this may be taken as an indication of a more serious breakdown in the Nazi Party than it really is.

What a dramatic episode in this whole fascinating hell!!

London buzzed with the name of Hess yesterday and in White's club where I lunched, the bar, the lounge and the restaurant were full of sibilants. It sounded like a basketful of snakes. The most interesting thing to me is the confused, contradictory and halting explanation given by the Germans. Here was something against which they had not planned and therefore their efforts to meet it have been stupid and confusing. Their successive hasty explanations will produce the worst possible result within Germany as they have already done so outside.

The Prime Minister made his usual epigram when he heard the news. 'The maggot is in the apple' he exclaimed!

General Raymond E. Lee

1941 [London]

I have absolutely no theory about the reason for Hess's arrival. It is completely mysterious. The one thing I know is that if a possibility exists of missing this propaganda opportunity, the British government will find it.

George Orwell

1941 [Rome]

The Hess affair sounds like a detective story. Hitler's substitute, his second-in-command, the man who for fifteen years had in his grasp the most powerful German organization, has made an airplane landing in Scotland. He fled, leaving a letter for Hitler. In my opinion, it is a very serious matter: the first real victory for the English. At the beginning, the Duce believed that Hess had been forced to make a landing while he was on his way to Ireland in order to start a revolt, but he very soon abandoned this thesis, and he now shares my impression of the exceptional importance of this event. Von Ribbentrop[1] unexpectedly arrives in Rome. He is discouraged and nervous. He wants to confer with the Duce and me for various reasons, but there is only one real reason: he wants to inform us about the Hess affair, which is now in the hands of the press all over the world. The official version is that Hess, sick in body and mind, was a victim of his pacifist hallucination, and went to England hoping to facilitate the start of peace negotiations. Hence, he is not a traitor; hence, he will not talk; hence, whatever else is said or printed in his name is false. His conversation is a beautiful job of patching things up. The Germans want to cover themselves before Hess speaks and reveals things that might cause a big impression in Italy. Mussolini comforted von Ribbentrop, but told me afterwards that he considers the Hess affair a tremendous blow to the Nazi regime. He added that he was happy about it because this will have the effect of reducing German stock, even among the Italians.

Count Ciano

1941 [London]

The wireless announces that Rudolf Hess, the third and most important personality in the German Reich, arrived alone and by plane in Scotland on Saturday night. A most hazardous journey and remarkable performance. All day people talked of a crack in the Nazi Government but I do not believe it. Hess once invited Honor and me to lunch in Berlin when we were there for the Olympic Games; we refused – but I remember that 'Duglo' Clydesdale [the Duke of Hamilton], as he then was, did go, as did Pat [Countess of] Jersey. The world does not know that the Duke [is] thus concerned in the story. He came to the Foreign Office yesterday and spent an hour with Anthony.[2]

'Chips' Channon

1943 [Paris]

The din of the explosions tears me from sleep at about nine. And while I am dressing in haste, new detonations much nearer make me rush to the window. In the direction of the harbour I see vast white

[1] Joachim von Ribbentrop, German Foreign Minister and Hitler's Special Representative.
[2] Anthony Eden, first Earl of Avon, Foreign Secretary.

clouds rising, which filled the sky for more than an hour. A very bright white glow continued for a long time to light up the horizon powerfully, the result no doubt of some tremendous fire. Amphoux, who had joined me in the living-room, judges that it is much closer to us than the harbour. I see another bomb fall on the left, in the direction of the Majestic, certainly less than a hundred yards from our house. And almost immediately afterwards people run in from the avenue Roustan, under our windows, carrying stretchers and hastening towards the scene. The wave of terror has passed; there is nothing to do but go back to bed, since I am beyond the age of being able to help the victims. But in expectation of a new wave that may perhaps strike us, remaining on the alert, I do not dare yield to sleep. No one can feel safe from such a blind aim; and why should I be spared? One feels the blast from near-by explosions pass over one like the flapping of a shroud.

André Gide

1967 [Bolivia]
Day of belching, farting, vomiting and diarrhoea; a real organ concert.

Ernesto 'Che' Guevara

14 May

1941 [Berlin]
After lunch we tried to buy a picture postcard of Hess, but they seem to have been withdrawn overnight and cannot be had for love or money. Indeed in one shop a woman said aggressively, 'Wozu brauchen Sie ihn denn? Er ist jan wahnsinnig geworden!' ['What do you need him for? He has clearly gone crazy!'] – the official version. To calm her down, we pretended we were interested in the whole zoo and bought one each of Goebbels and Goering.

Marie 'Missie' Vassiltchikov

1941 [Rome]
Ribbentrop left after having said good-bye to Mussolini during a brief meeting at the Palazzo Venezia. The Hess affair has had no developments so far. British radio says that he spends his time writing, which disturbs Ribbentrop. When Ribbentrop's four-engine plane was taking

off, Bismarck[1] said to Anfuso,[2] 'Let's hope that they will all crash and break their necks; but not here, or we'll have some unpleasant work to do.' That's German national solidarity for you!

Count Ciano

1943 [Tunisia]

I still feel as I did in the last war, that a dead steer, its head a swollen shapeless mass, its belly a great water sac, its legs galloping frantically through the sky, black blood drying on monstrous body cavities, gives one as real a picture of the 'horror of war' as anything I know. The smell and the buzzing of the flies – the vultures of Africa – are the sensory accompaniment of death.

George Biddle

1945 [Berlin]

Something dreadful – or eerie – is going on all around us. Every house door is locked. You can't visit your friends because no one opens to a knock. If you're lucky you run into someone you want to visit on his way home, and after a brief exchange he quickly slips behind the door, which is instantly locked behind him. Why? Because everyone is afraid of Russian soldiers, who try to force their way into homes at every opportunity. Granted, many of them are harmless, but many aren't, and those that just rob you aren't the worst. Above all people are afraid, and rightly so, that they'll rape the girls and women in the house. I wish I could prove that the people who tell stories about these sorts of rapes are liars. But I can't!

John Rabe

15 May

1864 [Georgia]

Today is Pentecost day. The battle lasted yesterday into the night and this morning it continues again. We were relieved last night. Our entire division is on the march to try to surround the enemy. We marched until noon and set up a battle line and moved out. Our

---

[1] Prince Otto Von Bismarck, Councillor at the German Embassy in Rome.
[2] Filippo Anfuso, Head of Count Ciano's Cabinet.

brigade attacked the enemy defences but we were thrown back. We regrouped and attacked again. Our regiment moved ahead in good formation, but the other regiments broke up and we had to retreat again. We attacked again but did not succeed. We received re-inforcements and took the defences. This was a horrible fight. Dead and wounded lay everywhere. We were taken to the rear and spent a quiet night, we are considerably disappointed since our regiment lost 70 men of 370 total.

Pvt Frederick C. Buerstatte, 26th Regiment, Wisconsin Volunteers

1915 [Gallipoli]

Our chaplain arranged an open air concert to take place after dark. It was the most weird concert I have ever attended. It went very dark and lightning was playing in the sky. The artillery were roaring a solo with a chorus of rifle fire, stray bullets even reaching the spot where we were. Every now and then Veras Lights were shot up from the French and our own lines, bursting into a shower of stars when in the air. All the while our fellows were in turn singing comic, secular and sacred songs. The limit however, was reached when Gilbert Wilson, a chum of mine, and who is a professional, sang Will o' th' Wisp. He sang it splendidly but the effect was almost unearthly. We piped down about 10 p.m. to dream of Turks, Germans, goblins and goodness knows what.

Pvt Horace Bruckshaw, Royal Marine Light Infantry

1915 [Gallipoli]

The knocking out of a sniper by some of the South Wales Borderers was described to me to-day by one of their officers. Two officers were standing up in their trench by a machine gun, one holding a periscope, when a bullet went through the sleeve of his coat, wounding the officer to whom he was talking. The first officer spotted a sniper bob down immediately after. He then got down in the trench beside the man working the machine gun, and pointed out to him the bush behind which the sniper had crouched. The machine gun was laid on to it. Then the man on the machine gun and the officer took cover, the man holding his hand up to the machine gun ready to pop off. The officer then cautiously raised the periscope over the trench and looked carefully at the lower mirror. He saw in the mirror, a head slowly appear above the bush about eight hundred yards away, then a rifle lifted. He said to the machine gun man 'Fire.' Pop-pop, and the sniper rolled over dead on his side beside the bush.

Major John Gillam, DSO

1918 [Gloucestershire]
Another piping hot day. These May days are indescribably beautiful. Dr Halliwell had given me a sleeping draught which I gulped, hoping to fall down like Juliet – I woke at three and then went off again until I was called at six, when I was fearfully sleepy.

On this morning I felt I won my spurs. I emptied my first bed-pan and had to see Harris's stump uncovered – his dressing having slipped off during the night. As usual the bite was not as bad as the bark. I did a good farce-act during the dressings whilst cutting a strip of plaster. I got my hand hopelessly stuck in it like a fly on flypaper. The dressing was delayed for several minutes whilst Sister and Stevens extricated me.

Lady Cynthia Asquith

1940 [Wiltshire]
We are told that parachute descents upon England 'are not extremely likely'. Everyone must shut up their cars every night or disconnect their engines. How MAD to be sitting listening to such things.

Frances Partridge

1940 [Rome]
Great excitement over the news of the breakthrough of the Maginot Line at Sedan. It is a piece of news that doesn't convince me completely, and I believe that it is dangerous to exaggerate information of secondary importance. Public opinion has now improved because of German victories, but the real feelings of the people have not changed.

Count Ciano

1940 [London]
New appeal last night for home defence – against parachutists. L[eonard, her husband] says he'll join. An acid conversation. Our nerves are harassed – mine at least: L. evidently relieved by the chance of doing something. Gun and uniform to me slightly ridiculous. Behind that strain: this morning we discussed suicide if Hitler lands. Jews beaten up. What point in waiting? Better shut the garage doors. This is a sensible, rather

matter of fact talk. A thunderous hot day. Dutch laid down arms last night. Ten days, we say, will settle it. I guess we hold: then dig in: about November the USA comes in as arbitrator. On the other hand – No, I don't want the garage to see the end of me. I've a wish for ten years more, and to write my book which as usual darts into my brain. L. finished his [*The War for Peace* yesterday]. So we've cleared up our book accounts – though it's doubtful if we shall publish this June. Hospital trains go by. A hot day to be wounded. Anyway, it can't last, this intensity – so we think – more than ten days.

This idea struck me: the army is the body: I am the brain. Thinking is my fighting.

Virginia Woolf

1941 [Carradale, Scotland]

Robbie [local fisherman] says that a plane came down in Belfast; the pilot was killed but they hanged him on a lamp post all the same; Robbie slightly shocked. Lachie Paterson [neighbour] thinks Hess should be hanged.

Naomi Mitchison

1941 [Berlin]

Yesterday: The Hess Affair has caused appalling damage. At home, according to the SD[1] report and other inquiries, the situation is one of complete débâcle. The public simply cannot understand what has happened. Some gratification among the reactionaries and in the Wehrmacht. The old, good-hearted Party comrades suffer most. The effect abroad is indescribable. It is the universal, almost the sole, talking-point. If Hess's senseless action was calculated to put him in the public eye, then it has succeeded brilliantly. Every possible kind of horror-story is being peddled. London is cunningly letting us wait for an official statement, and thus allowing free rein to the lies. But there is indication of an underlying grand strategy at this stage. I would be making more of it if I were the English Propaganda Minister. Churchill is being very reticent. The story is that he wants to talk to Hess personally. One piece of good news: official circles in London have said that Hess wanted peace, but on the basis of German strength. The main danger is that they will use him to give authenticity to faked atrocity-reports.

[1] The Sicherheitsdienst, 'Security Service'.

But this has not yet happened. He completely dominates the press in the USA. Child's play!

I outline the affair to the Ministerial Conference. Boundless amazement. Watchwords: at home, keep our nerve and say nothing for the moment; abroad, deny the lies and sketch out the background to the case.

Josef Goebbels

16 May

1915 [Paris]
I dreamed all night of Rupert Brooke. And to-day as I left the house he was standing at the door, with a rucksack on his back and his broad hat shading his face. So after I had posted a letter I did not go home. I went a long, very idle sort of amble along the quays. It was exquisitely hot: white clouds lay upon the sky like sheets spread out to dry. On the big sandheaps down by the river children had hollowed out tunnels and caverns. They sat in them, stolid and content, their hair glistening in the sun. Now and then a man lay stretched on his face, his head in his arms. The river was full of big silver stars; the trees shook faintly, glinting with light. I found delightful places – little squares with white square houses. Quite hollow they looked, with the windows gaping open. Narrow streets arched over with chestnut boughs, or perhaps quite deserted, with a clock tower showing over the roofs. The sun put a spell on everything.

I crossed and recrossed the river and leaned over the bridges and kept thinking we were coming to a park when we weren't. You cannot think what a pleasure my invisible, imaginary companion gave me. If he had been alive it would never have possibly occurred; but – it's a game I like to play – to walk and talk with the dead who smile and are silent, and *free*, quite finally free. When I lived alone, I would often come home, put my key in the door, and find someone there waiting for me. 'Hullo! Have you been here long?'

I suppose that sounds dreadful rubbish.

Katherine Mansfield

1940 [Surrey]
This morning at Molesey Police Station I enrolled in the Local Volunteer Force.

Walter Musto

1940 [Lewes, England]
Mrs Holman said that 12 young women at Barcombe were in the family way by soldiers. The battalion was assembled – and all the girls pointed to *one* man! What a valiant!

Mrs Henry Dudeney

1945 [Carradale, Scotland]
One doesn't seem to want to listen to the news now. And god knows, one now fails to see any road at all out of the mess we are in. I feel more and more depressed. However a long and delighted letter from Murdoch [her son, fighting in Italy], whose group has decided to 'sever our connection with the 8th Army' and who has been rushing round in his jeep, has been to Venice and Ferrara, and has been liberating hill villages and having parties with all the girls and partisans dancing jigs with loaded sten guns. Has finally fetched up in a German HQ which had just been deserted by its inhabitants and where they get as many hot baths as they want.

Naomi Mitchison

17 May

1940 [near Coventry]
Another glorious warm day, bright sun and lovely colouring every-where. Out early in the garden to make it look as it ought to be. The bird garden was sad-looking, the soil green-mouldy through lack of attention for months, and the tulips there devastated by a hailstorm the other day. So in an hour-and-a-half they were removed, along with the wallflowers, and the soil forked and freshened and given new life – redemption.

The war news is grave. The Germans have turned the salient into a bulge on the Western Front and great strength will be needed to flatten it again. The R.A.F. are doing magnificent work in preventing easy advance by bombing roads, railways, key points, etc. On the whole they are clever and, having done their work, the announcement says: 'All our aeroplanes returned safely.' Sometimes it is 'One of our aero-planes failed to return.' In a tremendous effort on a key position today, 'Eleven of our aeroplanes failed to return'.

Last night, just as I was in the half-dreamy stage of dropping off to sleep, I suddenly saw a face, rather white, against the dark background of my closed lids, and tried to keep it long enough to see whose face it was. As it faded away it seemed to be Alan, calmly asleep.

Clara Milburn

1982 [Kent]

This is *the* crisis. I am lucky to be in the House [of Commons] for it. Lucky, too, to be 'recognised' and allowed to 'achieve'. When one has seen this through, *then* one will have discharged one's duty.

Alan Clark

18 May

1940 [Paris]

Through a sense of decency I am concerned in this notebook only with what has nothing to do with the war; and this is why I go for so many days without writing anything in it. Those are the days on which I have not been able to rid myself of the anguish, not been able to think of anything but *that*.

André Gide

1942 [Holland]

The threat grows ever greater, and terror increases from day to day. I draw prayer round me like a dark protective wall, withdraw inside it as one might into a convent cell and then step outside again, calmer and stronger and more collected again. I can imagine times to come when I shall stay on my knees for days on end waiting until the protective walls are strong enough to prevent my going to pieces altogether, my being lost and utterly devastated.

Etty Hillesum

1943 [Rome]

Never have I seen a more lovely Roman May. The flower-stalls are piled high with irises and roses and madonna lilies, the fountains play, the cafés on the side-walk are thronged with pretty young women in summer hats ogling the tight-waisted young men who still, in astonishing numbers, walk up and down the pavements. In the *Giardino del Lago* the children sail their boats and watch the Punch and Judy shows and feed the swans, while an occasional plane swoops overhead. And yet the sense of menace is there. At night the streets, lit only by moonlight or starlight, are of an uncanny beauty – silent and deserted, with no eye to see.

Iris Origo

19 May

1916 [London]
Went to Downing Street for lunch. I sat beside a poor blinded officer who had been at the wonderful St Dunstan's institution for the blind. He was most pathetic and very nice, making one's heart ache. I had to cut up his food for him, and there was an awful moment when he thought his empty plate had got food on it.

Inexpressibly relieved to hear all our alarms on Tom's [her brother-in-law] account were false. He is safe at Jerusalem on the way to Damascus. Through the American Embassy we had asked for their two names and Tom's had been cabled, but alas not Ego's.[1] This is too cruelly disappointing. I'm afraid we have no idea where he is. There seems no reasonable doubt that he must have started with them from the battle-field, since all the bodies and badly wounded have been identified. As it was a twelve-hour march to the railway, the assumption is that he cannot have been very badly wounded, but of course he may have got worse and been obliged to be left somewhere – it's horrid not knowing. According to rumour, he was at first shot in the shoulder, and so slightly that, after having his wound dressed, he was able to go back into action. There is, however, a rumour that he was wounded a second time and someone has got hold of the idea that it was in the lung. This sounds mere *gossip*, though. Mamma terribly worried, over-tired, and nervy.

Mary Herbert[2] came in with lots of confusing Egyptian rumours. Apparently the poor Yeomanry made a magnificent fight of it, standing up against seven to one odds for about fourteen hours with only one machine gun. There was some disastrous headquarters blunder. One wounded man whom Mary Strickland [her sister] visited said he heard the man next to him say, 'There goes Elcho with the white flag.'

---

[1] Hugo Francis Charteris, Lord Elcho, her brother, later reported killed in action in Katia.
[2] Wife of Aubrey Herbert and daughter of 4th Viscount De Vesci.

If this were true, it would prove that Ego was still well enough to be active at the close of the battle.

Cynthia Asquith

1942 [POW camp, Java]
Change in command today. To Police Bureau at 1200 hours for the 'hand over', where a colourful monkey show. First, both officers took several pictures of the captive commanding officers on the steps, British CO (me) showing his natural modesty by standing in the gutter behind a fat Dutch colonel until dragged out with laughter, and then buried his nose under the peak of his cap and chin in his shirt. Next, assembled and did our attention and saluting display and were addressed by the old commander, who expressed his gratification at our previous reactions and the way we had carried out the orders. (My comment: bayonets are useful!) He then expressed the trite hope that we would continue to accord his successor the same enviable behaviour. The latter introduced, a picturesque character with a villainous shaven brachycephalic poll, a long drooping moustache, spectacles, a white tennis shirt, white cotton gloves – dandy what! He addressed us less eloquently, felicitating us upon the good reports given to him of our behaviour towards the departing and abjuring us to continue the good behaviour with him. Curtain, with more bowing and a very successful sortie (obtained food) on the way home. Rest of day somewhat uneventful.

Weary Dunlop

20 May

1940 [Aachen, Germany]
This has been a day in my life. To have seen the destruction of war, what guns and bombs do to houses and people in them, to towns, cities, bridges, railroad stations and tracks and trains, to universities and ancient noble buildings, to enemy soldiers, trucks, tanks, and horses caught along the way.

It is not pretty. No, it is not beautiful. Take Louvain, that lovely old university town, burned in 1914 by the Germans in their fury and rebuilt – partly by American aid. A good part of it is in shambles. The great library of the university, rebuilt by the donations of hundreds of American schools and colleges, is completely gutted. I asked a German officer what happened to the books. 'Burned,' he said.

I must have looked a little shocked as I watched the desolation and contemplated this one little blow to learning and culture and much that is decent in European life. The officer added: 'Too bad. A pity. But, my friend, that's war. Look at it.' I did. But it hurt.

William L. Shirer

1941 [Wiltshire]

For someone living in the Blitz, who finds herself among four country-dwellers, Hester's[1] tone was perfect. She discussed how to keep rabbits as if it were the most important thing in the world, but when she did start on her shelter stories they were fascinating. She described how one night as she lay huddled and terrified on a mattress in the shelter, listening to a series of appalling crashes and whizzes, she heard two voices discussing German airmen – 'They say they're heavily made-up, *you* know, red *nails, lip-stick* – I mean when men do *that* . . .' CRASH – BANG – WHIZZ from above. And a more outspoken voice put in loudly: 'Why, everyone knows Hitler himself is a Pansy!' CRASH. BOOM. BANG!

Frances Partridge

1969 [Bien Luc, Vietnam]

Halfway [searching for landmines] through our sector we came upon a woman and two children herding three water buffalo. I pointed in the direction of the village where we were to meet the Bravo commander. After much shouting and gesturing, I convinced her to lead the way. With the three buffalo and the locals walking in front of us, we felt a little safer from booby traps.

Using civilians in this manner is, of course, against Geneva Convention agreements. I really did not care. What are they going to do? Send me to Vietnam?

Michael Lee Lanning

1992 [Sarajevo]

Dear Mimmy,

The shooting has died down. Today Mummy felt brave enough to cross the bridge. She saw Grandma and Grandad, ran into various people she knows and heard a lot of sad news. She came back all miserable.

[1] Hester Chapman (Mrs R. L. Griffin), 1899–1976; novelist, biographer, historian.

Her brother was wounded on 14 May, driving home from work. Her brother is hurt and she doesn't find out about it until today – that's terrible. He was wounded in the leg and is in hospital. How can she get to him? It's like being at the other end of the world now. They told her he's all right, but she doesn't believe them and keeps crying. If only the shooting would stop, she could go to the hospital. She says: 'I won't believe it until I see him with my own eyes.'

Zlata Filipovic

21 May

1940 [Paris]
O incurably frivolous people of France! You are going to pay dearly today for your lack of application, your heedlessness, your smug reclining among so many charming virtues.

André Gide

1940 [London]
The only bright spot in the day [was] a remark by Mrs White my cook – 'I thought things must be hopeless when Mr Churchill started quoting Scripture.'

Violet Bonham Carter

22 May

1864 [Georgia]
One does not realize it, but today is Sunday. Tomorrow we march again. The heat is terrible and we are all almost 'finished'.

Pvt Frederick C. Buerstatte, 26th Regiment, Wisconsin Volunteers

1940 [Bisley, England]
Heavy rain all night and morning. Laura [his wife] returned to Street's Cottage. I lectured to the company upon the international situation and depressed myself so much that I could barely continue speaking.

In the evening a lecture from Fitzgerald who has just come off the *Curaçao* which was badly bombed in Norway. He described embarking a company and a half of the Leicesters who had the wrong baggage.

When that was adjusted they sailed, examined their stores at sea and found the anti-tank magazines empty. This battalion when fully assembled numbered 600 and returned 150 strong. Fitzgerald then described lying in the fjords round Andenes being bombed hourly day by day. RAF constantly flew without their distinguishing signs and neglected to give answering signals; were constantly fired on and sometimes brought down. Andenes had no anti-aircraft defences, but the Royal Marine garrison lost only one man killed and one wounded. In *Curaçao* a Vickers on a searchlight-mounting proved the most valuable weapon. She avoided being hit for some days by manoeuvre; keeping engine running, put full steam ahead or astern and wheel right over on approach of bomber. Bombs screamed. RAF several times came round ship stunting and showing off, and left her to shadowing Dorniers.

Evelyn Waugh

1942 [Portugal]
At San Vincenti, there got on the boat a fantastic Englishman, residing normally in Bournemouth, now Diplomatic Courier passing from place to place on sweltering African coast. Eye-glass in eye, he wandered watchfully about boat looking for girls; spoke of war, he had confidence in victory; wife in Bournemouth still, where he had with difficulty persuaded her to wear trousers for purpose of fire watching, with whom, when victory was won, Empire all regained, enemies all defeated, he would perhaps settle in Portugal procuring servants easily, reading *The Times* quietly in the sun, and after lunch taking a nap. Ancient playboy, very lecherous, another Knight with Woeful Countenance, strangely campaigning for justice, freedom and truth.

Malcolm Muggeridge

23 May

1871 [Paris]
Today the sound of firing came nearer and nearer. We could distinctly hear rifle-shots in the Rue Drouot. Suddenly a squad of workers appeared who had been ordered to block the boulevard on a level with the Rue Vivienne and to build a barricade under our windows. Their hearts were not in it. Some of them took up two or three paving-stones from the roadway, and the others, as if for form's sake, gave a

few blows with a pick-axe at the asphalt pavement. But almost immediately bullets started raking the boulevard and passing over their heads, and the downed tools. Burty[1] saw them disappear down the Rue Vivienne with a sigh of relief. We were both thinking of the National Guards who would have come into the house to fire from the windows, trampling our collections under their feet.

Then a large band of National Guards appeared with their officers, falling back slowly and in good order. Others followed, marching faster. And finally some more came rushing along in a general stampede, in the midst of which we saw a dead man with his head covered in blood, whom four men were carrying by his arms and legs like a bundle of dirty washing, taking him from door to door without finding a single one open.

The shells started falling again – this time shells fired by the Federates at the positions captured by the Versailles troops. We camped in the anteroom. Renée's [Burty] little iron bed was pulled into a safe corner. Madeleine [Burty] lay down on a sofa near her father, her face lit up by the lamp and silhouetted against the white pillow, her thin little body lost in the folds and shadows of a shawl. Mme Burty sank into an armchair. As for myself, I kept listening to the heartrending cries of a wounded infantryman who had dragged himself up to our door and whom the concierge, out of a cowardly fear of compromising herself, refused to let in.

The Brothers Goncourt

1916 [Scotland]

Lecture by S on maps. A sand model had been erected on a table by this person which occupied him an hour this morning. He had put tapes and flaps on it to signify contours and heights, and explained the features at enormous length; of course we all knew them and realised it was all eye-wash. He showed that he didn't know the difference between concave and convex, and bungled away for twenty minutes before a blackboard on which he had drawn an abominable map.

Arthur Graeme West

1943 [London]

Enormously worried about myself.

Lord Reith

[1] Philippe Burty, art critic.

1943 [Tunisia]
The Road to Enfidaville and Sousse showed here and there some tell-
tale evidence of what had swept through. The small, orderly, villages
of the dead, neat little piles of white sandstone. Occasionally they
were adorned by rows of empty gasoline cans, for no season's flowers
have bloomed since the recent killings. The usual decorations, however,
were the soldiers' helmets, or a German musket broken at the butt
before throwing it away, so that it would not be used to kill more
Germans. But the bodies will decompose as peacefully here as among
the white birch copses of Silesia or in the cool shadow of a Scotch
cemetery. And their dust will finally commingle with the dust of
Phoenicians, of Cato's army that surrendered here to Caesar, of the
vandal conquerors, the Moslems and the French. It is all one to the
grapevines of Algeria – the excreta of living bodies or the fertiliza-
tion of the dead.

George Biddle

24 May

1871 [Paris]
When I awoke I looked for the corpse of the National Guard who
had been killed yesterday. It had not been removed. It had simply been
partly covered with the branches of the tree under which he had been
killed.

The Brothers Goncourt

1940 [England]
Up to Leicester where there is a huge dinner of the 1936 Club. I get
an excellent reception and find that their morale is very good. It is not
mere complacency, since I give them a test question to vote on, namely,
'Should the Derby be put off?' They voted some 88 per cent in favour
of postponement.

Harold Nicolson

1940 [Kelvedon, Essex]
This evening we buried tin boxes three feet below the earth's surface
in the little churchyard under a tree near the brick wall – the West
wall, which divides the churchyard from Honor's private garden. The

larger, lower box contains my diaries, the smaller box my best bibelots, watches, Fabergé objects, etc. Mortimer, who dug the hole, is discreet, and he waited until all the gardeners had gone home; we watched the earth cover them over; may they sleep in peace. Mother Earth must hold many other such secrets in her bosom.

'Chips' Channon

1944 [London]

I suppose I am and always have been almost completely self-centred and that nothing interests me at all except what I am concerned in. I expect it is too late to change. I have no ordinary human kindliness or tolerance. I have brilliance, intellect and all sorts of things like that, energy, conscientiousness and thoroughness. About the only passion I show is in reviling politicians, Churchill especially. Never rise to any heights. Scornful of patriotism and honest efforts to serve the country. Loathing the common people. I will rarely admit greatness in others. This is the kind of thing that might be said about me. A good deal is true. I am obsessed by my own fate and by a desire for revenge for my treatment; by a sense of injury. Is my ambition just lust for power? (I don't think so; I never have.) I think no one is so unhappy or has had such hard treatment or is in such a bad way. The greatness that used to be there never now appears – nothing that shines. I only show a hopelessness and almost an acceptance of my own shortcomings. I have always known I had a horrid character and disposition. And now I am querulous and embittered and small and shrunken and can't see even the near horizon. Believing nothing and without faith or hope; stifled and strangled and submerged by the pettiness of my own pre-occupations. The inspiration and domination of my personality are gone.

Lord Reith

25 May

1864 [Virginia]

Were sent out on the front skirmish line. Shot at and was shot at by the Rebs but by the infinite mercy of God my life was spared, altho the bullets frequently came near me, but in God alone is our help to be found.

Samuel Findley Junkin, 100th Pennsylvania Volunteer Infantry

1940 [England]
Then we went up to what has been so far the worst week in the war. And so remains. On Tuesday evening the BBC announced the taking of Amiens and Arras. On Monday they broke through. It seems they raid with tanks and parachutists: roads crammed with refugees can't be bombed. They crash on. Now are at Boulogne. What are the great armies doing to let this 25 mile hole stay open? The feeling is we're outwitted. They're agile and fearless and up to any new dodge. The French forgot to blow up bridges. The Germans seem youthful, fresh, inventive. We plod behind. This went on the three London days. Rodmell burns with rumours. Are we to be bombed, evacuated? Guns that shake the windows. Hospital ships sunk. So it comes our way. Today's rumour is the Nun in the bus who pays her fare with a man's hand.

Virginia Woolf

1940 [USA]
Again bad weather, dark, cold, and damp. C [her husband, Charles] reads from the paper this morning – an article about Saint-Exupéry.[1] It was so nice to think he was still alive. What a curious world one lives in that we can be glad that *today* a man is alive, sitting at a café in Paris, writing an article, seeing his wife, when you know that yesterday he barely escaped death and that *tomorrow* he goes back again to it. Of course he has always lived like that.

Anne Morrow Lindbergh

1941 [London]
The news this afternoon confirms the sinking of the *Hood* (by the explosion of her magazine).[2] This is another event similar to what took place in the [First] World War, when in one of the earliest naval actions, three great ships went down in three successive bursts of flame, one minute after the other. This occasion brought forth the greatest

[1] Antoine de Saint Exupéry, French novelist, writer, pioneer airman, author of *Wind, Sand and Stars*. In 1940, after Germany invaded France, Antoine de Saint-Exupéry fled to the USA, where he met up with Anne Morrow Lindbergh and her husband Charles, with whom he shared an interest in aviation. His plane was shot down and he was killed on a reconnaissance mission in 1944.
[2] A shot from the German battleship *Bismarck* pierced the magazine of the *Hood*, which blew up. Only three of a crew of over 1400 survived.

example of understatement of which I know. Admiral Beatty, who was leading the attack in his flagship, after seeing the instantaneous destruction and engulfing of three of his most powerful units, sent for Admiral Chatfield, his Chief of Staff, and said, 'Chatfield, there seems to be something wrong with our bloody ships today.' What happened then was that the flaps between the turret and the magazine, which are supposed to prevent any flame going down the elevator which leads to the magazine, either did not exist or were not closed. I have no doubt that something like this happened with the *Hood*.

This has been a very black day, but upon reflection I still cannot believe that the Germans can win this war. It is, as I have often said before, a conflict between quality and quantity. If the Germans should win and dominate the world, it will mean the disappearance for ages of all our existing standards of morals, manners and elegance – in books, music, art, clothes, goods, ideas. I do not agree that the dark ages will return in the shape of a period of social confusion, for in any German domination there would be order – Teutonic – thoroughly uncomfortable and disagreeable order, but it would really be a dark age in the sense that the world would have to do without delicacy, sensitiveness and graciousness, for an indefinite period.

General Raymond E. Lee

1982 [London]
Heard on the 10 o'clock news this evening that another warship had been sunk.[1] Absolutely tragic loss of life. People are going to ask how long this madness will last – 26,500 men out there and a hundred ships, of which we have already lost four, for 1,800 Falkland Islanders who could all be brought safely to Britain if they would only come. Absolutely crazy.

Tony Benn

26 May

1915 [Gallipoli]
I dine with Ritchie at 7.30 p.m. in his dugout under our cliff, between our position and the bakery. Five other officers are there; among them

---

[1] HMS *Coventry*, on radar picket to the north of West Falklands.

is Major Huskisson, a charming 'Gypsy' Army A.S.C. man, who is in charge of the Main Supply Depot here, and also a man who was in the *River Clyde* at the landing and who saw Colonel Carrington-Smith killed. We play bridge after dinner, and I actually have a whisky. First game of bridge I have had since we landed, and it is weird playing in such surroundings. Outside, a perfect moonlight night.

Major John Gillam, DSO

1944 [Amsterdam]
Dearest Kitty,
I've asked myself again and again whether it wouldn't have been better if we hadn't gone into hiding, if we were dead now and didn't have to go through this misery, especially so that the others could be spared the burden. But we all shrink from this thought. We still love life, we haven't yet forgotten the voice of nature, and we keep hoping, hoping for . . . everything.

Let something happen soon, even an air raid. Nothing can be more crushing than this anxiety. Let the end come, however cruel; at least then we'll know whether we are to be the victors or the vanquished.

Anne Frank

27 May

1916 [France]
Sitting on the firestep in warm weather and sunshine about 10 a.m. with the lark above and the usual airmen. Can't remember Thursday night's show very clearly; it seems mostly rain and feeling chilled, and the flash of rifles in the gloom; and [Corporal Mick] O'Brien's shattered limp body propped up down that infernal bank – face ghastly in the light of a flare, clothes torn, hair matted over the forehead – nothing left of the old cheeriness and courage and delight in any excitement of Hun-chasing. Trying to lift him up the side of the crater, the soft earth kept giving way under one's feet: he was a heavy man too, fully six feet high. But he was a dead man when at last we lowered him over the parapet on to a stretcher; and one of the stretcher-bearers examined his wounds and felt for the life that wasn't there, and then took off his round helmet with a sort of reverence – or it may have been only a chance gesture. I would have given a lot if he could have

been alive, but it was a hopeless case – a bomb had given him its full explosion. But when I go out on patrols his ghost will surely be with me; he'll catch his breath and grip his bomb just as he used to do.

Siegfried Sassoon

1940 [London]

The Germans are in Calais. I don't seem able to react or to feel anything. I don't know what's real any more. I don't think I'm real or that this life is real. Before this last winter everything seemed real, but since then I seem to have been dreaming. I wanted to mix with artists so I rented a studio, and because of the studio I'm pretending to be an artist, when I don't even know what painting means. Ever since then I've been listening to people talking a new language, filth and blasphemy, and heard myself talking it too. I see myself acting like a tart, and men hurting me and sponging on me and trying to make love, and asking if they can pee in my sink, and telling me to take my clothes off and I really don't know whether I'm awake or asleep.

The bombs, which I know must come, hardly enter my fringe of consciousness. Bombs and death are real, and I and all the other artists around here are only concerned with unreality. We live in a dream, and it may be desperate but it's not dull.

Joan Wyndham

1945 [England]

Fine, but too cold to go out with any pleasure, so sat in the sun-room and diarised. 'Surely it's time people agreed to listen to Wagner's music and forget the bosh it's all about!' George had said at breakfast. I entirely agree. [Ernest] Newman writes in the *Sunday Times* today: 'If I know anything of him (Wagner), he would have stayed away ostentatiously from the performances (of his operas under Nazi patronage) and told Hitler and his storm-troopers frankly what he thought of them.' *Frankly,* Ernest? I think not – I just don't see that astute little monkey in the velvet jacket wishing to be sent to a concentration camp.

James Agate

1992 [Sarajevo]

Dear Mimmy,
SLAUGHTER! MASSACRE! HORROR! CRIME! BLOOD! SCREAMS! TEARS! DESPAIR!

That's what Vaso Miskin Street looks like today. Two shells exploded in the street and one in the market. Mummy was near at the time. She ran to Grandma's and Grandad's. Daddy and I were beside ourselves because she hadn't come home. I saw some of it on TV but I still can't believe what I saw. I've got a lump in my throat and a knot in my tummy. HORRIBLE. They're taking the wounded to the hospital. It's a madhouse. We kept going to the window hoping to see Mummy, but she wasn't back. They released a list of the dead and wounded. Daddy and I were tearing our hair out. We didn't know what had happened to her. Was she alive? At 16.00, Daddy decided to go and check the hospital. He got dressed, and I got ready to go to the Bobars' [their neighbours], so as not to stay at home alone. I looked out the window one more time and ... I SAW MUMMY RUNNING ACROSS THE BRIDGE. As she came into the house she started shaking and crying. Through her tears she told us how she had seen dismembered bodies. All the neighbours came because they had been afraid for her. Thank God, Mummy is with us. Thank god.

A HORRIBLE DAY. UNFORGETTABLE.

HORRIBLE! HORRIBLE!

Zlata Filipovic

28 May

1916 [the Russian Front]

We reached our quarters and prepared the bandaging-room without delay. An urgent message reached us: 'Prepare for burnt soldiers.' Laconic wording, but elaborated in some detail by the staff messenger. A disastrous fire had gutted a wine-cellar; several soldiers had been burnt to death; some were being brought for instant treatment. It seems that the men of the 101st Permski Regiment had that day marched through Buchach, singing lustily, on their way into reserve. During the evening, several had gone on a tour of exploration. They found a distillery in which casks of alcohol were still stored. They drank their fill and then, inebriated and elated, turned on the taps. But someone must have struck a match, for the cellar was suddenly swept with fierce flames. About a dozen men perished on the spot; others crawled out, but collapsed and died soon afterwards. Only two of them were able to stand and they were brought to us.

They came, both of them, *walking*: two naked red figures! Their clothes had been burnt off their bodies. They stood side by side in the large barn which we had converted into a dressing-station, raw from head to foot. Injections were immediately ordered, but we could find no skin and had to put the needle straight into the flesh. Their arms were hanging stiffly at their sides and from the finger-tips of the men were suspended what looked like leather gloves; these we were told to cut off which we did with surgical scissors. They were the skin of the hand and fingers which had peeled off and were hanging from the raw flesh of the finger-tips. Then we showered them with bicarbonate of soda and swathed their poor, burnt bodies with layers of cotton-wool and surgical lint. We laid them down upon straw in an adjoining shed. In an hour or two, the cotton-wool was completely saturated, but we could help them no further, save with oft-repeated injections of morphia which, we prayed, would deaden their sufferings. They died, both of them, before morning. And neither of them had spoken a single word! I don't think anything which I had ever seen touched me so keenly.

Florence Farmborough

1940 [near Coventry]

Up and round the household jobs so as to be ready to leave for Berkswell Rectory at 10 a.m., where we all worked hard making triangular bandages – nine dozen today – as well as an operation garment. We talk and work and the machines chatter too till at 12.45 we stopped for lunch (sandwiches), and then took a little breather outside. I bought a few toffees at the village shop, but on hearing the sad news of Belgium's capitulation through Leopold, their King, I forgot to eat them. This is indeed bad news and we were all overcome at first, but settled to work again, discussing parachutes and parachuters, etc., until 4 p.m.

The news at 9 p.m. was still very grave: the Belgian capitulation has increased the difficulties of the B.E.F. [British Expeditionary Force]. And the thought of Alan [her son] being with them in Belgium is almost more than one can bear tonight. It has been a hard day for us, though we do not say a great deal to each other, for one must keep up.

Clara Milburn

1940 [London]
This is the first day on which newspaper posters are definitely discon-
tinued. Half of the front page of the early *Star*[1] devoted to news of
the Belgian surrender, the other half to news to the effect that the
Belgians are holding out and the King is with them. This is presumably due to paper shortage. Nevertheless of the early *Star*'s eight pages,
six are devoted to racing.

People talk a little more of the war, but very little. As always hitherto, it is impossible to overhear any comments on it in pubs etc. Last
night E[ileen, his wife] and I went to the pub to hear the 9 o'clock
news. The barmaid was not going to have turned it on if we had not
asked her, and to all appearances nobody listened.

George Orwell

1941 [London]
America is in the war as near as makes no matter. Roosevelt is the
greatest jockey the human race has known.

James Agate

1969 [Vietnam]
Few of the platoon's men had been regularly employed before working
for Uncle Sam. Most, like Russell, had been 'on the street' before being
drafted. A couple of the men were volunteers, but not many. If one
joined the military by choice, signing up to be an infantryman was not
a popular option.

The Navy and Air Force, manned entirely by volunteers had little
problem filing their ranks. Those who chose the Army usually ended
up as grunts based on their failure to qualify for a support role in the
Military Occupational Speciality (MOS) testing upon entry with the
service.

There was, of course, no one in my platoon with a white-collar
background, or even an inclination in that direction. Few were from
that heritage by birth either. I never met an officer or soldier who
even knew anyone with an Ivy League education.

A high-school diploma was generally the highest degree attained.
Our generation was to become the most educated in our country's
history, but this did not apply to the Vietnam Veterans . . . All a man

---

[1] A London evening newspaper of the time.

had to do to avoid the draft was to stay in school with a deferment until he was twenty-six years old. At that magic age, he was no longer considered for conscription.

Michael Lee Lanning

29 May

1940 [New York]
It's true that the first casualty of war is truth. Peoria is polluted with rumors. The best restaurant in town is the Reiss German Restaurant on a bluff one block from the river. Now we're hearing vicious rumors about its owner, Karl Reiss: 'He dug a tunnel from his restaurant to the river so that he might provision Nazi submarines . . . He is broadcasting to Berlin from a radio in the basement of his restaurant . . . His body bears diagrams of American arsenals, written in invisible ink . . .'

On our staff we have an editor of monumental ignorance. When he heard these rumors, he ordered a reporter to go to the restaurant to *ask* Karl Reiss about them.

His eyes popping out, the reporter gasped, '*What?*'

Yes, the editor told him to go there right now and ask Reiss about the rumors. The reporter swore, balked, stamped around the city room, but at last did as he was told. Sheepishly.

What some people don't understand is this: most newspapers are conservative because publishers are wealthy. Most reporters are liberal because they are underpaid.

We reporters were so outraged by the stupidity and arrogance of that editor that we made a point of eating in that restaurant as often as possible. Karl changed its name from the Reiss German Restaurant to the Reiss Cosmopolitan Restaurant.

Edward Robb Ellis

30 May

1940 [Rome]
The decision has been taken. The die is cast. Today Mussolini gave me his message to Hitler about our entry into the war. The date chosen

is June 5, unless Hitler himself considers it convenient to postpone it for a few days. The message is sent in cipher to Ambassador Alfieri[1] at Berlin with orders to deliver it to Hitler personally. At the same time I inform von Mackensen:[2] although he was already prepared, the ambassador was overjoyed by the news. He had words of admiration for the Duce and praised my decision to take part in the war as a pilot. 'In Germany,' he said, 'the higher-ups in the Party have not set a good example. Baldur von Schirach,[3] at least until now, has been safely tucked away in the rear.'

Count Ciano

1940 [Germany]

What would I do if Hugo [her husband] were killed? War has seemed so remote from us. Somehow I've only thought of the *enemy* soldiers dying: in a way it's the fault of the newsreels. We see our soldiers alive, strong and jubilant, smoking after a battle. We hear what the enemy losses are – not ours.

Elisabeth von Stahlenberg

1942 [Middle East]

Stacy, the pilot who has been flying the Duke of Gloucester around, told me he had to go and identify the crew of an aircraft that burnt out at Heliopolis this morning. He said a well-cooked body is not too bad to look at – it's quite unrecognisable; it's when it's partially cooked, as these were, that you feel weak.

Cecil Beaton

31 May

1915 [London]

Grace [Dowager Countess of Wemyss] called for me at eleven and took me to Friary House, where we did a two hours 'shift' at making portions of respirators [type of gas mask]. There is a little machine with which you chop writhing, fish-like long strips of talc into the

---

[1] The Italian Ambassador to Germany.
[2] Hans Georg von Mackensen, German Ambassador in Italy.
[3] Baldur von Schirach, Hitler Youth Leader.

requisite lengths. You cut through five at a time and keep them in bundles of fifty. We worked at one machine, taking it in turns to work the machine or to feed the other with talc. We did about two and a half thousand together. Any manual labour has great fascination to me and I simply loved it. It is such fun feeling a factory girl and it gave one some idea of how exciting it must be to do piece-work for money. One felt so competitive even unrewarded. I must say I was very glad I hadn't got to do a twelve-hour day – it is quite tiring. The work isn't by any means quite automatic, as one can waste a lot of precious material by 'missing one's drive' or not getting the five thicknesses quite even, and with gross carelessness, one could cut off one's finger. There were quite a lot of other people working there at this and various other jobs. How one would have laughed incredulously at a vision of what we should all be doing in a year's time if it had been presented to one in 1914 – the wild tango year!

Lady Cynthia Asquith

1940 [Wiltshire]
Julia[1] and R. saw a lorry blazing through Hungerford, packed with uprooted signposts all pointing in different directions. We are told this is to confuse the invaders. Julia described it as 'A blood-curdling sight'.

Frances Partridge

1940 [London]
Struck by the fewness of the men who even now have been called up. As a rule, looking round the street, it is impossible to see a uniform . . . Barbed wire entanglements are being put up at many strategic points, e.g. beside the Charles I statue in Trafalgar Square . . . Have heard on so many sides of the shortage of rifles that I believe it must be true.

George Orwell

[1] Julia Gowling, née Strachey, sister of author Lytton Strachey.

JUNE

If we'd had as many soldiers as that, we'd have won the war!

Margaret Mitchell: on seeing the number of
Confederate troops in the film of *Gone with the Wind*

1 June

1940 [Wiltshire]

Anne and Heywood Hill to stay. Heywood expects to be called up before Christmas. He is taking a First Aid course, hoping perhaps to be able to join as a hospital orderly or stretcher bearer. All the morning, which was gloriously fine, they practised bandaging each other with a triangular handkerchief on which were printed parts of the body. So that one would see Anne with a small human bottom on her breast.

Frances Partridge

1941 [London]

The big news this morning is clothes rationing. Oliver Littleton [President of the Board of Trade] is only going to allow us 66 coupons per annum. A suit takes 26. Luckily I have got 40 or more. Socks will be the shortage. Apart from these, if I am not bombed, I have enough clothes to last me for years.

The evacuation of Crete is announced and we are told that over 15,000 men got away in our ships. I doubt whether the defence of the island was even worthwhile. It may have delayed the attacking forces in their downward march but it means also a further decline in our prestige. British Expeditionary Forces are now known as 'Back Every Friday'!

'Chips' Channon

2 June

1915 [London]

Went to see the Canadian Red Cross, and enlisted as visitors to wounded officers. I think it is the most embarrassing job one could possibly undertake. How will the unfortunate creatures be able to convey the fact that they don't like one, supposing that to be the case. The idea is that they are lonely having no relations in London.

Lady Cynthia Asquith

1940 [France]
Stayed all day [in camp]. Ate grass.

Sergeant L.D. Pexton, British Army

1940 [London]
Rough analysis of advertisements in today's issue of the *People*[1]:

Paper consists of 12 pages = 84 columns. Of this, just about 26½ columns (over ¼) is advertisements. These are divided up as follows:

> *Food and drink: 5¾ columns.*
> *Patent medicines: 9⅓.*
> *Tobacco: 1.*
> *Gambling: 2⅓.*
> *Clothes: 1½.*
> *Miscellaneous: 6¾.*

Of 9 food and drink adverts, 6 are for unnecessary luxuries. Of 29 adverts for medicines, 19 are for things which are either fraudulent (baldness cured etc.), more or less deleterious or of the blackmail type ('Your child's stomach needs –'). Benefit of doubt has been allowed in the case of a few medicines. Of 14 miscellaneous adverts, 4 are for soap, 1 for cosmetics, 1 for a holiday resort and 2 are government advertisements, including a large one for national savings. Only 3 adverts in all classes are cashing in on the war.

George Orwell

1942 [Holland]
I feel the end is near. Not my end, but the end of the war. I can't sleep. For the past hour squadrons of aeroplanes have been flying overhead. English planes. On their way to Germany. They have been coming for the past three nights. Cologne and Essen have been bombed. I wonder which city is going to get it tonight! It's a loud, constant drone. Some bombs have been dropped over The Hague as well. Even so, it's a comfort, to me.

Edith Velmans

---

[1] A Sunday newspaper.

1943 [London]

On my return [from Wiltshire] I was very ill, and crawled to see my doctor, Pierre Lansel. A recurrence of the old trouble and change of drugs, leading to shingles, retention of urine, catheters, germs in the bladder, high temperatures, agonies, despair, and bed for over four weeks. The worst affliction of the lot was a nurse who positively revelled in philistinism. One day she gleefully smashed the lid of my Worcester sugar bowl. When I remonstrated she got cross, and said it was ugly. 'Ugly?' I screamed at her. 'Ugly! Even if it were, it is old and precious. But it's beautiful. Surely you can see that.' 'I can't,' was the reply. And she added with a shrug, 'Oh well!' 'It isn't well,' I said. 'It's bad, very bad.'

Next morning she remarked through pursed lips, 'Any-wan mate sue-pose [this is how she spoke] yew pre-furred old ob-jects tew persons,' as though this were the most heinous charge she could bring against my morals. 'Anyone would be supposing perfectly correctly,' I snapped back. She was so flabbergasted by the barefaced admission that she left almost immediately. I got better.

James Lees-Milne

3 June

1915 [London]

Dance last night in aid of Blinded Soldiers and Sailors. About 40 people paid, and something over 30 came. Receipts about £11. Began at 9.15 and finished about 1.30. Curious method of sitting out. Couples went to sit out in the motor cars waiting in the stable yard. Coldish night. The earnest air of young couples, especially the girls, and the short-statured sitting about in my study, my bedroom, and M's rooms, also on the top stairs, was just as comic to me as ever it was. It is the small girls who seem to take the dalliance so seriously. I danced with six women, – a record.

Arnold Bennett

1916 [France]

I can imagine that, in a hundred or two hundred or two thousand years, when wars are waged in the air and under the ground, these French roads will be haunted by a silent traffic of sliding lorries and jolting wagons and tilting limbers[1] – all going silently about their business. Some staring peasant or stranger will see them silhouetted against the pale edge of a night sky – six mules and a double limber, with the drivers jigging in the saddle – a line of cumbrous lorries nosing along some bleak main-road – a battalion transport with the sergeant riding in front, and brake-men hanging on behind the limbers, taking rations to the trenches that were filled in hundreds of years ago. And there will be ghostly working-parties coming home to billets long after midnight, filing along deserted tracks among the cornlands, men with round basin-helmets, and rifles slung on their shoulders, puffing at ambrosial Woodbines – and sometimes the horizon will wink with the flash of a gun, and insubstantial shells will hurry across the upper air and melt innocuous in nothingness.

And the trenches – where the trenches used to be – there will be grim old bomb-fights in the craters and wounded men cursing; and patrols will catch their breath and crawl out from tangles of wire, and sentries will peer over the parapets, fingering the trigger – doubtful whether to shoot or send for the sergeant. And I shall be there – looking for Germans with my revolver and my knobkerrie[2] and two Mills-bombs in each pocket, having hair-breadth escapes – crawling in the long grass – wallowing in the mud – crouching in shell-holes – hearing the Hun sentries cough and shift their feet, and click their bolts; I shall be there – slipping back into our trench, and laughing with my men at the fun I've had out in no-man's land. And I'll be watching a frosty dawn come up beyond the misty hills and naked trees – with never a touch of cold in my feet or fingers, and perhaps taking a nip of rum from a never-emptying flask. And all the horrors will be there and agonies be endured again; but over all will be the same peaceful starlight – the same eternal cloudlands – and in those dusty hearts an undying sense of valour and sacrifice. And though our ghosts be as dreams, those good things will be as they are now, a light in the thick darkness and a crown.

Siegfried Sassoon

1916 [London]

What a bitter disappointment it is to realise that people the most intimately in love with one another are really separated by such a distance.

[1] A detachable two-wheeled vehicle containing ammunition, preceding the gun carriage.
[2] A round-headed stick used as a club or a missile.

A woman is calm knitting socks or playing Patience while her husband or sweetheart lies dead in Flanders. However strong the tie that binds them together yet they are insufficiently *en rapport* for her to sense even a catastrophe – and she must wait till the War Office forsooth sends her word. How humiliating that the War Office must do what love cannot . . . Human love seems then such a superficial thing. Every person is a distinct egocentric being. Each for himself and the Devil take the hindmost. 'Ah! but she didn't know.' 'Yes, but she *ought* to have known.' Mental telepathy and clairvoyance should be common at least to all lovers.

This morning in bed I heard a man with a milkcart say in the road to a villager at about 6.30 a.m., '. . . Battle . . . and we lost six cruisers'. This was the first I knew of the Battle of Jutland. At 8 a.m. I read in the *Daily News* that the British Navy had been defeated, and thought it was the end of all things. The news took away our appetites. At the railway station, the *Morning Post* was more cheerful, even reassuring, and now at 6.30 p.m. the battle has turned into a merely regrettable indecisive action. We breathe once more.

W.N.P. Barbellion

1940 [London]
Here is a story gleaned this week from the Café Royal. It was told me by a naval officer in charge of one of the ships during the Dunkirk episode. An English Army officer who was all in, finding no place to sit down, let alone lie, finally espied a life-boat containing flags and covered with a tarpaulin. Creeping under the tarpaulin, he fell into a deep and blissful sleep, from which he did not awake till some hours later. Lifting the tarpaulin and peeping over the edge of the boat, he found that he was back at Dunkirk. He had done the round trip!

James Agate

1940 [London]
[In a meeting with US Department of State Advisor, Herbert Feis]
Now there is a sudden interest in this war – the United States is profoundly aware of the consequences of an Allied defeat. The implication of all his remarks was that we should take a hand. He thought we ought to ship the Allies all our planes and guns now and make more for ourselves, but, he said, the War Department has so far opposed this, as it would leave us unarmed.

I asked him what attitude Kennedy [Joseph P, American Ambassador in Great Britain] was taking. He said, 'Defeatist, as he always has.' Because the war will lower the stock market, he said, and because Kennedy's securities are the only things he thinks about, he has been an appeaser all along. I said who does he see in London? 'Only appeasers,' was the reply.

General Raymond E. Lee

4 June

1904 [Yasnaya Polyana, Russia]

Haven't felt like writing for several days. Health not too good. The war,[1] the call-up of reserves – I suffer continually. Tried to write my memoirs yesterday – it was no good.

War is the product of despotism. If there were no despotism, there could be no war; there might be fights, but not war. Despotism produces war, and war supports despotism.

Those who want to fight against war should fight only against despotism.

Leo Tolstoy

1916 [London]

It has now become a victory.

W.N.P. Barbellion

1940 [Rome]

I have chosen my military position in the war. I shall take command of a bomber squadron in Pisa. I have chosen this airfield because it is closest to Corsica, and because it is dear to me to fight where I was born and where my father rests in peace. The Duce approved my decision to join up as well as that of leaving Rome for Pisa, because he prefers that I become 'a soldier minister' rather than a 'minister-soldier.'

Count Ciano

1940 [New York]

My feeling about the war is that Germans are made for conquering by nature and go to pieces, suicidal or insane under defeat, whereas English are made for dogged hang-on endurance which in the long

---

[1] The Russo–Japanese War which had begun on 27 January, 1904.

run conquers. One terrific defeat for the Germans and they will go to pieces, hysterical – the mechanized machinery of war will be no good under their personal defeat confusion.

Dawn Powell

1940 [Perth, Scotland]

It is inevitable that with the prolongation of warfare the writer who has given his allegiance to pacifism should experience with increasing intensity the constriction upon creative effort. Unable to share in the patriotic fervour, he is thereby self-excommunicated from the manifold tensions of battle which produce an emotional ferment, impure and febrific, but nevertheless procreative. But not only is he deprived of this general passion, he is also excluded from general mutuality; and with the growing concentration of the former, he becomes more and more conscious of his loss of the latter. His attitude, at first condoned, in time promotes an ever-deepening antagonism, and with it the necessity of a more and more conscientious watchfulness in himself, lest his ostracism betray him into bitter or sanctimonious response. Nor, being a man among men and a poet of their tragic moment, can he find in nature a substitute communication: since his vision, which must look steadfastly on the conflict to see beyond it, retains its images of strife even when turned upon the loveliness of the natural day.

William Soutar

1943 [Algiers]

There was an air raid over the city tonight, presaged by a long wailing shriek of fear from the sirens. Men ran along the docks lighting up the fuses for the smoke screens. The white smoke drifted lazily along the harbor, half submerging the shipping, and then lazily drifted back toward the shore as the ack-acks began to crack and the first series of tracer bullets shot graceful parabolas across the sky. Then all the guns opened with a roar. A devil's tattoo of angry, barking guns, chasing each other's syncopations through a mad symphony. The red tracer bullets followed and crisscrossed each other in the same unearthly dance. The heavy guns of the battleships from time to time would join in with a crash, following an explosion of light from the outer harbor. Two masses of curling flame floated down from the sky, like molten petals, to die out slowly in the ocean. Searchlights suddenly awoke from darkness, became interested apparently in nothing at all; seemed to adjust a monocle, focus a dozen eyes on a point in space, watch it intently for a moment, and then apparently losing interest, wander on aimlessly to observe and concentrate upon another atom in the firmament. I have never see a more magnificent display of fireworks or heard crazier, more intoxicating rhythms. The show lasted exactly half an hour and the curtain went down. Mitchell Siporin and Rudolf von Ripper had just arrived overseas to join our art unit. It was their second evening in Algiers. The four of us, including Fletcher Martin, had dined off shrimps and a bottle of wine at the Hôtel Oasis, and had front row seats on Fletcher's balcony at the Aletti.

I was told later that ten enemy planes had come over. Of the four that got through our air defense, two were shot down. The other two dropped bombs in the harbor in front of us and about the city. Two of our protective balloons were shot down by our own anti-aircraft. Several buildings were destroyed and I am told about one hundred and fifty people lost their lives. The fireworks probably cost about $1,000,000. On the whole a wasteful and expensive performance but fun to watch while it lasted.

George Biddle

1944 [on board USS *Montpelier*, in the Pacific]
This will be the first action for some of the new men. We got a lot of older men from the States in the forties and fifties, with big families, about three weeks ago. One of the new men by the name of Schaggs, from St Louis, let me read a letter he got from his wife and kids, and he is very proud of them. It is a tough blow to send a man with children overseas. The new men who just came aboard would give anything to be back with their families again. Now they appreciate them and see how lucky they were when they were at home with them. Some of the married men with children tell how they ran around when they were back home as civilians and how wrong they were. If they ever get back home again they will live a good life and spend more time with wife and children. They will not take everything for granted and will appreciate things more. They want to make up for all the trouble they caused to their wife and children. It reminds you of a person on his last day, telling his confession.

James J. Fahey, Seaman First Class

1982 [Yorkshire]

We (we!) drop leaflets on the Argentine troops besieged in Port Stanley, urging them to lay down their arms. Were such leaflets dropped on our troops we would consider them contemptible and ludicrous; our leaflets are represented as a great humanitarian gesture.

Alan Bennett

5 *June*

1918 [France]

When I rode into the transport lines this afternoon I saw Jim Linthwaite toiling at cleaning a limber, under the supervision of a military police-man. (He has still ten days to do of his twenty-eight Field Punishment No 2 for getting drunk at Marseilles.) But I gave him a cheery word and a grin, and he smiled at me, standing there in his grimy slacks and blue jersey. I wonder if he thought it a strange thing to do? I hadn't spoken to him since I talked to him like a father when he was awaiting his court-martial. Something drew me to him when I saw him first. 'Linthwaite, a nice name' I thought, when they told me he was a First Battalion man. Then I saw him, digging away at road-mending, and he'd got a rotten pair of boots, which were an excuse for conversation, and I've loved him ever since (it is just as well he's not in my present Company). And when he got into trouble I longed to be kind to him. And I talked to him about 'making a fresh start, and not doing anything silly again', while he stood in front of me with his white face, and eyes full of tears. I suppose I'd have done the same for any man in the Company who had a good char-acter. But there was a great deal of sex floating about in this particular effort. No doubt he dreams about 'saving my life'. I wish I could save his.

Siegfried Sassoon

1940 [London]

Winston is still full of offensive zeal and thinks that the Australians should be used for small forays on the coasts of occupied countries such as Denmark, Holland and Belgium. 'Enterprises must be prepared,' he minutes to Ismay,[1] 'with specially trained troops of the hunter class

---

[1] General Lord Ismay, Chief of Staff to Churchill as Minister of Defence, in 1940. He later served as Secretary General of NATO, 1952–57.

who can develop a reign of terror down these coasts, first of all on the "butcher and bolt" policy, but later on, or perhaps as soon as we are organised, we should surprise Calais or Boulogne, kill and capture the Hun garrisons and hold the place until all the preparations to reduce it by siege or heavy storm have been made, and then away.' Light armoured units must, he says, 'crawl ashore, do a deep raid inland cutting a vital communication, and then back leaving a trail of German corpses behind them. It is probable that when the best troops go on to the attack on Paris, only the ordinary German troops of the line will be left. The lives of these must be made an intense torment.'

Turning to more trivial subjects, the PM wrote this morning to Eden[1] suggesting the restoration to officers of the leather shoulder-strap, abolished by 'your foolish predecessor, [Leslie, Lord Hore-] Belisha'.

John Colville

1940 [Hampshire]

Churchill's remarkably frank and rhetorically eloquent speech summing up the events of the last five days will echo round the world. Over three hundred thousand Allied troops have been brought over the Channel from Dunkirk to English ports under perpetual German bombing and gun-fire, by some thousand ships and boats of all sorts and kinds escorted by the navy and air force. The BEF leaves behind them thirty thousand dead, wounded and missing. We have lost the whole of our armaments – guns, transport, tanks. Our small air force has proved itself, man for man, machine for machine, far superior to the Germans, who have lost four to one in the battle in the air. In a sense it is a glorious adventure; but from a realistic standpoint, Winston admits it, it is the greatest military disaster which has ever overtaken the British army. Today we have to defend our own island from invasion; he thinks that in this homely task we are invincible. But the French army – can it stand up against the German hordes, possibly reinforced by the Italians? That is left in doubt . . .

Beatrice Webb

[1] Anthony Eden, 1st Earl of Avon, at that time Secretary of State for War.

1944 [Scapa Flow]
I come down to breakfast and find Colonel Simpson there. He looked up at me and said in his Caithness accent, 'Heard the news? We entered Rome at 11pm. Last night.' Well, I never.

Harold Nicolson

1944 [London]
An Airforce honeymoon couple over my head made work impossible all day. Today I had the couple moved.

Evelyn Waugh

1967 [The White House]
This day began with that most dread and frightening sound that can happen in this house – the sudden ringing of the telephone in the middle of the night. It can never be good news. The insistent ring jarred me from the soft web of sleep.

I heard Lyndon's quick reaction, 'Yes.' Then a long silence interrupted on his part by a few crisp questions. He finally hung up and fell back on the pillow. With an almost unbearable wave of sympathy, I asked him what it was. He said: 'We have a war on our hands – in the Middle East.' I looked at the clock. It was about 4.30. An hour later the phone crashed the silence again. Once more there was talk with a few clipped questions on his side and then long silences. When it was over, I leaned over and kissed him.

I cannot say I slept anymore. Rather there was a long period of continuing nightmares in which I was lost and wandering, though sometimes the places were familiar. Finally I got up. Lyndon had been gone a long time. Not since that day in October 1962 (during the Cuban missile crisis) had I felt so tense and strained, known such a feeling of foreboding . . . I remember that other day, when I stood in the bedroom at The Elms – a beautiful clear, golden day – and looked out at the sunlight shimmering on the leaves of golds and crimsons and reds and wondered: 'Is this the last beautiful October day we shall see?' But there is nothing I can do about the great clash of powers – nothing at all, except be quiet and sympathetic and cheerful when Lyndon is home. And when he's not I might as well go on about my little business of the day. Today it was work on the speeches for the upcoming trip to New England, lunching with Lynda [her daughter], and planning the program for the award winners in beautification. Always, always, I feel that I would give a special prize to whoever would give us a better word than 'beautification'![1] It sounds institutional, clinical; it doesn't have any of the joy of the work in it.

Then I went back to work at my desk and turned on the TV. The news of the Middle East conflict was everywhere, but totally conflicting. The Israelis said the Egyptians started the fighting – the Egyptians said the Israelis had invaded their territory with planes and troops. The Israelis gave the numbers of the enemy planes – vast numbers – that they had knocked down. And the Egyptians claimed victories over the Israelis, citing the number of planes downed, though not as many as the Israelis claimed, with very little loss themselves. Then there was the news that a State Department official had used the phrase 'neutral in thought, word and deed' to define the United States' position in the Mideast conflict. Rusk[2] hastened onto TV to try to clarify the word 'neutral.'

The UN was struggling, with its major action arm, the Security Council, going into session for five or six hours, going out presumably for private talks among its members, and then promising to go back into session any minute. Like millions of others I strained with hope toward the UN and what it might produce. But I remembered with dismay the expressions of no confidence that I have heard applied to it these last months by many observers.

I turned off the TV and went over to the bowling lanes, where I used up my energy in three games, hurling a heavier ball than usual and running up scores in the 150s – all by myself. Not much fun, but exercise, and while I'm doing it I don't think much about anything else.

It was a little after 10 when Lyndon came home to dinner. He looked burdened and the lines in his face deeper, and I felt it would be the greatest cruelty for me to ask him to talk about the war in the Middle East. I tried some brisk, bright reports on what I had been doing today, and they sounded hollow.

At 12 his light was out. I prayed that he slept because last night he had had only about four hours.

The evening paper headlines were: 'War Rages in Mideast', 'UN Attempts to Get Truce In Israel Battle', 'Johnson Pushes UN Effort'. And so the anxious day came to an end.

Lady Bird Johnson

---

[1] Scheme involving the planting of trees, shrubs, plants etc.
[2] Dean Rusk, Secretary of State.

1992 [Sarajevo]

Dear Mimmy,

There's been no electricity for quite some time and we keep thinking about the food in the freezer. There's not much left as it is. It would be a pity for all of it to go bad. There's meat and vegetables and fruit. How can we save it?

Daddy found an old wood-burning stove in the attic. It's so old it looks funny. In the cellar we found some wood, put the stove outside in the yard, lit it and are trying to save the food from the refrigerator. We cooked everything, and joining forces with the Bobars, enjoyed ourselves. There was veal and chicken, squid, cherry strudel, meat and potato pies. All sorts of things. It's a pity, though, that we had to eat everything so quickly. We even overate. WE HAD A MEAT STROKE.

We washed down our refrigerators and freezers. Who knows when we'll be able to cook like this again. Food is becoming a big problem in Sarajevo. There's nothing to buy, and even cigarettes and coffee are becoming a problem for grownups. The last reserves are being used up. God, are we going to go hungry to boot???

Zlata Filipovic

6 June

1666 [London]

To St. James's [Palace]. There we all met and did our business as usual with the Duke. Thence after the Duke into the park walking through to White Hall, and there every body listening for guns, but none heard, and every creature is now overjoyed and conclude, upon very good grounds that the Dutch are beaten because we have heard no guns nor no news of our fleet. By and by an express to Sir W. Coventry, being the narration of Captain Hayward of the *Dunkirke*, who gives a very serious account; how upon Monday the two fleets [were] fighting all day till 7 at night, and then the whole fleet of Dutch did betake themselfs to a very plain flight, and never looked back again. That Sir Christopher Mings is wounded in the leg. That the Generall is well. That it is conceived reasonably, that of all the Dutch fleet, which, with what recruits they had, come to 100 sail, there is not above 50 got home – and of them, few, if any, of their flags.

We were all so overtaken with this good news that the Duke ran with it to the King, who was gone to chapel, and there all the Court was in a hubbub, being rejoiced over head and ears in this good news. Away go I by coach to the New Exchange, and there did spread this good news a little, though I find it had broken out before. And so home to our own church, it being the common fast-day; and it was just before sermon; but, Lord, how all the people in the church stared upon me to see me whisper to Sir John Minnes and my Lady Pen. Here after sermon comes to our office 40 people almost, of all sorts and qualities to hear the news, which I took great delight to tell them. Then home and found my wife at dinner, not knowing of my being at church. And after dinner my father and she out to Hale's where my father is to begin to sit to-day for his picture, which I have a desire to have. Bonfires were lighted all the town over. The joy of the city was this night exceeding great.

Samuel Pepys

1940 [near Coventry]

Still perfect hot weather. I never remember such a lovely spell, and the mornings are just grand.

The telephone rings at intervals all day with rumours and snippets of news from one or another, but nothing definite about our boys. As we sat down to dinner tonight, very tired and thirsty after digging and hoeing, Mrs Cutler rang up. She is just an acquaintance in Balsall Commons whom I knew through billeting. But she said: 'Mrs Milburn, I am going to Olton Monastery tomorrow and I am having candles lit and prayers said for the safe return of your son.' Surprised and touched, I could scarcely answer properly before the voice said 'Goodnight.' The kindness and sympathy everywhere is wonderful. After dinner a rest and then, as we were about to continue our gardening, Harry and Ethel Spencer came, and she and I talked of Neville and Alan, both thinking of them as our 'little boys' – mothers always do – and wiping away a tear or two. How drawn together we all are these dark days. Tonight, as they left, we all kissed each other like brothers and sisters. It is good to have so many real friends.

Clara Milburn

1940 [London]

Huge advert on the side of a bus: 'FIRST AID IN WARTIME FOR HEALTH, STRENGTH AND FORTITUDE. WRIGLEY'S CHEWING GUM'.

George Orwell

1943 [Kovno Ghetto, Lithuania]
The Ghetto population has continually decreased over the past twenty-two months. In the initial period, scores of Jews had already been murdered – individuals and groups. The Ghetto population was also reduced by arrests, and by transfer to Riga and other places. A high percentage of natural deaths has also played its part in this negative trend. Furthermore, there have been no births in the Ghetto. Giving birth is forbidden under pain of death.

Avraham Tory

7 June

1918 [England]
L. was told the other day that the raids are carried out by women. Women's bodies were found in the wrecked aeroplanes. They are smaller and lighter, and thus leave more room for bombs. Perhaps it is sentimental, but the thought seems to me to add a particular touch of horror.

Virginia Woolf

1944 [on board USS *Montpelier*, in the Pacific]
Got eight to midnight watch. We had a great time to ourselves. We had a free-for-all. We were throwing wet rags and paper at each other, one fellow would stick his head around the gun mount and get a big wet rag right in the face, it was like one of the old time comedies in the movies. Another fellow would get set to hit someone and he would get one in the back of the neck. You would never know that we are on our way to the largest invasion of the Pacific War.

James J. Fahey, Seaman First Class

8 June

1665 [Lowestoft]
Came newes of his Highnesse Victory over the Enemie, and indeede it might have ben a compleate one, and at once ended the War, had it ben pursued: but the Cowardize of some, Tretchery, or both frustrated that: we had however bonfires, bells, and rejoicing in the Citty etc.

John Evelyn

1667 [London]

Up, and to the office, where all the news this morning is that the Dutch are come with a fleet of 80 sail to Harwich, and that guns were heard plain by Sir W. Rider's people at Bednall Greene all yesterday noon. The King hath sent down my Lord of Oxford to raise the country there; and all the Westerne Barges are taken up to make a bridge over the River about the Hope, for horse to cross the river if there be occasion.

Samuel Pepys

1916 [London]

Came to London Tuesday morning for the Wounded Allies 'War Fair' at the Caledonian Market. Heavy shower. Great success. I sold books at M's stall. After 5.30, crowds of young women came to look at books and some to buy. One well-dressed man had never heard of Balzac. Demand for Kipling, Chesterton, Conrad, and me. Difficulty of selling autographs. Enthusiasm for Jepson's *Pillory*. Various estimates of profits of 2 days; but you can see the men keep estimating lower than their hopes. Thus Mr Henry – £8,000 to £15,000. Selfridge estimated attendance first day at from 25 to 30,000. I agree. Yet one man in charge of a gate said that through that gate alone he estimated that 30,000 people had passed. And so on. There were not enough goods, nor stalls. The place looked nearly empty when I arrived, and remained so. It was too big. I did a very good trade in books, but I brought down prices at the end considerably, and autographed favourites were going for 3s. and even 2s. 6d. Habit of women of squealing out in ecstasy over name of a book, and then refusing even to consider the purchase of it. Perhaps they were so startled to find that they recognised a title.

Arnold Bennett

1940 [Vichy]

The roads are cluttered by wandering families fleeing at random and without knowing where. Children have got lost, whom the wretched parents are seeking. Last night, through the open window of my room giving onto the end of the park, I thrice heard a heart-rending cry: 'Pierre! Pierre!' And almost went down to find the poor demented man who was uttering that call, desperately, in the night. And for a long time I could not go to sleep, ceaselessly imagining that distress . . .

This morning I spoke of it to Nalle. He too heard the cry all right; but, he tells me, it was the night watchman, who shouts: *'Lumière! Lumière!'* when he sees a lighted window, like mine.

André Gide

9 June

1917 [London]
Siegfried Sassoon lunched with me at the Reform yesterday. He expected some decoration for admittedly fine bombing work. Colonel had applied for it three times, but was finally told that as that partic- ular push was a failure it could not be granted. Sassoon was uncertain about accepting a home billet if he got the offer of one. I advised him to accept it. He is evidently one of the reckless ones. He said his pals said he always gives the Germans every chance to pot him. He said he would like to go out once more and give them a chance to get him, and come home unscathed. He seemed jealous for the military repu- tation of poets. He said most of the war was a tedious nuisance, but there were great moments and he would like them again.

Arnold Bennett

1940 [Berlin]
P.G. Wodehouse was taken prisoner near Abbeville while playing golf. The German High Command want him to edit a newspaper for British POWs and have brought him to Berlin.[1]

Marie 'Missie' Vassiltchikov

10 June

1916 [France]
At one in the morning, order for departure at 4 a.m. We are to march in the direction of Verdun. That gives us an extra day of life! We are billeted at Rosières near Bar.

Lieut. Henri Desagneaux, French 2nd Infantry Regiment

---

[1] This led to Wodehouse being persuaded to make broadcasts for the American Broadcasting System in Berlin – regarded as a collaborator, he was advised not to return to Britain.

1940 [London]

At Admiralty House the possibility of the French giving in, or being defeated, was of greater interest to all present than the approaching entry of Italy into the war. All Winston said about the latter event was, 'People who go to Italy to look at ruins won't have to go as far as Naples and Pompeii in future.'

John Colville

1940 [USA]

At night the radio announcer in Paris makes his last broadcast from Paris. It is quite moving. The French government is leaving Paris for Tours. Paris is being evacuated. The little iron chairs and tables on the side-walks are empty. 'The end of an era.' 'Goodbye from Paris.'

Roosevelt speaks, accuses Italy. 'The hand that held the dagger has struck it into the back of its neighbour.' Wild cheers! We certainly aren't neutral any more!

Anne Morrow Lindbergh

11 June

1940 [Poland]

Got our numbers today. 8806 is my number. This camp is called Stalag XXA (17). We shall go to work soon.

Sergeant L.D. Pexton, British Army

1940 [Surrey]

I came in from earthing up the potatoes to listen to the nine-o'clock news and heard that Italy had at long last declared war on England and France. Surely no nation in this world has ever drawn the sword so wantonly, with so little provocation.

Walter Musto

1940 [London]

I have not written for a whole week. Last Tuesday Winston made the greatest speech in my memory – one of the greatest speeches in history. Its candour & its courage were alike admirable. He admitted that we had had in Flanders a colossal defeat. We had lost enormous quantities of material – over 1,000 guns. Wars were not won by evacuations. But we shld fight to the end – if necessary alone. On the beaches – on the hills – in the fields – & even if part of England were invaded & subjugated – our Fleet & our Dominions wld bring the new world to the rescue of the old. This was only a breathing space. We must expect a new blow at any moment.

Violet Bonham Carter

1940 [Carradale, Scotland]

I had a talk today to Ian MacLaren, the plumber, who said there had been bad anti-Italian riots in Campbeltown; the three Italian shops had been broken up. The old man had been rather rash, saying that England needed a totalitarian govt and so on, but the younger ones were all decent, good citizens who gave money in charity and paid their taxes; one had contributed £50 to the Provost's fund; one of the youngest generation was in a mine sweeper. Ian had passed there early in the evening, and had seen a crowd hanging about and laughing, and wondered what was going to happen; people were beginning to get drunk; but he went home, then heard crashes and came out again and found the shops being broken up. If the tide had been in they would have put the old man into the harbour; the worst were Polish sailors. But mostly they were like 'grown-up boys', out for a bit of fun, and could easily be made to go the other way. Half of them were no good, on public assistance and so on. Someone had said it was a shame, and had promptly been knocked down. He, Ian, had stood by; you couldn't help thinking it was funny. But he would be as friendly as he could to the Italians next time he saw them.

Naomi Mitchison

1942 [London]

BBC Board. We discuss whether the clergy should use the microphone to preach forgiveness of our enemies. I say I prefer that to the clergy who seek to pretend that the bombing of Cologne was a Christian act. I wish the clergy would keep their mouths shut about the war. It is none of their business.

Harold Nicolson

12 June

1667 [London]

Up very betimes to our business at the office, there hiring of more fireships; and at it close all the morning. Ill news is come to Court of the Dutch breaking the Chaine at Chatham, which struck me to the heart, and to White Hall to hear the truth of it; and there, going up the park stairs, I did hear some lackeys speaking of sad news come to Court, saying that hardly anybody in the Court but doth look as if they cried.

So home, where all our hearts do now ake; for the news is true that the Dutch have broken the chain and burned our ships, and perticularly *The Royal Charles*; other perticulars I know not, but most sad to be sure. And the truth is, I do fear so much that the whole kingdom is undone that I do this night resolve to study with my father and wife what to do with the little that I have in money by me, for I give all the rest that I have in the King's hands for Tanger for lost. So God help us!

Samuel Pepys

1916 [the Russian Front]

Kulja, our driver, was a quiet middle-aged man, a very devout Moslem. When he came to himself, our head doctor told him quietly that his leg would have to come off. He shook his head: 'No!' Emphatically, 'No!' He would *never* allow his leg to be amputated. The doctor told him that he would wait until the next morning and hoped that by then he would have changed his mind; otherwise his life would be in jeopardy. Had he been a Russian, the situation would have been easier, but with a Moslem it was a different matter; they had rules which might prevent the amputation of a limb against the owner's will. The morning came and the doctors told Kulja in plain words that, unless his leg were taken off, he would certainly die, for gangrene had set in. Again he steadfastly refused an amputation. 'Good,' he said, 'I will die willingly, if Allah so wishes. The will of Allah be done.' He died in the evening, exactly 24 hours after he had been brought to us. I was with him at the end. He was quite happy: his simple Faith never wavered for a moment.

Florence Farmborough

1940 [Italy]

War raises the tone of life because it organises one's personal, inner life in accordance with a very simple pattern – the two opposing camps – giving one the idea that death is imminent and so investing the most banal actions with an air of importance more than human.

Cesare Pavese

1940 [London]

E. and I last night walked through Soho to see whether the damage to Italian shops etc. was as reported. It seemed to have been exaggerated in the newspapers, but we did see, I think, 3 shops which had had their windows smashed. The majority had hurriedly labelled themselves 'British'. Gennari's, the Italian grocer's, was plastered all over with printed placards saying 'This establishment is entirely British.' The Spaghetti House, a shop specializing in Italian foodstuffs, had renamed itself 'British Food Shop'. Another shop proclaimed itself Swiss, and even a French restaurant had labelled itself British. The interesting thing is that all these placards must evidently have been printed beforehand and kept in readiness.

Disgusting though these attacks on harmless Italian shopkeepers are, they are an interesting phenomenon, because English people, i.e. people of a kind who would be likely to loot shops, don't as a rule take a spontaneous interest in foreign politics. I don't think there was anything of this kind during the Abyssinian war, and the Spanish war simply did not touch the mass of people. Nor was there any popular move against the Germans resident in England until the last month or two. The low-down, cold-blooded meanness of Mussolini's declaration of war at that moment must have made an impression even on people who as a rule barely read the newspapers.

George Orwell

13 June

1666 [London]

Being invited to Sir Christopher Mings's funeral, I into the church and there heard the service, and stayed till they buried him, and then out. And there met with Sir W. Coventry (who was there out of great generosity, and no person of quality there but he) and went with him

into his Coach; and being in it with him there happened this extraordinary case. About a Dozen able, lusty, proper men came to the
coach-side with tears in their eyes, and one of them that spoke for
the rest, begun and says to Sir W. Coventry, 'We are here a Dozen of
us that have long known and loved, and served our dead commander
Sir Christopher Mings, and have now done the last office of laying
him in the ground. We would be glad we had any other to offer after
him, and in revenge of him – all we have is our lives. If you will please
to get his Royal Highness to give us a Fireshipp among us all, here is
a Dozen of us, out of all which choose you one to be commander,
and the rest of us, whoever he is, will serve him, and, if possible, do
that that shall show our memory of our dead commander, and our
revenge.' Sir W. Coventry was herewith much moved (as well as I, who
could hardly abstain from weeping), and took their names; and so parted,
telling me that he would move his Royal Highness as in a thing very
extraordinary, which was done.

Samuel Pepys

1667 [London]

Every minute some one or other calls for this order or that order; and
so I forced to be at the office most of the day. I did, about noon,
resolve to send Mr Gibson away after my wife with another 1000
pieces.

The King and Duke of York up and down all the day here and there;
some time on Tower-hill, where the City Militia was; where the King
did make a speech to them that they should venture themselfs no further
than he would himself. I also sent (my mind being in pain) Saunders
after my wife and father, to overtake them at their night's lodgings, to
see how matters go with them. In the evening I sent for my cousin
Sarah and her husband; who came, and I did deliver them my chest of
writings about Brampton [a family property], and my brother Tom's
papers, and my Journalls, which I value very much – and did send my
two silver flagons to Kate Joyce's [a cousin]. I have also made a girdle,
by which with some trouble I do carry about me £300 in gold about
my body, that I may not be without something in case I should be
surprised; for I think, in any nation but ours, people that appear (for we
are not indeed so) so faulty as we, would have their throats cut. Late at
night comes Mr. Hudson the cooper, my neighbour, and tells me that
he come from Chatham this evening at 5 o'clock and saw this after-

noon *The Royal James*, *Oake*, and *London*, burnt by the enemy with their fireships. I made my will also this day, and did give all I had equally between my father and my wife – and left copies of it in each of Mr. Hater and W. Hewer's hands, who both witnessed the will.

Samuel Pepys

1918 [Gloucestershire]
Very understaffed – and I had to tear round. Nurse – is a very good-natured little thing, but always breaking, dropping, knocking herself, barging into beds, spilling, or swathing herself in festoons of treacle. The men roar with laughter over her continued mishaps and so does she. All her pocket money must go in paying for her crockery casualties. We muddled the diet at lunch and Sister – whose fault it really was! apostrophised us as a lot of h'asses. It's very difficult not to giggle at her determined transposing of h's – she *never* forgets to do it. She got very over-excited at lunch about the 'hair-raids and hu-boats'.

A ghastly afternoon of blanket baths – such a strain on the brain! Some of the men had to be washed in bed, others given the where-withal and left, and others had to go to the bathroom; some had to be rubbed with methylated spirit in one place, some in two, and some not at all; and some had to be given clean top sheet and clothes, some clothes not sheets, and so on and so on. Nurse – went off and Nurse Jeanne (the little Belgian who got engaged to an Australian in the ward) had just come and knew nothing about the men, so I had to do all the staff work. All went well, except that naughty Hopkins – a gas gastric case – who should have been washed in bed, went off and had a bath on his own hook. Giving the blanket baths is rather difficult and I got tired of washing black toes.

Lady Cynthia Asquith

14 June

1918 [France]
I have seen a lot of soldiers at the war, but I have never seen a more well-behaved crowd than my present Company. They are living now in good billets, in a fairly good village. They are well fed. Their mental attitude is far less abject than is the case with the 1917–18 conscripts. But when their day's work is ended they have about four hours left

with nothing to do, nowhere to go. Not so much as a cinema or a YMCA hut. Perhaps they watch a football match till 6.30. There is only one ground, used by the Canadians as well.

So they go to the *estaminets*. I calculate that at least 10,000 francs are spent in *estaminets* (in this village by our battalion alone every week, probably £500 a week is the figure). And 50% of the battalion goes to bed drunk every night. Why do they do it? Because they all know that they will be in hell within a month; most of them have been away from home for nearly two and a half years. (Ten men go on leave each week from this battalion of eight hundred men.) They are having what is called a good time. Drink and death.

Siegfried Sassoon

1940 [Wiltshire]

A few days ago a friend of the [Gerald] Brenans living near Swindon tried to get his wife to sign a suicide pact because of the war. She was very tenacious of life and refused. So next morning he came in and shot her as she sat at her writing-table and afterwards shot himself.

Frances Partridge

1940 [Berlin]

Paris surrendered today. Strange how lukewarm the reaction is here. There is absolutely no feeling of elation.

Marie 'Missie' Vassiltchikov

1941 [Dresden]

After three months and against all expectation my plea of March 18 has been rejected, and so there remains a prison sentence of a full eight days, which I must begin on June 23. Reading and writing in *pencil* are supposed to be permitted. Keep smiling – I shall try.

Victor Klemperer

1944 [London]

Stuart told me that in his office the American soldiers speak with surprise about the familiarity of English girls, none of whom decline to sleep with them. They are convinced that all English women are tarts, and despise them accordingly, just as English soldiers despised the French girls during the last war.

James Lees-Milne

1967 [Bolivia]
I am now 39 years old. The time is inexorably approaching in which I will have to reconsider my future as a guerrilla fighter; for the time being I am 'all in one piece'.

Ernesto 'Che' Guevara

15 June

1940 [London]
I have been too rushed this historic week to write my diary in any detail. The events crowd thick and fast and each one seems worse than the other. Yet a curious psychological effect is produced. Fear and sorrow seem to give way to anger and pride. It may be because I know that I shall kill myself and Vita [Sackville-West, his wife] will kill herself if the worst comes. Thus there comes a point where Hitler will cease to trouble either of us, and meanwhile by every means in our power we will continue to worry him.

Then there is another state of mind which I notice. I am able almost entirely to dismiss from my thoughts any consideration of the future. I do not even have such pangs about the past as I had when the situation was less catastrophic. My reason tells me that it will now be almost impossible to beat the Germans, and that the probability is that France will surrender and that we shall be bombed and invaded. I am quite lucidly aware that in three weeks from now Sissinghurst [his home in Kent] may be a waste and Vita and I both dead. Yet these probabilities do not fill me with despair. I seem to be impervious both to pleasure and pain. For the moment we are all anaesthetised.

Harold Nicolson

1940 [Carradale, Scotland]
Young Dick [a local fisherman] was looking well and brown, his odd-coloured blue eyes showing magnificently; but he was jumpy. He had been posted to a boat after two days at Lowestoft; after some hesitation he confessed that it was called *Our Bairns!* They were sent off to mine-sweeping in the Channel and told to go to Le Havre; they expected nothing, but arrived to find half the town in flames and evacuation going on; they were bombed from the air; he said it was terrible being dived at; the planes were in the eye of the sun and they couldn't see them

properly till they were almost on them. There were no Allied planes. One bomb dropped close astern and cracked the condenser and did other damage – hence his leave. They all went ashore and looted the closed shops, as otherwise the Gerrys would have got the stuff; they got chocolate and wine 'which was awfully nasty', cheap champagne it sounded like, but the mate, older and wiser, filled a sack with coats and hats. The Old Man asked him where the hell he'd been and gave them all a lecture on looting, but it doesn't sound like strict discipline. The minesweepers are Harry Tate's Navy – none of the fishermen takes to discipline and all wear overalls on board. There is a crew of seven 'two Scots forby me and rest mostly from 'ull and Fleetwood'; he imitated Yorkshire dialect, thinking it very funny, but they used some Scots words.

Naomi Mitchison

1940 [England]

We arrived at Chequers in time to dine at 9.30. The party consisted of Winston, Duncan and Diana Sandys,[1] Lindemann[2] and myself. It was at once the most dramatic and the most fantastic evening I have ever spent. Before going into the dining-room Tony Bevir [of the War Cabinet Office] told me on the telephone that telegrams had been received from Bordeaux to the effect that the position was deteriorating fast and the request to be allowed to make a separate peace was being put in a more brutal form. I imparted this to Winston who was immediately very depressed. Dinner began lugubriously, W. eating fast and greedily, his face almost in his plate, and every now and then firing some technical question at Lindemann, who was quietly consuming his vegetarian diet. The Sandyses and I sat silent, because our spasmodic efforts at conversation were not well received. However champagne and brandy and cigars did their work and we soon became talkative, even garrulous. Winston, in order to cheer himself and us up, read aloud the messages he had received from the Dominions and the replies he had sent to them and to Roosevelt. 'The war is bound to become a bloody one for us now,' he said, 'but I hope our people will stand up to bombing and the Huns aren't liking what we are giving them. But what a tragedy that our victory in the last war should have been snatched from us by a lot of softies.'

---

[1] Winston Churchill's daughter and son-in-law.
[2] Professor F.A. Lindemann, Lord Cherwell.

Winston and Duncan Sandys paced up and down the rose garden in the moonlight while Diana, Lindeman and I walked on the other side of the house. It was light and deliciously warm, but the sentries, with tin helmets and fixed bayonets, who were placed all round the house, kept us fully alive to the horrors of reality. I spent most of the time telephoning, searching for Winston among the roses and listening to his comments on the war. I told him that fuller information had now been received about the French attitude, which appeared to be slipping. 'Tell them,' he said, 'that if they let us have their fleet we shall never forget, but that if they surrender without consulting us we shall never forgive. We shall blacken their name for a thousand years!' Then, half afraid that I might take him seriously, he added: 'Don't, of course, do that just yet.' He was in high spirits, repeating poetry, dilating on the drama of the present situation, maintaining that he and Hitler only had one thing in common – a horror of whistling – offering everybody cigars and spasmodically murmuring, 'Bang, Bang, Bang, goes the farmer's gun, run rabbit, run rabbit, run, run, run.'

Kennedy[1] telephoned and Winston, becoming serious for a minute, poured into his ears a flood of eloquence about the part that America could and should play in saving civilisation. Referring to promises of industrial and financial support, he said such an offer 'would be a laughing-stock on the stage of history', and he begged that 'we should not let our friend's (President R.) efforts peter out in grimaces and futility'.

About 1.00 a.m. Winston came in from the garden and we all stood in the central hall while the Great Man lay on the sofa, puffed his cigar, discoursed on the building up of our fighter strength, and told one or two dirty stories. Finally, saying 'Goodnight, my children', he went to bed at 1.30.

John Colville

1940 [London]

It has just occurred to me to wonder whether the fall of Paris means the end of the Albatross Library,[2] as I suppose it does. If so, I am £30 to the bad. It seems incredible that people still attach any importance to long-term contracts, stocks and shares, insurance policies, etc. in such

[1] Joseph Kennedy, American Ambassador in London.
[2] Parisian publishers who produced books in English for the continental market, several of which were banned in Britain.

times as these. The sensible thing to do now would be to borrow money right and left and buy solid goods. A short while back E made inquiries about the hire-purchase terms for sewing machines and found they had agreements stretching over two and a half years.

George Orwell

1943 [Kent]
Raining, aeroplanes droning, trees soughing.

Denton Welch

1982 [Yorkshire]
Mrs Thatcher announces the surrender of Port Stanley in well-modulated tones. Film follows of the funeral of the commandos killed at Goose Green, the simple service and the youth of the wounded unbearable. A pilot of one of the Harriers talks about the effectiveness of the Sidewinder missiles. 'A bit of an eye-opener' is how he puts it. A bit of an eye-closer too. Not English I feel now. This is just where I happen to have been put down. No country. No party. No Church. No voice.

And now they are singing 'Britannia Rules the Waves' outside Downing Street. It's the Last Night of the Proms erected into a policy.

Alan Bennett

1982 [London]
There has been an Argentinian surrender, and the reaction now is one of tremendous enthusiasm and support for Mrs Thatcher. However, this is not the moment to unbend but the time to reaffirm everything that we've said. It won't be popular, but if you take a principled position you don't withdraw from it.

I went to the House [of Commons] to hear the Prime Minister's statement announcing the surrender. Michael Foot congratulated her and her forces; somehow it was odious and excessive. I was called, and I asked if the PM would publish all the documents and the cost in terms of life, equipment and money of a tragic and unnecessary war. The Tories erupted in anger because this was Jingo Day. I said the world knew very well that the war would not solve the problem of the future of the Falkland Islands. 'Does she agree that in the end there must be negotiations, and will she say with whom and when she will be ready to enter into such negotiations?' She said she couldn't publish

the documents, she saw no reason to negotiate with Argentina, she
thought the war was tragic but not unnecessary, because the freedom
of speech which the Right Honourable Gentlemen made such excellent use of had been won for him by people fighting for it. Rubbish,
but the Tories loved it.

Tony Benn

16 June

1918 [France]

'What's the weight of *your* pig?' asked a witty Colonial. Coming up a
communication-trench, he squeezed himself against the chalky side of
the trench to make room for two men who were coming down; they
were carrying a dead body slung on a pole. This is how the Canadians
take their corpses away from the front-line. They tie the hands together
at the wrists; feet ditto. Then sling the body on a pole. What splendid
common-sense! And how jolly the War is! But I wish they'd put a
sandbag over the face.

Siegfried Sassoon

1940 [England]

G.J.[1] rang up – as he always does – to say awful things were happening which he couldn't tell me on the telephone. Just 'to warn' me.
Fat lot of good *that* does. Telephone call 4.45 – could I return to
London at once: I should be wanted to leave 'on a sea trip tonight'.
So I packed and had hurried tea and started 5.20. Car behaved splendidly and we got home 7.50. Orders are to leave with Winston and
others from Waterloo 9.40. Embark in 'Galatea' midnight Con-
carneau, or some point on coast of Brittany, to meet Reynaud[2].
Packed and dined. But at 8.50 Foreign Office rang up to say trip
off. 9.30 rang up to say trip on again. (I had kept my bag ready
packed!) Jumped into taxi and got to Waterloo at 9.55. Found
Winston had just gone back again to No.10 [Downing Street]. So
came home. Cabinet Offices warn me to be ready at a moment's

[1] Gladwyn Jebb, the Private Secretary to the Permanent Under-Secretary of State at
the Foreign Office.
[2] Paul Reynaud, French politician, who served as prime minister during the fighting
which preceded the fall of France in June 1940.

notice. Life rather like that of a fireman. (Only with no hope of putting out the fire!) Got into bed and at about 11.45 Cabinet Offices rang up to say Reynaud had resigned and Pétain[1] formed a Government. There might be a Cabinet meeting – would I stand by. I said I would 'lie by', in bed – turned out the light and went to sleep!

Sir Alexander Cadogan

1944 [Kent]

All night long, and just now too at breakfast, have been coming strange things, rocket planes, mechanical toys with thousand-pound bombs in them. They make a rude noise and the soldiers shoot off a little gun that sounds like pepper exploding. The rocket planes are radio-controlled, with no one in them, and when they crash they explode.[2] I wonder what will happen if the soldiers so near by will hit one.

Denton Welch

1982 [Yorkshire]

A cease-fire with 250 of our forces dead, one for every twenty civilians of the Falkland Islands – the price, Madam[3] says, of freedom. The ways the freedom of the Islanders seems to have been infringed before the outbreak of hostilities appear to be (i) they had to drive on the right, which, since their roads are mainly one-track, can scarcely have been a hardship; (ii) they were occasionally stood up against a wall, hands above their head, and searched, a humiliation suffered nightly by many citizens of this country – chiefly black – any protest about which is treated by the Conservative Party as humbug. The only actual atrocity seems to have been the death of a dairy cow. The man who would have had a field day with this war is Sydney Smith.[4]

Alan Bennett

---

[1] Marshall Henri Philippe Pétain, French Army officer, head of the Vichy State July 1940 – August 1944.
[2] V-1 flying bombs, nicknamed 'Doodlebugs'.
[3] Mrs Margaret Thatcher, Prime Minister.
[4] English cleric (1771–1845) and co-founder of the *Edinburgh Review*, famed for his wit.

17 June

1876 [Fort Lincoln]

We left Fort Lincoln on the 17th of May on a Campaigne against the Siux under the Command of General Terry the cavalry was Commanded by General Custer one month from the day we left Lincoln we struck the Rosebud, a creek that empties intoe the yellowstone. We passed in Review before General Terry an[d] Gibbons and they were highly pleased with the Warlike appearance of the officers and men. The[y] Cartonly a fine boddy of men. We left the Rose bud and marched up the stream 28 miles and Camped on the same the land along the stream is well timbered but as far as we have seen is entirely destitute of game.

Pvt Thomas W. Coleman, 7th US Cavalry

1916 [France]

At nightfall, the dead arrive on stretchers at the cemetery. In this, the Ravine of Death, they lay there, lined up, waiting to be put into the holes that are being hastily dug for them: Major Payen, his head red with blood; Major Cormouls black with smoke, still others unrecognisable and often in pieces. A sad spectacle, which is repeated here every day.

Lieut. Henri Desagneaux, French 2nd Infantry Regiment

1940 [London]

Winston was furious because the morning papers, which he likes to see before going to bed, had not arrived. In his emotion he upset his whisky and soda over all his papers. I asked him if he would see General Sikorski[1] tomorrow. 'I will see him,' he said, 'at noon,' and then went on to quote some entirely bogus quotation about that time of day, which he pretended was spoken by the nurse in *Romeo and Juliet*.

John Colville

1940 [London]

After a hilarious lunch at the café, with Jo [a boyfriend] doing imitations of Mussolini, I came home to find my mother as white as a sheet

[1] General Sikorski, Prime Minister and Commander in Chief of the Poles in exile in Britain. He died in an air crash in 1942.

and telephoning wildly. She said, 'France has surrendered – you'd better leave London tonight! Granny isn't well, so you can't go there, but your Aunt Lalla says she'll have you. I'll take you down there tomorrow.'

I fought tooth and nail but it wasn't any good – a lot of balls about being young and having your life before you – if London's going to be destroyed I'd rather stay with it as long as possible and go on working and being with my friends until we're all blown up. But my mother, who has no stamina, and is terrified of staying in London herself – she is staying on and sending *me* away, so that she won't have to worry about me! I think it's the bloodiest thing I ever heard of, being shuffled out of the way like this.

Joan Wyndham

1943 [Carradale, Scotland]

I talked a lot to Guy[1] who is extremely full of hate and wants to destroy all the Boches. I try to point out that historically nothing ever comes of revenge but at the same time, he's bound to talk like that – for I don't want him to feel embarrassed at talking to me. He's got to be able to talk, get all that into the open. He stood his two years of prison extremely well, I think. He also said that women in the army lost all their feminine charm and added that he was awfully shocked at the way women in London would sleep with four different men in one evening. I can't think where the French find these ladies! He added that I mustn't think *he* behaved like an American. They do hate the wretched *Amériques*. I keep trying to put in some pro-American propaganda but not much use. The French make up their minds and that's that.

Naomi Mitchison

18 June

1778 [Philadelphia]

About 8 o'clock this morning, the last Detachment of the Troops, consisting of about 5000 men, closed the Evacuation of Philadelphia & the Embarkation to the Jersies from Gloucester Point, about 2 miles

[1] One of seven Free French soldiers who stayed at Carradale.

below the Town, which was effected without the least molestation from the Rebels. The Precaution was taken to destroy the Bridge wch led over the marshes to Gloucester Point. The Bridge over Schuylkill, formed of cut masts, was destroyed a few Days before; and another Bridge, for the same place, constructed formerly by the Rebels, was burnt at Mud Island. In coming down, the Vigilant ran ashore upon the Spit opposite Mud Island, wch occasioned some Delay; though it was a happy Circumstance for a Detachment of about 180 men, whose Retreat was cut off from Billingsport by a party of 500 Rebels, & who were taken off by the Flat-Boats, however injurious the Delay was to the Sinking of the Vessels, filled with Stones, to obstruct the two narrow Channels, which Business was not so well effected by the strong Flux of the Tide.

Ambrose Serle

1876 [Fort Lincoln]

left Camp this morning at 6 A.M. and struck a large trail of Indians going in the direction of the big hor[n] river. But our Rattions giving out we had to turn back to the Yellowstone for supplies. We marched 28 miles and camped on the Yellowstone.

Pvt Thomas W. Coleman, 7th US Cavalry

1940 [Carradale, Scotland]

Went down to the Mission Hall to the LDV.[1]

It was a real farce; by the end of it I couldn't possibly believe there was a real war on, in fact I was in fits of giggles. Mr Baker was in the Chair and made some strange remarks about the Empire; it was a fullish meeting, about two thirds men. The speaker was a sweet man called Watson, I think a farmer, who began to read to us out of a document called SECRET. He told us which were danger zones for sea-planes, and produced a special reason why Carradale should be guarded. Rifles might be issued soon. Campbeltown seems to be held by what appears to us a rather small force, but they managed to get from Campbeltown to ———— in seven minutes, and 'wounded two men while they were at it' by letting off a gun accidentally. Most of the arms are going to the towns at present, but country districts would have their turn. Watchers were important;

[1] Local Defence Volunteers, later renamed the Home Guard.

when they saw something they were to ring up the police station and would then be asked 'a series of questions in set form' by the policeman.

He read us some more bits and then asked for questions. As there were none to start with, I asked if women could be watchers, as several had asked me. He said he thought it was what should be done but it couldn't be official. They could be runners too. I suggested it was a long run to Campbeltown. He said we should use cars if possible: 'the most people have plenty petrol here'. There was then an argument about the special reason, settled by Mrs Ritchie, who knew all about it. Alex said the best way to Campbeltown was by a speed boat if we had one. Cameron asked for duties and hours, which Watson was very vague about. He said that when we got the rifles (or even before!) we could have rifle instructions from one of the old soldiers here. Semple thought we had better get names, so it was decided to do that at once. So about seventeen men, probably about all who could go (they wouldn't take fishermen) went over to the table and had their names taken.

Naomi Mitchison

1941 [London]

In the evening I went to dine at a sort of buffet dinner at Grant Isaacs'.[1] There were about fourteen men there. His star guest was H.G. Wells, whom I had never seen before. He is well under middle height, has a rather pitched voice, is a most insignificant-looking individual, and one for whom I have a great deal of distaste, for taking him altogether I think he is fundamentally superficial, ignorant, and mischievous. I had no conversation with him, but listened to old Roberts, who was over here so long with Doubleday, Page & Company [publishers], and was a great friend of Walter Hines Page, talk about his experiences with Page during the World War.

I noticed that in the group which Wells gathered about, the conversation immediately became permeated with a hot discussion of the class war, revolution, and all the rest of the stock-in-trade which he has so profitably exploited over the last twenty years.

General Raymond E. Lee

[1] American Consul.

1943 [Zeralda, Algeria]

I work and swim and run a mile or two every afternoon on the beach. Life is idyllic. One feels ashamed to enjoy it thus to the full in a world full of death and hatred and suffering. Yet there are about two hundred thousand soldiers here in North Africa living an almost identical existence, eating the same chow, exercising in the sun and salt water, sleeping under blankets on the cool, grateful ground.

George Biddle

19 June

1876 [Fort Lincoln]

left camp this morning at 5 A.M. and marched down the river on the roughest Countery that I eaver saw a horse travel oaver got to Camp on the river at 3 P.M. feeling verry tired distance 28 miles to our camp is opposite the place we had the fight with the Indians in 73 and where the Suttler and the Regimental farrier got Killed.

Pvt Thomas W. Coleman, 7th US Cavalry

1916 [France]

We are expecting an attack at any moment. There is talk of recapturing the trenches with grenades. But what are our leaders doing? Ah, we don't see them here. We are left to ourselves, they won't come and bother us.

We try and make ourselves as comfortable as possible but the more we dig, the more bodies we find. We give up and go elsewhere, but we just leave one graveyard for another. At dawn we have to stop as the German planes are up above spying on us. They signal and the guns start up again, more furiously than before.

No sleep, no water, impossible to move out of one's hole, to even show your head above the trench. We are filthy dirty and have only cold tinned food to eat. We are not receiving supplies any more and have only been here for four days!

The afternoon and the evening are dreadful, it's an inferno of fire. The Germans are attacking our front line, we expect at any instant to be summoned to help. The machine-guns sputter; the ground trembles, and air is full of dust and smoke which scorch the throat. This lasts until 10 p.m. The fatigue party has to leave under a hail of fire to go and fetch our food just outside Verdun – 6 kilometres there and 6 more back. The men go without saying a word!

Lieut. Henri Desagneaux, French 2nd Infantry Regiment

1917 [In England, on leave]

Of the elderly male population I can hardly trust myself to speak. Their frame of mind is, in the majority of cases, intolerable. They glory in senseless invective against the enemy. They glory in mock-heroism of their young men. They glory in the mechanical phrases of the Northcliffe Press. They regard the progress of the war like a game of chess, cackling about 'attrition', and 'wastage of man-power', and 'civilisation at stake'. In every class of society there are old men like ghouls, insatiable in their desire for slaughter, impenetrable in their ignorance.

Siegfried Sassoon

20 June

1778 [New Jersey]

A rainy evening. Let me see, what company have we got within doors. – A pretty, full-faced, youthful, playfull lass. – The family quakers, meek and unsuspicious. – Hamilton, thou shalt not tread on this ground – I mark it for my own. Enter not this circle.

The pretty girl gives me some excellent milk, and sits and chats with me till bedtime. – She was too innocent a subject for gallantry, so I kissed her hand – telling her that we should be all gone before she got up – but not to forget that one man is often more dangerous to a woman than a whole army.

James McHenry

1855 [The Redan near Sebastopol]

Rode to Headquarters, where I heard that 95 officers and 1443 men were either killed or wounded. This is a most severe loss, and, added to those lost in the attack on the Quarries, makes an entire Brigade of our little Army, which can but ill be spared. All this too for nothing, except a couple of houses, and a slight advance to the left of the Left Attack gained by Eyre.

The men, I understand, did not behave well. But this, no doubt, arose from mismanagement of the attack, and is possibly a good lesson for some of our officers, who always seem to think that British pluck has done and can do everything. Now British pluck is not absolutely universal. When present it is as good as any pluck, and in some aspects better, but without *lead* is worth very little.

Lieut. General Sir Charles Ash Windham

1876 [Fort Lincoln]

today the long expected Steamboat Far West come to the landing and some of the boys got gloriously drunk we drawed 15 days Rattions and alsoe Tobacco the wead that a soldier likes eaven better than he does Whiskey.

Pvt Thomas W. Coleman, 7th US Cavalry

1917 [the Russian Front]

I went into the large tent where the heavily wounded were lying. Two torches provided a dim illumination and a lighted candle flickered on the small table in the middle of the tent. I sat at the little wooden table and tried not to be upset by the groans and cries of pain. There was a dreadful smell of pus and gangrene. Two men with smashed stomachs had just died; I called the orderlies to take them away, but they were busy in another tent. Now and then, I got up from my chair to give an injection, to pick up a blanket or sheet which had been thrown off by some restless form, to pour out a dose of medicine, or to feel the pulse of some poor man whose life was ebbing fast. From various corners of the tent came the repeated cries: 'Sestritsa [darling], please give water.' 'For the love of God, water!' 'Water, or I die!' I shut my ears to this living pain and tried to write a few words in my note-book, but I could not concentrate. The men with head wounds and whole stomachs were allowed to drink; but if a laparotomy patient lay alongside, I had to resort to strategy – hiding the mug in a fold of my overall, or kneeling between them. But it availed little, 'Sestritsa, give water!' The cry is taken up.

'Sestritsa, my *rodnaya* [own dear] Mother, water! Water! One drop! You can't refuse *one* drop!' I got up, pretending not to hear, and walked to the other side of the tent. A soldier with a smashed skull was breathing heavily with a funny, gurgling noise; his nostrils spouted out foamy matter with each gasping breath. An orderly, squatting by him, was constantly wiping his swollen face. Not far from him was a little stout man in a half-sitting position; the rattling noise in his throat was dreadful to hear. He had been shot through the right lung and his open wound was big enough to insert my fingers. The usual injection of morphia had had little or no effect and his frightened eyes were now gazing at me with a great pleading in them . . . If only I could help them! If only I possessed that magic 'healing touch' to soothe their anguish! '*Sestritsa*, don't you hear how I pray to you?' came a voice behind me. I hardened my heart and walked on.

Florence Farmborough

1941 [London]
Russia will be invaded on Sunday by Germany – if he is successful Hitler will be Master of Europe.

'Chips' Channon

1941 [London]
We have all been in a semi-melting condition for some days past. It struck me that one minor benefit of this war is that it has broken the newspapers of their idiotic habit of making headline news out of yester-day's weather.

George Orwell

1942 [Jersey]
This is a black day, for we have had to give up our wireless. Herbert packed it and took it to the parish hall. Everyone feels it very much as it is our only link with England. One feels so mad against the Germans (wrong as it is to feel so) for we have done nothing to deserve this. However, let us be thankful that it is only our wireless sets that have been taken and not our young men. We shall never be at rest until the Germans have gone – may they depart soon! Then, another disturbing thing: today in the *Evening Post* there is an Order from the German Commandant. He has arrested ten persons in Jersey, as hostages, because of leaflets with inciting contents, which have been printed and distributed; also for sabotage in connection with the telephone. If the perpetrators don't give themselves up, these ten persons are to be interned on the Continent. One has heard of this sort of thing in European countries under occupation and now it has come to this little island. Some girls had shown me one of these leaflets, trying to persuade people not to give up their wireless. I wish people would keep quiet, and not put us all into

trouble. It is no use going against the Germans unless it is a matter of conscience.

Well. We do feel depressed about everything tonight.

Nan Le Ruez

1944 [on board USS *Montpelier*, in the Pacific]

Most of the men are lying around getting some well needed rest. I had to clean up the Communication deck and did not get a chance to sleep, when I finished I wrote in the diary. I do not want to get behind with it. As I look around some of the men are out like a light, the sleep is better than food. Some of the fellows have a bucket full of clothes and are washing them, every man to his own taste. No doubt but I am the only sailor in the whole fleet who is writing a Diary.

James J. Fahey, Seaman First Class

1982 [Yorkshire]

The papers continue fatuous. Peregrine Worsthorne suggests that, having won this war, our troops emerging with so much credit, Mrs Thatcher might consider using them at home to solve such problems as the forthcoming rail strike or indeed to break the power of the unions altogether, overlooking the fact that this is precisely what we are supposed to object to about the regime in Argentina.

Since the war (the last war should we now call it?) there has been a noticeable increase in the use of the military metaphor in public debate. [Norman] Tebbit, the Employment Secretary, yesterday talked of campaigns, charges and wars of attrition. And the flag figures. The danger of such talk, of course, is that it presupposes an enemy.

Alan Bennett

21 June

1667 [London]

This day comes news from Harwich that the Dutch fleet are all in sight, near 100 sail great and small, they think, coming towards them; where they think they shall be able to oppose them. Sir H. Cholmly come to me this day, and tells me the Court is mad as ever and that the night the Dutch burned our ships the King did sup with my Lady Castlemayne at the Duchess of Monmouth's, and they were all mad in hunting a poor moth. All the Court afeared of a Parliament; but he thinks nothing can save us but the King's giving up all to a Parliament.

Samuel Pepys

1876 [Fort Lincoln]
left Camp this morning at the usual hour marched 15 Miles and Camped on the Rosebud the reason that it is Called so is the Banks ar[e] Coavered with Wild Rosies.

Pvt Thomas W. Coleman, 7th US Cavalry

22 June

1876 [Fort Lincoln]
Left Camp this Morning at 6 A.M. and travelled up the Rosebud. Our trail led across the stream Several times it was verry hot and Some of our horses gave out we marched 36 Miles and Camped on the Same Creek some of the Crow Scouts threw down Several of the Siux graves that had been Recently Erected the[y] had a gastley appearance laying on the Ground rapped up in their Buffaloe Robes with their Bowes and arrows at their head.

Pvt Thomas W. Coleman, 7th US Cavalry

1915 [the Russian Front]
One afternoon in Treschany as I was sitting near the dressing-tent, a peasant-cart driven by two soldiers and containing a coffin drew up on the road before me. Somewhat surprised at the sight of such a well-made coffin at a time when coffins were impossible to get, and thinking that the men had brought a dead soldier for burial in the brothers' cemetery, I directed them towards the hut where I knew Batyushka [Red Cross chaplain] had found a billet. 'No, *Sestritsa*,' said one of them. 'There is no dead man here. We have come to fetch the body of an officer.' And, producing a paper from his pocket, he handed it to me. They had come for the body of the student officer with the pale, serious face, who had spoken English with me.

'Is he really here?' I questioned. '*Tak tochno, Sestritsa* [Exactly so],' was the answer. 'We buried him here two days ago.'

I walked across the road and up the hill. The crosses stood starkly silhouetted against the sky. I went towards the newest graves and one after the other read the names inscribed on the crosses. Here was the one I had been searching for – 'Umer of ran . . . [Died from wounds]'.

The wooden cross was drawn out. 'Don't destroy it, the name can be erased and it will do for someone else,' said Smirnov, our head hospital-orderly. Carefully they dug away the earth. He was in his long military coat and his hands were crossed on his breast. So this was my 'red-hot revolutionary', who had loved his country over much and was ready to die for his countrymen! Was this the 'bad end' which had been playfully prophesied for him? I watched them drive down the hill, passing the golden cornfield and the field of dancing poppies on their way.

Florence Farmborough

1940 [England]

The inevitable news of Dick's[1] death came yesterday from Geneva: F/O Eric Richard Dennis Vaughan 65878 mort. Even M. [his mother] through the tearful wreckage of her grief could see the grim irony of that one word, understood in all languages, telegraphed across the battle-fields of Europe.

Keith Vaughan

1941 [Germany]

The Luftwaffe raids destroyed 1800 planes – Hitler has named Göring his successor in the event of his death. The news bulletins are so good, I know the war won't last for long. We have thousands of tanks on their way to Moscow and Leningrad.

This is the first time Michael has really been aware of what is happening, and he has a map in his room which he has pinned on the wall today. 'This is what we have conquered,' he said, for all the world like a school teacher. He showed me where our troops are, what we occupy, where we are *going* to occupy! He even told me we need *space* in Russia for '*Lebensraum*' and that their material resources were necessary for us. I said 'Where did you hear all that?' He said 'At camp and at school – but I have a mind of my own!' I said 'an excellent mind – but put it to use in your mathematics too.' His report last term was very poor.

Elisabeth von Stahlenberg

[1] Dick was his younger brother.

1942 [Fouglass]

Last night I had a nightmare that the Germans had arrived in Cairo, and had discovered my excessively indiscreet diaries left behind at Shepheard's Hotel, which were now receiving a very mixed reception among my friends, relayed over the air to England by Lord Haw-Haw.

Cecil Beaton

1944 [England]

At 4.30 one fine summer afternoon an aircraft dived out of the sky and sprayed a small village with machine gun fire. Such things happen every day, I know, but I want to consider this one particular instance. In two separate dives across the village, in the space of 38 seconds, 14 people were killed and 11 injured. The whole thing was photographed by one of the planes and we saw it in a newsreel.

In ten years' time the whole incident will be forgotten. The aircraft will be forgotten, the pilot forgotten. The girl who might have been a musician will be the matron at the local school. The old couple will be dead. The boy who was blinded will be well cared for by an institution. In 38 seconds on a summer afternoon seeds of misery and grief were sown which grow for more than one generation. Something atrocious has been done, and someone must be responsible.

Keith Vaughan

23 June

1665 [London]

The Duke of Yorke told us, that his dog sought out absolutely the very securest place of all the vessel, when they were in fight.

John Evelyn

1876 [Fort Lincoln]

Left Camp this Morning at the usual hour the trail led up the Creek My company B was in the advance after following the trail for four hours we Came to a Circular arbour about two hundred feet in Circumferance built with Crotches and strong poles their was a tree in the Centar 35 feet high around which was pilled a number of Buffaloe heads this place was devoted to Religious Cermony Called the Sun dance usually practised by this tribe before going on the War Path about 200 yards from here we found a fresh scalp supposed to have been taken from the head of one of General Gibbons Soldiers that was out hunting. We camped at ten A.M. for three hours after Marching 15 miles we got Coffee and resumed the March for 20 miles more we then went intoe Camp on the Rosebud and after supper we were in hoaps of having a good nights rest but we were saddly Disappointed for we again Marched at 11 and the night being so dark we could scarsely see the horses a head of us. My Company was rear guard and such Charging from Rear to front Keeping up the pack train I rearly seen it put me in mind of the Charge of the Black Horse Cavalry at the Battle of Bull run in 1861. We marched 8 miles and liquated our horses without unsaddling them and went to sleep several of the Companies lost suggar Bacon and Coffee we lost one Side of Bacon.

Pvt Thomas W. Coleman, 7th US Cavalry

1940 [Wiltshire]

Jimmy Bomford [a neighbour] was visited yesterday by a car containing eight policemen, one a Scotland Yard man. They thought it was about the German pianist, Peter Gellhorn, but 'Oh no,' they said, 'we've come about *you*.' They then went over the house from top to bottom, searched all the men bodily, and took away all Jimmy's papers and farm accounts. They would not say what were the grounds of suspicion, but they came to the conclusion it was village gossip, their having foreign friends, and Jimmy wearing a beard. When I tried to ring them up I was told the line was 'out of service'. I then tried to get onto the Wests[1] and got the same answer. Surely *they* can't be searched too? But they had been, and came to tell us so. The police were there for about six hours and took away all their foreign books, maps, guides, and even some toy soldiers belonging to Anthony! They took him to Marlborough police station, where the Chief of Police was hectoring and disagreeable: 'And by the way that's a pretty nasty shirt you're wearing.' One of the things the police had against him was that he knew the Bomfords and the Brenans! So I shan't be surprised if it's our turn to be searched next. I actually wandered round looking for things the police would be silly enough to carry

[1] Anthony West, writer, and his wife Kitty.

off if they came here. Hugo's *German* perhaps? Or Clive's[1] pacifist tract? Or this diary, I suppose.

Frances Partridge

1940 [Paris]

The armistice was signed yesterday evening. And now what is going to happen?

André Gide

1944 [Tuscany]

In the afternoon there is horrible news: a young partisan, who is accused of having shot a German at Chiusi (and who was caught in a cypress tree up which he had climbed for shelter) has just been publicly hanged on a lamp-post in the main street. He is to be left hanging there for twenty-four hours, in sight of the whole population, as an example. Bracci believes the poor wretch is innocent, but a German soldier says that he has recognized him, and the alternative is the execution of ten innocent hostages from the town. The German captain who gives these orders is a most sinister brute, elegant, hard and cruel. The bishop is present at the hanging and, in spite of a protest from the Germans, courageously imparts his benediction to the dying man. The corpse's presence hangs like a blight over the whole town, and the people who live in the main street dare not open their shutters on the horrible sight.

Iris Origo

24 June

1876 [Fort Lincoln]

Revelee at 4 A.M. after getting some Coffee we felt Much refreshed Left Camp at six and followed the trail that had now become large and fresh we marched 12 Miles and went into Camp every man feeling that the next twenty four hours would deside the fate of a good manny men and sure enough it did.

Pvt Thomas W. Coleman, 7th US Cavalry

---

[1] Clive Bell (1881–1964), writer and pacifist, a member of the Bloomsbury Group, he married Vanessa Stephen, Virginia Woolf's elder sister.

1915 [France]

House by roadside, roof damaged, contents taken away by G.'s [gendarmes]. Why? What they couldn't take they destroyed.

Trenches. Character of country: rolling upwards. Farms. Wheat, oats, *poppies*. Heavily wooded in places. High horizon of tree-lined roads.

Many tombs in wheat and hidden by wheat. Barbed wire on four stout posts (a bird on post), white wooden cross. Always a small white flag. Not always a name. On every side in these fields, the gleam of a cross or flag, as far as you can see. Scores and scores. Dark green-purple of distant wooded hills against high green of fields.

Cemetery used for firing from. Holes in wall.

Wheat absolutely growing out of a German.

General impression. How little is left. How cultivation and civilization have covered the disaster over!

Arnold Bennett

1916 [France]

Big German offensive on the right bank of the Meuse. This news arrived during the night. There is no question of our being relieved. Everything is silent and behind us, on Fleury ridge, the Boches continue infiltrating.

We have been turned! There is no longer any doubt, as we can see enemy columns invading the terrain and their machine-guns are attacking us from behind while our artillery has had to move back.

Now something worse: my men, who have been suffering all sorts of hardships for the last seven days, are becoming demoralized. The word 'prisoner' is being whispered. For many this would seem salvation. We must fight against this notion, raise morale. But how? We can't move around, and only those near us can hear. They are all good chaps, devoted, who won't leave us and will form a bodyguard.

What are we waiting for? We don't know. Yet we can only wait for it: perhaps the attack which will kill us, or the bombardment to bury us, or exile even. We spend some anxious hours without knowing how long this will last.

At 11 a.m. artillery is heard. Our batteries have taken up new positions and are opening fire, the Boches reply.

Impossible to eat, our nerves can't stand it. If we have a call of nature to satisfy, we have to do it in a tin or on a shovel and throw it over the top of our shell-hole. It's like this every day.

Lieut. Henri Desagneaux, French 2nd Infantry Regiment

1940 [Paris]

Yesterday evening we heard with amazement Pétain's new speech on the radio. Can it be? Pétain himself deliver it? Freely? One suspects some infamous deceit. How can one speak of France 'intact' after handing over to the enemy more than half of the country? How to make words fit those noble words he pronounced three days ago? How can one fail to approve Churchill? Not subscribe most heartily to General de Gaulle's declaration? Is it not enough for France to be conquered? Must she also be dishonoured? This breaking of her word, this denunciation of the pact binding her to England, is indeed the cruellest of defeats, and this triumph of Germany the most complete, by getting France, as she hands herself over, to debase herself.

André Gide

1940 [London]

I was called at 7, dressed and ate nervously; at 8.15 we set out for Euston. Honor and I had the child [son Paul, aged 5, about to be evacuated to the USA] between us; he was gay and interested. At the station there was a queue of Rolls-Royces and liveried servants and mountains of trunks. It seemed that everyone we knew was there.

We led our child to his compartment, and clung hungrily to him until the whistle blew and then after a feverish hug and kiss, we left him. I care more for Paul than for all of France, and mind his departure dreadfully. For the first time in my life I felt a surge of remorse for my own appallingly callous treatment of my parents, who perhaps once loved me as I love Paul.

'Chips' Channon

25 June

1876 [Fort Lincoln]

The sun rose this Morning with every appearance of it being verry hot and so it turened out we left Camp at Six A.M. our Company was rear guard we Marched 3 miles of the battle field and halted the

Scouts came in and reported a large village in our front the General [Custer] was highly pleased to hear it he then formed his plan of battle he took five Companies C commanded by his brother Tom, L commanded by his brother-in-law first Lieut Calehone, F commanded by Capt Yates I company commanded by Kehoe E Commanded by Capt Smith he gave Mageor Reno three Companies and Capt Benteen three he ordered Reno to Charge the village at the upper end and he would goe down and ford it at the lower end in order to Cut them Benteen he ordered well to the left so we were to bring up the pack train as quick as possible he struck the village at half past twelve and Reno Charged the Indians but he was entirely Surrounded and had to Cut his way back to the bluffs with the remnant of his Command the Indians following the[y] Came verry near Capturing My Company we were Moving so fast the packs would Slip off an[d] the packers had to put them on again My Company B, Capt McDougal got on the bluffs at 2 P.M. and foremed a Scirmish line and fought them untill dark when the[y] drawed off and left us in command of the bluffs we dug holes with our hunting Knives and awated the Indians in the Morning. As I said before Custer went below the Village in order to have them between two fires but he was surrounded and all of them killed to a man it was two and a half Miles from where we were that Custer Met his fate their was numbers of Indians between him and Mageor Reno.

Pvt Thomas W. Coleman, 7th US Cavalry

1916 [France]
Terrible day and night.

At 3 a.m., without warning, our own troops attack us from behind in order to recapture the terrain lost the day before on our right. These troops, without precise orders, without maps, without even knowing where our lines are, ventured off. They fell upon us, believing they had found the Boches. But the Boches were 100 metres in front, lying in wait and bursts of machine-gunfire cut them down in our trench. We thus have another heap of corpses and wounded crying out, but whom we are powerless to help. Trench! – well almost every evening we bury the dead on the spot and it's they who form the parapets!

At 6 a.m., the guns fire furiously and to add to our plight, our 75s fire at us. Terrible panic; six wounded at one go from a shell-burst, everyone wants to run for it. Agnel [a fellow officer] and I have to force these poor devils back by drawing our revolvers.

Major David is killed in turn by our 75s. Our green flares ask for the range to be lengthened, but with all the dust our artillery can't see a thing. We don't know where to put ourselves, we are powerless. Isolated from everything with no means of communication. There's blood everywhere; the wounded have sought refuge with us, thinking that we could help them; the blood flows, the heat is atrocious, the corpses stink, the flies buzz – it's enough to drive one mad. Two of the 24th Company commit suicide.

Lieut. Henri Desagneaux, French 2nd Infantry Regiment

1940 [London]

I had hardly got to sleep last night when the sirens sounded, and I went to the cellar where I was soon joined by 4 female servants in various stages of déshabille. The scullery-maid read the financial section of *The Times*!

The Duchess of Kent, Brendan Bracken[1] and others lunched. Brendan told us that he had been sitting in the garden at No. 10 last night with the PM when the sirens sounded; but they remained there drinking. From his conversational crumbs I gathered that all is far from well in Churchill's private paradise, and there are endless squabbles among the new ministers! Brendan attacked Attlee[2] and Greenwood[3] thus reflecting Winston's mind.

'Chips' Channon

1940 [London]

I saw in one of yesterday's papers that gas masks are being issued in America, though people have to pay for them. Gas masks are probably useless to the civilian population in England and almost certainly so in America. The issue of them is simply a symbol of national solidarity, the first step towards wearing a uniform . . . As soon as war started the carrying or not carrying of a gas mask assumed social and political implications. In the first few days people like myself who refused to carry one were stared at and it was generally assumed that

[1] A Conservative MP.
[2] Clement Attlee, Lord Privy Seal, later Prime Minister, 1945–51.
[3] Arthur Greenwood, MP.

the non-carriers were 'left'. Then the habit wore off, and the assumption was that a person who carried a gas mask was of the ultra-cautious type, the suburban rate-payer type. With the bad news the habit has revived and I should think 20 per cent now carry them. But you are still a little stared at if you carry one without being in uniform. Until the big raids have happened and it is grasped that the Germans don't, in fact, use gas, the extent to which masks are carried will probably be a pretty good index of the impression the war news is making on the public.

George Orwell

26 June

1776 [Virginia]
Last night after going to bed, Moses, my son's man, Joe, Billy, Postillion John, Mulatto Peter, Tom, Pantcove, Manuel and Lancaster Sam, ran away, to be sure, to Ld. Dunmore, for they got privately into Beale's room before dark and took out my son's gun and one I had there, took out of his drawer in my passage all his ammunition furniture, Landon's bag of bullets and all the Powder, and went off in my Petty Auger new trimmed, and it is supposed that Mr. Robinson's People are gone with them, for a skow they came down in is, it seems, at my Landing. These accursed villains have stolen Landon's silver buckles, George's shirts, Tom Parker's new waistcoat and breeches; and yet have not touched one thing of mine, though my door was open, my line filled with stockings and my buckles in my shoes at the door.[1]

Landon Carter

1876 [Fort Lincoln]
this Morning the Indians opened a Murderous fire on us with their long range Winchester Rifle[s] and one of our men got Killed and two baddley wounded we had now been 22 hours without water and we were Suffering verry Much for the want of it especially the wounded it was almost impossible for a Man to goe to the River without getting Killed or wounded Capt Benteen Made a Charge on them with his

---

[1] Carter attributed this to the fact that he had kept the slaves in their places and had never, in 6 or 7 years, used an angry word towards his slaves.

Company and drove them from the river he heald them in Check whilst Some of the Men went to get water in getting it one got Killed and two wounded at 10 A.M. the Indians Came so close to our lines that Captain McDougal of my Company B thought it necessary to Charge them mageor Reno led the Charge and we drove them back with loss the[y] Cept up a heavy fire on us from three different points and our horses and pack Mules suffered severly about four P.M. Their fire Slackened I suppose for the want of amunition and at dark the[y] left altogether their families going towards the big horn mountains and the warriors going towards the Yellowstone The[y] left us Masters of the field. But how dearly bought 42 Wounded and 14 Killed to night we got plenty of water for our Men and horses and we lay in the trenches with the Sky for a Covering and Slept Soundly untill Morning.

Pvt Thomas W. Coleman, 7th US Cavalry

1940 [London]
Yesterday the PM received the following letter:
  Dear Prime Minister
  Why not declare war on France and capture her fleet (which would gladly strike its colours to us) before A.H. recovers his breath?
  Surely that is the logic of the situation?

Tactically,
G. Bernard Shaw.

John Colville

1967 [Bolivia]
We captured two new spies; a lieutenant of the carabineers and one of his men. They were given a warning and set free, only wearing their underpants. This was done to a misunderstanding of my order to strip them of anything we could use. We left with nine horses.

Ernesto 'Che' Guevara

27 June

1876 [Fort Lincoln]
this Morning after sunrise i went oaver the Battlefield on this side of the river and the first person i saw was Lieut B.H. Hodgson of

my Company he was shot twise with Ball and once with arrow Several other boddies lay close by I buried the Lieut on a nice Knowl overlooking the River with a Cedar tree at his head he was a Brave officer and a true gentleman, about 10 A.M. General terry and gibbons Came to our reliefe the General was profoundly affected at the Sad disaster the[y] were welcome to us eaven after the battle was oaver this after noon a party of us went across the river to look for the boddy of one of our Company and we could not recognise him all of them were Scalped and otherwise horribly mutilated Some had their heads Cut off others arms and legs their hatred extended eaven to the poor horse the[y] cut and Slashed them before the[y] were dead this eavening we are mooving the Wounded across the river the poor fellows feel verry bad for the want of propper Care and nourishment.

Pvt Thomas W. Coleman, 7th US Cavalry

1943 [Algeria]

In wartime one is never alone but very spiritually lonely. It is natural then, that one's ego – though small, regimented, and totally unimportant – should bulk large. That is perhaps the reason why soldiers are so willing to have sketches made of them. It is as if they had a humble but steadfast faith in their own historical mission. It is also perhaps the reason why during war one so often has the desire to pray. Not that in wartime one particularly believes – or disbelieves – in god. The soldier is a skeptic. No; it is merely the sense of one's loneliness, of one's helplessness and at the same time – perhaps subconsciously – of one's abstract and historical import. One sees oneself objectively, as an atom, drifting senselessly yet relentlessly in a mathematically charted course.

George Biddle

1944 [Naples]

Del Giudice, a great amateur of local gastronomy, wanted me to taste the eels which at this time of the year are a speciality of the town. We visited what he said was the best restaurant along that part of the coast but I did not really enjoy the meal. Sea-food restaurants always seem to me more prone to evident and visual cruelty than others. The eels were being skinned alive in full view of the customers, chopped up and thrown into a frying-pan where they continued to squirm, and on one occasion a cook pulled a live octopus out of a tank, sliced off a testicle to add to some soup, and threw it back again. Del Giudice mentioned that the restaurant supplied short-time rooms for couples overcome by the aphrodisiac qualities of the food.

Norman Lewis

28 June

1876 [Fort Lincoln]

this morning we went to burry the[m] and Now Comes the Most hart rendering tale of all. As I have said before General Custer with five companies went below the Village to Cut them off as he Supposed but instead he was Surrounded and all of them Killed to a Man 14 officer and 250 Men Their the Bravest General of Moddern times met his death with his two Brothers Brother in law and Nephew not 5 yards apart Surrounded by 42 Men of E Company. Oh what a slaughter how Manny homes are Made desolate by the Sad disaster eavery one of them were Scalped and otherwise Mutiliated but the General he lay with a smile on his face the Indians eaven respected the great Chief My Company burried 30 of E Company the[y] were in line not 10 feet apart the[y] were so Disfigured by those female Monsters the squaws that i could not recognise one of them

Where the Village Stood and where the battle was fought is 24 miles from the big horn it is a lovely place the Valley is 1? Miles brade and four miles long the River winding like a Snake and dotted with Islands thickly studded with tim[b]er the water Clear as Christal as it comes rushing from the Mountains Oh what a pittey that Such a lovely place should be the abode of such a band of blood thirsty demons After burrying the dead we went across the river and went through the Village there was one funeral tent left standing filled with dead savage we left them as the[y] were their was all Kinds of culinary and Mechanical Instruments strewn around besides partley dressed Buffaloe Robes Showing the[y] were loaded with more valuable plunder and Could not Carry them along all the dead the[y] stript Completely naked we have moved our Camp Six Miles down the river the way we have of mooving the wounded is Novil there is two poles 16 feet Long tied to the Saddle one on each side the mules going in tandem the space in the Center from head to Croope there is two bars laid across the center is tide with Raw hide the wounded is placed on them the mules are lead and the poles swinging from side to side Make a comfortable Vehickle to ride an[d] i think it is preferable to an ambulance oaver a Rough Contery the reason that we Mooved Camp was in consequence of the Stench arising from the Battle field their was a number of their ponies dead in the Village.

Pvt Thomas W. Coleman, 7th US Cavalry

1940 [Berlin]

Today was the twenty-first anniversary of the signing of the Treaty of Versailles. And the world it created appeared to be gasping its swan-song today as German troops reached the Spanish border, and Soviet troops marched into Bessarabia and Bukovina. In Paris last week I learned on good authority that Hitler planned a further humiliation of France by holding a victory parade before the Palace of Versailles on this twenty-first anniversary. He would make a speech from the Hall of Mirrors, where it was signed, proclaiming its official end. For some reason it was called off. It is to be held, instead, in Berlin, I hear.

Official comment of Russia's grabbing Bessarabia and Bukovina from Rumania today was 'Rumania has chosen the reasonable way.'

William L. Shirer

1940 [London]

The PM is, as ever, actively interested in every small question relating to the war. This morning, 'Home Secretary: Let me see a list of prominent persons you have arrested.'

John Colville

1940 [London]

Horribly depressed by the way things are turning out. Went this morning for my medical board and was turned down, my grade being C in which they aren't at present taking any men in any corps . . . What is appalling is the unimaginativeness of a system which can find *no* use for a man who is below average level of fitness but at least is not an invalid. An army needs an immense amount of clerical work, most of which is done by people who are perfectly healthy and only half-literate . . . One could forgive the government for failing to employ the intelligentsia, who on the whole are politically unreliable, if they were making any attempt to mobilize the man-power of the nation and change people over from the luxury trades to productive work. This simply isn't happening, as one can see by looking down any street.

George Orwell

1940 [Perth, Scotland]

Bill Mackenzie appeared unexpectedly this forenoon – had been transferred to Leslie: certain troops concentrated in Fife, as the Germans may attempt a landing between the Forth and Tay. Bill looking very well; slimmer, and deeply sun-burned. Had got away from the Dunkirk dunes in comparative safety – and was surprised that the Germans hadn't bombed them more violently. However, he had been near enough death to retain a certain look in the eyes which is indefinable – a kind of impersonal glance that shows itself now and then.

William Soutar

29 June

1776 [Virginia]

[Col. Carter tells of the fugitive slaves.] At 7 in the morning after their departure some minute men at Mousquito Point saw the *Petty Auger* [Carter's boat] with ten stout men in her going very fast on the Middlesex shore. They pursued and fired at them, whereupon the negroes left the boat and took to the shore where they were followed by the minute men. By their firing they alarmed 100 King and Queen minute men who were waiting for the *Roebuck*'s men, should any of them come ashore there. It is supposed that Moses and many of the Negroes were killed.

Landon Carter

1876 [Fort Lincoln]

Today K and H Companies went to the village to destroy every thing that would be usefull to in one Revene the[y] found 150 dead Indians and it is supposed that their is a large number that was Carried away by their Squaws.

It is a principle of the Indians never to let the enemy get their dead for the[y] suppose that he Cannot goe to the happy Hunting grounds if he looses his Scalp We left Camp at 6 P.M. with our wounded for the Boat that lay at the mouth of the little horne distance 24 Miles it was a Melancholly Sight to See the poor fellows between two Mules Swaying from side to side as the[y] moved along we have one Crow Indian Scout that Killed 7 Sioux and got their Scalps he was wounded five times and Strange to relate he is in a fairway to recover he rode along in silence Never Complaining the next bad Case was an Irish Mon Madden of K Company his leg was shot all whilst he was in the act of getting water for the Wounded when we were Correlled on the bluffs although the litter he was on fell to the ground twice he never uttered a complaint we got to the boat at two A.M. of the 30th and put the wounded on board where the[y] were well taken Care of by the doctors we camped close by and lay down rapped our blankets around us and went to sleep not Caring for Sitting Bull or his Blood thirsty Wariors.

Pvt Thomas W. Coleman, 7th US Cavalry

1915 [Gallipoli]

The smell of dead bodies and horses is attracting the unwelcome attention of vultures from Asia. They are evil-looking birds, with ugly heads and enormous wings, and circle round and round overhead. Sometimes Tommies pot at them with their rifles, but get into trouble for doing so.

In the fire-trenches the Turks will not allow our men to bury the dead unless a special armistice is arranged. In consequence, in the dead of night our men volunteer to creep out, tie a rope round a body which may be too near them to make the atmosphere bearable, and then rush back, haul the body in, and bury it in the trench, or they will soak the body in petrol, go back to their trenches, then fire into the body – the white-hot bullets soon setting the petrol on fire, and the bodies in this dry climate quickly get cremated.

Major John Gillam, DSO

1950 [USA]

'From now on, I'll try to write every day. It will be a discipline – and these messages from the doomed ship may even be of some value, to somebody, later.'

It's nearly twelve years since I wrote those words, on August 20,

1938. And again I find myself having to declare my own private State of Emergency in order to be able to adjust to this Korean crisis.

The *Los Angeles Times* this morning carries an obviously press-agented account of how the veteran diva, General MacArthur, flew to the South Korean war front in an unarmed transport. 'The general summoned the newsmen to his office and told them his plans secretly last night. He said he did not know the war situation clearly and wanted a personal glimpse. Talking seriously and eagerly, he said the trip might be risky. "It will be an unarmed plane and we are not sure of getting fighter cover, not sure where we will land." He added: "If you are not at the airport I will know you have other commitments." One correspondent said, "There's no doubt we'll be there." MacArthur grinned and replied, "I have no doubt of your courage. I just wanted to give your judgement a chance to work."'

The great effort I must make is to realise that this fighting is actually taking place, that people are being killed, that the fighting may spread into a general war, that many people I know may be drafted, even that Los Angeles and other cities may be bombed – perhaps with atom bombs. It is very hard to realise the horror of all this – precisely because I have already spent most of one war right here in this city and so the prospect seems deceptively familiar and scarcely more than depressing. The danger of taking the war unseriously is a truly hideous spiritual danger. If I give way to it, I shall relapse into the smugness of the middle aged, who have nothing much to fear because they won't be drafted, or the animal imbecility of queens who look forward to an increase in the number of sailors around town.

Smog early, but it's sunny now.

Another day is going to be wasted. I have to review Lovell Naeve's *A Field of Broken Stones*. And get on with my novel.

Christopher Isherwood

30 June

1876 [Fort Lincoln]
We awoke this Morning after four hours good Sleep had our hard tack and Coffee fed our horses and felt verry good the boat left in the afternoon for Fort Lincoln with the Wounded 40 in all and to get supplies

for the Command we crossed the river was Mustered and went intoe Camp for the night.

Pvt Thomas W. Coleman, 7th US Cavalry

1914 [England]

There has been another assassination, this time of the heir of the Austrian Emperor.[1] I do not know how it affects the political situation.

Wilfred Scawen Blunt

1916 [France]

Myself, Agnel, and my orderly are squashed in a hole, protecting ourselves from splinters with our packs. Numb and dazed, without saying a word, and with our hearts pounding, we await the shell that will destroy us. The wounded are increasing in numbers around us. These poor devils not knowing where to go come to us, believing that they will be helped. What can we do? There are clouds of smoke, the air is unbreathable. There's death everywhere. At our feet, the wounded groan in a pool of blood; two of them, more seriously hit are breathing their last. One, a machine-gunner, has been blinded, with one eye hanging out of its socket and the other torn out: in addition he has lost a leg. The second has no face, an arm blown off, and a horrible wound in the stomach. Moaning and suffering atrociously, one begs me, 'Lieutenant, don't let me die. Lieutenant, I'm suffering, help me.' The other, perhaps more gravely wounded and nearer to death, implores me to kill him with these words, 'Lieutenant, if you don't want to, give me your revolver!' Frightful, terrible moments, while the cannons harry us and we are splattered with mud and earth by the shells. For hours, these groans and supplications continue until, at 6 p.m., they die before our eyes without anyone being able to help them.

At this moment, the hurricane of fire ceases, we prepare to receive an attack, but fortunately nothing happens.

Lieut. Henri Desagneaux, French 2nd Infantry Regiment

1940 [Chequers, Endland, official residence of the Prime Minister]

Looking through the Visitors' Book I saw that Marshal Foch had written in it: *Les affaires de l'Angleterre iront encore mieux quand son*

---

[1] Franz Ferdinand, Archduke of Austria, was assassinated by a group of young Serbian nationalists on June 28, 1914. Austria used the incident as a pretext for attacking Serbia, which precipitated WWI.

premier ministre pourra se reposer à Chequers. Let us hope he will not be as wrong about that as he was about Weygand[1]. ('When France is in danger send for Weygand.')

John Colville

[1] General Maxime Weygand (1867–1965) was in command of the French Army in the Middle East when he was asked to take charge of the Allied armies in France. However he did not live up to his high reputation, and was later sent to Algeria as Governor General. He was later imprisoned by the Germans for three years, and following that, he was imprisoned for a further three-year period by the French.

JULY

And 'mid this tumult Kubla heard from afar
Ancestral voices prophesying war!
Samuel Taylor Coleridge, Kubla Khan

1 July

1666 [London]
To Deptford to the yard, and so back to the Tower several times about the business of the pressed [press-ganged] men, and late at it till twelve at night, shipping of them. But, Lord! how some poor women did cry; and in my life I never did see such natural expression of passion as I did here in some women's bewailing themselves, and running to every parcel of men that were brought, one after another, to look for their husbands; and wept over every vessel that went off, thinking they might be there, and looking after the ship as far as ever they could by moonlight, that it grieved me to the heart to hear them. Besides, to see poor patient labouring men and housekeepers leaving poor wives and families, taking up on a sudden by strangers, was very hard, and that without press-money, but forced against all law to be gone. It is a great tyranny.

Samuel Pepys

1863 [Gettysburg]
At 4:30 P.M. we came in sight of Gettysburg, and joined General Lee and General Hill, who were on top of one of the ridges which form the peculiar feature of the country round Gettysburg. We could see the enemy retreating up one of the opposite ridges, pursued by the Confederates with loud yells.

Arthur James Lyon Fremantle

1871 [Paris]
At the Gare du Nord, prisoners of war were arriving back from Germany. Pale faces, thin bodies in greatcoats too big for them, faded red cloth and worn grey cloth: this is the sight to which the trains from Germany are treating Paris every day.

They walked along with little sticks in their hands, bent under grey canvas kitbags. Some of them were dressed in German breeches, and others were wearing a cloth cap in the place of the peaked cap they had left on some battlefield. Poor fellows! When they were turned loose, it was a pleasure to see them straighten up, it was a pleasure to hear their worn soles tread the pavements of Paris with a brisk, eager step.

The Princess[1] received me with that liveliness which is peculiar to her and which she puts into her handshake. She took me for a stroll in the park and started telling me about herself, about her stay in Belgium, about her sufferings in exile. She told me that for a long time she could not understand what was happening to her in Belgium, but that she knows now: she was present there in body but completely absent in mind, so completely indeed that she used to wake up in the morning thinking that she was in her Paris house. When I congratulated her on her good health, she said: 'Oh, it hasn't always been like that! There was a bad period, a peculiar period, during which my jaws set so hard, after all that I had been through, that sometimes I really had difficulty in eating anything.'

She spoke to me too of the Emperor, whom she had seen again, and whom she characterized as an *impersonal being,* a man whose fall did not seem to have affected him.

The Brothers Goncourt

1876 [Fort Lincoln]
left Camp this morning at 3 A.M. Marched 18 miles and camped on the big horn.

Pvt Thomas W. Coleman, 7th US Cavalry

1940 [London]
As I was free on Monday evening, I went, all alone, out to Hammersmith to see the D'Oyly Carte Company in *The Mikado.* They do it well and there are so many familiar tags and quotations recognizable that it is like listening to Shakespeare. The audience, in tweeds and gas masks, responded very well and I couldn't help but reflect that the English have changed very little since Gilbert and Sullivan's day. One hopes they have the same persistence and courage. All sorts of letters and articles are being printed now, pointing out that the young Englishman is lacking in the kind of training which affords a foundation for successful soldiering. Of course, this is a nice time to think about it.

General Raymond E. Lee

[1] Princess Mathilde, daughter of King Jerome.

1942 [Holland]

New measures again. Not only are we not allowed to cycle any more, we are not allowed to ride the trams either. We have to be off the streets by eight, and we are not allowed inside non-Jewish homes. Shopping is restricted for us to the hours between three and five p.m. It's a mess. I've moved back home; I couldn't stay at the Fernandez' [non-Jewish friends] any more. I did have a wonderful time there. At my last meal with them last night, I read them a poem of thanks I had written. We were all so moved and depressed because of the new measures, and crying so hard about everything, that we ended up sobbing with laughter. It was a comical tragedy, really.

Edith Velmans

2 July

1863 [Gettysburg]

At 7 A.M. I rode over part of the ground with General Longstreet, and saw him disposing of M'Laws's division for today's fight. The enemy occupied a series of high ridges, the tops of which were covered with trees, but the intervening valleys between their ridges and ours were mostly open, and partly under cultivation. The cemetery was on their right, and their left appeared to rest upon a high rocky hill. The enemy's forces, which were now supposed to comprise nearly the whole Potomac army, were concentrated into a space apparently not more than a couple of miles in length.

The Confederates enclosed them in a sort of semicircle, and the extreme extent of our position must have been seen from five to six miles at least.

Until 4:45 p.m. all was profoundly still, and we began to doubt whether a fight was coming off today after all.

At that time, however, Longstreet suddenly commenced a heavy cannonade on the right. Ewell immediately took it up on the left. The enemy replied with at least equal fury, and in a few moments the firing along the whole line was as heavy as it is possible to conceive. A dense smoke arose for six miles. There was little wind to drive it away, and the air seemed full of shells.

The Southern troops, when charging, or to express their delight, always yell in a manner peculiar to themselves.

When the cannonade was at its height, a Confederate band of music, between the cemetery and ourselves, began to play polkas and waltzes, which sounded very curious, accompanied by the hissing and the bursting of shells.

Major Fairfax arrived at about 10 P.M. in a very bad humor. He had under his charge about 1,000 to 1,500 Yankee prisoners who had been taken today; among them a general, whom I heard one of his men accusing of having been 'so G——d d——d drunk that he had turned guns upon his own men.'

Arthur James Lyon Fremantle

1876 [Fort Lincoln]
Revelee at 3 marched at 5 A.M. Made 29 miles crossed the Yellowstone on the s[t]eamboat Josephine and went into Camp.

Pvt Thomas W. Coleman, 7th US Cavalry

1917 [South Downs]
We hear from overseas the dull noiseless thud beating on the drum of the ear, hour after hour, day by day, telling of the cancelling out of whole populations on vast battlefield. One sometimes wonders how one can go on, eating and drinking, walking and sleeping, reading and dictating, apparently unmoved by the world's misery.

Beatrice Webb

1940 [Wiltshire]
The Arandora Star[1] has been torpedoed without warning in the Atlantic. It was taking German and Italian waiters, etc. to be interned in Canada, and about a thousand were drowned. That will make parents with American plans for the children quail for a little.

Frances Partridge

---

[1] The *Arandora Star*, a former cruise ship, was used to deport prisoners-of-war, mainly to Canada. On 2 July, 1940, it was struck by a torpedo from a German submarine. There were 734 Italians on board, of whom 486 died. Of the 479 Germans on board, 175 died.

3 July

1863 [Gettysburg]

At 6 A.M. I rode to the field with Colonel Manning, and went over that portion of the ground which, after a fierce contest, had been won from the enemy yesterday evening. The dead were being buried, but great numbers were still lying about; also many mortally wounded, for whom nothing could be done. Amongst the latter were a number of Yankees dressed in bad imitations of the Zouave[1] costume. They opened their glazed eyes as I rode past, in a painfully imploring manner.

The distance between the Confederate guns and the Yankee position – that is, between the woods crowning the opposite ridges – was at least a mile, quite open, gently undulating, and exposed to artillery the whole distance. This was the ground which had to be crossed in today's attack.

Pickett's division, which had just come up, was to bear the brunt in Longstreet's attack. Pickett's division was a weak one (under 5,000), owing to the absence of two brigades.

At noon all Longstreet's dispositions were made; his troops for attack were deployed into line and lying down in the woods; his batteries were ready to open. The General then dismounted and went to sleep for a short time.

A small boy of twelve years was riding with us at the time. This urchin took a diabolic interest in the bursting of the shells, and screamed with delight when he saw them take effect. I never saw this boy again, or found out who he was.

Finding that to see the actual fighting it was absolutely necessary to go into the thick of the thing, I determined to make my way to General Longstreet. It was then about two-thirty. After passing General Lee and his staff, I rode on through the woods in the direction in which I had left Longstreet.

I soon began to meet many wounded men returning from the front. Many of them asked in piteous tones the way to a doctor or an ambulance. The further I got, the greater became the number of the wounded. At last I came to a perfect stream of them flocking through the woods as great as the crowd in Oxford Street in the middle of the day.

[1] Soldiers belonging to a body of French infantry.

Some were walking alone on crutches composed of two rifles, others supported by men less badly wounded than themselves, and others were carried on stretchers by the ambulance corps; but in no case did I see a sound man helping the wounded to the rear unless he carried the red badge of the ambulance corps.

They were still under heavy fire; the shells were continually bringing down great limbs of trees and carrying further destruction amongst this melancholy procession. I saw all this in much less time than it takes to write it, and although astonished to meet such vast numbers of wounded, I had not seen enough to give me any idea of the real extent of the mischief.

When I got close up to General Longstreet I saw one of his regiments advancing through the wood in good order; so, thinking I was just in time to see the attack, I remarked to the General that 'I wouldn't have missed this for anything.' Longstreet was seated at the top of a snake fence at the edge of the wood and looked perfectly calm and unperturbed. He replied, laughing, 'The devil you wouldn't! I would like to have missed it very much; we've attacked and been repulsed; look there!'

For the first time I then had a view of the open space between the two positions and saw it covered with Confederates, slowly and sulkily returning towards us in small broken parties, under a heavy fire of artillery. But the fire where we were was not so bad as further to the rear, for although the air seemed alive with shell, yet the greater number burst behind us.

The General told me that Pickett's division had succeeded in carrying the enemy's position and capturing his guns, but after remaining there twenty minutes, it had been forced to retire.

Soon afterward I joined General Lee, who had in the meantime come to the front on becoming aware of the disaster. If Longstreet's conduct was admirable, that of Lee was perfectly sublime. He was engaged in rallying and in encouraging the broken troops and was riding about a little in front of the wood, quite alone, the whole of his staff being engaged in a similar manner to the rear.

His face, which is always placid and cheerful, did not show any signs of the slightest disappointment, care or annoyance; and he was addressing to every soldier he met a few words of encouragement, such as: 'All this will come right in the end; we'll talk it over afterwards; but in the meantime all good men must rally. We want all good men and true just now.'

He spoke to all the wounded men that passed him, and the slightly wounded he exhorted to 'bind up their hurts and take up a musket' in this emergency. Very few failed to answer his appeal, and I saw many badly wounded men take off their hats and cheer him.

He said to me, 'This has been a sad day for us, Colonel – a sad day. But we can't expect always to gain victories.'

I saw General Wilcox (an officer who wears a short round jacket and a battered straw hat) come up to him and explain, almost crying, the state of his brigade. General Lee immediately shook hands with him and said cheerfully, 'Never mind, General. All this has been *my* fault – it is I that have lost this fight, and you must help me out of it in the best way you can.'

Arthur James Lyon Fremantle

1864 [Confederate POW camp, Andersonville, Georgia]
Three hundred and fifty new men from West Virginia were turned into this summer resort this morning. They brought good news as to successful termination of the war, and they also caused war after coming among us. As usual, the raiders [fellow Union prisoners] proceeded to rob them of their valuables and a fight occurred, in which hundreds engaged.

The cut-throats came out ahead. Complaints were made to Captain Wirtz[1] that this thing would be tolerated no longer, and that these raiders must be put down, or the men would rise in their might and break away if assistance was not given with which to preserve order.

Wirtz flew around as if he had never thought of it before, issued an order to the effect that no more food would be given us until the leaders were arrested and taken outside for trial. The greatest possible excitement. Hundreds that have before been neutral and non-committal are now joining a police force. Captains are appointed to take charge of the squads, which have been furnished with clubs by Wirtz.

As I write, this middle of the afternoon, the battle rages. The police go right to raider headquarters, knock right and left, and make their arrests. Sometimes the police are whipped, and have to retreat, but they rally their forces and again make a charge, in which they are successful.

Can lay in our shade and see the trouble go on. Must be killing

---

[1] Captain Henry Wirtz, prison commandant, who was later found guilty of charges of mistreatment, cruelty and murder and was hanged November 1865.

some by the shouting. The raiders fight for their very life, and are only taken after being thoroughly whipped. The stockade is loaded with guards who are fearful of a break. I wish I could describe the scene today. A number killed. After each arrest a great cheering takes place.

Night

Thirty or forty have been taken outside of the worst characters in camp, and still the good work goes on.

John Ransom

1876 [Fort Lincoln]
the Boat left this morning for Fort Bufort for Supplies we are well supplied with Suttlers there is three in Camp one sells Whiskey but there is no drunkness in the Camp Suttlers are a Curse to the armey for the[y] do not Sell first Class goods in the first place then the[y] Charge exorbitant prices for everything. Whiskey Beer and all drinks 25 cents every othe[r] thing in proportion The[y] get all the Money the Soldiers have an[d] the[y] become Independent in a few yers if the[y] were not here the Soldiers would get along just as well if not better and he Could Save all his Money their was Muster of our Regiment this evening and it was found that their was but 250 men left fit to take the field and our horses are in poor Condition.

Pvt Thomas W. Coleman, 7th US Cavalry

4 July

1863 [Gettysburg]
Saturday. The great battle closed and quieted with the closing day – Some firing at various points –

Our Regt layed on arms with Pickets out – on the ground where we had put in some of the day – Rather expecting attack momentarily – Rained furiously during the night – We had fed, eaten, and were standing 'to horse' when about 6 o'clock NEWS CAME – 'The Rebs are falling back!' and 'Our forces are following them!' and our Regt went out towards Hunterstown reconnoitering. We found some confederates who had straggled, or were foraging, not knowing yet what had happened and was taking place – Of course, our Boys took them in – Making a little detour I captured two. Sergt Major J.T. Richardson and Private Cox 9th Va Cav – disarming them and bringing them in

– I guarded them – while the Regt gathered some others – P.M.
Captain Hughes came along and paroled them – and we were ordered
to camp near Hanover – where we first lay on arriving near Gettysburg
– Evening awfully muddy and disagreeable – I saw much of the destructiveness of the Johnies today.

Samuel Cormany, 2nd Cavalry Brigade, 2nd Division, Union Army

1864 [Confederate POW camp, Andersonville, Georgia]
The men taken outside yesterday are under Rebel guard and will be
punished. The men are thoroughly aroused now that the matter has
been taken in hand it will be followed up to the letter.

Jimmy Devers regrets that he cannot take a hand in, as he likes to
fight, and especially with a club. The writer hereof does no fighting,
being on the sick list. The excitement of looking on is most too much
for me. Can hardly arrest the big graybacks [insects] crawling around.

It is said that a court will be formed of our own men to try the
raiders. Any way, so they are punished. All have killed men, and they
themselves should be killed.

John Ransom

1876 [Fort Lincoln]
this morning there is nothing to distinguish it from anney other day
no firing of artillery no Speech making No demonstration whatever
not eaven a drunken man around Camp every thing quiet and everybody rapped up in his own thoughts and a great many in their blankets how different it is in 'Civilised Countery' it is a day of rejoicing
to boath young and old Oh Solitude where are thy Charms that sages
have seen in thy face.[1]

Pvt Thomas W. Coleman, 7th US Cavalry

1940 [London]
[House of Commons] I had a good seat in the Distinguished Strangers
gallery. Questions were being asked and answered. The House was full
and there was nothing to show in the rather ordinary-looking assem-
blage, lounging on the benches and laughing uproariously at every dextrous
exchange between Members and Ministers, that they were looking forward

[1] Line taken from *Verses Supposed to be Written by Alexander Selkirk* [the real-life *Robinson Crusoe*] by William Cowper (1731–1800).

to a historical moment. Finally the current business was disposed of, Churchill himself taking part in a most matter-of-fact way, and then there came a moment's pause. Churchill bounced to his feet, a most ordinary and undistinguished little rotund figure. He began quietly a stark recital of the events which had led up to the decision,[1] tracing them link by link with the utmost scorn for the successive breaches of faith upon the part of the Bordeaux government. He announced that this fateful decision had been, on the part of the Cabinet, completely unanimous and then, with the most dramatic effect and yet with the most superb composure, he narrated as a historian this vivid passage of history. He is a magnificent writer of history and I think the greatest political orator alive. The decision which may easily mark the turning point of Hitler's career, was not only his but was one which allowed him to identify himself with his great ancestor, Marlborough, and one could see how he revelled in this great moment and his complete competence in dealing it. Cheers from every corner of the chamber greeted his every point (and he knew how to make them), and when he finished, the decorum of the Parliament vanished. All were on their feet, shouting, cheering and waving order papers and handkerchiefs like mad. There was as much enthusiasm on the Labour side as the Conservative and the tumult endured for two or three minutes before there was enough quiet for him to move for a secret session in order that the matter might be debated.

General Raymond E. Lee

5 July

1776 [Virginia]

Hearing so many contradictory stories about Moses and his gang[2], I sent Beale off this morning to get fully informed either in Lancaster, Middlesex, or Gloster. I gave him 10 shillings to bear his expenses. The Gent. made a demur about his breeches being dirty. I told him dirty breeches are as certainly good to ride in as to stay at home in.

Landon Carter

---

[1] To prevent important units of the French fleet from falling into German hands, the decision was taken to present the French with an ultimatum to come over to Britain's side, sail into neutral ports or to scuttle their ships. The French refused and Britain sank a battleship and a battle-cruiser.

[2] Slaves belonging to Carter, and some of their friends, who had recently run away.

1863 [after Gettysburg]

Sunday. Rained awfully during the night. I got very wet –

Early we took up the march for Chambersburg – Crossing the battle-field – Cemitary Hill – The Great Wheat Field Farm, Seminary ridge – and other places where dead men, horses, smashed artillery, were strewn in utter confusion, the Blue and the Grey mixed – Their bodies so bloated – distorted – discoloured on account of decomposition having set in – that they were utterly unrecognisable, save by clothing, or things in their pockets – The scene simply beggars description – Reaching the west side of the Field of Carnage – we virtually charged most of the way for 10 miles – to Cashtown – Frequently in sight of the Rebel rear guard – taking in prisoners – in bunches – We captured some 1,500 wounded men, and 300 stragglers – we went as far as Goodyears Springs, where we rested for the night. (I had to guard a Reb all night.)

Samuel Cormany, 2nd Cavalry Brigade, 2nd Division, Union Army

1864 [Confederate POW camp, Andersonville, Georgia]

Boiling hot, camp reeking with filth, and no sanitary privileges; men dying off over a hundred and forty per day. Stockade enlarged, taking in eight or ten more acres, giving us more room and stumps to dig up for wood to cook with.

Have more mementoes than I can carry, from those who have died, to be given to their friends at home. At least a dozen have given me letters, pictures, &. to take North. Hope I shan't have to turn them over to someone else.

John Ransom

1942 [Lagos]

Everything is damp – the bed, clothing, papers. Soon one's luggage becomes mildewed. The earth is red, so that the swamps are like lakes of tomato soup. It is an uncomfortable billet too: the beds are granite, and the other men in the dormitory make such varied and horrible noises that one longs for earplugs. Even deep in the night there are continual disturbances with latecomers turning on lights and bawling at the top of raucous voices. Early calls start before dawn: again doors are banged, young men whistle bits of my least favourite ditties ('A Wandering Minstrel I' or 'She was poor but she was honest'), and the songs are accompanied by the most explosive gurglings and lavatory noises.

Cecil Beaton

6 July

1776 [Virginia]

Much is said of the slavery of Negroes, but how will servants be provided in these times? Those few servants that we have don't do as much as the poorest slaves we have. If you free the slaves, you must send them out of the country or they must steal for their support.

Landon Carter

1863 [after Gettysburg]

Monday. Had a good breakfast. Turned my prisoner over to others. We took up the march – via Fayeteville for Quincy – I told Corp. Netz I intended going on – to Chambersburg – To see wife and Baby – and would report in the morning again. He understood and I slipped away – and was soon making time for home – I got a fine '10 oclock piece' at Heintzelmans – on approaching Chambersburg I was assured there were still squads of rebs about town – Near town I was met by town folk inquiring about the battle. I was the first 'blue coat' they had seen – and the first to bring direct news of the Enemy's defeat – as communications had been cut. As I struck out of town, I was told 'The Rebel rear-guard has just left the Diamond.' So I ventured out 2nd Street and ventured to strike Main near where Darling and Pussy lodged – and behold They were at the door – had been watching the Reb Rear leaving town – and Oh, the surprise and delight thus to meet after the awful battle they had been listening to for passing days – My horse was very soon stabled. My Cavalry outfit covered with hay – and myself in my citizens clothes – So should any final 'rear' come along, I would not be discovered – To attempt to describe my joy and feelings at meeting and greeting my dear wife and little family must prove a failure – We spent the P.M and evening very sweetly and pleasantly, but only we had a few too many inquiring callers.

Samuel Cormany, 2nd Cavalry Brigade, 2nd Division, Union Army

1940 [Wiltshire]

Eleanor Rathbone in the *New Statesman*: 'This is no time to speak of women's rights – except one: to give their lives for their country.'

R. says Feminists are the only women with a castration-complex. They are mad with jealousy at not being allowed a 'weapon'.

Frances Partridge

1941 [Dresden]

I am trying to work up in outline on the typewriter the terrible week, no eight days, in prison, June 23 till July 1. Since my return on Tuesday exhausted, dazed, overjoyed, incapable of doing anything. Perhaps this was the good thing about the time of tribulation, that we became conscious again of belonging together, of our happiness, of the absolute unimportance of everything apart from being together. Short walks – an apple juice in the evening in the Toll House, chatting in the evening with Kätchen Sara [a neighbour], that's all. And housework of course, which after the nothingness now seems pleasant to me.

Victor Klemperer

7 July

1864 [Confederate POW camp, Andersonville, Georgia]

The court was gotten up by our men and from our own men; judge, jury, council. Had a fair trial, and were even defended, but to no purpose. It is reported that six have been sentenced to be hung, while a good many others are condemned to lighter punishment, such as setting in the stocks, strung up by the thumbs, thumbscrews, head hanging.

The court has been severe but just.

The prison seems a different place altogether; still dread disease is here, and mowing down good and true men. Would seem to me that three or four hundred died each day, though officially but one hundred and forty is told. About twenty-seven thousand, I believe, are here now in all. No new ones for a few days.

Rebel visitors, who look at us from a distance. It is said the stench keeps all away who have no business here and can keep away. Washing business good.[1] Am negotiating for a pair of pants. Dislike fearfully to wear dead men's clothes, and haven't, to any great extent.

John Ransom

[1] Ransom took in washing for other prisoners.

1915 [Essex, England]
8.45 a.m. this morning's post brought me a letter from my daughter [Mildred]:

> 4 July, 1915
> . . . I heard a lively story about a Scotch regiment to-day. They were burying the dead after an engagement and had begun to shovel earth on a German, when the man recovered consciousness and cried out 'Me no deaded, me no deaded.' 'Agh' cries the Scottie, 'Shovel some earth on him, Geordie. Them Germans is such liars that one can't believe a word they say!'

Andrew Clark

1940 [Dresden]
Yesterday Frau Haeselbarth [a friend and former student] came to see us in the late morning, in black: her husband fallen near St. Quentin, he 35, she 33, married for five years – 'four and a half really, then he was called for service' – three children. She brought me socks and shirt and briefs. 'You need it, it's of no use to me anymore.' We really did accept the things. Sympathy? Very great. But with it the dreadful 'Hurrah, we're still alive!' And the sympathy limited to the woman. The husband, whom I had not known, had first been a lawyer on his own account, and then for the Regional Farmers' Association, in the direct service of the Party therefore.

Victor Klemperer

8 July

1864 [Confederate POW camp, Andersonville, Georgia]
The camp is thoroughly under control of the police now, and it is a heavenly boon. Of course, there is some robbery, but not as before. Swan, of our mess, is sick with scurvy. I am gradually swelling up and growing weaker.

The swamp now is fearful. Water perfectly reeking with prison offal and poison. Still men drink it and die. Rumors that the six raiders will be hung inside. Bread today, and it is so coarse as to do more hurt than good to a majority of the prisoners.

The place still gets worse. Tunnelling is over with; no one engages in it now that I know of. The prison is a success as regards safety; no escape except by death, and very many take advantage that way.

Our quartette of singers a few rods away is disbanded. One died, one nearly dead, one a policeman and the other cannot sing alone, and so, where we used to hear and enjoy good music evenings, there is nothing to attract us from the groans of the dying.

Have taken to building air castles of late on being exchanged. Getting loony, I guess, same as all the rest.

John Ransom

1942 [Amsterdam]

Dearest Kitty,

At three o'clock, the doorbell rang. I didn't hear it, since I was out on the balcony, lazily reading in the sun. A little while later Margot appeared in the kitchen doorway, looking very agitated. 'Father has received a call-up notice from the SS,' she whispered. 'Mother has gone to see Mr van Daan.' (Mr Van Daan is Father's business partner and a good friend.)

I was stunned. A call-up: everyone knows what that means. Visions of concentration camps and lonely cells raced through my head. How could we let Father go to such a fate? 'Of course he's not going,' declared Margot as we waited for Mother in the living room. 'Mother's gone to Mr van Daan to ask whether we can move to our hiding place tomorrow. The van Daans are going with us. There will be seven of us altogether.' Silence. We couldn't speak. The thought of Father off visiting someone in the Jewish Hospital and completely unaware of what was happening, the long wait for Mother, the heat, the suspense – all this reduced us to silence. Suddenly the doorbell rang again. 'That's Hello,'[1] I said.

'Don't open the door!' exclaimed Margot to stop me. But it wasn't necessary, since we heard Mother and Mr van Daan downstairs talking to Hello, and then the two of them came inside and shut the door behind them. Every time the bell rang, either Margot or I had to tiptoe downstairs to see if it was Father, and we didn't let anyone else in. Margot and I were sent from the room, as Mr van Daan wanted to talk to Mother alone.

When she and I were sitting in our bedroom, Margot told me that the call-up was not for Father, but for her. At this second shock, I

---

[1] Hello Silberberg, one of Anne's suitors.

began to cry. Margot is sixteen – apparently they want to send girls her age away on their own. But thank goodness she won't be going; Mother had said so herself, which must be what Father meant when he talked to me about our going into hiding. Hiding . . . where would we hide? In the city? In the country? In a house? In a shack? When, where, how . . . ? These were questions I wasn't allowed to ask, but they still kept running through my mind.

Margot and I started packing our most important belongings into a satchel. The first thing I stuck in was this diary and then curlers, handkerchiefs, schoolbooks, a comb and some old letters. Preoccupied by the thought of going into hiding, I stuck the craziest things in the satchel, but I'm not sorry. Memories mean more to me than dresses.

Anne Frank

9 July

1776 [Virginia]
Beale returned but brought no account of Moses and his gang. He went to the King and Queen camp on the point between Rappahannock and Pianketank and talked with the commander. They had catched other people's Negroes but not mine.

Landon Carter

1864 [Confederate POW camp, Andersonville, Georgia]
Battese [an 'Indian' prisoner] brought me some onions, and if they ain't good, then no matter; also a sweet potato. One-half the men here would get well if they only had something in the vegetable line to eat, or acids. Scurvy is about the most loathsome disease, and when dropsy takes hold with the scurvy, it is terrible. I have both diseases, but keep them in check, and it only grows worse slowly. My legs are swollen, but the cords are not contracted much, and I can still walk very well.

Our mess all keep clean, in fact are obliged to, or else turned adrift. We want none of the dirty sort in our mess.

I still do a little washing but more particularly hair cutting, which is easier work. You should see one of my hair cuts. Knobby! Old prisoners have hair a foot long or more, and my business is to cut it off, which I do without regard to anything except to get it off.

A guard told me today that the Yanks were 'gittin' licked', and they didn't want us exchanged, just as soon we should die here as not. A Yank asked him if he knew what exchanged meant; said he knew what shootin' meant, and as he began to swing around his old shooting iron, we retreated in among the crowd.

John Ransom

1941 [London]
[Dining with General and Mrs John Scott Crawford]
Mrs Crawford told me in a perfectly inimitable and true way of her experience during the Battle of Britain. She said, 'I had sent my children on to a tennis party to join them later, and finally got on my bicycle and started. As I went along I thought I heard a most peculiar whistling sound but paid no attention to it until a lot of people who were leaning over their gates said, "Madam, Madam, you must not go up there because there are bombs falling."' She said, '"Nonsense, I don't believe a word of it, because I don't hear any bangs, and I am sure those are our own planes overhead."' She said, 'I went on and got to the party where I found the hostess somewhat perturbed because she heard that the planes overhead were not ours but Germans, so we thought we would put the children indoors. However, you know when you have ten children, you can never get them all in the house at once. If you have five in, there are always five out. Finally,' she said, 'the party was over and we shepherded the children home, and on the way I saw quite a lot of planes coming overhead doing the most peculiar things, and I thought to myself they will be severely disciplined for this, for they are not allowed to do aerobatics in wartime.' She said, 'I later found out this is what is called the victory roll, so they were coming home having defeated and destroyed a lot of Germans. It was not till a long time afterwards that I found out that this had been one of the critical moments of the Battle of Britain and there had been a great victory overhead and all the time I was thinking only of my children's tennis party. One does not know when one is in the midst of history.'

General Raymond E. Lee

1943 [Carradale, Scotland]
Curious evening. Jean[1] started talking about commando training and parachute jumping. It was partly a show-off, so as to make the French

---

[1] One of the Free French billeted in the Mitchison household.

girl and me say ooh, *les Hommes!* I didn't. I tried to take it all as a circus though sympathetically, because I think it's dangerous if women start admiring men for being brutal, taking risks and generally living in an unintellectual and insensitive way. But even allowing for exaggeration, the commando training sounds pretty tough. The parachute jumping sounds really beastly; obviously they find it hell and always have their hearts in their mouths.

I asked if they were volunteers and was told not exactly, they had to volunteer for the honour of France. If anyone just couldn't, he had to take back his still folded parachute to the girl who had made it. I said I thought that was awfully unfair, especially to the girl; they didn't look at it that way. It sounded to me as if Judo would be a great help for any of these things. They are all bothered about the suppression of the 'Marseillaise', though perhaps not so much as I am myself . . .

Naomi Mitchison

10 July

1666 [London]
To the office, the yard being very full of women (I believe above 300) coming to get money for their husbands and friends that are prisoners in Holland; and they lay clamouring and swearing and cursing us, that my wife and I were afeared to send a venison-pastry that we have for supper tonight to the cook's to be baked, for fear of their offering violence to it – but it went, and no hurt done. Then I took an opportunity when they were all gone into the fore-yard and slipped into the office, and there busy all the afternoon. But by and by the women got into the garden and come all to my closet window, and there tormented me; and I confess their cries were so sad for money, and laying down the condition of their families and their husbands, and what they have done and suffered for the King, and how ill they are used by us, and how well the Dutch are used here by the allowance of their masters, and what their husbands are offered to serve the Dutch abroad, that I do most heartily pity them and was ready to cry to hear them – but cannot help them, however, when the rest were gone, I did call one to me that I heard complaine only and pity her husband, and did give her some money, and she blessed me and went away.

Samuel Pepys

1776 [New York]

Orders were issued for one Brigade to be in readiness at 4 o'clock tomorrow Morning for a March. We all imagined that we were designed to make an Attack upon the Enemy on Staten Island, but on farther consideration we had reason to doubt of it as no particular Orders were Issued with Respect to our Baggage which would be Necessary to take with us if this was the Intention of the General. Last night the Statue on the Bowling Green representing George Ghwelps alias George Rex was pulled down by the Populace. In it were 4000 Pounds of Lead & a Man undertook to take 10 oz. of gold from the Superfices, as both Man & Horse were covered with Gold Leaf; the Lead we hear is to be run up into Musquet Balls for the use of the Yankies, when it is hoped that the Emanations from the Leaden George will make as deep impressions in the Bodies of some of his red-Coated and Torie Subjects, and that they will do the same execution in poisoning and destroying them, as the Super-abundant Emanations of the Folley and pretended Goodness of the real George, have made upon their Minds, which have, effectually poisoned and destroyed their Souls, that they are not worthy to be ranked with any Beings who have any Pretensions to the Principles of Virtue & Justice, but would to God that the unhappy contest might be ended, without putting us to the disagreeable necessity of sending them to dwell with those beings, for the Company of whom alone their Tempers and dispositions are not suitable.

Isaac Bangs

1864 [Confederate POW camp, Andersonville, Georgia]

Have bought off a new prisoner (quite a large thick, I mean) blank book, so as to continue my diary. Although it's a tedious and tiresome task, am determined to keep it up. Don't know of another man in prison who is doing likewise. Wish I had the gift of description, that I might describe this place. Know that I am not good at such things.

Nothing can be worse or nastier than the stream drizzling its way through this camp. On all four sides of us are high walls and tall trees, and there is apparently no wind or breeze to blow away the stench, and we are obliged to breathe and live in it. Dead bodies lay around all day in the broiling sun, by the dozen and even hundreds. It's too horrible for me to describe in fitting language.

Only those who are here will ever know what Andersonville is.

John Ransom

1941 [London]

There is nothing to indicate what is going on across the channel. The Nazis have evolved a perfect system of controlling the lands they seize. As soon as they take over, down come the window shades. Only the British air force keeps up a daily patrol by day, observing and photo- graphing and bombing at night. They come home with great tales of the damage they have done but it they haven't succeeded any better than the Germans, they have wasted their time. Fritz has been bombing the Bristol area every night now for two weeks but our consul there reports no material damage. There is a story told me today of a hearty air raid warden who was asked what damage had been done by a bomb in his neighborhood. 'None at all, sir' he said. 'Hit only 'it a soft-drink factory. But, blimey, if hit 'ad fallen a little further on, hit would 'ave 'it the brewery.'

General Raymond E. Lee

1942 [Amsterdam]

Dearest Kitty,

After we arrived at 263 Prinsengracht, Miep[1] quickly led us through the long passage and up the wooden staircase to the next floor and into the Annexe. She shut the door behind us, leaving us alone. Margot had arrived much earlier on her bike and was waiting for us.

Our living-room and all the other rooms were so full of stuff that I can't find the words to describe it. All the cardboard boxes that had been sent to the office in the last few months were piled on the floors and beds. The small room was filled from floor to ceiling with linen. If we wanted to sleep in properly made beds that night, we had to get going and tidy up the mess. Mother and Margot were unable to move a muscle. They lay down on their bare mattresses, tired, miserable and I don't know what else. But Father and I, the two cleaner-uppers in the family, started in right away.

All day long we unpacked boxes, filled cupboards, hammered nails and tidied up the mess, until we fell exhausted into our clean beds at night. We hadn't eaten a hot meal all day, but we didn't care; Mother and Margot were too tired and keyed up to eat, and Father and I were too busy.

Tuesday morning we started where we left off the night before.

[1] Miep Gies, one of her father's employees.

Bep[1] and Miep went shopping with our ration coupons, Father worked on our black-out screens, we scrubbed the kitchen floor, and were once again busy from morning to night. Until Wednesday, I didn't have a chance to think about the enormous change in my life. Then for the first time since our arrival in the Secret Annexe, I found a moment to tell you all about it and to realize what had happened to me and what was yet to happen.

Anne Frank

1943 [off Sicily]

On board a ship of the Castle Line. On deck till 3 a.m. Nothing to see from our beaches but Syracuse seems to be getting a most terrific plastering. Flares and ack ack, all through the night then lugubrious voice over the loud speaker ordering crews to their respective craft and craft convoy.

Up on deck at dawn. Sea dotted with vessels in the first light. Distant sky-line of mountains, flashes of gunfire and verey lights from shore. Sense of anxiety. Staff waiting news. Lovely view as sun rises. Noto on its hill, fire burning with cherry-coloured flames. Naval shelling. L.C.A.s [Landing Craft Assault] coming back, some with wounded on board, evidence of a great deal of sea sickness. Things sorting themselves out. More cheerful atmosphere. Still on board by 9.00. Sea dotted with warships, transports, L.S.M. [Landing Ship Medium], L.C.T.s [Landing Craft Tank] etc. Some shelling by warships. Little sign of activity on shore. Land looks very quiet and peaceful in the sunshine, contrast to this morning with its cold, lumy sea, L.C.A.s going off and wounded coming back, verey lights and bombs on shore. Extraordinary, no sign of enemy aircraft.

Arrive on shore in L.C.A., wade through surf up to knees. Tank landing craft, all manner of craft disembarking men and stores. Enemy aircraft, troops taking cover in high maize. Walk through walled olive and orange groves to Div. H.Q. Walk into Avola with Bob. Meet John [Polson], [John] Soboleff and [Ronnie] Monson, collect an aged revolver. Drink wine with some peasants. A few dead and wounded beside the road. Black-faced parachutists, some Yanks. Make a P.R. Encampment in orchard of lemons, really lovely. Go down to beach to make some drawings. Return to my grove just in time to miss some stuka raids. Soldiers digging slit trenches among the trees. Wash my feet

[1] Bep Voskuijl, another of her father's employees.

in very cold water running as an irrigation-ditch. Picnic supper to the sound of running water. Frequent raids on the beach and shipping.

Edward Ardizzone

1944 [England]

At the hairdresser the girl who washed my hair said that on Sunday she and her husband had gone round to tidy up her father's flat which had been blasted by bomb damage. They got the place into working order for him and started back home. At the end of the road wardens and firemen were still clearing up the street and from the windows of a big block of flats the people looked down on the street scene. 'They weren't sightseers, you understand,' she said, 'only ordinary people looking out at the fire engines. They were old women and children, girls and soldiers on leave.' Then suddenly she had seen the pilotless plane descending in an arc curve at great speed. She called out to her husband and flung her arms round a pillar box. Her husband had thrown her down the area steps and fallen after her. They heard the glass come crashing in around the area and when she looked up she saw her father running down the street waving his arms and calling out, 'My children were there.' The girl told me, 'All the time I see those people in my mind, with the plane coming down on to the roof and them not knowing anything about it.' She said several times, 'All those people – all those people. I don't seem able to forget them – all those people.'

Inez Holden

1944 [Germany]

This is no time for jokes, but two stories of 'Count Bobb' [popular figure of fun] illustrate how things are.

(1) He is drafted, and says to the staff surgeon: 'I would like to serve at the Führer's headquarters!'

'Are you crazy'

'Is that one of the requirements?'

(2) He is looking at a globe, and it is being explained to him that the large 'green area is Russia; the red area, the British Empire; the pale lilac, the United States; and the yellow, China' – all great areas.

'And that little blue spot?' he asks.

'That is Germany.'

'Hm. Does the Führer know how small it is?'

Ulrich Von Hassell

11 July

1864 [Confederate POW camp, Andersonville, Georgia]
This morning lumber was brought into the prison by the Rebels, and near the gate a *gallows* erected, for the purpose of executing the six condemned Yankees. At about ten o'clock they were brought inside by Captain Wirtz and some guards, and delivered over to the police force.

Captain Wirtz then said a few words about them having been tried by our own men, and for us to do as we choose with them; that he washed his hands of the whole matter.

After Wirtz made his speech, he withdrew his guards, leaving the condemned at the mercy of 28,000 enraged prisoners, who had all been more or less wronged by these men.

All were given a chance to talk. Munn, a good looking fellow in marine dress, said he came into prison four months before, perfectly honest, and as innocent of crime as any fellow in it. Starvation, with evil companions, had made him what he was. He spoke of his mother and sisters in New York, that he cared nothing as far as he himself was concerned, but the news that would be carried home to his people made him want to curse God he had ever been born.

Delaney said he would rather be hung than live here as the most of them lived, on their allowances of rations. If allowed to steal, could get enough to eat, but as that was stopped had rather hang. Bid all good bye. Said his name was not Delaney, and that no one knew who he really was, therefore his friends would never know his fate, his Andersonville history dying with him.

Curtiss said he didn't care a ———, only hurry up, and not be talking about it all day; making too much fuss over a very small matter.

William Collins, alias Moseby, said he was innocent of murder and ought not to be hung; he had stolen blankets and rations to preserve his own life and begged the crowd not to see him hung as he had a wife and child at home, and for their sake to let him live.

The excited crowd began to be impatient for the 'show' to commence, as they termed it.

Sarfield made quite a speech. He had studied for a lawyer; at the outbreak of the rebellion he had enlisted and served three years in the army, been wounded in battle, furloughed home, wound healed up, promoted to First Sergeant, and also commissioned; his commission as a Lieutenant had arrived but had not been mustered in when he was taken prisoner; began by stealing parts of rations, gradually becoming hardened as he came familiar with the crimes practiced; evil associates had helped him to go down hill, and here he was.

The others did not care to say anything. While the men were talking they were interrupted by all kinds of questions and charges made by the crowd, such as 'don't lay it on too thick, you villain,' 'get ready to jump off,' 'cut it short,' 'you was the cause of so and so's death,' 'less talk and more hanging.'

At about eleven o'clock they were all blindfolded, hands and feet tied, told to get ready, nooses adjusted, and the plank knocked from under. Moseby's rope broke and he fell to the ground with blood spurting from his ears, mouth and nose. As they were lifting him back to the swinging-off place he revived and begged for his life, but no use, was soon dangling with the rest, and died very hard.

I occupied a near position to the hanging, and saw it all from first to last, and stood there until they were taken down and carried away. Was a strange sight to see, and the first hanging I ever witnessed.

Rebel negroes came inside and began to take down the scaffold; prisoners took hold to help them, and resulted in its all being carried off to different parts of the prison to be used for kindling wood, and the Rebels got none of it back, and are mad.

John Ransom

1941 [Rome]

Naples was bombed – very bad. Not so much on account of the number of victims as because of the damage, of which the most serious was the fire of the Italian-American refineries. We lost 6,000 tons of oil, and God only knows how much we needed it. The Duce said, 'I am happy that Naples is having such severe nights. The breed will harden, the war will make of the Neapolitans a Nordic race.' Of this I am very sceptical.

Count Ciano

1942 [Amsterdam]

Dearest Kitty,

Last night the four of us went down to the private office and listened to England on the wireless. I was so scared someone might hear it that I literally begged Father to take me back upstairs. Mother understood my anxiety and went with me. Whatever we do, we're very afraid the neighbours might hear or see us. We started off immediately the first day sewing curtains. Actually, you can hardly call them that, since they're nothing but scraps of fabric, varying greatly in shape, quality and pattern, which Father and I stitched crookedly together with unskilled fingers. These works of art were tacked to the windows, where they'll stay until we come out of hiding.

Anne Frank

1943 [on board USS *Montpelier*, in the Pacific]
I think the rugged routine that we have had for the past 7 months has something to do with the way the men have been acting lately. The men have noticed it themselves doing it. Your mind goes blank and you find yourself walking around some part of the ship, some distance from where you want to go, and then it dawns on you that you are not supposed to be there. You forget what day it is, what you had for breakfast, what you did in the morning. You find yourself in the wash-room with no soap or towel. When you turn the water on, then it dawns on you. You forget to take your toothbrush and paste with you, until you begin to brush your teeth. You go in to take a shower without towel or soap. Some of the fellows have lighted a cigarette in their mouths and asked for a match to light theirs. When you wake up, you think it is time to go on watch etc. These things sneak up on you before you know it.

James J. Fahey, Seaman First Class

12 July

1864 [Confederate POW camp, Andersonville, Georgia]
Good order has prevailed since the hanging. The men have settled down to the business of dying with no interruption. I keep thinking our situation can get no worse, but it does get worse every day, and not less than one hundred and sixty die each twenty-four hours.

All day up to four o'clock p.m., the dead are being gathered up and carried to the south gate and place in a row inside the dead line. As the bodies are stripped of their clothing, in most cases as soon as the breath leaves, and in some cases before, the row of dead presents a sickening appearance. Legs drawn up in all shapes. They are black from pitch pine smoke and laying in the sun. Some of them lay there for twenty hours or more, and by that time are in a horrible condition.

At four o'clock a four or six-mule wagon comes up to the gate, and bodies are loaded on to the wagon and they are carted off to be put in trenches, one hundred in each trench, in the cemetery, which is eighty or a hundred rods away.

I was invited today to dig a tunnel, but had to decline. My digging days are over. It is with difficulty now that I can walk, and only with the help of two canes.

John Ransom

1915 [France]
Shelling going on, nothing very great. 7.30p.m. I clicked. I stopped about 20 pieces of a rifle grenade with my leg. Am bandaged up and taken to see advanced dressing station, where I arrive about 8.30. There I am re-dressed, taken to the dressing station at Vielle Chapelle by Motor Ambulance. Here I am examined by Doctor, dressed again. Spend the night here on a stretcher in a barn.

Pvt Montague S. Goodbar, 4th Battalion Cameron Highlanders

1941 [Egypt]
In T.'s flat again, we talked from midnight until 2 this morning, mainly of a project of his to go to, say, Yugoslavia after the war, a small colony of us (but not *called* a colony or anything precious), build our own cabins in the mountains, and live happily communally there, and work . . .

Erik de Mauny

13 July

1916 [France]
I keep reading *Tess* and *The Return of the Native* – they fit in admirably with my thoughts.

Siegfried Sassoon

1940 [London]
The Germans have been trying to convince us that they will invade us tonight. There is a goodish gibbous moon and fine weather. I go to bed without apprehension.

Ben [his son] has bought a Picasso portrait of a woman entirely composed of grey cubes. It was very expensive. It is a determined portrait and it says what it thinks. But I do not like these affirmations in art. I like art to be a relief and not a challenge. But Ben, who is far more expert than I am, regrets this sentimental approach. I am sure he is right.

Harold Nicolson

14 July

1776 [New York]

Mr Brown, another Lieutenant, was dispatched with a Flag of Truce to Washington at New York. He was stopped by three Boats at a little Distance from the Town, demanding his Business. Upon being told that he had a Letter from Lord Howe to their Commander, they ordered him to lay to, while one of the Boats went to the Shore for Directions. In a short time, three officers came off, and desired to know to whom the Letter was addressed. They would not touch it, but begged the Lieutenant to read it. As the Address was, *To George Washington Esq.* &c. &c. &c. they said, there was so such Person among them, and therefore would not receive it. Upon being asked what Address they required, it was answered that 'all the World knew who Genl. Washington was since the Transactions of last Summer.' So high is the Vanity and the Insolence of these Men! The Truth is, the Punctilio of an Address would never have retarded the Reception of a Letter from a Person, with whose Rank & Commission they were well acquainted, and whose Bravery & honor are so well known every where; if their Minds had been in the least disposed to the Duties of Humanity, Law and Allegiance. They have uniformly blocked up every Avenue to Peace, and whenever they have pretended to make Advances of that kind, they have always done it in a mode, that they knew well (and, because they knew, designed) was inadmissible, upon every Principle of Honor and Decency. There now seems no Alternative but War and Bloodshed, which must lay at the Door of these unhappy People: They pretend (or rather have pretended) to seek peace, and yet renounce it. The Faction have thrown aside all Appearances at length, and declare openly for Independence & War.

Ambrose Serle

1940 [England]

[At Chequers, the PM's official country residence] The PM has strong views on food rationing. He thinks it absurd to make it excessive when our supplies are as good as at present. In a letter to his Minister of Food, Lord Woolton, he says: 'Almost all the food faddists I have ever known, nut eaters and the like, have died young after a long period of senile decay. The British soldier is far more likely to be right than the scientists. All he cares about is beef . . . The way to lose the war is to try to force the British public into a diet of milk, oatmeal, potatoes, etc., washed down on gala occasions with a little limejuice.' The ideas are, I think, taken from Nat Gubbins in the *Sunday Express,* whom Winston and all his family read with avidity.

John Colville

1940 [London]

Jo [a boyfriend] joined up yesterday as a rear-gunner. The average life of an RG is supposed to be five flights.

'So what?' Jo says. 'Feed, fight, fornicate and die dramatically!' I told him he'd better be careful his wounds were dramatic ones, as he'd be sitting in the back of the plane. I still won't let Jo kiss me. 'Jesus,' he says, 'and this is the generation I'm going to die for?'

Joan Wyndham

1944 [on board USS *Montpelier,* in the Pacific]

After supper while we were out patrolling Saipan the fellows passed the time running from one side of the ship to the other, watching the Jap bodies float by. You could get a good look at them as they passed, because they were very close to the ship. Some were on their stomachs, others on their backs, they floated along like rubber balls. Some had army uniforms on, and others had no clothes on at all. They were bloated and their skin looked white. One looked like his back was all burnt. We counted 20 bodies just around our ship in no time at all and then stopped counting. If this was in the South Pacific those bodies would not be floating around very long, maybe the sharks are full.

James J. Fahey, Seaman First Class

15 July

1694 [London]

My Lord Berkely burnt Dieppe and Haverdegrace with the bombs in revenge of the defeat at Brest: This manner of destructive warring begun every where by the French, tho' it be exceeding ruinous, especialy falling on the poorer people, and is very barbarous, does not seem to tend to make any sooner [the] end of the War but rather to exasperate, and incite to revenge.

John Evelyn

1940 [London]

This is the date I have fixed in my own mind as the edge of the blitzkrieg season. I believe Hitler will attack this island with everything he has at any moment from now on. I also believe that if he is not successful by the fifteenth of September, he will never be.

General Raymond E. Lee

16 July

1776 [New York]

An American News Paper was put into my Hands, full of Bitterness and Malignancy. The following Sentence may serve for a Specimen. 'Be assured, the Sun, moon & Stars shall fall, the Ocean cease to roll, and all nature change its Course, before a few English, Scotch & German *Slaves* shall conquer this vast country.' There are several other Paragraphs in the Paper equally full of Nonsense, Madness & Fury.

Ambrose Serle

1916 [France]

Tonight I'm hungry for music. And still the guns boom, and the battle goes on three miles away. And Robert's[1] [Graves] somewhere in it, if he hasn't been shot already. He wants to travel with me after the war; anywhere – Russia for preference. And whenever I am with him, I want to do wild things, and get right away from the conventional silliness of my old life. Blighty! What a world of idle nothingness the

---

[1] Robert Graves, poet and novelist. He survived the war, dying in 1985.

name stands for; and what a world of familiar delightfulness! O god, when shall I get out of this limbo? For I'm never alone here – never my old self – always acting a part – that of the cheery, reckless sportsman – out for a dip at the Bosches. But the men love me, that's one great consolation. And some day perhaps I'll be alone in a room full of books again, with a piano glimmering in the corner, and glory in my head, and a new poem in my notebook.

Now the rain begins to patter on the tent and the dull thudding of guns comes from Albert way; and I've still got my terrible way to tread before I'm free to sleep with Rupert Brooke and [Charles Hamilton] Sorley[1] and all the nameless poets of the war.

Siegfried Sassoon

1940 [England]

After lunch and looking about the field, which is heavily barricaded, wired and fortified, we said goodbye to Beamish, the CO, and went on to see some new shell craters. One of the extraordinary things about all the German bombing so far is the little damage it has done. Here four large ones, presumably five hundred pounds, were dumped aimlessly. One fell within a hundred feet of a farmhouse. No windows were broken and no one hurt. The crater itself was thirty-five feet in diameter and thirty feet deep. On its edge was a barn containing a horse, a cow and a bull, none hurt. A pig was transfixed by a flying splinter of wood and a rooster was killed. That is all. The other three bombs fell in an open field and through some defect in their fuses, went off deep in the ground and did no damage at all, the only evidence being the smallish hole through which they entered the ground. We then went on to see a heavily defended port, which looks straight across the Channel. This was the front line but we put up at one of the fine and well-run railroad hotels. Ordinarily at this season it would be swarming with holiday-makers but now our party, with a few of the officers stationed there, were the only diners. We had a really good (British) dinner, with all our British guides and friends as guests. This was the most luxurious front line I had ever seen and about midnight, after having visited the AA [anti-aircraft] control room, we turned in in luxurious double rooms.

General Raymond E. Lee

[1] Sorley was killed in action in 1915.

1940 [Berlin]

Today at the office [Drahtloser Dienst (Wireless Service)] I received, by mistake, a blank sheet with a yellow strip across. These are usually reserved for specially important news. As I had nothing better to do, I typed out on it an alleged rumour about a riot in London, with the King hanged at the gates of Buckingham Palace, and passed it on to an idiotic girl who promptly translated it and included it in a news broadcast to South Africa. The boss, who has to vet any outgoing news item, recognised it as mine because of some German grammatical mistakes. As he was feeling mellow today, he took it well.

Marie 'Missie' Vassiltchikov

1943 [Kovno Ghetto, Lithuania]

Yesterday [SS Master Sergeant] Schtitz informed Dr Elkes – via Dr Kvitner – that he would be coming to the Ghetto at eight o'clock in the morning. He asked Dr Elkes to come to Lipzer's[1] room at that time; he would be waiting for Dr Elkes there. Schtitz feels unwell; he wants Dr Elkes to examine him.

The Nazi Race Laws forbid any such examination of a German by a Jew. But nothing is forbidden when Schtitz's health is at stake. The Nazi chiefs have a free hand in that respect. They are scrupulous in observing the regulations pertaining to the purity of the race as far as the German people are concerned, not to mention the Jews. There is, however, a world of difference between theory and practice. Every Nazi leader, large and small, maintains regular contacts with Jewish skilled workers: a seamstress making dresses for women: a cobbler who can make a pair of Prussian knee boots, etc. All this in addition to Jewish housemaids. Every Nazi everywhere does this: Jaeger of the Gestapo, General Wysocki of the German police, the German Army, the airfield administration, the civil administration, and, indeed, all other branches of the German government here.

Schtitz is in charge of Jewish affairs at the Gestapo. His attitude to the Jewish question is unyielding and cruel. He murders Jews and takes possession of their property. At the same time, he uses Lipzer to place orders in the Ghetto for toys to be made for the son of his mistress. He orders kitchen knives, rings, earrings and other pieces of jewelry

---

[1] Benno Lipzer, he worked with the Gestapo in order to help fellow Jews. He was eventually murdered by the Germans.

not only for his mistress and his wife, but also for numerous personal acquaintances.

Schtitz has not been feeling well recently. Although turning for help to a Jewish physician is against regulations, the regulations do not apply to a man like Schtitz or his friends.

Now Schtitz is sitting in Lipzer's room, consulting Dr Elkes about his health. He tells Dr Elkes that his powers are waning; also his kidneys are not in good repair. He asks the Jewish doctor to examine him and to prescribe medicine for his illness. He wants to be healthy, he wants to be as strong as he used to be. Dr Elkes listens seriously. He regards the man sitting in front of him, not as a cruel Nazi chief, but as a sick man in need of medical assistance.

Dr Elkes asks Schtitz whether he sleeps well at night. Schtitz replies that, yes, he does sleep well. 'Do you have dreams?' asks Dr Elkes. 'No,' replies Schtitz.

Dr Elkes is torn between his obligations as a Jew – as leader of the Jewish community in the Ghetto – and his sense of duty as a physician. But this inner conflict lasts only for a moment. The sense of duty gains the upper hand. Dr Elkes makes a diagnosis and prescribes the necessary medicines. He is discharging his duties as a physician.

At the end of the examination Schtitz attempts to play the part of an old friend of the Jews. 'Are things quiet now in the Ghetto?' he asks. Dr Elkes replies that the Ghetto is, indeed, quiet. 'After my last call on Jaeger and you,' he adds, 'the people here sighed with relief.' 'I am pleased,' says Schtitz, 'that I could make my own contribution towards the relaxation of tension in the Ghetto. Nothing bad is going to happen in the Ghetto in the future.'

Schtitz shakes Dr Elkes's hand and thanks him for the treatment. There are no grounds to believe that he meant what he said to a Jewish doctor, chairman of the Jewish community. Today I recalled the case of Erich Kohn. Schtitz sent him for a medical examination when the man was sick. When the man recuperated, he executed him. I believe that Schtitz's time will also come. Nobody will come to his aid then.

Avraham Tory

1943 [Italy]
Leave for Syracuse, however meet Laming between Carbentini and Lentini, change our minds and all have picnic on a little plateau. Terraces

with orange trees below us, the usual old olives . . . Tragedy, find Ronnie's bed roll lost.

I do some drawings and have a snooze. We drink a bottle of Ronnie's champagne. Heaven. Brought to earth by the smell of dead bodies hidden somewhere, a smell that haunts one everywhere. Head back for Syracuse, pass an open lorry of Italian prisoners in civilian dress, a dejected lot. The MP [Military Police] in charge told us they were paratroops wearing civis dress, they will probably be shot. I think by the look of them they realised that too.

Edward Ardizzone

17 July

1864 [Confederate POW camp, Andersonville, Georgia]
Succeeded in getting four small onions about as large as hickory nuts, tops and all, for two dollars, Confederate money. Battese furnished the money but won't eat an onion; ask him if he is afraid it will make his breath smell. It is said that two or three onions or a sweet potato eaten raw daily will cure the scurvy. What a shame that such things are denied us, being so plenty the world over. Never appreciated such things before, but shall hereafter. Am talking as if I expected to get home again. I do.

John Ransom

1941 [Rome]
Mussolini, as usual, speaks of the military men bitterly, and says that he likes only one general, I forget his name, who, in Albania, said to his soldiers, 'I have heard that you are good family men. That's fine at home, but not here. Here, you will never go too far in being thieves, murderers, and rapists.'

Count Ciano

18 July

1942 [Dresden]
Last Thursday the Marckwalds gave me a bag of potatoes – but they said they would hardly still be edible. Indeed, they stank and were

falling disgustingly apart. Nevertheless today I brushed and boiled about half of what I had lugged over here, the ones which were still just about holding together. And truly a few pieces of some were edible. Disgusting.

Victor Klemperer

1942 [POW camp, Java]

Slapping is rather in vogue again. About eight of the Australian *corvées* [fatigue parties] coming in today were slapped down for bringing in cigarettes, though this is often permitted. They were allowed to retain the cigarettes. The Nipponese who slapped them was very short and had to swing wildly, far uphill. The results were rather devastating actually – a ruptured eardrum, a broken tooth plate and a tooth knocked out. We have not had this sort of thing for some time.

Weary Dunlop

19 July

1915 [France]

Underwent another operation to have remaining pieces of shrapnel removed from leg.

Pvt Montague S. Goodbar, 4th Battalion Cameron Highlanders

1942 [Kovno Ghetto, Lithuania]

Israel Berlin, fifty-two, committed suicide by hanging himself. Lately he had been apathetic to his surroundings.

Avraham Tory

1943 [London]

In the afternoon I took the Polesden pictures to the National Gallery. Kenneth Clark met me in the vestibule to discuss their arrangement. Before I left he showed me a Rothschild collection of French pictures which he is housing. I urged him to exhibit them, but he said he couldn't.

On returning in the bus I was put into a paroxsym of rage on reading in the evening paper that Rome had been bombed. I was to have seen Harold [Nicolson] tonight. I did not go for I should have been hysterical and abused the Government. Instead I drank three Pimm's No. 1

with Jamesey at the Carlton Hotel. Together we vented our rage over the bombing. He said Churchill had sanctioned it, with 'I don't care a damn what buildings they destroy.' Then I dined with Johnny Dashwood at the Travellers' and drank a whisky and soda, a bottle of Burgundy and a glass of port – and came home sober.

James Lees-Milne

20 July

1776 [New York]
Read over [John] Adam's Pamphlet, entitled 'Common Sense.' A most flagitious Performance, replete with Sophistry, Impudence & Falshood; but unhappily calculated to work upon the Fury of the Times, and to induce the full avowal of the Spirit of Independence in the warm & inconsiderate. His Attempt to justify Rebellion by the Bible is infamous beyond Expression. That Religion, which renders Men bad Subjects and bad Citizens, can never be of GOD, who instituted Civil Government that all things might be done decently, and in order. He is not the author of Confusion, but of Peace.

Ambrose Serle

1861 [Washington]
The great battle [Bull Run] which is to arrest rebellion or to make it a power in the land, is no longer distant or doubtful. [General] McDowell has completed his reconnaissance in front of the enemy, and General Sutt anticipates he will be in possession of Manassas tomorrow night. All the statements of officers concur in describing the Confederates as strongly entrenched along the line of Bull's Run covering the railroad. The New York papers, indeed, audaciously declare that the enemy have fallen back in disorder. In the main thoroughfares of the city there is still a scattered army of idle soldiers moving through the civil crowd, though how they came here no one knows. The officers clustering round the hotels, and running in and out of the bar-rooms and eating-houses, are still more numerous. When I inquired at the head-quarters who these were, the answer was that the majority were skulkers, that there was no power at such a moment to send them back to their regiments or punish them. In fact, deducting the reserves, the rear-guards, and the scanty garrisons at the earth-works, McDowell

will not have 25,000 men to undertake his seven day's march through a hostile country to the Confederate capital; yet, strange to say, in the pride and passion of the politicians, no doubt is permitted to rise for a moment respecting his complete success.

William Howard Russell

1864 [Georgia]

Today we engaged in a terrible battle with the Rebs at Peach Tree Creek. At 2:00 o'clock PM our brigade which was at the left Rank of the corps, joined the 4th Corps in battle line. The enemy attacked at which time we advanced. Our regiment was always in the forward battle line. We advanced over a small hill and into a valley in which a small creek flowed. Then the Rebs came toward us down the hill in front of us. Now the firing really began. The gunfire exceeded anything I had ever heard before. We loaded and fired as fast as possible. The Rebs came to within 10 paces of us, at which time our musket balls became too thick for them. They turned to the right and retreated up the hill with us behind them. This was a sight which I had never seen before and hope never to see again. The entire field was scattered with dead, wounded and dying. The wounded moaned so much that I could hardly watch. However, we had no time and had to advance up the hill. There stood a fence behind which we petitioned ourselves. The Rebs tried to advance again but did not succeed, because a battery was placed on the hill behind us which greeted the enemy terribly with cannonballs. After 4 hours of firing, we were finally relieved and went to the second battle line. The firing lasted into the night. At night I helped carry more wounded from the field. We also captured a flag from the 33rd Mississippi Regiment.

Pvt Frederick C. Buerstatte, 26th Regiment, Wisconsin Volunteers

1940 [England]

I think that Hitler will probably invade us within the next few days. He has 6,000 aeroplanes ready for the job.[1] How strange it all is! We know that we are faced with a terrific invasion. We half-know that the odds are heavily against us. Yet there is a sort of exhilaration in the air. If Hitler were to postpone invasion and fiddle about in Africa and the Mediterranean, our morale might weaken. But we are really proud

[1] The actual number was 2,670 fighters and bombers deployed in the West.

to be the people who will not give way. The reaction to Hitler's speech yesterday[1] is a good reaction. Yet I know well that we shall be exposed to horrible punishment. It is so strange that in this moment of anxiety there is no hatred of Hitler or the Germans. Opinion slides off into oblique animosities such as criticism of the Old Gang and rage that the LDV [Local Defence Volunteers] are not better equipped. All this is dangerous, since it is in essence a form of escapism and appease-ment. We are really frightened of Hitler, and avoid the dynamic resist-ance to him which is uniform hatred. 130 years ago all this hatred was concentrated against Bonaparte. We flinch today from central enmity. If we are invaded we may become angry.

Harold Nicolson

1944 [England]
An attack on Hitler's life, but unfortunately the bastard wasn't killed.

Joan Wyndham

21 July

1861 [Washington]
The calmness and silence of the streets of Washington this lovely morning suggested thoughts of the very different scenes which, in all probability, were taking place at a few miles' distance. One could fancy the hum and stir round the Federal bivouacs, as the troops woke up and were formed into column of march towards the enemy. I much regretted that I was not enabled to take the field with General McDowell's army, but my position was surrounded with such difficulties that I could not pursue the course open to the correspondent of the American newspapers . . . Hence, all I could do was to make a journey to see the army in the field, and to return to Washington to write my report of its first oper-ation . . . There was no *entente cordiale* exhibited towards me by the members of the American press; nor did they, any more than the gener-als, evince any disposition to help the alien correspondent of the *Times* . . . General McDowell, on giving me the most hospitable invitation to his quarters, refrained from offering the assistance which, perhaps, it was not in his power to afford; and I confess, looking at the matter calmly,

---

[1] To the Reichstag, hinting at the possibility of discussing peace terms with Britain.

I could scarcely expect that he would, particularly as he said, half in jest, half seriously, 'I declare I am not quite easy at the idea of having your eye on me, for you have seen so much of European armies, you will, very naturally, think little of us, generals and all.'

William Howard Russell

1864 [Georgia]

This morning our regiment, after a sleepless night, had to bury the dead Rebs which laid before our regiment. They were all from the 33rd Mississippi regiment. Our regiment lost 9 dead and 36 wounded. We buried over 50 Rebs, among them Colonel Drake and most of the officers of the 33rd Miss. Regiment. Now we had to clean our guns.

Pvt Frederick C. Buerstatte, 26th Regiment, Wisconsin Volunteers

1941 [London]

While the barber, a very serious artist, was shaving me this morning, I said, 'This moustache of mine is getting to be too bushy, too umbrageous. What are we going to do about it?' 'Well, sir,' he said, 'you will remember that you put me in charge of it when you returned here last year, and I advised you to let it alone. It has grown beautifully ever since, sir, and in fact it is nearly perfect.' 'I think so, too,' I replied, 'but the fact remains that it is too luxurious, and when it comes down over my lip I can't abide it, something must be done.' He tried to pass this off and said that it was too important a matter to deal with in my bath, and at that time of day. 'However,' he said, 'we might discuss it further when you come to have your hair cut, and that certainly will be some time this week.'

I stopped in at six o'clock, and had my hair trimmed, and then to his dismay, said, 'The moment is now come for the operation on the moustache, or the amputation, if you prefer to regard it seriously.'

He tried again to dissuade me from tinkering with it, but found me adamant and so began, very unwillingly, to singe it gently here and there. Then he brought the mirror, but to me it looked exactly as before. Therefore I said firmly, 'It must be reduced in size.' 'But, General,' he said, plaintively, 'if we go any further with it that moustache will get completely out of our control.' After some discussion, I made him cut it back and prune it rather relentlessly, but he is as unhappy and glum as can be. I think he feels that this moustache belongs to him more than it does to me, and that I am quite unworthy of having such an ornament.

After I paid my bill and he said good-bye, he added, 'I am very unhappy because I feel that we are going to have trouble with that moustache.'

General Raymond E. Lee

22 July

1861 [Washington]

I perceived several waggons coming from the direction of the battle-field [Bull Run], the drivers of which were endeavouring to force their horses past the ammunition carts going in the contrary direction near the bridge, a thick cloud of dust rose behind them, and running by the side of the waggons, were a number of men in uniform whom I supposed to be the guards. My first impression was that the waggons were returning for fresh supplies of ammunition . . . But every moment the crowd increased, drivers and men cried out with the most vehement of gestures, 'Turn back! Turn back! We are whipped.' They seized the leads of the horses and swore at opposing drivers. Emerging from the crowd a breathless man in the uniform of the office with an empty scabbard dangling by his side, was cut off by getting between my horse and cart for a moment. 'What is the matter, sir? What is all this about?' 'Why it means we are pretty badly whipped, that's the truth,' he gasped, and continued. The crowd up front continually increased, the heat, the uproar, and the dust were beyond description, and these were augmented when some cavalry soldiers, flourishing their sabres, and preceded by an officer, who cried out, 'Make way there – make way there for the General,' attempting to force a covered waggon in which was seated a man with a bloody handkerchief round his head, through the press.

William Howard Russell

1915 [France]

Doc came round and put a 'B' on my board, which I find stands for 'Boat' – not Blighty although it's the same thing. Well of course my spirits rose to boiling point.[1]

Pvt Montague S. Goodbar, 4th Battalion Cameron Highlanders

---

[1] He was shipped home to convalesce after an operation to remove the rifle grenade shrapnel from his leg.

1940 [Berlin]
Hitler has given Mussolini a birthday present. It's an anti-aircraft armoured train.

William L. Shirer

1941 [Rome]
Dummy air raids continue at Rome. It was the Duce who personally ordered an air raid in the capital every time there is one in Naples. He does this because he wants to give the country the impression that a war is taking place. He has also ordered that at the first opportunity anti-aircraft should fire in order to make it more exciting. Is all this worthwhile?

Count Ciano

23 July

1776 [New York]
Gvr. Tryon called upon us this Morning. Adml. Shuldham and the Captains of the Fleet dined with us. In the Evening the Chaplain and myself took a Walk upon Staten Island for a considerable Way. The Scenes were romantic to the Eye, though barren for the most part in the Soil. We met several People who had just escaped out of Long Island from the Tyranny of those insolent Demagogues, who, under pretences of superior Liberty, are imposing upon all about them the worse of Bondage. It excited one's Sympathy to see their poor meagre Faces, and to hear their Complaints of being hunted for their Lives like Game into the Woods and Swamps, only because they would not renounce their allegiance to their King and affection for their Country; These are some of the choicest Blessings of the Faction, which pretends to Religion, Patriotism, and a hundred other Virtues, but knows nothing of any of them but by their Name.

Ambrose Serle

1861 [Washington]
I awake from a deep sleep this morning, about six o'clock. The rain was falling in torrents and beat with a dull, thuddy sound on the leads outside my window; but, louder than all, came a strange sound, as if of the tread of men, a confused tramp and splashing, and a

murmuring of voices. I got up and ran to the front room, the windows of which looked on the street, and there, to my intense surprise, I saw a steady stream of men covered with mud, soaked through with rain, who were pouring irregularly, without any semblance of order, up Pennsylvania Avenue towards the Capitol. A dense stream of vapour rose from the multitude, but looking closely at the men, I perceived they belonged to different regiments, New Yorkers, Michiganders, Rhode Islanders, Massachusetters, Minnesotians, mingled pell-mell together. Many of them were without knapsacks, cross belts, and fire-locks. Some had neither greatcoats nor shoes, others were covered with blankets. Hastily putting on my clothes, I ran downstairs and asked an 'officer' who was passing by, a pale young man, who looked exhausted to death, and who had lost his sword, for the empty sheath dangled at his side, 'Where from? Well, Sir, I guess we're all coming out of Verginny as far as we can, and pretty well whipped too.' 'What! the whole army, sir?' 'That's more than I know. They may stay like that. I know I'm going home. I've had enough of fighting to last my lifetime.'

William Howard Russell

1940 [London]

There are many things about London which the war has changed. There is much less traffic in town and very few cars on the country roads. Policemen and LDV's are much more inquisitive and one is scrutinized by everyone more carefully. Perhaps it is my straw hat.

The clubs have waitresses instead of men.

No one dresses any more. Most of the men are in uniform.

Most people carry gas masks and everyone must have identification and ration cards.

One gets only a lump of sugar and a thin little flake of butter.

No more iced cakes. Fewer kinds of cheese.

Only six pages in the newspapers. All paper is saved. Iron railings are being torn down and all metal junk is salvaged.

Many women are in uniform, driving cars and ambulances. Others are bus conductors, landworkers, munitions workers.

Lights are all cut off or shaded after dusk on pain of heavy fines or even a month's imprisonment.

Theaters are mostly closed and the hotels have only the merest handful of guests. Claridge's is like a lamb except at luncheon.

At every road junction or bend there is some sort of pillbox and there are barriers of concrete at frequent intervals along them.

A belt of coast about twenty miles wide has had all foreigners removed and most of the natives who have no business there evacuated. No one is allowed on the beaches, which are, in fact, mostly covered with barbed wire entanglements.

No radios are allowed in cars and any car which is left must have both ignition and windows locked. If not, the police come along and let the air out of the tires.

General Raymond E. Lee

1940 [POW camp, Germany]

Got a basinful of macaroni from German cook. Had been a prisoner in England during the last war. Very decent chap. Thinks war will soon be over now. France has given in. Hope he is right. He was as fed up as me with it.

Sergeant L.D. Pexton, British Army

1941 [Lewes, England]

Margaret Hill said that all the Lewes girls were having babies by the French-Canadian soldiers in the town. She cynically added that if they must 'sin' they might just as well have babies, as we should want as many as we could get after the war and these soldiers are 'good stock'.

Mrs Henry Dudeney

1942 [Worcestershire]

We are going to have to increase our consumption of potatoes by 20 per cent, so it is said. Partly to save bread, and partly to dispose of this year's potato crop, which is enormous.

George Orwell

1943 [London]

This evening I walked home – about three miles – across Hyde Park and down Exhibition Road, listening to the voices of Czech, Polish and French soldiers. I love the present cosmopolitanism of London. Summer nights in London are soft and velvety even if the previous day has been grey. At nights the colourlessness disappears, and the savage emptiness of the black-out is filled with pools of violet, blue and yellow light. I am at last feeling well again and have a zest for living.

James Lees-Milne

1966 [Kentucky]

. . . Then we were off for Fort Campbell, Kentucky, for the most memorable scene of the day. There Lyndon awarded medals to twenty-two veterans of the 101st Division returned from Vietnam, saw weapons captured in Vietnam, and spoke as Commander in Chief. What I remember most was a simulated attack – helicopters coming in at treetop height in lines as precise as ballet dancers, the swiftness with which men debarked, picked up soldiers where the big pink flares had been left burning, and were off in seconds. It was breathtaking and frightening. I remember the huge parachute, mottled green and brown for camouflage in the jungle, used to drop such material as a truck. And I remember the sense of awed silence I felt when I tried to speak to the wounded men in wheelchairs.

Soon it was time to fly on. (This is what I would call 'a four-shirt day'. After every speech Lyndon is wringing wet, and at least four times today he changed shirts.)

We went by Convair to Lawrenceville, Illinois, for an airport rally. Once more, thousands of people, in this heartland of America that's not supposed to be our territory. Only once did I think I saw an unfriendly sign. I believe it had the words 'PRESIDENT GOLDWATER'.[1]

Lady Bird Johnson

24 July

1861 [Washington]

To-day the aspect of Washington is more unseemly and disgraceful, if that were possible, than yesterday.

As I returned to my lodgings a scene of greater disorder and violence than usual attracted my attention. A body of Confederate prisoners, marching two by two, were with difficulty saved by their guard from the murderous assaults of a hooting rabble, composed of civilians and

---

[1] Senator Barry Goldwater, a Republican politician. He contested the 1964 presidential election but was heavily defeated by Lyndon Bird Johnson.

men dressed like soldiers, who hurled all kinds of missiles they could lay their hands upon over the heads of the guards at their victims, spattering them with mud and filthy language. It was very gratifying to see the way in which the dastardly mob dispersed at the appearance of a squad of mounted men, who charge them boldly, and escorted the prisoners to General Mansfield.

Soon afterwards a report flew about that a crowd of soldiers were hanging a Secessionist. A senator rushed to General McDowell, and told him that he had seen the men seemingly with his own eyes. Off went the General, *ventre à terre,* and was considerably relieved by finding that they were hanging merely a dummy or effigy of Jeff. Davis, not having succeeded in getting at the original yesterday.

Poor McDowell has been swiftly pummelled for his defeat, or rather for the unhappy termination of his advance. As soon as the disaster was ascertained beyond doubt, the President telegraphed to General McClellan to come and take command of his army. It is a commentary full of instruction on the military system of the Americans, that they have not a soldier who has ever handled a brigade in the field fit for service in the North.

– William Howard Russell

1915 [England]

Am excited at being home again.[1]

Pvt Montague S. Goodbar, 4th Battalion Cameron Highlanders

1940 [near Coventry]

A letter from the War Office Casualty Branch giving us Alan's [her son] address: 'Stalag XXA', Germany. That cheered us up a bit, for now we can write to him. And, of course, it was not long before I wrote him a stilted little letter on a single sheet of notepaper, which is all one may do at a time. One can write as often as one likes – but how little one can really say! For one thing news is scarce when one cuts out the war, and one may not say anything to give any information to the enemy. So things have to be carefully sifted till there is very little said. However one can send love and give facts in a veiled way, as I did today when I wrote: 'Little Bert Austin takes your father

---

[1] Goodbar recovered and later transferred to the Royal Flying Corps. He was killed in action in 1917.

to his daily work', which meant 'Father has an Austin 7 to drive into Coventry, where he has taken a job at the Labour Exchange'. And then continued: 'and Maria stays with me at Burleigh. She is as good a girl as ever and behaves nicely, so I am glad to have her with me'. That meant: 'I have the Rover car for my use', because we call the Rover 'Maria'. He knows that and will put two and two together.

Clara Milburn

1943 [Palermo]

Waked at six-thirty by the noise of tanks and troop-laden trucks rumbling by. We eat tinned ham and eggs and chocolate. Sicilian donkey carts, piled with tomatoes and onions, mingle with the motorized vehicles. Refugees returning to the city with bundles on their heads. Four Italian soldiers come up to Tom Henry and very politely offer to surrender. He explains to them that he has no authority to accept prisoners. One of them pulls out a box of cigars and offers it to us, if we will only take them in. They hang around until we leave.

George Biddle

25 July

1864 [Confederate POW camp, Andersonville, Georgia]

At my earnest solicitation was carried to the gate this morning, to be admitted to the hospital. Lay in the sun some hours to be examined, and finally my turn came and I tried to stand up, but was so excited I fainted away. When I came to myself I lay along with a row of dead on the outside. Raised up and asked a Rebel for a drink of water, and he said, 'Here, you Yank, if you ain't dead yet, get inside there!' And with his help was put inside again.

John Ransom

1917 [London]

[The Yacht Club]

Went to dine at [J.M.] Barrie's with Thomas Hardy and his wife. Barrie has an ugly little manservant, and the finest view of London I ever saw. Mrs Hardy a very nice woman, with a vibrating attractive voice. Hardy was very lively; talked like anything. Apropos of Tchekoff he started a theory that some of Tchekoff's tales were not justifiable because they told nothing unusual. He said a tale must be unusual and the people interesting. Of course he soon got involved in the meshes of applications and instances; but he kept his head and showed elasticity and common sense, and came out on the whole well. He has all his faculties, unimpaired. Quite modest and without the slightest pose. Later in the evening Barrie brought along both Shaw [George Bernard] and the Wellses [H.G.] by phone. Barrie was consistently very quiet, but told a few A1 stories. At dusk we viewed the view and the searchlights. Hardy, standing outside one of the windows, had to put a handkerchief on his head. I sneezed. Soon after Shaw and the Wellses came Hardy seemed to curl up. He had travelled to town that day and was evidently fatigued. He became quite silent. I then departed and told Barrie that Hardy ought to go to bed. He agreed. The spectacle of Wells and G. B. S. talking firmly and strongly about the war, in their comparative youth, in front of this aged, fatigued and silent man – incomparably their superior as a creative artist – was very striking.

Arnold Bennett

1942 [Perth, Scotland]

Now is the season when the war is most openly exposed in contrast with natural living. Again the generosity of life is revealed in the abundance of fruit and grain now ripened to fullness: an abundance from which all may be satisfied without struggle or craft. And added to the joy of bodily sufficiency is the joy given to the mind which looks upon the coloured beauty of autumn. Against this world of beauty and beneficence, the havoc of the striving nations destroys the comeliness of common earth. Harvest lands are blasted into fields of desolation, and where the harvester had rejoiced is barren soil littered with twisted metal and riven bodies. When faith in life degenerates, then death becomes our certainty.

William Soutar

26 July

1940 [Berlin]

[Count] Albert Eltz dropped in this evening. He brought us cake and Kolynos toothpaste – a valuable item which one can get now only at Siemensstadt. He is an anti-aircraft gunner on the roof of the factory there and was locked up recently for having been caught reading an English novel instead of scanning the skies for English planes.

Marie 'Missie' Vassiltchikov

1941 [London]

I had a ludicrous conversation yesterday with honest, British Franks, my chauffeur. 'Don't you think, sir,' he asked me politely, 'that you notice a gradual rise of interest in the United States?' 'Why, yes, a trifle,' I replied. 'But how do you notice it?' 'Well, sir, I can't quite say. It is not that people read more about America, or think about it so much more, sir, but if I might put it so, sir, one might say there is a little more bonhomie about. Don't you think that might be so, sir?' 'Well, yes,' I agreed. 'Perhaps you might describe it that way, but it is only natural, don't you think, that for $7,000,000 (that's nearly 2 million pounds) we ought to be entitled to a little bonhomie!' 'Oh yes, sir, yes, sir, quite. That's just what I mean, sir. I should say there is quite a bit more bonhomie in the air, sir.'

General Raymond E. Lee

1943 [Tuscany]

The long-expected news has come at last: Mussolini has fallen. The news was given by radio last night, but we did not hear it until this morning. Mussolini has resigned, the King has appointed Marshal Badoglio in his place and has himself taken over the command of the Army. A proclamation of Badoglio's announces: 'Italy will keep her pledge; the war continues.'

As the broadcast closes E. burst into my room: 'Have you heard? After twenty years – after twenty years . . .' We all have a lump in our throat. Hope – perplexity – anxiety – doubt – then hope again – infinite relief. A weight has been lifted, a door opened; but where does it lead? We spend the day in speculation, fed by driblets of news. First a proclamation of martial law, with the institution of a curfew at sunset and a prohibition of any public meetings: moreover, it is forbidden to carry firearms or to circulate in any private vehicle; a few hours later we hear with delight of the disbanding of the Fascist militia; its members are to be incorporated in the regular Army. In the evening comes the list of the new Cabinet; mostly permanent officials or under-secretaries. It is clearly to be a moderate, traditional government of administrators, not of 'great men'. Italy has had enough of heroes. But still innumerable questions are unanswered. What has happened to Mussolini and his satellites? And above all – increasingly with every hour – what about Germany?

Iris Origo

27 July

1943 [Berlin]

On our way to lunch we [her sister and a friend] were followed by a man who moved from tram to bus and kept behind us until we got quite worried. We tried to get rid of him by diving into a house, but he waited outside until we came out, finally buttonholed me and gave me to understand that he objected to our speaking French. This sort of thing used not to happen, but the bombings are making people more bitter.

Marie 'Missie' Vassiltchikov

2000 [Chechnya]

Klavdia[1] tries from memory to repeat the Moscow telephone number of her one and only son who, it turns out, is in charge of the fire brigade at Mytishchi near the capital: 'But you must say that everything [her situation] is fine.'

'I'll tell him what I saw.'

'Not under any circumstance! He'll be upset. And he's a very important man, always at work and that's why he can't come to get me.'

Anna Politkovskaya

28 July

1916 [the Russian Front]

More than 100 wounded came during the night. They have been arriving in numbers all day and in the late evening were still being

---

[1] Klavdia Anufryeva, a blind 73-year-old woman, dirty and underfed, had to reach her home via landmines.

brought in. We have all been working in tremendous haste; most of the bandaging has been left to our hospital-orderlies; we, the surgical staff, have been cleaning, operating, dressing. Austrians of all ranks were among the wounded. All night long, the operating table was occupied: eight major operations had been performed before daylight. Candles, kerosene lamps and torches supplied the only available light. Stomach wounds were by far in the majority. Our surgeons never flagged; they were chain-workers. Prostrate form replaced prostate form on the table. The room was filled with agonising groans, stentorious breathing, the rustle of moving arms, the murmur of voices, the clink of surgical instruments, the slash and click of surgical scissors, and always the deeply-drawn breathing of men performing a task of intense importance.

Florence Farmborough

1940 [London]

This evening I saw a heron flying over Baker Street. But this is not so improbable as the thing I saw a week or two ago, i.e. a kestrel killing a sparrow in the middle of Lord's cricket ground. I suppose it is possible that the war, i.e. the diminution of traffic, tends to increase bird life in inner London.

George Orwell

1940 [Surrey]

A long bright day of useful and entertaining activity. Having volunteered for service in the Esher war-salvage scheme with six others, including the dustman and his driver, I paraded for duty at the council yard at 8.30 a.m. for instructions. Arranging the fourteen roads on our list in topographical sequence we loaded the lorry then drove away to find the first and commence operations. So early on a Sunday morning many people were still asleep but it was the womenfolk, with a dressing-gown or coat thrown over their nightclothes, who appeared shyly at the doors to direct us to the cellars and outhouses where we found, in little heaps, the accumulated odds and ends of old iron which it was our job to collect. The response to the council appeal was remarkable and unexpectedly generous. In the first two roads we collected well over twenty old cycles and almost as many perambulators and push-chairs. Of old baths, buckets, fire-irons, flat-irons and stair-rods, there were plenty. From another road we collected copper preserving pans, much brass and aluminium ware and almost a ton of broken iron railings. Each of the four roads canvassed produced a load to capacity. Among the curious finds was a German cavalry sword of fine workmanship taken in the last war, a griddle plate over a century old and a set of old-fashioned servants' hall bells complete with springs and sprockets, which jingled merrily on their way to the lorry. In the afternoon two charming old ladies provided most welcome tea and entertained us with reminiscences of earlier years when the griddle plate was in daily use somewhere in the far north of Scotland. But perhaps no incident of the day was more indicative of willing sacrifice than when an elderly widow, having handed over her contribution to the junk, as an after-thought produced a bright shining brass and iron fender on which she said her husband loved to rest his slippered feet on winter evenings – he had been killed in action during the last war. 'But,' said she, 'you cannot have it whole.' She took a large hammer, shattered it with vengeful blows and, on her late husband's account, handed me the pieces – for Hitler.

Walter Musto

1940 [London]

'You realise', said Jack Bergel, 'what bringing this out now means?' *This* was *Ego* 4.[1] 'It means that you regard your Diary as more important than the war.' I said, 'Well, isn't it? The war is vital, not important.'

James Agate

1942 [Holland]

7.30 a.m. I shall allow the chain of this day to unwind link by link. I shall not intervene but shall simply have faith. 'I shall let You make Your own decisions, oh, god.' This morning I found a buff envelope in my letter box. I could see there was a white paper inside. I was quite calm and thought, 'My call-up notice, what a pity, now I won't have time to try repacking my rucksack.' Later I noticed that my knees were shaking. It was simply a form to be filled in by the staff of the Jewish Council. They haven't even issued me with an identity number yet. I shall take the few steps I have to. My turn may not come for a long time. Jung and Rilke will go with me in any case. And if my mind should be unable to retain very much later on, nevertheless these last

[1] Volume 4 of his diaries, published annually from 1935 onwards, under the title of *Ego*.

two years will shine at the edge of my memory like a glorious landscape in which I was once at home and which will always remain part of me. I feel that I am still tied by a thousand threads to everything I treasure here. I will have to tear myself away bit by bit and store everything inside me, so that when I have to leave, I shall not abandon anything but carry it all with me.

Etty Hillesum

1943 [Sicily]
At Sperlinga we passed a car carrying a stretcher. A man was tied down to the stretcher, lying on his back. He watched us as we passed. He had a look of quiet contentment on his red dusty face. A little later we passed three of our tanks of the Seventieth Tank Battalion. They were put out of action last night by enemy fire, while on a reconnaissance tour. Under the first tank were the fragments of a man's trousered legs. We passed a dead Italian soldier lying in a ditch. His face was green, a whitish green against the neutral gray green of his uniform. Behind him a bush of green thorn stood out from the yellow earth and yellow grass. The whole thing was a green symphony, in beautiful subdued tones with patches of black blood to throw it into relief. A little farther on lay a dead horse, his belly all inflated, and then a burnt truck. Completely burnt, with two charred helmets below the chassis.

George Biddle

29 July

1864 [Confederate POW camp, Andersonville, Georgia]
Alive and kicking. Drink some soured water made from meal and water.

John Ransom

1940 [Wiltshire]
News of a terrific air battle over Dover harbour, with fifteen German aeroplanes shot down. Also that Mr. Chamberlain[1] is doing well after his operation. R.: 'Has he had his appeasement out?'

Frances Partridge

---

[1] Neville Chamberlain, who had recently resigned as Prime Minister, had had an operation for cancer – he died on 9 November, 1940.

1942 [Lewes, England]

Letter from Margery [her daughter in America]. She said: 'What's the matter with the British? One defeat after the other.' I wrote back: 'I am *very* angry with you. The matter with the British is that they saved the world in 1940, fighting alone while America was sitting back and licking her chops!'

Mrs Henry Dudeney

1999 [Moscow]

'To whom does a dead body belong?' Ask any normal person and they will answer without a moment's thought: 'To the relatives, of course, and no one else.'

Try as he might, Colonel Slipchenko could not clearly formulate an answer to this question. He is the general director of Military Commemoration Ltd: not long ago he was a colonel serving on the General Staff. Today the remains of more than 400 soldiers and officers are still lying in unmarked graves somewhere in Chechnya, and several hundred other corpses are awaiting identification at Forensic Laboratory No 124 in Rostov-on-Don, but Slipchenko, a military man himself, finds nothing particularly shocking about this.

'So they're lying there! We must work effectively, and not rush things. It'll take years yet to finish the job,' Slipchenko assured us.

He quickly changed the subject and began to talk about the American experience. Even today, he believed, not all the US participants in the Vietnam War had been found and identified. As a businessman, though, Slipchenko's odd attitude is entirely understandable. The longer the process of exhumation continues, the more profit there is for him. He earns his money from the exhumation and identification of those officers and soldiers of the Russian armed forces who died in Chechnya: his firm, Military Commemoration Ltd, where this interview took place, is located in the same Moscow building as the Chief Military Prosecutor's office. It is, to be sure, a very curious kind of commercial enterprise. And there is, of course, nothing accidental about their proximity. The Military Prosecutor's Office, as we all know, bears part of the responsibility for locating the unmarked graves. It should be doing this job during working hours and is paid to do so. But it cannot always find the time.

Anna Politkovskaya

30 July

1864 [Confederate POW camp, Andersonville, Georgia]
Hang on well, and no worse.

John Ransom

1943 [London]
I joined Jamesey at Rule's restaurant. We drank quantities of Pimm's and enjoyed ourselves hugely. There is no one with whom I can be happier. We can be as one. I say 'can be'. We were tonight. As we talked and laughed in an animated way two very tough-looking men at a neighbouring table were staring at us critically and discussing us. I then realized how we must have struck them, both youngish and out of uniform, both enjoying ourselves, which in their eyes we had no right to do. In truth they had no right to judge us, for James is in the army, and I was.

We walked out of the restaurant into the heat, and down the embankment. We crossed London Bridge to the south side of the river, and ambled along Cardinal's Wharf. Jamesey was extolling in the most candid and engaging manner his age – he is twenty-six – his good looks and his successes, saying he did not believe he could ever die. He said, 'Our relationship is such a one that can never have existed in the past. I don't think anything marks the progress of civilization so vividly as improved personal relations.' I said, yes, I felt certain that before our time personal relations could never have been so intimate, though of course we could never tell what, for instance, Byron and Hobhouse talked about at nights in a tent during their travels in the Morea. I said that more people ought to keep diaries, but the trouble was that the most unscrupulous diarists were too scrupulous when it came to putting personal truths on paper. James said that Cecil's [Beaton] diary would be the chronicle of our age, that we would only live through it. I said Eddy Sackville-West kept one. James said, 'We could not be hoisted to posterity on two spikier spikes.' We looked at bombed churches and sat in churchyards, and drank shandies in City pubs.

James Lees-Milne

31 July

1916 [London]

This War is so great and terrible that hyperbole is impossible. And yet my gorge rises at those fatuous journalists continually prating about this 'Greatest War of all time', this 'Great Drama', this 'world catastrophe unparalleled in human history', because it is easy to see that they are really more thrilled than shocked by the immensity of the War. They indulge in a vulgar Yankee admiration for the Big Thing. Why call this shameful Filth by high sounding phrases – as if it were a tragedy from Euripides? We ought to hush it up, not brag about it, to mention it with a blush instead of spurting it out brazen-faced.

Mr Garvin,[1] for example, positively gloats over the War each week in the *Observer*. 'Last week was one of those pivotal occasions on which destiny seems to swing' – and so on every week, you can hear him, historical glutton smacking his lips with an offensive relish.

W.N.P. Barbellion

---

[1] James Louis Garvin, editor of the *Observer* (1908–42), a strong supporter of Lloyd George.

AUGUST

And when we clear away
  All this debris of day-by-day experience,
What comes out to light, what is there of value
  Lasting from day to day?
Louis MacNeice, Autumn Journal

1 August

1914 [London]
All Europe is mobilising.

W.N.P. Barbellion

1940 [London]
Priestley[1] has sent the PM an article he has written pleading for Government benevolence towards the people's recreation. We will give up our Bank Holidays, but let us have laughter and fun and untaxed books (the Chancellor in his much-criticised budget proposes to tax books and has aroused a justifiable storm of protest). Priestley declaims against the drift towards dreariness. What is far more dangerous, as Mother points out, is the film-fed public's insatiate longing for sensation. It has often been said that the Dictators could only survive if they took some dramatic action every six months, and now the British public, drugged by Hollywood and by the stirring events of recent months, seems to need incessant change and excitement.

John Colville

2 August

1914 [London]
Will England join in?

W.N.P. Barbellion

1914 [Germany]
Germany has declared war on Russia. – Swimming in the afternoon.

Franz Kafka

---

[1] J.B. Priestley, English novelist, who during WWI made a significant contribution to national morale through his broadcasts.

1916 [England]

Lying in a hospital train on his way to London he looks out at the hot August landscape of Hampshire, the flat green and dun-coloured fields – the advertisements of Lung Tonic and Liver Pills, the cows-neat villas and sluggish waterways – all these came on him in an irre-sistible delight, at the pale gold of the wheat-field and the faded green of the hazy muffled woods on the low hills. People wave to the Red Cross train – grateful stay-at-homes – even a middle-aged man, cycling along a dusty road in straw hat and blue serge clothes, takes one hand off the handlebars to wave feeble and jocular gratitude. And the soul of the officer glows with fiery passion as he thinks, 'All this I've been fighting for and now I'm safe home again I begin to think it was worth while.' And he wondered how he could avoid being sent out again.

Siegfried Sassoon

1941 [London]

Times are changing. I took my favorite brown suit down to Scholte's today to see if he could make me another pair of trousers, because the present pair has two large holes in the seat. [He] could not find any of the same material and advised me to have the seat patched, for, he said, 'I could make it last for you quite a while longer.' The sleeve linings also were frayed, and I said, 'What about new sleeve linings?' He said, 'You will have to produce two coupons before I can do it. Why not go on and wear it that way for, although they are frayed, they will last quite a long while yet.' Before the war, neither one of us would have considered wearing trousers with a big patch in the seat, and a coat with torn and worn sleeve linings. Now it is the thing to do.

General Raymond E. Lee

1943 [Berlin]

Notices have been put up in every house, ordering the immediate evac-uation of all children and of those women who are not doing defence work. There is a tremendous rush on the stations and great confusion, as many evacuated Hamburgers are coming through Berlin on their way elsewhere. There are also rumours that government offices will be moved out of town *in corpore* and we have been given orders to pack, but I am not taking this very seriously. Mamma now spends the nights out in the country and has at last agreed to join Tatiana [her daugh-ter in Dresden] soon.

Lunched with Ambassador von Hassell. He told me interesting stories about Mussolini, who he knew well. He is retired now and writes articles on economics, which he keeps sending me. I confess I don't understand much.

Later I dragged a suitcase over to Potsdam and went to bed early, as I was very tired. Unfortunately sleep was postponed by the arrival of Gottfried Bismarck, Loremarie Schönburg and Count Helldorf, who is Polizeipräsident [Chief of Police] of Berlin. He comes to Potsdam often and they all confer late into the night. It is all very hush-hush, but Loremarie, who has also moved out to Potsdam, keeps me informed about what I call 'the Conspiracy'. She is feverishly active, trying to bring various opposition elements together and acts often in a headstrong and imprudent way. Gottfried, however, never breathes a word.

Marie 'Missie' Vassiltchikov

1943 [Kent]
We go to the village fête at Sissinghurst. All the village children dress up and there is one little boy who impersonates [Field Marshal] Montgomery riding on a tank. There are many side-shows. One of them is a dart contest, in which people are invited to throw darts at large cartoons of Hitler, Tōjō[1] and Mussolini. Captain Reed is in charge of the Mussolini target and does no business at all. Hitler and Tōjō attract great crowds, but people do not want to throw darts at Mussolini as they say he is 'down and out'. Really the English are an amazing race.

Harold Nicolson

3 August

1943 [Leningrad]
(Evening) I was nearly killed today.

At a quarter to eight, at sunset, I went to our allotment to pick some dill. I wanted to have everything ready by the time my people arrived. Marietta [her friend] was at a lecture, I.D. [her husband] had gone to the District Committee. I had given him my word not to go

---

[1] General Tōjō Hideki (1884–1948), Japan's political and unlikely leader during the greater part of WWII in the East.

out in the street, as the shelling hadn't stopped since early morning. I promised, but our allotment isn't the street. It's right in our courtyard, on the banks of the Karpovka. I can remember when it was still a wilderness, rusty junk was buried there, and remains of artificial limbs, broken-up mattresses. Now it's covered in greenery bulging like a wood seen from a plane.

It was watering time. Home Sister, girl orderlies, the upholsterer (his cabbages are the best of all) were there. It was all so summery, peaceful. The Karpovka reflected the charm of the Botanical Gardens in its waters.

Anfisa Semenovna, the so-called 'Professor Farro', wife of the chief book-keeper, Ivan Zakharovich Krutikov, strolled between the beds. Krutikov isn't young any more. He has worked in the hospital for forty years. He has a pale narrow face and a toneless voice. He is one of the quietest people I have ever known.

Anfisa Semenovna is mentally ill. She used to work in the hospital as a paediatrician, and she suddenly went out of her mind. Since then, she is put in a mad-house during her worst periods, and at others let out, at the request of her husband. They are tenderly attached to each other, in a gentle, old-fashioned way.

Anfisa Semenovna wore a bonnet under her hat, pince-nez on her nose, and carried a small suitcase. She is energetic, talkative, domineering, knows about everything, and is, on the whole, harmless. Only she insists on being called 'Professor Farro'. She very skilfully steals keys from doors and cupboards and hides them in her little case. It's impossible to retrieve them from her, so various ruses have to be adopted.

When I came into the allotment 'Professor Farro' was just finishing something like a public lecture on how the rats which were nibbling the turnips, allegedly spread typhoid.

I gathered some dill, and had just bent down towards a large ripe marrow when there was a noise like a thunder-clap. It was a shell falling near the second surgical [ward]. It was followed by a second – in our allotment, this time – and then a third.

I saw (so far I'd only seen such a thing so close in a movie) a pillar of fire, smoke and earth – all of it from base to crumbling apex. Hot air blew in my face. I squatted down on the bed, trying to hide my head amongst the big leaves . . . I don't remember any more – what and how. Later, when things quietened down, I picked the marrow, after all, and ran towards home, my legs shaking.

As I ran, people came running towards me from the second surgical ward, shouting that Krutikov had been injured in another distant part of the allotment. He was carrying a can to water his cucumbers. His left hand was torn off. Later, more wounded were brought to us from the street.

And what is so disturbing is the fact that the Germans seem to have found the range for our hospital. The last few days they have been getting closer and closer, more and more accurate. Now they are hitting their target.

At present the night around me is quiet, close, cloudy and brooding. There is a continual rumble of gun-fire in the distance.

We thought we might go elsewhere to spend the night, but we dropped the idea.

It doesn't matter now.

Vera Inber

4 August

1941 [Kovno Ghetto, Lithuania]
Only six weeks have elapsed since the beginning of the blitzkrieg of the German Army which rolled through Lithuania. Dozens of Jewish settlements, firmly rooted on Lithuania soil for hundreds of years, have already been obliterated from the face of the earth as if they had never existed. They were replaced by mounds of poisonous earth covering large pits – fresh mass graves, without tombstones, without inscriptions or any identifying marks – in the forests and fields beyond the town and village boundaries.

In Slobodka, the Jewish houses, looted and boarded up, have already been emptied of the last corpses, which had been lying inside ever since the 'bloody prologue' which took place on the night of June 25–26, 1941. No fewer than 700 Jewish martyrs were put to death that night by the Lithuanian murderers. Some of them breathed their last in the flames engulfing their homes, which had been surrounded from all sides and set on fire. Only a mound of wet sand covered the hastily piled up bodies of the victims of the first pogrom: it became the new 'sand hill' on the shore of the Vilija river, Slobodka's bathing spot.

At the garage of the Agricultural Cooperative Society on Vytauto

Boulevard, no trace is left of the fifty-two Jews, tortured and then torn to pieces during an outburst of savagery – a fiendish spectacle which for four to five hours provided entertainment to the crowd of Lithuanian onlookers on one of the first days of the war. The victims' bodies have already been haphazardly buried somewhere in a pit.

Quiet has already returned to Kovno prison and to the Seventh Fort, that horrible slaughter-field. Thousands of Jews who were crammed in there in the first weeks, and squeezed into the long passage-ways of the fortress, have already been slaughtered by the Lithuanian 'freedom fighters', some were killed in small groups, others *en masse*. The gray fortress barracks, permanently dank, which until recently was brimming over with Jewish women and children rounded up together, has already been emptied. Night after night the Lithuanian henchmen would proceed to select their victims: the young, the pretty. First they would rape them, then torture them, and finally murder them. They called it 'going to peel potatoes'.

Avraham Tory

5 August

1901 [The Boer War]

That is the infantry soldier's battle – very nasty – very tiring – very greasy – very hungry – very thirsty – everything very beastly. No glitter – no excitement – no nothing. Just bullets and dirt.

Lieutenant David Miller

1914 [London]

It was a strange London on Sunday: crowded with excursionists to London and balked would-be travellers to the Continent, all in a state of suppressed uneasiness and excitement. We sauntered through the crowd to Trafalgar Square, where Labour, socialist and pacifist demonstrators, with a few trade union flags, were gesticulating from the steps of the monument to a mixed crowd of admirers, hooligan warmongers and merely curious holiday-makers. It was an undigni-fied and futile exhibition, this singing of the 'Red Flag' and passing of well-worn radical resolutions in favour of universal peace. We turned into the National Liberal Club: the lobby was crowded with men, all silent and perturbed. Sidney [her husband] went up into the smoking-room and brought down Massingham[1] and Hammond.[2] Both these men were bitter and depressed. We argued with them that if Belgian neutrality was defied we had to go to war – they vehemently denied it. On Monday the public mind was cleared and solidified by Grey's[3] speech. Even staunch Liberals agree that we had to stand by Belgium. But there is no enthusiasm about the war: at present it is, on the part of England, a passionless war, a terrible nightmare sweeping over all classes, no one able to realize how the disaster came about.

Beatrice Webb

1914 [Paris]

Germany declares war on Belgium, and England on Germany.

André Gide

1940 [Rome]

The Duce is ranting against 'the Italians', which happens whenever he encounters opposition to his projects. The main points he made were: decrease in the birth rate, the tendency toward alcoholism, and complacency. He says that one day he will make a sweeping speech entitled 'The Secret Wounds of Italy'. He will do this in order to force the nation to face its own weaknesses. He said that the main reason for the reforestation of the Apennine regions is to make the climate of Italy more rigorous. This will bring about the elimination of the weaker stock and an improvement of the Italian race.

Count Ciano

1942 [POW camp, Java]

The Dutch members of the camp had a visit from St Nicholas bringing gifts.

Weary Dunlop

1945 [London]

The world has been electrified, thrilled and horrified by the atomic bomb; one has been dropped in Japan today. It devastated a whole

---

[1] Henry William Massingham (1860–1924), Liberal journalist and editor.
[2] J.L. Hammond, journalist and writer.
[3] Sir Edward Grey (1862–1933), third baronet and Viscount Grey of Fallodon, Foreign Secretary 1905–16.

town and killed a quarter of a million people. It could mean the end
of civilisation.

'Chips' Channon

6 August

1870 [Paris]

From the Print Room of the Bibliothèque Impériale I saw people
running along the Rue Vivienne; I promptly ran after them.

The steps of the Stock Exchange, from top to bottom, were a sea
of bare heads, with hats flung into the air and every voice raised in a
tremendous *Marseillaise*, the roar of which drowned the buzz of noise
from the stockbrokers' enclosure inside the building. I have never seen
such an outburst of enthusiasm. One kept running into men pale with
emotion, children hopping around in excitement and women making
drunken gestures. Capoul[1] was singing the *Marseillaise* from the top of
an omnibus in the Place de la Bourse; on the Boulevard, Marie Sasse[2]
was singing it standing in her carriage, practically carried along by the
delirium of the mob.

But the dispatch announcing the defeat of the Crown Prince of Prussia
and the capture of twenty-five thousand prisoners, the dispatch which
everybody claimed to have read with his own eyes, the dispatch which I
was told had been posted up inside the Stock Exchange, the dispatch
which, by some strange hallucination, people thought they could actually see, telling me: 'Look, there it is!' and pointing to a wall in the distance
where there was nothing at all – this dispatch I was unable to find.[3]

The Brothers Goncourt

1914 [Paris]

The idea of a possible collapse of Germany gains strength little by
little; one struggles against it, but one does not convince oneself that
it is impossible. The wonderful behaviour of the government, of everyone, and of all France, as well of that of the neighbouring nations,
leaves room for every hope.

[1] Victor Capoul, a singer.
[2] Marie Sasse, a Belgian opera singer.
[3] In an attempt to rig the market, a false rumour was started at the Stock Exchange
on the 6th August, that the Crown Prince of Prussia's army had been defeated.

One foresees the beginning of a new era: the United States of Europe bound by a treaty limiting their armaments; Germany subjugated or dissolved; Trieste given back to the Italians, Schleswig to Denmark; and especially Alsace to France. Everyone talks of this remaking of the map as of the forthcoming issue of a new serial.

André Gide

1914 [Thorpe-le-Soken, England]

On arriving at Brightlingsea on Monday afternoon, I was told that petrol could not be got in the district; that it was fetching up to 10s. a tin at Clacton; and that Baggaley, the regular hirer of motorcars at B'sea, had gone forth in an attempt to get petrol. At Clacton yesterday the price was 2s. 3d. or 2s. 4d. a gallon. I have 60 gallons in stock.

A great crowd of holidaymakers at Clacton in the showers yesterday. No difficulty in getting change for a £10 note in gold and silver. At the fish shop, slight increases of price in poultry and eggs. The man said there was no chance for him to make money. He said he expected to get no more fish after that day.

Yesterday we heard noise of explosions destroying inconvenient houses at Harwich. The sensations of Harwich people must be poignant. Nevertheless the GER [Great Eastern Railways] in yesterday evening's papers was advertising its Hook of Holland service (with restaurant cars etc.) exactly as usual, and I believe the boat left last night. We also heard thunder; and the children affirm that they distinctly heard the noise of firing – not explosions. (Report of action in the North Sea in evening papers.) I saw one warship in the offing at Clacton; but an ordinary steamer coming to the pier; and a barge sailing northwards.

An officer came yesterday to complain of a fox terrier (?ours) which flew at despatch-riders on motor bicycles. He said it would be shot if found loose. These despatch-riders are the most picturesque feature of the war here. They rush through the village at speeds estimated up to 50 miles an hour. I am willing to concede 40.

I agree that Russia is the real enemy, and not Germany; and that a rapprochement between England and Germany is a certainty. But I doubt whether it is wise, in the actual conduct of affairs, to try to see so far ahead. I think that the belligerency of England is a mistake – for England. Yet if I had had to choose, I believe my instinct would have forced me to make war.

Sir Edward Grey's astounding mistake, in his big speech, was his assertion that the making of war would not much increase our suffering. It will enormously increase it. The hope for us is in the honesty and efficiency of our administration. The fear for France springs from the fact that the majority of French politicians are notoriously rascals, out for plunder. The corruption of Russian administration is probably even worse. The seriousness of the average French private will atone for a lot, but it will not – for instance – create boots for him. The hope for France is that the German army, arrogant in its traditions etc., may be lower than its reputation.

After reading the diplomatic papers leading up to the rupture between England and Germany, this morning, one has to admit that Sir E. Grey did everything he could once he had stated his position. The war is a mistake on our part, but other things leading to it were a mistake, and, these things approved or condoned, the war must be admitted to be inevitable. Judged by any current standard Sir E. Grey is a man of high common sense. He has not yet grasped the movement of social evolution; but then very few people have. And you cannot properly or fairly try to govern a country on a plane of common sense *too* high above its own general plane.

Apart from Germany two countries are pre-eminently suffering at the beginning of the war – France and Belgium. Both are quite innocent; Belgium touchingly so. I can imagine the Germans among them if they get the upper hand. The Germans are evidently quite ruthless and brutal and savage in war. This is logical; but a large part of their conduct is due to the arrogant military tradition, which will one day be smashed. If Germany is smashed in this war, the man most imperilled will be the German Emperor. If she is not smashed the man most imperilled may be the Tsar.

Arnold Bennett

1916 [France]
We moved out of trenches to 'TARA' HILL. 4th Div. Relieved us, & just as we were preparing to go to sleep Fritz lobbed shells around & one went into the deserted gun pit where COL. R. WATSON, Mjr. MANNING, CAPT. TATNAL, CAPT. PLANT & Lt. CARVISK were asleep. Only COL. WATSON escaped with severe shell shock, the others were killed, 4 of our best officers gone in a second.

Lance Corporal Thomas Part, 6th Infantry Battalion, 2nd Division,
Australian Imperial Forces

7 August

1940 [London]

Desmond Morton[1] tells me the Secret Service have absconded with £13,000,000 in francs which they discovered in the courtyard of a French bank in occupied France. This money will be used to finance de Gaulle. So the Secret Service are not entirely useless.

John Colville

1942 [Kovno Ghetto, Lithuania]

[SS Master Sergeant, Helmut] Rauca, accompanied by Garfunkel [a Ghetto resident and former public figure] toured the institutions of the Ghetto. During the tour he noticed a pregnant woman, in her seventh month. Rauca said: 'This embryo must perish. If not, it will be taken away from its mother right after the birth.'

Avraham Tory

1942 [Leningrad]

The city is quiet and deserted to an extent that is shattering.

Even the kitchen gardens hurt. The vegetables aren't growing as they should, the cabbage seedlings weren't thinned out. So huge, absurd leaves are growing without any body. They have such a bitter taste that even our hospital horses refuse to eat them. People carry away these tragic leaves, these shattered hopes, in the tram.

Quiet. Even the shelling has stopped. How can anyone write in such a city! It was easier even under the bombing. And what is it going to be like next winter?

On the 9th Shostakovich's Seventh Symphony is going to be performed in the Philharmonic Hall. Maybe that will dispel all this quietness.

Vera Inber

8 August

1943 [POW camp, Java]

We trod for a time along the Nipponese railway [the Burma–Thailand

---

[1] Major Sir Desmond Morton (1891–1971), Winston Churchill's liaison with the Foreign Office.

railway], the cause of it all, and smile with bitter humour at its crude and snake-like course. Every possible fault exists except that for the most part the rails are parallel. At times the rails are up in the air above the sleepers; sometimes the sleepers are up in the air attached to the rails! The sleepers are not even faintly regularly laid – just like so many matches tossed down by a giant hand. The rails are spiked down approximately 1 in 5 sleepers. There is a curious switchback railway effect in places supposed to be level. Often one rail is higher than the other and to look along the rails is to see a most disconcerting zigzag – a 'Snakes and Ladders railway'.

At one place, the rail is carried over a ravine by a most crazy wooden bridge which has repeatedly fallen down and is now held up by stays. At this new point, a new embankment and cutting are being built by Tamils to skirt and avoid the bridge. However, the rail has passed on and trucks drawn by diesel engines are carrying fresh rails and sleepers up to Kinsayok. In the wake of the railway is left a wreckage of humanity, stupidly broken by inefficiency and design.

Weary Dunlop

9 August

1915 [the Russian Front]
Four sharp attacks were made in the night by the enemy and were repulsed by our men. The ambulance-vans arrived early in the morning and, after depositing their load of wounded, made their way back to the Front. Some hundred or so walking cases had gathered outside our dressing-tent and were lying about on the ground, awaiting their turn, for, as usual, the stretcher-cases claimed our immediate attention. One man walked slowly up to me in the tent; I told him: 'You must go outside and await your turn.' He said nothing, but lifted up his blackened shirt and showed his left hand supporting a mass of his own intestines which had spilled out from a cruel gash in his abdomen. In that condition he had walked nearly three versts! [about 2 miles]

Among the severely wounded, head injuries were the most numerous. At one time I had thought it a most terrible thing to have a man's brains bespattering my hands and white overall; but, as the Retreat continued, I grew accustomed to it. No fewer than three instances of wounds caused by a *razryvnaya pulya* [dumdum bullet] came to our notice that day – for the first time in our Front-Line work. In two or three cases, several small particles of metal were extracted from the wounds; they proved without doubt that they had belonged to those barbaric explosive bullets.

Florence Farmborough

1916 [on the Eastern Front with the German Army]

Senhöfer, a perfect comrade, promoted Corporal only to-day, was shot. He had been four years with the regiment. The bullet went in through his mouth and came out through the back of his head. I remained remarkably calm and cool; one has got so accustomed to the thought of death; one is on familiar terms with fate; one must be hard – remorselessly hard; but later on I felt it very much, for I was very fond of this comrade. I must admit though I couldn't bear to look long at the dead man, with his face now so set, pale and covered with blood, when only that morning we had sat together, chatting and laughing . . .

Adolf Sturmer

1940 [London]

The money situation is becoming completely unbearable . . . Wrote a long letter to the Income Tax people pointing out that the war had practically put an end to my livelihood while at the same time the government refused to give me any kind of job. The fact which is really relevant to a writer's position, the impossibility of writing books with this nightmare going on, would have no weight officially . . . Towards the government I feel no scruples and would dodge paying the tax if I could. Yet I would give my life for England readily enough, if I thought it necessary. No one is patriotic about taxes.

George Orwell

1945 [Japan]

Today another sailor and I picked our way through the ruins of what once had been the town of Shuri in the southern part of Okinawa. Its former population was 16,000, the size of my home town in Illinois, but then American bombers obliterated it. This was first time I ever saw a city leveled by war.

In mounting horror I climbed through the debris, through one shattered house after another, the odor of death in my nostrils, seeing here a broken vase, there a child's coloring book, and on the lawn a severed hand fingering black and white pebbles like piano keys. My mind reeled. Nauseated, in need of fresh air, I stumbled out of that row of jagged dwellings and walked onto a coral road. There I stood and trembled, unable to comprehend the magnitude of the holocaust to which I was witness, and suddenly within my skull I heard the music of a famous symphony. What was it? I *had* to know the name of that composition, for otherwise I might never expel it from my mind. So I froze on the road by the ruins and thought and thought and thought, and at last remembered. The symphony I was hearing in my brain was written by Sibelius and is entitled *Valse Triste* – Sad Waltz.

Edward Robb Ellis

10 August

1914 [London]
Every one is excited and perturbed; and most of us are haunted by the horrors that we know are taking place a few hundred miles away.

Beatrice Webb

1940 [London]
At lunch Winston gave me his own views about war aims and the future. He said there was only one aim, to destroy Hitler. Let those who say they do not know what they are fighting for stop fighting and they will see. France is now discovering what she was fighting for. After the last war people had done much constructive thinking and the League of Nations had been a magnificent idea. Something of the kind would have to be built up again: there would be a United States of Europe, and this Island would be the link connecting this Federation with the new world and able to hold the balance between the two. 'A new conception of the balance of power?' I said. 'No,' he replied, 'the balance of virtue.'

John Colville

1941 [England]
There are certain peculiarities about staying in a country house in wartime. One is the problem of the black-out. When you retire to your room for the night you find that it has been most thoroughly blacked out in several layers. First the extremely tall heavy windows have been securely closed and fastened (these can only by opened by

pulling on two long cords with white bobbles attached to the ends of them). Then the shutters have been closed and fastened with mighty crossbars fitting into grooves. The black-out curtains which also can only be made to come apart by pulling the correct pulleys, so that one gazes in dismay at the number of possible cords all twined around knobs. If you pull the wrong combination of pulleys (i.e. one of the curtain cords and one of the cords that open the windows) you are involved in a breathless struggle which yields no results save frustration. It must be remembered that the business of opening the windows has to be done in the pitch dark as the light must be turned out before you begin playing about with curtains. One night staying at Stansted I was completely defeated by the combination of obstacles and panting with exhaustion after wrenching at shutters and pulling at cords I took to my bed and tossed all night in breathless confinement. But at Waddesdon I triumphed, and what a relief to hear the wind sighing in the trees and to feel the soft night air! Then, of course, fumbling your way by the light of a small hand-torch along black corridors filled with unfamiliar furniture to the WC (which one had failed to mark by daylight) or alternatively to the bedroom of your girl-friend is another country-house hazard. At Waddesdon the valet asked me what I would like for breakfast. 'Coffee,' he suggested, 'toast or anything cooked, sir?' What a question in any English country house! But I stood out for an egg – felt the Rothchilds should be able to manage it – somehow!

Charles Ritchie

1943 [Sicily]

We move again forward down the new German road, passing through a battalion of Goums [gendarmarie]. Shaven heads, black beady eyes between heavy eyebrows, and short black beards. They carried long sheath knives, rifles, tommy guns, and trench tools. It was cold and they wore the hood of the black and brown and narrow white striped *gelaba*. I made a sketch of one of them. In Africa the Ninth Division had had them on their flank at Segenay. The officers used to make a price with the Goums and the Goums would go out at night and bring them back German lugers for $10 or $20. One officer wanted a pair of German boots. The Goums brought him back a pair. The boots had legs in them.

George Biddle

11 August

1776 [New York]
The Lords Day is come once more. But the Sabbath is scarcely known in the Army. Profaned is all religious Exercise. Dreadful is the thought that Men who expect an Engagement every Day with a obstinate, wise & powerful Enemy, should be so ungodly. But the God of this World has blinded the Mind.

Philip Vickers Fithian

1940 [England]
A lovely clear morning but rather cold. I bathe nonetheless. A great heron flaps away from the lake. The cottage garden is ablaze with yellow and orange and red. A real triumph of gardening. Vita, who is so wise and calm, asks the unspoken question which is in all our minds, 'How can we possibly win?'

Harold Nicolson

1943 [on board USS *Montpelier*, in the Pacific]
The men are having a lot of trouble with skin rash from the heat. This has been going on for some time. Out here you sweat 24 hours a day, and that makes it impossible to cure the heat rash. Some of the fellows are in bad shape but the Dr. cannot help them. Some of the men's rash have turned into big sores. Many of the men also have trouble with their eyes, they are full of pus.

We have been eating bread that is full of little hard bugs for quite some time and this will not change because of the heat. When you put a slice of bread in front of you, there seems to be as many bugs in it as there is bread.

James J. Fahey, Seaman First Class

1943 [Leningrad]
News cameraman K. told me some terrifying details of the Sunday shelling of the Nevsky and Sadovaya streets: the tramway-stop was bathed in blood. Bits of bodies were lying in the street all mixed up with cans, shopping bags, spades, vegetables. Many people were on their way to the allotments outside the city, or on their way back. K. saw a torn-off arm with a cigarette in the fingers, still smoking. Beetroots

and carrots were swimming in blood. Later, firemen hosed down the streets and pavements to wash the blood away.

I must frankly admit that I'm very much afraid of this tramstop. It was a favourite target even at the time when shelling was still a rarity.

Vera Inber

12 August

1914 [London]

We all await the result of a battle between two millions of men. The tension makes me feel physically sick.

W.N.P. Barbellion

1916 [Essex]

When Kitchener's[1] death was first told to the troops in France they did not believe it, but thought it was one of the many rumours they got out there. Kitchener and the King had each been killed about four times. The men in the camps and trenches joked over the report and in the trenches they had mock funerals. It was a week or ten days later before the death was officially announced to the troops in France.

Andrew Clark

1940 [Scotland]

Came over to Wemyss Bay in the very crowded boat. All the mouth of the Clyde filled with mixed shipping. Submarines and things. On the line up the small, sad and nameless stations[2]; one slept for a moment, and tried to guess where one was on waking, but no clues. Some oat fields cut already. Ours will be early too. Somewhere a new works with buried and isolated shops, presumably for explosive of some kind. The new 'Mightier Yet' poster. The only nice things the strips of stuff on the windows of the waiting rooms at Paisley(?) making clean patterns. A bit unnecessary to take off the names at Glasgow Central?

In the streets, strange uniforms, Polish mostly, and camouflaged cars

---

[1] Lord Kitchener (1850–1916), secretary for war in WWI, drowned on 5 June 1916, when the cruiser taking him to Archangel in Russia on a fact-finding mission struck a mine off Orkney.

[2] To confuse the enemy, most place names had been removed from railway stations.

and lorries. Odd and dizzy being in a crowd again. Few people take their gas-masks. We go to a flick and see half a Marx brothers: great fun. The newsreel with the horrible commentator making frightful jokes and encouraging morale I suppose: Pathé. How I hate it all. How I should like to see united effort for construction, for peace (but would the same man still do the newsreel propaganda?); how I should like to look out of a train some day, spotting new constructive things instead of new war things.

Naomi Mitchison

13 August

1943 [London]

Some of us went to James's flat where we drank gin. Cecil had the previous night been at a bomber command station from which the raiders over Germany and Italy set forth. In the control room he followed the full course of the raids. The planes were absent eight hours and all returned safely. Cecil heard the orders given to each crew before they flew off. In talking to him many of the men expressed sympathy with the 'poor I-ties' because their ack-ack defences were so very inadequate. Cecil said it was useless to appeal to their sentiment where historical monuments were concerned. Such things meant nothing to them at all. On the other hand their distaste for taking life unnecessarily was genuine. He said that unlike soldiers and sailors the airmen harboured no feelings of hatred or revenge against the Germans.

James Lees-Milne

1944 [Naples]

Today a begrimed and bedraggled waif calling herself Giuseppina appeared at the office. This alert 12-year-old would tell me nothing about herself other than her age, that her parents had been killed in the great bombing, and that she lived 'under a house' down by the river. There are boy-orphans by the hundred like her, barefooted, ragged and hungry, but somehow managing to survive and fill the gaunt streets with their laughter, but this was the first abandoned girl I had seen. Giuseppina told me she had come for her blanket as usual.

I was astonished. Blankets are one form of currency in this Italy in ruins – but currency of a fairly high denomination, good Australian or Canadian specimens fetching the equivalent of a low-grade factory-worker's weekly wage. I told her I had no blankets to give away, and offered her a packet of army biscuits, which she gracefully refused. 'Isn't this still the police station?' she asked. I agreed that it was, and she told me that the man who had been here before – clearly my Canadian predecessor – had given her a blanket once a week.

Only at this point did I realize the tragic significance of the request, and that this skinny, underdeveloped little girl was a child prostitute. The *scugnizzi* [slum children] of Naples and Benevento are intelligent, charming and above all philosophical – notably more so than children from protected homes – and this female version of the breed was in no way different from her male counterparts. Much as she may have been disappointed by my rejections of her services, nothing but good humour showed in her face. She bobbed something like a curtsy. 'Perhaps I'll take the biscuits after all,' she said. Then, with a wave, she was off.

Norman Lewis

14 August

1939 [Rome]
I find Mussolini worried. I do not hesitate to arouse in him every possible anti-German reaction any way I can. I speak to him of his diminished prestige and his playing the none-too-brilliant role of second fiddle. And, finally, I turn over to him documents which prove German bad faith on the Polish question. The alliance was based on premises which they now ignore, they are the traitors and we must not have any scruples in ditching them. But Mussolini still has many scruples. I am going to do my level best to convince him, because in so doing I am sure that I shall render a great service to him and to my country. Meanwhile, I tell Starace[1] not to withhold the country's true state of mind, which is clearly anti-German, from the Duce. Tomorrow I shall also discuss this with the head of the police force. He must be made aware that the Italian people do not want to fight alongside Germany in order to give it that power with which one day it will threaten us. I no longer harbour any doubts about the Germans. Tomorrow it will be Hungary's turn, and then ours. We must act now while there is time.

[1] Achilles Starace, Secretary of the Fascist Party (PNF).

I meet the Polish ambassador at the beach. I speak with him in vague terms and advise moderation. Our counsellor at Warsaw tells us that Poland will fight to the last man. The churches are filled. The people pray and sing a hymn, 'O god, help us save our country.' These people will be massacred by German steel tomorrow. They are completely innocent. My heart is with them.

Count Ciano

1940 [Oswestry, England]

I have been reading Virginia Woolf's *To the Lighthouse*. Although I have read her before this is the first time I have really taken note of her special technique. It is one that commends itself to me – I find it attractive and believe I could do it – indeed, I already have, in a mild way. Sitting by the kitchen fire drying my hair, a cat, a basket chair and a willow tree and Mr Churchill and President Roosevelt meeting in the middle of the ocean to discuss War and Peace Aims.

Barbara Pym

1940 [Hampshire]

Yesterday morning, as I was enjoying my hot bath, there opened a roar of aeroplanes overhead, then machine guns and rapid explosions, shaking the walls and the roof. 'I must not be found naked,' I thought, and hurriedly put on my underclothing.

Beatrice Webb

15 August

1914 [Paris]

The sky clouded over during the night, and in the early morning a big storm broke east of Paris.

The first rolling of the thunder at about four o'clock seemed enough like the explosion of bombs to make one think a flight of zeppelins had raided Paris. And in my half-sleep I imagined for some time that Paris was being bombarded and that it was even the end of the world. From my lack of emotion I realized I was ready for anything and everything; but it was only a dream. Yet can I know how I might react when faced with real danger? Of what simple stuff are they made, the people who can guarantee their reactions at any hour of day or night!

How many soldiers anxiously wait for the event that will prove whether or not they are brave? And he who doesn't react as *he would like to* – whose will alone is brave! . . .

André Gide

1943 [Tuscany]

My birthday, which we celebrate together with [her daughter] Benedetta's by having a children's party. In the middle of Blind Man's Buff a military lorry drives up and two German officers come clanking down the garden path. They belong to the division, encamped beneath Radicofani, which crossed the Brenner on July 28th. Their own company, however, is to go in a few days to Salerno – where, they tell us, the Allied landing is now expected. They deny that the first line of defence is to be along the Apennines; it is to be, they say, from Salerno to Brindisi, to prevent the Allies from cutting across Italy to the Adriatic. Several divisions, however, will still remain in Tuscany. As they sit, very correct and polite – drinking their glasses of wine and proposing a formal toast – I feel that they are the most highly specialized human beings that I ever encountered: the 'fighting man'. Both of them (one from Mecklenburg, one from the Saar) are under twenty-five; both have taken part in the campaigns of Poland, France, Russia – and now Italy. One of them, risen from the ranks, commanded for six months a company of Russian deserters, who are now fighting against Russia (he says that there are now two hundred thousand of them) under German and Russian officers; the other was at Stalingrad. To one of them I say: 'You must have gone into the Army straight from school.' 'No,' he replies. '*Schon in der Schule war ich Soldat.* (I belonged to the Hitler Jugend.)'[1] We ask about the Russian front. 'We'll hold them back all right; we *must*.' It is impossible to convey the depth of the conviction in his voice, both then and later, while he expounded to us the familiar doctrines which had been taught him: the needs of *Gross Deutschland*, Nordic racial superiority, the inevitability of Germany's entry into war (in spite of all Hitler's efforts to make peace with England), his pride in his country and his men, and above all his unshakeable certainty, even now, of victory. He was not being

---

[1] Hitler Jugend – Hitler Youth – was an organisation for young men aged from 14 to 18. According to Hitler, its members were required to be 'slim and slender, swift as greyhounds, tough as leather and hard as Krupp steel'. Membership was compulsory.

a propagandist, but simply stating a creed, a creed to which he brought an absolutely single-minded, self-denying devotion, with no half-shades of humour, self-criticism or doubt. Add to this, admirable health, iron discipline, and the vigour and courage of youth, and arm and clothe such an army well – and the results are formidable: the results that Hitler intended to produce, and that fifty Mussolinis could not produce here.

Iris Origo

1945 [USA]

When the end of the war was announced last night I was in my office, working on my record of my magazine days. My first news of it came with the blowing of factory whistles and ringing of church bells. Even the nuns of the House of [the] Good Shepherd clanged their bell, though only briefly. This was at 7.05 p.m. The uproar went on inter-mittently for two hours, with morons dashing by in their automobiles, blowing their horns. At 8.50 I went to Baltimore and Gilmor streets to mail letters. A few dozen neighbourhood oakies, lintheads and other such vermin were gathered there in ragged groups, but they were making no noise. At 9.10 the celebration in West Baltimore ceased abruptly, and after that there were only an occasional toot of an automobile horn. I heard a couple of shots about midnight: they seemed to come from the linthead barracks in the 1500 block of Baltimore Street.

The *Sun* this morning reports that the crowd in Baltimore Street, from Eutaw to the Fallsway, ran to 200,000. For 200,000 read 50,000: such estimates are always grossly exaggerated, especially when made by the police. In my reportorial days I often counted a crowd, and then asked the cops to estimate it. They always at least doubled it, and usually tripled or quadrupled it. Any number above 1,000 staggers the police.

H.L. Mencken

16 August

1776 [New York]

Our Situation, & Living now are most fine. A genteel, sober, patriotic Family, of which, in order to be agreeable, I need say no more. We have a small neat Room, free of Noise, well furnished, & with a good Bed – But our Situation – ! From the door of our Room, we have a good View of the Fleet – A perfect View of New York; Governor's Island; Powles-Hook; & Red-Hood – We live on the very Bank of the Water opposite to Governor's Island.

Some say our Situation is dangerous; but all places in the Neighbourhood of York are, I think, equally dangerous – We fear not Tory *George*, & his War-worn Army! – We fear them not. I prefer my Situation here, where I can discover the first Motions of his Fleet, & trace them along to their Place of Action, or out of the Harbour – To any Situation whatever of *Elegance, Safety*, or *Ease*.

Philip Vickers Fithian

1940 [POW camp, Germany]

Went 10K to work today with Poles. Girls as well. I love to hear them sing while they work, although what they find to sing about beats me. They're as badly off as us. Bed means straw, no blanket. Just lay down in what you work in, except taking these awful clogs off. We haven't a towel or soap, and only clothes to stand up in, shirt and thin drawers. All lousy. Even our uniform is full of them. Can't keep them down no how.

Sergeant L.D. Pexton, British Army

1940 [Boulogne]

Our officers and officials have been careful to see that we do not talk with any returning German pilots. But I talked to a number of navy and army men in charge of the coastal guns yesterday and this morning and was surprised that they all thought the war would be over in a few weeks. One naval captain in charge of a big gun at Cap Blanc-Nez, half-way between Calais and Cap Gris-Nez, took me this morning into his little dug-out, scooped out of the side of the slope, to show me how he had fixed it up. It was very cozy. He had slung a hammock between the two walls and had a little table crowded with German books and magazines. He was a straw-blond, clean-cut young man from near Hamburg, and extremely intelligent.

'You've got a nice little place here,' I said. 'Only –'

'Only what?' he laughed.

'Well, I know Normandy in winter, and from the end of October until April it's damned cold here and it rains every day. Your dug-out is all right now, captain, but it won't be so comfortable over the winter.'

He looked at me in complete amazement.

'Why, I haven't the slightest intention of spending the winter here,' he said, deadly serious now. 'Why, the war will be over long before then. You were kidding, I think, isn't it?'

'No, I wasn't kidding,' I said, a little taken back by his dead certainty. 'Do you mean you think the invasion will be completed and England conquered before Christmas, captain?'

'I shall be at home with my family this Christmas,' he said.

William L. Shirer

1940 [Ashcombe]

Only a few minutes after the 5 o'clock to Salisbury had left Waterloo the air raid sirens sounded. Then the guard, a little man of over fifty years, came along the corridor crying 'All blinds down'. Above the noise of the train we hear thumps and bangs. We went on reading or minding our own business with lowered eyelids. The English behave with unpassitivity even in the face of disaster. Imagine this carriage filled with Latins! The screams! The hysteria!

Cecil Beaton

1967 [The White House]

Early in the day I had been to a ceremony in the East Room – a Vietnam Civilian Service Awards Ceremony – that was very moving. Former Ambassador Lodge was with us on the stage. A small group of civilians, workers in AID and members of a church group, received citations for their bravery and their dedication and their long hours in constructive work in Saigon hospitals and schools – a gigantic effort quite apart from the war. Were there ever such people as Americans?

Lady Bird Johnson

17 August

1942 [Jersey]

The Germans have now got to our field making their railway, and today they have Russians working on it. Hundreds have arrived, even women. It is said that people in town wept to see them pass. One

Russian, at work today, asked John if he were English: 'I Soviet, You English,' and he clapped his hands joyfully! It is a strange thing that we should be allied with Russia. One does not know what to think about these things. Yet we feel so sorry for these Russians – far from home, half-starved and half-naked. Then, the fact of us all being under the Germans is a link. One feels friendly towards all who are suffering in the same way as oneself.

Nan Le Ruez

1943 [POW camp, Java]

We are replacing the decrepit Dutch crosses over their ten graves in the cemetery and have an excellent signboard on a large tree. 'Hintok, Australian and NEI POWs' [Netherlands East Indies] Cemetery', surmounted by a rising sun.

Weary Dunlop

18 August

1940 [Surrey]

A glorious summer day, the peace and serenity of which was rudely interrupted by two raids, one at lunchtime, the other during tea, which obliged us to suspend our enjoyment of it and seek shelter in our 'hide' in the passage. Revelling in a nude sunbathe in a quiet spot in the garden when the second raid was announced, I had to dress hurriedly as I felt, curiously enough, that I didn't want to find myself in trouble, unclothed. Nevertheless, I had a good session of gardening in the morning and a quiet, restful afternoon. In spite of enemy attention the day was well and agreeably spent.

Walter Musto

1940 [London]

Sunbathed on Rupert's [a boyfriend] roof in brassière and trousers, reclining like an odalisque on a rose-pink pillow, with Henry Miller purring on my stomach. I could hear Leonard and Agnes quarrelling through the window overhead. We read aloud from back numbers of *The Booster* monthly, run by Gerhardt [a German boyfriend] and his Paris friends, which has poems like 'Out of the gorse came a homosexual horse'.

Air-raid siren while we were cooking lunch, and lots of planes came over. I went on frying baked beans and Rupert went on reading *Madame Bovary*. No one took much notice except for Leonard and Agnes who rushed into the shelter carrying chairs. Next day we read in the papers that it had been the biggest day-time air battle since the war started, with 185 German planes destroyed over England.

Joan Wyndham

1992 [Sarajevo]
Dear Mimmy,
Mummy is carrying home the water. It's hard on her, but she has to do it.[1] The water hasn't come back on. Nor has the electricity.

I didn't tell you, Mimmy, but I've forgotten what it's like to have water pouring out of a tap, what it's like to shower. We use a jug now. The jug has replaced the shower. We wash dishes and clothes like in the Middle Ages. This war is taking us back to olden times. And we take it, we suffer it, but we don't know for how long.

Zlata Filipovic

19 August

1916 [London]
I so loathed the idea of rejoining the Army that I determined to desert and hide away somewhere.

This was so strong with me on Saturday, August 19th, when rather against my family's wishes, I went down to Tiverton for the last time. Never was the desire to desert and to commit suicide so overriding, and had it not been that I knew I would pain many people, I would certainly have killed myself that night. I imagined myself getting a knife, putting its point carefully between two ribs, and driving it home with the intensest of pleasure and no feeling for the pain.

Arthur Graeme West

---

[1] Her father had been diagnosed with a hernia and was forbidden to lift heavy weights.

20 August

1942 [Kent]

And as I walked by the river today all the corn had been cut, and there were no barges left where the soldiers would work like slaves to get them in and out of the water while the officer sat on the bank, not even watching, but paring his nails. The soldiers were dressed in flimsy football shirts and dirty singlets or nothing, but the officer had on his neat uniform and a white jersey which he must once have had for school sports.

Now those barges were not there. They and the men must have crossed the channel to take part in the great battle of the day before yesterday. Each barge would hold a tank so snugly and the men would sweat and strain just as they did here, only now it would be to get the monsters on to a French beach, and overhead there would be bombers and gusts of machine-gun fire.

Then there is death and dying over there still and agony all night for some.

The five labourers forking the corn into the lorry see me by the river's brim and shout. I think one waves. It is so far away that I dare not answer for fear of a mistake or insults. I just watch the rhythm of the blue shirted and white shirted ones playing to each other with their movements like flute and oboe. I think that being still by the river with prunes and biscuits and coffee and precious chocolate is almost to be easy. To take your shirt off and lie back against the spiky satin grass! To feel the first heavy drops of rain on your skin and to know that no one will come near you. Yet how I loathe nature lovers! My thoughts are never on nature though I go out to roam for hours in the fields every day. My thoughts always go to history, to what has happened century after century on each spot of earth. To lovers lying on the banks, young men that are dead.

On a torn piece of note-paper that I found was an eagle coming out of a circle on which was written Per Ardua ad Astra,[1] then in washed-away ink an address of some aircraftman. And I remembered how a month ago I had found the same piece of paper, only then I could read his address. Now I couldn't. What was the letter about?

Denton Welch

[1] By steep and toilsome ways to the stars. The motto of the RAF.

21 August

1942 [Amsterdam]

Dearest Kitty,

There's little change in our lives here. Peter's[1] hair was washed today, but that's nothing special. Mr van Daan and I are always at loggerheads with each other. Mummy always treats me like a baby, which I can't stand. For the rest, things are going better. I don't think Peter's got any nicer. He's an obnoxious boy who lies around on his bed all day, only rousing himself to do a little carpentry work before returning to his nap. What a clot!

Anne Frank

1942 [London]

This afternoon I came upon Rick talking to a lodger who is a Commando and was in the Dieppe raid this week. He is young, bronzed and incredibly tough. When introduced he shook my hand in a vice-like grip. I felt so shy in his presence, and humble, and inferior, that I could find nothing to say. Nor did I much care for him. He casually remarked that a man in his troop had shot two of his officers for cowardice, one at Dunkirk and the other during a recent cross-Channel raid.

James Lees-Milne

22 August

1941 [Dresden]

LTI. Lightning war [Blitzkrieg], *final battle* – superlative words. War and battle are no longer enough. At the same time the megalomania of numbers.

Frau Paul [a neighbour], whose 2nd or 3rd husband was Jewish, who is going through divorce proceedings with the 3rd or 4th, talks in despair about her mother, 89, who is showing signs of senile dementia. 'I cannot put her in a hospital, she'll be killed there.' There is widespread talk now of the killing of the mentally ill in the asylums.

Victor Klemperer

---

[1] Peter van Daan, young son of Mr and Mrs van Daan.

1943 [POW camp, Java]

I called to have a last powwow[1] with the local Korean No.1 Yamamoto, and told him of arrangements tomorrow, to which he agreed. I then thanked him for having been a very kind No.1 and that I hoped he would soon be made a general – to which bait he responded, by producing a pommelo, bananas and cigarettes, etc. and made all sorts of kind enquiries re my wife and seven children [fictitious for prestige]. He asked if I had only one wife, as seven children seemed rather of lot to ask of one woman. He has, on his own part, a wife and three children whom he has not seen for three years. People in Japan are very tired of war, he said, and never thought it would be so long – 'Now, perhaps – another three years? What did I think of Nipponese men?' Answer: 'Sama sama all men – some good some bad.' He said: 'Yes some very bad men in Nippon – but some good.'

Weary Dunlop

23 August

1915 [the Russian Front]

Finger and hand cases came to the fore again; many of them had walked in themselves, despite the fact that they had been warned to apply for aid only at the divisional Unit, where the medical staff had its own harsh methods of treatment for self-inflicted wounds. One old soldier, with grey threads in his beard and pathetic brown eyes, held out a trembling, blood-stained hand; I washed it, and under the thick blood-coating, there was revealed the dark tell-tale stain of a wound received at close quarters. I looked at him and he knew that I *knew*, but nothing even akin to cowardice could be read in that haggard face; I saw in it only despair and a great exhaustion of mind and body. I painted the wound quickly with iodine; the dark stain faded somewhat under the yellow tincture. He was trembling all over now; I bandaged him; the necessary details of name and regiment were written down and he was despatched, together with other walking cases, to the Base. A man with a self-inflicted wound is a difficult person to deal with; one could not hastily condemn

---

[1] Dunlop and his men were being moved to another camp and were making special arrangements for cholera patients.

him, for so many conflicting influences would first have to be taken into consideration and we became sensitive to the signs from which we could detect those cases which were the outcome of cowardice. On the other hand, it was not difficult to distinguish the soldiers whose excitable nature and raw-edged nerves could induce them, in a weak moment, to seek the outlet as a definite means of deliverance from the scene of their physical suffering and mental anguish.

Florence Farmborough

1940 [London]
Have got my Home Guard uniform, after 2½ months.

George Orwell

1943 [Surrey]
Reported missing recently, my colleague's neighbour's lad was given up for lost. Their airman son had lately set out on a bombing mission to Milan.

Approaching the Alps one of his crew mentioned that he felt a little sick, due, he thought, to the hearty meal of fish and chips he had taken with the rest before the trip. Soon, another of the crew became sick, and another. Then the pilot, a Norwegian, complained of nausea. One of them, checking on the oxygen supply, found that it had exhausted itself through a leak in the apparatus, just when most needed. Already above the safety limit of 9000 feet it was decided, on consultation with the pilot, who declared his intention of attaining his objective, if at all possible, that they would severally transfer to him their personal emergency oxygen supplies to enable him safely to ascend the 16,000 feet required to clear the mountain range in the hope that all would eventually survive the ordeal of impaired respiration and all its attendant evils. Getting safely over and the crew restored, the pilot descended to 9000 feet which, at Milan, exposed him to attack by flak from below and the hazard of falling bombs from our own aircraft above. He duly released his bombs on the target. Turning away he reflected that, without oxygen, he couldn't return via the Alps as briefed, and without charts for an alternative route they were in a quandary. But, rising to the occasion, the navigator declared that they might make the 700 miles to North Africa. Arriving safely at Tripoli they decided to go on to Algiers, finally to land at Gibraltar. There, they reported to HQ and were given two days' leave with a fortnight's pay in advance. Off the chain for a couple of days while the plane was re-serviced they were made much of and thoroughly enjoyed the visit. Meanwhile, London had been advised of the safe arrival of the missing plane and its crew. Laden with bananas and lemons, the crew returned to the airfield for take-off to find it contained eight passengers for London, a large parcel and mail which, together with the quantities of fruit stowed on board, exceeded their original payload by a thousand pounds in weight. And so a cheerful party started off with a still-leaking oxygen apparatus and, never rising above 9000 feet, they crossed the Bay of Biscay and home to England. Whistling loudly along the home road at 11.30 p.m. the following evening, to the inexpressible delight of his parents, came the son, and later, telling his story, he placed in his mother's hand – a lemon!

Walter Musto

1944 [New York]
Mercedes de Acosta[1], whose voice I have not heard for seven years, telephoned, as if the past had never existed, to tell me the news of the liberation of Paris.

From my hotel bedroom I could see paper flying like confetti from the tall buildings. At the Rockerfeller Center ticker-tape streamers were floating in the breeze like octopuses, while sheets torn from telephone books looked like doves or miniature aeroplanes.

Cecil Beaton

24 August

1914 [Essex]
At Little Waltham troops are billeted for the night. Mrs Suckling, a widow, had expressed her willingness to have two. She found immediately a big '4' chalked on her door. A house-holder is allowed 2s. a day for each soldier, in return, he has to find them shelter of roof and two meals (breakfast and a weak supper). They sleep on the floor of a room, with their own blankets.

Andrew Clark

[1] Poet, playwright and author (1896–1968), one of the most celebrated lesbians of her generation. She claimed: 'I can get any woman from any man.' Among her many lovers were Greta Garbo and Marlene Dietrich.

1941 [Kovno Ghetto, Lithuania]
DOCUMENT: Order of SS Captain Jordan

The Jews of the Ghetto are forbidden to keep dogs unless they are on a leash; or to let cats into the streets.

Avraham Tory

25 August

1776 [New York]
Another holy Sabbath presents to our View. No social Worship to be performed this Day – Carts & Horses driving every Way among the Army – Men marching out & coming in to & from the front Camp – Small Arms & Field Pieces continually firing; all in tumult.

Philip Vickers Fithian

1914 [London]
We are going away for ten days' or a fortnight's holiday to walk ourselves into a quieter state of mind . . .

Beatrice Webb

26 August

1916 [Essex]
Notes of the Zeppelin raid of Thursd. night 24 Aug. as told in the Cadet camp at Little Waltham today: outside Ipswich is a heath. When the Ipswich folk heard the Zeppelins were coming they plunged the town in total darkness. Then some went out on the common and lit a bonfire here and there to look (as seen from a great height) like the flare of big works. They also put up a few acetylene-gas lamps on bushes here and there, to look like lamps at street corners. They lit off a few squibs to attract attention. Then they went back to Ipswich, and waited. Presently a Zeppelin passed right over Ipswich, hovered over the illuminated common, dropped a ton-load of bombs about it. Then, having got rid of the cargo, turned and went back seaward, to report in Germany that it had destroyed a great town.

Andrew Clark

27 August

1776 [New York]
O doleful! doleful! doleful! – Blood! Carnage! Fire! Our People drove
this Morning within their Lines! The Alarm Guns were fired a little
before Day. Many Battalions, of excellent Men, went out into the
Woods on the right & left Wing of the Enemy; – Alas! Numbers were
never to return! – the Enemy surrounded them. Those who could,
retreated within the Lines. Those who could not were obliged to fight
their Way thro the Enemy at every Hazard – But many, many we fear
are Lost. General Lord Sterling's Brigade, in special, excited our tender-
est Pity; A Savage would have pitied them – They stood formed in a
large Body, on a good Eminence, in our plain View, but where we
could give them no Relief! – On three Sides of them were the Enemy
– on the other Side was a broad Marsh, & a Creek. There the brave
Men stood more than four Hours – they found their Enemies surrounding them more, at last they divided placed a body to attack the Enemy
while a Part crossed over the Water – Here was a desperate Fire. But
it was the best they could do. The Officers swam their Horses over,
the Men some swam & some passed in Boats, but many stood behind;
among these is Lord Sterling. Gen. Sullivan also is yet missing! The
daring Britains came up boldly to our Works twice, & twice they were
beat off – But such a dreadful Din my Ears never before heard! – And
the distressed wounded, came crying into the Lines! We have taken
upward of thirty of them.

Philip Vickers Fithian

28 August

1776 [New York]
By account recd. this Morning the Number of the Killed, Wounded
& Prisoners of the Rebels is considerable indeed: Exact Returns are
not yet made.

In the Afternoon, our People penetrated farther upon the Rebels
about Brookland and the Ferry: The Firing was very continual & very
hot, and lasted till dark night. We could only see imperfectly at a
Distance, and impatiently wait to know the Event.

How melancholy is the Reflection, that the Folly & Wickedness of Man, under the abused Titles of Prudence & Patriotism, shall ruin the finest Countries, and proceed, as far as they may, to desolate the Earth! A little Pains & a little common Honesty might have induced a meeting with the King's Commissioners, and have settled all Differences with Amity & Ease. But – *Quos Deus perdere, prius dementat.*

Ambrose Serle

1914 [Sussex]

There are two perturbing moral paradoxes in this war. There has been a disgusting misuse of religious emotion in the assumption of the Almighty's approval of the aims of each of the conflicting groups of combatants. France, it is true, has kept herself free from this loathsome cant, and our 'religiosity' has been tactfully limited to formal medieval phrases and to an Erastian prayer for the use of the established Church. But the Kaiser and the Tsar have outdone each other in fervent appeals to their tribal Gods: the German vulgar and familiar, the Russian dignified and barbaric. The theologians of Europe have disgrace themselves. No Eastern mystic would be guilty of such vulgar blasphemy . . .

The other disturbing reflection is that war is a stimulus to service, heroism and all forms of self-devotion. Hosts of men and women are willing to serve the community under this coarse stimulus who, in ordinary times, are dully immune to any other motive but self-interest qualified by self-indulgence. War, in fact, means an increase of corporate feeling and collective action in all directions. An unholy alliance, disconcerting to the collectivist who is also a believer in love as the bond between races as well as between individuals. I am beginning to loathe the newspapers – with their bombast and lies about atrocities, or their delighted gossip about the famine and disease in 'enemy' countries.

Beatrice Webb

1940 [England]

Christopher Hobhouse's[1] widow comes. She tells me that he left her on Monday evening at 4.30 in their little bungalow at Hayling island. He

---

[1] Christopher Hobhouse, author and one of Nicolson's closest friends.

went down to the Fort [at Portsmouth] and half-an-hour later there was a bombing attack and Christopher and three fellow officers were blown to pieces. They would not let her even attend the funeral since there was so little left. Poor girl. She is to have a baby in March and wants me to be godfather. She is left without a bean. I feel so sad about it.

Harold Nicolson

1940 [Berlin]

We had our first big air-raid of the war last night. The sirens sounded at twelve twenty a.m. and the all-clear came at three twenty three a.m. For the first time British bombers came directly over the city, and they dropped bombs. The concentration of anti-aircraft fire was the greatest I've ever witnessed. It provided a magnificent, a terrible sight. And it was strangely ineffective. Not a plane was brought down; not one was even picked up by the searchlights, which flashed back and forth frantically across the skies throughout the night.

The Berliners are stunned. They did not think it could happen. When the war began, Göring assured them it couldn't. He boasted that no enemy planes could ever break through the outer and inner rings of the capital's anti-aircraft defence. The Berliners are a naïve and simple people. They believed him. Their disillusionment today therefore is all the greater. You have to see their faces to measure it. Göring made matters worse by informing the population only three days ago that they need not go to their cellars when the sirens sounded, but only when they heard the *flak* going off near by. The implication was that it would never go off. That made people sure that the British bombers, though they might penetrate to the suburbs, would never be able to get over the city proper. And then last night the guns all over the city began pounding and you could hear the British motors humming directly overhead, and from all reports there was a pell-mell, frightened rush to the cellars by the five million people who live in this town.

William L. Shirer

1941 [Lake District, England]

We are in the Belleville Hotel right on Lake Windermere, sleeping in bunks. Every morning at crack of dawn we have to hit the parade ground and all day long there are lectures in the Nissen huts on how to be an administration officer.

Here is a typical day's programme – parade (and at least four things found wrong with my appearance – 'Ropy do, Wyndham, your collar is filthy!'). Then a lecture on VD and scabies, followed by compulsory hockey in a thunderstorm – then another lecture on pregnant WAAFs. As if this wasn't enough we have a compulsory cello concert after dinner – can you imagine, after all that a *cello* concert?

Joan Wyndham

1941 [Lewes, England]

Parson Newbury and his wife from Barcombe at Mrs Jervis's. Such dear people. Mrs Newbury voluble about the immorality at Barcombe, as everywhere. Girls and married women 'expectant mothers' by soldiers. She also said that a German plane came down at Barcombe. A dead German in it. 'We hoped to just pop him quietly into a corner of the churchyard but, would you believe it, when the Rector arrived to read the funeral service there were 300 bicycles *outside* the church and the place *packed* with people!'

Mrs Henry Dudeney

29 August

1940 [Berlin]

I had my own troubles at the radio [station] last night. First, the censors announced that we could no longer mention a raid while it was on. (In London Ed Murrow not only mentions it, but describes it.) Secondly, I got into somewhat of a row with the German radio officials. As soon as I had finished my broadcast, they ordered me to the cellar. I tried to explain that I had come here as a war correspondent and that in order-ing me to the cellar they were preventing me from exercising my profes-sion. We exchanged some rather sharp words. Lord Haw-haw,[1] I notice, is the only other person around here, except the very plucky girl secre-taries, who does not rush to the shelter after the sirens sound. I have avoided him for a year, but have been thinking lately it might be wise to get acquainted with the traitor. In the air-raids he has shown guts.

William L. Shirer

---

[1] The sobriquet of William Joyce (1906–46), who was born in New York but fled to Germany in 1939 to avoid internment as a fascist. He was infamous for broadcasting German propaganda. In 1945, he was arrested, tried, convicted and hanged for treason.

30 August

1776 [New York]

Once more our Army is in New York – the prevailing Opinion is we cannot keep the Capital more than two or three Days. The Winds are northerly & have been since they came on Shore but the huge Ships beat up a little nearer every Tide, & we hourly expect them before the Town.

Philip Vickers Fithian

1862 [Manassas, America]

Got with the Regt about 10 a.m., we lay in line of battle until 3 p.m. when the greatest battle of the war commenced in earnest. Regular skirmishing had been kept up all day. The battle opened right in our front. We were ordered immediately forward. We met a desperate fire but pushed forward until we gained the old rail road. Soon got the Yanks in full retreat. [General] Longstreet closed in from the right and did some desperate fighting, finally got them to running. We followed in pursuit about an hour after dark, encamped the night near Stone Bridge. We had two days fight and I am now left with not over 15 men present in my Company.

Captain Michael Shuler, Company H, 33rd Virginia Volunteer Infantry,
CSA

1914 [Essex]

Reports from Braintree: twenty-eight men of Courtauld's Braintree crape-works, after a recruiting meeting, volunteered for service. The government is said to allow – per week – to each man 8s. 9d., to his wife 7s. 7d. and 1s. 2d. for each child. The hospital of the Red Cross at Braintree was very much out of pillow cases. Mrs Lave of Gosfield Hall, a very wealthy but most eccentric widow-lady, had lent four, all carefully marked with her name and stringent orders that they should be returned when no longer needed.

On my way to Church for a Christening at 6 p.m., Miss Lucy Tritton, elder daughter of H. L. M. Tritton of the Hole Farm, Great Leighs, met me, jumped off her bicycle and told me that her father had heard from someone in the 'Home' office (she said) that a large Russian force from Archangel had landed in Scotland and was being speeded south by rail to take its place in the theatre of war in Belgium.

I mentioned the report of Saturday's evening paper, that a train-load of 200 Russians escaped from Germany into Switzerland and France, had reached England. But Miss Tritton was positive that her information was authentic and correct.

My elder daughter, Mary Alice, attended the evening service at Fairstead, one of the ring of parish churches which lie round Great Leighs. The Rector, Thomas Sadgrove, preached a horrifying sermon, on the horrible scenes of the battlefield and exhorted all the young men to join the army. He had a big Union Jack hung in front of the pulpit, instead of the pulpit-hanging.

Andrew Clark

1939 [London]
We wait still; war or peace. The governments have locked themselves in and continue exchanging letters; only we no longer know what they are saying. Tension has relaxed, simply because it was impossible to remain at that pitch of anxious fever for long. But the situation is the same. One hopes blindly for some miracle, but one dare not speak about it. People seem resigned, almost cheerful. 'I think we're going to have a slap at him this time.'

Keith Vaughan

1940 [London]
I went about with my camera. At the Natural History Museum near by, the curator showed me the wreckage. *The Times*, he complained, had minimized the damage. Why, the herborium had been burnt out by an incendiary bomb! And that was the centre of interest of all the botanists of the world!

Cecil Beaton

31 August

1862 [Manassas, America]
Wrote a letter home this morning and made a detail to bury the dead. Knapsacks, blankets, and oil cloths are strewn in all directions. Cooked some rations and took up the march in the direction of Leesburg.

Captain Michael Shuler, Company H, 33rd Virginia Volunteer Infantry,
CSA

1916 [the Russian Front]

My temperature this morning was 38.1°. Marching-orders have reached us and our *Letuchka* [Flying Column] is to leave on the morrow! I feel desperate. Could anything be worse for me at the present moment? Two staff doctors came to see me. I was to be transferred without delay to the Base hospital in Podgaytsy. I knew the name; it was miles away and long, long, miles from the Fighting Lines. I wept bitterly and protested vehemently, but tears and protests were of no avail. So this was the end; a miserable, humiliating end to all my longed-for Red Cross work. I lay helpless in my bed, torn by misery and fever.

Florence Farmborough

1939 [Perth, Scotland]

Learned from the air this morning (Sep.1st)[1] that Germany has invaded Poland at dawn – already many cities are suffering bombardment; the first bomb fell among civilians hours ago. Now we await our own evacuees and the intimation that the first bomb has fallen upon London. The greatest catastrophe which has erupted in the world is already a fact, although the oncoming surge of it has not as yet broken over us. Outside in the overcast day, the familiar sounds rise up through the quiet. Children are at play nearby, a tradesman's bell is ringing, someone rattles a pail. And in the garden the autumnal beauty still lingers, halted at this hour in stillness – scarcely a leaf moves on the sycamore tree, under the dark green of the hawthorn are still the blue and yellow blooms, a bird skims silently across the smooth stretch of grass. The peace which we have broken so barbarously abides here for yet another day.

William Soutar

1940 [Italy]

I went hunting with Ribbentrop.[2]

Count Ciano

1942 [Russia]

All our talk concerns two subjects: leave and women, yes, women even here in Russia. You often hear such talk from comrades as 'I consider

---

[1] Soutar was writing his diary for the 31 August in the early hours of the following day.

[2] Joachim von Ribbentrop (1847–1934), German Foreign Minister, Hitler's Special Representative.

myself married only in Germany . . .' One can readily imagine how these fellows spend their leisure time.

Pvt First Class Wolfgang Knoblich, 7th Company, 2nd Battalion, 513th Infantry Regiment, Wehrmacht

1944 [London]

The Allies march on to victory, more triumphs everywhere. What a fortnight it has been. 'Key towns', of which one has never heard, fall daily, and Paris has been liberated twice in three days. Coats are turning inside out in the Balkans, and old Hindenburg[1] must be turning, too, in his grotesque tomb at Tannenburg.

'Chips' Channon

---

[1] Field Marshal Paul von Beneckendorff und Hindenburg (1893–1946), commanded the German Eighth Army with Ludendorff as his COS, and initiated the futile offensives in the spring of 1918. Elected president of the Weimar Republic in 1925.

SEPTEMBER

The unmentionable odour of death
Offends the September night.

W.H. Auden, 'September 1, 1939'

1 September

1854

Arrived at Constantinople this morning; and heard that the Army was embarking for Sebastopol, and would probably sail on the 3rd.

The French and English have suffered severely from sickness in Bulgaria. For my part I never felt better, and I sincerely hope I may be preserved to return home: but, above all things, I do earnestly pray that God will grant me strength and courage to behave as becomes a man and a soldier, come what may.

It will be my first battle, and no man can say what effect that may have on him, so I repeat that, above all things, I pray for a stout heart and a clear head when the battle rages fiercest, particularly *should we be unsuccessful*.

Lieut. General Sir Charles Ash Windham

1939 [Carradale, Scotland]

Woke from nightmare to realise that at least it [declaration of war] hadn't happened yet; so until after breakfast. Got the news at 10.30. Two of the boys had been out all night herring fishing so were asleep still; the others came in and listened. At the end Dick [her husband] said That's torn it. Thought I had better at once return the cups and saucers borrowed from the WRI [Womens' Rural Institute] and the school urn, and see what news there was of the children to be evacuated. Felt a bit sick. Went into the garden, and saw Willie, very white; he had been listening to Hitler, 'working them up' – Willie himself conducts a choir. Talked a little to him and James Downie, all felt it had got to come now.

We talked of the ordinary people in Germany and tried to hope this would mean the end of privilege everywhere. So to the stables; Lachie was filling up the car, so I waited talking to Eddie and Taggie, both of them curiously without enmity towards Germany; we discussed ploughing up the fields for potatoes, and they argued as to whether they would bear two crops in succession and I said I hoped they wouldn't have to. Taggie talked about his young brother who is a C.O.

[conscientious objector] said They'll shoot him before he goes, and It's no free country where they can do that. I said I thought it important that there should be some real pacifists in any community, and they agreed; I said I would do what I could for the boy. Both agree that the ordinary people in Germany don't want this. Lachie brought the car back; I said Bad news, and he soberly said Aye.

Naomi Mitchison

1939 [Perth, Scotland]

Jenny [the maid] had just started to clean my window when the 10.30 a.m. news-bulletin began intimating that Germany had invaded Poland. Mother passed on the news to Jenny who, on returning to her window-cleaning, exhibited such an increased acceleration that she was done in less than half her normal time. With a like exuberance she tackled the summer-house windows; dashing up and down the steps, and now and then sticking out her chest like a belligerent bantam. Evelyn [sister] remarked in the evening that the public-houses were crowded with young fellows, and numerous militia-men rolling along the streets. My own recollection of a personal reaction prompted by a similar mood takes me back to June, 1916. On the afternoon when the report of Kitchener's death was made public, I was crossing from the Academy to the North Inch where, on a strip of grass bordering the path to the left of the old cannon, a number of senior boys were practising putting the weight in preparation for the approaching sports. Before I had joined them, somebody informed me that Kitchener had been drowned. This bit of news immediately galvanized me into a mindless exuber-ance, and I instantly set off towards the potential athletes leaping and running and shouting, 'Hurrah! Kitchener's dead!' Then, on joining the starting party, I picked up the weight and gave it a mighty heave, out-distancing all the previous throws. I suppose the unconscious thought expressing itself in such a display of animal boisterousness is: 'Look, Death, look; here is somebody alive and very much alive.'

William Soutar

1940 [London]

Slept late, office till half-past one, then [Col. Michael] Scanlon and I went to get in a few holes of golf at Addington, selecting that course because it is not far from Croydon, which the Jerries frequently attack and we thought we might see a battle. What a queer way to go golfing, with tin hats and field glasses strapped onto our caddy bags. It was a beautiful afternoon but, although British fighters were quartering the sky far above us, the only excitement of the afternoon was when I holed a niblick approach from well off the green to win a hole which Scanlon already counted as his.

General Raymond E. Lee

1940 [London]

Recently bought a forage cap . . . It seems that forage caps over size 7 are a great rarity. Evidently expect all soldiers to have small heads. This tallies with the remark made by some higher-up to R.R.[1] in Paris when he tried to join the army – 'Good God, you don't suppose we want intelligent men in the front line, do you?' All the Home Guard uniforms are made with 20-inch necks . . . Shops everywhere are beginning to cash in on the Home Guard, khaki shirts etc. being displayed at fantastic prices with notices 'Suitable for the Home Guard'. Just as in Barcelona [during the Spanish Civil War], in the early days when it was fashionable to be in the militia.

George Orwell

1941 [Leningrad]

We have ten or fifteen alerts each day. It seems more like one continuous alert with short breaks. But it is quiet – we do not even hear the anti-aircraft guns. Everything seems to be happening far away, beyond the horizon. We feel that the Junkers circle the outskirts of the city, but cannot break through . . . but the day will come when they will break through, as they did in Moscow.

I would take my typewriter and start down the stairs to the air-raid shelter. Once I met a woman on the stairs; she had gone out of her mind. Her husband was dead, but she thought he had stayed behind in the flat, alive. As she walked down, the cried, 'He was with me all the time, and then suddenly he lagged behind . . . How is he managing without his overcoat?'

I went on down. In the shelter there was a woman – a stranger to us – who was rushing to and fro in a frenzy, looking for her baby, asking if any of us had seen it. All the time the baby was in her arms, wrapped in a shawl.

---

[1] Richard Rees, writer, painter, critic.

I never locked the door of my Moscow flat because of the danger of incendiary bombs. I was on the top floor, and, besides, the fire-watchers on the roof occasionally came for a drink of water.

Once I went up before the All Clear was sounded. Two of our tenants stood at the open window, speaking in low voices. Above the Kremlin walls the stars shone brilliantly; they shone with that particular brilliance we see in the hour before dawn, as if they are moist from dew. And in the distance the sky was scarlet from raging fires . . . the three of us stood for a long time watching the distant inferno.

Vera Inber

1943 [London]
At an S.P.A.B. [Society for the Protection of Ancient Buildings] meeting I found a small attendance considering a matter of the first importance, whether or not to protest in the press against the night bombing of historic German cities. Maresco Pearse and Marshall Sisson were uncompromisingly in favour of protesting. [Viscount] Esher took the view that to do so would have no effect whatever; that the Government would not be the least deterred and many members of the public would be antagonized. I dare say he is right in saying that protest would be fruitless, nevertheless I am in favour of our making some gesture of disapproval of the indiscriminate bombing. I had come unprepared for such a discussion and thought the committee should have been warned in advance. After much talk it was decided that no letter of protest should be sent by the Society to the press, but that Esher should submit to the Secretary for Air a list to be prepared by Sisson of historic German towns with the recommendation that the Air Ministry might spare them as far as possible.

James Lees-Milne

2 September

1870 [Paris]
Coming out of the Louvre, I met Chennevières,[1] who told me that he was leaving for Brest tomorrow, to escort the third trainful of

---

[1] Philippe de Chennevières, writer.

pictures from the Louvre, which are being taken out of their frames, rolled up and sent to the arsenal or the prison at Brest to save them from the Prussians. He described to me the melancholy, humiliating spectacle of this packing operation, with Reiset[1] crying like a baby over *La Belle Jardinière*[2] lying at the bottom of her crate, as if over a loved one about to be nailed into her coffin. This evening, after dinner, we went to the station at the Rue d'Enfer, and I saw the seventeen crates containing the *Antiope*, the finest Venetian paintings, and other treasures – pictures which one had imagined fixed to the walls of the Louvre for all eternity and which were now nothing but parcels, protected against the hazards of removal by the word *Fragile*.

The Brothers Goncourt

1939 [London]

Arrived in London by air, with Hugh [her husband]. Hugo rescuing me, anxious, possessive: 'How good it is to have you. It took a war to make you come home.' London. This dismal city of monsters, fair of ugliness and deformities, the man and woman without magic, fleshy like meat in butcher shops, and every wart, every blackhead, dandruff, magnified a hundred times because they make no effort to be beautiful, employ no artifice or stratagems. A skeleton thinness that one sees nowhere else, bones and muscles showing as in a medical chart, pimples, nonhuman eyes. The proof? Their only connection is with the animal. They are only human with carts, dogs, horses.

Anaïs Nin

1939 [London]

Awful news: they are planning to close the theatres! I rushed straight off to the New to see John and Edith Evans for the last time doing *The Importance [of Being Earnest]*. Sat in the gallery. People in the street seemed really quite cheerful, and all the people in the gallery queue were talking to each other, which is unusual for the English!

When I got home Mummy and Sid were absolutely furious with me for going to the theatre. They seemed to think it was a dreadfully frivolous thing to do at such a time.

Joan Wyndham

[1] Marie-Frederick de Reiset, art collector.
[2] By Raphael.

1939 [Saltsjöbaden, Sweden]

Up at 7.30. Cool, rainy, then better. Battles, bombardments in Poland
. . . After tea took a walk with the Frenchman who had come to
Sweden to buy precision instruments and is now cut off from Paris;
he has three sons in the army. After dinner read proofs. Then listened
to the broadcast from London. England's ultimatum. The determination to put an end to the National Socialist regime. Declarations
of loyalty from the dominions. A comment by a university German
teacher, simple and effective, summarising world press opinion. Now
they are speaking our language, calling Hitler a madman. Late, very
late . . . If the wretched man had a spark of that 'love for Germany'
that allegedly started him on the course of his crimes, he would put
a bullet through his head and leave orders that they pull out of
Poland.

Thomas Mann

1940 [Kent]

There is a tremendous raid in the morning and the whole upper air
buzzes and zooms with the noise of aeroplanes. There are many fights
over our sunlit fields. We go up to see Gwen [his sister] at Horserace
and suggest improvements to her garden. Raids continue the whole
time. It is evident that the Germans are sending more fighters to protect
their bombers, and our losses are therefore in higher proportion.

In the evening Vita [his wife] and I discuss the high-spots in our
life. The moment when I entered a tobacconist's shop in Smyrna, the
moment when we took Ebury Street, our early days at Long Barn,
the night that Nigel was born, the night at Kermanshah, and so on.
Vita says that our mistake was that we remained Edwardian for so
long, and that if in 1916 we had got in touch with Bloomsbury, we
should have profited more that we did by carrying on with Mrs George
Keppel,[1] Mrs Ronald Greville[2] and the Edwardian relics. We are amused
to confess that we had never even heard of Bloomsbury in 1916. But
we agree that we have had the best of both the plutocratic and the
Bohemian worlds, and that we have had a lovely life.

Harold Nicolson

---

[1] Alice Keppel, one-time mistress of King Edward VII and London hostess.
[2] Maggie Greville, famous London hostess.

3 September

1777 [Pennsylvania]

A wounded man who was left on the field was found to be quite drunk. It seems the whole had received an extraordinary quantity of strong liquor, and that the detachment was composed of Volunteers and looked upon as a Corps from which great exertions were to be expected. They were commanded by a General Maxwell.

John André

1939 [England]

I am going to keep a journal because I cannot accept the fact that I feel so shattered that I cannot write at all.

Stephen Spender

1939 [London]

At eleven o'clock this morning England declared war on Germany. The insane calamity whose fear has overshadowed most of my conscious life has happened; has become actual, real and present. And it takes all my will to convince myself that it is so. The moon is high and full and the sky is starred with stillness. There is a peace over the land more profound that anything I can remember.

Keith Vaughan

1939 [Saltsjöbaden, Sweden]

Again more summery weather. I wrote my pages as usual, awaiting events. At noon took a walk along the cliffs of the bathing island, and while sitting on a bench spoken to by a Swedish teacher, with whom I conversed for some time. The English ultimatum ran out at noon. Since that moment England and France have been at war with Germany. The German radio is playing marches, which is their response to the English demand (their usual obstinate mendacity), and Hitler's announcement to the troops in the East that he is on his way to inspect them. Fate now taking its course. They plan to bring Poland to her knees within two weeks and turn away the enemy from the West Wall. There are comments about months 'and years' to come. Will the people of Germany be prepared to wait out those years?

Thomas Mann

1939 [Surrey]

At 11.15 a.m. today the Prime Minister announced over the wireless that a state of war exists between England and Germany from this moment. Dreadfully disappointing for him. God grant that right shall prevail over might. At 11.31 the first real air-raid warning. At 5 p.m. a state of war came into existence between France and Germany. At 6 p.m. the King made an affecting speech over the radio and gave this our crusade of right over might his blessing.

Walter Musto

1939 [London]

This morning war was declared by the Prime Minister over the radio.

Five minutes after the National Anthem, while we were still sitting around feeling rather sick, the air-raid warning went. For a moment we didn't believe our ears – we hadn't had time to realise we were at war – then we went down to our gas room and began damping the blankets with pails of water.

When the room was ready we went and sat on the front doorstep waiting for the first gun. The balloon barrage looked too lovely in the sun against the blue sky, like iridescent silver fish swimming in blue water. After a bit the all-clear sounded. We heard afterwards that it had all been a mistake.

Joan Wyndham

1939 [Rome]

At 11:00 the news arrives that Great Britain has declared war on Germany. France does the same at 5 p.m. But how can they fight this war? The German advance in Poland is overwhelming. It is not impossible for us to foresee a very rapid finish. In what way can France and England bring help to Poland? And once Poland is liquidated, will they want to continue a conflict for which there is no longer any reason? The Duce doesn't think so. He tends to believe in peace in the short term, since he feels that the clash itself, being militarily impossible, will not take place at all. On the other hand, I think it will; I don't know which course the war will take, but it shall play itself out and will be long, uncertain, and implacable. The participation of Great Britain makes this certain. England has declared war on Hitler. The war can end only if Hitler is eliminated or Great Britain is defeated.

Count Ciano

1939 [Dresden]

This torture of one's nerves ever more unbearable. On Friday morning blackout ordered until further notice. We sit in the tiny cellar, the terrible damp closeness, the constant sweating and shivering, the smell of mould, the food shortage, makes everything even more miserable. I try to save butter and meat for Eva and Muschel [his wife and cat], to make do myself as far as possible with still unrationed bread and fish. This in itself would all be trivial, but it is all only by the way. What will happen? From hour to hour we tell ourselves, now is the moment when everything is decided, whether Hitler is all-powerful, whether his rule will last indefinitely, or whether it falls, now, *now*.

On Friday morning, September 1, the young butcher's lad came and told us: there had been a radio announcement, we already held Danzig and the Corridor, the war with Poland was under way, England and France remained neutral. I said to Eva that a morphine injection or something similar was the best thing for us, our life was over. But then we said to one another, *that* could not possibly be the way things were, the boy had often reported absurd things (he was a perfect example of the way in which people take in news reports). A little later we heard Hitler's agitated voice, then the usual roaring, but could not make anything out. We said to ourselves, if the report were even only half true they must already be putting out the flags. Then down in town the dispatch of the outbreak of war. I asked several people whether English neutrality had already been declared. Only an intelligent salesgirl in a cigar shop on Chemnitzer Platz said: No – that would really be a joke! At the baker's, at Vogel's, they all said, as good as declared, all over in a few days! A young man in front of the newspaper display: the English are cowards, they won't do anything! And thus with variations the general mood, vox populi (butter seller, newspaper man, bill collector of the gas company etc., etc.). In the afternoon read the Führer's speech. It seemed to me pessimistic as far as the external and internal position was concerned. Also all the regulations pointed and still point to more than a mere punitive expedition against Poland. And now this is the third day like this, it feels as if it has been three years: the waiting, the despairing, hoping, weighing up, not knowing. The newspaper yesterday, Saturday, vague and in fact anticipating a general outbreak of war: England, the attacker – English mobilization, French mobilization, they will bleed to death! etc., etc. Still no declaration of war on their side. Is it coming or will they fail to resist and merely demonstrate weakness?

Victor Klemperer

1939 [England]

This is I suppose certainly the last hour of peace. The time limit is out at 11. Prime Minister to broadcast at 11.15. L. and I 'stood by' ten minutes ago. We argued. If we win − then what? L. said it's better to win. I suppose the bombs are falling on rooms like this in Warsaw. No children yet come. Maynard[1] has given Quentin[2] a job as tractor driver. This is a relief. No one knows how we're to fight. Rumours beginning. A flurry of people shopping in Lewes yesterday. Shops rather empty. People buying stuff for windows. Little girl says if we have a chink they'll spy us out. Two hours sewing [black-out] curtains. An anodyne: pleasure to do something: but so tepid and insipid. One's too tired, emotionally, to read a page.

It's now about 10.33. Of course I shall have to work to make money. That's a comfort. Write articles for America. Keep the [Hogarth] Press going. So far plenty of petrol. Sugar rationed. So I shall now go in.

Virginia Woolf

1939 [Peoria, USA]

Early this Sunday afternoon Lee [his wife] and I took a nap, but about 2:30 she nudged me and said : 'Eddie, something's happening! They're selling extras!' I awakened instantly. I heard newsboys nearing our place yelling words I couldn't understand. I ran downstairs and bought a paper, an extra edition of the *Journal-Transcript*, with this headline:

BRITAIN FRANCE
MARCH TO WAR

I took the paper up to Lee and we stared at one another, dumb with horror. Chamberlain proclaims a state of war exists with the German Reich . . . President Roosevelt and his aides scan war situation . . . Berlin quickly accepts envoy from Moscow . . . giant German

---

[1] John Maynard Keynes (1883–1946), economist.
[2] Quentin Bell (1910–1996), writer, nephew of Virginia Woolf.

liner in peril at sea . . . text of fateful radio speech . . . Chamberlain message text . . . war bulletins . . .

I asked my wife: 'If you could kill Hitler, would you?'

'Gladly!'

Then she added she is so afraid I might have to go to war that she may shoot off one of my toes.

Edward Robb Ellis

1939 [Germany]

England has declared war on Germany. Hugo has just telephoned me from Berlin. I had to have a strong drink, and now I can't write any more. My head is splitting and I feel ill with nerves.

Elisabeth von Stahlenberg

1940 [London]

The desire to make this journal grew out of the sense of my failure to live a life. When war came I felt that all further hope of success or achievement was over and that there remained only one task, to keep a log book of the last remaining days of the stricken vessel and try to discover what went wrong. If I could do that I felt that failure would lose some of its bitterness. From the rather melodramatic conception of war current at the time I thought it unlikely that I should have very much longer to live. I didn't consider the span in terms of actual weeks or months, but I thought it unlikely that I would see another birthday. The fact that I now find myself alive does not appear extraordinary, nor would it appear extraordinary if I were to die tonight. Life and death are concepts of equal probability. Expectation of life as a natural birthright is something we seem to have outgrown. Announcements declaring the value of War Bonds in 1950 seem rather ridiculous, like taking a house on a ninety-nine year lease. Time in the future is as difficult to comprehend as interstellar space. One lives in an extending and dimensionless present.

Keith Vaughan

1940 [London]

Went to a service at Westminster Abbey to commemorate the first anniversary of the war. The King and Queen were to have gone, but an air-raid warning sounded just before the service began. However the PM [Churchill] and a good many Ministers attended. I rescued [Sir

Anthony] Eden and [Sir John] Dill[1] from a garden where they had been isolated by an over-zealous verger and where they would otherwise have been left and forgotten.

Bishop Hensley Henson, the new Canon, preached an eloquent fighting sermon, containing much alliteration, many fiery denunciations, a good deal of politics and no Christianity – which was what Winston had come to hear.

John Colville

4 September

1854 [Varna]
That the French and English Armies should have been here for months doing nothing, and that now, when they are out of health and spirits, and have lost in effective strength at least one-third of their force, they should undertake to beard in his den the lion that they were afraid of in the open, is certainly wonderful . . .

Only fancy if we fail in this expedition. To say nothing of the bloodshed, look at the loss of reputation to our armies, to the apparent certainty, or at least, stray probability, of a split with France; for a defeat would assuredly produce the most bitter disputes; lastly, consider the defencelessness of our island in the event of the Army being destroyed. And what, I ask, are we to gain? Sebastopol! And in what respect will Russia be injured if we have to return it to her at the end of the war?

We shall, if unsuccessful, be further off peace than ever, in my opinion; and, if unsuccessful, it is better to run, unless we fall back on Odessa, and declare the Crimea attack to have been only a feint. God is merciful, and spares many who little expect or deserve it . . .

All I can say is that, as I am firmly convinced of the folly of the attack, undertaken to gratify the vainglory of a lot of foolhardy men, I will never expunge a word.

Lieut. General Sir Charles Ash Windham

[1] Field Marshal Sir John Greer Dill, Commander of the 1st British Corps. He later became the representative of the British Chiefs of Staff committee in Washington and his work in cementing Anglo–American relations led to the posthumous honour, in 1944, of being the only foreigner to be buried in Arlington cemetery.

1941 [Leningrad]

I was at the editorial offices of our war newspaper when the editor and two of our Moscow writers and their driver returned from the front line. They came into the room, all of them wearing greatcoats and each had a hand-grenade behind his belt. The driver had four grenades and carried a portable machine-gun, which he put down on a table. One of the typists got up, and as she did, she shook the table, and the gun fell off with a clatter. What a mercy the safety catch was in place.

When they had put the grenades on the table the party unrolled a map and studied it with great attention. They were all very gloomy; their trip had been a failure, our troops have been pushed back, the Germans were bombing the Army HQ. And they were all hungry.

Suddenly the telephone rang, and it was reported that one of our anti-aircraft batteries had shot down fifteen enemy planes . . . An unheard-of figure!

And all of them forget their gloom and their hunger, they pick up their grenades and their machine-gun and they rush out. They are to pay a visit to the battery.

Vera Inber

1942 [Berlin]

After lunch – in the office canteen – went with Tatiana [her sister] to see the film G.P.U. This was very well done. But they were also showing a long newsreel about the attempted British landing at Dieppe and seeing that, we were nearly sick; hour after hour of close-ups of torn and mangled bodies. When I next meet one of those responsible for their news films, I will give him a piece of my mind. When in so many countries nearly everyone has already lost a brother, or a son, or a father, or a lover, to go on to show that kind of horror, presumably in order to prop up German morale, is not only shocking but plain idiotic, as it is bound to be counter-productive. And if it is shown abroad, the effect will probably be even more disgraceful. And with good reason!

Marie 'Missie' Vassiltchikov

1943 [Tuscany]

A friend writes: 'There is a patrimony common to all humanity, made up of decency, sensibility and civilized behaviour, which is every day diminishing and will soon be bankrupt. I envy the only people whose hands are still clean, the Swiss, with ideologies which are reflected in the simple acts of everyday life.'

Iris Origo

5 September

1917 [France]

I rejoice in the beauties of Nature; in this summer-like Renoir autumn of the canal and the Aisne; in the ever-shimmering, ever-rustling avenue of elms. The hedge-bordered meadows take on a bluish tinge from the rising mist on the brink of the water, and a faint, blue-green reflection is mirrored below. This green, flourishing wilderness is woven in summer's threads of autumn-tinted soft-toned wools. One can hardly look into the dazzling blue sky. In the tangled grass blooms – an exquisite miracle – the autumn crocus. Long, slender, pale-lilac flowers, with their wonderfully varying lengths of petal, and the pistil, thickly coated with scented yellow pollen, shining through the frail calyx. Their delicate stems are snow-white. The ruins of the town are pastel-white in the heat. Sometimes one sees here the 'classic' landscape of Poussin or Böcklin. I realize how art is determined by landscape. I have drunk all that my eyelashes could encircle of the world's gold superabundance.

Helmut Zschuppe

1939 [London]

The third day of the war and it feels more like the third year. I've sat all day in the noise of ping-pong balls, the tap of billiard cues and incessant vulgar music on the radio. Reading about severed arteries, fractured femurs, dislocated shoulders in the aloof impersonal prose of a first-aid manual. And listening to the stories of the last war by the decrepit old veterans who have suddenly become leaders again. Sitting and waiting. Waiting and doing nothing. The sun has been hot and the sky blue and innocent. Where is this war? If there is a war let us see it and know it for what it is. If there is no war let us stop playing these idiotic parlour games.

Keith Vaughan

1939 [London]

The evening broadcast says that the Germans claim to have captured a Polish town only 56 miles from Warsaw. It looks as if the Polish resistance was nothing at all. We had foreseen that, but it is distressing to get no real news.

I was glad to attend Jessica's [his niece] wedding, since it made me feel that there was something outside this present horror. But in fact I am in a mood of deep depression. I do not really see how we can win this war, yet if we lose it, we lose everything. It may be that I am old and sad and defeatist. But one thing I do know and it comforts me. I would rather go down fighting and suffering than creep out after a month or two at the cost of losing our pride. That may be the only thing left to us.

Harold Nicolson

1940 [Sussex]

Hot, hot, hot. Record heat wave, record summer if we kept records this summer. 2.30 a plane zooms; ten minutes later air raid sounds; twenty minutes later, all clear. Hot, I repeat; and doubt if I'm a poet. An idea. All writers are unhappy. The picture of the world in books is thus too dark. The wordless are happy: women in cottage gardens. Now, in my nightgown, to walk on the marshes.

Virginia Woolf

1942 [Lewes, England]

When I was in my bath and Winnie [her maid] in her bed 2 police-men arrived and said the bathroom light was showing and must go out at once or they would report me. Winnie, at the bathroom door, very voluble and would have burst in if I hadn't hastily burst *out* of the bath and locked the door. So out went the light and I had to dry myself, get into some garments and fumble upstairs in total darkness. Reminded me of the lovely story: Policeman to lady of the house: 'You've a chink showing upstairs.' Lady: 'Why he told *me* he was the Japanese Ambassador'!

Mrs Henry Dudeney

6 September

1914 [Essex]

Another day of intense heat – deep blue sky – only the faintest white clouds; pastures and gardens burnt up by the long drought. Apples, pears and acorns falling prematurely. Mr T. Stoddart, Rector's Churchwarden, tells me that although it is a time of stress and sorrow of war, it is the wish of the parish that the Harvest Festival shall be held next Sunday just as usual in thankfulness for the extraordinary bounty of this year's harvest and unbroken harvest weather.

Andrew Clark

1939 [London]

I used to agree with Hazlitt's 'Egotism is an infirmity that perpetually grows upon a man, till at last he cannot bear to think of anything but himself, or even to suppose that others do.' In war-time this does not hold. I realise that I have become a person of no distinction, and it is this which I find disconcerting. *Per contra*, all sorts of people one had regarded as amiable noodles now turn out to be of immense importance. They burst upon the club in uniform and hold forth where they used to listen. I feel like Kipling's Eustace Cleever, 'decorator and colour man in words', who found himself abashed in the company of young men of action.

James Agate

1939 [England]

I wake up on a lovely morning and lie there thinking how foul it is that this late summer dawn should be bruised by fear and horror. I am thinking these uplifting thoughts when Vita flings open the door and announces, 'There is an air-raid.' It is such a lovely morning that we do not take the air-raid too seriously and remain outside in the sunshine looking at the Alpine plants. Then off I go to catch the train. We are stopped by air-raid wardens in Sissinghurst and Staplehurst but I tell them that I am going to London to execute my functions as Member of Parliament. They are much impressed by this information and pass me on.

I go down to the House and find that it has risen. In the smoking-room I find Bob Boothby[1] talking to Arnold Wilson.[2] The latter is putting it about that Germany will mop up Poland and that we must then make peace. He is a dangerous, well-meaning but slightly insane person. Not that his view is incorrect. I feel perfectly certain that

[1] Sir Robert Boothby (1900–86), MP.
[2] Sir Arnold Wilson (1884–1940) MP, originally known for his pro-Fascist views, he later volunteered and was killed in action.

Germany will mop up the Poles in a week or so. She may also seize the Rumanian oil-fields, solidify her agreement with Russia, and then offer us the most favourable terms of peace. It will then be that our ordeal (and when I say 'our', I mean the Eden Group)[1] will arrive. If we insist upon the continuance of battle, we may condemn many young men to death. If we urge acceptance, we are ending the British Empire. The appeasers will gamble upon the defection of Russia and Italy and good terms with Germany. Again one comes back to the point that Chamberlain did not want this war, and is continually thinking of getting out of it. He may be right. But he has not behaved with sufficient honesty and moral courage to carry the country with him.

Harold Nicolson

1942 [England]

Miss O'Sullivan and I walked to the Blicking mausoleum through the park this morning. She is a weird, embittered woman, whom life has obviously treated unkindly. It is sad how many people there are whose natural goodness can only be brought to light by persistent delving beneath an unpromising surface. So often one has not the time, or energy, or circumstance for the operation, and consequently a false impression of a person may remain with one for a lifetime. During our walk we talked about the war. Miss O'S., who is a regular churchwoman and churchwarden at Blicking, said that the English did not deserve to win, for it was idle to presume we were fighting for the Christian ideal; and that the young, having been brought up without any religious instruction to fend for themselves, which meant to make money, were spiritually barren. These sentiments are, I dare say (although I am not absolutely sure), irrefutable. I told her that I was still fundamentally a pacifist, and only decided to join the army and fight when I realized – not till six months after war had broken out – that no amount of pacifism would stop the war, and the only way to stop it was to win it, which involved the killing of as many Germans as possible. She replied that my decision showed a lack of principle.

James Lees-Milne

[1] Group of MPs, including Nicolson, who were critical of Britain's failure to help the Poles, and who believed that Winston Churchill should succeed Chamberlain as Prime Minister.

7 September

1704 [London]

This day was celebrated the Thanksgiving for the late great victory with the utmost pomp and splendor by the Queene, Court, greate officers, Lord Major, Sheriffs, Companys etc the streets scaffolded from Temple-barr (where the L. M[ayor] presented her Majestie with the Sword, which she returned), every Company ranged under their Banners, and Citty Militia with out the rails, which were all hung with Cloth suitable to the Colour of the Banner, the L. Mayor, sherifs and Aldermen in their Scarlet roobs on their Caparisoned Horses: The knight Martiall and pensioners on horse, the Footguard: the Queene in a rich Coach with 8 Horse, none with her but the Dutchesse of Marlbrow, in a very plaine garment, The Q: full of Jewells, Musique and Trumpet[s], at every Citty Company: The greate officers of the Crown and nobility and Bishops all in Coach of 6. Horses, besides innumerable Spectators in this order went to S. Paules where the Deane preched etc after which the Queene went back in the same order to St. James: The Citty and Companys, feasting all the Nobility and Bonfires and Illuminations at night: Note that there was Musick composed by the best masters of that art, to accompany the Church musique and Anthems etc to all which (after a[n] exceeding wet and stormy day) succeeded one of the most serene and Calmest bright-day[s], as had ben all the yeare.

John Evelyn

1939 [London]

I came to London this morning to fix up our small flat so that we can let it furnished at a moment's notice if necessary. Mrs Sparrow [her charlady] helped me pack up our few treasures and our wedding presents – it seemed strange to be sending them to store. She asked me all the questions I have been asking myself: How long will it last? Will they bomb London? What shall I do now? I promised her I will 'let' her with our flat or not let it at all – so she may be sure of work.

I lunched with Grannie Cooper, who told me that this morning she put her name down for war work and described herself as 'Eighty but active'. We talked of Poland. Afterwards I walked to the gun shop in Pall Mall and bought a small .25 Colt revolver. The shopkeeper said I may not take possession of it until I get a licence. Then I went to Whitaker's [her husband's valet, who had accompanied him to war] flat near Tottenham Court Road and arranged for all his things to be stored. The piano he was buying on the instalment system from Selfridges will have to be returned. On my way home I bought two 'safari' beds made of canvas with slim detachable steel feet. They fold into a neat bundle and are lighter than the old wooden ones. Tomorrow I begin training to be an ambulance driver – in gumboots and gas-mask.

Countess of Ranfurly

1940 [England]

At Tonbridge, where we change trains, there are two German prison-ers. Tiny little boys of 16 they are, handcuffed together and guarded by three soldiers with fixed bayonets. They shuffle along sadly, one being without his boots, shuffling in thick grey socks. One of them just looks broken down and saturnine; the other has a superior half-smile on his face, as if thinking, 'My Führer will pay them out for this.' The people on the platform are extraordinarily decent. They just glance at them and then turn their heads away, not wishing to stare.

Harold Nicolson

1940 [London]

Midnight. Well here I sit in the air-raid shelter with screaming bombs falling right and left, and Sir John Squire, roaring tight, sitting oppo-site me next to his Scotch Presbyterian cook. Squire's breath fills the shelter and the cook looks as if she's going to be sick. Sid is reading Maxim Gorky and I'm trying to write this diary, though I can't see very well as there is only a storm lantern. Squire keeps on saying he wants to read Wodehouse's *Uncle Fred in Springtime* once more before he dies.

I can't help feeling that each moment may be my last, and as the opposite of death is life, I think I shall get seduced by Rupert tomor-row. Rowena has promised to go to a chemist's with me and ask for Volpar Gels, just in case the Reanch thingummy isn't foolproof.

Another bomb, quite near this time. Squire leapt to his feet and is making for the exit. 'I want some cigarettes. I'm going to the pub –'

'Oh no you're not,' says Sid, clutching his arm. 'You're not leaving this shelter until the all-clear goes!'

'Ma'am,' says Squire, evading her with dignity, 'I am!' He climbs over her, remarking indistinctly that he has never stepped over a lady before, and disappears into the shell-scarred night, walking with difficulty.

Joan Wyndham

8 September

1870 [Paris]
Empire or Republic, nothing really changes. It is annoying to hear people saying all the time: 'It is the Emperor's fault.' If our generals have shown themselves to be inefficient, if our officers are ignorant, if our troops have had their moments of cowardice, that is not the Emperor's fault. Moreover, a single man cannot have so great an influence on a nation, and if the French nation had not been disintegrating, the Emperor's extraordinary mediocrity would not have robbed it of victory. Let us not forget that sovereigns always reflect the nation over which they rule, and that they would not remain on their thrones for three days if they were at variance with its soul.

The Brothers Goncourt

1914 [Essex]
Miss Tritton tells me a charming story of Mrs Bearman, a deafish woman in Fuller Street, one of whose sons (who used to work at Lyons Hall farm) has been called out. The old lady said she 'did not know exactly where her son was, but he was at the front; he was at the front for sure.' In answer to an enquiry whether she did not feel very anxious about him, she said 'Ah, but Miss, I have one great comfort. He sends his wash to me every week.' He is apparently as far off as Warley [eighteen miles away].

Andrew Clark

1939 [Gloucestershire]
It seems a very long time since the war began. No one seems anxious to take this house or to employ me on National Service. The discontent among the evacuees has increased. Seven families left the village amid general satisfaction. Those who remain spend their leisure scattering waste paper round my gates. Diana Awdry stopped in to say that

a German submarine was lying berthed on the sand at Lyme Regis and was offended by our incredulity.

Evelyn Waugh

1940 [London]

I took a walk over toward Victoria; the station is closed but one can see that a bomb came through the roof all right and knocked things about badly. The sign said, with true British restraint, 'Closed on account of obstructions'.

General Raymond E. Lee

1942 [London]

A sergeant air-gunner writes: 'I don't suppose you have spent eighteen months in a desert. Or sat in a gun-turret for four thousand and fifty hours, eight hours at a stretch. Or been shot down and wounded. If you had, perhaps you would take more kindly a view of the enclosed poem.' I have replied: 'No, I shouldn't. Your poem, badly rhymed and worse scanned, did its job when it took your mind off the desert and the gun-turret. Having done this, it became waste paper.'

James Agate

1976 [Pagsanjan, the Philippines, on the set of *Apocalypse Now*]

Late in the afternoon I was standing on the main steps of the temple with Francis and Marlon [Brando]. The two of them were talking about Kurtz. Francis had asked Marlon to reread *Heart of Darkness*. Now Marlon was saying how his character should be more like Kurtz was in the book. Francis said, 'Yes, that's what I've been trying to tell you. Don't you remember, last spring, before you took the part, when you read *Heart of Darkness* and we talked?' Marlon said, 'I lied. I never read it.'

Eleanor Coppola

9 September

1939 [England]

Yesterday morning while I was waiting for a bus, some soldiers passed down the road singing 'It's a long way to Tipperary.' An unshaved and very ragged old tramp wearing the ribbons of several medals so loosely attached to his coat that they were almost falling off, said to me, 'They're singing now, but they won't be singing when they come back. Hearing 'em sing reminds me of when I went out to fight in them trenches. We went out singing, but we didn't sing for long.'

Stephen Spender

1939 [Italy]

War makes men barbarous because, to take part in it, one must harden oneself against all regret, all appreciation of delicacy and sensitive values. One must live *as if those values did not exist*, and when the war is over one has lost the resilience to return to those values.

Cesare Pavese

1943 [Italy]

Landed on 'Red Beach', Paestum, at 7 p.m. Boatloads had been going ashore all day after a dawn shelling from the ships and a short battle for the beach-head. Now an extraordinary false serenity lay on the landward view. A great sweep of bay, thinly pencilled with sand, was backed with distant mountains gathering shadows in their innumerable folds. We saw the twinkle of white houses in orchards and groves, and distant villages clustered tightly on hill-tops. Here and there, motionless columns of smoke denoted the presence of war, but the general impression was one of a splendid and tranquil evening in the late summer on one of the fabled shores of antiquity.

We hauled the motor-cycles off the landing-craft, started them easily, and rode up over the wire-mesh laid across the sand, making for the cover of a wood. The corpses of those killed earlier in the day had been laid out in a row, side by side, shoulder to shoulder, with extreme precision as if about to present arms at an inspection by death. We numbered eleven: ten sergeants and a sergeant-major. Captain Cartwright, the Field Security Officer, badly smashed up in a car crash the day before we embarked, was presumably still in hospital in Oran. We had been given no briefing or orders of any kind, and so far as the Americans were concerned we might as well not have existed. This was the greatest invasion in this war so far – probably the greatest in human history – and the sea was crowded to the horizon with uncountable ships, but we were as lost and ineffective as babes in the wood. No one knew where the enemy was, but the bodies on the beach at least proved that he existed. In place of the guns, tanks, armoured cars, barbed wire we had expected to see, all that had been landed in this sector of the beach were pyramids of office equipment for use by Army Headquarters. We had been issued with a Webley pistol and five rounds of ammunition apiece. Most of us had never fired a gun.

As the sun began to sink splendidly into the sea at our back we wandered at random through this wood full of chirping birds and suddenly found ourselves at the wood's edge. We looked out into an open space on a scene of unearthly enchantment. A few hundred yards away stood in a row the three perfect temples of Paestum, pink and glowing and glorious in the sun's last rays. It came as an illumination, one of the great experiences of life. But in the field between us and the temple lay two spotted cows, feet in the air. We crept back into the depths of the sheltering wood, burrowed into the undergrowth, and as soon as night fell, slept. At some time during the night I awoke in absolute darkness to the sound of movements through the bushes, then a mutter of voices in which I distinguished German words. The voices died away, and I slept again.

Norman Lewis

10 September

1854 [SS *Harbinger*, Varna]
The men are ordered to land with their knapsacks, great-coats, and three days' provisions, and to leave their blankets behind them. In my opinion, the knapsack is a perfectly useless thing.

I have walked under weight, and have carried my own provisions for many days, and I am sure that, provided you took a blanket, and put in it a spare shirt, a pair of shoes, and a towel, you might leave your knapsack and great-coat behind you for a fortnight.

A great-coat is a great-coat and nothing more, but a blanket is a blanket and great-coat too, and when men lie down in twos and threes, they can, with good blankets, make themselves comfortable; at least, I always find this to be the case in my hunting trips in North America, where I have gone through more real hard work than falls to the lot of most men.

Lieut. General Sir Charles Ash Windham

1855 [Balmoral]

Albert said they should go at once and light the bonfire. In a few minutes Albert and all the gentlemen, in every species of attire, sallied forth, followed by all the servants, and gradually by all the population of the village – keepers, gillies, workmen – up to the top of the cairn. We waited, and saw them light it; accompanied by general cheering. The bonfire blazed forth brilliantly, and we could see the numerous figures surrounding it – some dancing, all shouting. About three-quarters of an hour after, Albert came down, and said the scene had been wild and exciting beyond everything. The people had been drinking healths in whisky, and were in great ecstasy. The whole house seemed in a wonderful state of excitement. The boys were with difficulty awakened, and when at last this was the case, they begged leave to go up to the top of the cairn.

We remained till a quarter to twelve; and, just as I was undressing, all the people came down under the windows, the pipes playing, the people singing, firing off guns, and cheering – first for me, then for Albert, the Emperor of the French, and the 'downfall of Sebastopol'.[1]

Queen Victoria

1884 [Khartoum]

Spy came in from south front, and one from Halfaya reports Arabs will not attack, but will continue the blockade.

Sent off two sets of telegrams by a spy, who will go to Shendi.

Yesterday, when the messenger went out to deliver my answer to the Arabs, in response to Mahdi's letter, though he had a white flag, they fired on him, and tried to capture him. They use the white flag and find it respected by us, and that we let their men go back. They chain any men we send to them.

General Charles George Gordon

1914 [Essex]

Luckin Smith, the Chelmsford Provisioners, say that they no longer call the well known thick smoked wurtz, 'German Sausage' but 'Dunmow Sausage'. W. Ketley's son says that in Chelmsford and district there are now 17,000 troops. The men are supposed to have a pound

---

[1] 67,000 British, French, Turkish and Sardinian troops began the Siege of Sevastopol on 25 September 1854. It eventually fell on 8 September 1855.

of meat a day and the housekeeper in whose home they are billeted is paid 9d a day for cooking their meals for them. Young Ketley says that, by fault of the butchers, some of the men quartered on him have not had more than 8 oz apiece of meat, the weight being made up of bones.

Andrew Clark

1939 [London]
Ever since war was declared the sun has shone with unremitting splendour, and there is nothing about the gaily dressed smiling crowds in the streets to remind us of this great catastrophe – except perhaps for the gas-masks slung across their backs and the number of men in uniform.

John Colville

1939 [Essex]
I went to Kelveden on Saturday afternoon in lovely weather in the hope of a peaceful perfect Sunday but it was not to be. There were endless decisions to be made; papers to be stored; fuss and confusion; irritated servants; neglected dogs; plate-room and cellar complications. We packed up all our jewelled toys, our Fabergé bibelots and gold watches, etc., and counted the wine, then we welcomed the refugees, all nice East End people, but Honor was depressed and worn out, and our Sunday not as happy as I had hoped.

On my way I looked in at Bucks and saw several swaggering officers with highly polished belts stuffing themselves with oysters ... All morning I went about carrying an absurd gas-mask in a canvas bag, which I found a bore ...

'Chips' Channon

11 September

1939 [France]
War is here. In order to escape its obsession, I am going over and learning long passages of *Phèdre* and of *Athalie*. I am reading the *Atheist's Tragedy* of Cyril Tourneur and Eichendorff's *Taugenichts*. But the oil lamp throws a poor light; I must close the book and my mind returns to its anguish, to its interrogation: is this the twilight or the dawn?

André Gide

1939 [England]

When I drew the blinds I felt the autumn chill in my bones, and because of the decision I have taken which is simply a recognition of existing facts, I had a sense of the desolation of the world. Above all, the world should be home, it should be somewhere where everyone has his place, is surrounded by the simple machinery, the task, the house, the furniture, the companion, the river, the trees or streets which assure him that he is loved. Everyone should be rooted. This is the simplest thing in life, it is the cocoon that surrounds childhood, it is the simple security of the flesh and the kiss and the fireplace and the setting sun which brings him home. The lands that destroy this homeliness whether in children or grown-up people are ripping the child in all of us that never leaves the womb away from the womb, and tearing the belly of the mother into ribbons. No one should want anything except to find this place in life, the centre of his potential to love and be loved.

Stephen Spender

1943 [Italy]

The Fifth Army Headquarters has moved, and we – helplessly parasitic as we are – with it, to Albanella Station, just south of the Sele. This is in a delicate fusion of landscapes: apple orchards full of glowing fruit, vineyards, and olive groves haunted by multitudes of brilliant blue grasshoppers. A few hundred yards away both the road and railway line are carried on a bridge over the river. This, somewhat damaged, is under repair by a team of British engineers, and it is assumed that sooner or later we shall cross it to advance. Fifteen miles or so away to the north a greyish bruise on the otherwise faultless sky indicates a conflict of which we see or hear nothing, and which in our perfumed Arcadia seems remote and unreal.

For all that, an uneasy feeling is beginning to grow that the present unnatural calm cannot last and that the Fifth Army does not altogether realize what it is doing here. There are still no tanks in sight, no artillery but a few ack-ack guns, and no signs of any defences being prepared. The only urgent activity in our neighbourhood is that of hundreds of soldiers streaming like ants to bring typewriters and filing cabinets up from the beach. Those not occupied in this way hang about in desultory street-corner groups, many of them unshaven. We get the impression that they have slight confidence in their leaders and we are frequently asked when we expect Montgomery and the Eighth Army to arrive. Unfortunately Montgomery is still a hundred miles away. So far the only evidence of German interest in our presence here is an occasional visitation by five FW 190s. These cause great alarm but do no damage, as their target is the great armada of ships anchored in the bay.

This afternoon we proceeded with our private exploration of the neighbourhood. We are surrounded by a beautiful desolation. All the farms are abandoned, the trees are heavy with apples, and the ripe tomato crop will soon wither. Unhappy animals mooch about looking for water. Two Americans, tired of their packet K rations containing the ham, cheese, biscuits and sweets that seem so desirable to us, chased after a cow that first galloped, then limped, then staggered as they fired innumerable bullets from their pistols into it. Finally they brought it down and hacked off a hindquarter, with which they departed. We took over an empty farmhouse, littered everywhere with the debris of a hasty departure: articles of clothing strewn about, unmade beds, a pink-cheeked doll on the floor. Italian soldiers who had walked away from the war were plodding along the railway line in their hundreds on their way to their homes in the south. Their feet were usually in terrible shape, with blood sometimes oozing through the cracked leather of their boots; they were in tremendous spirits, and we listened to the trail of their laughter and song all through the day. I spoke to one of these and gave him a few pieces of cheese salvaged from K ration packs jettisoned by the thousand after the candies they contain had been removed. In return he presented me with a tiny scrap of tinselly material torn from a strip he pulled from his pocket. This was from the mantle of a miracle-working Madonna in Pompeii, and by carrying it on my person I would be rendered bullet-proof for a year. 'You never know when it might come in handy,' he said, and I agreed. I thanked him profusely, and we shook hands and parted.

Lining up for chow this evening we were told by Americans belonging to the 45th Division that they have been ordered by their officers not only to take no German prisoners, but to use the butts of their rifles to beat to death those who try to surrender. I find this almost incredible.

Norman Lewis

12 September

1776 [New York]

One daily hears mortifying Accounts of the bitter Tyranny of the Rebels over the loyal Subjects in their Power. Such men are no Enemies to absolute Rule: they only hate it in others, but ardently pursue it for themselves. From the beginning, as soon as they had the least Authority, they have been uniformly Persecutors, though (strange to tell) they pretended to leave their mother-Country upon the Account of Persecution. A flagrant instance of this appeared in the infant State of the New England Colonies; for to these I chiefly allude; so early as the Year 1657. The Assembly at Boston made a Law against Quakers, the Substance of wch was; 'That whoever brought any Quaker, knowing him to be such, should pay 40 Shillings an Hour for such Concealment; and any Quaker there should forfeit £100. That those who concealed a Quaker, after the first Conviction, if a man, was to lose one Ear, and a second Time the other; A Woman, each Time to be severely Whipped, and the third Time man or woman, to have their Tongues bored through with a red hot Iron: Besides, every Quaker, who should become such in the Colony was subjected to the like Punishments.' At length, finding this not enough, they made it Death for a Quaker to appear in the Province; and accordingly hanged some. Yet these, and men like these, are our noisy Advocates for civil & religious Liberty!

Ambrose Serle

1884 [Khartoum]

It is most dispiriting to be in the position I am, if it was not good for me, when I think that *when I left* I could say, 'no man could lift his hand or foot in the land of the Sudan without me' (Gen. XLI 44) and now we cannot calculate on our existence over twenty-four hours. The people are all against us and what a power they have; they need not fight, but have merely to refuse to sell us their grain. The stomach governs the world, and it was the stomach (a despised organ) which caused our misery from the beginning. It is wonderful that the ventral tube of man governs the world, in small and great things.

During our blockade we have often discussed the question of being frightened, which, in the world's view, a man should never be. For my part I am always frightened, and very much so. I fear the future of all engagements. It is not the fear of death, that is past, thank God; but I fear defeat, and its consequences. I do not believe a bit in the calm, unmoved man. I think it is only that he does not show it outwardly. Thence I conclude no commander of forces ought to live closely in relation with his subordinates, who watch him like lynxes, for there is no contagion equal to that of fear. I have been rendered furious when, from anxiety, I could not eat, I would find those at same table were in like manner affected.

General Charles George Gordon

1918 [Essex]
A munition-girl came into the Aldiss' shop, the draper's, Braintree, to buy a hat. She was shown one at 12s. 11d. That, she said, was not nearly good enough for her. Aldiss said he had no better but could trim one up for her. She said she would call in and see it that evening. He took the flower out; put another flower in; and priced it at 18s. 11d. She was entirely pleased with it.

Andrew Clark

1939 [London]
I had lunch with T.S. Eliot a few days ago at his club. He said it was very important that one should, at all costs, go on writing now . . . I mentioned that I hadn't been able to work, so had started this journal. He said, 'Yes, that's an excellent idea. Just writing every day is a way of keeping the engine running, and then something good may come out of it.'

Stephen Spender

1939 [London]
Mother came up from Badminton for the day with Queen Mary. She is furious at being marooned in the country and talks as though she were Ovid eating her heart out at Tomi. She was extremely funny about the effect of the air-raid alarms on the Queen. Apparently they so upset the old lady that she had acute and urgent stomach trouble, with disastrous and undignified results on the motor-drive from Sandringham to Badminton. They were forced to stop at a lonely inn, where the inn-keeper was most helpful. The Queen sent him a small silver knife as a thank-offering, and he replied by sending her a beautiful little carved silver chain (which, as Philip [his brother] remarked,

was a most suitable souvenir!). When they reached Badminton the Queen, who has spent three sleepless nights owing to air-raid warnings and thunderstorms, looked forward to a welcome rest, but was aroused the next morning at 6.00 a.m. because the kitchen-maid turned on the private air-raid warning by mistake for the electric light.

John Colville

1940 [London]

Mummy had made cold meat fritters with the bits left over from the joint, but I felt sick and couldn't eat them – surely I can't be pregnant already. I was beginning to think nervously about taking quinine, which is what the girls in Redcliffe Road drink when they get pregnant, but my mother told me it is something nervous called 'Siren Stomach', very prevalent at the moment!

Joan Wyndham

1941 [London]

Dylan Thomas comes to see me. He wants a job on the BBC. He is a fat little man, puffy and pinkish, dressed in very dirty trousers and a loud check coat. I tell him that if he is to be employed by the BBC, he must promise not to get drunk. I give him £1, as he is clearly at his wits' end for money. He does not look as if he had been cradled into poetry by wrong.[1] He looks as if he will be washed out of poetry by whisky.

Harold Nicolson

1941 [Germany]

Saw *Ich klage an* ['I Accuse', a film about euthanasia] last night, the best film I have seen this year. It really made one think – not just be entertained. Hugo didn't seem impressed, and said it was angled and melodramatic . . . but I do see the point made by the story, that *sometimes* (not always) it is right to kill, *painlessly*, genetic undesirables. There was a family in one village in which almost every child had a defect, and the father was in and out of prison. We used to say the mother ought to be sterilized – now I wonder if at least two of the children who were mentally deficient and couldn't even

---

[1] 'Most wretched men/ are cradled into poetry by wrong/they learn in suffering what they teach in song.' Shelley, *Julian and Maddalo*.

go to school, ought to have been 'allowed to sleep' at birth. When I said this to Hugo he became very angry and refused to discuss it, which I think is stupid. Everything should be discussed, *especially* questions like this.

Elisabeth von Stahlenberg

1967 [Bolivia]
The day began with a tragic-comic episode: at 0600 precisely, time for reveille, Eustaquio came to warn us that some men were advancing along the stream; he called us to arms and everybody mobilised. Antonio had seen them and when I asked how many there were of them, he held up his fingers to show there were five. In fact, it turned out to be a hallucination, dangerous for the morale of the troop as the men immediately started to talk psychosis. Later, I talked to Antonio and evidently he wasn't normal; tears came to his eyes, but he denied that there was anything on his mind and said that he is only affected by lack of sleep, because he has had six days' extra duty for falling asleep at his post and then denying it.

Ernesto 'Che' Guevara

13 September

1939 [Dresden]
On Monday, September 11, *house search* again. For a radio. Amiable child's play for 30 minutes, but nevertheless house search. A fat country police lieutenant from Gittersee and *our* police constable. Friendly, sympathetic people. 'And why aren't you abroad yet?'

Victor Klemperer

14 September

1884 [Khartoum]
It is curious how quick the people forget their disasters and losses; it is only ten days ago that we lost nearly one thousand men, yet no one speaks of it now; it takes about four or six days to obliterate the bitterness of a disaster.

General Charles George Gordon

1917 [Germany]

Yesterday the Iron Cross of the Second Class was sent to me. The pleasure this gave me was some small compensation. To-morrow I start back to the Company. To-day I am in the Convalescent Section getting ready. Well, and what now? When one thing is over one begins to ask, what next? I wait for what fate may bring; am low-spirited, pale and love the dusk. It seems as if many sleepless nights had made one ultra-sensitive. When I was left alone for a few minutes with the Cross, I had quite different thoughts from those that were in my mind before. It seemed as if the Cross were made of shell-splinters – black blood encrusted with pus – the strangled cries of hoarse voices – flaccid, gangrened flesh on the stump of a leg. But all that shall not make me hold back!

Helmut Zschuppe

1940 [London]

On the first night of the barrage, which was the heaviest, they are said to have fired 500,000 shells, i.e. at an average cost of £5 per shell, £2? millions worth. But well worth it, for the effect on morale.

George Orwell

1940 [Wiltshire]

Mrs. Hill on the telephone again! 'I've just heard that twenty refugees are arriving in half an hour. Could you have some more?' R., Burgo [their son] and I drove down to the village and waited. Then the bus came lumbering in, and children ran to gape and stare. One very small child thudded along screeching out 'VACU-*EES! VACU-EES!*' As soon as they got out it was clear they were neither children nor docksiders, but respectable looking middle-aged women and a few children, who stood like sheep beside the bus looking infinitely pathetic. 'Who'll take these?' 'How many are you?' 'Oh well, I can have these two but no more', and the piteous cry, 'But we're *together.*' It was terrible. I felt we were like sharp-nosed housewives haggling over fillets of fish. In the end we swept off two women about my age and a girl of ten. And then fetched the other two members of their party and installed them with Coombs the cowman. Their faces at once began to relax. Far from being terrified Londoners, they had been evacuated against their will from Bexhill, for fear of invasion, leaving snug little houses and 'hubbies'.

Frances Partridge

1942 [Scotland]

Ten days at Ardrossan playing dice and drinking a great deal.

Evelyn Waugh

2000 [Chechnya]

There was firing during the night and many heard cries. When they reached the site of this tragedy, half of the dead man's hand had already been chewed away by the thin and hungry dogs of Argun.

Anna Politkovskaya

15 September

1776 [New York]

This Morning about 7 o'clock, the Renown of 50 Guns, Capt. Banks, the Repulse of 32 Guns, Capt. Davis, & the Pearl of 32 Guns, Capt. Wilkinson, with the Schooner, Lieut. Brown, sailed up the North River. The Morning was fine, the Tide flowed, and there was a fresh breeze. The Rebels began their Canonade as furiously as they could, but apparently with very little Effect, as their Guns were but poorly served. The Ships, as these were the grand Batteries of the Enemy, returned a heavy Fire, and struck the Walls of the Batteries and the Sods of the Earth, which the Rebels had raised, very frequently. What other Damage our People did them, we as yet know not; but, 'tis observed, that, except for beating down particular Structures, or clearing the Way for other operations, Cannon have but a very small or precarious Effect. The great Business is always accomplished by the minor Implements of War.

Above a Quarter before 9, the Ships came to an Anchor in the North River, in view of the Fleet, at about 4 or 5 Miles Distance above it, and beyond the principal Works of the Enemy.

A Transport, during the Affair upon the North River, went up the East river & joined the other Ships, almost without Molestation.

The whole Scene was awful & grand; I might say, beautiful, but for the melancholy Seriousness which must attend every Circumstance, where the Lives of Men, even the basest Malefactors, are at Stake. The Hills, the Woods, the River, the Town, the Ships, and Pillars of Smoke, all heightened by a most clear & delightful morning, furnished the finest Landscape that either art and nature combined could draw, or the Imagination conceive.

After this affair had subsided for a little while, a most tremendous Discharge of Cannon from the Ships began (as was concerted) in the East River, in order to cover the Landing of the Troops upon New York Island. So terrible and so incessant a Roar of guns few even in the Army & Navy had ever heard before. Above 70 large Pieces of Cannon were in Play, together with Swivels & small arms from the ships, while the Batteries added to the uproar upon the land. The Rebels were apparently frightened away by the horrid Din, and deserted the Town & all their Works in the utmost Precipatation. The King's Forces took Possession of the Place, incredible as it may seem, without the Loss of a man. Nothing could equal the Expressions of Joy, shewn by the inhabitants, upon the arrival of the King's officers among them. They even carried some of them upon their Shoulders about the Streets, and behaved in all respects, Women as well as Men, like overjoyed Bedlamites. One thing is worth remarking; a Woman pulled down the Rebel Standard upon the Fort, and a Woman hoisted up in its Stead his Majesty's flag, after trampling the other under Foot with the most contemptuous Indignation. I first espied both Circumstances from the Ship, and could not help paying the first Congratulations to Lord H. upon the Occasion. The Spirit and Activity of the Troops & Seamen were unequalled: Every man pressed to be foremost, consistent with Order, and to court Distinction. The dastardly Behaviour of the Rebels, on the other Hand; sinks below Remark. The Ground, where our People landed, was far from being advantageous; the Tide rapid, the Current unequal, the Shore shallow; and themselves obliged to march up on Ground where these Poltroons had been at Work to entrench themselves for several months. Providentially, the Wind coming in with a fine Breeze from the S.W. wch it had not done before since we have been here, and wch was the most favourable Circumstance our People could have desired, enabled the Boats to carry over the Forces almost in a Direct Line, and return in like manner for the second Division, notwithstanding the Rapidity of the Current. Thus this town and its Environs, wch these blustering Gentlemen had taken such wonderful pains to fortify, were given up in two or three Hours without any Defence, or the least appearance of a manly Resistance.

In the Evening the Admiral ordered up the Mercury of 24, and the Fowey of 20 guns, to lie close to the Town, to prevent the Transport Boats from going ashore & plundering wch many of them appeared very ready to do.

Ambrose Serle

1777 [New York, the Saratoga Campaign]

Moved about 3 miles nearer the enemy, and took post on a strong position late in the evening, and had just time to pitch our camp before dark; about 11 at night we received orders to stand to our arms, and about 12 I returned to my tent and lay down to get a little rest, but was soon alarmed by a great noise of fire, and on running out saw Major Ackland's tent and markee all in a blaze, on which I made the greatest haste possible to their assistance, but before I could arrive, Lady Harriot Ackland, who was asleep in the tent when it took fire, had providentially escaped under the back of it; but the major was much burned in trying to save her. What must a woman of her rank, family and fortune feel in her then disagreeable situation; liable to constant alarms and not knowing the moment of attack; but from her attachment to the major, her ladyship bore everything, with a degree of steadiness, and resolution, that could alone be expected from an experienced veteran.

William Digby

1864 [Marine Hospital, Savannah]

A great change has taken place since I last wrote in my diary. Am in heaven now, compared with the past. At about midnight, September 7th, our detachment was ordered outside at Andersonville, and Battese picked me up and carried me to the gate.

The men were being let outside in ranks of four, and counted as they went out. They were very strict about letting none go but the well ones, or those who could walk. The Rebel Adjutant stood upon a box by the gate, watching very close. Pitch-pine knots were burning in the near vicinity to give light.

As it came our turn to go, Battese got me in the middle of the rank, stood me up as well as I could stand, and with himself on one side and Sergeant Rowe on the other, began pushing our way through the gate. Could not help myself a particle, and was so faint that I hardly knew what was going on.

As we were going through the gate the Adjutant yelled out: 'Here, here! Hold on there, that man can't go, hold on there!'

And Battese[1] crowding right along outside. The Adjutant struck over

---

[1] Despite making many inquiries, Ransom was unable to trace the kind Indian (or 'Native American' as he would now be termed) from Minnesota, who disappeared after visiting Ransom in hospital.

the heads on the men and tried to stop us, but my noble Indian friend kept straight ahead, hallooing: 'He all right, he well, he go!'

And so I got outside, the Adjutant having too much to look after to follow me. After we were outside, I was carried to the railroad.

John Ransom

1940 [Kent]

A slack morning with the usual air raid going on overhead. After luncheon there is a terrific dog-fight above us. Two 'planes come down near Sissinghurst village and one crashes in flames at Frittenden. We see a parachute descending slowly with the man below it wriggling as if on a pendulum. They take four German prisoners. The station at Staplehurst has been laid flat by a Spitfire which crashed upon its roof. A Spitfire comes down in Victor Cazalet's[1] park, only a hundred yards from Swift's [a mile from his house]. In the evening we have the news. They say we have brought down 185 of the enemy against 30 of ours. They have again bombed Buckingham Palace. We are told that Goering is directing this campaign. If so, he must be a stupider man than I thought. There is another raid at night. Poor Vita worries about my going up tomorrow [to London]. As Priestley said tonight, London is in effect in the front line. Thank God they have got the delayed bomb out from under St Paul's.

Harold Nicolson

1940 [London]

If there was ever a time when one should wear life like a loose garment, this is it. I particularly admire the little tarts who wander about the streets of Mayfair every afternoon and evening in their finery. When everyone else is hurrying for the air raid shelters, they are quite indifferent and continue to stroll unperturbed.

General Raymond E. Lee

1941 [Dresden]

The Jewish armband, come true as Star of David, comes into force on the nineteenth. At the same time a prohibition on leaving the envi-

---

[1] Peter Victor Cazalet (1907–73), Conservative MP.

rons of the city. Frau Kreidl Sr. was in tears, Frau Voss had palpitations. Friedheim said this was the worst blow so far, worse than the property assessment. I myself feel shattered, cannot compose myself. Eva, now firmly on her feet, wants to take over all the errands from me, I only want to leave the house for a few minutes when it's dark. (And if there is snow and ice?) Perhaps by then the public will have become indifferent, or *che so io*? The newspaper justification: after the army had got to know, through Bolshevism, the cruelty, etc, of *the* Jew, all possibility of camouflage must be removed from the Jews here, to spare the comrades of the people all contact with them. – The true reason: fear of Jewish criticism because things look bad in the East or at least are at a standstill. And: rule of the terror people, of Himmler, because things look bad in the East. Wild rumours: Goering is a prisoner after an argument with Hitler. – Hitler has been shot in the stomach by a general. He had reviled the general, he had lain raving on the carpet and 'chewed the tassels'.

Victor Klemperer

1942 [Jersey]

What a blow has fallen on the island again tonight. In the *Evening Post* there is an Order from a higher authority (Hitler!) saying that all Englishmen, aged 16–70 years, are to be evacuated with their families to Germany. There is no word bad enough to describe the cruelty and beastliness of the Germans. Of course they give no reason whatever for this. Then, to spring this upon us so suddenly; tonight people had orders to leave tomorrow. We have so many friends amongst the English people – it is too dreadful, one can hardly think.

Nan Le Ruez

1943 [Sicily]

My cook has strange ideas as to what to do with oatmeal and currants. I get soup which is a sort of savoury porridge and a sweet of currants in their syrups with condensed milk, the latter so awful I have had to put a stop to it. Also getting heartily tired of peppers.

Edward Ardizzone

16 September

1854 [Sevastopol]

Self-assurance and effeminacy: these are the main, sad features of our army – common to all armies of states that are too big and too strong.

Leo Tolstoy

1939 [England]

Wake up early and have a bad gloom. I try to think of something which is not painful, and all I can manage to think of are the telephone numbers of my friends. It is always the worst time, this early awakening. I get a letter from John Sparrow,[1] who has joined up as a private in the Oxford and Bucks Light Infantry. His idea is (a) that although a Fellow of All Souls, he is not a good military man and that it is better to obey orders than have to give them; (b) that it is less painful if one breaks entirely with one's previous life. He is not too unhappy. I daresay he is right about all this. My appalling depression may be due to the fact that I am living my former life with all the conditions altered. Rob Bernays[2] told me yesterday that all the front-bench people [in Parliament] keep exclaiming, 'I wish I were twenty. I cannot bear this responsibility.' What they really mean is, 'I wish I did not know how bad things are!' The whole world is either paralysed or against us. These are the darkest hours we have ever endured.

Harold Nicolson

1940 [London]

I drove back to London via the East End, which is a scene of desolation; house after house has been wrecked, debris falls from the remaining floors, windows are gone, heaps of rubbish lie in the pavements. A large hospital and a synagogue still stand, but they are windowless. Some streets are roped off because of time bombs. The damage is immense, yet the people, mostly Jewish, seemed courageous. I gave many of them lifts.

Everyone still seems cock-a-hoop in the face of almost certain invasion: I am less so, for the German machine is very thorough and very successful; there are ships of all kinds congregated along the French coast,

---

[1] A Fellow, later Warden, of All Souls College, Oxford.
[2] Liberal National MP for Bristol North.

enough, they say, to transport half a million men: luckily a gale is blowing.

'Chips' Channon

1940 [London]

This morning Sid and I nearly got bombed in the bus on our way to the first-aid post. Two dropped very close and we saw the smoke. Dovehouse Street first-aid post was short of clerks so we stayed till the all-clear at eleven. Lots of casualties streaming blood, very messy. There was a nice little doctor in gum boots who looked like Nero.

Came back to the studio to find Prudey [a girlfriend] in Madame A's room. She has been staying in Oxford. We all drank tea and told our various experiences. Then Prudey and I went off to try and salvage some more of her stuff. I went too, hoping to find my *Apes of God*,[1] which Leonard had borrowed.

When we got there it looked very dangerous, and Prudey said, 'Don't go in, you can't die a virgin!'

'But I'm *not* a virgin,' I announced proudly. Prudey did a double take.

'Oh really! Well that's fine, I expect you feel much better for it, don't you?'

'Well yes, I suppose I do.'

'I'm so pleased – did you use Volpar Gels?'

'No, but I'm going to.'

'You were lucky to have Rupert, of course. He's very sweet isn't he? It's terribly important to be poked by someone nice the first time. Most girls get awful men, and it puts them off poking for good.'

We climbed up into the ruins; my share of the pickings were a vacuum cleaner, an abstract picture by Gerhardt, a bottle of mayonnaise, two pairs of camiknickers and a roll of Jeyes paper. Prudey saved all her clothes and crockery, also her rubber douche and her copy of *Black Spring*, which is the most indecent book ever written, but she feels sentimental about it because of having slept with Henry Miller. We also found Prudey's will. She leaves £500 to Rupert, her carving tools to Gerhardt and her green silk Chinese dressing-gown to a tart in Bramerton Street.

Back in the studio we emptied the stones out of Rupert's gramophone and wound it up and it worked. We were playing 'I've got my love to keep me warm' when Madame A. came up to lend Pru her novel, *The Hieroglyph*. It starts, ' "Are you a sadist or a masochist?" asked

---

[1] A novel by Wyndham Lewis.

Iris Langford, idly burning the wrists of her companion with her cigarette end.' Great stuff!

Just then there was a rumbling noise like a landslide and we rushed
to the window. Some of the ruins at number 34 had collapsed and
white smoke hung over the street. Prudey and I ran downstairs squeaking with excitement.

The warden was standing in the street, looking distraught. 'There
are two women under there,' he cried, dramatically. 'Oh no, they're not,'
we said, 'we're here!' What a narrow escape!

Then the warden started shouting, 'Get back everyone! This may
set the time bomb off!' So we thought we'd had enough and turned
and ran back through the rubble into the studio. Prudey looked through
her clothes, but couldn't find anything clean to change into. It was
terribly hot and close.

'Have to eat dinner with the Princes Lowenstein tonight in these
filthy trousers,' she said gloomily, dabbing 'Amour, Amour' under her
armpits. 'Hell, I've sweated into my best jersey!'

Joan Wyndham

1940 [London]

Franks [his chauffeur], who was pretty harried on Saturday, showed up
this morning, rather chipper after a weekend of sleep in the country.
Lose sleep and you get down quickly. There are all sorts of effects of
this war. We tried to take an elevator to Beaverbrook's[1] office. 'Sorry,
sir,' said our guide, 'but the lift man's house has been demolished and
he's digging for his wife. Will you please use the other lift?' Private
cars are held up by people who want to get home and cannot be
accommodated by the subway, which shuts down during the air raids
and therefore cannot haul passengers who bank up during that time.
Queen Anne's Mansions was hit by a bomb which went straight down
through every floor, blowing the wall out so one could look into it as
in a doll's house. The big new Shell-Mex building next to the Savoy
had its tower blown off and top floor collapsed. A really large amount
of damage was done last night. But none of it was vital. It is all of it,
or nearly all, just aimless, random battering.

To Hell with Hitler, I say.

General Raymond E. Lee

---

[1] Lord Beaverbrook (1879–1964), owner of the *Daily Express*.

1941 [London]

I have been asked to approve £450 odd for wines etc. on the *Prince of Wales* for Churchill and Co., under guise of entertainment of foreigners.[1] I wonder how much of it Roosevelt drank. Today I was asked to approve £1300 for a special train for Beaverbrook and Co. going to the north of Scotland en route for Moscow. I hope Beaverbrook gets killed en route. It would be a splendid release and escape for this country. And this also is under guise of entertainment of foreigners.

Lord Reith

1941 [Leningrad]

It gave me a strange feeling when the phone rang, and a fresh young voice said: 'The telephone is disconnected until the end of the war.' I tried to raise a protest, but knew in my heart it was useless. In a few minutes the phone clicked and went dead . . . until the end of the war.

And immediately the flat, too, became dead, frozen and tense. We were cut off from everyone and everything in the city. And that is how all the telephones in Leningrad were cut off at the same time. Only very special offices, clinics and hospitals are excepted.

Vera Inber

1942 [Jersey]

What a day! The evacuation to Germany begins. I went to see if Uncle Gordon had heard anything about himself. It was a shock, as I walked up to the door, to see his small suitcase packed and to hear women's voices saying, 'Well, best of luck Mr Amoore,' and so on. Oh, I thought, he's going. And yes, there he was, just leaving. I couldn't believe it! He has been in Jersey for 40 years. Last night, at 9 o'clock, two Germans, with Constable Crill, arrived to tell him that he must be off by the 4 o'clock boat today. I put his suitcase on my carrier and we walked to the place where a good number were waiting, so brave, with a smile on their faces as if they were going for a holiday, instead of what I fear, to their deaths perhaps. It is cruel and wicked. Fine boys and girls from our Colleges, waiting there with blankets on their arms, and their parents with them. One, a typical Englishman, a Mr Fenton, I think, leaning against the wall, with a careless nonchalant air, as if it did not matter at all! Not a

[1] Reith was Minister of Works from October 1940 until February 1942.

sign of what he really felt. As some women were saying to me: 'We must not on any account show the skunks what we feel. We will keep a cheerful face.' How wonderful those English folk are. At last, after an hour's wait, the bus came, and they were all herded in by German soldiers to be driven to the pier. I couldn't help crying a little as the bus went and Uncle waved goodbye. His neighbours took my arm and told me to be brave.

Nan Le Ruez

1943 [Amsterdam]
Dearest Kitty,
I've been taking valerian every day to fight the anxiety and depression, but it doesn't stop me from being even more miserable the next day. A good hearty laugh would help more than ten valerian drops, but we've almost forgotten how to laugh. Sometimes I'm afraid my face is going to sag with all this sorrow and that my mouth is going to permanently droop at the corners. The others aren't doing any better. Everyone here is dreading the great terror known as winter.

Anne Frank

17 September

1939 [Essex]
A glorious September day at Kelvedon where I bathed in the pool, and then in a bath towel rang up the FO to be told the grim news that the Russians had definitely invaded Poland. Now the Nazis and the Bolsheviks have combined to destroy civilisation, and the outlook for the world looks ghastly.

'Chips' Channon

18 September

1916 [London]
Not till the end of the war will there be any time for art or love or magic again. Perhaps never.

Mary Butts

1941 [Dresden]
The 'Jewish star', black on yellow cloth, at the centre in Hebrew-like lettering 'Jew,' to be worn on the left breast, large as the palm of a hand, issued to us yesterday for 10 pfennigs, to be worn from tomorrow. The omnibus may *no* longer be used, *only* the front platform of the tram. – For the time being at least Eva will take over all the shopping, I shall breathe in a little fresh air only under shelter of darkness.

Victor Klemperer

1942 [on board USS *Montpelier*, in the Pacific]
Today was a very outstanding day for the men who went over to the beach in the afternoon. We saw our first woman in almost 10 months and it happened to be the First Lady of the United States. It was President Roosevelt's wife, Mrs Franklin D. Roosevelt. She spoke to hundreds of sailors and marines who are stationed on the ships here. Her talk lasted about 10 minutes, then she walked around to see what the place looked like, she was with some officers and a woman from the Red Cross. The outfit she wore was very nice, she is much better looking in person.

James J. Fahey, Seaman First Class

19 September

1917 [Zürau]
In peacetime you don't get anywhere, in wartime you bleed to death.

Franz Kafka

1918 [Essex]
In Braintree today I noticed this war-placard outside F. A. Dancer's, fruiterer's: 'National Salvage Council: We are asked to collect fruit-stones and hard shells needed in the manufacture of anti-gas masks. Save them and bring them here, however few. You may save a soldier's life.'

Andrew Clark

1939 [Scotland]
To adopt a pacifist attitude were hypocritical presumptuousness if one believed that the life of man was a self-contained process; it is only out of the conviction that the activities of humanity are centred

in cosmic purpose, and meaningful when obedient to living law, that pacifism is freed from false-assumption. It is not that the pacifist is more human or more magnanimous than his fellows, but that he has become more conscious of the nature of reality, and accordingly able to act with full awareness of the need of the hour. He is not blind to his dependence upon the community, but he is as deeply sensible of the gifted nature of life and that his ultimate allegiance is to the source. His strength is not his own but maintained by his assurance of life's pervading presence, essential in his trust, and manifested daily in nature and in the many unrecorded words and acts of goodwill which he partakes from his common mingling with men.

William Soutar

1941 [Leningrad]
Bravery is as contagious as cowardice.

Vera Inber

20 September

1776 [the Burning of New York]
A little after 12 o'Clock last night a most dreadful fire broke out in New York, in three different places in the South, and windward part of the town. The Alarm was soon given, but unfortunately there was a brisk wind at South, which spread the flames with such irresistible rapidity, that notwithstanding every assistance was given which the present circumstances admitted, it was impossible to check its Progress 'till about 11 this day, when by preventing it from crossing the Broadway at the North part of the town, it was stopped from spreading any further that way, and about 12 it was so far got under that there was no danger of its extending beyond those houses which were then on fire. It broke out first near the Exchange, and burnt all the houses on the West side of Broad Street, almost as far as The City hall, & from thence all those in Beaver Street, and almost every house on the West side of the town between the Broad way and the North River, as far as The College, amounting in the whole to about 600 houses, besides several Churches, particularly Trinity Church, the principal one in town.

From a variety of circumstances which occurred it is beyond a doubt that the town was designedly set on fire, either by some of those fellows who concealed themselves in it since the 15th Instant, or by some Villains left behind for the purpose. Some of them were caught by the Soldiers in the very act of setting fire to the inside of empty houses at a distance from the fire; many were detected with matches and combustibles under their Clothes, and combustibles were found in several houses. One Villain who abused and cut a woman who was employed in bringing water to the Engines, and who was found cutting the handles of the fire buckets, was hung up by the heels on the spot by the Seamen. One or two others were found in houses with fire brands in their hands and were put to death by the enraged Soldiery and thrown into the flames. There is no doubt however that the flames were communicated to several houses by means of the burning flakes of the Shingles, which being alight, were carried by the wind to some distance and falling on the roofs of houses covered with Shingles, (which is most generally the case at New York) and whose Inhabitants were either absent or inattentive, kindled the fire anew. The Trinity Church, a very handsome, ancient building, was perceived to be on fire long before the fire reached the adjacent houses, and as it stood at some distance from any house, little doubt remained that it was set on fire wilfully.

During the time the Rebels were in possession of the town, many of them were heard to say they would burn it, sooner than it should become a nest for Tories – and several Inhabitants who were most violently attached to the Rebel cause have been heard to declare they would set fire to their own houses sooner than they should be occupied by The King's troops.

No assistance could be sent from the Army 'till after daybreak, as the General was apprehensive the Rebels had some design of attacking the Army.

It is almost impossible to conceive a Scene of more horror and distress than the above. The Sick, The Aged, Women, and Children, half naked were seen going they knew not where, and taking refuge in houses which were at a distance from the fire, but from whence they were in several instances driven a second and even a third time by the devouring element, and at last in a state of despair laying themselves down on the Common. The terror was increased by the horrid noise of the burning and falling houses, and pulling down of such wooden buildings as served to conduct the fire, (in which the Soldiers and Seamen were particularly active and useful) the rattling of above 100 wagons, sent in from the Army, and which were constantly employed in conveying to the Common such goods and effects as could be saved; – The confused voices of so many men, the Shrieks and cries of the Women and children, the seeing the fire break out unexpectedly in places at a distance, which manifested a design of totally destroying the City, with numberless other circumstance of private misery and distress, made this one of the most tremendous and affecting Scenes I ever beheld.

Frederick Mackenzie

1854 [Battle of the Alma]

We advanced again early in the morning, and after a slow, loitering march, arrived at the Alma about mid-day. When I first saw the village on its banks it was in flames, but the smoke from it was soon equalled, if not eclipsed by the fire from the Russian artillery.

The Light and Second Divisions crossed first, and were soon followed by the First. The Third and Fourth Divisions acted in support, and were neither of them engorged during the day, though under fire.

It was my first fight, and I was quite astounded at my coolness. I didn't feel a bit more nervous than I should have done in Hyde Park.

The great slaughter was at the large *battery*, about half-way up the hill, six hundred yards from the river. Here the enemy lay thick, both on the inside and outside of it, but more on the outside. As to myself, I had nothing to do. I was never exposed to a close musketry fire. The shells and round shot flew about fairly, but nothing much. At the end, when I *was* near enough, the enemy was making off too fast to put one in much danger.

Lieut. General Sir Charles Ash Windham

1939 [England]

Today I left by the 10.30 a.m. wartime train for Leeds, no dining or buffet car, an interminably long journey, arriving at Peterboro' first stop at 12.30 p.m. For some of the crowd of passengers, a scramble for tea at the refreshment room; others besieged the tea trolley – no coffee available. Except that tea – and very poor tea – in bulk was ready, there was no organization for dealing with the rush, which should have been anticipated. Not until it was over did someone think to make ready several dozen cups at once for quick distribution, almost every one of which, because too late and unwanted, I saw poured back into large enamelled tin jugs – presumably for future use. At 3d. per cup – it was ghastly stuff to have to scramble for. Eventually my train drew into Leeds at 4 p.m. I thought to listen to the radio commentary, repeated by the press this morning, on Hitler's Danzig speech made earlier in the day. I felt that in whatever contempt his utterances may be held in this country, we at least should not descend to the indignity of wrangling and recrimination like some ignorant slut of a fishwife, propaganda or no propaganda. If, as I believe, we are conducting this crusade for a principle, let us do so without stooping, be war never so terrible, lest in the wrangling we forget what we are fighting for.

Walter Musto

1939 [London]
Chris[1] remarked that for ten years in Napoleonic wars we stayed at war with France without firing a shot; when pressed dropped to six years; when pressed admitted there might have been some fighting; when pressed admitted Finisterre and Trafalgar as incidents during his period of unbroken peace.

Evelyn Waugh

1941 [Leningrad]
Yesterday bombs were dropping in the Novaya Derevnya, on the market place. Fifty people were brought in, one of them a child of about seven years old. She kept complaining that the rubber tourniquet on her leg was hurting her. People comforted her, telling her that the pain would soon be easier. Then she was anaesthetised, and her leg amputated. She came round and said, 'Everything is marvellous. It doesn't hurt any more.' She had no idea that she had lost her leg.

Vera Inber

1941 [Kovno Ghetto, Lithuania]
DOCUMENT: Order of SA Captain Jordan
Each Ghetto family must hand over one piece of toilet or shaving soap.

Avraham Tory

---

[1] Christopher (Maurice) Hollis (1902–1977), writer.

1943 [Italy]

We finally got through by jeep to Salerno, but found a battle still going on in the outskirts of the town. German mortar bombs were exploding in the middle of a small square only a few hundred yards from Security Headquarters. Here I saw an ugly sight: a British officer interrogating an Italian civilian, and repeatedly hitting him about the head with a chair; treatment which the Italian, his face a mask of blood, suffered with stoicism. At the end of the interrogation, which had not been considered successful, the officer called in a private of the Hampshires and asked him in a pleasant, conversational sort of manner, 'Would you like to take this man away, and shoot him?' The private's reply was to spit on his hands, and say, 'I don't mind if I do, sir.' The most revolting episode I have seen since joining the forces.

Norman Lewis

21 September

1937 [Nanking, during Japanese invasion]

All the rich or better-off Chinese began some time ago to flee up the Yangtze to Hankow. In courtyards and gardens, in public squares and on the streets, people have feverishly been building dugouts, but otherwise everything remained calm until two days ago, when I received my baptism by fire during four air raids on Nanking.

Many Americans and Germans have departed as well. I've been seriously considering the matter from all sides these last few nights. It wasn't because I love adventure that I returned here from the safety of Peitaiho, but primarily to protect my property and to represent Siemens'[1] interests. Of course the company can't – nor does it – expect me to get myself killed here on its behalf. Besides, I haven't the least desire to put my life at risk for the sake of either the company's or my own property; but there is a question of morality here, and as a reputable Hamburg businessman, so far I haven't been able to side-step it.

Our Chinese servants and employees, about 30 people in all including immediate families, have eyes only for their 'master'. If I stay, they will loyally remain at their posts to the end. I saw the same thing happen before in the wars up north. If I run, then the company and

[1] Rabe was head of the local branch of Siemens, the German electrical company.

my own house will not just be left deserted, but they will probably be plundered as well. Apart from that, and as unpleasant as that would be, I cannot bring myself for now to betray the trust these people have put in me. And it is touching to see how they believe in me, even the most useless people whom I would gladly have sent packing during peacetime. I gave Mr. Han, my assistant, an advance on his salary so that he could send his wife and two children to safety . He quite frankly admits: 'Where you stay, I stay too. If you go, I go along!'

The rest of the poor servants, most of whom are actually from northern China, simply don't know where to go. I wanted to send off the women and children at least, offered their husbands money for the trip, but they don't know what to do. They want to go back home to the north, but there's a war there, too, and so they would rather just huddle here around me.

Under such circumstances, can I, may I, cut and run? I don't think so. Anyone who has ever sat in a dugout and held a trembling Chinese child in each hand through the long hours of an air raid can understand what I feel.

Finally – subconsciously – there's a last, and not the least important reason that makes my sticking it out here seem simply a matter of course. I am a member of the NSDAP [National Socialist German Workers Party], and temporarily even held the office of local deputy leader. When I pay business calls on the Chinese agencies and ministries who are our customers, I am constantly asked questions about Germany, about our party and government, and my answer always is:

Yes, indeed –

We are soldiers of labour;

We are a government of workers,

We are friends of the working man,

We do not leave workers – the poor –

in the lurch when times are hard!

To be sure, as a National Socialist I was speaking only about German workers, not about the Chinese; but what would the Chinese think? Times are bitterly hard here in the country of my hosts, who have treated me well for three decades now. The rich are fleeing, the poor must remain behind. They don't know where to go. They don't have the means to flee. Aren't they in danger of being slaughtered in great numbers? Shouldn't one make an attempt to help them? Save a few at least? And even if it's only our own people, our employees?

I've equipped the dugout with my personal first-aid supplies, plus some from the apothecary in the school, which closed down some time ago. We plan to use vinegar compresses as face masks in the case of gas attack. I've also stored food and drink in baskets and thermos bottles.

John Rabe

1940 [Rome]
I went with Ribbentrop to Villa d'Este and to Villa Adriana. In the last few days Ribbentrop has wanted to meet many people both inside and outside political circles. Everybody disliked him.

Count Ciano

1940 [Berlin]
X came up to my room in the Adlon [hotel] today, and after we had disconnected my telephone and made sure that no one was listening through the crack of the door to the next room, he told me a weird story. He says the Gestapo is now systematically bumping off the mentally deficient people of the Reich. The Nazis call them 'mercy deaths'. He relates that Pastor Bodelschwingh, who runs a large hospital for various kinds of feeble-minded children at Bethel, was ordered arrested a few days ago because he refused to deliver up some of his more serious mental cases to the secret police. Shortly after this, his hospital is bombed. By the 'British'. Must look into this story.

William L. Shirer

1940 [Sussex]
We've just bottled our honey. Very still and warm today. So invasion becomes possible. The river high; all softly blue and milky; autumn quiet – twelve planes in perfect order, back from the fight, pass overhead.

Virginia Woolf

1942 [Amsterdam]
Dearest Kitty,
There's something happening every day, but I'm too tired and lazy to write it all down.

Anne Frank

22 September

1776 [after the Burning of New York]

A person named Nathaniel Hales, a Lieutenant in the Rebel Army, and a native of Connecticut, was apprehended as a Spy, last night upon Long Island; and having this day made a full and free confession to the Commander in Chief of his being employed by Mr Washington in that capacity, he was hanged at 11 o'clock in front of the Park of Artillery. He was about 24 years of age, and had been educated at the College of Newhaven in Connecticut. He behaved with great composure and resolution, saying he thought it the duty of every good Officer to obey any orders given him by his Commander in Chief; and desired the Spectators to be at all times prepared to meet death in whatever shape it might appear.

Frederick Mackenzie

1939 [London]

In France there is calm but fixed determination: '*il faut en finir*'.

John Colville

1939 [London]

Honor [his wife] came up yesterday and I took her to luncheon at the Ritz which has become fantastically fashionable; all the great, the gay, the government; we knew 95% of everyone there. But Ritzes always thrive in wartime, as we are all cookless. Also in wartime the herd instinct rises.

'Chips' Channon

1940 [Kent]

We dine with the Drummonds.[1] There is, as always, that sense of mahogany and silver and peaches and port-wine and good manners. All the virtues of aristocracy hang about those two crippled and aged people, and none of the vulgarity of wealth. We listen to the news while distant bombardments thump and crunch over the hills and plains of Kent. Priestley gives a broadcast about the abolition of privilege, while I look at their albums of 1903 and the Delhi Durbar and the Viceroy's train. Priestley speaks of the old order which is dead and of the new order which is to arise from its ashes. These

[1] Major General Laurence Drummond, neighbours at the Nicolsons' home at Sissinghurst.

two old people listen without flinching. I find their dignity and distinction and patriotism deeply moving. I glance at the pictures of the howdahs and panoply of the past and hear the voice of Priestley and the sound of the guns. We go out into the autumn night and see the searchlights swinging their shafts across the sky. There are clear stars and a moon struggling in eastern clouds. I write this before going to bed. A butterfly with white outstretched legs and dark closed wings has settled upon the black cloth of the screen across my window. Beyond it I can hear the drone of an aeroplane. Tomorrow I return to London and the bombardment which goes on and on and on.

Harold Nicolson

1941 [Leningrad]
I am moved by the thought that while the bombs rain down on this besieged city Shostakovich is writing a symphony. *Leningrad Pravda's* report on it is tucked away between communiqués of the southern front and reports of petrol bombs. And so, in all this horror, art is still alive. It shines and warms the heart.

Vera Inber

23 September

1884 [Khartoum]
The men who went out to drive back the marauders between Halfaya and Shoboloha have come back. They drove back the Arabs and captured a lot of things.

During the blockade here, viz., from say March 12th till to-day September 22nd we have expended –

3,240,770 Remington . .}
1,570 Krupp gun   . .} cartridges
9,442 Mountain gun . .}

Of the Remington cartridges perhaps 240,000 may have been captured by enemy, so that we fire 3,000,000 away; and I expect the Arabs lost perhaps 1000 in all. Each Arab killed needed 3,000 cartridges. We have left here –

2,242,000 Remington . .}
660 Krupp gun   . .} cartridges

8,490 Mountain gun . .}
and we turn out 50,000 Remington cartridges a week.

Fifty Arab horsemen came down on our foraging party who were outside Bourré, but the steamer drove them back.

General Charles George Gordon

1915 [the Russian Front]

Dead animals were lying here and there about the fields and road-sides; cows, sheep, pigs, all in various stages of decomposition. I remember having seen many large droves, in which more than one suffering animal was panting from exhaustion; while many limped painfully. I remembered seeing a horse fall during the early months of the Retreat; I think it was in the dreadful sands of Molodychi. The men cut it hastily out of the gun-carriage harness and left it lying by the roadside, without so much as a word of regret. As we passed, I remember how its sides heaved and its eyes looked at us like the eyes of a human being forsaken, and left to suffer and die in solitude.

A molar which had been worrying me of late started suddenly to ache violently and persistently. I covered my face with my black travelling veil and nursed the pain in silence. Only once I uncovered it – and that for a fraction of a minute – when an indescribably repugnant odour permeated the air and penetrated to my nostrils. 'What is that dreadful smell?' asked more than one voice. 'Carcasses!' Answered our Tatar driver phlegmatically. Later, we were told by a Divisional Doctor that the plain was a pitiful sight to behold; near the spot where we had noticed the offensive smell, some twenty dead animals were lying, among them several horses; they had been there for more than two weeks.

Florence Farmborough

1939 [near Portsmouth]

After lunch I went by train to Stansted [Park] to spend the week-end with the Bessboroughs. They were just *en famille*, Lord and Lady Bessborough,[1] and Moyra,[2] There were also sixty or more orphans,

[1] Vere, 9th Earl of Bessborough, Govenor General of Canada, 1931–35. Married to Roberte de Neuflize.
[2] Lady Moyra Ponsonby. Afterwards married to the distinguished surgeon, Sir Denis Browne, and herself superintendent in Chief of St John's Ambulance Brigade.

who played cricket happily on the lawn in front of the house but were carefully excluded from the main part of the house itself, which remains as cheerful and comfortable as ever.

John Colville

1939 [Sussex]

Civilisation has shrunk. The amenities are wilting. There's no petrol today: so we are back again with our bicycles at Asheham in 1915. And once more L. and I calculate our income. How much must we both earn? Once more we are journalists. Then one begins stinting paper, sugar, butter, buying little hoards of matches. The elm tree that fell has been cut up. This will see us through two winters. They say the war will last three years. We had an SOS from Kingsley.[1] He came for the night. What was it he couldn't say on the telephone? Nothing. Should he come out in favour of peace? Chamberlain has the terms in his pocket. All in the know say we are beaten.

Virginia Woolf

1944 [Naples]

When I first moved into the hotel I noticed that Don Enrico, enthroned in his wicker armchair in a position in which he could keep under observation every person who entered or left the hotel, occasionally groped in his pocket to touch his testicles on the appearance of a stranger. This, Don Ubaldo explained to me, was a precaution – commonplace in the South, but frequently practised by Northerners, including Mussolini himself – to ward off the evil eye. On two or three occasions in the last week I have noticed women hastily cover their faces with a scarf or a veil at my approach, and scuttle past with averted faces. This, apparently, is how women deal with the problem. Now, this evening, coming into the hotel, I found a row of half a dozen regulars – Don Enrico included – sitting under the palms, and at the sight of me I seemed to notice a sly movement of every left hand towards the right side of the crotch. A disconcerting confirmation of loss of favour.

Norman Lewis

---

[1] Kingsley Martin (1897–1969), editor of the *New Statesman and Nation*.

24 September

1937 [Nanking, during the Japanese invasion]

In the long hours of crouching in the dugout during the recent bombardment, I turned on Radio Shanghai to take my mind off things with a little music, and they were playing Beethoven's Funeral March, then to make matters worse they announced to their listeners: 'This music is kindly dedicated to you by the Shanghai Funeral Directors.'

John Rabe

1940 [Wiltshire]

R. went to Aldbourne and came back with the news that Gerald has been in trouble with the police *again*. He spent a whole day at the Marlborough Police Station, and R. got to Bell Court just in time this morning to interview a Scotland Yard man and vouch for Gerald's character. Apparently when Sir Oswald Mosley[1] was in danger of being arrested at the beginning of the war he made a bonfire of his papers, but one or two floated over a wall and came into the hands of the police. On one was written among other notes: 'Gerald Brenan, Bell Court, Aldbourne.' The Scotland Yard man told R. that if Gerald hadn't been able to explain this he would quietly have been interned for the duration of the war. The explanation was that he had written a letter to the *Telegraph* urging that Sir Oswald be arrested, and was therefore an enemy of the Fascist Party and his name and address noted as such.

Frances Partridge

1941 [Rome]

I saw a report by Cecchi[2] on the treatment of our labourers in Germany. In some camps, in addition to beatings, large watchdogs are used which are trained to bite the legs of those workers who are guilty of only slight transgressions. If a report of this kind became known to the Italian people they would revolt with a violence that few can imagine.

Count Ciano

---

[1] Sir Oswald Mosley (1896–1980), sixth baronet. Politician and Fascist leader.
[2] Emilio Cecchi, a diplomat.

25 September

1812 [Iberian Peninsula]

One howitzer opened today but without effect – the wheel broke. The sapping goes on but slowly as they have but few who can work at it. The Engineers give a shilling apiece for all the large French shot that are brought and sixpence for the smaller. The men go out to look for them and stand watching the places where they hit, running the chance of being hit for the chance of getting a shilling or two. We are very well supplied here with the gross necessaries of life. Butter, bread, vegetables, country wine, etc. There is no claret to be got in Burgos now, as the Spaniards when they entered the town destroyed almost everything. The usual price of it is three and sixpence per bottle.

Ensign John Mills, 1st Battalion, Coldstream Guards

1899 [Pretoria]

[Loreto Convent] There is not much study going on. Everybody is excited, expecting war to break out, and almost every class is divided into pro-Boers and pro-Britishers. We discuss, argue and quarrel, and sometimes almost fight. Our Lady Superior today called us together and told us that in future the discussion of politics was forbidden.

But who on earth can stop us talking politics? At night, when all the girls are in bed, the lights out, and the Dormitory Sister gone downstairs, an argument might begin between two or three girls; at first very quietly, then more loudly, and then several others would wake and join in. The discussions ranged from the landing of Van Riebeek at the Cape in 1652 to the latest dispatch from Joseph Chamberlain, Secretary to the Colonies.

Soon the whole dormitory is awake. Some of the little ones, thinking that war has already broken out and that they would be killed immediately, begin to cry. Others wake up thinking they have had a nightmare but, hearing our familiar voices, they go to sleep again, relieved at the thought that there are no regiments marching through the dormitory.

Freda Schlosberg

1939 [Dresden]

From today cards for bread. Chocolate confiscated.

Victor Klemperer

1939 [London]

Allen Lane[1] comes to see me, and it is agreed that I do a Penguin Special for him on why Britain is at war.

Harold Nicolson

1940 [London]

Dined at home and then went to call on Zara[2] and Betts.[3] Zara told me she was engaged to Ronald Strutt,[4] after knowing him for only ten days. Betts said all people in love were intolerable, but Zara had a dreamy, blissful unconscious look on her face which it did me good to see. Betts talked much nonsense about religion and the ineffectiveness of our propaganda in American, her remarks on the latter being based entirely on hearsay. It is a waste of time, and exasperating, to talk to most women on serious subjects. Sex, the Arts and the Abstract seem to me the only topics to discuss with women.

John Colville

26 September

1812 [Burgos, Iberian Peninsula]

The siege of this place promises fair to rival that of Troy in duration. Every day shows the deficiency of our means, the strength of the place, and the ingenuity of the garrison – in the refinements of war they far exceed us. We are stubbornly brave, they are gallant in spirit, but in all inventions and devices we must be content to copy, and the experience costs us dear. An acting Engineer was killed, an artillery officer wounded. The sap [engineering work] goes on well. They are so near that the garrison roll down live shells and throw hand grenades.

---

[1] Sir Allen Lane (1902–1970), Chairman and Managing Director of Penguin Books Ltd.

[2] Zara Mainwaring, daughter of Sir Harry and Lady Mainwaring. Married first Ronald Strutt and secondly Peter Cazalet, well-known trainer of steeplechasers.

[3] Lady Elizabeth Montague, daughter of the 9th earl of Sandwich.

[4] Ronnie Strutt, later Lord Belper.

We keep up a heavy fire of musketry which keeps their heads under. The 6th Division have a working party near the river, not connected with our works. I believe the object is to make a place for musketry.

Ensign John Mills, 1st Battalion, Coldstream Guards

1914 [Essex]

1.30 p.m. at lunch at Lyons Hall: the Coldstreams, having suffered so heavily, are now withdrawn from the front. The Guards are in terrible want of socks. With the constant marching, each man wears out a pair a week. To help the Coldstream Guards some friends of the Regiment are 1,000 of each shirts, socks, tins of boracic ointment, packets of peppermints.

Sir Richard Pennyfeather plumes himself that he has caught a spy. An elderly woman with a strong German accent, selling lace at Little Waltham, was arrested by his order. She said her husband was a doctor, in a small way, at one of the East Coast towns, but by Sir Richard's order she was imprisoned for the night. In the morning her account of herself was confirmed but Sir Richard, still suspicious, has ordered her to be kept under public surveillance. This is probably the lace seller who caused great alarm to the Tufnell household at Langleys, Great Waltham. She made in the neighbourhood the most minute enquiry as to the number and character of the rooms in the mansion and as to the age and habits of all its inmates. The Langley people imagined she was a militant suffragette, planning an incendiary outrage.

Andrew Clark

1937 [Nanking, during the Japanese invasion]

Yesterday evening Mr. Chow, an engineer from Shanghai, arrived after spending 26 hours on the train. He has been ordered here by Mr. Tao of the Communications Ministry to repair the telephone system. Chow is one of our best people.

When I asked if his family was worried that something might happen to him on the trip, he answered – and a remarkable answer it is. 'I told my wife, if I am killed you can expect nothing from Siemens [his employers] and should go to my relatives in the north where you and the children can live from the yield of our little parcel of land there. I undertook this trip not only in the company's interest, but also, and above all, in the interests of my fatherland.'

It reveals an attitude one generally doesn't credit the Chinese with having, but it is there, and it is gaining ground, especially in the lower and middle classes.

John Rabe

1939 [London]

The Prime Minister [Neville Chamberlain] gets to make his statement. He is dressed in deep mourning relieved only by a white handkerchief and a large gold watch-chain. One feels the confidence and spirits of the House dropping inch by inch.[1] When he sits down there is scarcely any applause. During the whole speech Winston Churchill had sat hunched beside him looking like the Chinese god of plenty suffering from acute indigestion. He just sits there, lowering, hunched and circular, and then he gets up. He is greeted by a loud cheer from all the benches and he starts to tell us about the Naval position. I notice that *Hansard* does not reproduce his opening phrases. He began by saying how strange an experience it was for him after a quarter of a century to find himself once more in the same room in front of the same maps, fighting the same enemy and dealing with the same problems. His face then creases into an enormous grin and he adds, glancing down at the Prime Minister, 'I have no conception how this curious change in my fortunes occurred.' The whole House roared with laughter and Chamberlain had not the decency even to raise a sickly smile. He just looked sulky.

The effect of Winston's speech was infinitely greater than could be derived from any reading of the text. His delivery was really amazing and he sounded every note from deep preoccupation to flippancy, from resolution to sheer boyishness. One could feel the spirits of the House rising with every word. It was quite obvious afterwards that the Prime Minister's inadequacy and lack of inspiration had been demonstrated even to his warmest supporters. In those twenty minutes Churchill brought himself nearer to the post of Prime Minister than he has ever been before. In the Lobbies afterwards even Chamberlainites were saying, 'We have now found our leader.' Old Parliamentary hands confessed that never in their experience had they seen a single speech so change the temper of the House.

Harold Nicolson

---

[1] Russia had invaded Poland, and Britain's guarantees to Poland and Rumania were now seen as acts of folly – blamed on a weak Chamberlain – and there were calls for him to resign.

1940 [Berlin]

It burns me up that I cannot mention a raid that is going on during my broadcast. Last night the anti-aircraft guns protecting the *Rundfunk* [radio station] made such a roar while I was broadcasting that I couldn't hear my own words. The lip microphone we are now forced to use at night prevented the sound of the guns accompanying my words to America, which is a pity. Noticed last night too that instead of having someone talk to New York from the studio below to keep our transmitter modulated for the five minutes before I began to talk, the RRG substituted loud band music. This was done to drown out the sound of the guns.

As soon as I had finished my broadcast at one a.m., the Nazi air-wardens forced me into the air-raid cellar. I tried to read but the light was poor. I became awfully bored. Finally Lord Haw-Haw and his wife suggested we steal out. We dodged past the guards and found an unfrequented underground tunnel, where we proceeded to dispose of a litre of schnapps which 'Lady' Haw-Haw had brought. Haw-Haw can drink as straight as any man, and if you can get over your initial revulsion at his being a traitor, you find him an amusing and intelligent fellow. When the bottle was finished we felt too free to go back to the cellar. Haw-Haw found a secret stairway and we went up to his room, opened the blinds, and watched the fireworks.

Sitting there in the black of the room, I had a long talk with the man. Haw-Haw, whose real name is William Joyce, but who in Germany goes by the name of Froelich (which in German means 'Joyful'), denies that he is a traitor. He argues that he has renounced his British nationality, had become a German citizen, and that he is no more a traitor than thousands of British and Americans who renounced their citizenship to become comrades in the Soviet Union, or than those Germans who gave up their nationality after 1949 and fled to the United States. This doesn't satisfy me, but it does him. He kept talking about 'we' and 'us' and I asked him which people he meant.

'We Germans, of course,' he snapped.

William L. Shirer

1942 [Russia]

We have again been relieved by Italians. Those wonderful, dreamlike days at Post V. are a thing of the past. The order to prepare for immediate departure came to us like a bolt out of the blue.

To-day we are stationed at a small town about 10 miles from Kaprin and about the same distance from Rossosh. No one knows what is to become of us, and we least of all. We can give free rein to our fancy.

I'm afraid we may be disillusioned in our new assignment! Everybody says that winter will find us fighting, though nobody is sure of it. On the other hand, everyone in the innermost recesses of his heart cherishes the dream of returning to Germany or at least to the occupied regions. Anywhere to get away from Russia.

Pvt First Class Wolfgang Knoblich, 7th Company,
2nd Battalion, 513th Infantry Regiment, Wehrmacht

1943 [Bari, Italy]

We get up at 6.00 to find my jeep and Jim's bicycle disappeared. We tramp the town interviewing *carabinieri* and making enquiries. The difficulty of not knowing the language, no M.P.s to help. Hear a rumour that an RAF officer had taken them. As a last resort take a taxi to the airport. Hang about there for two hours while Admin officer very grudgingly makes a search. To our intense surprise and relief he finds them. Some bibulous RAF officers had loaded the bicycles on to a three-tonner and towed the jeep away, then painted them to obliterate the markings. They had not the grace to apologise or even offer us a drink, the prize shits.

Edward Ardizzone

27 September

1939 [London]

Warsaw has surrendered after a heroic defence against overwhelming odds. Hitler is therefore free to turn his attention westwards, but it remains to be seen whether he will have the courage and stupidity to strike the first serious blow. For the moment the position can be best summed up in the words of the Italian Ambassador in Paris to Sir Eric Phipps:[1] 'I have seen several wars waged without being declared; but this is the first I have seen declared without being waged.'

John Colville

---

[1] British Ambassador in Berlin, 1933–37, and in Paris 1937–39.

1940 [near Coventry]

A boatload of children and grown-ups have been found drifting in a lifeboat from *The City of Benares*, the evacuee ship which the Germans torpedoed without warning. A woman escort massaged the children (all boys) and kept them interested for eight days, on and off, with a long serial story which she made up more or less, beginning with John Buchan's *Thirty-nine Steps* and carrying on with anything she could remember or make up. On the eighth day a little boy who was a scout suddenly called out: 'Oi – a Sunderland!' and there, overhead, was a flying boat. The Sunderland saw the lifeboat and a small boy waving a handkerchief. The pilot saw the child was signalling *City of Benares*. He soon understood, and went off to get help. When they dropped food by parachute, the boatload was near the end of its rations. When, eventually, a warship arrived to pick them up, the children were too weak to climb the ladder and had to be carried aboard. A great story!

The days go by and no news of Alan. Today I have just heard of someone who has been waiting longer than we have and had news of her prisoner son yesterday. Hope is a great thing and patience a real virtue in these times, but difficult for me.

Clara Milburn

1940 [Berlin]

The pact[1] is signed. The signature takes place more of less like that of the Pact of Steel. But the atmosphere is cooler. Even the Berlin street crowd, a comparatively small one, composed mostly of school children, cheers with regularity but without conviction. Japan is far away. Its help is doubtful. Only one thing is certain: that it will be a long war. This does not please the Germans, who had come to believe that with the end of the summer the war would also end. A winter of war is hard to take. More so since food is scarce in Berlin, and it is easy to see that the window displays of the stores promise much more than what is actually inside.

Another thing contributing to the depressed spirit of Berlin life is the constant recurrence of air raids. Every night citizens spend from four to five hours in the cellar. They lack sleep, there is promiscuity

---

[1] The Tripartite Pact, negotiated in Tokyo and signed in Berlin by Germany, Italy and Japan.

between men and women, cold, and these things do not create a good mood. The number of people with colds is incredible. Bomb damage is slight; nervousness is very high. At ten o'clock in the evening every-one looks at his watch. People want to return home to their loved ones. All this does not yet justify the pessimism in certain quarters where the first war is being remembered and they are beginning to think of the worst.

But it is a fact that the attitude in Germany today is not like last June or even last August.

Count Ciano

28 September

1940 [SS *Empress of Britain*]
This is Hades. We are clamped down below decks because we are passing enemy territory. The purser told me that the last convoy which came through took a terrible pasting from Italian planes based in Eritrea and Italian Somaliland. For four days we will be in danger. The heat is unbelievable. The swimming pool has been emptied for this perilous period.

At midday, when the bar opens, the rush for it is astonishing. Toby[1] says we are in a floating inebriates' home. The officer commanding troops confided in me today that the lower decks are fast turning into a brothel. He has had to post sentries to try to restore order.

Toby keeps trying to persuade me to go home with her but I am adamant that somehow I will get back to the Middle East. I am reading a lovely book called *Sand, Wind and Stars* by St-Exupéry.[2] He tells a delightful story about flying over the Andes and carrying a bowl of goldfish in his place so as to be sure which way up he was. Quite a lot of people are 'enjoying the voyage'. The officers and crew of this ship are quite remarkable. They have superb discipline, manners and

---

[1] Toby Wallace, a 'Yeomanry wife', and close friend of Ranfurly. She had followed her husband, Dandy Wallace, to war, leaving two young children behind in Scotland, but was now returning to Britain. Shortly after this entry the SS *Empress of Britain* was bombed (Ranfurly was no longer on board) and it was believed that Mrs Wallace, lying badly injured, on the upper deck, could not be moved, and so went down with the ship.

[2] *Wind, Sand and Stars*, by Antoine de St-Exupéry.

kindness but they have incessant problems – they are often in danger and they must be worried for their own families in England.

Mrs Chitty, a very senior AT [Auxiliary Territorial], who has just surfaced after being seasick since Suez, is being sent home to recruit shorthand typists for the Middle East. She has kindly promised to recruit me if I return to England!

Countess of Ranfurly

29 September

1939 [Yorkshire]

Warsaw has surrendered. Poland is being partitioned by Germany and Russia. I telephone Jan Smeterlin [Polish pianist] in London. He was so upset he could hardly speak. 'Hold on,' he said. 'I'll put the receiver down on my piano.' He played me a little sad Chopin and then came back on the line – 'That's how I feel,' he said, and hung up.

Firearms Certificate No.2802 has arrived from the Leicestershire Police. A note was enclosed: 'We had a good laugh over your application – "For use against parachutists"'. Now I can collect my revolver and ten rounds of ammunition.

Countess of Ranfurly

1942 [Amsterdam]

Dearest Kitty,

The plumber was at work downstairs on Wednesday, moving the water pipes and drains from the office lavatory to the passage so the pipes won't freeze during a cold winter. The plumber's visit was far from pleasant. Not only were we not allowed to run water during the day, but the lavatory was also out of bounds. I'll tell you how we handled this problem; you may find it unseemly of me to bring it up, but I'm not so prudish about matters of this kind. On the day of our arrival, Father and I improvised a chamber pot, sacrificing a preserving jar for this purpose. For the duration of the plumber's visit, preserving jars were put into service during the daytime to hold our calls of nature.

Anne Frank

30 September

1915 [Buxton]

I did expect I should at least hear something to-day but no news came. Again I wandered about but every telegraph boy I saw going in the direction of the Park made me hasten home, and every loud ring at the bell when I was in the house made my heart beat so fast that I felt choked & stifled. From all sides I heard that people had been getting news of casualties during the last few days, and *The Times* obituary list was long with the names of people who had fallen in France & Flanders, chiefly on the 25th and 26th. But in a war like this no news does not necessarily mean good news – quite the reverse. It simply means that in certain parts of the line there has been more confusion than in others. Loos is probably one of those places as the most vigorous part of our attack took place there. It makes me so angry to think that so many people are hearing news of their relations & friends – are even getting them back wounded, but *I* can hear nothing of my one dear soldier. It is impossible he can have come through unharmed; he may be flung unidentified on a pile of forgotten dead, or perhaps dying in some French hospital among strangers who know nothing about him beyond the information on his identity disc.

The Allies' advance seems to be waning somewhat in fury. Well, I wonder if yet *another* day will pass & leave me still in suspense.

Vera Brittain

1942 [Germany]

The Führer said in a speech today that this war will bring about the destruction of the European Jews. I wonder if he is right?

Elisabeth von Stahlenberg

OCTOBER

Frankly, I'd like to see the government get out of war altogether and leave the whole field to private industry.

Joseph Heller, *Catch-22*

1 October

1870 [Paris]

Horse-meat is sneaking slyly into the diet of the people of Paris. The day before yesterday, Pélagie [their housekeeper] brought home a piece of fillet which, on account of its suspicious appearance, I did not eat. Today, at Peter's restaurant, I was served some roast beef that was watery, devoid of fat, and streaked with white sinews; and my painter's eye noticed that it was a dark red colour very different from the pinky red of beef. The waiter could give me only a feeble assurance that this horse was beef.

The Brothers Goncourt

1899 [South Africa]

We were awaked last night by Field Cornet Piet Uys who has come to Bronkhorstspruit with a commando of about 200 men, and he demanded sleeping accommodation. He is an old friend of ours and Father gave him the spare room, and about thirty of his men were given the unfinished storerooms we are building; but the rest of the men had to sleep in the yard under the trees. These young men are very arrogant and say that they will drive the English into the sea; and after that all the *uitlanders* [foreigners], who, they say, are intruders and not welcome. This saddens us, for we are *uitlanders*. When Mr Uys heard this talk he was very grave and filled with dark thoughts regarding the future of his country.

His commando is divided into sub-commandos of thirty men, each commanded by an assistant field cornet. These young commandos are very audacious and seemed always to be looking at me, and Mother told me to stay in the house.

Freda Schlosberg

1939 [Santa Monica]

Exactly one month since England's declaration of war. The unimaginable has happened – and, of course, it's utterly different from anything we had pictured. One looks ahead to a war and imagines it as a single, final, absolute event. It is nothing of the kind. War is a condition, like peace, with good days and bad days, moods of optimism and despair. The crisis of August was actually, for us in Santa Monica, worse than this month which has followed the outbreak. I see Frau Frank's face, contorted with hate. I hear Gottfried Reinhardt yelling, Klaus Mann chattering like an enraged monkey. Berthold snoring like a war-horse. The night war was declared, Vernon sat listening to our radio at home. It was as though neither of us were really present. The living room seemed absolutely empty – with nothing in it but the announcer's voice. No fear, no despair, no sensation at all. Just hollowness.

Christopher Isherwood

1943 [Naples]

Find a room on the first floor of an hotel. Floor above, a brothel. Girls in kimonos on its balcony and American troops going up and coming down looking rather sheepish. Man with a blowpipe goes round my bed to kill bugs, a bad omen.

People very hungry, any lengths to get food. Women will lie with you for a packet of biscuits. In the evening share a bottle with American correspondent and artist. The chambermaid, in pyjamas, in the room too, tells us that the girls and men throw grenades at the Germans. Her feet bound up – said she was wounded by a bullet. Don't believe a word of it.

Edward Ardizzone

2 October

1944 [Palestine]

After a typical cup of Naafi tea – dark with beige-coloured milk – Viola and I wandered in search of the beach. 'Officers' Lido is good,' the proprietor had told us. I haven't got a bathing suit but I thought a pair of fairly opaque lock-knit knickers and a bandana skilfully tied around my chest would do. However when we finally reached the beach it was entirely covered by swarms of all-sized high-legged and incredibly speedy crabs. We took against bathing after this and sat on a marooned raft gazing at the sunset over the sea. Washing in a tin saucer-sized basin requires talent but I have it and made a complete toilet before supper. The club was quite active. Three girls in civilian clothes, six or seven rather nondescript officers. We ate our meal, and then went for a stroll under the moon. It was hot and still. The breeze doesn't rise in the evening here as it does in Cairo. I must say I will always have a very special feeling for Cairo, but I don't think Samson missed much being eyeless in Gaza. It is remarkably unremarkable.

Joyce Grenfell

3 October

1812 [the Siege of Burgos in the Iberian Peninsula]
At one a.m. I went into the trenches and remained till six. We finished the embrasure of a four howitzer battery. We have now about eight times as many batteries as guns. A great deal of rain fell during the night and the trenches are full of mud.

Ensign John Mills, 1st Battalion, Coldstream Guards

1870 [Paris]
Paris has never known an October like this. The clear, starry nights are like nights in the south of France. God loves the Prussians.

The Brothers Goncourt

1939 [Perth, Scotland]
During a conversation which Mr M had shared lately with a certain Mrs B (the wife of an undertaker), the lady confided that her husband had been advised to take in an enormous stock of timber so that he should be able to cope with the mortality of air-raids; a possible enough eventuality in a town on the Forth. Mr M commented that this must have entailed a big expenditure, and concluded: 'I suppose it would mean a loss if all that stuff were left on his hands.' 'Oh yes!' innocently answered the good lady: 'It would be a dead loss.'

William Soutar

1942 [Massachusetts]
I enlisted in the US Navy today. It looks like the Navy got the makings of a very poor sailor when they got me. I still get carsick and cannot ride on a swing for any length of time. I took my physical examination

at the Post Office Building in Boston, Mass. A fellow next to me was rejected because he was color blind. They told him the Sea Bees[1] would take him. On the way home I relaxed in the old trolley car and felt like the Fleet Admiral himself.

James J. Fahey, Seaman First Class

1943 [American 16th Evacuation Hospital, Paestum, Italy]
A gale of the kind no one ever expects of Italy blew down our tent in the middle of the night. Pitch darkness, hammering rain, the suffocating weight of waterlogged canvas over mouth and nostrils, muffled cries from all directions. A lake of water flooded in under the beds, and gradually rose to the level of the bottom of the mattress. It was several hours before we could be rescued. All my kit stowed under the bed was lost, and only my camera and notebooks in the drawer of the bedside table survived. One patient was killed by the main tent-pole falling across his bed.

Norman Lewis

4 October

1999 [Chechnya]
That evening nothing was as usual in Unit 52157B. The officers were uncharacteristically kind. Numerous crates of vodka were carried through the guardhouse quite openly, even escorted by a corporal. The experienced soldiers, seeing this, hid themselves away as best they could and did not appear again. When the green young conscripts staggered out for a breath of fresh air they were not met by the usual obscenities. On the contrary, they were given cigarettes and hints were dropped that soon some of the regiment might be sent to Daghestan. Sergei [surname withheld] and the hundred or so 18-year-olds like him decided that they would not be affected, since they had been called up late in June and had only once since then been shown how to use an automatic rifle.

After the evening meal the officers invited the soldiers to join their table, something that had never happened before. There was a great

---

[1] Name derived from the initials CB (construction battalions) – a force of 8,000 and 250,000 men who constructed naval bases, handled cargo, etc, in the Pacific.

deal of delicious homemade food there and an impressive number of bottles.

By 10 p.m. all had drunk their fill. The next day 50 men were missing from the barracks. Half of those who disappeared were among the new recruits who had fired a gun only once in their lives. At 2 a.m. the officers had woken them up when they were still completely drunk and ticking names off a list, loaded them on to trucks; at 3.30 a.m. they despatched them to Daghestan.

These ominous drunken parties would happen again at the unit. But now none would drink themselves senseless, since they all feared being sent off to fight. The scenario remained the same, however. Each time at the dead of night, more groups were woken, rapidly assembled and despatched.

Anna Politkovskaya

5 October

1917 [London]
Six successive raids have wrecked the nerves of Londoners, with the result of a good deal of discreditable panic even among the well-to-do and the educated. The first two nights I felt myself under the sway of foolish fear. My feet were cold and my heart pattered its protest against physical danger. But the fear wore off, and by Monday night's raid, the nearest to us, I had recovered self-possession and read through the noise of the barrage with the help of an additional cigarette.

Beatrice Webb

1939 [Rome]
Hitler announces that tomorrow morning he will let us have the text of the speech he is to deliver at twelve o'clock. According to Attolico,[1] it seems that appearances have been saved with respect to Poland. It is certain that tomorrow will be the fateful day: either peace or real war. I should not be surprised if Hitler became a little more yielding. Determined as he is to face events with force, a bit of the old socialist still remains in him, making him hesitate at the prospect of

---

[1] Bernardo Attolico, Italian Ambassador to Germany.

a European conflagration. Not so Ribbentrop. He is an aristocrat, or rather worse, a *parvenu*, and the shedding of the people's blood does not worry him. The case of Hitler is different. He was a worker, and he still feels repulsed by bloodshed. He would prefer victories without spilling blood. Therefore I think that a faint though very feeble hope still exists.

Count Ciano

6 October

1917 [London]

In fits of maudlin self-compassion I try to visualise Belgium, Armenia, Serbia, etc., and usually cure myself thereby.

W.N.P. Barbellion

1941 [Hampshire]

Yesterday afternoon, when he and I were sitting in the garden, I asked Sidney: 'Do you wish to go on living?' He sat silent, surprised at the question, then slowly said '*No*.' He is physically comfortable, he is always reading and not actually bored; he loves and is loved, he is mildly interested in other people and keen to hear the news. But he resents not being able to think and express his thoughts, and thus help the world he lives in.

Beatrice Webb

1941 [Kovno Ghetto, Lithuania]

All the patients in the surgical and therapy ward were evacuated, including Dr. Feinberg and his wife, who had nursed him, and Dr. Zvi Elkes, the brother of the Council Chairman.

In the maternity ward, which housed eight women, preparations got under way for the evacuation of the patients. Women who could not leave unaided remained in their beds, waiting to be carried out on stretchers.

Two Germans entered the room. They asked what type of patients were there, and why they were not ready for transfer. The women replied that they had just given birth and that their ardent wish was to get up quickly from their beds so as not to delay the operation.

The Germans wanted to see the babies who had just been born.

They came up to the ledge by the window on which the six babies were lying. They stood there for a while watching the babies. The eyes of one of the Germans grew misty. 'Shall we leave them?' he asked his friend. They both left the room, letting the mothers and the babies stay. This time they survived.

The Germans then started taking the children out of the children's home. Out of 153 children, only 12 were left in the Home. They were simply overlooked. The nurses were also taken away. Those children who were in swaddling clothes were taken out and placed on the ground in the stone-paved hospital courtyard, their tiny faces turned skyward. Soldiers of the third squad of the German Police passed between them. They stopped for a moment. Some of them kicked the babies with their boots. The babies rolled a little to the side but soon enough regained their belly-up position, their faces turned toward the sky. It was a rare spectacle of cruelty and callousness.

Avraham Tory

1942 [Jersey]

At dinner-time lots more Russians came. When too many come, we can't give them much, but they all had a big handful of boiled pig potatoes each. One of them appeared very ill (we had noticed him lying in the field all morning) and we gave him a cup of hot milk and water.

Another little lad sat on a box in the yard for about three-quarters of an hour eating potatoes and what he could find of bits of raw vegetables we had thrown there for the pigs. Mother asked him his age and he said 15 (on his fingers). Then he began to say 'Kaput, Kaput', trying to show, I think, how many of his family were gone, then the poor little fellow burst into tears. We all wept to see him. Mother put her hand on his shoulder. He showed me an immense hole in his trousers, so we gave him a needle and thread and he mended it and was quite pleased with himself.

Finally, John felt so sorry for him that he gave him a cigarette and a match, and how pleased he was! He stroked John's coat and kissed his hand. As we were leaving, tonight, the same little fellow was working with the squad in Mr Bisson's field. He recognised us and gave us a broad smile. I winked at him, making sure the Tod [enemy] was not looking. One has to be so careful.

Nan Le Ruez

7 October

1665 [London]

Up and to the office. Did business, though not much, because of the horrible crowd and lamentable moan of the poor seamen that lie starving in the streets for lack of money, which do trouble and perplex me to the heart; and more at noon when we were to go through them, for then a whole hundred of them followed us, some cursing, some swearing, and some praying to us. And that that made me more troubled was a letter come this afternoon from the Duke of Albemarle, signifying the Dutch to be in sight with 80 sayle yesterday morning off of Solebay, coming right into the bay. God knows what they will and may do to us, we have no force abroad able to oppose them, but to be sacrificed to them.

Samuel Pepys

1812 [Iberian Peninsula]

It rained incessantly during the day and night. They [the French] dismounted another eighteen pounder this morning so that there is now but one left and yet the siege is continued though the chance of success must be very remote. At three in the morning the garrison made another sortie. They advanced under favour of a very heavy rain and got up to the breach without being perceived, and drove our men from every part of the wall. The Germans were on the covering party. After some time the Germans succeeded in regaining the wall after a most obstinate defensive, being so closely engaged that they knocked each other about with their butt ends. Major Cocks, of the 79th, the Field Officer in the trenches, was killed at the beginning of the business. His loss is irreparable. He was one of the greatest promise and during the three years he had been in the country had greatly distinguished himself. Every officer present was either killed or wounded, and the loss of men is about a hundred and fifty. They levelled all our works and buried some of the sappers alive. Two officers and 50 men were in my post behind the shot. They [the French] got into their rear – the officers were killed and hardly a man escaped. I cannot help thinking myself very fortunate in having escaped.

Ensign John Mills, 1st Battalion, Coldstream Guards

1939 [London]

I am indulging in an orgy of spending, in the belief that materials will grow worse in quality and more expensive. This morning I tried on a new suit and an overcoat at my tailor's, and two ruinous pairs of shoes at Peal's [they cost £2.10.0].

John Colville

1942 [Boston to Naval Training Station, Great Lakes]

I got up early this morning for my trip to Boston, on my way to the Great Lakes Naval Training Station in Chicago, Illinois.

Before leaving I shook my father's[1] hand and kissed him goodbye.

It was a clear cool morning as my sister Mary, brother John and I headed for the bus at the corner of Cedar Street. The bus and trolley car were crowded with people going to work. When we reached the Post Office Building in Boston I shook John's hand and kissed Mary goodbye.

With a big band leading the way we marched through downtown Boston before thousands of people. It took about half an hour to reach the North Station and at 5.30 p.m. we were on our way.

When the train passed through my city it was beginning to get dark and I could picture the folks at home having supper. There would be an empty place at the table for some time. It would have been very easy for me to feel sad and lonely with these thoughts in my mind but we should not give in to our feelings. If we always gave in to our feelings instead of our judgment we would fall by the wayside when the going got rough.

It will be a long tiresome trip and our bed will be the seat we sit in, two to a seat.

James J. Fahey, Seaman First Class

1943 [Tuscany]

Much as the Germans are disliked and dreaded, however, these sentiments are as nothing compared with those awakened by the members of the new Fascist Party – and with reason. Here is a true story. A few days ago, at the bar of the Excelsior, the radio played *Giovinezze*. One of the men present (a business man called Piaggio) remained seated. 'Get up,' ordered one of the Fascists. The other shrugged

---

[1] Orphaned at the age of three, Fahey had been brought up by a cousin and his wife whom he looked on as his parents.

contemptuously. Whereupon the Fascist drew a revolver and shot him. Most of the other people in the room ran away, but some Germans picked up the wounded man and took him to hospital, where he lay for some days at the point of death, having been hit in the kidneys. No one attempted to arrest the Fascist, who is still at large.

Iris Origo

1944 [London]

Charwomen and the young sluts who are so much in evidence these days conduct their conversation in the shape of all screaming simultaneously and continuously at the top of their raucous voices, quite oblivious of what any others of the party are saying and periodically emitting hyena-like yells of laughter. There can be no attention to content – only volume and continuity. It is a melancholy and miserable spectacle.

Lord Reith

1967 [Bolivia]

We have completed the eleventh month since the guerrilla began. It was a day without complications, even bucolic, until 12.30, when an old woman, herding her goats, entered the canyon where we were camped and we had to take her prisoner. The woman had not given us any trustworthy news about [Bolivian government] soldiers, saying to every question that she doesn't know and that she hasn't been past here for a long time. She only gave us information about the trails; as a result of her information, we estimate we are about one league from Higueras, one from Jaqüey, and about two leagues from Pucará. At 17.30 Inti, Aniceto and Pablito went to the old woman's house, where she had one crippled and one dwarf daughter. She was given 50 pesos and charged with not speaking a word; we don't have much hope she will keep her promises.

The seventeen of us set out under a small moon, and the march was very tiresome and we left a lot of traces in the canyon where we were; it has no houses nearby, but there are some potato fields irrigated by ditches from the same stream. At 0200 we halted because it was useless to go on advancing. El Chino [a wounded guerrilla] is becoming a real burden when we have to travel at night.

The army issued a strange report about the presence of 250 men in Serrano, to stop the passage of the encircled men, who are said to number 37; they located our hiding-place between the Acero and Oro rivers. The item appears to be a red herring.[1]

Ernesto 'Che' Guevara

8 October

1915 [London]

The window rattled behind me: then all the windows rattled and we became conscious of the booming of guns getting nearer, 'At last the Zeppelins', Sidney said, with almost boyish glee. From the balcony we could see shrapnel bursting over the river and beyond, somewhat aimlessly. In another few minutes a long sinuous airship appeared high up in the blue sky, lit up faintly by the searchlights. It seemed to come from over the houses just behind us, we thought along Victoria Street, but it was actually passing along the Strand. It moved slowly, seemingly across the river, the shells bursting far below it. Then there were two bursts that seemed to nearly hit it and it disappeared. I imagine it bounded upwards. The show was over. It was a gruesome reflection afterwards that while we were being pleasantly excited, men women and children were being killed and maimed. At the time it was impossible not to take it as a 'Sight'.

Beatrice Webb

1940 [London]

Go round to see Julian Huxley at the Zoo. He is in an awkward position since he is responsible for seeing that his animals do not escape. He assures me that the carnivores are perfectly safe, although a zebra got out the other day when its cage was bombed and bolted as far as Camden Town. While we are at supper a fierce raid begins and the house shakes. We go on discussing war aims. He feels that the future of the world depends upon the organisation of economic resources and the control by the U.S.A. and ourselves of raw materials. The raid gets very bad, and at 8.30 he offers to drive me back. It is a heavenly moonlit night, and the searchlights are swaying against a soft mackerel sky and a great calm moon. The shells light up their match-flares in

---

[1] This is the last entry in the diary. On 8 October 1967, 'Che' Guevara was wounded and captured. He was later shot.

the sky. A great star-shell creeps slowly down over the city under a neat parachute. We hear loud explosions all round as he drives me bravely back to the Ministry [of Information].

Harold Nicolson

1942 [Naval Training Station, Great Lakes]
We spent four weeks of training and lived in barracks. A Chief Petty Officer was in charge of each company and our chief was liked by all.

Some of the Chiefs are hated because they go out of their way to make it as miserable as possible. They enjoy getting the fellows up at two in the morning and have them stand at attention in the cold for a long time with very little clothing.

You learned that your days of privacy were over while you were in the Navy and they would not return until you were back in civilian life again. When you ate, slept, took a shower, etc., you were always part of the crowd, you were never alone.

James J. Fahey, Seaman First Class

1943 [Naples]
Contact with the military units brought its inevitable consequences. The phone started ringing first thing in the morning and rarely stopped. An excited officer was usually on the line to report the presence in his area of an enemy agent, or a secret transmitter, or a suspected cache of abandoned loot. All this information came from local civilians who poured into the nearest army HQ, anxious to unburden themselves of secrets of all kinds, but not even phrase books had been issued to help with the language problem, mistakes were frequent. Today, being the only section member left in the office, I was sent hurriedly on the motor-bike, in response to the most urgent request, to Afragola, where an infantry major was convinced from local reports that a village woman was a spy. In this case evidence had been transmitted mostly by gestures which the major had failed to interpret. It turned out that what the villagers had been trying to explain was that the woman was a witch, and that if allowed to cast her malefic gaze on the unit's water supply, she would make it undrinkable.

On my way to resolve this misunderstanding I saw a remarkable spectacle. Hundreds, possibly thousands of Italians, most of them women and children, were in the fields all along the roadside driven by their hunger to search for edible plants. I stopped to speak to a group of them, and they told me that they had left their homes in Naples at daybreak, and had walked for between two and three hours to reach the spot where I found them – seven or eight miles out of town. Here a fair number of plants could still be found, although nearer the city the fields had been stripped of everything that could be eaten. There were about fifteen different kinds of plants which were worth collecting, most of them bitter in flavour. All I recognized among their collections were dandelions. I saw other parties netting birds, and these had managed to catch a few sparrows and some tiny warblers which they said were common at this time of year, attracted by the fruit in the orchards. They told me they faced the hostility of the local people, on whose lands they were trespassing, and who accused them of raids on their vineyards and vegetable patches.

Norman Lewis

9 October

1916 [London]
Clegg brought a Capt. B. (of his Battery) to lunch. Had been out at Ypres ten months and then wounded in the head, in front of right ear. He carries a good scar. He talked well, and said he should like to write if he could. I told him he could.

He said the newspaper correspondents' descriptions of men eager to go up over the parapet made him laugh. They never were eager. He related how he had seen a whole company of men extremely pale with apprehension and shaking so that they could scarcely load their rifles. Then he said that men who nevertheless *did* go over in that state were really brave. He told us how his battery saw hundreds, thousands, of grey figures coming along only 1,000 yards off, and every man thought he would be a prisoner in ten minutes, when suddenly thousands of Canadians appeared from nowhere, and the Boches fled. The cheering was delirious. He told this very dramatically, but without any effort to be effective. For a long time the fellows wrote to him regularly once a fortnight, and every letter ended with: 'When are you coming back?' He said they had had glorious times now and then, glorious. He said that to sit on a factory chimney and see the Boches going over was better than big game shooting. He said the Boches had any amount of pluck and grit. Both Clegg and B. facetiously contrasted the rough, anyhow, bumping treatment the wounded get on their way from the firing line (when they really *are* ill) with the hushed, tender, worshipping treatment they get on arriving in London when many of them are doing pretty well.

Arnold Bennett

1917 [London]

We had a horrid shock. L came in so unreasonably cheerful that I guessed a disaster. He has been called up. It was piteous to see him shivering, physically shivering, so that we lit his gas fire, and only by degrees became more or less where we were in spirits; and still, if one could wake to find it untrue, it would be a mercy.

We had a short walk by the river. As it is a fine, fairly still evening, perhaps I shall have a raid to describe tomorrow. We have a liver and bacon Clumber [spaniel] in view, the property of a man taken for the army.

Virginia Woolf

1942 [Amsterdam]

Dearest Kitty,

Have you ever heard the term 'hostages'? That's the latest punishment for saboteurs. It's the most horrible thing you can imagine. Leading citizens – innocent people – are taken prisoner to await their execution. If the Gestapo can't find the saboteur, they simply grab five hostages and line them up against the wall. You read the announcements of their death in the paper, where they're referred to as 'fatal accidents'.

Anne Frank

1942 [England]

Took a Hector up to-day. Wings flap, struts shake, all the instruments rattle. Am sure I've overlooked some remote fuel cock somewhere. Sergeant 'Whitey' White in the back seat amusing himself dropping various objects on passing targets below. 'Whitey', quite irrepressible, a merry little Cockney. His Pa drives a cab, I hope with less abandon than his son pilots an aircraft.

Desmond Leslie

1943 [Naples]

This afternoon another trip along the sea-front at Santa Lucia provided another spectacle of the desperate hunt for food. Rocks were piled up here against the sea wall and innumerable children were at work among them. I learned that they were prising limpets off the rocks, all the winkles and sea-snails having long since been exhausted. A pint of limpets sold at the roadside fetched about two lire, and if boiled long enough could be expected to add some faint, fishy flavour to a broth produced from any edible odds and ends. Inexplicably, no boats were allowed out yet to fish. Nothing, absolutely nothing than can be tackled by the human digestive system is wasted in Naples. The butchers' shops that have opened here and there sell nothing we would consider accept-able as meat, but their displays, of scraps of offal, are set out with art, and handled with reverence; chickens' heads – from which the beak has been neatly trimmed – cost five lire; a little grey pile of chickens' intestines in a brightly polished saucer, five lire; a gizzard, three lire; calves' trotters, two lire apiece; a large piece of windpipe, seven lire. Little queues wait to be served with these delicacies. There is a persist-ent rumour of a decline in the cat population of the city.

Norman Lewis

10 October

1870 [Paris]

This morning I went to get a card for my meat ration. It seemed to me that I was looking at one of those queues in the great Revolution which my poor old cousin Cornélie used to describe to me, in that patient line of heterogeneous individuals, of ragged old women, of men in peaked caps, of small shopkeepers, cooped up in those improvised offices, those whitewashed rooms, where you recognized, sitting round a table, omnipotent in their uniforms of officers of the National Guard and supreme dispensers of your food, your far from honest tradesmen.

I came away with a piece of blue paper, a typographical curiosity for future Goncourts and times to come, which entitles me and my housekeeper to buy every day two rations of raw meat or two portions of food cooked in the municipal canteens. There are coupons up to 14 November: a good many things may happen between now and then.

The Brothers Goncourt

1940 [Berlin]

In the afternoon I inspect the dance troupe established by me at its first appearance at the *Volksbühne*. I can only stay for a few minutes. But the whole thing is rather too forced and intellectual for my taste. Dance must glide, as if on wings; it must express beauty and embody grace, but not make ideology. Modern dance suffers greatly from this tendency.

Josef Goebbels

1942 [England]

A diversion this afternoon. A Tigermoth arrives and discharges a most pukka-looking type in a natty Irving jacket. The pukka-looking type is preceded by a black cigarette holder of immeasurable length. He looks the last word in Wing Commanders, and raises a fluster of salutes wherever he goes. The Duty Pilot's office jump smartly to attention, but he graciously waves them down. He removes his Irving jacket to reveal dirty sergeant's stripes beneath. He is Sergeant Ollie Moxon. Ollie and I get on rather well.

Desmond Leslie

11 October

1812 [Iberian Peninsula]

General Paget arrived from England this morning to act as second in command in the room of Sir Thomas Graham. The round shot is entirely expended and 'Thunder' the only eighteen-pounder, 'Nelson' being in the mud and 'Lightning' ditched. Rain.

Ensign John Mills, 1st Battalion, Coldstream Guards

1940 [Berlin]

Midday with the Führer, who is back from Munich. I show him the newest examples of Italian 'art'. His only response is a contemptuous smile.

Josef Goebbels

12 October

1914 [London]

Am better today. My better self is convinced that it is silly and small-minded to think so much about my own puny destiny – especially at times like these when – God love us all – there is a column of casualties each day. The great thing to be thankful for is that I am *alive* and alive *now*, that I was alive *yesterday*, and even may be to-morrow. Surely that is thrilling enough. What, then, have I got to complain of? I'm a lucky dog to be alive at all. My plight is bad, but there are others in a worse one. I'm going to be brave and fight on the side of Nietzsche. Who knows but that one day the dancing star may yet be born!

W.N.P. Barbellion

1940 [London]

Londoners have had one month of this [bombing] so far, and they must look forward to a whole winter of it. The planes arrive each night at dusk. One hears the drone, then the bangs, zumphs of the bombs. The AA gunfire, which is gay and heartening, is like a firework fiesta: and then an interval. During the lull one tries to read a book, but one's thoughts wander, and soon the hum of more approaching planes is heard. The zumphs come perilously near, and one leaves the chair for a vantage point under the lintel of a door. The restless night continues.

By degrees many people have grown accustomed to being frightened. For myself, most evenings I have beetled off to the Dorchester. There the noise outside is drowned with wine, music and company – and what a mixed brew we are! Cabinet ministers and their self-consciously respectable wives; hatchet-jawed, iron-grey brigadiers; calf-like airmen off duty; tarts on duty, actresses (also), *déclassé* society people, cheap musicians and motor-car agents. It could not be more ugly and vile, and yet I have not the strength of character to remain like Harold Acton,[1] with a book.

In the infernos of the Underground the poor wretches take up their positions for the night's sleep at four o'clock in the afternoon. The winter must surely bring epidemics of flu, even typhoid. The prospect is not cheering, and Churchill makes no bones about the ardours of the future. The electric trains are bombed, so typists fight their way on to extra buses. Telephone exchanges are out of order, and hardly a clock has its face intact. Yet the life of the city manages, more or less, to continue as if in normal times. Nothing can really dash the spirits of the English people, who love to grumble, and who, in spite of their complaints, are deeply confident of victory.

Cecil Beaton

[1] Historian and aesthete (1904–94).

1940 [England]
[At Lord and Lady Astor's estate, Cliveden]

He [Lord Halifax] described his visit to Hitler, when the latter started off with a terrific diatribe against the democratic system and the democracies. Finally Halifax told him that he had not come to Germany to debate the relative merits of their two forms of government and that if this was the only course their conversation was to take he might as well go home. Hitler stopped short, appeared somewhat flustered, and immediately moderated his tone. Halifax said it was evident that very few people called his bluff this way but that the same thing had happened with the British Ambassador, Sir Nevile Henderson, who on one occasion completely lost his temper and assailed Hitler in the same tone and terms that the Führer himself was using, with the result that Hitler immediately became almost deferential. The conclusion, of course, is that there is only one way in which the Germans can be dealt with successfully. Their only respect is for naked force.

General Raymond E. Lee

1942 [Germany]
Herr Rust arrested for serving Jews with more than their ration. Hope this doesn't mean the shop will be closed down.[1] I rely on him for extra fats.

Elisabeth von Stahlenberg

13 October

1915 [London]
A Zeppelin raid last night. I am down with a temperature but our little household remained quite calm, thank God. We heard guns going off, and I had a fit of trembling as I lay in bed. Many dead of heart failure owing to the excitement.

W.N.P. Barbellion

1915 [London]
We dined at Queens' Restaurant, Sloane Square. Just as we had finished and were emerging, there was a bustle and we heard the magic word

[1] It was.

'Zeppelin'. We rushed out and found people in dramatic groups, gazing skywards. Some men there said they saw the Zeppelin. Alas, I didn't! But our guns were popping away and shells bursting in the air. I felt excited pleasurably, but not the faintest tremor and I longed and longed for more to happen. Bibs [her husband] was the only member of the family who had sufficient imagination to be frightened. My only words were: 'Something for my diary!'

Lady Cynthia Asquith

1939 [London]
This war really isn't at all bad. We make the best of things, putting our trust in god and Arthur Askey [popular light entertainer]. This week's 'Bandwagon' was the best ever. We all felt so cheered and reassured after it. We have the radio on all the time, news bulletins mostly – our expeditionary army is going to France – and we listen to a lot of music too. I shall never think of the war without thinking of Chopin's 'Tristesse' – they played it all through the crisis, and now they've turned it into a jazz song as well.

Joan Wyndham

1939 [Germany]
The English have *turned down* Hitler's offer for peace. One good thing, I have a *fur coat!* Hugo arranged it (left by Jews in Berlin, so we were able to buy it at about a third of its real price), it has never been worn I should think. Arctic fox – creamy silver – lined with satin. Ostentatious on one of *them*, but I look like a film star!

Elisabeth von Stahlenberg

1940 [London]
Winston's only noteworthy remark during lunch was, 'A Hun alive is a war in prospect.'

John Colville

1941 [Dresden]
The cobbler in Habsburger – no: Planettastrasse: 'Please, let your wife come from now on. The guild has strictly forbidden us to do work for Jews – you are to go to the Jewish cobbler: But you are an old customer of mine.'

Victor Klemperer

1942 [England]
Jimmy, still slightly sozzled after a night on the tiles, does his dive approach and runs out of airspace three fields short. There's an awful crash, a hole in a hedge, a large one in a cowshed and Jimmy, walking back rather dazed, muttering 'I had a glider a minute ago. I'm sure I had a glider, I *know* I had a glider.' The best way to collect that glider would be with fifty large wastepaper baskets.

Desmond Leslie

14 October

1780 [South Carolina]
Twelve field officers were chosen to try the military prisoners[1] – particularly those who had the most influence in the country. They condemned thirty – in the evening they began to execute Lieut.-Col. Mills, Capt. Wilson, Capt. Chitwood, and six others, who unfortunately fell a sacrifice to their infamous mock jury. Mills, Wilson, and Chitwood died like Romans – the others were reprieved.

Anthony Allaire

1939 [Berlin]
Great debate about supplies of fat. In hotels, too much meat continues to be given out without ration cards. I take steps against it.

Josef Goebbels

15 October

1917 [the Russian Front]
In the early evening, a man was led in who had been wounded by a German bullet. He soon came to know that he was the only soldier in that ward who had received a wound from an enemy. He strutted up and down feeling quite a hero among the many who had self-inflicted or accidental wounds.

Florence Farmborough

---

[1] Allaire was amongst a group of Loyalists, officers and men, captured by the Rebels.

1940 [Gibraltar]
Reached Gibraltar 6am. The last ten days very tedious. We've all read all the books in the library, drunk nearly all the wine, smoked all the cigars, and eaten most of the food. The buggery trials were the only thing of interest. I defended Marine Florence. He got eight months. His companion in pleasure got eleven. I did quite well for him.

Evelyn Waugh

16 October

1942 [POW camp, Java]
I have seen during the last two days some excellent specimens of deficiency disease – pellagra-type scrotal dermatitis (Bandoeng balls),[1] perlèche[2] – typical tongue. Rash on hands, ulnar border of forearms and elbows. A characteristic, though, is that great numbers of troops are troubled by *intense burning of the feet* and an exquisite sensitiveness which scarcely enables them to walk and they cannot sleep or get any rest. I have seen one case who has also a slight burning of hand on ulnar side (one hand only). He is the only case that shows a tendency to the unilateral. In general, these cases show slight exaggeration of knee jerks, but one or two cases exhibiting the phenomenon have lost their ankle jerks. It is disconcerting how long it takes for improved food and yeast (of which we have great hopes) to do any good. We use a thick paste, black specimen of yeast (up to date we have only been able to afford about two teaspoonsful per case daily).

Weary Dunlop

1944 [North of England]
It was hardly light when I went over to breakfast. The air was a cold colourless grey. One of the prisoners who had arrived the day before was sitting on the low stone parapet outside the cookhouse. He had been sent to work there and was waiting for someone to tell him what to do. The ginger cat was crouched on his lap and he ran his fingers through the thick creamy fur, over and over as though he would

---

[1] A deficiency disease manifested by a raw, weeping scrotum.
[2] Rawness and ulceration at the corners of the mouth.

absorb all the softness into them. The cat received this unusual attention with placid indifference.

When I came by half an hour later he was in the same position,
his hands buried in the cat's softness. His head was sunk low on his
chest and the wind blew on the top of his skull and caught locks of
fair hair and flung them one after another across his forehead sharply
like the leaves in a book. The morning flight of bombers was crossing the sky, low and invisible above the hanging cloud and filling the
air with a throbbing blanket of sound. As I passed he raised his head
and looked up. His face was white and smooth like a child's and his
eyes, sunk in craters of darkness, were brimming with tears.

But the morning was cold with a sharp wind that brings tears easily
to the eyes.

Keith Vaughan

17 October

1780 [South Carolina]

Moved at eight o'clock in the morning. Marched fifteen miles; halted
at Capt. Hatt's plantation. Three prisoners attempted to make their
escape this night; two succeeded – the other was shot through the
body.

Anthony Allaire

1914 [Essex]

11.30 a.m. Notice up at the Police Station, opposite the Post Office
that:

(a) no lamps must show in shops;
(b) as few lights as possible may show in the streets;
(c) no lights must shine from windows of upper storeys;
(d) no lobby lights to be used, unless shaded, so as not to show outside.

1p.m. the Policeman served a copy of this notice to the Rectory. He
says this house is on the line along which hostile airships are expected
to travel.

Andrew Clark

1941 [Rome]

At the Attolicos[1] in honor of Frau Goebbels, who is passing through, accompanied by a sister-in-law. This is how Bismarck[2] addressed Anfuso[3] on the subject: 'Frau Goebbels is the typical wife of a high Nazi official. She was first married to a crook, and earned money through prostitution. Later she became the friend of Goebbels, but this did not prevent her from going to bed with many of the frequenters of the party meetings at the Sports Palace. Goebbels married her one night when he was drunk. They have several children together, and maybe not together, because Frau Goebbels has continued her former ways. Now she goes around looking for men, and when there are not enough, there is also her sister-in-law, who is another whore. I am ashamed to think that my wife has anything to do with such people.' This is how a Bismarck talks about the wife of one of the most outstanding men in the Nazi regime.

Count Ciano

1942 [Kovno Ghetto, Lithuania]

This morning brought the bitter surprise: at 7 a.m. a Gestapo car arrived. The wives of Krieger and Reibstein [both had been police officers] together with their children, were taken urgently to the Ghetto command. A woman and her two little children were also taken there; her husband had been arrested on charges of black-racketeering and was imprisoned in the Ghetto detention center.

Schtitz [SS Master Sergeant] also ordered Erich Kohn to be taken there. Kohn was a sick man. He had been in the hospital for a long time and had to be taken to the Ghetto command headquarters on a stretcher. Kopelman [fellow inmate] pleaded with Schtitz to leave the man in peace on account of his illness. He said, 'Why should he be troubled; after all, he is unable to run away.' Erich Kohn was returned to the hospital.

Schtitz told the women and children that they were going to join their husbands and fathers on a journey to Riga. He put them in the car which drove off in the direction of the Ninth Fort. There they were executed that same morning. The German Ghetto commandant, Litschauer, attended the execution.

---

[1] Bernardo Attolico, Italian Ambassador to Germany.
[2] Prince Otto von Bismarck, Councillor at German Embassy in Rome.
[2] Filippo Anfuso, head of Garo's cabinet.

Taking the people to the Ninth Fort and then murdering them brutally was unheard of until now. It boggles the mind. Why lie? Why didn't they say: 'These people are condemned to death'? Or, as has always been the case, not say anything? And the most ominous question of all: why do the children have to die for the real or imaginary offences of their parents, or women for the sins of their husbands? Ever since human beings stopped eating the flesh of their own species, such horror has been unheard of. And all this because a number of people made a wrong step: not to get rich, but to bring home some flour!

Avraham Tory

18 October

1780 [South Carolina]

About five o'clock in the morning the Rebels executed the man who unfortunately got wounded in attempting to make his escape. We moved at eight o'clock in the morning, and marched eighteen miles to Moravian creek, and halted.

Anthony Allaire

1812 [Iberian Peninsula]

The Coldstream formed the covering party in the morning. Harvey was killed whilst visiting his party. The battery continued firing upon the breach and succeeded in making it very good. At three o'clock it was communicated to us that the place was to be stormed at 4 o'clock. The signal was the explosion of the mine, on which a flag was to be held up on the hill. The mine exploded – the explosion was attended with so little noise that though we were anxiously expecting it, we could hear no noise. The earth shook a little, we looked to the hill and saw the flag. The 300 Germans stormed the breach and got well up it. They then attempted the third line, by a place in the wall which was broken down. It ended in their being beat out of the whole with the loss of 7 officers and a great many men. Our party was to escalade the wall in front. Burgess ran forward with 30 men, Walpole and myself followed with fifty each and ladders. Burgess got up without much difficulty, Walpole and myself followed. The place we stood on was a ledge in the wall about three feet from the top. A most tremendous fire opened upon us from every part which took us in front and rear.

They pour down fresh men and ours kept falling down into the ditch, dragging and knocking down others. We were so close that they fairly put their muskets into our faces, and we pulled one of their men through an embrasure. Burgess was killed and Walpole severely wounded. We had hardly any men left on the top and at last we gave way. How we got over the palisades I know not. They increased their fire as we retreated, and we came off with the loss of more than half our party and all the badly wounded were left in the ditch. Burgess behaved nobly – he was first up the ladder and waved his hat on the top. I found him lying there wounded. He begged me to get my men up and in the act of speaking a stone hit him, he fell on the ledge and was shot dead. The time we were on the wall was not more than six minutes. The fire was tremendous, shots, shells, grape, musketry, large stones, hand grenades and every missile weapon was used against us. I reckon my escape particularly fortunate. A party of sixty men attempted to escalade on our right. They were met by a very superior force and were immediately driven back but with very little loss. The mine destroyed a small church on the right. Colonel Brown with some Portuguese got possession of it. It completes our possession of the whole of the first line which was before incomplete. The failure of this is to be ascribed entirely to our want of men. Had we but double the number we could have maintained ourselves but they dropped off so fast and none coming to supply their place, we failed from sheer weakness. Crofton was slightly wounded in the arm whilst waiting with the support. Walpole had his arm shattered with a grape shot, which struck him likewise in the side, but the shot was most providentially glanced, striking and tearing Ninon de L'Enclos[1], which he happened to have in a side pocket at the time, otherwise it must have killed him. Thus finished this trying day. I was slightly wounded in the arm by a stone, but not the least hurt.

Ensign John Mills, 1st Battalion, Coldstream Guards

1938 [Spain]

A lieutenant and a *guardia civil* sat for hours in the surgery seeing the men who had shot themselves and writing down their signed statements

---

[1] *The Life of Anne Lenclos* (1616–1706), a French courtesan, who had many lovers and two sons, one of whom, not realising she was his mother, grew passionate towards her and, when informed of their real relationship, blew out his brains.

of how it happened. I cannot help feeling terribly sorry for them as unless their stories can be proved true they will be shot. I am certain that some of them are perfectly innocent. One, for instance, is only twenty and has been twenty-one months at the front. His hand is all shot to bits by an explosive bullet. He says he picked up a Red's gun instead of his own during a battle and it exploded in his hand.

Priscilla Scott-Ellis

1939 [Lewes, England]
I said to Mrs Pinyoun at 10 Castle Banks that either she or Mrs Richardson at 9 showed a light in the kitchen window. Mrs Pinyoun said : 'Not me, M'm. I'm so nervous that I even take my false teeth out in the dark.'

Mrs Henry Dudeney

1940 [London]
Travelling by underground is revolting now. Trains are sparse and travellers are legion.

John Colville

19 October

1899 [London]
I addressed them a few parting words as follows: 'I desire to wish you Godspeed. May God protect you! I am confident that you will always do your duty, and will ever maintain the high reputation of the Gordon Highlanders.'[1] The men then gave three cheers, and I called up Captain Kerr, who seemed much moved, and could hardly speak. I shook hands with him, and wished him a safe return, and also spoke to the two Lieutenants. It was very touching, and I felt quite a lump in my throat as we drove away, and I thought of how these remarkably fine men might not all return.

Queen Victoria

1917 [the Russian Front]
I saw one of our young doctors dressing a wound before the dirt and grime around it had been washed off. I gave way to my wrath and

[1] Bound for South Africa and the Boer War.

told him that he was asking for serious trouble if he had dressed the wound before first cleansing it. He rudely told me to mind my own business. I told him that it was *my* business to see that our soldiers' wounds were cleansed before bandaging. We exchanged many angry, resentful words. But I know that I was right; he knew that he was wrong. But he was a doctor and I was only a Sister!

I worked it out before I went to sleep. I knew that I was growing coarse, bad-humoured and fault-finding. At first, I ascribed it to the pressure of warfare, the many hardships and humiliations, the conditions of our everyday life at the Front, when for days we could not undress, or even have a good wash. I decided that there were, indeed, good reasons for my bad temper; yet I began to feel ashamed of myself. Before I became a Red Cross nurse, I had been fully aware that there would be many exasperating moments, but I had been certain that I would overcome them – even welcome them in order to prove the strength of my will. I would often repeat those words of Goethe: '*Es bildet ein Talent sich in der Stille, sich ein Charakter in dem Strom der Welt*' ['Talent is developed in tranquillity, but character is moulded in the tumult of the world']. I had wanted my character to be strengthened and to come through, as victor in the struggle. But recently there have been times when the knowledge that I was rude and ill-tempered did not even bother me.

Some of our Sisters and Brothers were not noted for their self-control and when they began to throw nasty, biting words at each other, I would tell myself: 'It is lack of education,' or 'It is the Russian temperament.' And now, I am doing the same thing! And I am English! We English have a reputation here for having our feelings well under control. I really am ashamed of myself and must take myself in hand.

Florence Farmborough

1939 [Berlin]

Yesterday: We launch swingeing attacks against England in the press. I write a furious article aimed against Churchill, packed with crushing facts. That charming gentleman won't be able to hide this behind the mirror.

Josef Goebbels

20 October

1937 [Nanking, during the Japanese invasion]

Herr Hoth from the German embassy is lying in Kulou Hospital. On a hunting trip in a sampan on the Yangtze, the man behind put a load of buckshot in his calves. He was not given first aid until they were on board an English warship. The things that can happen to a person in war! In the calf of all places! I've been wondering whether I ought to award him the Order of the Garter for his ailing legs. I think I'll do it!

John Rabe

1940 [Berlin]

Evening at Wolly Saldern's in Grünewald. He is on leave and lives with his family. The house is crammed with good books and good music. We had just started for home in Zichy's car when the alarm sounded. As only diplomats are allowed in the streets after the sirens, Zichy drove us back to Wolly's, where we sat listening to records until about 2 a.m. Then I set out for home with Konstantin of Bavaria, a walk of over three miles. After we had crossed the Halensee bridge, the sirens again started to howl. As nobody stopped us, we went on, but the shooting soon became unpleasant and on the Kurfürstendamm a policeman shoved us into a cellar. We sat there on the floor, shivering with cold, for three hours. I had no coat, so we both huddled under Konstantin's raincoat. Part of the time we dozed or listened to the others talking. Berliners are at their best in times of crisis and can be very funny. At 6 a.m. the all-clear sounded. No trams or taxis, of course, anywhere, so we ran a race down the Kurfürstendamm to warm up and finally found a taxi which brought us home. We had to make a detour near my house – two ambulances had collided just after having dug some people from the house next to ours, which is now pulverised, and three people who had survived the bomb were killed in the crash.

On getting home, I found Tatiana very worried about me, for that bomb had just barely missed our own building. I pulled on a sweater, lay down for half an hour and then had to take off for the office. I could not work. I was so tired. At Katie Kleinmichel's suggestion I stretched out on a camp bed (which is there for emergencies) and woke up only three hours later to find my boss studying me with disapproval.

Marie 'Missie' Vassiltchikov

1940 [London]

Sunday morning. It was a lovely fall day and I had got up a little late, read the papers at breakfast, and was being shaved in the barber's shop when suddenly we heard the sirens wailing. Almost at once I heard a bomber overhead and had just started to remark that it had arrived undetected when the whistling scream of the descending bomb was evident. The barber fell flat on the floor and then as the first bomb went off we heard another coming down, scrambled to his feet and shouting for me to come with him. With my face covered with lather I followed him into a strong niche or passageway at the end of the barber's shop, where we waited while a third bomb came down and went off. Then as all was quiet, we emerged and he resumed shaving me. He had seemed so distraught at first that I wondered whether it was safe for him to wield the razor, and after he had finished I congratulated him on having such a steady hand. He held it out for a moment and contemplated it with satisfaction, for it did not waver in the least. I could not but reflect that there are all sorts of indirect results from this bombing business. If he had been a very nervous individual, it might easily have made his hand jerk while he was shaving me and I might have lost my nose completely.

General Raymond E. Lee

21 October

1899 [Bronkhorstspruit, South Africa]

Several balloons are rumoured to have been seen over Johannesburg, Pretoria and Standerton and it is said that the Government has given orders to shoot at them; so several stars are shot at.

Freda Schlosberg

1939 [Port Jefferson, USA]

The plump, humorous-faced little man, contentedly sipping his beer at one end of the bar – shabby, working clothes, but coat on and soiled felt hat. A young man in garage mechanic clothes, big Sinko sign on back of shirt, came in. He looked at the clock, 'Ten minutes to five,' he said. 'I never can drink till five. Never till after work.'

'Saving to get married, eh?' said the plump man. 'Can't have a beer until after five, eh?'

'Yeah, and what'll we do for that good Czecho-Slovakian beer now that Hitler's got my country?' evaded the young man.

'Hitler and Roosie,' said the little man.

'And Mussolini.'

'Ah, Mussolini is too smart,' said the little man.

'Like Stalin, they wait till Hitler's got his moustache shaved off, then they step in and divide it all up.'

'Roosia. There's a country I'd like to see wiped off the map.'

'Mussolini'll fall in line soon enough,' said the little man, 'then us.'

'Hitler don't want us or the Eyetalians; he don't even want the French,' said the young man. 'All he's after is the limeys.'

'He wants to knock the handle off Chamberlain's umbrella,' chuckled the little man.

'Not only Chamberlain,' said the young man. 'He wants all the limeys. Those limeys are what gets his goat.'

'Sure, Mussolini'll fall into line,' said the little man. 'Then our boats will be sunk, then we'll fall into line. I wish John Pershing[1] were a little younger, we'd have nothing to worry about.'

A traveling salesman, blue suit, gray hat, blue tie, with beer at other end of bar, spoke up. 'The brains is still there,' he said.

'That's right. The brains is still there.'

'He could run a war from here, if the brains is still there,' said the young man, and looked at the clock again.

'Saving up to get married, eh?' teased the little man, watching him fondly. 'No beer till five o'clock. Well, Johnny, what about it? You got no country now, Hitler's took it away. You got no country, like a Jew. What're you going to do now?'

The young man lazily unwound himself from the stool, yawned and stretched.

'Well, I can always go back to Brooklyn, where I was born.'

'Brooklyn's good country, alright,' said the traveling salesman.

---

[1] General John Pershing (1860–1940) commanded the American Expeditionary Forces in France in World War I.

'Nothing the matter with Brooklyn,' said the little man. 'Brooklyn's all right.'

Dawn Powell

1942 [England]

First day with no wind only no one noticed it at the time. – Not till it happened. The Flight Commander, F/lt. R. has wanted to take off on instruments ever since the Masters arrived. He announces his intention of talking off under the hood with a glider in tow. However, F/O. M. does a normal tow first to see what it is like to-day. He finds with no wind he barely clears the trees. Quickly he gets rid of his glider and comes down to warn R. But just as he is landing he sees R. taking off. He waves frantically but it is no good. R.'s plane begins to hobble across the field, very slowly, so damn slowly to us onlookers. Just then a phone rings in the C.I.'s office. A strangely agitated voice at the other end. Something in its tone freezes the C.I. as he answers it. 'This is Mrs. R. speaking. Please tell my husband not to fly today, I beg you don't let him fly. He mustn't, he mustn't. Please stop him.'

Across the field the C.I. sees people running and something large and black rising up from the trees, tall and mushroom-like, its base licked with orange. A beastly job for him to have to tell her she is just too late.

Desmond Leslie

1945 [New York]

[At a party] One lady said the uniforms of the men made their slim hips look so fine and Coby [a close friend] said 'Nobody but a lecherous female would notice that. Slim hips, for Christ's sake! Who cares whether hips are slim or as big as Brooklyn Bridge?' 'You don't mean women's hips can be that big?' 'Sure,' he said, 'women's hips *ought* to be as big as Brooklyn Bridge.' He complained that all the younger men he knew – pallid, nearsighted chaps – had gone to war, been lost in jungles, in prisons, wounded in combat, riddled with jungle fever, pellagra and Bombay duck, and come back looking better than they ever had in their life – an argument for war as a health measure.

Dawn Powell

1940 [London]
The PM [Churchill] made a gaffe. He is speaking on the wireless in French tonight, and just before dinner he came into the room, where the French BBC expert and translator, M. Duchesne was standing, and exclaimed: 'Where is my frog speech?' M. Duchesne looked pained.

John Colville

1965 [Washington]
On the way out[1] we stopped in a ward full of Marines wounded in the fighting in Vietnam. Those who could stand and one in a wheel-chair gathered around Lyndon, and most of those in bed propped themselves up on elbows. What followed was touching. Lyndon told them simply and movingly how proud he was of them all. 'And when I feel pretty blue at night, and I issue the orders that you carry out, I do it with a heavy heart.' And then, 'Whenever we cease to love it [our country] and whenever we cease to be willing to die for it, and whenever we are willing to throw in the towel, why then some other society will come along and take us over.' I could not read the expression in the eyes of all of them. There was tense interest everywhere and in many, I believe, strong emotions. I could not hold back my tears.

Then we wheeled and started down the corridor fast and out the door, saying good-bye to all the hospital heads on the steps. Up on the left we heard voices, and there were streamers hanging out the windows, and heads stuck out and hands: 'Good luck, Mr. President – from the boys in 4-C.' 'Vietnam, O.K.' 'Good luck from Ward 4-D, LBJ.' They were waving and shouting, 'We're with you.' 'The military is behind you.' Lyndon called back, 'They fixed me up. I'm in good shape. Now *you* get well.'

Lady Bird Johnson

22 October

1917 [London]
The moon grows full and the evening trains are packed with people leaving London. We saw the hole in Piccadilly this afternoon. Traffic

---

[1] Lyndon Johnson had just been discharged from the hospital after an operation.

has been stopped, and the public slowly tramps past this place. Swan & Edgar has every window covered with sacking or planks; you see shop women looking out from behind: 'business goes on as usual' so they say. Our London Library stands whole, however, and we found our books, and came home in the tube, standing the whole way to Hammersmith, and have just come in.

Virginia Woolf

1939 [Exbury]

I walked round the garden, which was a sight of unparalleled beauty with its blaze of autumn red and gold, and talked to Lionel de Rothschild,[1] who was at his most agreeable. He suggested that our war aim should be to give Germany to the Jews, and divide up the Germans among the races of the world: in other words to make the two races change their position. But then, I said, the Jews in Germany will complain that the Germans control world finance!

John Colville

1943 [Naples]

There is no relief in sight to the near-famine conditions in the city and surrounding country.

Friday, at least ten jobs come up, among which was the visit to a peasant house near Aversa where the people had been assaulted by deserters. Having found nothing lootable, they had molested all the womenfolk, subjecting them to every conceivable indignity, including attempted buggery. The women were evidently spared from outright rape by the fear many of our soldiers share of contracting syphilis. One of the girls involved in the nightmarish business was outstandingly pretty, although spoiled by a puffiness – a sogginess of the flesh showing particularly about the eyes. This I've noticed so often in people close to starvation. I did my best to pacify the sufferers with vague promises of redress. There was nothing else to do.

Today the same girl appeared at the HQ, eyes downcast, and shaking. She brought a letter from her father, which, from its unusual literacy, I suspected might have been put together by the village priest.

---

[1] A friend from Harrow and Trinity. Later senior partner of N.M. Rothschild and Son.

Sir,

I noticed when your honour was good enough to call that from the way you looked at my daughter she made a good impression on you. This girl as you know, has no mother, and she hasn't eaten for days. Being out of work I can't feed my family. If you could arrange to give her a good square meal once a day, I'd be quite happy for her to stay, and perhaps we could come to some mutually satisfactory understanding in due course.

Your humble servant.

Norman Lewis

1939 [Sussex]

We have spent a week in London. The poster read, at Wimbledon: 'The War begins . . . Hitler says, Now it's on.' So as we drove to Mecklenburg Square I said 'It's foolish to come to London the first day of the war.' It seemed as if we were driving open eyed into a trap. The flat was oh in such a mess – very small, very crowded. Whistles sounded. The dark was thick as Hell. One seemed cut off. No wireless. There we sat.

You never escape the war in London. People are all thinking the same thing. All set on getting the day's work done. Hitches and difficulties hold one up. Very few buses. Tubes closed. No children. No loitering. Everyone humped with a gas mask. Strain and grimness. At nights its so verdurous and gloomy that one expects a badger or a fox to prowl along the pavement. A reversion to the middle ages with all the space and the silence of the country set in this forest of black houses. A torch blinks. An old gentleman revealed. He vanishes. That red light may be a taxi or a lamppost. People grope their way to each other's lairs. We were talking in our lair about six hours daily. Great caterpillars dug up the Square. Gradually the sense of siege being normal replaced the fear – the individual fear. One's temper was rubbed by the sheer discomfort and perpetual need for clearing drawers, arranging furniture. The kitchen very small. Everything too large. Stairs bad. No carpets. The clerks scream like parrots. Rain poured – profuse unbridled mediaeval rain. Did nothing – was indeed in fretful useless distraction. So we came down and the world rises out of dark squalor into this divine natural peace. Alone today and for many days. It was an odd morbid week of many disagreeable sensations.

Virginia Woolf

23 October

1943 [POW camp, Java]

I returned to normal duties feeling rather feeble and ineffective [he had suffered a malaria attack]. I finished the evening in reprobate fashion, Bill Wearne and I being thoroughly ticked off for playing chess after lights out.

Weary Dunlop

24 October

1914 [London]

In the Strand you may buy war maps, buttonhole flags, etc., etc. I bought a penny stud. One shop was turned into a shooting gallery at three shots a penny where the Inner Temple Barristers in between the case for the defence and the case for the prosecution could come and keep their eye in against the time the Germans came.

W.N.P. Barbellion

1939 [Berlin]

We chat with the Führer about the changeableness of our conception of feminine beauty. What was considered beautiful forty years ago is now fat, plump, dumpy. Sport, gymnastics and the fight against sexual can't have changed people's attitudes, probably for the better. We are taking huge, swift strides towards a new classical age. And we are the trail-blazers of this revolution in all respects.

Josef Goebbels

1944 [Syria]

Two small signal corps units last night at Homs, and the night before. The first disguised in hive-huts. My background was a wall entirely covered in pin-up girls, mostly stark naked. Princess Elizabeth in pale blue looked rather overdressed among them. Cheese sandwiches and sweet tea to follow the performance and I was shown the works. Last night's groups were housed in small tin huts. The one we used for the show was a round one with a tin roof. Someone had rigged up a light for the piano and a little tin-reflected spot for me.

Three Armenians from the nearby village came to see the show – mother and two daughters of about sixteen and ten. They sat in a row on the front bench, dead still, with their hands folded in their laps, their wax white faces entirely without expression and their beetle black eyes on us both without blinking for the whole session.

Afterwards in solemn procession and without smiles they shook us by the hand and filed out in silence. I wonder what they made of it all.

Joyce Grenfell

25 October

1854 [the Battle of the Alma]
Horsford [of Rifle Brigade] had just pointed out the confused masses of French to our right, and I had just gone to point out the same to the General [Sir George Cathcart], when up galloped Captain Ewart, of the 93rd, and ordered us (the 4th Division) off to Balaclava.

We got under Arms immediately, and, on arriving at the scene of action, were informed that the Turks had run off to a man without firing a shot [not true], running straight through our Cavalry Camp. The Russians instantly took possession of the position, but abandoned the greater portion of it on our approach.

The cavalry instantly went into action and the Heavy Brigade did very well. Unfortunately the Light Brigade was ordered to charge, and they did so gallantly; but, being received by three times their number and three batteries of artillery, besides rifle-men, they got cut up and driven back, losing about half their number.

The 4th Division got there just as this charge was being made, and the Russians abandoned two of the redoubts, retaining only the one furthest to the eastward.

Captain Nolan, who took the orders to Lord Cardigan, was killed, charging at the Head of the Light Cavalry. Although a good fellow, from all I can learn, his conduct was inexcusable. His whole object appears to have been to have a charge at any cost; but he could not have chosen a worse time.

After the fight was over, and we had been packed for the better portion of the day, we returned at night to camp, abandoning our original line as too extensive.

My leg wonderfully painful all day, but I held on.

Lieut. General Sir Charles Ash Windham

1940 [London]

The other night examined the crowds sheltering in Chancery Lane, Oxford Circus and Baker Street stations. *Not* all Jews, but I think, a higher proportion of Jews than one would normally see in a crowd of this size. What is bad about Jews is that they are not only conspicuous, but go out of their way to make themselves so. A fearful Jewish woman, a regular comic-paper cartoon of a Jewess, fought her way off the train at Oxford Circus, landing blows on anyone who stood in her way. It took me back to old days on the Paris Métro.

George Orwell

1941 [Berlin]

I arrive at headquarters. I am welcomed at the station by von Ribbentrop and Hitler at the entrance of his fortified cabin. They had told me that he was looking tired and old. This is not true. I found him in top form, physically and mentally. He is very courteous, or perhaps I should say chummy. He quickly has me come into his study, together with von Ribbentrop and [General Arthur] Schmidt. I have made a report of the conference to the Duce, and it is filed elsewhere. I have also candidly added my own observations, but now I shall limit myself to jotting down a few episodes and impressions.

Von Ribbentrop speaks in a strangely confidential tone. Usually he is very reserved and dignified, so all this surprises me. He goes so far as to busy himself about my personal comfort, and has sent to my room warm, sweetened milk to help my cough. In Tuscany they say that when people are making more of a fuss than usual is when they are about to cheat you, or you have already been cheated.

He doesn't trust the monarchy. While we were hunting in the woods, von Ribbentrop asked me point-blank, 'What is your King doing?' 'He is hunting,' I answered.

'No, I mean in politics.'

'Nothing that is particularly interesting. The King is informed about politics, but does not meddle.'

'Yet in court circles they intrigue.'

'I can deny that most emphatically. Perhaps, at times, they gossip, and even this is to a limited extent. If you knew the people at court, you would soon realize that but for one or two exceptions they are not even worth suspecting.'

'I am pleased to hear this. But you will not say the same about the Prince of Piedmont. That fellow is hostile.'

'Not at all. I can give the most ample assurances regarding the Prince of Piedmont. He is young. He has neither prestige nor the experience of his father, but he is very respectful of the regime, and is devoted to the Duce. I beg you, my dear Ribbentrop, don't listen to gossips. They flourish in every country, but are of no account. One must not fish up information from the gutter of public gossip.'

The shoot was very beautiful. Everything was perfectly organized. The game was driven by 400 soldiers commanded by their officers, and they all took their task seriously, as if it were a question of ejecting the Russians from the forests of Viasma or Briansk.

If in Italy a party leader dared to assign soldiers for a similar purpose, there would be a tremendous scandal.

At the final dinner Ribbentrop took the floor and spoke very tactfully to the guests and to the organizers of the shoot. He concluded thus: 'Next year, my dear Ciano, our game will be better, not only because we shall kill double the number of animals, but also because England will have finally realized that she can no longer win the war. The bag of 1943 will, in the end, be that of peace.' For a man like Ribbentrop, who has always, from 1939 on, been announcing victory in fifteen days, this was a big jump to take.

Roosevelt's speech made a big impression. The Germans have firmly decided to do nothing that will accelerate or cause America's entry into the war.[1] Ribbentrop, during a long lunch, attacked Roosevelt.

'I have given orders to the press to always write "Roosevelt, the Jew"; I wish to make one prophecy: that man will be stoned in the Capitol by his own people.' I personally believe that Roosevelt will die of old age, because experience teaches me not to give much credit to Ribbentrop's prophecies.

On our way to the station Ribbentrop repeated something that I have heard many times: 'Hitler's New Order in Europe will ensure peace for a thousand years.' I remarked that a thousand years is a long time.

---

[1] America declared war on Japan on 8 December, 1941, and Germany and Italy retaliated, declaring war on America, three days later.

It is not easy to hand a couple of dozen generations on the achievements of one man, even if he is a genius. Ribbentrop ended by making a concession: 'Let's make it a century,' he said. For my peace of mind I was satisfied with the reduction, which was certainly considerable.

Count Ciano

26 October

1942 [USA]

Edna [St Vincent] Millay's poem 'Lidice',[1] 'We Refuse to Die' – written for the Office of War Information. Put over the radio. Is it great poetry? Can one write great *occasional* poetry? If I were asked to write on Lidice it would not be a poem about them – whom I know nothing about, whose suffering I cannot even comprehend, so horrible was it. No, it would have to be about how Lidice affected me, an ordinary person sitting at home far away from tragedy. It would have to say a worm has eaten into the apple of happiness – everybody's apple and forever – because it happened. And I cannot escape it. The most perfect morning is tinged with it – the freshest rose.

Anne Morrow Lindbergh

1943 [London]

The happiest day of my life – without any doubt or comparison. Little Andrew [her grandson] came thro' in the morning from Scotland. I lunched with him & went out afterwards to shop. When I came in & went into Miss T's room she looked as if she had seen a seen a ghost. She said 'Lady V. who do you think telephoned *3 minutes ago*? MARK [Bonham Carter, her son]. He said he was in England & wld probably be home tonight. He has escaped.' About an hour later he walked in – I heard his voice in the hall saying 'Is her Ladyship in?' – & then he ran up the stairs. He looked well – very thin – *amazingly* alive. He had walked 500 miles – from Modena to Termoli – right thro' the German lines & joined our forces. It is a miracle. Mark

---

[1] The Lidice massacre was ordered by Hitler on 9 June 1942 to avenge the assassination of Deputy Reichsprotektor of Bohemia and Moravia, Reinhard Heydrich. Lidice, near Prague, was completely destroyed. The men were shot, the women sent to prisons or concentration camps and the children thought to be 'racially useful' given to German families for adoption.

talked to me till nearly 3. I lay awake all night tense with the greatest happiness I have ever felt.

Violet Bonham Carter

27 *October*

1777 [New York]

We received the unwelcome news that a letter from Gen Clinton to Gen Burgoyne (it was not an answer to his of the 21st) had fallen into the hands of the enemy. On the express being taken he swallowed a small silver bullet in which the letter was, but being suspected, a severe tartar emetic was given him which brought up the ball.

William Digby

1941 [London]

The sights – the long tree-lined avenue in Hyde Park at dusk echoing with the noise of soldiers' boots as they come strolling, swinging, whistling, singing, or alone looking for a girl, and the girls plain – most of them – little working girls in short skirts and sweaters with fancy handkerchiefs around their necks. They know they are wanted – they twist and turn as they walk and break into sudden gusts of giggles and cling to each other's arms. The whole length of the avenue is alive with desires. There are satyrs behind every tree. Silhouetted against the half-lights soldiers with their girls sit on the deck-chairs on the grassy stretches that border the avenue. The flicker of a cigarette lighter reveals for a long second – the pose of a head – the movements of hands. Near the park gates the Military Police in their rose-topped caps stand in groups of twos and threes hoping for trouble, longing to exercise summary justice.

In the expensive restaurants at this hour pink, well-scrubbed school-boys masquerading in Guards uniforms are drinking bad martinis with girl-friends in short fur capes and Fortnum and Mason shoes, who have spent the day driving generals to the War Office or handing cups of tea and back-chat to soldiers in canteens. Grass widows in black with diamond clips or pearls are finding the conversation of Polish officers refreshingly different from that of English husbands. Ugly vivacious A.T.S. [Auxiliary Territorial Service] are ordering *vin rosé* at the Coquille. A film actress (making the best of a patriotic part at present) is just going through the swinging door of the Apéritif with David Niven at her elbow. Ageing Edwardian hostesses whose big houses are now shuttered and silent are taking little naps in their hideouts on the third floor ('so much the safest floor, darling') at Claridges or the Dorchester. Cedric (in a yachtsman's jacket) and Nigel are hipping their way through the crowd of pansies at the Ritz bar (they all have the most madly peculiar jobs in the Ministry of Information or the B.B.C.). At the Travellers' Club Harold Nicolson in his fruity voice is embellishing a story as he settles on the leather sofa. Anne-Marie is sitting on the side of her bed at the Ritz making eyes at herself in the mirror and trumpeting down the telephone in Romanian French. It is a world of hotels and bars and little pubs that have become the fashion overnight – of small drinking clubs run by gangsters who make a nice profit out of prostitutes and the dope racket – packed with R.A.F. pilots, Canadian officers, blondes and slot-machines and perhaps a baccarat table in the upstairs rooms.

And along Piccadilly from the Circus to Hyde Park Corner is an incessant parade of prostitutes, and out of the black-out an acquisitive hand on your arm and 'Feeling lonely, dearie?' 'Hello, my sweet' (in a Noël Coward voice), or '*Chéri*.' In Berkeley Square the railings are down. An old man is making a bonfire of dead leaves beside the little pavilion in the centre of the garden.

Charles Ritchie

1942 [Germany]

Hugo back – thank GOD. I said 'I'd have divorced you if you hadn't come to your own party.' He said 'It's your party' . . . He's not what I would call full of life at the moment.

Everyone says Stalingrad will surrender by November 10th at the latest – and then it will *all be over*. England will surrender.

I am terrified something will go wrong tomorrow. I'm having my hair done early – first appointment. I've told Michael he's allowed to stay up. I *think* he's guessed.

Every time the phone rings I think it is going to be a message to say that *he can't come*. I don't care if the [Josef and Magda] Goebbels don't turn up – but I will DIE if AH [Adolf Hitler] isn't here. I am sure it will be the turning point of our lives.

Elisabeth von Stahlenberg

28 October

1917 [London]

Still no raids, presumably the haze at evening keeps them off, though it is still and the moon perfectly clear. The numbers who have gone out of London this week must feel a little foolish.

Virginia Woolf

1917 [the Russian Front]

During the day, gunfire started again. Two shells fell perilously near our *Lazaret* [hospital] and our cow received a small leg wound.

Florence Farmborough

1942 [England]

My 39th birthday. A good year. I have begotten a fine daughter, published a successful book [*Put out More Flags*], drunk 300 bottles of wine and smoked 300 or more Havana cigars. I have got back to soldiering among friends. This time last year I was on my way to Hawick to join 5 RM. I get steadily worse as a soldier with the passage of time, but more patient and humble – as far as soldiering is concerned. I have about £900 in hand and no grave debts except to the Government; health excellent except when impaired by wine; a wife I love, agreeable work in surroundings of great beauty. Well that is as much as one can hope for.

Evelyn Waugh

1942 [Germany]

I know how the Disciples felt when Jesus picked them!

The summit of my life.

First Strauss's Capriccio – the poor old fellow looked very frail – then the official party.

Afterwards *my* supper. The Führer ate the Dordogne truffles and *a great deal* of raspberry dessert. (No dentures?)

I had one glass of champagne, then left – everything was perfect at home – I had candlelight mainly, and lit them at five to eleven.

Michael was waiting – and I told him, 'As far as I know, the Führer is going to come.' His eyes were brighter than the footlights! I told him not to be disappointed if he didn't arrive – but I thought he would.

He did. He was charming. The guests were *stunned*. He talked to Michael about school – and afterwards said to me, 'What a handsome boy – it makes me feel overjoyed when I think of the new generation. We are producing fine men of the proper type.'

He left at 12.17 – and the others had all gone by one o'clock.

Even the collapse of Stalingrad won't compete with tonight.

A triumph.

I did it.

Elisabeth von Stahlenberg

1943 [Naples]

Neapolitans take their sex lives very seriously indeed. A woman called Lola, whom I met at the dinner-party given by Signora Gentile, arrived at HQ with some denunciation which went straight into the waste-paper basket as soon as her back was turned. She then asked if I could help her. It turned out she had taken a lover who is a captain in the RASC, but speaks no single word of Italian, communication can only be carried on by signs, and this gives rise to misunderstanding. Would I agree to interpret for them and settle certain basic matters?

Captain Frazer turned out to be a tall and handsome man some years Lola's junior. Having his hands on military supplies, he could keep her happy with unlimited supplies of our white bread, which for Neapolitans in general – who have been deprived of decent bread for two years – has come to symbolize all the luxury and the abundance of peace. She was also much impressed by his appearance. The Captain was a striking figure. His greatcoat had been specially made for him and it was the most handsome coat I had ever seen. His hat was pushed up in front and straightened with some kind of stiffener. This, although Frazer worked at a desk, made him look like an officer in a crack German SS formation. She wanted to know all about his marital status and he hers, and they lied to each other to their hearts' content while I kept a straight face and interpreted.

She asked me to mention to him in as tactful a way as possible that comment had been caused among her neighbours because he never called on her during the day. Conjugal visits at midday are *de rigueur* in Naples. This I explained, and Frazer promised to do better.

When the meeting was over we went off for a drink, and he confided to me something that was worrying him too. On inspecting her buttocks he had found them covered with hundreds of pinpoint marks, some clearly very small scars. What could they be? I put his mind at rest. These were the marks left by *iniezione reconstituenti*: injections which are given in many of the pharmacies of Naples and which many middle-class women receive daily to keep their sexual powers at their peak. Frequently the needle is not too clean, hence the scars.

She had made him understand by gestures one could only shudderingly imagine that her late husband – although half-starved, and even when in the early stages of tuberculosis from which he died – never failed to have intercourse with her less than six times a night. She also had a habit, which terrified Frazer, of keeping an eye on the bedside clock while he performed. I recommended him to drink – as the locals did – marsala with the yolks of eggs stirred into it, and to wear a medal of San Rocco, patron of *coitus reservatus*, which could be had in any religious-supplies shop.

This seemed the moment, as Lola had offered her services as an informant, to check on her background in the dossiers section on the top floor of the Questua. It appeared from her *fasciolo* that since the death of her husband she had been the mistress of a Fascist hierarch, and there were sardonic references in typical police style to other episodes of her love-life. It seemed extraordinary to me that a Fascist leading light could do nothing to shield his private life from invasion by the police.

Norman Lewis

29 October

1777 [New York]
About day break our piquet was fired on from the wood in front, but the damage was trifling. I suppose seldom two armies remained looking at each other so long without coming to action. A man of theirs in a mistake came into our camp in place of his own, and being challenged by our sentry, after recollecting himself, 'I believe,' says he, 'I am wrong and may as well stay where I am.' That he might be pretty certain of.

William Digby

1854 [the Battle of the Alma]
All quiet; the only news I have heard is that the Russians, in reply to our flag of truce, said that they had only two officers of the Light Cavalry Brigade prisoners. All the men and other officers were killed.

This looks like foul play to the poor wounded fellows who fell, and corroborates what many of the men said at the time, namely, 'They are sticking them in the ground.'

Lieut. General Sir Charles Ash Windham

1940 [England]
Today I cycled to Newhaven – city of the Dead. Sepulchred shops empty; silent, dour men. Baker boasted of the raid – at 5.30 yesterday twenty-five Germans descended: dropped twenty-five bombs – houses ruined – little girl killed. 'And not a Spitfire anywhere near. . .' The gloomy self-confidence of the newly bombed.

Virginia Woolf

1940 [England]
A butcher's shop caught alight. The fire cooked the meat, it had not yet crept near enough actually to burn it. For a while then, the shop was bright with the savour of fine brown sides of beef and good crackling pork. But only for a while: at last the meat caught fire, and once more the old smell of hot disintegration swept the shop like a cloud.

A hundred other stores and factories each cook the firemen their own sweet dishes . . . a sugar factory – acres of boiling sweet molasses . . . a paint factory – and the poisonous fumes of blistered chemicals . . . a rubber depository . . . a toffee warehouse – which delighted me particularly because here again was the exciting smell of the schoolday kitchen, the warm nut brown and gold smell of the toffee pan broiling away on a dark winter's afternoon. In dockland, in 1940, on a night of smoke and noise and flying steel, it was comforting to find this treasured nostalgia a thousand times magnified.

William Sansom

1943 [Amsterdam]
Dearest Kitty,
Mr and Mrs van Daan have had more raging battles. The reason is simple: they're broke. They wanted to sell an overcoat and a suit of Mr van D.'s , but were unable to find any buyers. His prices were much too high.

Some time ago Mr Kleiman was talking about a furrier he knows. This gave Mr van D. the idea of selling his wife's fur coat. It's made of rabbit skin, and she's had it for seventeen years. Mrs van D. got 325 guilders for it, an enormous amount. She wanted to keep the money herself to buy new clothes after the war, and it took some doing before Mr van D. could make her understand that it was desperately needed to cover household expenses.

Anne Frank

1944 [Paris]
[The British Embassy] At drinks-time a few old cronies assembled in *le salon vert* to forge severed links of friendship. Although Diana[1] takes her own unconventionality with her wherever she goes, awe of the British Embassy is obviously paramount in the minds of the Parisians. As they mounted the imposing staircase the men, in black coats and striped trousers, were excessively formal, bowing from the waist and kissing hands. All seemed to have a conservative, even ceremonial, attitude that made one realize how much more relaxed and at ease would be their equivalents in London. Little wonder that an elderly Frenchman, arriving unexpectedly early, was surprised when Diana, unbuttoning her trousers to change into a skirt, asked him point blank: 'And what can I do for you?'

The women were a curiously dressed bunch in a fashion that struck the unaccustomed eye as strangely ugly – wide, baseball-players' shoulders, Düreresque headgear, suspiciously like domestic plumbing, made of felt and velvet, and heavy sandal-clogs, which gave the wearers an added six inches in height but an ungainly, plodding walk. Unlike their austerity-abiding counterparts in England these women moved in an aura of perfume. Women and men alike were all avid for the unaccustomed bounty, now presented on a marble-topped table, of chippolatas, *petits fours* and cheese biscuits garnered from the Naafi stores. 'What we have suffered!' they exclaimed, prodding their sausages with little picks.

Cecil Beaton

30 October

1939 [London]
Seventeen days of sitting up till four and five in the morning working at my anthology for the Forces, *Speak for England*. Clemence Dane[2]

---

[1] Lady Diana Cooper (1892–1986), whose husband Duff was British Ambassador in Paris.
[2] Pseudonym of playwright and novelist Winifred Ashton.

gave me the title; it is a phrase shouted in the House the other day when Arthur Greenwood[1] got up to speak on the declaration of war. After wasting a lot of time and going through agonies of indecision I drew up a set of rules which I then rigidly adhered to:

1. War to be background only.
2. Connecting thread of anthology to be Rupert Brooke's 'The thoughts by England given'.
3. Anthology must hang together.
4. Must be intelligible to the average soldier.
5. Nothing to bore or depress.
6. The note to be R.B.'s sonnet transposed into the key of 'If he, *i.e.*, another, should die . . .'

I found snags everywhere. Modern poetry too grim. Sassoon's horrors put him out of the question. I tried hard to have that moving poem of Wilfred Owen with its exquisite concluding line, 'And each slow dusk a drawing-down of blinds.' But then there was that first line, 'What passing-bells for these who die as cattle?' Hardly encouraging to open an anthology at a poem called *Anthem for Doomed Youth!* Tom Driberg[2] thought the sailors might like Hopkins's *Wreck of the Deutschland.* Just don't see how the average A.B. [Able Seaman] is going to cope with a rigging full of nuns, or the gushing of a 'lush-kept plush-capped sloe mouthed to flesh-burst'. The prose selections were just as difficult. I had decided upon Thackeray's magnificent passage in the ninth chapter of *Esmond* beginning 'Why does the stately Muse of History', but had to reject it in view of General Staff's susceptibility in the matter of a C.-in-C., who would steal 'a portion out of a starving sentinel's three-farthings'. However, I got the anthology done at last, and delivered to the hour.

James Agate

1942 [Barrow, England]

One nice Australian sergeant pilot will not come into the canteen again, and tell us tantalizing yarns of bright warm sun, surf-bathing and lovely cheap fruit. He crashed last Monday and was buried today.

---

[1] MP, elected deputy leader of the Labour Party, 1935, member of war cabinet 1940–42.
[2] Tom Driberg (1905–1976), journalist and later MP.

How hard – or is it philosophical? – we are growing. Beyond a 'Poor lad, I thought he was late', and pity for the wasted lives, no remarks were passed. Things that would have shocked us to our heart's core now receive no more than a passing remark.

Nella Last

1942 [California]
Here I am with Denny [friend] in Palm Springs, staying at the Estrella Villas – one of those luxurious bungalow courts with a swimming pool and a bright green lawn that looked as if it had been ordered from a Los Angeles furniture store and unrolled like a carpet. It is crossed by paths of colored crazy pavement. Each cottage has a rustic fireplace, tasseled ropes draped around the windows, Japanese prints, brass marine lamps, fluffy white rugs, cream upholstery with lemon cushions. We've already gotten into trouble with the landlord for bringing in puncture-weed thorns on the soles of our shoes: the ground is covered with them.

All around the village and the airfield with its winking light, spreads the untidy desert with its dry silvery bushes alive in the heat, as seaweed is alive in the sea. In the late afternoon, when Palm Springs is already in shadow, the mountain range across the valley turns mauve and violet in the setting sunshine. It shines in the distance like the landscape of another planet, unearthly, beautiful and dead. Actually – like the mountains behind us – it is nothing but a huge litter of ugly, smashed stones: nature's lighting effects supply all the glamor. Overhead, the P-38s whine and drone. Since the outbreak of war, the desert seems to belong naturally to the army. It is dotted with airfields and camps, where troops are trained in warfare under North African conditions. The sterile activity of war drill finds here its ideal setting.

We go back to Los Angeles the day after tomorrow. Denny is restless and bored, but he really needed the change. While he was in hospitals he got terribly thin, with long sinister birdlike legs. A change has come over him – not in the way Gerald hoped and expected, and yet somehow due to Gerald's influence. He wants to become a psychologist. But before he can even begin to study for his medical degree, he must first get his high school diploma. He left school without graduating, and now he must start again where he left off all those years ago: one never really dodges anything. As soon as we're home, he'll go to the UCLA and arrange to take a correspondence course. He can do this in his spare time at camp.

Christopher Isherwood

1944 [Carradale, Scotland]

I am getting awfully tired of this diary. I never seem to write about what is really happening in my mind, and the various jealousies and resentments and fears that seem to get into me and the idiotic worries in the night, and thinking I've paid the tinks [tinkers] too much and wondering if I'm making the hell of a muddle of the farm or if I'm getting enough work out of people or if everyone is really laughing at me and if my various boy friends are really double crossing me. Or for that matter this plain god-awful feeling that one is getting old, that the only pleasures of the flesh left to one are eating and drinking – which I have never taken very seriously, that one regrets all lost opportunities, and oh god being fed-up with Carradale.

Naomi Mitchison

31 October

1939 [England]

They are saying, 'The generals learned their lesson in the last war. There are going to be no wholesale slaughters.' I ask, how is victory possible except by wholesale slaughters?

Evelyn Waugh

1940 [Lille, France]

I attended a large lunch party given by the Prefect of Lille. The guests were Gort[1], Prince Henry [Duke of Gloucester], Dill, Pownall,[2] Pagézy, General [illegible] of the French Mission, Mr and Mrs Gudgeon of the British Council in Lille, and a lot of others. Champagne lunch consisting of oysters, lobster, chicken, pâté de foie gras, cheese, and fruit, coffee liqueurs etc. We sat down at 1 pm and got up about 3 pm! The ladies comprised Madame the Prefect, Madame the Sous

---

[1] Field Marshal John Standish Vereker Gort (1886–1946), 6th Viscount, Commander-in-Chief, British Expeditionary Force.
[2] Lieutenant General Sir Henry Royds Pownall (1887–1961), British Expeditionary Force.

Prefect, Mrs Gudgeon and the Prefect's daughter. Madame the Prefect worked very hard with 'Son Altesse', but did not get much response out of him. He told me that by the time he has thought of a good sentence and translated it into French inwardly it is too late and he has to start on a new one!

Field Marshal Lord Alanbrooke

1943 [Devon]

A drizzly, muggy, drab day. I had breakfast downstairs with Charles Ritchie and [Baron] Philippe de Rothschild, the latter in his dressing-gown. He looks like Johnny Churchill[1] and is 'galant'. Takes the women's arms and paws them. He escaped from unoccupied France only this year and said that the English here have no idea of conditions on the Continent. He was pained by the bland way in which the English criticize the behaviour of various French men and women in France. They do not realize the pressures put upon them, or the motives behind their behaviour. They may be perfectly honourable ones. We discussed our different ideas for the preservation of peace in the post-war world. The two men favoured the creation of a federal bloc in Western Europe for practical purposes. By this means future war might be averted for longer than the interval between Wars I and II. (So far so good.) By the end of that period the weapons of war would be so devastating that with the growth of armaments in the opposing blocs, the likelihood of an outbreak would surely be nil. I disagreed with this notion, although I felt bound to admit the interesting fact that in this war gas has not so far been used simply because both sides realize the deadliness of a weapon which would rebound on the side which first used it. We all agreed that meanwhile the peoples of the whole world must be indoctrinated against the war spirit, and its futility.

James Lees-Milne

1968 [the White House]

About 7 I went first to the map room and then to Lyndon's office. There, a little past 7, we watched Lyndon on all three TV channels making the announcement of the bombing halt [in Vietnam].

The next hour was a ludicrous mixture of grave and heavy, and warm and funny. Lyndon and I sat side by side and watched the story

[1] John George Spencer-Churchill, artist.

of the bombing halt unfold. Staff members came in and out. And in the midst of it all, Lyn [her sixteen-month old grandson] arrived dressed in his Halloween suit – a red-and-white costume that said 'SUPER PRESIDENT' – and in his fat little hand, a pumpkin. He and his mother had stopped by the office on their way to 'trick or treating' at some friends' houses. Lyn kept trying to attract his grandfather's attention. Finally he went over and gave Lyndon's face on the TV screen a big kiss, first on one screen, then another, then another, looking up for our approval. When the announcement was over, we watched the commentators. Most of them were good. What a change! But there were some acid calls from the public, calling the halt a political move, on one of the open telephone programs.

Lady Bird Johnson

NOVEMBER

To the general everything was so simple. The road to military glory ran according to the recipe: at 6 p.m. the soldiers get goulash and potatoes, at half past eight the troops defecate it in the latrines and at nine they go to bed. In the face of such an army the enemy flees in panic.

Jaroslav Hašek, *The Good Soldier Svejk*

1 November

1703 [London]

There was now a full account of the particulars of the Successe of both our Land forces with the Confederates, our taking of so many fortified Townes and Territorys which the French had usurpt in Flanders and nearest parts of Germany, with the happy escape of my L.[ord] Maborow our Generall, surprised by a party, as he was returning to Holland after this Winter Campagne: But as the Duke of Ormond (coming from Cales) taking sinking and destroying a greate part of the Spanish Plate-Fleete at Vigo, by a very bold and gallant attacking them in that harbour to the number of 38 or 40 Ships, Gallions, Men of Warr and all their Equipage and of neer 1000 Cannon, plate and rich Lading etc, for which a day of publique Thanksgiving is appointed thro the whole nation: So as this summers Actions by these and the vast number of prizes (with little losse) and unwonted agreements of the Parliament, now met and sitting, such a concurrence of blessings and hope of gods future favour, has not ben known in 100 yeares.

The forces also in Italy and on the Rhine prosperous beyond Expectation. Add to these the rich and numerous Returne of our Ships from the E. Indys and all other places.

John Evelyn

1775 [Quebec]

Our greatest luxuries now consisted in a little water, stiffened with flour, in imitation of shoemakers' paste, which was christened with the name of Lillipu. Instead of the diarrhoea, which tried our men most shockingly in the former part of our march, the reverse was now the complaint, which continued for many days. We had now arrived as we thought to almost the zenith of distress. Several had been entirely destitute of either meat or bread for many days. These chiefly consisted of those who devoured their provisions immediately, and a number who were in the boats. The voracious disposition many of us had now arrived at, rendered almost any thing admissible. Clean and unclean were forms now little in use. In company was a poor dog, who had hitherto lived through all the tribulations, became a prey for the sustenance of the assassinators. This poor animal was instantly devoured, without leaving any vestige of the sacrifice. Nor did the shaving soap, pomatum, and even the lip salve, leather of their shoes, cartridge boxes, &c., share any better fate.

Isaac Senter

1940 [Carradale, Scotland]

My mother sent me a knife for my birthday – and I have sent her back a ½d stamp! I hope I shan't lose it. She says Oxford with a normal population of 90,000 has 150,000 and no new houses. 'People simply won't stay in the country and drift back here, some of them back into the institutions they were drafted from, but others, with plenty of money, bribing people to take them in. There has been a good deal of that, lodgers turned out (people with work here) to make room for well-to-do East End Jews and it isn't good for anti-Semitic feeling to be allowed to spread. I never heard a murmur of it before down here.' She says she isn't going to bother to open windows for the next raids, as it makes the house so cold. She has liked all the people who are billeted on her, mostly Army and families, very much, and sounds quite cheerful.

Naomi Mitchison

1940 [London]

After the PM [Churchill] had had his afternoon sleep we left for Chequers. I travelled with him in his car and after a sticky beginning found him most affable. He was dressed in his R.A.F. uniform and we stopped at Northolt to inspect the Hurricane Squadron, No. 615, of which he is Honorary Air Commodore. They had been up four times today and told us of their experiences in the Mess while we drank whisky and soda. When we continued our journey the PM talked about the Italians, whose impertinence in sending bombers to attack this country has much annoyed him. He said he intended to attack Rome before long, as soon as we had enough Wellingtons at Malta. Last night our bombers successfully attacked Naples from there and today the press, ignorant of the truth, is chortling about the magnificent 3,000 mile flight from England to Naples and back. I said to the PM that I hoped if we bombed Rome we should be careful to spare the Coliseum. The

PM answered that it wouldn't hurt the Coliseum to have a few more bricks knocked off it and then, becoming pensive, quoted:

> *While stands the Coliseum Rome shall stand*
> *When falls the Coliseum Rome shall fall . . .*[1]

John Colville

2 November

1775 [Canada]

Long ere this necessity had obliged us to dismiss all our encamping equipage, excepting a small light tin kettle among a number; but nothing to cut our wood, &c. According to our strength and spirits, we were scattered up and down the river at the distance of perhaps twenty miles. Not more than eight miles had we marched, when a vision of horned cattle, four footed beasts, &c. rode and drove by animals resembling Plato's two footed featherless ones. Upon a higher approach our vision proved real! Exclamations of joy. – Echoes of gladness resounded from front to rear! With a te deum. Three horned cattle, two horses, eighteen Canadians and one American. A heifer was chosen as victim to our wants; slain and divided accordingly. Each man was restricted to one pound of beef. Soon arrived two more Canadians in B. Canoes, ladened with a coarse kind of meal, mutton, tobacco, &c. Each man drew likewise a pint of this provender. The mutton was destined for the sick. They proceeded up the river in order to the rear's partaking of the same benediction. We sat down, ate our rations, blessed our stars, and thought it luxury. Upon a general computation we marched from 20 to 30 miles per day. Twenty miles only from this to the settlements. Lodged at the great falls this night.

Isaac Senter

1854 [Odessa]

Since the landing of the Anglo–French troops we have had three engagements with them. The first was at Alma on 8 September in which the enemy attacked and defeated us; the second was Liprandi's action on 13 September in which we attacked and were victorious,

---

[1] From Byron's *Childe Harold's Pilgrimage*.

and the third was Dannenberg's terrible action in which we attacked again and were beaten again. It was a treacherous, revolting business. The 10th and 11th divisions attacked the enemy's left flank, drove them back and spiked thirty-seven guns. Then the enemy put forward 6,000 riflemen – only 6,000 against 30,000 – and we retreated, having lost about 6,000 men. And we had to retreat, because half our troops had no artillery owing to the roads being impassable, and – God knows why – there were no rifle battalions. Terrible slaughter! It will weigh heavy on the souls of many people! Lord forgive them. The news of this action has produced a sensation. I've seen old men who wept aloud and young men who swore to kill Dannenberg. Great is the moral strength of the Russian people. Many political truths will emerge and evolve in the present difficult days for Russia. The feeling of ardent patriotism that has arisen and issued forth from Russia's misfortunes will long leave its traces on her. These people who are now sacrificing their lives will be citizens of Russia and will not forget their sacrifice. They will take part in public affairs with dignity and pride, and the enthusiasm aroused in them by the war will stamp on them for ever the quality of self-sacrifice and nobility.

Leo Tolstoy

1939 [Lodz, Poland]

Lodz: Seyss-Inquart[1] meets me and delivers a short report. A thousand questions and problems. Lodz itself is a hideous city.

Drive through the Ghetto. We get out and inspect everything thoroughly. It is indescribable. These are no longer human beings, they are animals. For this reason, our task is no longer humanitarian but surgical. Steps must be taken here, and they must be radical ones, make no mistake.

Josef Goebbels

1941 [POW camp, Germany]

Due to lack of washing facilities in hot water, many have had their head shaved. The result is grotesque to look at, but quite likely wiser. For myself, I am today feeling delightfully clean having last night, just before getting into bed, had a hot tub – I must explain. One stands up in a zinc wash basin which just takes the feet, in 1½" of really hot water, when the

---

[1] Artur Seyss-Inquart (1892–1946), Deputy to Hans Frank, 'Chief Civilian Officer' and later Governor of German-occupied Poland.

feet are in, and by dint of scouring oneself and standing as erect as possible so as not to splash clothes, beds, readers, writers, etc., attains a state of cleanliness which had for weeks seemed unredeemable. Finished off with a powder all over, with foot powder and climbing into clean pyjamas, to be followed by a hot drink of Ovaltine, was simply marvellous.

I enjoyed a most rare sensation today, which was jumping clear of traffic – i.e. a lorry on one of the Camp tracks. Having for so long walked dreamily knowing well that barbed wire protected me from vehicles, I was quite staggered by this incident. I wonder what it will feel like to get into a car again.

Captain John Mansel

3 November

1942 [POW camp, Java]
Evening. British Theatricals Ltd had a delightful little wind-up ceremony[1] with several stage skits. Sgt Wynne and P/O Abbott both dressed as whores and looking the part; Berny Weller and his band. Some very pleasant Nip solders gave money to players, tried the instruments and eventually came back loaded with cakes! They overlooked the lateness of the hour.

Weary Dunlop

4 November

1939 [London]
There is no real war. Hitler is indeed shrewd. Is he trying to bore us into peace?

'Chips' Channon

1939 [France]
Wet and dreary day again. Went up with Monty[2] to 7th Guards Brigade front to try out experiment of fumes in a closed pillbox. Eighteen of

---

[1] Australian POWs were being moved from Bandoeng to a camp at Batavia.
[2] Field Marshal Bernard Law Montgomery (1887–1976), Commander of 3rd Division, BEF.

us got into pillbox, closed down all openings and then fired an anti-tank gun and a Bren gun through the apertures for five minutes to make certain that the fumes and gases from the firing would not be such as to affect the garrison of the pillbox. None of us felt any the worse, but it would have assisted promotion considerably if it had been otherwise as there were 1 Lt Gen, 1 Maj Gen, 2 Brigadiers, 1 Colonel and 3 Lt Colonels amongst those in the pillbox! Expensive 'white mice' for such a trial!

Field Marshal Lord Alanbrooke

5 November

1854 [Battle of Inkerman]
Marched the relief down to the trenches at 4 a.m., and, on returning, mounted my horse and went into action with my Division: 2225 under arms. Felt quite calm and collected during the fight; nervous and unhappy after it. Loss and carnage fearful.

Lieut. General Sir Charles Ash Windham

1938 [Spain]
After lunch Consuelo went to ask Maruja something, found the door of the doctor's room locked. After a bit Maruja came out saying she had shut the door as she had a headache and wanted to rest, but Consuelo saw Torrigos legging it down the stairs out of the corner of her eye. Romance in the hospital between a jellified skeleton and a prize sow.

Priscilla Scott-Ellis

6 November

1941 [Tuscany]
As I was driving up the road yesterday afternoon, in a light mist which gave a somewhat unreal aspect to the landscape, I suddenly beheld striding before me tall, fair, well-shaped men in sporting jackets and short breeches, a costume easily Neolithic. For part of a second I was transported to the Scottish Highlands and wondered whether I had not Fingal and other Ossianic heroes before me. Then I recalled that

there were superior British officers being held as prisoners in the castle I had just passed. Sure enough little fellows in greenish-grey coats with guns in their hands ran along before, behind and at the sides of these Northern giants. So the Normans must have looked who, though a handful, conquered Apulia, Calabria and Sicily, establishing an empire that lasted long enough to decide West Mediterranean history for centuries.

Bernard Berenson

1944 [Carradale, Scotland]

We had an awful argument in the evening about 'punishing war crim-inals'. What I mind is the attitude of the CP [Communist Party], being so smug about showing everyone that Nazi-ism doesn't pay. They won't achieve that end unless the people to whom this salutary thing is to be shown, agree that the procedure is reasonable. Otherwise it's just revenge. And I can't help thinking of Hang the Kaiser. Revenge may be necessary but I don't like talking about trials and crime, as though this were anything like criminal law. I only hope it will happen soon enough to get counted as one more bloody awful bit of the war, not as anything 'legal'.

Naomi Mitchison

7 November

1939 [Berlin]

With the Führer. He is of the opinion that England must be given a k.o. blow. Quite right, too. England's power is simply a myth these days, no longer a reality. All the more reason why it must be destroyed. Otherwise there will be no peace in the world.

Josef Goebbels

1939 [France]

Everywhere – in schools, post-offices or town-halls – where there are women's lavatories and men's lavatories, the officers comman-deer the women's lavatories and 'Officers' is marked up under the sign 'WC'. This gives them a rather girlish air, that very well suits their uniforms with their high waists. I am quite ready to grant that the officers are the feminine element in the army. And that we, the squaddies, with our long boots and our dumb expressions are the males. But Pieter [a fellow reservist], reverently, always goes into the Officers' toilets, so much tenderness is there in his heart and his big bum.

Jean-Paul Sartre

8 November

1939 [Rome]

The Duce is very much impressed by what General Liotta told him about the German tendency toward alcoholism. The General went as far as to say the 'German peril can be held back by means of the alcoholization of Germany,' and 'that tomorrow's world will belong to the people who drink water'. However, I have wondered whether it is worthwhile taking that Sicilian peasant, Liotta, seriously, who, because he offered some bottles of bad wine to the Germans, believes that he has won their confidence.

Count Ciano

1942 [Cairo]

Each morning I breakfast on a balcony overlooking the Nile and gloat over the news: Alexander's[1] soldiers are pressing the Germans back. American and British Forces have landed in French North Africa. Surely this must be the beginning of the end of the war in North Africa.

So the days begin – on peaks of optimism. But as the hours wear on and I visit the Cairo hospitals I sink back into chasms of gloom. The price of this news is so terrible: you see it in the leg wards where some of the tallest are the shortest now – poor Richard Wood has lost both his legs; you see it in the long ward where the burn cases lie so still – sometimes even their eyes are bandaged; it glares at you from screened-off beds where people are dying. You put on your gayest frock, paint your face, collect sweets and magazines and determine to be cheerful. Then at the hospital, the smell of rotting flesh meets you in the long dark corridors, and you begin thinking again. You owe them so much but there is nothing you can do except try not to talk

[1] Field Marshal Sir General Harold Alexander (1891–1961).

of things they will never do again. Today when I took down letters in shorthand for those that cannot write I sat with my back to them so they should not see my eyes. They all wrote of victory; not one of them mentioned the price.

Countess of Ranfurly

1943 [Tuscany]

The first snowfall. Bitter cold. How will the prisoners and other fugitives in the woods survive the long winter? The boy from the G.I.L.E.,[1] who is now settled at one of our farms, comes up to ask for clothes – having nothing on but a linen jacket and a thin vest. There is also a constant stream of fugitive soldiers and evacuated women and children, all begging for clothes. We are giving what we can of our own, and are making jerseys and baby-jackets with every scrap of wool, using the fringes off old counterpanes; slippers with old strips of carpets and curtains; and babies' nappies with old sheets – but soon it will all be exhausted.

Iris Origo

1944 [Paris]

Perhaps partly in order to get rid of them he [Picasso] escorted the [visiting] soldiers down the street to the neighbouring studio of Adam, a sculptor and engraver. When he returned alone to his place he discovered that some of the GIs had left anonymous gifts: a package of cigarettes by the bed, a cake of soap on the rim of the bath. 'They often do that,' he smiled.

Picasso seemed far removed from the war and spoke of it in fairy-tale simplifications. But when I showed him M[inistry] of I[nformation] photographs of the destruction in London he was obviously moved. '*C'est épouvantable!* And that is happening all over the world?' I asked him if I might do some sketches of him. He sat in profile and laughed that I should not make him look like Whistler's mother. Then a Hindu silence fell between us. He said: 'How refreshing not to talk! It is like a glass of water.'

Cecil Beaton

---

[1] A school for Italian children evacuated in 1940 by the Fascists from Tunis, Cairo, Malta, etc.

9 November

1899 [Bronkhorstspruit, South Africa]

We heard today the sad news that our friend, Mr Wolters, was killed in the first battle of the war near Ladysmith. He was a gallant gentleman and died a heroic death. We mourn for you, noble friend.

Then we had a worse shock. The *landdrost* [magistrate], Mr Schutte, told Father that he had received an anonymous letter about us saying that we were against the Boers, that we do nothing to help them, that we hope the British will win, and so on. The writer evidently wanted us deported. The *landdrost* sent the letter to the Field Cornet,[1] who said that he had known Father for twelve years, and was sure that nothing in the letter was true, that his farm was the most up-to-date in the district, that he was growing forage and mealies which he was supplying to the Boers, that he had many horses, mules, cattle and sheep and would not want to lose all this by being disloyal.

I think that Father is too honest and completely without guile to do anything that is not right, but we are worried about Joseph and Robert [her brothers] as the Boers think they should be fighting for them.

When Mr Schutte asked Father today why they do not join a commando, he replied: 'I need them on the farm. You know very well that every Boer commando that passes through Bronkhorstspruit receives food and shelter from me, forage for their horses, and goods from the shop.'

'But you do well out of this,' the *landdrost* said. 'You get paid and make a good profit.'

Father is really a very simple man and he replied that he had never asked payment for food and shelter. 'As for the forage and goods,' he said, 'I have a box full of receipts signed by the field cornets. What do you think, Mr Schutte, will I ever get paid?'

I was present and said, 'You will get paid if the Boers win. But can they win?'

'Hold your tongue,' Father said angrily. 'Go to your room.'

As I walked away I heard Father say, 'She is only a child, though she looks grown up.'

---

[1] Junior officer equivalent to lieutenant. Usually elected by the members of a commando. Sometimes applied to the police officer of the district.

Mr Schutte mounted his horse and rode off. I noticed that he was very grave. And so was Father.

Freda Schlosberg

1939 [Berlin]

At Nuremberg comes bad news. There the Führer is handed a telegram, according to which an explosion took place at the Bürgerbräu hall shortly after he left. Eight dead, sixty injured. The whole roof crashed down. At first the Führer thinks this must be a mistake. I check with Berlin, and the entire report is correct. There had been unsuccessful attempts to stop the train. The extent of the damage is enormous. An assassination attempt, doubtless cooked up in London and probably carried out by Bavarian separatists.[1]

Josef Goebbels

1939 [Rome]

The attempt on Hitler's life at Munich leaves everybody quite sceptical, and Mussolini is more sceptical than anyone else. Actually, many details of the matter do not altogether convince us of the accuracy of the account given in the papers. Either it is a master plot on the part of the police, for the purpose of creating anti-British sentiment among the German people, who are quite indifferent, or, if the attempted murder is real, it is a family brawl of people belonging to the inner circle of the Nazi party; perhaps a carry-over of what took place on June 30 [1934] which cannot have been forgotten in Munich. The Duce has had a hard time composing a cable expressing his delight that the danger has been avoided. He wanted it to be warm, but not too warm, because in his judgement no Italian feels any great joy over the fact that Hitler has escaped death – least of all the Duce.

Count Ciano

1939 [London]

An attempt on Hitler's life unfortunately failed. It was probably genuine, but I should not be surprised if Hitler made use of the occasion for a great internal purge. He may even use it as a pretext for beginning the war in earnest. Let us hope it will not increase his popularity at home, as did the Rye House Plot that of Charles II.

[1] In fact, it was the work of one man, George Elser, a joiner.

The PM [Neville Chamberlain] has gout, rather badly. This may give a useful handle to those who think he is too old for the job and ought to retire. But there is really nobody to take his place: Halifax has not the forcefulness and Winston is too unstable.

John Colville

1940 [London]

I decided to have the afternoon to myself and went to lunch at the Guards Club. When people talk about shortage of food, I must say that it is not very apparent. For lunch I had a rather large portion of lobster mayonnaise, some roast beef and Yorkshire pudding, with brussels sprouts and potatoes, and after that an apple tart with cheese, all of which cost me only three shillings (about sixty cents), to which must be added a shilling for a bottle of cider. The Germans have got to go a long way before they starve this country out.

General Raymond E. Lee

1941 [Dresden]

On Saturday evenings we are often downstairs with the Kreidls now or they come to us. Paul Kreidl, doing heavy laboring work constructing railway lines, the Jew's star on his sackcloth smock, can get a good sleep on Sunday. He talks a lot about life as a businessman (inherited sporting goods shop), something of a snob, but very interesting.

The deportations to Poland continue, the Jews everywhere deeply depressed. I met the Neumanns [friends] outside the teacher training college in Teplitzer Strasse, these usually plucky, optimistic people were utterly downcast, considering suicide. The possibility of getting to Cuba had just been offered to them when the complete ban on emigration came into force. Frau Neumann's uncle, Atchen Fink's older brother, a man late in his sixties committed suicide with his wife in Berlin, when they were to be deported. Neumann said to me he would rather be dead and know his wife dead, than see her 'louse-ridden and rebuilding Minsk'. Frau Neumann in tears: 'We were just discussing where we could obtain veronal [a barbitone]' . . . I roused them with such fine words that I quite raised my own spirits.

Victor Klemperer

1942 [USA]

Call Milles[1] at night. I say, 'This is Anne Lindbergh.' He says, 'Ach, my dear . . .' in his soft Swedish voice. We are going to see him on Wednesday evening. He says, 'We will talk about Art – nothing but Art and beauty – and we will forget all the terrible things in the world.' He lives in a world of his own. But he can afford to. He is old, he has lived his life and fought his battles and produced his great work. It is all before us.

Anne Morrow Lindbergh

1942 [Leningrad]

When I told Efronsiniya that the Germans have been stopped near Stalingrad she answered:

'Oh, Vera Mikhailovna, it makes me tremble all over to hear such things.'

I understand her very well. When I hear that the Germans are being beaten, I too shiver all over with happiness. At times I pray I shan't die of joy on the day the Germans are finally beaten.

Heard only the second half of Stalin's radio speech, as there was a meeting at the 'Red Army House' at the same time. But as soon as the meeting was over we ran into the office of the head of the club. The reception was remarkable. It was as if Stalin were speaking in the same building, in the hall that we had just left.

There is something irresistible about Stalin's voice. You can feel from the sound of it that its owner knows everything, and that he will never be a hypocrite.

Vera Inber

10 November

1937 [Spain]

I have enjoyed today so much. It is now 3 o'clock but I don't feel in the least sleepy. I went to the hospital as usual this morning and we all worked fast and got the whole ward finished by 10.30. So that we could go and watch the doctor operating. It was the first time I had seen an operation and I was enthralled. There were two. The first was

---

[1] Carl Milles (1875–1955), Swedish sculptor.

amputating a leg below the knee and the other removing astragalus. The amputation was given chloroform and was very neat and tidy. It looked so odd to see the foot detached from the rest of the man, sitting on the floor by itself. The second man was scared stiff. He would not have chloroform as he said he would die, so he was given an injection in the spine to deaden his lower half. He could not feel anything much, but looked and screamed and moaned the whole time. I never knew anyone could make such a noise. He was quite mad and shook and fought until finally they forcibly chloroformed him. The most unpleasant thing was the heat and the smell of anaesthetic.

Priscilla Scott-Ellis

1943 [Italy]

The sexual attitudes of Neapolitans never fail to produce new surprises. Today Prince A., now well known to us all and an enthusiastic informant from our first days at the Riviera di Chiaia, visited us with his sister, whom we met for the first time. The Prince is the absentee landlord of a vast estate somewhere in the South, and owns a nearby palace stacked with family portraits and Chinese antiques. He is the head of what is regarded as the second or third noble family of Southern Italy. The Prince is about thirty years of age, and his sister could be twentyfour. Both are remarkably alike in appearance: thin, with extremely pale skin and cold, patrician expressions bordering on severity. The purpose of the visit was to enquire if we could arrange for the sister to enter an army brothel. We explained that there was no such institution in the British Army. 'A pity,' the Prince said. Both of them speak excellent English, learned from an English governess.

'Ah well, Luisa, I suppose if it can't be, it can't be.' They thanked us with polite calm, and departed.

Last week a section member was invited by a female contact to visit the Naples cemetery with her on the coming Sunday afternoon. Informants have to be cultivated in small ways, whenever possible, and he was prepared to indulge a whim of this kind, in the belief that he would be escorting his friend on a visit to the family tomb, expecting to buy a bunch of chrysanthemums from the stall at the gate. However, hardly were they inside when the lady dragged him behind a tombstone, and then – despite the cold – lay down and pulled up her skirts. He noticed that the cemetery contained a number of other couples in vigorous activity in broad daylight. 'There were more people above ground than under it,' he said. It turned out that the cemetery is the lovers' lane of Naples, and custom is such that one becomes invisible as soon as one passes through the gates. If a visitor runs into anyone he knows neither a sign nor a glance can be exchanged, nor does one recognise any friend encountered on the 133 bus which goes to the cemetery. I have learned that to suggest to a lady a Sunday-afternoon ride on a 133 bus is tantamount to solicitation for immoral purposes.

Norman Lewis

1943 [Germany]

This time he [Josef Goebbels] *was* there, and took my call.

Dr. G: My dear Frau von Stahlenberg, what can I do for you?

Me: I need your help.[1]

Dr. G: In any way I can.

Me: May I come and talk to you?

Dr.G: Do you want to come to Berlin?

Me: Anywhere.

Dr. G: I'll send a car for you. You can fly from Nuremberg. I'll have you informed of the arrangements.

I said to myself when I put down the telephone, remember to wear your French perfume, your crêpe de chine underwear and your Dutch cap.

Elisabeth von Stahlenberg

11 November

1854 [Sevastopol]

Troops who have never been under fire can't *retreat*; they run away.

Leo Tolstoy

1915 [London]

Oh why was I born for this time? Before one is thirty to know more dead than living people? Stanway, Clouds, Gosford – all the settings of one's life – given up to ghosts. Really, one hardly knows who is alive

---

[1] Goebbels, who had propositioned Elisabeth von Stahlenberg on a previous occasion, was an incorrigible philanderer. She allowed him to seduce her in the hope that he would transfer her husband back to Germany. It worked.

and who is dead. One thing is that now at least people will no longer bury their dead as they used. Now they are so many one *must* talk of them naturally and humanly, not banish them by only alluding to them as if it were almost indelicate.

Lady Cynthia Asquith

1918 [Lewes, England]
Armistice signed. I was typing in the middle bedroom when Ernest [her husband] called up from the yard: 'Alice, it is over.' I tied on Nelson's red, white and blue bow and off we went into the High Street. Everything and everyone was delirious. All the dogs out, all with bows and all twisting round your legs in the crowd. A lot of soldiers outside the Town hall collared Mackay Clarke, the Rector of All Saints, bundled him up on to an impromptu platform, roared at him to make a speech. So there he was, with his ginger moustache and his sweating carrot red face, waving his arms about, moving his lips, and nobody heard one blessed word for the shouting and laughing and roaring. And lots of people were crying and one old woman outside Stone's shop said: 'But think of them poor boys what 'ull never come back.'

Mrs Henry Dudeney

1918 [England]
I was walking in the water-meadows by the river below Cuddesdon this morning – a quiet grey day. A jolly peal of bells was ringing from the village church, and the villagers were hanging little flags out of the windows of their thatched houses. The war is ended. It is impossible to realise. Oxford had much flag-waving also, and signs of demonstration.

I got to London about 6.30 and found masses of people in streets and congested Tubes, all waving flags and making fools of themselves – an outburst of mob patriotism. It was a wretched wet night, and very mild. It is a loathsome ending to the loathsome tragedy of the last four years.

Siegfried Sassoon

1918 [Germany]
Today the dreadful armistice terms have been signed. Langwerth [a diplomat] says that anything else was out of the question: our Front has cracked completely. The Emperor has fled to Holland.

Count Harry Kessler

1918 [London]

Twenty-five minutes ago the guns went off, announcing peace. A siren hooted on the river. They are hooting still. A few people ran to look out of windows. The rooks wheeled round, and wore for a moment the symbolic look of creatures performing some ceremony, partly of thanksgiving, partly of valediction over the grave. A very cloudy still day, the smoke toppling over heavily to the east; and that too wearing for a moment a look of something floating, waving, drooping. So far neither bells nor flags, but the wailing of sirens and intermittent guns.

Virginia Woolf

1918 [London]

Peace!

London today is a pandemonium of noise and revelry, soldiers and flappers being most in evidence. Multitudes are making all the row they can, and in spite of depressing fog and steady rain, discords of sound and struggling, rushing beings and vehicles fill the streets. Paris, I imagine, will be more spontaneous and magnificent in its rejoicing. Berlin, also is reported to be elated, having got rid, not only of the war, but also of its oppressors. The people are everywhere rejoicing. Thrones are everywhere crashing and the men of property are everywhere secretly trembling. 'A biting wind is blowing for the cause of property,' writes an Austrian journalist. How soon will the tide of revolution catch up the tide of victory? Will it be six months or a year?

Beatrice Webb

1939 [Berlin]

A number of Berlin Party comrades have been beating up harmless passers-by for absolutely no reason. I send them to a concentration camp.

Josef Goebbels

1939 [France]

The suspense continues, more threats to Belgium and Holland, but no further moves on the part of the Germans. This morning I took part in an Armistice ceremony at the Canadian Memorial at Vimy Ridge. We had two guards of honour, a French one formed by the 51st

Division, and a British one from the Black Watch. General Pagézy came from Lille for the ceremony. He and I laid wreaths of poppies on the Memorial, the French guard then presented arms whilst their bugles sounded a 'Sonnerie', this was followed by the Black Watch guard presenting arms whilst their pipers played 'Flowers of the Forest'. The ceremony ended with inspection of each other's guards, and by a march past of the guards.

I felt throughout the ceremony as if I were in a dream. The white tall pillars of the monument standing out against the ashy grey sky seemed entirely detached from this earth, whilst the two red wreaths of poppies looked like two small drops of blood on that vast monument. They served as a vivid reminder of the floods of blood that had already been spilt on the very ground [on which] we were standing, and of the futility of again causing such bloodshed. I suppose that it is through such punishments that we shall eventually learn to 'love our neighbours as ourselves'.

Field Marshal Lord Alanbrooke

1942 [USA]
This should teach the human race never to designate another 'Armistice day'.

Anne Morrow Lindbergh

1942 [Lewes, England]
The railings went and the gate.[1] Two dogs at once rushed in assuming it to be a public lavatory!

Mrs Henry Dudeney

1942 [London]
Today, the anniversary of the Armistice, Hitler has announced that he is to occupy all France. All of lovely France gone.

There was a great fog today. The most impenetrable in human memory. There were accidents, delays, late trains and general dislocation. Of course it quite threw my day out of joint. I tried to walk to the House of Commons, since taxis were unobtainable, but I couldn't see, and so turned back. Thus I missed the formal opening

[1] Railings, gates, etc were removed from both domestic and public areas to provide metal for the munitions industry.

of the new session by their Majesties. In the afternoon when I finally got there, I was in time to see Peter Thorneycroft,[1] looking a mere boy, rise and with very little shyness, though just enough, hold the House as he seconded the Gracious Speech. It was an admirable performance. Winston followed and for 76 minutes we had a dramatic treat, as he described the African landings, the victory in Egypt, etc. But whilst vivid and boisterous, he said nothing, or little, that one had not heard on the wireless. Indeed, events just now seem to happen with such dramatic celerity and frequency that we are breathless. The Germans have occupied Tunisia, the Italians have taken the Riviera. Darlan[2] is rumoured to be treating with us. We listened enthralled. At last I crept away, and slept solidly in the library for 20 minutes, and when I returned, Winston was winding up. It was a creditable, indeed amazing performance for an overworked man of 68. He was cheered when he sat down, and the House emptied, or almost. The announcement that the Church bells are to be rung on Sunday in celebration of the Egyptian victory, was enthusiastically received, and I was reminded of the Greek bells which I heard announcing victory of Klissura, when I was in that ghastly train between Athens and Belgrade in January 1941.

'Chips' Channon

1944 [Paris]

After lunch Mrs [Anthony] Eden asked if I'd go with her to see the rooms at the Quai d'Orsay, and Mrs [Winston] Churchill said she'd like to join us. It was an interesting experience walking through the crowds – none of whom recognized Mrs Churchill who was buffeted by *gendarmes*, bystanders, jeeps, etc. But she was thrilled to be in Paris again, and like most women, could not resist taking an interest in the shop windows. She thought the Düreresque hats hideous.

Outside the Quai d'Orsay the *gendarmes* challenged our approach and told us to go to a side entrance, but Mrs Churchill pleaded: 'My name is Churchill' – at which moment a jeepful of American GIs drove up: 'Say, if you're English can you tell us the way to . . . ?'

Cecil Beaton

[1] Conservative MP.
[2] Admiral Jean Darlan (1881–1942), Vice-Premier and Minister of Defence of the Vichy regime, co-operated with General Eisenhower after the General Invasion of North Africa.

12 November

1775 [Quebec]

On the chapel door at Point Levi, I found the following pompous proclamation to ensnare the ignorant:

'Conditions to be given to such soldiers as shall engage in the Royal Highland Emigrants. They are to engage during the present troubles in America only. Each soldier is to have 200 acres of land in any province in North America he shall think proper. The king to pay the patient fees, secretary's fees and surveyor general, beside twenty years free of quit rent. Each married man gets fifty acres for his wife, and fifty for each child, on the same terms, and as a gratuity besides the above great terms, one guinea levy money.

Allen Mclean, Lt. Col.

Quebec, Aug . 3, 1775. Commandt.

Isaac Senter

1918 [Berlin]

Spent the afternoon at the Reichstag in the quarters of the 'New Fatherland League'. I agreed to join its executive. Clubs like the 'New Fatherland League', the 'Activists', and so on, formed to discuss and decide important political questions beforehand, just as in the French Revolution, have taken over the Reichstag committee-rooms and hold their sessions alongside the Soldiers' and Workers' Councils. Although entry to the Reichstag is now under strict control (it is impossible to get in without the Soldiers' Council red pass), its appearance inside has not altered since the first night of the revolution except for the even greater accumulation of filth. Cigarette butts everywhere; waste paper, dust, and dirt from the streets litter the carpets. The corridors and lobby teem with armed civilians, soldiers and sailors. In the lobby rifles are piled on the carpet and sailors lounge in the easy chairs. The disorder is vast, but quiet reigns. The old attendants, in their parliamentary finery, flit about, helplessly and shyly, last relics of the former regime. The members of the bourgeois parties have completely disappeared.

In the city everything is peaceful today and the factories are working again. Nothing has been heard of shootings. Noteworthy is that during the days of revolution the trams, irrespective of street fighting, ran regularly. Nor did the electricity, water, or telephone services break down for a moment. The revolution never created more than an eddy in the ordinary life of the city which flowed calmly along on its customary course. Moreover, though there was so much shooting, there were remarkably few dead or wounded. The colossal, world-shaking upheaval has scurried across Berlin's day-to-day life much like an incident in a crime film.

Count Harry Kessler

1942 [USA]

The Germans have occupied all of France. Rumors are wild. Darlan has commanded the French to stop fighting, to give over the fleet. The American troops are successful all over Africa. The papers are soaring buoyantly. One doesn't know what's true or not. Pat[1] says her art teacher said, 'It'll all be over in three weeks!' and C. [Charles, her husband] says a man at the factory said, 'There'll be no need of these bombers now!'

Anne Morrow Lindbergh

1967 [Williamsburg, Virginia]

This morning we went to the old Bruton Parish Episcopal Church. It's a venerable building, and in the past I've spent hours with Lyndon's mother in the graveyard and walking through the interior where the names of so many of the signers of the Declaration of Independence adorn the walls. We sat in George Washington's own pew in the front row. The choir was absolutely lovely. And then came the sermon.

The Reverend Cotesworth Pinckney Lewis gave short shrift to any Biblical text and launched into a general discussion of the state of the Union and of the world – touching on Civil Rights, disorder in the streets, and the general upheaval in the nation. And then I froze in my seat as I heard him say, 'And then there is the question of Vietnam. But there is a rather general consensus that something is wrong in Vietnam – a conviction voiced by leaders of nations traditionally our friends, leading military experts and the rank and file of American citizens – we wonder if some logical, straightforward explanation might be given?' . . . And on and on. 'It is particularly regrettable that to most nations of the world the struggle's purpose appears to be neo-colonialism.' He then veered 180 degrees. 'We are mystified,' he said, 'by

---

[1] Pat Troy, her secretary.

news accounts suggesting that our brave fighting units are inhibited by directives and inadequate equipment from using their capacities to terminate the conflict successfully. While pledging our loyalty, we ask humbly: "Why?"'

I turned to stone on the outside and boiled on the inside. I thought of Lyndon's asking for equal time and rising to the pulpit to explain to him 'why'. But no, if I thought *he* shouldn't use the pulpit for what he is doing, how much less would it become a visiting worshipper to rise and answer? Lyndon had just spent two days and traveled thousands of miles across the country answering exactly his questions – why are we there?

All things end. Finally the beautiful choir raised its great voice, and then we were walking stiffly out the door. There, of course, was that inevitable melee – the flashing cameras, the crowds of casual tourists and visitors lining the streets, smiling, cheering, reaching out their hands. Off in the distance to the left, I noticed a very small group of protesters with banners. I could only see the word 'Peace'. And there was Reverend Cotesworth Pinckney Lewis – hand extended. Be it said for my husband that he shook hands briefly with a smile while I said, 'The choir was beautiful.' We stepped into the waiting car with a wave to the crowd.

Later Lyndon looked at me with a wry smile and said, 'Greater love hath no man than that he goes to the Episcopal Church with his wife!'

Lady Bird Johnson

13 November

1918 [London]
We got an authentic version of the armistice terms. To think of our being able to talk like that to the Hun. It leaves one dizzy. The men took it all amazingly calmly. There was hardly any open exultation, but everybody wore an air of complete if somewhat bewildered, satisfaction, as one who rises from a thoroughly good dinner. Small wonder it took some time to assimilate; even now the immensity of what we have done leaves me gasping. That within five months of that nightmare of last spring the Beast should be broken body and soul; that his armies should be in rout, his emasculated fleet in English harbours, and

Kaiser in exile, the Crown Prince the jape of Europe, Ludendorff[1] a broken imbecile; that all the wild jingo-hopes we used to toy with in the early years before jingoism died and stank, and hope itself almost withered, should in one thunderclap become stark reality; that, most unbelievable of all, the answer had come to our 'Lord, how long?' of so many endless nights – can you wonder that we were dazed and slow of comprehension?

Other things, too, made revelry difficult; for, at the gathering of this stupendous harvest, too many of the sowers were not there. Even when you win a war, you cannot forget that you have lost a generation.

Sir Alan 'Tommy' Lascelles

1942 [Kent]

Now I hear that Freddie[2] has been killed in action. Freddie was always dirty, and, one felt, faintly slippery all over, with brown polished skin and a mind which leapt about and coloured itself according to the company. All things seemed almost equal to him. Broad, narrow, high, low, fat, thin; all were inquired into, laughed about. There was no sort of restraint or selection at all. Everything was made to be enjoyed as much as possible.

Only in the summer we had that lemon gin at Penshurst and I told them of my *Horizon* acceptance.[3] Now with the notice of his death comes another fabulous letter from Edith Sitwell, praising my book with such a wealth of careful thought and expression. It is lovely and blossoming and budding and it comes with Freddie's death note. In an aeroplane in a blinding flash with burning hate and sights too horrible to dream of he must have died. He never meant anything to me, he was only someone who seemed miraculously unfettered by his sordid upbringing and by fear.

Three years ago when we went hunting for his ancestors' tombs in my little red car, to Biddenden, to Benenden, to the farms and other houses, picking up lean fragments about [Freddie's family], it was strange to imagine any sort of settled background with Freddie, any worthy burghers, prosperous farmers, gone-off squires. Yet his family was supposed to have a sort of trashy romance about it. They

---

[1] General Erich von Ludendorff (1865–1937), who promulgated the idea of 'total war'.
[2] Freddie Beale, an old friend.
[3] *Horizon* published Welch's article on Walter Sickert, which launched his literary career.

had lived for centuries in this part until they rotted away to Freddie's father who was always away from home 'on the booze', a mysterious figure whom nobody ever met. And his mother? Well, she, it was said, would come to the door and then divest herself of her clothes as the visitor waited. There was obviously madness and instability on both sides.

Freddie saying aloud with childish fervour, 'I want to be able to play Bach and Chopin better than anyone else in the world.'

Denton Welch

1942 [California]
Went to Metro [film studios], to talk to Lesser Samuels about Maugham's *The Hour Before Dawn*, which Lesser may be going to write for Paramount. He wants me to help him – chiefly a sort of technical adviser on the scenes for the conscientious objector.

A surprisingly large number of elevator boys and messengers were still at their jobs, despite the draft. There are now exits to air-raid shelters at the ends of the corridors. A writer told me how Victor Saville [film executive] had reprimanded him for writing a scene in which a man runs in and takes his hat and coat from a bedroom chair. 'My dear fellow,' said Saville, 'surely you know that the only place a man leaves his coat on the back of a chair is in a whorehouse?'

I had tea with Saville. He was much excited by the favorable war news from Egypt. 'Isn't it marvellous,' he said to me, 'to think you and I were sitting in this office at the fall of Dunkirk?' He wants to see Italy not only invaded but thoroughly bombed – 'to soften them up'. And he'd have Darlan shot as soon as the war is over: 'that Goddam turncoat sonofabitch.'

Christopher Isherwood

14 November

1854 [Battle of Inkerman]
At 6 a.m., the breeze freshened; at 8 a.m., our tent went; and by 9, it was blowing a perfect hurricane. Every tent down; and what with snow, rain, and wind, all in camp were thoroughly miserable. I can hardly imagine men living through a worse day; indeed, many did not.

Lieut. General Sir Charles Ash Windham

1939 [Berlin]
I order some investigations of astrology. A lot of nonsense is talked and written in this field. Strangely enough, however, all of it speaks in our favour.

Josef Goebbels

1940 [Westminister Abbey, London]
The Abbey, as the Service[1] has been kept so secret, was far from crowded. There had been some uneasiness lest the Germans would stage a raid and get Winston and the entire Government with one bomb. However, nothing occurred, and there was no alert during the actual service, which was long, dignified, and moving. Rab[2] and I were put in the second pew.

There in the Abbey, and it angered me to see them, were all the little men who had torpedoed poor Neville's heroic efforts to preserve peace, and made his life a misery: some seemed to be gloating. Winston, followed by the War Cabinet, had the decency to cry as he stood by the coffin, and Mr Speaker and others too seemed deeply stirred . . . The service was long, and the Abbey was cold, that terrible ecclesiastic cold known only to English churches.

Afterwards I heard that after everyone had left the Abbey, poor Horace Wilson,[3] the once all-powerful eminence grise of the Chamberlain régime, was seen alone, his face contracted with grief, praying for his dead friend.

'Chips' Channon

15 November

1917 [Essex]
The Taylors at the Post Office are officially asked to collect razors to be sent to the army. The general public are not asked but the PO people are to canvas quietly. C. Cole, the Policeman, has given them one which he took from a man who tried to cut his throat with it.

Andrew Clark

[1] Neville Chamberlain's Memorial Service. He died on 9 November, 1940.
[2] Rab Butler (1902–1982), Under Secretary of State for Foreign Affairs, 1938–41.
[3] Sir Horace Wilson (1887–1972), civil servant and adviser to Chamberlain.

1918 [London]

Peace is rapidly dissolving into the light of the common day. You can go to London without meeting more than two drunk soldiers; only an occasional crowd blocks the street. But mentally the change is marked too. Instead of feeling that the whole people, willing or not, were concentrated on a single point, one feels now that the whole bunch has burst asunder and flown off with the utmost vigour in different directions. We are once more a nation of individuals. Some people care for football; others for racing; others for dancing; others for – oh well, they're all running about very gaily getting out of their uniforms and taking up their private affairs again. The streets are crowded with people quite at their ease; and the shops blazoning unshaded lights. Yet it's depressing too. We have stretched our minds to consider something universal at any rate; we contract them at once to the squabbles of [Prime Minister] Lloyd George, and a General Election. The papers are unreadable.

Virginia Woolf

1941 [Leningrad]

Yesterday a large high-explosive bomb fell next to the mortuary. A second fell in the Botanical Gardens. All the glass in the hot-house was blown out, and cold air rushed in. And in the morning all the palms were dead.

Vera Inber

1942 [London]

Church bells rang this morning – in celebration for the victory in Egypt. The first time that I have heard them in over two years.

George Orwell

1992 [Sarajevo]

Dear Mimmy,

An awful lot of people have left Sarajevo. All of them well known. Mummy said: 'Sarajevo is leaving.' Mummy and Daddy know a lot of them. They talked to them and when they said goodbye, everyone kept saying: 'We'll see each other again somewhere, sometime.' It was sad. Sad and upsetting. November 14th, 1992 is a day Sarajevo will remember. It reminded me of the movies I saw about the Jews in the Second World War.

Zlata Filipovic

16 November

1899 [Bronkhorstspruit, South Africa]

An armoured train is wrecked near Estcourt and an important man by the name of Winston Churchill is taken prisoner.[1]

Freda Schlosberg

1940 [England]

Audrey[2] and I rode for an hour and then I took her, lovely in her new M.T.C. Uniform, to Cambridge where I lunched in Hall at Trinity with the Master and Fellows on the occasion of the installation of George Trevelyan as Master.

John Colville

17 November

1940 [England]

Butter stolen yesterday; Louie says 'You are too well liked for any villager to take it.' This flatters us. The butter disappeared when we were playing bowls. A man's voice heard, and the card of St Dunstan's found in the door. Assumption then that the voluntary Collector took it.

Virginia Woolf

1942 [Kovno Ghetto, Lithuania]

DOCUMENT: From SA Colonel Cramer, City Governor, Kovno

To the Jewish Council, Kovno-Vilijampolé

It is henceforth forbidden to use horses within the Ghetto, except for the acquisition of materials.

Funeral hearses and all other types of wagon must henceforth be pulled by the Jews themselves.

Avraham Tory

---

[1] Churchill, having recently been defeated in his first attempt to enter Parliament, was a correspondent for the London *Morning Post*.

[2] The Hon. Audrey Paget. She was a driver for the Polish officers as a member of the Military Transport Corps. Colville added, '"What is it like?" I asked her one day. "Well," she replied, "I have to say Yes, Sir, all day and No, Sir, all night".'

18 November

1939 [Berlin]

Discuss book-collection for the front. Fifteen million books have poured in. We add some National Socialist literature, which has been rather lacking until now.

Josef Goebbels

1943 [London]

I attended Kenneth Clark's lecture at Greek House, the Greek Ambassador in the chair. The subject of the lecture was the influence of Greek art upon British art, in particular architecture. K. must be the most brilliant of lecturers – superhuman learning worn with ease, diction perfect – because he makes me concentrate as though I were immersed in a book. I can say this about no other lecturer, except Harold [Nicolson]. He sat beside me for a few moments before the lecture, talking most graciously. Gracious is the word. He makes me feel like a nurserymaid addressed by royalty. He makes me feel a snob because I record that he spoke three words to me. Is he a very great man, and am I a very small one? The answer to both questions must be Yes.

James Lees-Milne

19 November

1942 [Amsterdam]

Dearest Kitty,

Mr Dussel[1] has told us much about the outside world we've missed for so long. He has sad news. Countless friends and acquaintances have been taken off to a dreadful fate. Night after night, green and grey military vehicles cruise the streets. They knock on every door, asking whether any Jews live there. If so, the whole family is immediately taken away. If not, they proceed to the next house. It's impossible to escape their clutches unless you go into hiding. They often go around with lists, knocking only on those doors where they know there's a big haul to be made. They frequently offer a bounty, so much per head. It's like the slave hunts of the olden days. I don't mean to make light of this; it's

[1] Albert Dussel had recently joined the Franks in hiding.

much too tragic for that. In the evenings when it's dark, I often see long lines of good, innocent people, accompanied by crying children, walking on and on, ordered about by a handful of men who bully and beat them until they nearly drop. No one is spared. The sick, the elderly, children, babies and pregnant women – all are marched to their death.

Anne Frank

20 November

1942 [POW camp, Java]
Continuing with the investigation of all the deficiency diseases group. Trying hard to get some yeast: Ns [Japanese soldiers] have been approached from several angles, but in vain. Seem to be interested only in infectious disease which might spread to them. Indian supply agent with monopoly here is a greasy, shifty, avaricious blob named Seth – a Hindu. Of course there is a N racket here, too; they fix the exorbitant prices and the one or two local price contacts made have shown us how excessive this is. I was told that he couldn't get yeast since [it's] all controlled and not for sale.

Weary Dunlop

21 November

1914 [Furnes, Belgium]
I am up to my eyes in Soup! I have started my soup-kitchen at the station, and it gives me a lot to do. Bad luck to it, my cold and cough are pretty bad!

It is odd to wake in the morning in a frozen room, with every pane of glass green and thick with frost. When I can summon enough moral courage to put a foot out of bed I jump into my clothes at once; half dressed, I go to a little tap of cold water to wash, and then, and for ever, I forgive entirely those sections of society who do not tub. We brush our own boots here, and put on all the clothes we possess, and then descend to a breakfast of Quaker oat porridge with bread and margarine. I wouldn't have it different, really, till our men are out of the trenches; but I am hoping most fervently that I shan't break down, as I am so 'full of soup'.

Sarah Macnaughtan

1942 [POW camp, Java]
Lovely weather continues. Ns actually laid on 5½ bags of *katjang idjoe*
today. There is a catch as usual: these beans are not *katjang idjoe*, but a
larger, worm-eaten variety, white in colour and with a bitter, rather
unpleasant taste. 1000 kilos – the 5½ bags delivered – is our issue for
a month, and according to the lump of grease that supplies us, they
have now controlled all supplies of *katjang idjoe* so that we will not be
able to go on buying our usual 80 grams a day per man. Also, today
we get our medical supplies (for the month presumably): approx. 500
creosote tablets, quinine tablets and some yellow tablets said to be
wonderful for typhoid – acriflavine. They seem to think they have
done wonders in supplying these and that we ought to be very happy,
though of course they bore no relationship to our requirements or
requests.

Weary Dunlop

22 November

1939 [Somerset]
The Marines have sent me a long questionnaire asking among other
things if I am a chronic bedwetter. It seems probable that I am going
to get a commission there.

Evelyn Waugh

1944 [Naples]
Worked very hard, did [censored] 213 letters, a lot for Naples, but how
unlike the weeks before D Day. Had dinner at Jimmy's Mess. The Major
came in with lipstick on his face.

Barbara Pym

23 November

1864 [in the woods, near Doctortown, Georgia]
During the night the cars ran very slow, and sometimes stopped for
hours on side tracks. Two guards at each side door, which was open
about a foot. Manage to get near the door, and during the night talked
considerable with the two guards on the south side of the car.

At about 3 o'clock this a.m., and after going over a long bridge which spanned the Altamaha River and in sight of Doctortown, I went through the open door like a flash and rolled down a high embankment. Almost broke my neck, but not quite. Guard fired a shot at me but did not hit me.

Am happy and hungry and considerably bruised and scratched up from my escape.[1]

John Ransom

1939 [France]

Started the day by having to 'tell off' Monty for having issued a circular to his troops on the prevention of venereal disease worded in such obscene language that both the C of E and RC senior chaplains had complained to the Adjutant General! The latter had shown this circular to Gort [Field Marshal], who had instructed him to come and see me. I had already seen the circular and told Monty what I thought of it, namely that by the issue of such a document he had inevitably undermined the respect and esteem of the division for him, and thus seriously affected his position as commander. The AG originally suggested that Monty should be made to withdraw the document he had issued. I was dead against such a procedure. Monty had already sufficiently undermined his position as a commander through the issue of the document; to make him withdraw it now would be a clear indication of superior authority disapproval which would remove any vestige of respect they might have for him. I told AG that instead I would have him up again, express the C-in-C's [Commander-in Chief] displeasure to him and impress on him again the magnitude of his blunder. I therefore pointed out to Monty that his position as the commander of a division had been seriously affected by this blunder and could certainly not withstand any further errors of this kind. I also informed him that I had a very high opinion of his military capabilities and an equally low one of his literary ones! He took it wonderfully well, and I think it ought to have done him good. It is a great pity that he spoils his very high military ability by a mad desire to talk or write nonsense.

Field Marshal Lord Alanbrooke

---

[1] Ransom, was recaptured and sent to a prison camp at Blackshear. He escaped again on another train journey and went into hiding, helped by negroes. On 22 December, he and two other escapees met up with the Union army and were able to join the troops of the 80th Ohio Regiment.

1944 [near Coventry]

The French have reached Strasbourg, where the Marseillaise was composed – the ancient capital of Alsace. The French Chamber was much moved on hearing this news this morning. They rose and sang the Marseillaise and the session was dissolved. Along the rest of the front there is progress and we push on, it seems, beyond the places taken yesterday and check and beat off counter-attacks. Grim fighting continues at the northern end of the battle-front, while the Germans are faced with a vast turning movement as the French drive north. The Siegfried line will most likely prove a difficult obstacle everywhere. It was meant to be!

Our great news today is of *three letters from Alan*, dated 31.8.44, 11.9.44 and 10.10.44, so it certainly is our lucky day. In the last he says: 'Next month we shall start digging and so it will go on until we are told "you can go home now."' He tells of the progress of the onions, tomatoes and beetroot, the runner beans – with black fly, which were then disposed of by ladybirds – and then a bit about games. 'Are gardening and games all the lad thinks about? No, but it's a good topic for letters!' He sounds just the same 'lad', anyway.

Clara Milburn

24 November

1914 [Furnes, Belgium]

We are beginning to get into our stride, and the small kitchen turns out its gallons and buckets of liquid. Mrs.— has been helping me with my work. It is good to see anyone so beautiful in the tiny kitchen, and it is quaint to see anyone so absolutely ignorant of how a pot is washed or a vegetable peeled.

I have a little electric lamp, which is a great comfort to me, as I have to walk home alone at midnight. When I get up in the morning I have to remember all I shall want during the day, as the villa is a mile from the station, so I take my lantern out at 9.30 a.m.!

I saw a Belgian regiment march back to the trenches today. They had a poor little band and some foggy instruments, and a bugler flourished a trumpet. I stood by the roadside and cried till I couldn't see.

Sarah Macnaughtan

1943 [Tuscany]

Return from a week in Florence, having gone there by car. During my visit several acquaintances, who belonged to an association for helping British prisoners (guiding them in the hills from one band to another, and furnishing them with clothes and arms), were suddenly arrested – betrayed by a spy to whom they had idiotically entrusted the driving of an ambulance in which [some] of the prisoners had been hidden. Consequently all the members of the organization whom this spy happened to encounter are now under arrest – and the others are afraid that their names may be given away too. Among those arrested are several whose share in the work was very slight and whose motives were un-political – kindly, naive people, with English connections or friends, who wanted to 'help the boys' – and scarcely even realized the danger they were running. One elderly man, whose only share was to allow some of the clothes to be deposited in his house, has suffered a most brutal examination – after a night in the punishment cell – which is so narrow and low that one can neither stand up nor sit in it, but merely squat. His wife came to us, begging for candles, since all his life the poor man has been afraid of the dark. One little boy of twelve, who had helped his mother in guiding the prisoners in the hills, on going one day to his aunt's house, opened the door to find an SS man standing there, who pointed his revolver at him, and took him in charge. Eventually he was allowed to go home, where he reported all that had occurred, and his aunt's arrest, with complete self-control and clarity – only that night, as he was going to bed, his mother noticed that his pants were moist. He blushed. 'When that man pointed his revolver at me, I couldn't help it!'

Iris Origo

25 November

1937 [Spain]

There was an enthralling operation at the hospital this morning when I went out. They were removing a bullet from a man's back. The X-ray gave the impression that it was lying on the ribs, but when they opened him up it turned out to have gone through the ribs and lodged in the left lung. It was fascinating watching it being hooked out.

Priscilla Scott-Ellis

1939 [Kent]

How curious are the moods through which one passes! I sit here in my room at Sissinghurst thinking back on the days since 3rd September. The acute depression and misery of the first weeks has passed. I have accepted the fact that we are at war, and I suppose I am physically relieved by the fact that there are not likely to be any raids during the winter upon London and that the Germans have not made a dash through Holland. Yet the fact that this war is costing us six million pounds a day and that I am not really certain that we shall win it, fills me with acute sadness at times. We all keep up a brave face and refuse to admit that defeat is possible. But my heart aches with apprehension.

Harold Nicolson

1939 [London]

Went straight to the medical board which was in a flat in St James's. In a tiny outer room there were three or four youths waiting and two bloods, already in the Navy, who were undergoing an intensive examination for the Air Arm. Doctors in shabby white coats strode in and out smoking cigarettes. I went first to have my eyes tested and did deplorably. When asked to read at a distance with one eye I could not distinguish lines, let alone letters. I managed to cheat a little by peering over the top. Then I went into the next room where the doctor said, 'Let's see your birthday suit. Ah, middle-aged spread. Do you wear dentures?' He tapped me with a hammer in various organs. Then I was free to dress. I was given a sealed envelope to take to the Admiralty. In the taxi I unsealed it and found a chit to say that I had been examined and found unfit for service. It seemed scarcely worthwhile going to the interview. I went and found the same youths waiting in another waiting-room. They went in nervously, one by one, and came out jointly. Finally myself. A colonel in khaki greeted me in the most affable way, apologized for keeping me waiting and gradually it dawned on me that I was being accepted. He said, 'The doctors do not think much of your eyesight. Can you read that?', pointing to a large advertisement across the street. I could. 'Anyway most of your work will be in the dark.' Then he gave me the choice between Marine Infantry, a force being raised for raiding parties, and Artillery, an anti-aircraft unit for work in the Shetlands. I chose the former and left in good humour.

Evelyn Waugh

1940 [Berlin]

I have at last got to the bottom of these 'mercy killings'. It's an evil tale.

The Gestapo, with the knowledge and approval of the German government, is systematically putting to death the mentally deficient population of the Reich. How many have been executed probably only Himmler and a handful of Nazi chieftains know. A conservative and trustworthy German tells me he estimates the number at a hundred thousand. I think that figure is too high. But certain it is that the figure runs into the thousands and is going up every day.

William L. Shirer

1943 [Naples]

Food, for the Neapolitans, comes even before love, and its pursuit is equally insatiable and ingenious. They are almost as adaptable, too, as the Chinese in the matter of the foodstuffs they are prepared to consume. A contact from Nola mentioned that the villages in his area had lost all their breeding storks because last year the villagers eked out shortages by eating their nestlings. This is regarded as a calamity by those who did not benefit directly, as there is a widespread and superstitious aversion in Italy, as elsewhere, to molesting storks in any way.

Another example of culinary enterprise was provided by the consumption of all the tropical fish in Naples' celebrated aquarium in the days preceding the liberation, no fish being spared however strange and specialized in its appearance and habits. All Neapolitans believe that at the banquet offered to welcome General Mark Clark[1] – who had expressed a preference for fish – the principal course was a baby manatee – the most prized item of the aquarium's collection – which was boiled and served with a garlic sauce. These two instances demonstrate a genius for improvisation. But some of the traditional local cooking is weird enough in its own right. On Vesuvius they make a soft cheese to which lamb's intestine is added. Shrove Tuesday's speciality is *sanguinaccio*, pig's blood cooked with chocolate and herbs.

My experience of Neapolitan gastronomy was expanded by an

---

[1] Mark Clark, US Army officer whose Fifth Army captured Rome during the Italian campaign.

invitation to a dinner, the main feature of which was a spaghetti-eating competition. Such contests have been a normal feature of social life, latterly revived and raised almost to the level of a cult as a result of the reappearance on the black market of the necessary raw materials.

Present: men of gravity and substance, including an ex-Vice-Questore, a director of the Banco di Roma, and several leading lawyers – but no women. The portions of spaghetti were weighed out on a pair of scales before transfer to each plate. The method of attack was the classic one, said to have been introduced by Fernando IV, and demonstrated by him for the benefit of an ecstatic audience in his box at the Naples Opera. The forkful of spaghetti is lifted high in the air, and allowed to dangle and then drop into the open mouth, the head being held well back. I noticed that the most likely-looking contestants did not attempt to chew the spaghetti, but appeared to hold it in the throat, which, when crammed, they emptied with a violent convulsion of the Adam's apple – sometimes going red in the face as they did so. Winner: a 65-year-old doctor who consumed four heaped platefuls weighing 1.4 kilograms, and was acclaimed by hand-clapping and cheers. These he cheerfully acknowledged and then left the room to vomit.

Norman Lewis

26 November

1775 [Quebec]
A proclamation came to hand issued by General Carleton, commanding all the citizens of Quebec, that would not take arms to defend the city, to disappear within four days; that if found after that they would be treated as spies. In consequence of this order several came out to our army.

Isaac Senter

1943 [Cairo]
The story goes that Randolph Churchill woke his father yesterday morning saying, 'Twinkle, twinkle little star, how I wonder where you are.' Anyhow the Prime Minister[1] suddenly demanded to know why

[1] Churchill, Roosevelt and Stalin met for talks in Tehran.

some of our soldiers were not wearing the Desert Star Medal. Churchill had taken trouble over this medal: the yellow on it is for sand, the blue for the sea, and so on. Few have yet been issued – hence the dilemma. Now all the ribbon in existence has been made up and any desert soldier who sees Churchill will wear it but will have to return it at the gate on departure for others to wear.

Countess of Ranfurly

27 November

1915 [London]
Today, armed with a certificate from my Doctor in a sealed envelope and addressed 'to the Medical Officer examining Mr W.N.P. Barbellion', I got leave to attend the recruiting office and offer my services to my King and Country. At the time, the fact that the envelope was sealed caused no suspicion and I had been comfortably carrying the document about in my pocket for days past.

Of course I attended merely as a matter of form under the pressure of the authorities, as I knew I was totally unfit – but not quite *how*. After receiving this precious certificate, I learnt that K [a friend] was recruiting Doctor at W, and he offered to 'put me thro' in five minutes', as he knows the state of my health. So at a time agreed upon, I went today and was immediately rejected as soon as he had stethoscoped my heart. The certificate therefore was not needed, and coming home in the train I opened it out of curiosity . . .

I was quite casual and thought it would be merely interesting to see what M— [his doctor] said.

It was.

'Some 18 months ago,' it ran, 'Mr Barbellion shewed the just visible symptoms of —' and altho' this fact was at once communicated to my relatives it was withheld from me and M therefore asked the MO [Medical Officer] to respect this confidence and to reject me without stating on what grounds. He went on to refer to my patellar and plantar reflexes, by which time I had had enough, tore the paper up and flung it out of the railway carriage window.

I then returned to the Museum [his place of work] intending to find out what — was in Clifford Allbutt's System of Medicine. I wondered whether it was brain or heart; and the very thought gave me palpitations. I hope it is heart – something short and sharp rather than lingering. But I believe it must be — of the brain, the opposite process of softening occurring in old age. I recall M's words to me before getting married: that I had this 'nerve weakness', but I was more likely to succumb to pneumonia than to any nervous trouble, and that only 12 months' happiness would be worth while.

On the whole I am amazed at the calm way in which I take this news. I was a fool never to have suspected serious nerve trouble before. Does dear E [his wife] know? What did M tell her when he saw her before our marriage?

W.N.P. Barbellion

1940 [Berlin]

Dined at Savarin's. Ate lobster and other unrationed plutocratic delicacies.

Marie 'Missie' Vassiltchikov

1944 [on board USS *Montpelier*, in the Pacific]

During a little lull in the action the men would look around for Jap souvenirs and what souvenirs they were. I got part of the plane. The deck near my mount was covered with blood, guts, brains, tongues, scalps, hearts, arms etc. from the Jap pilots. One of the Marines cut the ring off the finger of one of the dead pilots. They had to put the hose on to wash the blood off the deck. The Japs were splattered all over the place. One of the fellows had a Jap scalp, it looked just like you skinned an animal. The hair was black, cut very short, and the color of the skin was yellow, real Japanese. I do not think he was very old. I picked up a tin pie plate with a tongue on it. The pilot's tooth mark was into it very deep. It was very big and long, it looked like part of his tonsils and throat were attached to it. It also looked like the tongue you buy in the meat store. This was the first time I ever saw a person's brains, what a mess. One of the men on our mount got a Jap rib and cleaned it up, he said his sister wants part of a Jap body. One fellow from Texas had a knee bone and he was going to preserve it in alcohol from the sick bay.

James J. Fahey, Seaman First Class

28 November

1915 [France]

Walked into Béthune for tea with Robert Graves, a young poet, captain in Third Battalion and very much disliked.[1] An interesting creature, overstrung and self-conscious, a defier of convention. At night went up again to Festubert with working-party. Dug from 12 to 2 a.m. Very cold. Home 4.15.

Siegfried Sassoon

1941 [Leningrad]

The future of Leningrad fills me with anxiety. The burning of the Badayev Stores was no joke. Fat going up in heavy smoke – the carbohydrates necessary to maintain life. Protein – meat – we hardly see at all. Recently Professor Z. told me, 'Yesterday my daughter spent all day in the attic searching for the cat.' I was prepared to be deeply touched by such love for animals, but Z. added: 'We eat them.'

Vera Inber

1941 [Wiltshire]

Drove to Oxford, where R. and I dined at the George. Watching airmen and their girls, R. and I discussed whether it was possible to be in love when one is risking one's life in a war. R. said no, it was not, only in lust. Yet one of the airmen gazing with froglike eyes at his unsensual-looking blonde was, I believe, in love with her in a way. Lust was certainly the bond between another stocky red-haired fellow and his sophisticated little friend, to whom he was talking shop all the time.

Frances Partridge

1943 [Tuscany]

Antonio returns from Florence with the news that the Jew-hunt still continues. Last night they searched even the convents, hunting out and capturing the last poor wretches who had taken refuge there, including even a two-months' baby, which had been deserted by its panic-stricken mother. A new law has now declared all Jews to be enemy aliens, and their property, consequently, is confiscated, while

---

[1] Sassoon based his character David Cromlech in *Memoirs of an Infantry Officer* on Robert Graves.

they themselves are being deported, in sealed vans, to 'concentration camps'. Some will not arrive there. When the closed vans of one train which left Rome on Friday were not opened until Tuesday at Padova, one of them contained the corpse of an old man, another a new-born baby. No one was allowed to get out, and the train went on to Germany.

Every Italian I have met, irrespective of political opinion, is horrified and disgusted by this brutality – which is equalled by that of the new Republican police. At Palazzo Braschi (their headquarters in Rome) young men armed with whips stand about openly in the courtyard. We are being governed by the dregs of the nation – and their brutality is so capricious that no one can feel certain that he will be safe to-morrow.

Iris Origo

1944 [London]
London much less crowded than in Feb, quite a few Americans. I notice that hairdos are simpler, more like mine sometimes – I shall tell the Carradale girls so! For the first time for ages I am in fashion with a hanky over my head, and very used to it as I often wore one in the old days when it wasn't fashionable. I got a grey-blue Liberty one, as I don't think the printed ones are my line. It's quite odd getting a thing for oneself. I went to get Val a frock. Some lovely ones at Harrods. But at a price!

Naomi Mitchison

29 November

1916 [Lewes]
The young man at the Westgate Stores I had unkindly taken for a 'Conchie' came out, in the course of a brief affable conversation, that he had been torpedoed three times!

Mrs Henry Dudeney

1939 [England]
The soldier's budget must be laid out carefully. As I am married I make an allotment of pay to my wife, and am left with 7s.6d. per week. Out of this I am expected to buy metal polish, boot polish, soap, dusters, button-stick, and other extras from the N.A.A.F.I., also to replace lost

mugs, and so on. Then I may buy cups of tea at a penny each, and cakes, also a penny, at 10.30 every day, if I am lucky enough to reach the counter before the half-hour 'break' is up. Our food is good, not always well-cooked, but more often so than not, and yet not *quite* enough. We may, and do, therefore eat suppers at the N.A.A.F.I., costing anything from 3d. to 6d. For example, meat and potato pie with chips is 5d. Add to that the cost of tobacco, cigarettes and occasional chocolate, and it will be seen how little if anything is left of the traditional shilling a day.

J.F. Hendry

1939 [Berlin]

The English King opens a new session of Parliament with a completely ridiculous and colourless speech containing absolutely nothing.

Josef Goebbels

30 November

1941 [Germany]

Hilde [her maid] daily threatens to leave me for more 'useful' work . . . I wish she'd think of me as her war effort. Her brother was killed in Russia and she went home for *two weeks* to comfort her mother – it couldn't have taken that long.

Elisabeth von Stahlenberg

1944 [near Coventry]

An eventful day, with visitors to lunch. This was the day arranged for Mrs Greenslade and Edward[1] to come and see us, and so it was interesting to lay the table for four and to use the best glass again. It is so long since we used wineglasses on the table that I did not know in which box to look. However they were found and polished up, as well as the table. It all looked very nice, with the yellow mats and the jasmine and the cassinea in a cut-glass vase. Our guests arrived just before 1 p.m., Edward walking slowly with his two sticks, and soon we were toasting him, Alan and each other in a good glass of sherry. Then we did full justice to the Greenslade duck and Milburn wartime trifle and apple tart.

[1] Mother and son, old family friends. The son had been injured in action.

Edward says the mud colour of everything and the khaki is dreadfully monotonous in prison camp and how he enjoys the colour he finds everywhere here. That is just as I thought. Behind everything there is always the monotony of prison life. The lack of privacy, never, never to be alone, is also very wearing, he says. We spent the afternoon talking and hearing things. No knives and forks for prisoners of war – a bowl and spoon – and no tablecloths, of course. How deadly sick of it all they must be!

It is Mr Churchill's 70th birthday.

Clara Milburn

1939 [New York]

I'm hearing more and more jokes about President Roosevelt. Here's one of them: a man dies and his soul goes to the Pearly Gates. St. Peter asks what he did when alive on earth. The man says he was a psychiatrist. St. Peter cries: 'Come in! Come in! You're just the man we need. God thinks he's Franklin D. Roosevelt!'

Edward Robb Ellis

DECEMBER

We, the survivors, are not the true witnesses.
Primo Levi, *The Drowned and the Saved*

1 December

1899 [Intombi Camp, near Ladysmith, South Africa]

The Scots as usual celebrated St Andrew's night, though whisky was scarce and haggis out of the question; but a very pleasant and social evening was spent. The orators, being Scotsmen, spoke about the virtues of their race, the magnificent grandeur of their country and the prowess of Scotland's sons. We English felt small and looked small, but being polite and their guests, we remained quiet and did not deprive them of their conceit.

Dr James Alexander Kay

2 December

1862 [Virginia]

I was ordered under arrest by General Lee for shooting my pistol at a squirrel when we stopped this evening.

Captain Michael Shuler, Company H, 33rd Virginia Voluntary Infantry,
CSA

1915 [France]

Quiet day. Rode with R. Ormrod after lunch. Tried to make black pony jump a ditch and failed utterly. Saw a heron, which sailed slowly away across the misty flats of ploughed land; grey, still evening, gleaming dykes, willows and poplars; a few lights here and there as we rode home, and flicker of star-shells in the sky beyond Béthune. Robert Graves lent me his manuscript poems to read; some very bad, violent and repulsive. A few full of promise and real beauty. He oughtn't to publish yet. [Quartermaster] Cotterill[1] and Ormond to dinner, and the servants produced an awful repast, worst ever known. Moving again to-morrow. Very wet night. I dreamed of a sudden death.

Siegfried Sassoon

---

[1] Sassoon based his character Dottrell in *Memoirs of an Infantry Officer* on Cotterill.

1939 [Sussex]
I saw a Kingfisher and a cormorant the other day's walk in rubber boots.
Planes very active. Russia attacking Finland. Nothing happens in England.
There's no reason anywhere. Brutes merely rampant. It's like being in
a temporary shelter with a violent storm raging outside. We wait.

Virginia Woolf

3 December

1915 [Gallipoli]
We now hear a rumour that we are not evacuating at all, and that only
the 29th [Division] are going, but I do not believe this. We learn this
rumour from Sergeant Jones, of Jones's water dump. Every day rumours
are circulated from Sergeant Jones's dugout on 'A' Beach. All day officers and men who pass call in here and say, 'Good -morning [or good-
evening], Jones; what is the latest rumour?' They are invited to sit down
while Jones tells the latest and best that he had heard from all sources
– trenches, Navy, and beaches. I have seen at one time in Jones's dugout
a Brigadier, Major, and two Captains and a corporal all sitting round
the oil-stove fire while Sergeant Jones, at his table, is eating his supper.
As an officer comes in, Jones stands up, saying, 'Good-evening, sir; what
can I do you for?' If it is water required, then that worry has to be
settled; if it is an ordinary call at this half-way house, then the officer
is invited to sit down by the fire, Jones adding, if he should be at
supper, 'You will excuse me going on with my supper, won't you sir?'
One night he said to me, 'May I press you to a plate of porridge, sir?'
We do not look upon him as a soldier or an N.C.O. It is difficult to
describe how we regard him. Personally, I feel my relations with him
are as they would be to the landlord of a familiar roadside inn.

Major John Gillam, DSO

4 December

1914 [Essex]
Patriotic concert last night in village schoolroom. Full. All the toffs of the
village were there. Rev. Mathews and family dined with us before it. Most
of the programme was given by soldiers, except one pro. It was far more

amusing than one could have expected. Corporal Snell, with a really superb bass voice, sang two very patriotic, sentimental songs, sound in sentiment but extremely bad in expression. They would have been excruciating in an ordinary voice; but he was thrilling in them. Our Lieutenant Michaelis was there, after mining the roads, together with a number of his men. The great joke which appealed to parsons and everyone was of a fat lady sitting on a man's hat in a bus. 'Madam, do you know what you're sitting on?' 'I ought to. I've been sitting on it for 54 years.'

This morning, with an endorsement by G. B. S. [George Bernard Shaw] himself, I received a suggestion from Mark Judge that I should edit Shaw's Manifesto [*Common Sense about the War*] for volume publication.

Arnold Bennett

1937 [Spain]
The cinema tonight was thrilling. All about a war in Bavaria against Napoleon and everyone was killed. It is silly how in the middle of a war everyone flocks to the nearest gruesome film for a thrill.

Priscilla Scott-Ellis

1941 [Dresden]
The diary must be out of the house. Yesterday Paul Kreidl brought news that a circular was on its way: *Inventory of household effects.* That means confiscations, perhaps also deportation. A house search can be expected immediately after the inventory statement. Eva is therefore to take my diaries and manuscripts to Annemarie [Köhler, a surgeon friend]. If necessary I shall have to stop the diary notes altogether. – Today I shall also leave my personal documents to be photographed since all documents are likely to be confiscated.

Victor Klemperer

5 December

1940 [Wiltshire]
The Christmas catalogues appear, much as usual, except for such things as a toby jug, representing Mr. Churchill, round which is written 'We will fight on the sea, we will fight in the hills', and for this wonderful historical memento the price is five guineas.

Frances Partridge

1941 [Dresden]

Nine tenths a false alarm: The circular merely contains the obligation to report every testamentary disposition of 'movable goods', that is all Jewish property (every piece of furniture, etc.) is being *fixed*, nothing can be got to safety anymore. Bad enough – but not quite as bad and immediately threatening as an inventory. – But the 'evacuations' continue, it can hit us any day. Also numerous house searches for food-stuffs, soap and skin cream are said to be taking place. At all events diaries since 1933 will be out of the house today. And some manu-scripts. And personal papers which, so it is said, the Gestapo like to take away with them.

Victor Klemperer

6 December

1915 [France]

A straight, wide road with tall trees on either side; through a village – up a hill – then the road got bad. We passed a few villages, but very few isolated farms. Twice I saw our shadows thrown on to a white wall by a transport lamp in rear of the column. Once it was a few colossal heads, with lurching shoulders and slung rifles, and again, on a dead white wall, a line of *legs only*, huge legs striding along, as if jeering at our efforts. And all the while we slogged on to the steady beat of the drums in front – up hill down dale; about 3.30 the sky cleared, and we marched under the triumphant stars, plough and bear and all the rest – immortal diadems for humble soldiers dead and living.

Siegfried Sassoon

1939 [USA]

The war gets crazier every day. Italy denounces Russia, sends bombers against them to help the Finns – apparently with Hitler's sanction. Russia reported demanding Bessarabia. No fighting on the Western front. No air raids on London. No peace. 'Very soon,' I told Berthold, 'Britain and Germany will sign a mutual aggression pact – to keep at least five divi-sions facing each other on the Maginot line for the next ten years – while they both attack Russia.' As poor Toller predicted, 'Nie wieder Frieden' [there will never be peace again] is the new slogan.

It is silly, old-fashioned, nowadays to write: 'I wish I were dead.' I wish I were alive.

Christopher Isherwood

1999 [Chechnya]

We were standing outside the village of Muzhichi, in the distant foothills of Ingushetia. For no reason whatsoever this army general had just shot dead a skinny young brown cow that provided the milk for one Ingush family. It's not far from the border with independent Georgia and no distance at all, across the pass, to rebellious Chechnya. So the troops and howitzers have long been billeted in the village and the children sleep badly at night, disturbed by the crash of the artillery.

The cow met its end as follows. She was ambling back from the pasture through the twilight with the other cattle towards her familiar shed. She could already see the fence, where she enjoyed scratching herself, and her owner, Khadizhat, whose warm hands would gently pull at her stubborn teats each evening. Suddenly the path to her familiar and understandable world was blocked by the General. (We know his name and surname, but are not publishing them because he has children of his own, and they are not to blame.)

He was young and handsome, a striking figure. A real fighter. Bear-chested, camouflage hat at an angle, he had fury in his eyes and was as full of testosterone as any teenager after three months at the front. Leaving his men behind him he placed his (by local standards) Very Important Person in the middle of the path and faced the herd. The General was obviously selecting a target. Then, he rapidly fired his machine-gun one-handed and from the hip. Khadizhat screamed and the village shuddered. Tomorrow they would be burying someone else they thought.

First the General shot the cow with his own gun. Then he lifted the body onto the armoured vehicle and, to the wails and laments of the cow's owner, ordered his men to drag it back to the field-kitchen.

'You had nothing to eat?' I asked.

'No, I'm not hungry. It's just that those ***** aren't paying me any money!'

'Who? The Ingush from Muzhichi?'

'No, the Muscovites in Internal Affairs.'

The soldiers listen very attentively to this conversation.

'What's your name?'

'It's a military secret.' The cow-conqueror smelled of stale alcohol. 'We are forbidden to associate with journalists. One more question and I'll arrest you for spying.'

Anna Politkovskaya

7 December

1941 [New York]
Early this Sunday afternoon Lee and I sat in the front room listening to a news broadcast from WMBD by George Barrett, my boss, the editor of the *Journal-Transcript*. Suddenly he hesitated, paused, then said rapidly: 'Ladies and gentlemen, we have a flash from the United Press: Japan has attacked Pearl Harbor!'

With a reporter's reflex, I looked at my watch. The time was 1:33 p.m. Lee, who had been chewing something, stopped chewing. Our eyes met. I remember gasping. Then I walked over and took my wife in my arms. She had a far-away look in her blue eyes but she had resumed chewing. She said: 'I'm sorry, Eddie, but I don't feel it yet.'

I ran to the phone to call the office. The boy on the switchboard said nobody was there. When I called the home of my city editor, his wife said he was out hunting. As I hung up, the enormity of this event hit me so hard that my profanity suffered. In astonishment I heard myself say 'Pooh!' Sort of a Gilbert and Sullivan reaction to a world crisis.

I pulled out an encyclopedia and maps to look up Pearl Harbor, then recent issues of *Time*, *Life* and *Newsweek*, cluttering up the floor with the stuff. While trying to absorb as much data as possible, I kept listening to the radio spew out one bulletin after another. Lee had to attend a rehearsal of the string section of the Peoria Philharmonic, so I decided to ride downtown with her to take some data to my office.

When I got there I found Vic Kaspar, who said an extra would be published and that other staffers were on their way to the building. Barrett, who had come from the studio, was in his office. I walked in and dumped an armload of information about Hawaii, Japan and the Philippines on his desk. Vic sent me to the composing room to read proof, the first time I've done this in years, and there I remained, the only proof-reader, until the paper was put to bed. Our managing editor is such a mild man that I was surprised when, for the first time, I heard him say *hell*! As soon as I got my hands on a copy of the extra, I was sent into the streets to show it to pedestrians to get their reactions – which were varied. Some people were surprised, some not. Some were excited, some calm. Some made intelligent comments, most did not. But what all had in common was one idea: Kick the hell out of Japan! Two young women said they had come downtown for Cokes, but after hearing the war news they decided Scotch and soda were more in keeping with the crisis.

Back in the office I wrote my story, then telephoned around town to try to find a list of names of Peoria boys in service in the Pacific. A woman who belongs to the Peoria Sailors and Marines Mothers' Club has such a list and offered it to me. When she arrived she said her son is on an American gunboat that has just been captured. Her black eyes were moist. In our own office there is a young woman whose husband is at Pearl Harbor, and I saw her tremble.

At last I ran across the street to a Greek restaurant for a bowl of chili and its juke-box was playing symphonic music. As I began to relax I heard a newsboy racing past shouting: 'War is declared!' I sat there, bathed in the beauty of a masterpiece by Tschaikovsky, while beauty leaked out of this world.

In the office again I learned that Japan has declared war against the United States. Its attack on Pearl Harbor astonished me because I thought it was bluffing. For many months I have been an isolationist; now I know that we isolationists were wrong, dead wrong! Nothing could have unified the American people so much as that sneak attack. If I were single I might enlist. My sister Fran said on the phone that she's terrified because her boy friend plans to enlist. My sister Kay said the war news had brought on a fresh attack of ulcers. My friend Max Bosler said that when he heard the flash he thought it was just another radio stunt by Orson Welles. Worst of all was the reaction of seven-year-old Mickey Gearhart, the son of a friend, who screamed: 'I'm going to kill myself! I don't want to get blown up by a bomb!'

Edward Robb Ellis

1943 [London]
Everyone is talking of the imminence of the Germans' rocket shells. The Germans themselves announced over the wireless on Saturday that these shells would shortly rain upon London and totally destroy it. The War Office takes them very seriously, and soldiers are commanded to carry steel helmets again.

James Lees-Milne

8 December

1899 [Intombi Camp, near Ladysmith, South Africa]

We have managed to blow up one of the Boer guns. General Hunter led 500 men of the Imperial Light Horse and the Natal Carbineers up Gun Hill, a hill between Lombard's Kop and Bulwana. They got to the foot of the hill at about 2 a.m. and passed within a few feet of a sentry asleep whom they never saw. Only a hundred men ascended the hill, led by Hunter himself. While on the way up the sentry awoke and yelled out, and the fifty or so Boers asleep round him woke up too and commenced firing. Hunter shouted 'Fix bayonets, and give them cold steel!' But there wasn't a bayonet amongst them. The Boers retreated.

Dr James Alexander Kay

1915 [London]

I find it ever-increasingly difficult to read the newspapers, and the last dregs of the voluntary system are rather sickening. What a farce it is – 'Come along *willingly*! Or we'll fetch you!'!

Lady Cynthia Asquith

1941 [USA]

On Sunday I drove up to Woods Hole – a beautiful day, clear and cold and a tearing wind.

Listening to the radio in the early afternoon I heard the news – that Japan has attacked Pearl Harbor, Manila, Guam Island, Wake Island. It is the knell of the old world. All army officers all over the US ordered into uniform. Espionage kit involved. I listen all afternoon to the radio. I am listening to the Philharmonic, a beautiful concerto of Brahms. But it is interrupted every ten minutes with bulletins about the war. This is what life is going to be from now on, I think.

Anne Morrow Lindbergh

1941 [Germany]

The Japanese have attacked the American fleet at a place called Pearl Harbour.

Elisabeth von Stahlenberg

9 December

1939 [Dresden]

On Monday I was in the Jewish Community House, 3 Zeughausstrasse, beside the burned-down and leveled synagogue, to pay my tax and Winter Aid. Considerable activity: The coupons for gingerbread and chocolate were being cut from the food ration cards: in favor of those who have family members in the field. The clothing cards had to be surrendered as well: Jews receive clothing only on special application to the Community. Those were the kinds of small unpleasantnesses that no longer count. Then the Party official present wanted to talk to me: We would in any case have informed you in the next few days, you must leave your house by April 1; you can sell it, rent it out, leave it empty: that's your business, only you have to be out; you are entitled to a room. Since your wife is Aryan, you will be allocated two rooms if possible. The man was not at all uncivil, he also completely appreciated the difficulties we shall face, without anyone at all benefiting as a result – the sadistic machine simply rolls over us. Then on Thursday he was here with Estreicher, the responsible Jewish Community official, to inspect the place. Again friendly and helpful: You will find it impossible anyway to carry on here, from January 1 you will have to fetch all provisions from one specified place in the city. Estreicher told me I should discuss the details with him. Eva [his wife] much more collected than I, although she will be hit so much harder. *Her* house, *her* garden, *her* activity. She will be like a prisoner. We also lose the last bit of property, because to rent the house out would leave us open to harassment, and if we sell it, once the mortgage has been deducted we are left with a tiny amount that will go into a blocked account and we shall never be able to put our hands on it again. And what to do with our furniture, etc.? And our little tomcat will have to be poisoned.

Victor Klemperer

1943 [on board USS *Montpelier*, in the Pacific]

On the way to the Solomons, you could smell the flowers. On the eight to midnight watch, one would have thought the water was full of lilacs. All of the flowers in the jungle must be blooming now.

James J. Fahey, Seaman First Class

10 December

1775 [Quebec]

The enemy, spying our battery, opened a brisk cannonade of their heavy cannon, in order to demolish it, likewise rushed out of St. John's gate in the cover of their cannons, burnt a number of houses, in one of which was a sick woman consumed. This was a distressing circumstance to the poor inhabitants, who were obliged to abandon their houses, notwithstanding the dire inclement season, and seek a shelter in the different parts of the country, where the humanity of the people would admit them. The view of the enemy in this *incineration* was to prevent our troops making a lodgement in them, and facilitating the operation of a general storm upon the city, which they had too much reason to apprehend.

Isaac Senter

1939 [London]

An intoxicating day spent with someone I have hardly seen alone since January, i.e. Myself. There is no such blissful companionship, no such satisfactory or stimulating friendship. I got up late, wrote many letters, tidied up and telephoned. The war is 100 days old, and a damned bore it is, though no-one seems to talk about it now. It might be somewhere very remote, and I feel that there is a definite danger in such detachment.

'Chips' Channon

1941 [London]

An unhappy day. I begin by glancing at Gerald Berners' new novel *Far from the Madding War*, and am horrified to feel that Mr Lolypop Jenkins must be a portrait of myself.[1] Ben [his son] sees no resemblance, but I do. Then a Viennese actress comes to see me and wants a job, but what can I get for her? She stinks the room out with her exotic scent. Then I go to see Sir Kenneth Goadby [his doctor]. He finds me tired. I have only taken off one pound in three weeks. I walk away from him, and as I cross into Oxford Circus, I see a poster, '*Prince of Wales* and *Repulse* sunk'. The whole circus revolves in the air and I lose my breath. I feel sick. To the Beefsteak [a gentleman's club] as quick as I can, where I have a glass of sherry to revive me.

[1] Lord Berners denied this.

When disaster comes, we always flock to the Beefsteak to comfort each other.

Harold Nicolson

1943 [London]

Lying in the bath this evening, with the hot tap gently running and the water making throaty noises down the waste-pipe – a thing one is strictly enjoined not to allow in war-time – I thought how maddening it is that the worst sins are the most enjoyable. I wondered could it possibly be that these sins would recoil upon me in my old age. For at present they don't seem to do my soul much harm. And the lusts of the flesh, instead of alienating me from God, seem to draw me closer to him in a perverse way. He on the other hand may not be drawn to me. Can it be that he is too polite, as I am when Clifford Smith[1] button-holes me at party and I am longing to escape? How oddly one's body behaves in the bath as though it did not belong to one. Admiring my slender limbs through the clear water I thought, what a pity they aren't somebody else's.

James Lees-Milne

11 December

1940 [Berlin]

Wagner[2] is resisting the new charter of the Bavaria company. But I cannot help him. We must have order and clarity. Only one person can give the orders, and in this case it must be me.

Josef Goebbels

1941 [Germany]

We have declared war on America (I wonder if Liz will be able to send me any more parcels – the coffee was like nectar after the Muckefuck [ersatz coffee] we've had to drink).

Elisabeth von Stahlenberg

---

[1] H. Clifford Smith, Keeper of the Department of Woodwork at the V & A Museum before WWII.
[2] Adolf Wagner, Gauleiter of Munich-Upper Bavaria.

12 December

1899 [Intombi Camp, near Ladysmith, South Africa]
We have managed to blow up another gun, this time on Surprise Hill.
Our men got to the top of the hill without firing a shot and charged
with the bayonet. In one spot there were seven dead Boers and it is
thought we killed about thirty. Blowing up the gun took half an hour
as the first fuse wouldn't burn. The Boers massed below and had a
cross fire on our men as they came down the hill, and we lost 4 officers and 30 men killed and wounded. However, we must break eggs
when we make omelettes.

Dr James Alexander Kay

1914 [Furnes, Belgium]
Such a nice boy died tonight. We brought him to the hospital from
the station, and learned that he had lain for eight days wounded and
untended. Strangely enough he was naked, and had only a blanket over
him on the stretcher. I do not know why he was still alive. Everything
was done for him that could be done, but as I passed through one of
the wards this evening the nurses were doing their last kindly duty to
him. Poor fellow! He was one of those who had 'given even their
names'. No one knew who he was. He had a woman's portrait tattooed
on his breast.

Sarah Macnaughtan

1940 [London]
Mrs [Clementine] Churchill having a migraine, Mary[1] and I dined
alone with the PM. He began by saying he was going to read his
book (Boswell's *Tour to the Hebrides*) – 'you children can talk' – but
the tastelessness of the soup so excited his frenzy that he rushed out
of the room to harangue the cook and returned to give a disquisition
on the inadequacy of the food at Chequers and the fact that ability
to make good soup is the test of a cook.

Talking of the future he sketched the European Confederations that
would have to be formed ('with their Diets of Worms') and shuddered as he thought of the intricate currency problems, etc. He did
not understand such things and he would be out of it. He did not

[1] Churchill's daughter, later Lady Soames.

wish to lead a party struggle or a class struggle against the Labour leaders who were now serving him so well. He would retire to Chartwell [his private residence] and write a book on the war, which he already had mapped out in his mind chapter by chapter. This was the moment for him; he was determined not to prolong his career into the period of reconstruction. I said I thought he would be demanded by the people; there was no other leader. (This was not just Boswellian; there is not at present any man of the right calibre, nor any sign of one on the horizon.)

John Colville

1940 [Berlin]
My interview with the Paris correspondents has been grotesquely distorted by Unipress. I have a denial rushed out for foreign consumption. Journalists are almost always reptiles.

Josef Goebbels

1942 [London]
I am having domestic difficulties with my staff, as the Ministry of Labour wish to call up both my butler and the cook. I mustn't grumble as I have had three years and three months of comfort, even luxury, while everybody else has pigged it.

At dinner at Emerald's [Cunard], Duff [Cooper] was in a violent, vehement, tipsy mood, and attacked everybody and everything, particularly Mr Chamberlain. He still harps on that, and finally I gently asked him how long he had served under him. Duff, rather nettled, went red in the face. He can be so difficult and opinionated.

'Chips' Channon

13 December

1782 [South Carolina]
Had been expecting, every day for a month past, to hear of the intended evacuation of Charleston. The Governor's guard was a object at this time, as the officer commanding would, of course, accompany or escort him into the city. I was so fortunate as to have the guard this day, when advice was received that the British would embark next morning. A few hours for the Governor to get ready, we set

out in the evening with one tumbrel, containing books, papers, &c., and reached the city early next day. Saw the last of the enemy embark in their boats and put off to the shipping. An immense fleet lay in sight all day; found the city very quiet – houses all shut up. A detachment from the army had marched the day before to take possession as soon as the English would be off. Guards stationed at proper places, and small parties, conducted by an officer, patrolled the streets. Charleston a handsome town, situated on neck of land between the confluence of Ashley and Cooper rivers; Cooper river, however, appears to be the only harbor. Town here fronts the east; business all done on this side. Second and third day people began to open their houses and show themselves, and some shops opened. Stayed a week, and returned to our old encampment.

Ebenezer Denny

1937 [Spain]

A completely blank day. There are no interesting wounds.

Priscilla Scott-Ellis

1940 [London]

Coming out into Leicester Square a huge bit of shrapnel whizzed on to the road in front of me and I was running to pick it up when another bit cracked down just where we'd been standing! All the people sheltering in the cinema made a rush to grab, but we got there first. It was still hot when we picked it up.

Felt very sexy going home in the bus. I get like that some days, especially on buses.

Joan Wyndham

1941 [England]

Quiet morning. Cannot help being delighted about America being so dumbfounded at the Japanese attack [on Pearl Harbor]. This feeling is not malice but a genuine relief that (a) they have at last been forced to realise that this war is theirs as well as ours, and (b) that whatever the future brings they will never be able to say that they came in to pull our chestnuts out of the fire, as they were quite obviously caught with their trousers down.

Noël Coward

14 December

1899 [London]

After tea saw Lord Rowton.[1] Had much talk with him about the [Boer] war and our want of preparedness, which has existed for a long time, and which is very culpable. Also asked him to see Lord Salisbury [Prime Minister], to try and impress upon him the importance of having no official enquiry into the conduct of the war until it is over. It would only be repeated back to the Boers and to foreign countries, and would do us a great deal of harm.

Queen Victoria

15 December

1777 [Forge Valley, America]

Quit. Eat Pessimmens [persimmons], found myself better for their Lenient Operation. Went to a house, poor & small, but good food within – eat too much from being so long Abstemious, thro' want of palatables. Mankind are never truly thankfull for the Benefits of life, until they have experienced the want of them. The Man who has seen misery knows best how to enjoy food. He who is always at ease & has enough of the Blessings of common life is an Impotent Judge of the feelings of the unfortunate.

Albigence Waldo, First Connecticut Infantry Regiment

1914 [Germany]

The defeats in Serbia, the stupid leadership.

Franz Kafka

1939 [Germany]

A friend said that not long ago several people had gathered at the home of an acquaintance and had indulged in some critical utterances. Suddenly there was a call from the Gestapo: 'You are warned not to continue this conversation.' The call was prompted by his own daughter (a member of the Hitler Youth). She had eavesdropped at the door and informed the Gestapo by telephone.

Ulrich Von Hassell

---

[1] Lord Montague William Corry Rowton (1838–1903), politician and philanthropist.

1940 [London]

We saw *Gone with the Wind* which lasted till 2.00 a.m. I thought the photography superb. The PM said he was 'pulverised by the strength of their feelings and emotions'.

After some conversation between the PM and [Anthony] Eden about N. Africa I got to bed at 3.00 a.m.; but the PM, throwing himself on a chair in his bedroom, collapsed between the chair and the stool, ending up in a most absurd position on the floor with his feet in the air. Having no false dignity, he treated it as a complete joke and repeated several times, 'A real Charlie Chaplin!'

John Colville

16 December

1940 [Berlin]

Last night bombs fell on the Tauentzienstrasse, a main Berlin shopping artery, smashing most of the windows. The whole street is littered with broken glass.

Marie 'Missie' Vassiltchikov

1944 [near Coventry]

This not-so-cold day was started with a very cheerful letter from Alan dated 31.10.44. He says he is 'well and not bored and I have a good appetite'. I hope there will be enough food to satisfy the latter, because I am sure he is working hard at gardening and taking it out of himself, from what he says. The car took me to the butcher's and Twink [her dog] afterwards took me to the grocer's! At the latter a mysterious small bag was put into my basket with the words 'twopence ha'penny'. I did not know what this under-the-counter treasure was until I got home and found *two lemons!* Great excitement.

Clara Milburn

17 December

1915 [France]

I am happy, happy; I've escaped and found peace unbelievable in this extraordinary existence which I thought I should loathe. The actual life is mechanical; and my dreams are mine, more lonely than ever. We're safe for another year of war, too, so next summer ought to do something for me. Anything but a 'cushy' wound! That would be an awful disaster. I must endure, or else die. And it's nice to look back on my childhood which lasted so long (until I was twenty-three, anyhow). What a confused idea I had of everything, except beauty; was that time *all* wasted? Lovely now seem the summer dawns in Weirleigh garden [his home in England]; lovely the slow music of the dusk, and the chords of piano-music. Loveliest of all, the delight of weaving words into verses; the building of dream on dream; oh the flowers and the songs, now so far away. The certainty of my power to touch the hearts of men with poetry – all faded now like a glorious sky. And then the July days, the afternoons of cricketing, and the silly joy I had when I managed to stay an hour or two at the wicket. And oh the quiet winter mornings when I rode to meet the hounds – and the dear nights when the tired horse walked beside me. Days at Ringmer – days at Witherley – good rides in Kent and Sussex – and the music of the hounds in the autumn woods – and talks by the fire with good old Gordon [Harbord], and my Nimrod. Good-bye to life, good-bye to Sussex.

Siegfried Sassoon

18 December

1777 [Virginia]
Universal Thanksgiving – a roasted Pig at Night. God be thanked for my health which I have pretty well recovered. How much better should I feel, were I assured my family were in health. But the same good Being who graciously preserves me, is able to preserve them & bring me to the ardently wish'd for enjoyment of them again.

Our Brethren who are unfortunately Prisoners in Philadelphia meet with the most savage and inhumane treatments that Barbarians are capable of inflicting. Our Enemies do not knock them in the head or burn them with torches to death, or flay them alive, or gradually dismember them till they die, which is customary among Savages and Barbarians. No, they are worse by far. They suffer them to starve, to linger out their lives in extreem hunger. One of these poor unhappy men, drove to the last extreem by the rage of hunger, eat his own fingers up to the first joint from the hand, before he died. Others eat the Clay, the Lime, the Stones of the Prison Walls. Several who died in the Yard had pieces of Bark, Wood, Clay and Stones in their mouths, which the ravings of hunger had caused them to take in for food the last Agonies of Life! 'These are thy mercies, O Britain!'

Albigence Waldo, First Connecticut Infantry Regiment

1940 [Berlin]
The other day we drew up a list of food served in our office canteen. It is short and not very imaginative.

Monday: Red cabbage with meat sauce.

Tuesday: Meatless day. Codfish in mustard sauce.

Wednesday: Stonefish patties (this tastes exactly as it sounds)

Thursday: Assorted vegetable dish (red cabbage, white cabbage, potatoes, red cabbage, white cabbage)

Friday: Mussels in wine sauce (this is a 'special dish' which vanishes within minutes, so that one has to fall back on potato dumplings in sauce)

Saturday: One of the above

. Sunday: Another of the above

Dessert all through the week: vanilla pudding with raspberry sauce.

Marie 'Missie' Vassiltchikov

19 December

1864 [Georgia]
We received ½ rations again.

Pvt Frederick C. Buerstatte, 26th Regiment, Wisconsin Volunteers

1917 [England]
Came to Litherland on December 11. Since then have eaten, slept, played a few rounds of golf at Formby, walked on the shore by the Mersey mouth, and am feeling healthy beyond measure. I intend to lead a life of light-hearted stupidity. I have done all I can to protest against the war and the way it is prolonged. At least I will try and be peaceful-minded for a few months – after the strain and unhappiness of the last seven months. It is the only way by which I can hope to face the horrors of the front without breaking down completely. I must try to think as little as possible. And write happy poems. (Can I?)

Siegfried Sassoon

1939 [Berlin]
I am forced to have a number of church publications seized. The priests are becoming rather too insolent.

Josef Goebbels

1940 [England]
1940 is undoubtedly coming to an end. The shortest day comes this week: then the days draw out. It would be interesting if I could take today, Thursday, and say exactly how the war changes it. It changes it when I order dinner. Our ration of margarine is so small that I can't think of any pudding save milk pudding. We have no sugar to make sugar puddings: no pastry unless I buy it ready made. The shops don't fill until midday. Things are bought fast. In the afternoon they are often gone. Meat ration diminishes this week. Milk is so cut that we even have to consider the cat's saucer. I spent an hour making butter from our skim of cream – a week's takings provide about half a pound. Petrol changes the day too. All prices rise steadily. The screw is much increased since the summer. We buy no clothes but make do with the old. These are inconveniences rather than hardships. We don't go hungry or cold. But luxury is nipped off, and hospitality. It takes thought and trouble to feed one extra. The post is the most obvious inconvenience perhaps. It takes two days to get a London letter, four to get a parcel. I bicycle to Lewes instead of driving. Then the black out – that's half an hour daily drudgery. We can't use the dining room after dark. We are of course marooned here by the bombs in London. This last week the raids are so few that we forgot to listen for a siren. That used to come at 6.30 punctually. What's Hitler got up his sleeve next – we ask? A certain old age feeling sometimes makes me think I can't spend force as I used. And my hand shakes. Otherwise we draw breath as usual. And it's a day when every bough is bright green and the sun dazzles me.

Virginia Woolf

20 December

1940 [Rome]
Jealousies among generals are worse than among women. One should hear Soddu's telephone calls to Sorice. He demolishes all the generals.

Geloso has softening of the brain, Perugi is a disaster, Trionfi is bank-rupt. Today, for some unknown reason, he speaks well of Vercellino, saying, 'Poor Vercellino. He is such a dear. He came to see me and he wept.'

Count Ciano

21 December

1777 [Pennsylvania]

Preparations made for hutts. Provisions scarce. Sent a letter to my Wife. Heartily wish myself at home, my Skin & eyes are almost spoil'd with continual smoke. A general cry thro' the Camp this Evening among the Soldiers, 'No Meat! No Meat!' – the Distant vales Echo'd back the melancholy sound – 'No Meat! No Meat!' Imitating the noise of Crows & Owls, also, made a part of the confused Musick.

What have you for your Dinner Boys? 'Nothing but Fire Cake & Water, Sir.' At night, 'Gentlemen the Supper is ready.' What is your Supper Lads? 'Fire Cake & Water, Sir.' Very poor beef has been drawn in our Camp the greater part of this season. A Butcher bringing a Quarter of this kind of Beef into Camp one day who had white Buttons on the knees of his breeches, a Soldier cries out – 'There, there Tom is some sort of your fat Beef, by my soul I can see the Butcher's breeches buttons through it.'

Albigence Waldo, First Connecticut Infantry Regiment

1941 [London]

I was in a vile temper with the hopelessness of things at home and in the office. I was feeling in dreadful bad form, inclined to scrap my whole diary. I kicked this volume across the study last thing at night.

Lord Reith

1944 [London]

The question is not what we are to do with Germany after the war but with this country. My idea is to sentence the upper classes to the same fate as the lower – perpetual hard labour without imprisonment.

James Agate

22 December

1775 [Quebec]

Lay excessive Cold & uncomfortable last Night – my eyes are started out from their Orbits like a Rabbit's eyes, occasion'd by a great Cold & Smoke.

Albigence Waldo, First Connecticut Infantry Regiment

1914 [Essex]

1.15p.m. the infant-boy of Fred Cloughton was christened in Great Leighs Church, receiving the baptismal names Eric Charles Mons. The only reason I could discover for the *Mons* was that the child's mother's sister's husband's brother is 'at service on the water!'

Andrew Clark

23 December

1775 [Quebec]

The Party that went out last evening not Return'd to Day.

Albigence Waldo, First Connecticut Infantry Regiment

1939 [France]

The further I go, the more I see that men deserve war – and deserve it more, the more they wage it. It's like the song of Adam that each individual, according to Kierkegaard, freely adapts as his own. The declaration of war, which was the fault of certain men, we all adapt as our own, with our freedom. This War – we have all declared it at one moment or another.

Jean-Paul Sartre

1943 [Verona]

Within a few days a sham tribunal which makes public a sentence which has already been decided by Mussolini under the influence of that circle of whores and pimps which for some years have plagued Italian political life and brought our country to the brink of the abyss. I accept calmly what is to be my infamous destiny. I take some comfort in the thought that I may be considered a soldier who has fallen in battle for a cause in which he truly believed. The treatment inflicted upon me during these months of imprisonment has been shameful and inhuman. I am not allowed to communicate with anyone. All contacts with persons dear to me have been forbidden. And yet I feel that in this cell, this gloomy Verona cell where I am confined during my last days of earthly life, I am surrounded by all those whom I have loved and who love me. Neither walls nor men can prevent it. It is hard to think that I shall not be able to gaze into the eyes of my three children or to press my mother to my heart, or my wife, who in my hours of sorrow has revealed herself a strong, reliable, and faithful companion. But I must bow to the will of God, and a great calm is descending upon my soul. I am preparing myself for the Supreme Judgement.

Count Ciano

1944 [Lewes, England]
Met Mrs Jervis. She gave me – secretly – one of her 8 toilet rolls. I am to tell no one.

Mrs Henry Dudeney

24 December

1854 [Battle of Inkerman]
Weather last night and to-day, shockingly bad; cold rain and sleet. Ten men of the 63rd died in the night, and three of the other regiments. Today the 57th had five men killed and two wounded in the advanced trenches. This arose from the poor fellows having to lie down in the wet until perfectly numb with cold. They were then obliged to rise to warm themselves, when five of them were instantly shot.

Lieut. General Sir Charles Ash Windham

1939 [Dresden]
This Christmas and New Year's Eve we are decidedly worse off than last year, we are threatened with the confiscation of the house – despite that I feel better than I did then; there is movement now, and then everything was stagnating. I am now convinced that National Socialism will collapse in the coming year. Perhaps we shall perish with it – but

it will certainly end, and with it, one way or another, the terror. Shall we manage to save house and tomcat, however? – We have lit our nice Christmas tree every night and intend to do so again today.

Victor Klemperer

1940 [London]
After lunch the PM signed a number of books, which he is giving us all as Christmas presents, and sent off presents to the King and Queen: a siren-suit for the King and Fowler's *English Usage* for the Queen! As he left the room he said, remembering our plea for a Christmas holiday, 'A busy Christmas and a frantic New Year.'

John Colville

1940 [Rome]
It is snowing. The Duce looks out of the window and is glad that it is snowing. 'This snow and cold are very good,' he says. 'This is how our good-for-nothing men and this mediocre race will be improved. One of the main reasons I have requested reforestation of the Apennines has been to make Italy colder and more snowy.'

Count Ciano

1942 [on board USS *Montpelier*, Panama Canal]
We reached the entrance to the Panama Canal at twelve noon. It took eight hours for the ship to go through the locks. It was quite an experience going through the locks and the thick green jungle all around us was beautiful. They say every known animal in the world can be found here. If you go deep into the jungle you will come across savage tribes. If they leave the tribe and return they are killed because the rest of the tribe thinks he will be civilised. We could see some alligators on the beach in this beautiful spot.

James J. Fahey, Seaman First Class

25 December

1864 [Georgia]
Christmas morning inspection. We received a ½ unit crackers, rice and meat.

Pvt Frederick C. Buerstatte, 26th Regiment, Wisconsin Volunteers

1915 [France]
Christmas night was jolly, by the log fire, the village full of maudlin sergeants and paralysed privates.

Siegfried Sassoon

1940 [London]
The unofficial Christmas truce has been kept by both sides. We have not bombed Germany, nor they us.

John Colville

1940 [Wiltshire]
I don't believe the war was mentioned once all day.

Frances Partridge

1940 [London]
Woke to carols on the wireless, and an orgy of present-opening. I got Damon Runyan, Wodehouse and Thurber, a book on Surrealism, a record by Scarlatti, some new green trousers, milk chocolates and cigarettes, a book on chess problems, cold cream and stockings.

Mummy had to go on duty, so Yurka [an Armenian boyfriend] took me to the Brasserie for lunch. We had turkey and plum pudding, and I wore my new pink shirt and grey beret and was looking particularly glamorous and old. He wore a brown double-breasted overcoat with a velvet collar and dark-grey knitted gloves. His nose is always pink in cold weather.

Over lunch he trotted out some real old chestnuts to go with the turkey, like 'You are the sort of girl who should be met at dawn by fifty outriders with drawn sabres glittering', which added to my enormous appetite. I drank quite a lot of beer too, although I can't stand it, in the hope that it might make me tight. It didn't.

Walking back to the post for night duty the pubs were all full of happy, drunken people singing 'Tipperary' and the latest Army song which goes 'Cheer up my lads, fuck 'em all'. I spent a dreary night in an unheated room, sleeping in my clothes on a hard bed. Talk about Christmas night in the workhouse!

Joan Wyndham

1943 [Casablanca]

Christmas day lunch. Spam, bread and coffee.

Technical Sergeant Harry Schloss, 17th Bomb Group, 34th Bomb
Squadron, USAAF

1943 [Delhi]

The bearer, white-turbaned and bare-footed, pulls back the curtains to let in a blaze of sun. Outside, the fountains are playing, the birds are shrieking. Cascades of stocks, carnations and petunias hang over the edges of ornamental pools. Someone is practising on bugle, and sentries clear their throats with resounding rasps to spit, then stamp their bulbous boots on the gravel. A bearer, in scarlet tunic, comes in, salaams and gives me a parcel tied with ribbon. Another servant, in an enormous cheese-cloth puggaree, brings in a necktie wrapped in coloured paper. It is Christmas Day in Viceroy's house . . .

I was allowed into the War Room of South East Asia Command. The chiefs of all departments, American and English, 'breezed in' for what is known as 'early morning prayers' (a study of the latest maps, the day's reports and a short lecture given by half a dozen specialists). The Supreme Commander, Admiral Lord Louis Mountbatten, who had arrived in this theatre not long before, seemed as yet unaffected by the climate. 'We mustn't let it be a damper on effort – we've got to galvanize everyone, got to teach 'em to hustle,' he said – and he appeared to have impregnated his immediate entourage with his own robust brand of enthusiasm.

Cecil Beaton

1966 [on board the *Patch*, bound for Vietnam]

Today is Christmas. But you wouldn't know it by the mood on the ship. Everyone knows we're getting nearer to Nam. It is unusually quiet today. Now and then we saw a ship on the horizon, and an island off in the distance. I seem to be gathering strength as we approach Vietnam. It's hard to explain, but it is so.

There are a few guys who are anxious to get there. Take Ashwork, for instance; he's already horny for the Vietnamese women. Yet there are guys like Yost, who sits for hours without saying anything. You know he's worrying. And you know what he's worrying about.

David Parks

26 December

1916 [England]

Great adventure! I did a day's nursing at the Winchcomb Hospital from eight to eight. I went in some trepidation, but I hadn't realised the tremendous psychological effect of a uniform. Directly I stepped into the ward I felt an entirely new being – efficient, untiring, and quite unsqueamish – ready to cut off a leg, though generally the mere sight of a hospital makes me feel faint. It's wonderful how right it puts one with the men, too. I feel so shy as a laywoman, but was absolutely at my ease as 'Nurse Asquith'. I loved hearing myself called 'nurse' and would certainly go on with it if I were free. I felt all the disciplined's fear of the Sister and the experienced V.A.D. [Voluntary Aid Detachment], and most terribly anxious to acquit myself well.

First I was put down to wash an oilskin table. It looked so clean at first, and appeared dirtier and dirtier under my attention. Then I washed all the lockers, etc., etc. The morning in my memory is a long blur of mops, taps, brooms, and plates. The unpleasant moments are when one can't find anything to do. One can't bear to stand idle and yet one feels a fool when one ostentatiously attacks a quite irreproachable counterpane. My most serious breach of etiquette was that I spoke to a soldier while the doctor was in the ward. We had a meal of cocoa and toast and butter at 9.30, to which I brought a ravenous appetite. It seemed an eternity to 12.30 when we had our lunch.

There really wasn't enough to do. Most of the cases were trench feet – quite raw, a horrible sight. I assisted at the dressing of them, feverishly obeying curt orders. The men were delightful. Made lots of beds after tea, tidied up lockers, etc., etc. Only got tired in the last hour. Got home at 8.30 feeling excited, and wound up, and very well. Far less tired than after an ordinary London day.

Lady Cynthia Asquith

1939 [Berlin]

Get to know the inner rottenness of English society by reading Maugham. This society will collapse if it is pushed hard enough. And we shall make sure of that.

Josef Goebbels

1941 [POW camp, Germany]

I can safely say that I have never imagined a more miserable Christmas Day. One as a prisoner is possibly a novelty, but the 2nd is indescribable. There is no sign of any Christmas feeling and there is nothing to drink – which we did at least have last year. But I am going too fast. We all in our room rose early – Ted and I for Communion Service, the remainder to prepare for a Christmas breakfast. Unfortunately, things didn't go quite *planmässig*. There were only 2 padres at the Service and at least 500 chaps turned up. With the natural running out of supplies early on, it was soon evident that we shouldn't be finished by Appell [roll call] and would at the same time would miss our Christmas breakfast. In fact only about ½ of the service was finished. Appell was ages in length due to many being absent and no one knowing who. The little Rittmeister was naturally in a bad temper and Ted & I had to sit down after Appell, after the special Christmas breakfast party was over, to what had been left for us – sausage roll and bacon (the treat) now cold, and tea (now cold). I fear I was not feeling seasonably charitable as the day was cold, and the mud deeper than ever. When we went to church in the Dining Hall in the grey light of dawn, you could only see water and mud for miles. In the wash-house it was pitch dark, with scores of officers – and orderlies – falling over one another, feet squelching on the mud-covered concrete floor. 'Peace on earth, goodwill towards men.' 'Comfort and joy, comfort and joy' etc. All very ironical. No Red X Christmas parcels and run out of tobacco. Our hosts have provided not a drop of drink, but have provided extra rations in the form of sauerkraut.

Added to this, if you looked like greeting people, they were apt to warn you of the forceful result and the only apparently permissible greetings were 'A Good Christmas' or 'A Happy Christmas next year'. Tempers were frayed, as it had blown a hurricane and rained all night and the huts had literally rocked. All told a happy start for a festive day.

Captain John Mansel

1944 [Lewes, England]

Mrs Brough said that the shortage of Toilet Rolls is because the Air Force had collared the lot, 2 rolls to each pilot. Something to do with scattering leaflets.

Mrs Henry Dudeney

27 December

1915 [Buxton]

I had just finished dressing when a message came to say that there was a telephone message for me. I sprang up joyfully, thinking to hear in a moment the dear dreamed-of tones of the beloved voice.

But the telephone message was not from Roland [her fiancé] but from Clare [his sister]; it was not to say that Roland had arrived, but that instead had come this telegram;

> T.223. Regret to inform you that Lieut. R.A. Leighton, 7th Worcesters Died of wounds December 23rd. Lord Kitchener sends his sympathy. Colonel of Territorial Force, Records, Warwick.

Vera Brittain

28 December

1777 [Virginia]

Yesterday upwards of fifty officers in Gen Greene's Division resigned their Commissions – Six or Seven of four Regiment are doing the hike to-day. All this is occasion'd by Officers Families being so much neglected at home on account of Provisions. Their Wages will not buy considerable, purchase a few trifling Comfortables here in camp, and maintain their families at home, while such extravagant prices are demanded for the common necessaries of Life – What then have they to purchase Cloaths and other necessaries with? It is a Melancholy reflection that what is of the most universal importance, is most universally neglected – I mean keeping up the Credit or Money. The present Circumstances of the Soldier is better by far than the Officers – for the family of the Soldier is provided for at the public expense if the Articles they want are above the common price – but the Officer's family, are obliged not only to beg in the most humble manner for the necessaries of Life – but also to pay for them afterwards at the most exorbitant rates – and even in this manner, many of them who depend entirely on their Money, cannot procure half the material comforts that are wanted in a family – this produces continual letters of complaint from home.

When the Officer has been fatiguing thro wet and cold and returns to his tent where he finds a letter directed to him from his Wife, fill'd with the most heart aching tender Complaints, a Woman is capable of writing . . . What man is there – who has the least regard for his family – whose soul would not shrink within him? Who would not be disheartened?

Albigence Waldo, First Connecticut Infantry Regiment

1939 [Berlin]

The Führer pours scorn on teachers. I have no objection to that. Today they have as little right to be called 'creators of the race' as they had yesterday to be called 'popular educators'. They are and will ever remain arse-whackers.

Josef Goebbels

1940 [Dungannon, Ireland]

I am writing this on the counter at the Central Bar. Larkins is playing darts with the landlord and beating him. Larkins seems in a fair way to become my 'mate'. He is a barber from Limehouse and cuts our hair for three pence. He looks like Charles Boyer[1] as Napoleon or perhaps like Napoleon himself and eats garlic, leeks, onion and bottled sauce and pickles whenever he can get hold of them. Highly flavoured foods are his main interest in life. His second string is beer. He is rather dirty, and Barry Sanderson [lance-bombardier] has threatened him with disciplinary action if he does not wash himself within the next three days.

Rayner Heppenstall

1944 [London]

Overheard in a bar:

AMERICAN SOLDIER: 'You can't argue with me. I'm ignorant!'

James Agate

1992 [Sarajevo]

As I sit writing to you, my dear Mimmy, I look over at Mummy and Daddy. They are reading. They lift their eyes from the page and think about something. What are they thinking about? About the book they are reading or are they trying to put together the scattered pieces of

---

[1] Popular film star of the time.

this war puzzle? I think it must be the latter. Somehow they look even sadder to me in the light of the oil lamp (we have no more wax candles, so we make our own oil lamps). I look at Daddy. He really has lost a lot of weight. The scales say twenty-five kilos, but looking at him I think it must be more. I think even his glasses are too big for him. Mummy has lost weight too. She's shrunk somehow, the war has given her wrinkles. God, what is this war doing to my parents? They don't look like my old Mummy and Daddy any more. Will this ever stop? Will our suffering stop so that my parents can be what they used to be – cheerful, smiling, nice-looking?

This stupid war is destroying my childhood, it's destroying my parent's lives. WHY? STOP THE WAR! PEACE! I NEED PEACE!

I'm going to play a game of cards with them!

Zlata Filipovic

29 December

1775 [Quebec]

Continued the Work. Snow'd all day pretty briskly – The party of the 22nd return'd – lost 18 men, who were taken prisoners by being decoyed by the Enemies Light Horse who brought up the Rear, as they Repass'd the Schuylkill to the City. Our party took 13 or 14 of their Horsemen. The Enemy came out to plunder – & have strip'd the Town of Derby of even all its Household furniture. Our party were several times mixed with the Enemy's horse – not knowing them from our Connecticut Horse – their Cloaks being alike.

Albigence Waldo, First Connecticut Infantry Regiment

1940 [Dungannon, Ireland]

I had put myself down as an agnostic and so did not have to go on church parade. I stretched out on my bed and congratulated myself. The orderly sergeant came into the billets and put me on cleaning hurricane lamps. This was not so good. While the others sat clean and comfortable in church, I stood in the rain and cold wind and covered myself with soot and paraffin.

Rayner Heppenstall

1940 [Italy]
In Venice I saw little and can say little about how the people feel.
Some degrees below freezing, and the lagoons are covered with ice;
therefore the Venetians are unwilling to show any interest in politics.

Count Ciano

30 December

1940 [London]
We went to St Paul's to offer our prayers for its miraculous preservation. Near the cathedral is a shop that has been burned unrecogniz-
ably; in fact, all that remains is an arch that looks like a vista in the
ruins of Rome. Through the arch could be seen, rising mysteriously
from the splintered masonry and smoke, the twin towers of the cathedral. It was necessary to squat to get the archway framing the picture. I
squatted. A press photographer watched me and, when I gave him a
surly look, slunk away. When I returned from photographing another
church, he was back squatting and clicking in the same spot as I had
been. Returning from lunch with my publisher, my morning's pictures
still undeveloped in my overcoat pocket, I found the press photographer's picture was already on the front page of the *Evening News*.

Cecil Beaton

1940 [London]
The Germans in their four-hour blitz last night did an immense amount
of damage, mostly by fire. The main attack centred on the City, which,
of course, is not a military objective at all, and terrific conflagrations
were burning all over it. Seven churches have been burned out, including four of Sir Christopher Wren's which were the glory of London.
The Guildhall is likewise gutted, and so disappears this ancient
fifteenth-century building which, more than any other one, has been
the cradle of individual liberty from which the citizens of London
have defied all kings, from the Normans down, and forced the written
acknowledgement of their rights from William the Conqueror. The
great and mysterious statues of Gog and Magog have been destroyed
in the conflagration, together with many of the other ancient records
and souvenirs of the history, running back to the days of the Conquest.
There is no measure of the value of the carving by Grinling Gibbons

and others which have gone up in smoke. The grand library of the Guildhall, up the aisle of which Jeanette [his wife] and I walked when we first came, to be received by the Lord Mayor in his robes and accompanied by all his retinue, is only a mass of smouldering ruins. All this is plain arson and has nothing to do with anything military.

General Raymond E. Lee

1941 [Leningrad]
Recently, at one place, twenty-seven powders of ascorbic acid (Vitamin C) were exchanged for a live dog. (The dog to be eaten.) Marietta said, reasonably, 'Why not, if the dog is a large one? It is a profitable exchange.'

Vera Inber

31 December

1665 [London]
The Duch war goes on very ill by reason of lack of money.

Samuel Pepys

1870 [Paris]
In the streets of Paris, death passes death, the undertaker's waggon drives past the hearse. Outside the Madeleine today I saw three coffins, each covered with a soldier's greatcoat with a wreath of immortelles on top.

Out of curiosity I went into Roos's, the English butcher's shop on the Boulevard Haussmann, where I saw all sorts of weird remains. On the wall, hung in a place of honour, was the skinned trunk of a young Pollux, the elephant at the Zoo; and in the midst of nameless meats and unusual horns, a boy was offering some camel's kidneys for sale.

The master-butcher was perorating to a group of women: 'It's forty francs a pound for the fillet and the trunk . . . Yes, forty francs . . . You think that's dear? But I assure you I don't know how I'm going to make anything out of it. I was counting on three thousand pounds of meat and he has only yielded two thousand, three hundred . . . The feet, you want to know the price of the feet? It's twenty francs . . . For the other pieces, it ranges from eight francs to forty . . . But let me recommend the black pudding. As you know, the elephant's blood is the richest there is. His heart weighed twenty-five pounds . . . And there's onion, ladies, in my black pudding.'

I fell back on a couple of larks which I carried off for my lunch tomorrow.

The Brothers Goncourt

1915 [Gallipoli]

The last day of a damnable year. Honours in favour of the enemy. Luck all against us. But our turn will come before another year is out. In the morning the Turks heavily shell our front line reserve areas; and D.H.Q., of course, being only just in rear, get it badly. All day the beaches suffer. Life on the beaches is like a game of musical chairs. Instead of sitting down on a chair when the music stops, you promptly fling yourself behind cover when a shell arrives. I am a perfect tumbler now, and after the war will give exhibitions of the many different antics that one performs when dodging shells. A New Year's dinner, as cheery as the Christmas dinner, but broken by visits to the Main Supply depot to send off the rations by trams, and then to bed.

Major John Gillam, DSO

1915 [Buxton]

This time last year He [her fiancé] was seeing me off on Charing Cross Station after *David Copperfield* [play] – and I had just begun to realise I loved Him. To-day He is lying in the military cemetery at Louvencourt – because a week ago He was wounded in action, and had just 24 hours of consciousness more and then went 'to sleep in France'. And I, who in impatience felt a fortnight ago that I could not wait another minute to see Him, must wait till all Eternity. All has been given me, and all taken away again – in one year.

So I wonder where we shall be – what we shall all be doing – if we still *shall* be – this time next year.

Vera Brittain

1916 [the Russian Front]

We were sitting quietly in our common-room when a knock came on the door. An officer appeared. 'Ah! here you are!' he ejaculated, 'I have some news for you! Grigory Rasputin[1] has been murdered.' We were all looking at him agape with curiosity and suspense, and not a word

[1] Monk well known for his dissolute manner of living and believed to have had great influence over the Russian Imperial family and especially over the Tzarina, Alexandra.

was spoken. 'Yes,' he said slowly, 'strange as it may sound, it is true. We received the news from a reliable source this afternoon.' In the buzz of conversation which followed, question after question was asked; everyone was eager to hear every available detail of such an amazing crime. We heard that the monk had been missing for several days, but his disappearance had been hushed up; nevertheless, it was known that the Secret Police, together with Rasputin's friends and the Court Officials who had openly supported him, had been searching for him high and low. Now his body had been discovered, half-embedded in ice in the River Neva. The newspapers referred to the 'mysterious crime' in guarded terms; they dared not do otherwise; and the names of the conspirators – even that of Rasputin himself – had not been mentioned. 'Have you any idea who the murderers might be?' someone asked. Our friend hesitated and then replied: 'We all have our suspicions, but it would not be right to brand a couple of patriotic men as murderers until we have proof. One thing we do know – the world is well rid of this treacherous man, who was doing all in his power to bring about the downfall of Russia and to sell his country to the enemy.'

Florence Farmborough

1939 [London]
I just hope 1940 turns out to be a bit more exciting than 1939.

Joan Wyndham

1939 [Princetown]
Listened to all kinds of things on the radio and read more on India. – Bitter cold. – More on Hitler's New Year's message: it will be essential to dismantle the sovereign states, and England's long-standing threat to the world must come to an end . . . 'The new world, socialistic.' The wretch, the wretch.

Thomas Mann

1939 [Germany]
Tonight we're going to have dinner in the Vier Jahreszeiten Cellar. I wonder what 1940 will be like. Hugo said that Hitler thinks it's more important for actors to entertain than go into the army. I was surprised but it is good sense if you think about it.

Elisabeth von Stahlenberg

1939 [Rome]

Mussolini is still suffering from the usual recurrent waves of pro-Germanism. Now he would like to send Hitler some advice (his previous advice made no impression), informing him that Italy is continuing to arm. But what are we preparing for? The war at the side of Germany must not be undertaken and never will be undertaken. It would be a crime and the height of folly! As for war against Germany, for the moment I do not see any reason for it. In any case, if necessary I acquiesce in war against Germany but not in her company. This is my point of view. Mussolini's point of view is exactly the opposite. He would never have war against Germany, and, when we are ready, he would fight on the side of Germany against the democracies, who, in my opinion, are the only countries with which one can deal seriously and honestly.

Count Ciano

1940 [Surrey]

Said a neighbour's wife to him, in her flat, toneless drawl, in reference to the bombed-out area in York Road, Wandsworth, which we passed in his car on our way up to town together, 'I once thought it was nice to have houses all in a row, to save trailing about collecting rents, but when so many can be destroyed by one bomb, it isn't so good.' I was shocked by her outlook, and a further shock awaited me later when she remarked that it were better that the National Gallery had been bombed instead of Hampton Showrooms, as the destruction of all their beautiful furniture almost made her cry. And again, what did the wrecking of London's Guildhall matter? After all, it was an old building. Her chief regret at the end of the day's town shopping was the neglect, through her own indecision, of a bargain offer of a large lampshade, going cheap from a partly wrecked store, 'Oh, it was marvellous!'

Said her husband, 'You already have a good one in use at home, why want another?'

Walter Musto

1941 [Kent]

We stay up late listening to the wireless and hearing Maisky,[1] Wellington Koo[2] and John Winant[3] exchanging polite messages. Then there is a

[1] Ivan Maisky, Soviet ambassador in London.
[2] Chinese ambassador in London.
[3] American ambassador in London.

Scottish service, in the middle of which Big Ben strikes and 1941 is finished. Not a year on which I shall look back with any pleasure. I shall say no more about it than that. It has been a sad and horrible year.

Harold Nicolson

1941 [POW camp, Germany]

The day has been rather uneventful as far as I am concerned, tho' the Scotsmen are making as much of it as they can. Tonight they start their celebrations at 9.00 and continue till after midnight. Special permission has been granted by the Kommandant for lights out to be put back till 1.00.

A new order came round today saying that no one will be allowed out to the latrines after 10.45 p.m. – back to the delights of the thunder box!

I found an old stick of plug tobacco in a box tonight. This will last me tomorrow, and will see the New Year in – and, today brought me my 500th letter.

Well, let 1941 go to hell. It has certainly been eventful for us. Poland and this place have taken 6 months of it – an incredible thought. I say I'll be home in 1942. Is that absurd optimism? Yes, I suppose it is. 1941 – TAKE A RUNNING JUMP AT YOURSELF.

Captain John Mansel

1942 [London]

I go down to the House to fire-watch. I sit in the map-room feeling pretty glum. I hear Big Ben strike out the old year. There are distant shouts of *Auld Lang Syne*, sung with an American accent. Then the snoring in my dormitory resumes its sway.

Harold Nicolson

1943 [Tuscany]

Return from two days in Florence. On the surface it is quieter than a few weeks ago. The Fascist SS are less active, and their leader, whose singularly inappropriate name is Carità,[1] has been removed. During his rule, however, the number of arrests, followed by torture, was sufficiently large. Among his victims was a little hairdresser (of pro-Allied

---

[1] It means charity, love, compassion.

sympathies) whose shop was frequented by some ladies who had helped British prisoners, or merely chattered about them. He was tortured to supply a list of their names, but remained silent – and was finally taken to the prison of Le Murate in such a condition that the Government refused to take him in, and sent him off to the hospital instead.

The rounding-up of the Jews appears now to be completed – though no doubt many unfortunate women and children are still hidden. The Archbishop of Florence, Cardinal della Costa, has taken a courageous stand. When some of his nuns were arrested, in consequence of having given shelter to some Jewish women in their convent, the Cardinal, putting on his full panoply, went straight to the German Command. 'I have come to you,' he said, 'because I believe you, as soldiers, to be people who recognize authority and hierarchy – and who do not make subordinates responsible for merely carrying out orders. The order to give shelter to those unfortunate Jewish women was given by me: therefore I request you to free the nuns, who have merely carried out orders, and to arrest me in their stead.' The German immediately gave orders for the nuns to be freed, but permitted himself to state his surprise that such a man like the Cardinal should take under his protection such people as the Jews, the scum of Europe, responsible for all the evils of the present day. The Cardinal did not enter upon the controversy. 'I look upon them,' he said, 'merely as persecuted human beings; as such it is my Christian duty to help and defend them. One day,' he gave himself the pleasure of adding, 'perhaps not far off, *you* will be persecuted: and then I shall defend you!'

Iris Origo

1943 [London]

Having dined with Geoffrey[1] I walked home and went early to bed. I read, but the Battersea church bells started pealing across the river, contrary as I thought to the regulations. It was more than I could bear, so I went downstairs to put cotton wool in my ears. Still I heard them. At midnight I stuffed my fingers into my ears in order not to listen to the striking of the little tortoise-shell and silver clock at my bedside. The loneliness of this moment, wholly artificial though it be, harrows me. When it had passed I went on reading. At 12.30 the telephone rang. I threw the sheets back and leapt out of bed. Book, paper and

---

[1] Geoffrey Houghton-Brown, connoisseur and old friend of JLM.

pencil clattered to the floor. It must, I thought, be the voice I longed for. It would be contrite, solicitous, loving. No such thing. It was that bore Dr Dietmar[1] to wish me a Happy New Year, as though 1944 could augur anything but the direst misery of our lives. Only a German could be so obtuse. I was not very friendly, and pretended that he had woken me up.

James Lees-Milne

---

[1] Dr Dietmar, a young secondary-school teacher who had been in an internment camp but had been recently freed, due to the intervention of Harold Nicolson.

Biographies

Note: where birth and death dates are unknown we have used *fl.* to indicate when the extracts were written.

AGATE, JAMES EVERSHED (1877–1947) English drama critic, born in Lancashire, the son of a cotton manufacturer's agent. Through the two decades separated by the World Wars he was the liveliest and most influential theatre critic in London. From 1923 until his death he contributed to the *Sunday Times*. But while his journalism was voluminous it paled in comparison with the detailed diary of his life which he started in 1932. He was not an entirely attractive man. According to Arnold Bennett he was rather coarse-looking with a reputation for sexual perversity. Capable of meanness and malice he was probably right when he said of himself: 'His enemies will miss him.'

ALANBROOKE, FIELD MARSHAL LORD (1883–1963) British Chief of the Imperial General Staff (CIGS) from December 1941 to January 1946. He attended Woolwich Military Academy, after which he joined the Royal Artillery and during the First World War rose from lieutenant to lieutenant-colonel. Throughout the Second World War he had a particularly close relationship with Churchill. His diary, which he addressed to his second wife, was written initially out of love and loneliness. When not concerned with military matters, he was a keen ornithologist.

ALLAIRE, ANTHONY (1755–1839) Lieutenant on the American side during the War of Independence. He was born in New Rochelle, New York. He sailed for Georgia at the end of 1779 and saw action during the Charleston campaign. He was charged with the murder of a fellow Loyalist officer during a quarrel but was acquitted at court martial. After the war, he emigrated to Canada and settled in New Brunswick.

ANDRÉ, JOHN (1750–80) The son of a Swiss merchant, born in London. He purchased a commission in the British army in 1771. He was captured by Americans at St Johns, near Montreal, in 1775 and exchanged at the end of the following year. He was captured by New York militia in September 1780 while attempting to return to British lines in civilian disguise, condemned as a spy and hanged.

ANON (*fl.* 1864) A private in the 6th United States Colored Infantry, who described himself as 'Bought and Sold'.

ARDIZZONE, EDWARD JEFFREY IRVING (1900–79) British illustrator and author, born in Vietnam to an Italian father and a Scottish mother. After taking evening classes at the Westminster School of Art, he worked as a freelance artist. His first book for children, *Little Tom and the Brave Sea Captain*, published in 1936, made his name. In total, he illustrated more than 170 books. He became a war artist in February 1940 when a 2nd Lieutenant in an anti-aircraft battery in Clapham Common, and was posted to France and Egypt. The start of his diary coincided with the invasion of Sicily in the summer of 1943.

ASQUITH, LADY CYNTHIA (1887–1960) The daughter of the 11th earl of Wemyss, she was the second wife of Herbert Asquith, who was Prime Minister from 1908 to 1916. From 1918 to 1937 she was private secretary to J.M. Barrie, most of whose fortune she inherited. She knew many writers and artists and was herself an author of note. Her works include three volumes of autobiography, anthologies of ghost and children's stories, novels and biographies. Her *Diaries 1915–18*, published posthumously in 1967, are remarkable for the death toll of the 'golden generation'.

BANGS, ISAAC (1752–80) Born in Harwich, Massachusetts, he graduated from Harvard in 1771, after which he practised medicine. In 1776, he joined the Massachusetts militia regiment as a 2nd Lieutenant and served in the siege of Boston. In 1779, he joined the crew of the frigate *Boston* as doctor's mate.

BARBELLION, W.N.P. (BRUCE FREDERICK CUMMINGS) (1889–1919) English diarist and biologist, born in Barnstaple in the West Country, where his father was a newspaper reporter. Leaving school at sixteen, he joined his father as an apprentice but quickly abandoned journalism to work at the Marine Laboratory, Plymouth. In 1912, he joined the staff of the Natural History Museum in London. A sickly child, he grew increasingly ill and in early manhood learned he was doomed to an incurable and progressive paralysis. He kept a diary, the candid, introspective and moving testimony of a self-styled 'disappointed man', from the age of thirteen to his death.

BEATON, SIR CECIL (1904–80) English photographer and designer, born in London and educated at Harrow and Cambridge. His love of photography was spurred after spotting a photograph of Lily Elsie (the 'Merry Widow') lying on his mother's bed. He was soon dressing up his two younger sisters as models. His breakthrough came when he met Stephen Tennant, who paved his way into glamorous society. As well as photographing various members of the Royal Family and stars such as Greta Garbo, Katherine Hepburn and Mick Jagger, he designed sets for theatre, opera, ballet and film. Once described as 'that rare creature, a literate photographer', his diaries are waspish, befitting a man dubbed by Jean Cocteau 'Malice in Wonderland'.

BENN, (ANTHONY WEDGWOOD) TONY (1925–   ) British politician, the son of Viscount Stansgate. A Labour MP from 1950 to 1960, he was debarred from the House of Commons on succeeding to his father's title. On renouncing it in 1963, he was re-elected to Parliament the same year. An outspoken and eloquent maverick on the left wing of the Labour Party, he nevertheless held various senior Cabinet and party posts. He remained an MP until 2001. His diaries, which he dictates into a tape recorder, run from 1940 to the present day. He was named Pipe Smoker of the Year in 1992, arguing in his acceptance speech that 'pipe smoking stopped you going to war'.

BENNETT, ALAN (1934–   ) English playwright and actor, born in Leeds, Yorkshire, where his father was a butcher. He first appeared on stage in *Beyond the Fringe* at the Edinburgh Festival. His stage plays include *Forty Years On, Habeas Corpus, The Old Country, Enjoy, Kafka's Dick* and *The Madness of George III*. He has also written extensively for television. He has kept a 'sporadic' diary since the early 1970s and in *Writing Home,* a miscellaneous collection of work, he published excerpts from 1980 to 1990, thus encompassing the Falklands War.

BENNETT, (ENOCH) ARNOLD (1867–1931) English novelist, playwright and critic born in Staffordshire, the son of a solicitor. Destined for the law, he failed his exams and departed for London where he soon began to earn a living as a journalist and writer. His novels include *Anna of the Five Towns*, *The Old Wives' Tale* and the Clayhanger series. At one time he was the most successful English writer, in print and on the stage. His journal, begun in 1896, was modelled partly on that of the Goncourt brothers, and was kept daily, running originally to a million words. During the First World War he was invited by Lord Beaverbrook, then Director of the Ministry for Information, to become head of the section devoted to propaganda in France.

BERENSON, BERNARD (1865–1959) Art critic and connoisseur, born in Lithuania. He went to Boston at the age of ten and graduated from Harvard in 1887. In 1900, he acquired I Tatti, at Settignano near Florence, which he transformed into a cultural shrine and bequeathed to Harvard University. He was a scholar pre-eminent in Italian art and a discriminating collector. He kept a daily diary for much of his life, including the duration of the Second World War, which he spent mostly in Italy.

BIDDLE, GEORGE (1885–1973) American sculptor, painter and graphic artist. Born in Philadelphia, he studied at Groton and Harvard. He helped organise the Public Works of Art Project 1933–34 with support from Franklin and Eleanor Roosevelt, and was an active participant in the first American Artists Congress. He was appointed to the influential Fine Arts Commission by President Truman. He organised and chaired the War Department Art Advisory Committee and took charge of the Art Unit covering the North African front and kept a diary of his time there. His works hang in many galleries in America and Europe.

BLUNT, WILFRID SCAWEN (1840–1922) British traveller, politician and poet, noted Arabist and anti-imperialist, who, in 1869, married Annabella King-Noel, Byron's granddaughter. In 1872, he inherited Crabbet Park, Sussex. With his wife, he penetrated the mysterious territory of Nedj. His first collection of poetry, *Sonnets and Songs of Proteus*, published in 1875, contains passionate addresses to women in keeping with his Byronesque inclinations. A renowned conversationalist and welcoming host, his friends included William Morris and Lady Gregory. He was later championed by T.S. Eliot and Ezra Pound.

BONHAM CARTER, VIOLET (1887–1969) The only daughter, from his first marriage, of Prime Minister Herbert Asquith, whom she worshipped. She was a close friend of Winston Churchill – whom she described as 'that brilliant politician who eludes all categories and defies classification' – and bitter opponent of Lloyd George. During the Second World War she was an air-raid warden. Although a career in politics seemed a distinct possibility, she devoted herself almost exclusively to her private life until the mid-1930s, after the Nazis rose to prominence, when she joined an inter-party and non-party group to fight appeasement. Her diaries, which run from the beginning of 1914 to the end of 1945, vividly capture one of the most exciting epochs in British history.

BRITTAIN, VERA MARY (1837–1970) The daughter of a wealthy manufacturer, she was brought up in the north of England and educated at Oxford University. During the First World War she served as a nurse. Grieving for her fiancé, Roland Leighton, who was killed in France at the end of 1915, she wrote *Testament of Youth*, a moving account of her childhood and desire for education. Her diary, comprising more than 250,000 words, was maintained from 1913 to 1917. *Wartime Chronicle: Vera Brittain's Diary 1939–1945*, recorded her experiences during the Second World War.

BRITTEN, SERGEANT S.V. (*fl.* 1915) As a member of the Canadian Division at Ypres, Britten was witness to the first use of poison gas in the First World War.

BRUCKSHAW, HORACE (*fl.* 1915) A private in the Royal Marine Light Infantry, he volunteered in August 1914. His diary details some of his experiences at Gallipoli, Churchill's doomed attempt to force open the Dardanelles in the Mediterranean, held by Germany's ally, Turkey. He was later transferred to the Western Front. He was killed during the battle of Arleux in 1917.

BUERSTATTE, FREDERICK C. (*fl.* 1864) A private in the 26th regiment Wisconsin Volunteers. Not yet eighteen, he enlisted in the Union Army in February 1864, and kept a diary until his discharge in October 1865. The extracts, from enlistment to the winter of 1864, include his participation in General William T. Sherman's historic march on Georgia, the so-called 'March to the Sea'.

BUTTS, MARY (1890–1937) British feminist writer born in Dorset into an upper-middle-class family. She led an unconventional life and knew many of the most famous figures in early twentieth-century literature, music and art, including T.S. Eliot, Virginia Woolf, James Joyce and Man Ray. Aleister Crowley initiated her into the world of magic. Butts's journal runs from 1916 till towards the end of what she called her 'sapphic life', February 1937, a month before she died of peritonitis, a perforated duodenal ulcer and diabetes.

BYRON, GEORGE GORDON, SIXTH BARON (1788–1824) The son of 'Mad Jack' Byron (1756–91), he was born in London with a club foot. His hysterical mother took him to Aberdeen where he was abused by a nurse. At the age of ten, he became Lord Byron and he and his mother moved south where he continued his education at Harrow. A handsome young man, he had a dissipated time at Cambridge but managed to publish his first collection of poems in 1807. He took up his seat in the House of Lords in 1809 and began to travel extensively. *Childe Harold* was published in 1811 and Byron 'woke up to find himself famous'. He left England in 1816 on the collapse of his marriage and never returned, ceaselessly writing, pursuing amorous adventures, living riotously, and engaging in political causes, notably in Greece where he predicted, accurately, that he would die. He was an inveterate writer of letters and journals, many of which were intended for public consumption.

CADOGAN, SIR ALEXANDER GEORGE MONTAGU (1884–1968) The younger son of the 5th Earl Cadogan, he was educated at Eton and Balliol and entered the Diplomatic Service in 1908. He had a distinguished career in the public service, including postings to Peking and the United Nations and was Chairman of the Governors of the BBC 1952–57. As adviser to three Foreign Secretaries, he had privileged access to the centre of power. His diaries cover the years 1938–45, when he was head of the Foreign Office.

CARTER, LANDON (1710–78) The son of a wealthy Virginian landowner, he was educated in England. On the death of his father in 1732, he inherited several plantations. He served as a justice of the peace, 1734–78, and in the Virginia assembly, 1752–68. He built a large mansion at Sabine hall, his plantation in Richmond County. He opposed the Stamp Act and wrote numerous newspaper articles in defence of American rights. He kept a diary from 1752 to 1778, including the first three years of the American War of Independence.

CHANNON, SIR HENRY (1897–1958) Invariably known as 'Chips', he was an American, Chicagoan born. He arrived in Europe in 1918, oozing charm, ability and social ambition. He married Lady Honor Guinness, became a member of parliament and served in the Foreign Office, 1938–41. From the late 1920s he was ubiquitous in London salons, his circle including King Edward VIII, the Duke and Duchess of Windsor and Lady Cunard. His diary, which spans 1934 to 1958, is a model of indiscretion.

CIANO, COUNT GALEAZZO (1904–43) Italian Fascist politician, born in Livorno, the son of a First World War hero. He married Mussolini's daughter Edda and ran the Fascist propaganda office before becoming Foreign Minister in 1936, from which post he was sacked in 1943, then tried and executed on his father-in-law's orders. Given to crass behaviour – at the coronation of Pius XII in 1939 he caused a scandal when he strutted down the nave of St Peter's in Rome giving the Fascist salute and waving to the crowd – Hitler referred to him as 'that disgusting boy'. In some quarters, however, he was reckoned to have a keener political judgement than Mussolini.

CLARK, ALAN (1928–99) The eldest son of Kenneth Clark, the aesthete and author of *Civilization*. He was Conservative MP for Plymouth (Sutton) from 1974–92, Minister of Trade 1986–92, Minister of State, Minister of Defence, 1989–92, and Conservative MP for Kensington and Chelsea from 1997 to his death. Though he wrote three novels, he made his reputation as a military historian. His diaries, published in three volumes, which start in 1972, make a virtue of indiscretion, relating with candour his lustful longings and politically incorrect views. He is regarded alternatively as a cad and a character. When he learned of the invasion of the Falkland Islands by Argentina his reaction, relayed to his long-suffering wife, Jane, was typically hyperbolic: 'It's all over,' he said. 'We're a Third World country, no good for anything.'

CLARK, REVEREND ANDREW (1856–1922) English vicar with a village parish in Essex, born near Dollar in Clackmannanshire, the son of a farm labourer. When he was fifteen he went to St Andrews University and from there to Oxford, where he took a double-first in Greats. In 1886 he married Mary Pearson Walker, a daughter of the Provost of St Andrews. When news of Germany's declaration of war against Russia reached England, he began to keep a diary. He described the contrasts between his peaceful village and the battle-fields of Europe, between the quiet, slow, ordered life of rural England and the horrors of twentieth-century warfare. By the end of 1914 he had eight volumes; by the time of the ceasefire on 11 November 1918 he was on his eighty-fourth volume. In March 1915, he wrote to the Bodleian Library, saying he was keeping 'an extraordinary

"War Diary" – but very voluminous'. Throughout his life he retained a fervent interest in history.

CLARK, OSSIE (1942–96) Fashion designer, born in Liverpool, the youngest of six children. Academically undistinguished, he had a flair for art and entered Manchester Regional Art College in 1958 at the age of 16. He then moved to London and the Royal College of Art. Between 1965 and 1974 he was one of the leading fashion designers, fêted by celebrities and crowned the 'King of the King's Road'. Homosexual, he was sexually promiscuous, addicted to drugs and drink, and given to violence. His diaries begin in 1974 and continue until the day before he died, murdered by his lover, Diego Cogolato.

COLEMAN, THOMAS W. (*fl.* 1876) Private in the 7th US Cavalry, who fought at Little Big Horn in June 1876, serving under Captain McDougall, in 'B' Company. He wrote his account of the battle in a small, leather-bound notebook which contained a letter to his sister, dated 26 October 1876, suggesting that he transcribed a copy of his battlefield diary three months after the event.

COLVILLE, SIR JOHN (RUPERT) (1915–87) British diplomat and author, born in London. He was educated at West Downs School, Harrow, and Trinity College, Cambridge. In 1937, he joined the Diplomatic Service and within two years was seconded to Downing Street as Private Secretary to Neville Chamberlain. After the outbreak of the Second World War, however, he was determined to enter the armed forces and in 1941 joined the Royal Air Force Volunteer Reserve. In spite of Churchill's best efforts to woo him back to Westminster, he remained with the air force until the end of 1943, when he was allowed to rejoin his unit for the invasion of France. He returned to Downing Street in August 1944. His diaries, published in two volumes titled *The Fringes of Power*, are peppered with affectionate anecdotes about Churchill among many others.

COPPOLA, ELEANOR (1936–) In 1976 Eleanor Coppola, her film director husband Francis and their three children left California for the Philippines, where Coppola's film about the Vietnam War, *Apocalypse Now*, was to be filmed. As the months stretched into years, her diary became an extraordinary record not only of the making of a movie but of the emotional and physical price exacted from all who participated in it.

CORMANY, SAMUEL (*fl.* 1863) A member of the 2nd Cavalry Brigade, 2nd Division, Union Army.

COUGLIN, SEAN T. (1969–) A US marine, he graduated from the US Naval Academy in Annapolis, Maryland, and received his commission as a 2nd Lieutenant in the US Marine Corps in May 1987. Throughout the first Gulf War, he worked with a Special Staff officer and was thus in a privileged position to observe the campaign. For services rendered during the conflict in Saudi Arabia, Couglin received the Kuwaiti Campaign Medal with three bronze stars, an Overseas Development Medal, the Kuwaiti Defense Medal, and a Navy Achievement Medal. He received his Master of Fine Arts Degree from the University of California in LA in 1995 and is now a film director working in Santa Barbara, California.

COWARD, NOËL (1899–1973) Born in Middlesex the son of a piano salesman, he was encouraged by his mother to make a career of the theatre. Renowned for his comic talent, he wrote a plethora of popular plays, including *Hay Fever*, *Private Lives* and *Blithe Spirit*. He also wrote the screenplay of the hit wartime film, *Brief Encounter*. In the 1960s, he enjoyed a new lease of life as a cabaret artiste. His diaries, which span 1941 to 1969, give a master-class in name-dropping.

CRESSWELL, NICHOLAS (1750–1804) The son of a landowner and sheep farmer, born in Derbyshire, England. He arrived in Virginia in 1774 intending to buy western land. In March 1775, he wrote letters condemning American resistance to British authority that were intercepted and given to the Alexandria Committee of Safety. He was threatened with imprisonment in October 1775 but was released when a friend posted bond. He went to New York City in early September 1776 but was unable to reach British forces. He returned to Virginia where he remained at liberty on parole. Along with a Scottish friend, he seized a boat at pistol point in May 1777 and escaped to a British warship in Chesapeake Bay. He reached England in August 1777 and returned to Derbyshire.

CROCKETT, DAVY (1786–1836) American frontiersman, soldier and politician, known as 'the King of the Wild Frontier'. Though he was from Tennessee, he fought and died at the Alamo defending the cause of Texan independence. His diary, the authenticity of which has been questioned by some, is a record of that much-mythologised event. In the film *The Alamo*, Crockett was played by

John Wayne, an inspired piece of casting. Crockett gave his name to the M-388 'nuclear bazooka', an 'inherently destabilising' weapon which was employed by the US army in the 1960s.

CURRY, FRANK (*fl.* 1939) A member of the Royal Canadian Navy during the Second World War. He was an Asdic (Allied Submarine Detection Investigation Committee, an Anglo-French organisation which used a system of detecting submarines by sound) operator on board a corvette escorting convoys across the Atlantic.

DENNY, EBENEZER (1761–1822) Born in Carlisle, Pennsylvania, he was commissioned as ensign in the Pennsylvania Continental regiment in 1781. He fought at Green Spring, July 6, and at the siege of Yorktown. After the war, he remained in the army and served in the Northwest Territory. He survived the defeat of the St Clair expedition in November 1791, and carried news of the disaster to President Washington. He resigned from the army in 1794 and settled near Pittsburgh. He was elected the first mayor of Pittsburgh in 1816.

DESAGNEAUX, HENRI (*fl.* 1916) French infantryman during the First World War. In 1916, he took part in the battle of Verdun, which in terms of casualties and suffering has been described as 'one of the most terrible battles of history'. His diary graphically describes what it was like to be there. There is no definitive number of casualties but each side lost more than 300,000 men, with more on the French side than the German. The determination of the French to halt the German advance was summed up by Marshal Pétain, who declared, 'Ils ne passeront pas' – They shall not pass.

DIGBY, WILLIAM (*fl.* 1777) An ensign in the British army, which he joined in 1770. He was promoted to lieutenant in 1773 and landed in Canada on 1 June 1776. He fought at Trois Rivieres on 8 June 1776, and served in the advance on Crown Point in October 1776. He spent the winter in Canada before moving south with the Burgoyne expedition in June 1777. With Burgoyne's army at Saratoga, he surrendered on 17 October 1777. In 1786 he retired from the army.

DUDENEY, MRS HENRY (1866–1945) An English writer of short stories and novels which brought her high praise. She was once described as 'a rival to Thomas Hardy'. She kept a diary from 1910 until her death, with only a short gap for the years 1914–15. Publication, however, was withheld for forty years, in deference to local sensibilities. Her pre-war diaries were written during her turbulent marriage and her affair with a married man. By the outbreak of the First World War, the Dudeneys had reconciled and were living in Lewes, but Mrs Dudeney also moved in other circles – she became a life-long friend of Sir Phillip Sassoon and as his guest mingled with more illustrious society in his London and country homes. Her war diaries record the difficulties of day-to-day living as well as her somewhat uneasy relationship with her husband, and after his death, the re-emergence of her former lover.

DUNLOP, E.E. (1907-93) Sir Edward Dunlop. Australian commanding officer and surgeon whose diaries record the harrowing conditions of life in Japanese POW camps in Java, and on the Burma–Thailand railway. A tall man, he was constantly stooping, which gave him a tired look, hence his nickname 'Weary'. Dunlop kept detailed records of camp life – the treatment of the men at the hands of their captors, how the wounded were looked after, the cholera epidemics, and the constant fear of the sick being drafted into the Japanese work parties. Dunlop himself suffered from several ailments, including malaria, dysentery and ulcers, but carried on regardless. When he and his men went on to work on the infamous Burma–Thailand railway his courage earned him the respect of thousands of fellow Australians. After the war he returned to civilian life but later he went back to southeast Asia to take up the post of Team Leader, Australian surgical team, caring for civilians during the Vietnam War. Back in Australia he had a distinguished career in medicine as well as being a national hero. In 1977 he was voted Australian of the Year.

ELLIS, EDWARD ROBB (1911–98) American journalist, born in Kewanee, Illinois. His newspaper career spanned nearly four decades but his extensive diary is his true legacy, a one-man history of twentieth-century America. It is listed in *The Guinness Book of Records* as the world's largest, comprising 42,000 pages and 21 million words. The cast of characters includes Mae West ogling Mr America, Eleanor Roosevelt and Greta Garbo, Paul Robeson, Grace Kelly and Al Jolson. Only about one per cent of the entire diary has been published, under the title *A Diary of a Century*.

EVELYN, JOHN (1620–1706) The second son of a wealthy Surrey landowner, he was always a man of substance, though not independently well off until 1699, when he inherited the family estate at Wotton. He went to Balliol College, Oxford, then read law before travelling extensively on the Continent. Throughout his long life he was an eye-witness to many epochal happenings, including the Restoration of Charles II, the Second Dutch War, the Plague and the Great Fire of London. His epitaph described this era as 'an age of extraordinary events and revelations'. In 1664 he published *Sylva, or a Discourse of Forrest Trees*, which was highly influential and made him a celebrity. Of his eight children, only one survived him. His immense *Diary* extends from 1620 in the reign of James I to 1706 in the reign of Queen Anne, a time of enormous transformation.

FAHEY, JAMES J. (1918–1991) An American sailor, he enlisted on 3 October 1942 and within four days he was on his way to his training at the Great Lakes. He served as a Seaman First Class on the USS *Montpelier*, on duty in the Pacific, and despite regulations to the contrary, he kept a diary, written on loose sheets of paper, for over three years. When his diary was published after the war it became a bestseller and Fahey donated all his earnings to the construction of a cathedral in southern India. At the dedication of the cathedral he was greeted by a crowd of over 100,000. A modest man, he drove a sanitation truck for a living, which he continued to do until he retired in 1979.

FARMBOROUGH, FLORENCE (1887–1978) English nurse who, in 1908, at the age of 21, went to work in Russia as a governess. When war broke out she joined the Red Cross and was sent to the Front. In 1917, when the Russian Revolution started, she was ordered to return to Moscow. A year later she came home via Siberia and the United States. Her diary, which she kept between 1914 and 1918, originally ran to some 400,000 words. She marvelled at 'how much a human being can endure without any outward sign of having broken up into pieces'.

FILIPOVIC, ZLATA (*b.*1980) A Bosnian refugee of mixed ethnic heritage. She began her diary when she was eleven years old, and continued to keep it as the war closed in. She records the loss of friends, the hardships and the effects of the war on her family. Her diary was published throughout Europe by UNICEF, and in 1993 Zlata and her parents were allowed to leave Sarajevo and relocate in France.

FITHIAN, PHILIP VICKERS (1747–76) Army chaplain, born in Greenwich, New Jersey. He graduated from the College of New Jersey (now Princeton) in 1772 and became a tutor to the children of wealthy Virginia planter Robert Carter. He was ordained as a

Presbyterian minister in 1775 and was appointed the following year as chaplain to the New Jersey militia serving with the Continental army. He died of dysentery in New York.

FRANK, ANNE (1929–45) Of German-Jewish stock, she was born in Frankfurt. She fled from the Nazis to Holland in 1933 with her family. After the Nazis invaded Holland she hid with her mother, father, sister and four others in a sealed-off back room – the Secret Annexe – in Amsterdam until they were betrayed in 1944. Her diary, the moving story of their concealment, was first published in Holland in 1947. She died while imprisoned at Bergen-Belsen concentration camp, three months short of her sixteenth birthday.

FREMANTLE, ARTHUR JAMES LYON (1835–1901) A British soldier who, in America as a tourist, 'spyglass slung over his shoulder, diary in his pocket', talked his way into the company of General Lee's Confederate forces at Gettysburg. On the second day of the battle, Southern officers were amazed to see the Englishman in their midst. Fremantle witnessed the battle, which he recorded in his diary, first published in London in 1863.

GIDE, ANDRÉ (1869–1951) French novelist and man-of-letters, born in Paris. A lonely only child whose father died when he was eleven, he was educated privately. Bisexual, he married his cousin in 1892. Key books include *The Immoralist*, *Strait is the Gate* and *The Counterfeiters*. He wrote over fifty books, including an autobiography and witty, candid and compelling diaries which run from 1889 to 1949. He was awarded the Nobel Prize for Literature in 1947.

GILLAM, JOHN (1883–1965) The seventh of eight children, he was born in Brighton and was raised after the early deaths of his parents by his sisters, who doted on him. He joined Duckhams, a chemical manufacturer in 1900 – the same year he joined the Honourable Artillery Company – and rose to become manager. On 4 August 1914, the day Britain declared war on Germany, he returned to London, re-enlisted in the HAC and was posted to their Reserve Battery. He served in Gallipoli with the 29th Divisional Train. His Gallipoli diary was first published in 1918. *The Times'* reviewer wrote, 'who were not there, and who care to know what it was really like, could do no better than read this unaffected and graphic diary'. After the war he married a sales assistant who sold him a toothbrush in Gamages department store.

GILLESPIE, ANDREW (*fl.* 1991) After attending the Royal Military Academy, Sandhurst, he received his commission in the Royal Artillery in 1974. A graduate of the Army Command and Staff College and Cranfield University, he saw service in Germany, Northern Ireland, the Middle and Far East, and also served with the UN in Cyprus and Korea. He commanded O Battery (The Rocket Troop), 2nd Field Regiment Royal Artillery in the 1991 Gulf War, for which he was awarded Commander 4 Armoured Brigade's Commendation for Outstanding Service. His diary records the build-up and training leading up to the war and its immediate aftermath.

GOEBBELS, PAUL JOSEF (1897–1945) German Nazi politician, the son of a Rhenish factory foreman. He was born with a deformed foot and was therefore able to avoid military service. Through scholarships he attended eight universities. Unemployed and lacking direction, he became an enthusiastic supporter of Hitler and edited the Nazi newspaper *Völkische Freiheit*. Ultimately he was head of the ministry of propaganda and popular enlightenment. Vain, rabidly antisemitic, a womaniser and ruthlessly ambitious, he retained Hitler's confidence to the end. A day after the Führer committed suicide, Goebbels followed him. He had his children killed first, after which he commanded an orderly to shoot him and his wife. His diaries reflect his personality.

GONCOURT, EDMUND DE (1822–96) and JULES DE (1830–70) French authors, brothers, who collaborated closely. Originally artists, they turned to the novel, being primarily interested in manners. Their greatest novel is *Madame Gervaisais* but they are best remembered for the Prix Goncourt, France's most prestigious literary award, and their journal, a lively, irreverent record of forty-five years of their lives, beginning on the day of Napoleon III's coup d'état in 1851 and ending with Edmund's death in 1896. Flaubert, Zola, Baudelaire, Rodin, Degas and George Sand are just a few of the many famous people who swam into their orbit.

GOODBAR, MONTAGUE S. (d.1917) A private in the 4th Battalion Cameron Highlanders, he was wounded at the battle of Neuve Chapelle but recovered and later transferred to the Royal Flying Corps. He was killed in action in 1917.

GORDON, MAJOR GENERAL CHARLES GEORGE (1833–85) English soldier, born in Woolwich, he served during the Crimean War. He later became known as 'Chinese Gordon' when he took command of a Chinese force from 1863–64 and fought numerous actions against the Taipings, taking many walled towns and ultimately crushing a formidable rebellion. A tumultuous career ended in Khartoum, where help arrived too late to relieve the prolonged siege of the city. After his murder on the steps of the governor's palace, the uproar in Britain nearly brought down the government. A complex character, he was the subject of a debunking biographical essay by Lytton Strachey, included in *Eminent Victorians*.

GRENFELL, JOYCE (1910–75) English actress famed for her comic monologues, born in London. She was one of the best-loved stage performers of her day. She made her debut in *The Little Revue* in 1939. She entertained the troops throughout the war as part of the Entertainments National Services Association (ENSA), a period lovingly recreated in her journals. Her autobiography, *Joyce Grenfell Requests the Pleasure*, appeared in 1976.

GUEVARA, ERNESTO (1928–67) Argentine-born Cuban revolutionary, known as Ché. He was the archetypal guerrilla warrior. In 1965 he left Cuba and spent several months in the Congo in Africa, returning to Cuba secretly in July 1966. In November 1966 he arrived in Bolivia where he established a guerrilla detachment fighting that country's military dictatorship. An athlete as well as a scholar, he was appalled by the poverty he witnessed in Latin America and elsewhere. Following several months of skirmishes with the Bolivian army, he was captured on 8 October 1967, and executed the following day. A year later he was adopted by revolting students keen to emulate his sexual promiscuity and ill-disciplined spontaneity, inspired by his rebellious idealism.

HASSELL, ULRICH VON (1881–1944) German diplomat who was involved in plots to assassinate Hitler. He served in the German army during World War I but was wounded at the Marne and returned to the Diplomatic Service. By 1919 he was unhappy with the political situation in Germany but remained in the Service, working overseas in the Foreign Office. However, his opposition to the Anti-Comintern Pact in 1937 cost him his post and he returned to Germany where he worked for an organisation in Berlin. His job allowed him to travel abroad, lecturing and studying the economic situation in Europe, and it was during this time that he became increasingly involved in schemes to get rid of Hitler. His diaries of these times were carefully written; names and places, for example, were changed to ensure secrecy. He was arrested in 1944 for his involvement in the failed attempt on Hitler's life on July 16. He was sent to Ravensbrück camp, where he was hanged.

HENDRY, JAMES FINDLAY (1912–86) Scottish poet and novelist, born in Glasgow. He is perhaps best remembered for his novel *Fernie Brae*, based on memories of his childhood spent in the west of Scotland. During World War II he served in the Intelligence Corps. He later worked as translator for agencies connected with the United Nations.

HEPPENSTALL, RAYNER (1911–81) English writer, born in Huddersfield, Yorkshire. For many years he was a producer for the BBC. His circle of friends included George Orwell, who once impressed Heppenstall by sending back a bottle of red wine in restaurant because it was over-chilled. He wrote several novels, the last of which was *The Pier*, published post-humously, a murder story set in a small seaside town.

HERZBERG, ABEL J. (1893–1989) Born in Amsterdam, he grew up in a non-orthodox but religious home. His father was a broker in uncut diamonds. During the First World War he enrolled as a volunteer in the Dutch army though he did not have Dutch nationality. He qualified as a lawyer and played a prominent role in the Dutch Jewish community. After the occupation of Holland in 1940, Herzberg, his wife and three children were forced to go into hiding, but later returned to Amsterdam where they were arrested. In January 1944 they were taken to Bergen-Belsen but amazingly the whole family survived. His diary was written during their time in the concentration camp. After the war, he wrote many books, most of them on the theme of the persecution of the Jews.

HILLESUM, ETTY (1914–43) The daughter of a teacher, she was born in Holland, and studied law before turning to psychology. Julius Spier, a psychochirologist, was a formative influence and she became, in turn, his assistant, lover and intellectual equal. She started keeping a diary when she was 27, at a time when Holland was increasingly under the sway of German terror. She reached Auschwitz on 10 September 1943, the very day her parents were gassed. Her death was reported by the Red Cross just two months later.

HITCHCOCK, ETHAN ALLEN (1798–1870) An American soldier, one of the most influential members of Abraham Lincoln's war councils, described by one historian as 'the most intelligent officer in the highest ranks of the army'. In 1847, he was one of the principal architects of the audacious capture of Mexico City. In 1862, told he could have any position he wished, he chose to remain in Washington as military adviser to Lincoln. He was never happier than among his books.

HOLDEN, INEZ (1904–74) British novelist and journalist, a familiar figure among the London *demi monde* between the two wars. Her acquaintances included Evelyn Waugh, H.G. Wells, in whose garage she lived for a while, George Orwell, to whom she was devoted, and Anthony Powell, who described her as 'an unusual person', 'torrential talker', 'accomplished mimic' and 'fantastical' gossip. Her passionate hatred of the Communist Party, speculated Powell, suggested close knowledge of its methods. Her books include *Born Old; Died Young* and *It Was Different at the Time*, her diary of the Second World War.

INBER, VERA (1890–1972) Soviet writer who published her first collection of poems, *Objective and the Way*, in 1923. Her poem 'Five Nights and Days' written in memory of Lenin, brought her wide recognition. After travelling extensively around the country in the 1930s, she wrote a number of essays and stories describing the changes occurring in the young Soviet republics of Central Asia. She lived almost three years in Leningrad at the time of the siege during World War II and wrote of the blockaded city's heroism in her diary *Almost Three Years*.

IRAQI SOLDIER (ANONYMOUS) (*fl.* 1991) The soldier's diary begins at the commencement of the air war and concludes just before the liberation of Kuwait. The notebook in which the soldier wrote his thoughts was found in a ditch by the wires of the marine mines in Amghara, south of Kuwait City. It is not known if the soldier ever returned home. Though he never revealed his name we know that he was from Baghdad.

ISHERWOOD, CHRISTOPHER (1904–86) Born in Cheshire, England, he was a friend from boyhood of W.H. Auden, with whom he collaborated on several works. Educated at public school and Cambridge, he was much influenced by his experience of living in Berlin in 1929–31. His first novel, *All The Conspirators*, was published in 1928 but it pales in comparison to *Mr Norris Changes Trains* (1935) and *Goodbye To Berlin* (1939), both of which give a vivid portrait of

Germany during the rise of Nazism. The latter was dramatised in 1951 by John van Druten as *I am a Camera* and was later turned into the stage and film musical *Cabaret*. *Christopher and his Kind* (1977) is a frank account of his homosexual adventures as a young man. In 1939, he went with Auden to America, and became an American citizen in 1946.

JOHNSON, CLAUDIA ALTA TAYLOR (LADY BIRD) (1912–) The wife of Lyndon Baines Johnson, the 36th president of the United States, following the assassination of President Kennedy. Johnson was President from 1963 to 1968, when he retired from politics. His period in office co-incided with the war in Vietnam. He died in 1973. Lady Bird, so named because of her pretty petiteness, married LBJ in 1934 after a whirlwind romance. As First Lady, she became known for her work to improve the appearance of America, which became known as her 'beautification'. An astute businesswoman and sophisticated and charming hostess, she was the author of *A White House Diary*, of which she said: 'I was keenly aware that I had a unique opportunity, a front row seat, on an unfolding story, and nobody else was going to see it from quite the vantage point that I saw it.'

JUNKIN, BINGHAM FINDLEY (*fl.* 1864) Union army soldier, mustered at North Liberty, Pennsylvania, on 8 March 1864. In June 1865, he was wounded, his thigh shattered by gunshot. He was honourably discharged from service on 8 July 1865.

KAFKA, FRANZ (1883–1924) German-speaking Jew, born in Prague, one of the twentieth century's most influential writers. His reputation rests on the posthumous publication of three novels: *The Trial*, *The Castle* and *America*; and a body of short stories, including 'Metamorphosis'. His diaries, published in two volumes, cover the years 1910–23 and detail his misery at having to work in a job he detested, his fractious relationship with his father and mother and his tortured liaison with Felice Bauer, to whom he was twice engaged but never married.

KAY, DR JAMES ALEXANDER (1849–1914) Born in Plymouth, the son of a Royal Navy surgeon. In his final year studying medicine at Aberdeen University he joined a whaling ship and spent ten years in the Antarctic. He was in Durban when the Zulu War broke out and he joined the Royal Army Medical Corps. After the defeat of the Zulus he was stationed in Pretoria with the British troops during the first occupation of the Transvaal and left in 1881, when the

Convention was signed, following the defeat of the British at Bronkhorstspruit and Majuba. He returned to England, married, then returned to Pretoria to set up practice. After a spell in Dublin where he gained further qualifications, he returned to Pretoria in 1894, to discover that his practice had been destroyed, and his journals begin from this event. He later returned to Pretoria in 1900 as a war correspondent.

KESSLER, COUNT HARRY (1868–1937) Born in Paris, the son of a Hamburg banker and an Irish beauty. In World War I he was an officer in the German army and later oversaw the withdrawal of more than 100,000 German troops from the Eastern Front. He was both a purveyor of gossip and an intellectual. He kept a diary for thirty-five years, assuming from the beginning that the events of his time would be worth recording, revealing as they did the German nation in a time of unprecedented crisis.

KLEMPERER, VICTOR (1881–1960) The son of a rabbi, he studied in Munich, Geneva, Paris and Berlin, where he became a journalist. He taught at the University of Naples, and received the Distinguished Service Medal as a volunteer in the German Army in World War I. Subsequently, he was a professor of Romance Languages at Dresden Technical College until he was dismissed as a consequence of antisemitic edicts in 1935. He also lost his house, many of his friends and even his cat, as Jews were not allowed to have pets. He managed to escape the concentration camps for many years, largely because he was married to an 'Aryan'. In 1945, as he was about to be summoned for deportation, he was able to escape in the Allied bombing of Dresden and spent the remaining months of the war in hiding and on the run. He survived the Holocaust and the war and taught in East Germany until his death. His diaries, published in two volumes, are an unvarnished portrayal of life under Nazi rule.

KNOBLICH, WOLFGANG FINDLEY (*fl.* 1942) A private in the Wehrmacht, the German armed forces. He dedicated his diary, which he began on 25 March 1942, to his parents, prefacing it with the epitaph: 'Conquer the heritage of your fathers/ So that you may have the right to possess it.'

LANNING, MICHAEL LEE (*fl.* 1969) An American platoon leader in Vietnam, where he spent a year, an account of which is given in *The Only War We Had*. In a prefatory note, he wrote: 'It was popular among many who fought to say that Vietnam "wasn't much of a war, but it was the only war we had". I can only say that it was enough of a war for me, for I am neither old nor young enough to experience another one.'

LASCELLES, SIR ALAN 'TOMMY' (1887–1981) A nephew of the fifth earl of Harewood, he read Greats at Oxford. In World War I he fought as a cavalry officer in the Bedford Yeomanry, was wounded and received the Military Cross. From 1931 to 1935 he was Secretary to the Governor General of Canada and Private Secretary to George VI from 1943 to 1952.

LAST, NELLA (1909–66) A housewife from Barrow, England, she started keeping a diary in September 1939 and maintained it for almost thirty years. Writing initially for Mass Observation, an organisation set up to 'record the voice of the people', she left a detailed record of her life comprising over two million words.

LEE, GENERAL RAYMOND E. (1886–1958) American general who between 1940 and 1941 was military attaché and head of intelligence in London, during which period he kept a journal. Born in St Louis, Missouri, his parents put great emphasis on learning and reading. Throughout his military career he travelled with a library of books complete with collapsible shelves. In London's blitzed streets he cut a dashing figure, often wearing a straw hat, unafraid of the bombs, exhibiting 'a divine folly of honour, and a splendid carelessness of life'.

LEES-MILNE, JAMES (1908–97) English author and rescuer of decaying country houses, born in Worcestershire. He was educated at Eton, from which he made an unscheduled early exit, and Oxford. His life was beset by ogres, among them his father. A man with no military talents, he managed to remove a whole company of Irish Guards from the army's strength before they had left the parade ground. He was invalided out in 1941. He found his métier in the infant National Trust and spent most of World War II visiting country houses. *Another Self*, has been described as 'one of the briefest and most self-deprecating' of autobiographies. His published diaries, which he began in 1942, have to date reached 1987.

LE RUEZ, ANNIE MARGARET ('NAN') (1915–) Born on a farm on Jersey in the Channel Islands, she was the second of ten children. She left school at sixteen to work on the family farm. She kept a diary 'on and off' throughout her schooldays and continued to do so during the German occupation. At the end of the war she placed the volumes in a Red Cross box, where they remained unopened for fifty years.

LESLIE, DESMOND (1921–) Spiritualist, science fiction writer and World War II Spitfire pilot. He wrote a number of books, including the bestselling *Flying Saucers Have Landed*, which he co-authored with George Stransky. It was translated into more than fifty languages. He once punched the BBC drama critic, Bernard Levin, on the nose on *That Was The Week That Was*, after Levin wrote a damning review of a show starring his first wife.

LEVI, PRIMO (1919–87) Italian writer and chemist, born in Turin to Jewish parents. He studied chemistry at Turin University because he believed 'the nobility of Man . . . lay in making himself the conqueror of matter'. During the war he fled into the mountains, where he formed a small guerrilla force. Towards the end of 1943 he was betrayed, arrested and sent to Auschwitz. 'It was my good fortune to be deported to Auschwitz only in 1944,' he wrote in the preface to *If This Is a Man*, 'that is, after the German government had decided, owing to the growing scarcity of labour, to lengthen the average life span of the prisoners destined for elimination'. He spent ten months in the concentration camp, a horrific experience which may have driven him to take his own life. *If This Is a Man*, published in 1947, is a first-hand account of life in this human abattoir. It ends with a diary of the last days of Auschwitz, which was liberated by Soviet forces in January 1945. Between 1.2 and 1.5 million people were murdered there, of whom approximately 800,000 were Jews.

LEWIS, NORMAN (1918–2003) British travel and thriller writer born in London. His credentials as a travel writer were established with *A Dragon Apparent*, published in 1951. His novel, *The Volcanoes Above Us*, based on personal experiences in Central America in revolt, sold six million copies in Russia. His experiences as an intelligence officer in Naples in Italy during World War II form the basis of *Naples '44*, where the citizens were so destitute that all the tropical fish in the city's aquarium were devoured and even respectable women were driven to prostitution.

LINDBERGH, ANNE MORROW (1906–2001) Her father was an American ambassador in Mexico, where she met Charles Lindbergh in 1927. She learned to fly, operate radios and navigate, and accompanied her husband on his survey flights over North America in

1931 and 1933. She wrote books about flying and her travels. She had five children, one of whom became the famous Lindbergh Baby, who, kidnapped in America in 1932, was later found dead. Her husband made several pre-war visits to Germany and he received a decoration from the Third Reich. On his return to America in 1939, he became the leading spokesman for the America First isolationist movement, challenging President Roosevelt in a bitter debate over American involvement in World War II. As his wife's diaries make plain, it was not an easy row to hoe.

McHENRY, JAMES (1753–1816) Born in Ballymena, Ireland, and educated in Dublin, he emigrated in 1771 to Philadelphia, where he studied medicine. In 1776, he joined the medical staff of the military hospital in Cambridge, Massachusetts, and was subsequently appointed surgeon of the Pennsylvania Continental regiment. He was captured at Fort Washington in November 1776, paroled in January the following year and exchanged in March 1778. Two months later he was appointed secretary to George Washington, who in 1796 appointed him secretary of war, a position he retained under John Adams until May 1800 when he was asked to resign. He retired to his estate in Baltimore.

MACKENZIE, FREDERICK (d. 1824) The son of a Dublin merchant, he arrived in Boston in 1774 as a lieutenant in the British army. He was promoted to captain the following year and was made major in 1780. His diary records his service in Rhode Island, 1777–78, and New York City, 1781. He was promoted to lieutenant colonel in 1781. He died in Teignmouth, Devonshire.

MACNAUGHTAN, SARAH (1850?–1916) She was the daughter of a JP, of Scottish descent. There is doubt over her date of birth as she went to great lengths to conceal it. A suffragette of independent means, she never married and, having some training as a nurse, she was in a position to offer her services to tend the wounded of the Balkan wars, the Boer war and the First World War, where she worked as a volunteer with the Red Cross. Back in England she did voluntary work, lecturing at munitions centres. She went on to establish soup kitchens, working in Russia and Persia, where she fell seriously ill and had to return to England, where she died.

MANN, THOMAS (1875–1955) German novelist and essayist, born in Lübeck. After giving wholehearted support to the German cause in World War I, he recanted, vigorously attacked Fascism and was among the first to be declared *persona non grata* by the Nazis. When Hitler came to power he went into exile and spent most of his time in the United States. His first novel was *Buddenbrooks*, subtitled 'The Death of a Family', which was published in 1902. Other key works include *Death in Venice*, *The Magic Mountain*, and *Tonio Kröger*. He was awarded the Nobel Prize for literature in 1929.

MANSEL, CAPTAIN JOHN (1900–74) The son of a stockbroker, he was born in London. He attended Winchester College and Liverpool University, where he qualified as an architect. He joined the Territorial Army in 1935 and was mobilized in 1939. His diaries describe his five years as a German prisoner of war.

MANSFIELD, KATHERINE (1888–1923) A renowned short-story writer born in Wellington, New Zealand, and educated at Queen's College, London. Her personal life was chaotic and brought her much distress, which informed the stories in her first collection, *In a German Pension*, published in 1911, the year she met the critic and editor John Middleton Murry, whom she married in 1918. Through him she was introduced to the Bloomsbury Group but was never totally accepted by it. In her diaries Virginia Woolf revealed a deep dislike of Mansfield. 'Her mind,' wrote Woolf, 'is a very thin soil, laid an inch or two upon very barren rock.' Murry published an expurgated version of her diary in 1927. A fuller version, offering a more painful picture of their often strained relationship, was published in 1976.

MAUNY, ERIK DE (*fl.* 1941) New Zealand writer and translator, the author of several books, including *The Huntsman in his Career*. It was said of him that he was 'one of the few New Zealand writers who responded positively to existentialist ideas'.

MENCKEN, H(ENRY) L(OUIS) (1880–1956) Prolific American journalist and polemicist, critic and lexicographer. He was born in Baltimore and associated with *The Smart Set*, for which he was first literary editor, then co-editor with George Nathan, with whom he also worked on *The Black Mask*, a magazine of detective fiction. An iconoclast, he loudly advocated the virtues of American authors. In 1924, he co-founded *The American Nation*. He started his diary in 1930, when he was fifty, and made his last entry in 1948. He was given to sweeping generalisations, such as 'nearly all white men dislike the Japs and like the Chinese'. Gore Vidal wrote of him: 'Like Puck, Mencken found most mortals fools.'

MILBURN, CLARA (1883–1961) English middle-class housewife who lived with her husband six miles from Coventry, which suffered badly from German bombing during the Second World War. Her diary, published in 1979, gives an intimate portrait of life in Britain during the war. Mrs Milburn, as she was known, was much concerned for the safety of her son, Alan, who went missing but was later revealed to be a prisoner of war. He returned home safely, married, and was killed in a car accident.

MILLER, DAVID (*fl.* 1901) An infantryman in the British Army during the Boer War.

MILLS, JOHN (*fl.* 1812) An ensign in the British army, he served with Wellington in the Iberian Peninsula from 1811 to 1814. He kept a diary throughout and recorded the siege of Burgos.

MITCHISON, NAOMI (1897–1999) Prolific Scottish writer, born in Edinburgh and educated at Oxford. Her brother was the scientist J.B.S. Haldane. She married G.R. Mitchison, a barrister and later Labour MP and life peer. Her early historical novels, including *The Conquered, The Bull Calves*, and *The Corn King and the Spring Queen*, are among her best. She also wrote science fiction, biography and memoirs. Her circle included E.M. Forster, W.H. Auden and Aldous Huxley. She was an official tribal mother to the Bakgatla of Botswana and a member of the Highlands and Islands Advisory Panel. She kept a full diary for the duration of the war. It was begun at the request of the social research organisation, Mass Observation. The diary's setting is the fishing village of Carradale on Kintyre, where the Mitchisons bought a biggish house and a smallish farm.

MUGGERIDGE, MALCOLM (1903–90) English journalist and provocateur, born in London. After a spell lecturing in Egypt, he joined the *Manchester Guardian* as its Moscow correspondent. During the Second World War, he served with the Intelligence Corps and received the Legion of Honour and the Croix de Guerre with Palm. After the war he resumed his career in journalism and was editor of *Punch* before drifting into television, where he was a pungent and iconoclastic interviewer. He was also rector of Edinburgh University, resigning over student liberalism and promiscuity though he was no stranger himself to the latter. He wrote many books, including novels and two volumes of memoirs. His diary, which he kept in a desultory way from 1924, grew to more than three-quarters of a million words.

MUSTO, WALTER (1879–1952) English eccentric and civil servant. He served in the army during the First World War. Though too old to fight in World War II, he joined an ARP (Air Raid Precautions) Unit, for which he helped to organise a fire patrol. His diary, which he began to keep on 1 January, 1939, is on occasion reminiscent of *Dad's Army* as scripted by Pooter. 'To be average is not to be mediocre or static,' he once wrote. 'It is to eschew extremes.' The opening entry is typical of the man. Waiting for a kettle to boil he stands naked in his snow-covered garden 'vigorously rubbing my body and limbs until I am aglow in the cold sweet air – delicious moments'. He was an enthusiastic knitter.

NICOLSON, SIR HAROLD GEORGE (1886–1968) English writer and politician, born in Tehran. He was educated at Wellington College and Balliol College, Oxford, and had a distinguished career as a diplomat before turning to journalism. In 1913 he married Vita Sackville-West, and their open relationship was controversially described by their son, Nigel, in *Portrait of a Marriage*. Nicolson was briefly a supporter of Oswald Mosley, leader of the British Union of Fascists, and was a Member of Parliament from 1935 to 1945. He was a prolific writer, concentrating on biography, politics and history. He kept a diary from the moment he left the Foreign Office at the end of 1929 until 1964. 'A diary,' he said, 'should be written for one's great-grandson. The purely private diary becomes too self-centred and morbid. One should have a remote, but not too remote, audience.'

NIN, ANAÏS (1903–77) Born in Paris, partly of Spanish origin, she lived there until she was eleven, when she emigrated to the United States. On her marriage to Hugo Guiler, a banker, she returned to Paris where she encountered many artists and writers, including Henry Miller. A voluminous writer, she published novels, criticism and erotica. Ultimately her fame rests on her *Journals*, which span the years 1931–74.

ORIGO, IRIS (1902–88) Though born in England, her childhood was divided between the United States, Ireland and Italy where, in 1924, she married Antonio Origo, the illegitimate son of a cavalry officer, painter and sculptor, who loved football and Wagner. Together they bought La Foce, a vast, untamed estate in Val d'Orcia in Tuscany, which they energetically rescued from ruin. When the war started, she worked for the Italian Red Cross and then turned her attention to sheltering refugee children, feeding Italian partisans and hiding and guiding Allied prisoners-of-war during the German occupation, all of which is described in *War in the Val d'Orcia: 1943–1944*. Her other books include *Images and Shadows*, subtitled 'Part of a Life', and *The Merchant of Prato*. Her biography, written by Caroline Moorehead, appeared in 2000.

ORWELL, GEORGE, pseudonym of ERIC ARTHUR BLAIR (1903–50) British novelist, essayist and social commentator, born in Bengal and educated at Eton. During the Spanish Civil War he threw in his lot with the Republicans. He was wounded in the throat. His version of the events of that period is told in *Homage to Catalonia*. He was the author of several seminal novels, including *Animal Farm* and *Nineteen Eighty-Four*, which appeared the year before his death. Other notable books include *The Road to Wigan Pier* and *Down and Out in Paris and London*. Some of his best work appeared during the Second World War, which he spent largely in London. His diary covers the period 28 May 1940 to 28 August 1941, then resumes from 14 March to 15 November 1942.

PARKS, DAVID (*fl.* 1966–67) An American soldier in Vietnam, the son of Gordon Parks, a photo-journalist and filmmaker. His diary is a record of his maturation as a soldier and coming-of-age as a black man during the escalation of the war in Vietnam and his encounters with racism and corrupt military top brass.

PART, THOMAS (d.1918) An Australian infantryman during the First World War. He arrived in France on 26 March 1916, reaching the front line a fortnight later. He continued writing his diary until April 1917 and his first leave. He was killed in France on 25 April 1918, the first anniversary of Anzac Day.

PARTRIDGE, FRANCES (1900–2002) Born in Bloomsbury, London, one of six children. Friends of the family included Conan Doyle, Henry James and the Stracheys. She was educated at Bedales School and Newham College, Cambridge. She married Ralph Partridge in 1933. Closely associated with the members of the Bloomsbury Group, her diaries, written without thought of publication, chronicle a long and remarkable life. During World War II she and her husband, both pacifists, opened their home in Wiltshire to refugees, as well as various friends and members of the Bloomsbury Group.

PAVESE, CESARE (1908–50) Italian novelist and poet, born on a farm in Piedmont. He had a hard upbringing, not least because his father died when he was six. Renowned for the novel *The Moon and the Bonfires*, published the year in which he committed suicide after a woman with whom he had fallen in love left him. His diaries, covering the troubled years 1935–50, reveal his thoughts on 'This Business of Living'.

PEPYS, SAMUEL (1633–1703) The son of a tailor, he was educated at St Paul's School, London, and Magdalene College, Cambridge. He married Elizabeth St Michel, who was fifteen years old, in 1655. Initially through patronage, he pursued a successful career in the Admiralty. His diary opens on 1 January 1660, and closes on 31 May 1669, when he erroneously believed that he was going blind. However, he also wrote an interesting diary when he was posted to Tangier in 1683. His career effectively came to an end in 1688 with the 'Glorious Revolution'. He was sent to the Tower in 1699, accused of complicity in the 'Popish Plot', but was soon set free. His diary remained in cipher at Magdalene College until 1825, when the code was broken. An unexpurgated edition was published 1970–83 in eleven volumes.

PEXTON, SERGEANT L.D. (*fl.* 1940) A sergeant in the British army in the Second World War. He served with the British Expeditionary Force sent to France to counter a German invasion. He was taken prisoner in May 1940. He decided not to continue his diary after 18 September 1940.

POLITKOVSKAYA, ANNA (1959–) Russian journalist, renowned and – in some quarters in her homeland – reviled, for her reports of atrocities in Chechnya. Since 1999 she has been a special correspondent for *Novaya gazeta*. After graduating from the journalism faculty of Moscow University in 1980 she worked for *Izvestiya*, a daily newspaper. Subsequently, she wrote for two weeklies, *Megapolis Express* and *Obshchaya gazeta*. From July 1999 to January 2001 she reported from Chechnya on a war that was supposed to be over. For her pains, she was held overnight in torture cells, was accused of being a Western agent, received death threats and was forced to flee the country.

POWELL, ANTHONY (1905–2000) Fêted as the author of the twelve-volume *roman fleuve*, *A Dance to the Music of Time*, he was educated at Eton and Oxford. Before embarking on a career as a novelist, he worked in publishing. As well as novels he wrote a biographical study of John Aubrey and a four-volume autobiography. He began writing a journal in 1982, when he became 'stuck' on a novel, and continued into the 1990s.

POWELL, DAWN (1897–1965) Born in Ohio, she ran away from home at the age of twelve and was brought up by an aunt. She graduated from Lake Erie College in 1918 and moved to New York, where she lived and worked for the rest of her life. She married the advertising executive Joseph R. Gousha, with whom she had a son. She published fifteen novels, which at the time of her death were all out of print. However, an article on her by Gore Vidal in the *New York Review of Books* sparked a revival and many of her books are now available. Her voluminous diaries cover the period from 1931 to 1965.

PYM, BARBARA (1913–80) British novelist, educated at St Hilda's College, Oxford. Her father was a Shropshire solicitor. Her work centres mainly on life in the professions, drawing on her experience as an editor of anthropological journals, and on machinations within the Anglican Church. In 1963 her publisher rejected *An Unsuitable Attachment* and she consequently suffered a prolonged period of neglect. In 1977, however, David Cecil and Philip Larkin mentioned her in a symposium in the *Times Literary Supplement* on neglected writers and her work gradually came back into print. She was subsequently shortlisted for the Booker Prize in 1977 for *Quartet in Autumn*. Her journals and letters appeared in 1984, entitled *A Very Private Eye*.

RABE, JOHN (1882–1949) In 1937, as the Japanese army closed in on Nanking, then the capital of China, all members of the foreign community were ordered to leave. One man, a mild-mannered fifty-five-year-old German, John Rabe, head of the local branch of the Siemens electrical firm and a member of the Nazi Party, refused to go. It is estimated that he saved between 250,000 and 300,000 lives by his efforts. Each night in Nanking, he wrote up his diary, which was published in 1998. He was arrested by the Gestapo on his return to Germany because there was a question-mark over his sympathies; he gave lectures in Berlin telling of Japanese atrocities towards the Chinese and wrote to Hitler about them, believing him to be unaware of the truth. However, he was released once the Gestapo realised that his intention was not to stir up sympathy for the Chinese or work against German policy. He survived the war and died in obscurity.

RANFURLY, COUNTESS OF (1914–) 'Since I was about five years old I have kept a diary' wrote the Countess in the introduction to her wartime diaries, *To War with Whitaker*. When the Second World War broke out her husband, Dan Ranfurly, was dispatched to the Middle East with his faithful valet, Whitaker. Defying the War Office, she ran off in pursuit of her husband. Her diaries, covering the six years of the war, include cameo appearances by Churchill and Eisenhower.

RANSOM, JOHN (1843–1919) A brigade quartermaster sergeant in the 9th Michigan Cavalry. He was captured on 6 November 1863 and sent to the Confederate prison at Belle Island, near Richmond, Virginia, and later transferred by train to Andersonville, Georgia, where nearly 50,000 men were taken. Over 13,000 died in the terrible conditions, compounded by lack of proper shelter and sanitation. He escaped twice and was recaptured each time. Eventually, however, he made a successful escape, recovered his health and rejoined a Union regiment. In later years he moved to Chicago, Long Beach, California and eventually lived in Pasadena, where he died. The books in which he kept his diary were destroyed by a fire a few years after the war but the text was saved, as it had previously been published in Ransom's home-town newspaper, the *Jackson, Michigan Citizen*.

REEVES, ENO (d. 1807) During the American War of Independence he enlisted in the Continental army as a private. He was commissioned ensign in 1777 and promoted to lieutenant in 1778. He served in Pennsylvania Continental regiments. After the war, he moved to South Carolina.

REITH, LORD (JOHN) (1889–1971) Politician, pioneer broadcaster and staunch Presbyterian, born in Stonehaven in the northeast of Scotland, where his parents were on holiday at the time. He was educated at Glasgow Academy. After serving an engineering apprenticeship, he entered the field of radio communications. In 1922, he became the first general manager of the British Broadcasting Corporation and was its Director-General from 1927 to 1938. Thereafter he entered politics, but his career at the BBC is his claim to posterity, for he was largely responsible for defining its didactic, paternalistic tone. He published an autobiography, *Into the Wind*, in 1949. His diaries, which show him to be deeply troubled and vulnerable, were published posthumously. He did not get on with Churchill.

RITCHIE, CHARLES (1906–95) Canadian diplomat and author, educated in Canada and at Oxford. He joined the Canadian Department of External Affairs and was posted to London in 1939. Until his retirement from the Foreign Service in 1971 he represented Canada in Germany, the United Nations, Washington and London. According to the biographer Victoria Glendinning, he was 'no one's idea of a Canadian'. He was elegant, stylish and wore his learning lightly. He owed his introduction into English high society in part to John Buchan, who helped pave his way. During the Second World War, he began an affair with the novelist Elizabeth Bowen, which she drew on for her celebrated novel, *The Heat of the Day*. Ritchie's own book, *The Siren Years: A Canadian Diplomat Abroad, 1937–1945*, was a revelation.

RODNEY, THOMAS (1744–1811) Born on a plantation in Kent County, Delaware, he became a farm manager for his older brother in 1762. He was appointed a Justice of the Peace in 1770 and from 1772–74 he kept shop in Philadelphia. He became a captain of the militia in 1775 and served during the Trenton campaign and at Princeton, after which he returned to Delaware. He was appointed Associate Judge of the Delaware supreme court in 1802, from which he resigned the following year when Thomas Jefferson named him US Judge for Mississippi territory.

RUSSELL, SIR WILLIAM HOWARD (1820–1907) British war correspondent, born in Dublin. From an early age he was attracted to the military life and used to get up at dawn to watch soldiers drilling at a nearby barracks. He tried several times to enlist but was stopped by his grandfather. Instead he became a journalist and is generally regarded as 'the first and greatest' war correspondent. He applied the phrase 'the thin red line' to the British infantry at Balaclava, called attention to the sufferings of the British army there, and inspired Florence Nightingale. In 1854, he gave a first-hand account of the Charge of the Light Brigade. He reported from several conflicts, including the Zulu War, the Indian Mutiny, the American Civil War (his vivid account of the Battle of Bull Run made him highly unpopular) and the Prusso–Russian War. He single-handledly spawned an industry. Having been the only war correspondent at the Crimean War, he was one of 500 to observe the American Civil War.

SALAM PAX (1974–) Pseudonym – a play on the word for peace in Arabic and Latin – of a young Iraqi who kept a 'blog' (an Internet diary) during the US invasion in 2003. He began his blog as a means of keeping in touch with a friend who have moved to Jordan, but soon his website attracted attention for his candid comments on the Iraqi regime, the Americans and life in general. He sent his blogs from his office in Baghdad where he worked as an architect, or from 'Hotel Pax' – the nickname for his home which had become a refuge for many of his relatives during the war. He wrote about everyday life – from watching American sitcoms to the quality of Egyptian soap – and corresponded with a large number of fellow bloggers and Internet buffs. His writings appeared in a fortnightly column in the *Guardian* newspaper and by the end of the conflict his celebrity was such that his name could be found on a range of merchandising.

SANSOM, WILLIAM (1912–76) English short-story writer and novelist, born in Camberwell, London. His stories tend to evoke a drab, seedy, post-war London. His novels include *The Body*, published in 1949, in which we are led into the deranged mind of a middle-aged barber consumed by jealousy. He joined the National Fire Service at the outbreak of war and witnessed the bombing raids on London.

SARTRE, JEAN-PAUL (1905–80) French philosopher, dramatist and novelist. He was born in Paris and studied at the Sorbonne with Simone de Beauvoir. He taught philosophy in France and Germany in the early 1930s and at the outbreak of World War II he joined the French Army, and was later captured by the Germans. Upon his release he joined the Resistance in Paris, and later became a leading member of the intellectual life in the city. He founded and edited an avant-garde monthly, *Les Temps modernes* and published an autobiographical novel, *La Nausée* in 1938, the same year in which he wrote a collection of short stories, *Le Mur*. He wrote several plays, *Les Mouches*, *Huis clos*, and *Les Mains sâles*, which was filmed as *Crime Passionnel*. His other works include novels such as *Les Chemins de la liberté*, the play *Les Séquestrés d'Altona*. He declined to accept the Nobel Prize for literature, awarded to him in 1964, and later became opposed to American policies in Vietnam.

SASSOON, SIEGFRIED (1886–1967) English poet and memoirist, born in Kent and educated at Cambridge. His mother earmarked him at an early age as a poet. He enjoyed country sports, particularly hunting. In the First World War he was awarded the military cross but discarded it. Supposedly suffering from shell-shock, he was sent to a hospital in Edinburgh, where he met Wilfred Owen, whose poetry he helped polish. Revered as a war poet, he was also celebrated for his autobiographical trilogy, *Memoirs of a Fox-Hunting Man* (1928), *Memoirs of an Infantry Officer* (1930) and *Sherston's Progress* (1936). His diaries span ten years, from 1915 to 1925.

SCHLOSBERG, FREDA (1885–1922) A farmer's daughter living at Bronkhorstspruit, she was fourteen years old and attending a convent boarding school, when the Anglo–Boer war broke out. Her home was eventually destroyed and her family moved to Pretoria in 1900. She later married and had a family, and when a young nephew (who later edited her journals) asked to read her journals for a history project she replied that she had to keep house for a husband and two infants and was too busy to search them out. She was, she said, 'a prisoner of love'.

SCHLOSS, HARRY (*fl.* 1943–44) A waist gunner on a B-26 Marauder bomb Group, 17th Bomb Group, 34th Bomb Squadron, USAAF (United States Army Air Force). He survived the war.

SCOTT, SIR WALTER (1770–1832) Born in Edinburgh, he was the first international bestselling author. He virtually invented the historical novel, influenced countless authors, including Balzac and Goethe, and is credited with popularising a romantic vision of Scotland which is still potent. In 1826, at the height of his fame, his printer and publisher, Ballantyne and Constable, suffered a financial crash, dragging Scott down with them. Determined to pay off his debts – which he succeeded in doing before his death – he threw himself even more strenuously into his writing. These difficult times are recorded in his diary, his 'Gurnal'. 'I have all my life regretted that I did not keep a regular [journal],' he wrote in his first entry on 20 November 1825. 'I have myself lost recollection of much that was interesting and I have deprived my family and the public of some curious information by not carrying this resolution into effect.'

SCOTT-ELLIS, PRISCILLA (1916–83) She was born during an air raid on London. The daughter of the 8th Lord Howard de Walden and Seaford, she went to Spain in 1937 as a nurse on the Nationalist side, and in 1939 she went to France with an ambulance outfit. She later set up and ran a hospital for Poles in Scotland, becoming a colonel in the Polish Army, and learned to speak fluent Polish. She married José Luis de Vilallonga, the son of a Spanish marquis, in 1945, and later became a successful novelist and actress.

SENTER, ISAAC (1753–99) Born in New Hampshire, he moved to Newport, Rhode Island, and studied medicine. During the American War of Independence, he volunteered as a surgeon for Benedict Arnold's expedition to Quebec in 1775 and was appointed Surgeon General of Rhode Island Militia in 1779. After the war he established a practice in Pawtucket, before returning to Newport, where he died.

SERLE, AMBROSE (1742–1812) Prior to the War of Independence he served as Under Secretary to Lord Dartmouth, Secretary of State for the American colonies. In 1775 he published a pamphlet, *Americans Against Liberty*. In 1776 he was appointed Private Secretary to Admiral Lord Howe, Peace Commissioner for the colonies. He wrote for the Loyalist *New-York Gazette* from September 1776 to July 1777, and returned to England in 1778. He later became a commissioner for the care and exchange of prisoners of war.

SHEHADEH, RAJA (1951–) Palestinian lawyer living under Israeli occupation. He was educated at a Quaker school in Ramallah and at the American University of Beirut. He was called to the Bar in London, then returned to Ramallah and private practice with his father, Aziz. He is the founder of Al Haq (Law in the Service of Man), a non-partisan organisation, and the author of several books, including *The Third Way: A Journal of Life in the West Bank*.

SHIRER, WILLIAM L. (1904–93) American journalist, author and broadcaster, born in Chicago. His father was a lawyer. He was educated in the US and Paris. Throughout the Second World War he was a war correspondent based in Germany. From this experience came his *Berlin Diary: The Journal of a Foreign Correspondent*. His other books include *The Rise and Fall of the Third Reich* and several volumes of autobiography.

SHULER, MICHAEL (*fl.* 1862) A captain in the Union army, he kept a diary from June to December 1862. It finished abruptly on the same day that the Battle of Fredericksburg commenced. The Union side lost 12,600 men. 'Our poppy corn generals,' wrote a Massachusetts private, 'kill me as Herod killed the innocents.' The Confederates lost 5,300, most them missing, gone home for Christmas.

SOUTAR, WILLIAM (1898–1943) Scottish poet, born in Perth. His parents were of farming stock and his father was a master joiner. During the First World War, Soutar contracted a spinal disease which left him bedridden from 1930 onwards. From then until his death he kept a day-by-day record of his experiences and observations. As a poet he specialised in 'bairnrhymes', charming poems for children written in Scots. His diaries were first published in 1954 titled *Diaries of a Dying Man*. Reviewing it in the *Observer*, fellow diarist Harold Nicolson greeted it as a 'brave and animating book'.

SPENDER, SIR (HAROLD) STEPHEN (1909–95) English poet, novelist and critic, a contemporary of W.H. Auden, Louis MacNeice and Christopher Isherwood. After leaving Oxford he lived for a spell in Germany. His first collection of poems appeared in 1930. During the Spanish Civil War he wrote propaganda for the Republican side. In the Second World War he was a member of the National Fire Service. At the outset of the war he wrote, 'I am going to keep a journal because I cannot accept the fact that I feel so shattered that I cannot write at all.' His autobiography, *World Within World* was published in 1951; his *Journals: 1939–83* appeared in 1985.

STAHLENBERG, ELISABETH VON (*fl.* 1939–43) A fictional diarist, created by Gillian Freeman who wrote *Nazi Lady: The Diaries of Elisabeth von Stahlenberg*, first published in 1978 with no acknowledgement of its real author. Various authorities, including Alan Clark, believed it was authentic and reviewed it accordingly, but the *Evening Standard* later revealed it to be a spoof and in subsequent editions it was described as 'a novel'. Its protagonist is a young German actress and Nazi sympathiser who, in order to have her husband, a film-maker, returned from the Eastern Front, invites Josef Goebbels to seduce her, a plausible if imaginary scenario.

STURMER, ADOLPH (d. 1916) A former law student, he served in the German army on the Eastern Front. He was killed on 23 October 1916.

THOMAS, (PHILIP) EDWARD (1878–1917) Welsh poet (though born in London) and critic, educated at Lincoln College, Oxford. He was a solitary man, 'a quiet rambler', wrote Martin Seymour-Smith, 'in search of the sources of his own melancholy'. He was killed at Arras, where 150,000 British soldiers fell in six days. Thomas's diary, which he kept from New Year's Day to 8 April in 1917, the final entry written only a few hours before he died, is one of the most moving testimonies of the First World War. It was written in a small pigskin pocket-book which still bears its own Arras scars in the form of creased and crumpled pages.

TOLSTOY, COUNT LEO (1828–1910) Russian novelist and moral-ist, born at Yasnaya Polyana, 130 miles from Moscow. Both his parents died young. Inclined to dissolution, he abandoned his studies and ran up huge debts. In 1852, he joined the army and saw action in the Caucasus, Silistria and the Crimea. His marriage to Sofia Behrs in 1862 marked a turning point in his life. In 1863, the first of their thirteen children was born. He is famed as the author of *War and Peace* and *Anna Karenina*. A keen self-improver, he gave up his title, the copyright to his works, alcohol, tobacco, blood sports and eating meat. His family was not in sympathy with his views and after forty-eight years of marriage he left home for good, only to die on an obscure railway station.

TORY, AVRAHAM (1909–) Israeli lawyer, born Avraham Golub in Lithuania. His father qualified as a rabbi though he never practised. During the Second World War he lived in the Jewish ghetto of Kovno and kept a diary of the atrocities carried out there. The diary was used in 1982 to prove that Kazys Palciauskas was mayor of Kovno at the time and had acted with the Germans in the mass murder of tens of thousands of Jews. In 1947, Tory arrived in Palestine and two years later changed his name, abandoning Golub (which means 'dove' in Russian) and taking a Hebrew equivalent, Tory, from the biblical phrase, 'The voice of the turtledove is heard in the land.'

TREECE, HENRY (1911–66) English poet and novelist, born in Staffordshire and educated at the University of Birmingham. He was a schoolteacher before becoming a full-time writer. With J.F. Hendry, he is credited with founding the 'New Apocalypse' school of writing, a romantic literary movement. His *Collected Poems* was published in 1946. He wrote numerous historical novels, especially for young people.

VASSILTCHIKOV, MARIE ('MISSY') (1917–78) The fourth child (and third daughter) of Prince Illarion and Princess Lydia Vassiltchikov, she was born in St Petersburg but spent much of her life in exile. At the start of the Second World War she was in Germany; she first found a job in Berlin with the Broadcasting Service and then with the Foreign Ministry's Information Department. There she worked closely with a hard core of anti-Nazi resisters who were involved in Count von Stauffenberg's abortive plot to assassinate Hitler. She was a compulsive diarist, daily typing out in English a summary of events. In 1976, after much soul-searching, she agreed to make her diary public. A definitive version was completed by her just weeks before she died of leukaemia in London.

VAUGHAN, KEITH (1912–77) English painter, educated at Christ's Hospital, London. His father died when he was a child and he was brought up by his mother. He worked for an advertising agency until 1939. Initially a conscientious objector, he later served in the Pioneer Corps and as an interpreter for German POWs. His diary, which he kept from 1939 until he took his own life, is, in the words of its editor, Alan Ross, 'a self-portrait of astonishing honesty: devoid of disguise in any shape or form, or hypocrisy'.

VELMANS, EDITH (1925–) Born in Holland, she led a carefree life until the summer of 1942, when it became clear that her family's Jewish background might prove fatal. She was sent into hiding with a Christian family in the south of Holland. Her diary, published as *Edith's Book* in 1998, tells the story of how she survived the war, after which she became a psychologist specialising in gerontology and went to live in the United States.

QUEEN VICTORIA (1819–1901) Born at Kensington Palace, she succeeded to the throne on 20 June 1837 at the age of eighteen and was crowned the following year on 28 June. She became Empress of India in 1877. In 1840, she married Prince Albert of Saxe-Coburg-Gotha, who took the title of Prince Consort. He was a major influence on her and when he died in 1861 she was inconsolable. She remained in retirement for a long time and never ceased to mourn him. Throughout her reign Britain waged several wars, including the Afghan, the Crimean and the Boer. She kept a diary from when she was thirteen until just a few days before she died.

WALDO, ALBIGENCE (*fl.* 1775–77) A surgeon in the Connecticut Infantry Regiment in September 1777, during the American War of Independence he found himself in the midst of the agony of Valley Forge in Pennsylvania, which was the winter headquarters of George Washington's troops.

WAUGH, AUBERON (1939–2001) Novelist and journalist, the son of Evelyn Waugh. At Downside school he held the record for the most-ever beatings in one term. He did his National Service in Cyprus, where, trying to unblock a jammed machine-gun, he shot himself six times in the chest. He lost a lung, his spleen, his forefinger and various ribs. He wrote five novels before abandoning fiction and embracing journalism. A wilful controversialist and indefatigable mischief-maker, he wrote prolifically, principally for the *Daily Telegraph* and the *Spectator*. He also edited the *Literary Review*. He was *Private Eye*'s diarist for sixteen years, the second volume of which, *A Turbulent Decade*, from 1976 to 1985, he regarded as his finest work of journalism.

WAUGH, EVELYN (1903–66) Widely regarded as one of the foremost English novelists of his generation, he was born in London and educated at Lancing and Hertford College, Oxford. After an early sortie into teaching, he produced his first novel, *Decline and Fall*, in 1928. Other notable books include *Scoop*, a newspaper farce, the 'Sword of Honour' trilogy, which follows the wartime career of Guy Crouchback, and *Brideshead Revisited*. He was a dyspeptic wit, as revealed in his letters and diary, which he kept almost continuously from the age of seven until the year before his death.

WEBB, BEATRICE (1858–1943) Notable as a social reformer and researcher (among other things she worked as rent-collector for a philanthropic housing association and was the author of a book on the Co-operative movement), she married Sidney Webb, who shared her passionate interest in improving living conditions for ordinary people. Both were prominent in the Fabian Society. She wrote two acclaimed autobiographies: *My Apprenticeship* and *Our Partnership*. Her exhaustive diaries, in which she details her obsessive and self-thwarted passion for Joseph Chamberlain and her work as a young woman in London's East End, are a remarkable record of nearly seventy years at the heart of British political and intellectual life.

WELCH, (MAURICE) DENTON (1915–48) English novelist, born in Shanghai. Originally, his ambition was to be an artist but his training was cut short at the age of twenty when he was knocked off his bicycle by a motorist. The repercussions dominated the rest of his life. He kept a journal from 1942 until he died, writing in longhand in a series of school exercise books. It was first published in an abridged form in 1952.

WEST, ARTHUR GRAEME (1891–1917) The author of the posthumously published *Diary of a Dead Officer*, which has been described as 'the naked grapplings of a man with his own soul'. Born and brought up in the countryside in the south-west of England, he moved with his family to London. He attended Balliol College, Oxford, and enlisted at the outbreak of war, convinced of the justness of the cause.

After two years, however, his view changed and he became a pacifist, hating violence and abhorring army life. He was struck by a sniper's bullet as he left his trench. The value of his diary is in its absolute frankness.

WILLIAMS, KENNETH (1926–88) Much-loved English actor, broadcaster and comedian, born to the north of King's Cross railway station. His father managed a hairdresser's. He was best known for his roles in the *Carry On* films, which made an art of innuendo. For over forty years he kept a diary in which he made pen portraits, often poisonous, of colleagues. 'You'll be in my diary!' he would threaten, and not hollowly. As Russell Davies, the editor of his diaries, published five years after his death observed: 'Williams took against strangers instinctively until proved wrong.'

WINDHAM, SIR CHARLES ASH (1810–70) British soldier and politician, educated at Sandhurst. In 1826 he joined the Coldstream Guards, rising to colonel in 1854. In the Crimean War, he saw action at Alma, Balaclava and Inkerman. He became Liberal MP for East Norfolk in 1857, the same year he commanded the troops at Cawnpore, which he was unsuccessful in holding.

WOOLF, VIRGINIA (1882–1941) Novelist and essayist, born in London. She was the daughter of Sir Leslie Stephen, the first editor of the *Dictionary of National Biography*, and the wife of Leonard Woolf, a writer and publisher. Her social circle encompassed many of the leading intellectuals of the day, including members of the Bloomsbury Group. Her novels include *Mrs Dalloway*, *The Waves* and *To the Lighthouse*. Her essay *A Room of One's Own* is a landmark of feminist literature. With James Joyce, of whom she was not a fan, she is regarded as one of the innovators of the modern novel in English. *A Writer's Diary*, edited by her husband, was published in 1958. A five-volume edition of her diaries, edited by Quentin Bell, appeared in 1977–84.

WYNDHAM, JOAN (1922–) Brought up a strict Catholic and educated at a boarding-school convent, she went to the Royal Academy of Dramatic Art (RADA). She was in the Women's Auxiliary Air Force (WAAF) for five years, a time described in her wartime diary, *Love as Blue*. Among the many colourful characters she encountered was Dylan Thomas, who told her poetry was not the most important thing in life. 'Frankly,' he said, 'I'd rather lie in a hot bath sucking boiled sweets and reading Agatha Christie.' She also had a fling with a Highland laird. After the war she opened Oxford's first espresso bar, cooked at pop concerts and dabbled in journalism.

ZSCHUPPE, HELMUT (d. 1917) A German soldier who was wounded in the First World War. He was awarded the Iron Cross Second Class four days before he was killed on the Western Front.

Wars In Brief: A Chronology

ANGLO–DUTCH WARS (1652–54, 1665–67, 1672–72 and 1680–84) Four naval wars fought between the Dutch Republic and England, caused mainly by commercial and colonial rivalry between the two great sea powers. The first three, in the second half of the seventeenth century, did not result in the supremacy of either nation; the fourth, from 1680 to 1684, shortly before the French revolutionary period, was heavily lost by the Dutch, and signalled the end of their claims to commercial domination. The wars were the occasion of great naval heroics on both sides. Pepys's diary covers the period from May 1665 to August 1667 but, as his biographer Claire Tomalin noted, 'it is often easy to forget this', since those years also encompassed the plague and the Great Fire of London as well as Pepys's personal and domestic concerns.

AMERICAN INDEPENDENCE WAR (1775–83) The war that established the thirteen American colonies as independent from Britain, often called the American War of Independence or the War of the Revolution. In the years 1763 to 1775 relations between the North American colonies and Britain became increasingly strained as Britain began taking measures to tighten control over the colonies. Colonial resistance was especially strong over the issue of whether the British parliament had the right to tax colonies without their representation.

Anti-British sentiment was more organised in the major port towns, with considerable support coming from the elected assemblies. The tension during this period was reflected in the Stamp Act crisis, resistance to the Townsend Act, the Boston Massacre, the burning of the cruiser *Gaspé*, and the Boston Tea Party, when resistance to British attempts at direct taxation resulted in the destruction of 342 chests of dutied tea by workmen disguised as Indians.

The British Parliament's passing of the Intolerable Acts in 1774 to punish Massachusetts for the Tea Party led to the calling of the First Continental Congress. In April 1775 fighting broke out between British troops and the colonial militia, known as the Minutemen, at the battles of Lexington and Concord in Massachusetts. Other military engagements followed, including the colonial capture of Fort Ticonderoga in May 1775, the Battle of Bunker Hill, and the unsuccessful American expedition in Quebec, Canada.

In June 1775 the Second Continental Congress elected George Washington to command the Continental Army and in July adopted the Declaration of Independence. Following the British evacuation of Boston in May 1776, the main theatre shifted to New York, New Jersey, and Pennsylvania. Washington's troops suffered a number of defeats in the New York area, including the Battle of Long Island in August, 1776, but his surprise attacks at Trenton on Christmas day the same year and at Princeton in January, 1777, though small victories, did much to reinvigorate the colonial cause.

At the Battle of Brandywine in Pennsylvania, in September, 1777, however, Washington's troops again suffered a setback. In June 1777 British troops had begun to move down from Canada and at first seemed assured of victory, but shrewd American manoeuvring resulted in defeat of the British and the surrender of Burgoyne following the Battle of Saratoga in upstate New York.

This American triumph convinced the French to enter the war officially, bringing to the colonists badly needed material support, troops, monetary credit and a fleet. During the winter of 1778 Washington's troops suffered great hardship while wintering in Valley Forge. By the spring the colonial forces had regrouped and Washington's men made a good showing at the Battle of Monmouth in June, 1778. Later that year fighting shifted southward, when Sir Henry Clinton commanded an invasion of South Carolina.

Clinton's successor, Lord Cornwallis, led the army gradually north until Washington and the French Admiral de Grasse trapped him on the Yorktown Peninsula in Virginia, where he surrendered in 1781. The defeat resulted in the fall of the British prime minister, Lord North, who had prosecuted the war, and ended British will for further fighting. After almost two years of negotiating, the Treaty of Paris was signed in September 1783, recognising the independence of the USA.

It was a war fought in the difficult, heavily wooded back country, terrain troops found hard to negotiate. Indians were enlisted on both sides as allies, though their tactics and *modus operandi* – ambush, raiding, wanton killing, and the taking of hostages, many of whom were forced to go native – were anathema to the colonists.

The revolution had an impact far beyond the battlefield. Although support had not been universal – many loyalists fled at the war's end and formed the core of English-speaking Canada – the various coalitions uniting entrepreneurs, professionals, planters, farmers, and urban working people had given shape to the most advanced political hopes of their time. The newly created republic was an institution that political thinkers of the day had doubted was capable of governing a large area or even of surviving at all. The new country, founded by a democratic movement and based on the ideology of 'equal rights', opened the way for the long-term decline of monarchy in the rest of the world.

THE NAPOLEONIC WARS (1803–15) In 1779, the French overthrew the *ancien régime* of Louis XVI, to install in its place a radical democratic republic under the National Assembly. By inclination the French Revolution was anti-militaristic; its survival, however, obliged it to arm itself with something more than the untrustworthy remnant of the regular army it had inherited. Tens of thousands of citizens in the grip of revolutionary fervour rallied to the defence of the republic against its enemies from within and without, but when their numbers proved insufficient conscription was introduced. Freed from aristocratic hindrances – officers were promoted on merit not class or wealth – and fired up on a transcendent political ideology, the new model French army defeated all comers.

Pre-eminent among the generals who brought victory was Napoleon Bonaparte, a Corsican. As military success fell into Bonaparte's hands, so did political power. In the 1799 coup d'état, he appointed himself First Consul of France. Five years later he crowned himself Emperor, before leading out the *Grande Armée* on an epic decade of campaigning. Half of Europe was conquered. Only in Spain, where it encountered a determined British expeditionary force under Wellington, did it suffer defeat.

The turning point in the Napoleonic Wars came in 1812 when France invaded Russia. Caught by the early onset of winter, the French army froze and starved to death. Pushed back into Germany, Napoleon was defeated at Leipzig by allies-turned-enemies, Austria and Prussia, and he was forced to abdicate in 1814.

In 1815 he returned to power to head the remnant of his armies against an Allied force under Wellington and the Prussian Blücher. The two sides met in Belgium near the village of Waterloo, the last battle of the Napoleonic Wars. Though he had more men and even more fire power, Napoleon was out-thought and out-fought.

THE SIEGE OF THE ALAMO (1836) One of the most celebrated and mythologised battles in American history, and a symbol of Texan independence from Mexico, which was established in 1821. By 1836, Texas was in open revolt, and had become an independent republic. But Mexico was determined to bring it to heel and dealt brutally with those who took up arms against it. On 6 March 1836, General Antonio López de Santa Anna, in command of a force of several thousand Mexicans, stormed the Alamo, a walled compound in San Antonio, killing everyone inside it. Around 180 Texans and other Americans, under the command of Jim Bowie and William Travis, and including the famous Davy Crockett, defended the Alamo for twelve days until the last survivors were overwhelmed. The victorious Mexicans lost over 600 soldiers in the battle.

CRIMEAN WAR (1853–56) Once described as 'one of the bad jokes of history', one of its ostensible causes was a dispute between Russian Orthodox and Roman Catholic churches over privileges in holy places in Palestine. The war arose from the conflict of great powers in the Middle East and was more directly caused by Russian demands to exercise protection over the Orthodox subjects of the Ottoman sultan.

It was fought between Russia and a coalition of Great Britain, France, the Kingdom of Sardinia, and the Ottoman Empire (now Turkey); it was a major turning point in the political history of post-Napoleonic Europe.

The roots of the conflict lay in the Eastern Question posed by the continuing decay of the Ottoman Empire. Since the late eighteenth century,

Russia had become more eager to take advantage of this situation to increase its influence in the Balkans and to seize control from the Turks of the straits between the Black Sea and the Mediterranean Sea. After their victory in the Russo–Turkish War of 1823–29 and especially with the Treaty of Unkiar-Skelessi in 1833, the Russians moved towards the establishment of a unilateral protectorate over the Ottoman Empire.

Britain and France saw these developments as a threat to their own interests in the Middle East. Austria too, despite a long tradition of diplomatic co-operation with Russia, was uneasy about the increasing Russian influence in the Balkans. In 1841, the European powers and the Ottoman Empire managed to replace the Unkiar-Skelessi agreement with a general European protectorate.

By the early 1850s, however, Czar Nicholas I of Russia believed he saw another opportunity to further Russian influence by intervening in Turkish affairs. In particular, he felt he could count on support from Austria in return for the aid Russia had given the Habsburg dynasty during the revolutions of 1848–50. He also believed, mistakenly, that the British government would collaborate in a partition of the Balkan territories controlled by the Turks.

In December 1852 the Ottoman sultan, responding to French pressure, decided in favour of the Roman Catholics. Nicholas, the protector of Orthodoxy, immediately dispatched a mission to Constantinople (now Istanbul) aimed at a new settlement in favour of the Orthodox Christians and a treaty guaranteeing the rights of the Orthodox population of the Ottoman Empire. At the same time, in discussions with the British ambassador to Russia, Nicholas raised the possibility of a partition of the Balkans and a 'temporary' Russian occupation of Constantinople and the straits.

The British ambassador to Constantinople helped to arrange an amicable settlement of the holy places question, but persuaded the Turks to reject the other Russian demands as a threat to their sovereignty. Russia responded on 1 July 1853 by occupying the Turkish principalities of Moldavia and Walachia. Attempts at a compromise by the European powers proved futile. On 4 October, confident of British and French support, Turkey declared war.

At the end of November Russia destroyed the Turkish fleet at the Black Sea port of Sinope, resulting in a public outcry in Britain and France. In March 1854, after Russia ignored their demand to evacuate Moldavia and Walachia, Britain and France declared war. On 3 June Austria, to Russia's dismay, also threatened to declare war. Russia complied on 5 August, and Austrian troops occupied the principalities.

The allies then decided on a campaign against Sevastopol in the Crimea, headquarters of Russia's Black Sea fleet, and their forces landed in the Crimea in September 1854. Despite victories over the Russians at the Alma river, Balaklava and Inkerman, the war dragged on, as the Russians refused to accept the allies' peace terms. Finally, on 9 September 1855 Sevastopol fell, but Russia only agreed to make peace after Austria threatened to enter the war.

The Treaty of Paris, signed on 30 March 1856, was a major setback for

Russia's Middle Eastern policy. Russia was forced to return southern Bessarabia and the mouth of the Danube to Turkey; Moldavia, Walachia and Serbia were placed under an international rather than a Russian guarantee; the sultan limited himself to vague promises to respect the rights of all his Christian subjects; and the Russians were forbidden to maintain a navy on the Black Sea.

In military terms, the war was a blundering, needlessly costly affair. The commanders on both sides proved remarkably inept, squandering lives in senseless engagements such as the Charge of the Light Brigade, in which a British unit suffered severe losses during the Battle of Balaclava. Supply services for both armies were hampered by inefficiency and corruption, and medical services were appalling. The British nurse Florence Nightingale won fame by her efforts to improve the care of the sick and wounded – an angel in the ward, she was as tough as old boots in her dealings with the military hierarchy. Nevertheless more men died of disease than in battle.

The war was an event of major significance in European history. It marked the collapse of the arrangement whereby the victors of the Napoleonic Wars – Britain, Russia, Austria and Prussia – had co-operated to maintain peace in Europe for four decades. Russia's reputation as a superpower was in shreds, and the break-up of the old coalition permitted Germany and Italy to free themselves from Austrian influence and emerge as nations in the decade that followed.

The Crimean War was also notable because it was the first to be reported by a war correspondent. William Howard Russell's graphic despatches for *The Times* managed to turn public opinion against a war which, when it broke out, was – in the estimation of Queen Victoria – 'popular beyond belief'.

INDIAN MUTINY (1857–58) A serious rebellion against British rule, prompted in part by the belief among Indian troops in British service that new cartridges had been greased with a mixture of cow and pig fat – something which would have been abhorrent to both Hindus and Muslims. The first violent protests took place at Meerut, to the north-east of Delhi, on 10 May 1857. There men of the Third Native Light Infantry were court-martialled for refusing to use the new greased cartridge that was being issued to units of the Bengali Army. As a result, eighty-five of the mutinous sepoys were sentenced to ten years' hard labour.

Queen Victoria, in a perceptive letter to Lady Canning, wife of the Governor-General of India, wrote: 'I think that the greatest care ought to be taken not to interfere with their religion – as once a cry of that kind is raised amongst a fanatical people – very strictly attached to their religion – there is no knowing what it may lead to and where it may end.'

At the same time, however, there was resentment among the old governing class over the reduction in their power, and Western innovations. The uprising at Meerut on 10 May 1857 spread throughout northern India, with both urban and rural populations rising in revolt. Delhi quickly fell, and Cawnpore and Lucknow garrisons were besieged. The British finally regained full control in mid-1858. The immediate result was the transfer of government from the British East India Company to the British Crown, but the long-term result was a legacy of bitterness on both sides. Moreover the episode provided a source of inspiration for later Indian nationalists. It also caused considerable damage to Victorian self-esteem and struck a chilling blow at European security by putting at risk the lives of thousands of British men, women and children.

AMERICAN CIVIL WAR (1861–65) The greatest war of the nineteenth century, the most brutal, the longest lasting, the most traumatic and divisive. It began at 4.30 a.m. on 12 April 1861, when General Pierre Gustave Toutant Beauregard ordered his Confederate gunners to open fire on Fort Sumter in Charleston harbour in South Carolina. A little less than a day and a half later, a white flag was raised over the fort, bringing an end to the bombardment. The only casualty was a Confederate horse. As Ken and Ric Burns, the documentary film-makers wrote, 'It was a bloodless opening to the bloodiest war in American history.'

The war has been given many different names, including the War Between the States, the War Against Northern Aggression, the Second American Revolution, the Lost Cause, the War of the Rebellion, the Brothers' War, and the Late Unpleasantness. Call it what you will, say the brothers Burns, 'it was unquestionably the most important event in the life of the nation. It brought an end to slavery and the downfall of a southern planter aristocracy . . . It was the first modern war and, for Americans, the costliest, yielding the most American casualties and the greatest domestic suffering, spiritually and physically. It was the most horrible, necessary, intimate, acrimonious, mean-spirited, and heroic conflict the nation has known.'

It was conflict demarcated geographically, between Northern states – the Union – and Southern states that had seceded – the Confederacy, the *soi-disant* 'Rebels'. The causes of the war included a disagreement over slavery, which was then only extant in the south, and conflict over how much control the federal government should exert over individual states. The election as president in 1860 of Abraham Lincoln, who was hostile to slavery and opposed its extension to new territories (although he did not believe at first that he could interfere with it where it already existed) precipitated the conflict.

South Carolina seceded almost once from the Union, followed shortly thereafter by another ten states. These eleven states formed the Confederacy early in 1861. Most of the Civil War battles were fought in the South, and the Confederacy won some early victories, particularly at Bull Run, the first battle of the war, and Fredericksburg and in the Peninsula Campaign. But Antietam, in 1862, was a victory for the North. In a single day, the Union side lost 2,108 dead and 10,293 wounded or missing while the Confederates under General Robert E. Lee had fewer casualties – 10,319 – but, because they represented a higher percentage of their total army, suffered a more telling blow.

Shortly after Antietam, President Lincoln signed the Emancipation

Proclamation freeing all slaves in the Confederacy. This further reduced the available manpower in the South and as the war continued, the Union, with its far greater manpower, and industrial resources, slowly took control. The Battle of Vicksburg in 1863 was a major victory, and the Battle of Gettysburg, followed by Lincoln's Gettysburg Address, on 19 November, marked a turning point in the war.

'Fourscore and seven years ago,' said Lincoln, 'our fathers brought forth on this continent a new nation, conceived in liberty, and dedicated to the proposition that all men are created equal.

'Now we are engaged in a great civil war, testing whether that nation, or any nation so conceived and so dedicated, can long endure. We are met on a great battlefield of that war. We have come to dedicate a portion of that field as a final resting place for those who here gave their lives that that nation might live.'

By 1864, Union forces had captured Atlanta and completed a march of destruction through Georgia to the sea. The war ended on 9 April 1865, when General Lee surrendered to Ulysses M Grant at Appomattox Court House, having agreed two days earlier 'to avoid useless effusion of blood'.

SIEGE OF PARIS (1870–71) After the battle of Sedan, on the Meuse near the Franco–Belgian border, and the capture and abdication of Napoleon III, the Prussians then besieged Paris. Attempts by the National Guard from inside the city, and by the new armies raised by Léon Gambetta (Minister of the Interior in the Government of National Defence) south of the River Loire failed to lift the siege. Gambetta escaped from the Siege of Paris by balloon and ruled France as Leader of the Tours Delegation until the government were forced, due to the shortage of food, to ask for an armistice at the end of January 1871. The hysterical atmosphere of the siege, and the existence of the National Guard, which was not disarmed by the terms of the armistice, were important causes of the insurrection of 18 March, leading to the Paris Commune.

EGYPTIAN AND SUDANESE CAMPAIGNS (1882–98) Mohammad Ahmed, the Mahdi of the Sudan, joined the Samaniyya dervish order, but around 1872 he proclaimed privately that he was al-Mahdi al-Muntazar ('the awaited or expected Mahdi'), who promised believers that a new order was imminent. He made a tour of the Sudan from Dongola to Sennar, from the Blue Nileto Kordofan, and convinced himself of the people's disaffection and discontent with the established order.

In 1881 he made his first public appearance as Mahdi and Mahdism spread from Kordofan and Bahr al-Ghazal to the eastern Sudan. His forces annihilated the large Egyptian army led by Col. William Hicks in 1883 and the British government decided to evacuate the Sudan, sending in General Gordon in 1884 to superintend the evacuation of the Egyptian garrisons.

Gordon was besieged at Khartoum for ten months by the Mahdi's forces, and was killed two days before a relief expedition arrived. Mohammad Ahmed died the same year (1885) but the Sudan remained under Mahdist control until 1898, when Kitchener defeated Ahmed's successor, Khalifa Abdullah, at Omdurman, in a battle which claimed the lives of an estimated 11,000 'dervishes'.

All Gordon's admiration, wrote Lytton Strachey in a controversial essay, was reserved for his enemies. The meanest of the Mahdi's followers, he realised, was 'a determined warrior, who could undergo thirst and privation, who no more cared for pain or death than if he were a stone. Those were the men whom, if the choice had lain with him, he would have wished to command.'

BOER WARS (1880–81 and 1899–1902) The two Boer Wars were the culmination of two and a half centuries of Afrikaner expansion and conflict between the Africans and the British. In 1877, Britain annexed the Transvaal in an attempt to unify South Africa, eventually leading to the outbreak of the first Boer War. This annexation was overturned in 1881, after Paul Kruger, 'Oom Paul', led a rebellion, which culminated in the defeat of the British at the Battle of Majuba Hill. Subject to certain conditions, the Transvaal's independence was restored, including British supervision of its foreign policy.

The second Boer War was declared by the Boers on 11 October 1899. According to Rudyard Kipling, it gave the British 'no end of a lesson'. In a letter to Lord Salisbury, the prime minister, Queen Victoria wrote:'I sincerely hope that the increased taxation, necessary to meet the expenses of the war, will not fall upon the working classes; but I fear they will be the most affected by the extra sixpence on beer.'

It was widely expected by the British public that the war would be over in a matter of months. In fact, it ran on for two and three-quarter years, cost over £200 million, and resulted in almost 60,000 casualties: 20,000 British, 25,000 Boer and 12,000 African.

There were three distinct phases. From October 1899 to January 1900, the Boers claimed a number of successes, including the sieges of Ladysmith, Kimberley and Mafeking, as well as victories at Stormberg, Modder River, Magersfontein, Colenso, and Modderspruit. From February to August 1900, however, Lord Roberts led several counter-offensives, raising the sieges, claiming victory at Paardeberg Drift, and capturing Pretoria. Finally, from September 1900 to May 1902 there was a period of guerrilla warfare when Kitchener attempted to prevent Boer commando raids on isolated British units and lines of communication.

The Boers effectively won the peace. They maintained control of 'native affairs', won back representative government in 1907, and federated South Africa on their terms in 1910. On the other hand, British interests in South Africa were protected and, despite internal strains, the Union of South Africa entered both World War I and World War II on the British side. 'In money and lives,' wrote Thomas Packenham in *The Boer War* (1979), 'no British war since 1815 had been so prodigal.'

WORLD WAR I (1914–18) Its origins lay in the increasingly aggressive foreign policies as pursued by Austria-Hungary, Russia and, most significantly, Germany. The assassination of the heir to the Habsburg throne, Franz Ferdinand, at Sarajevo in Bosnia on 28 June 1914, triggered the war which soon involved most European states following Austria's declaration of war on Serbia towards the end of July. Shortly thereafter Russia mobilised in support of Serbia, and Germany declared war on Russia and France.

The German invasion of neutral Belgium on 4 August brought the British into the war on the French side. Japan joined Britain, France and Russia under the terms of an earlier agreement with Britain, and Italy joined the Allies in May 1915. In November 1914, Turkey allied with Germany, and they were joined by Bulgaria almost a year later. Military campaigning centred on France, Belgium and, later, Italy in Western Europe, and on Poland, western Russia and the Balkans in Eastern Europe.

The French Army prevented the Germans from executing the Schlieffen Plan – named after Count Alfred von Schlieffen, a Prussian field marshal, who drew it up. This envisaged a German breakthrough in Belgium and the defeat of the French within six weeks. Germany would then turn its attention eastwards to confront and subdue the Russians, who would sue for peace. Schlieffen, however, was over-optimistic and ignored the long-term implications of British entry into the war.

By the end of 1914, a static defence line had been established from the Belgian coast to Switzerland. From April 1915 to January 1916, the Allies attempted to break the stalemate by the Gallipoli Campaign aimed at re-supplying Russia and knocking out Turkey, but failed.

On the eastern and southeastern fronts, the Central Powers occupied Russian Poland and most of Lithuania, and Serbia was invaded. After staunch resistance, Serbia, Albania and, latterly, Romania were overrun. For three years, an Allied army was involved in a Macedonian campaign, and there was also fighting in Mesopotamia against Turkey. Naval competition had played a crucial role in heightening tension before 1914, but in the event, the great battle fleets of Germany did not play an important part in the war. The only significant naval encounter, at Jutland in 1916, proved indecisive.

The Allies organised a large offensive for the Western Front in 1916, but were forestalled by the Germans, who attacked France at Verdun. To relieve the situation, the Battle of the Somme was launched on 1 July, but was inconclusive. On the first day alone the loss of life was appalling. Of the 100,000 British troops who entered no-man's land, 20,000 did not return and 40,000 were wounded. Four weeks later, the writer Gerald Brenan, then a young British officer, found the bodies of soldiers wounded on 1 July who had 'crawled into shell holes, wrapped their waterproof sheets round them, taken out their bibles and died'.

In January 1917, the Germans then unleashed unrestricted submarine warfare to cripple Britain economically before the USA could intervene. The USA declared war on Germany on 2 April 1917, by which time British food stocks were at emergency levels, and the German submarine menace was finally overcome by the use of convoys. By 1917, the Russian armies were broken and revolution broke out in St Petersburg and Moscow. In late 1917 Lenin's Bolshevik government sued for peace and in March 1918 Germany and her allies imposed the punitive peace of Brest-Litovsk on the USSR, which was subsequently annulled. Following this, in the spring of 1918, the Germans launched a major attack in the west, but after several months of success were driven back, with the USA providing an increasing number of much-needed troops.

By September 1918, the German Army was in full retreat, and signified its intention to sue for peace on the basis of President Wilson's Fourteen Points. Two months later, when the armistice was signed, the Allies had recaptured western Belgium and nearly all French territory. Military victories in Palestine and Mesopotamia resulted in a Turkish armistice on 31 October 1918; Italian victories and a northward advance by Franco–British forces finished Austria-Hungary and Bulgaria.

The death toll was horrendous. Over a million citizens of the British Empire died, 1,700,000 French, 1,500,000 soldiers of the Habsburg Empire, two million Germans, 460,000 Italians, 1,700,000 Russians and hundreds of thousands of Turks. The number of wounded has been estimated at double the above totals. 'Little wonder,' wrote John Keegan in *The First World War: An Illustrated History*, 'the post-war world spoke of a "lost generation", that its parents were united by shared grief and that the survivors proceeded into the life that followed with a sense of inexplicable escape, often tinged by guilt, sometimes by rage and revenge'. Among them was one Adolf Hitler who in a photograph taken in 1914 can be seen amidst a crowd in Munich joyfully celebrating the outbreak of war.

SPANISH CIVIL WAR (1936–39) 'No other war in recent times,' wrote Phillip Knightley in *The First Casualty*, 'with the possible exception of Vietnam, aroused such deep commitment, such violent partisanship as the Civil War in Spain.' On one side were the representatives of the old order, the Nationalists – bankers, landlords, conservative Catholics, the army and monarchists; on the other, the Republicans, including peasants and workers, writers and intellectuals, and a democratically elected government. 'In essence it was a class war,' wrote George Orwell. 'If it had been won, the cause of the common people would have been strengthened. It was lost, and the dividend-drawers all over the world rubbed their hands.'

The armed forces were divided. Both sides attracted foreign assistance: the Republic from the USSR and the International Brigades; the Nationalists from Fascist Italy and Nazi Germany. The Nationalist victory was due to the balance of foreign aid; to 'non-intervention' on the part of the Western democracies; and to greater internal unity, achieved under the leadership of General Franco.

The war took the course of a slow Nationalist advance. In July 1936, the Nationalists seized much of north-west Spain and part of the south-west, and advanced on Madrid but did not manage to take control of it. However, they captured Malaga in March 1937 and the north coast (March–October 1937) and advanced to the Mediterranean, and by April 1918 had succeeded in cutting Republican Spain in two. From December 1938 to February 1939, the Nationalists overran Catalonia and finally occupied Madrid and south-east Spain in March 1939.

Nationalist forces numbered in the region of 600,000 while the Republicans had approximately 450,000. Losses in battle were 110,000 and 175,000 respectively but to them must be added the 80,000 Nationalist sympathisers who were caught on the wrong side of the lines and executed, and the 40,000 Republicans who were executed during and after the war. Often misleadingly described as a dress rehearsal for WWII, it included the bombing by the German Air Command in 1937 of Guernica, a small town 32 kilometres from Bilbao, then in the hands of the Republicans. It was seen as an example of 'terror bombing' and became the subject of an iconic painting by Pablo Picasso. Originally, it was reported that 1,000 civilians had died here; 300 is probably a more accurate figure.

The Republicans attracted many foreign artists and intellectuals to their cause, including Orwell and Ernest Hemingway. 'Civil war,' observed Hemingway, 'is the best war for a writer, the most complete.' 'The fact is that Hemingway was never a very good war correspondent,' wrote Anthony Burgess. 'His fiction-writer's talent impelled him to invent, organise reality into aesthetic patterns.'

WORLD WAR II (1939–45) For some historians and politicians the origins of World War II could be dismissed in two words: Adolf Hitler. For the historian AJP Taylor, however, that was much too simplistic. For him, the story of WWII was one without heroes 'and perhaps even villains'. Hitler, however, was a convenient demon on whom to heap the world's opprobrium. 'The blame for everything,' wrote Taylor in *The Origins of the Second World War*, 'could be loaded on to his uncomplaining shoulders.'

Its origins lay in three different conflicts which merged after 1941: Hitler's desire for European expansion and perhaps even world domination; Japan's struggle against China; and a resulting conflict between Japanese ambitions and US interests in the Pacific.

The origins of the war in Europe lay in German unwillingness to accept the frontiers laid down in 1919 by the Treaty of Versailles and the National Socialists' expansionist foreign policy. After the German invasion of rump Bohemia-Moravia in March 1939, Britain and France pledged support to Poland. Germany, meanwhile, entered into an alliance with the USSR in August the same year and a month later invaded Poland. Britain and France promptly declared war on Germany, but could not prevent Poland from being overrun in four weeks.

For six months there was a period of 'phoney war', when there was little fighting. But in April 1940 the Germans occupied Norway and Denmark, followed by Belgium and Holland. France was next to fall. A combination of German tank warfare and air power brought about the surrender of Holland in four days, Belgium in three weeks, and France in seven weeks. Italy declared war on France and Britain in the final stages of this campaign.

In May 1940, Field Marshal Lord Gort ordered the evacuation of the British Expeditionary Force from Dunkirk at Normandy. The expedition began on 26 May and over the following days vessels of all sorts were commandeered. In total, 338,000 men, 120,000 of them French, were evacuated. Of the 693 British ships which took part, about 200 were sunk and many were damaged. Over a hundred aircraft were also lost. Though Winston Churchill warned that 'wars are not won by evacuation', the success of the operation was psychologically and materially vital to the British war effort. There followed the Battle of Britain, also known as the 'Spitfire summer', in which Germany tried in vain to achieve air supremacy over Britain. Ultimately, German attempts to force Britain to come to terms came to nothing, not least because of Churchill's obduracy.

Germany then launched submarine U-boat attacks against British supply routes, but then moved east and invaded Greece and Yugoslavia in the spring of 1941 and, following an Italian military fiasco there, Greece. British military efforts were concentrated against Italy in the Mediterranean and North Africa. After early reverses for Italy, Rommel was sent to North Africa with the German Afrika Korps to reinforce Italian military strength, and fiercely-contested campaigning continued here for three years until Allied troops finally ejected German and Italian forces in mid-1943, invaded Sicily and then Italy itself, and forced Italy to make a separate peace in September 1943.

In June 1941, in line with Hitler's historical hostility to the USSR, and in his quest for Lebensraum ('living space'), Germany invaded her ally Russia along a 2,000 mile front, and German armies advanced in three formations; to the outskirts of Leningrad in the north, towards Moscow in the centre, and to the Volga river in the south. After spectacular early successes, the Germans were held up by bitter Soviet resistance, and by heavy winter snows and Arctic temperatures, for which, despite the example of Napoleon, they were completely unprepared. From November 1942 they were gradually driven back, suffering decisive reverses at Stalingrad, where 60,000 Germans died and 110,000 others were captured, and Kursk.

Leningrad was under siege for nearly two and a half years, and about a third of its population died from starvation and disease. But by August 1944, the Germans were finally driven out of the USSR. A second front was launched against Germany by the Allies, through the invasion of Normandy, and Paris was liberated on 25 August. Albert Camus, then working for the Resistance newspaper *Combat*, wrote in an editorial: 'The greatness of man lies in his decision to be stronger than his condition.'

Despite German use of flying bombs and rockets against Allied bases, the Allies continued their advance into Germany in February 1945 and connected with the Russians on the River Elbe two months later. The Germans surrendered unconditionally at Rheims in May.

In the Far East, Japan's desire for expansion, combined with a US threat of economic sanctions against her, led to her attack on Pearl Harbor and other

British and US bases on 7 December 1941. A day later the USA declared war on Japan. Japan's allies, Germany and Italy, promptly declared war on the USA. Within four months, Japan controlled south-east Asia and Burma. Not until June 1942 did naval victories in the Pacific stem the advance, and Japanese troops defended their positions grimly. Bitter fighting continued until 1945, when, with Japan on the retreat, the USA dropped two atomic bombs on Hiroshima and Nagasaki, on 6 and 9 August. Japan then surrendered on 14 August. Between 130,000 and 200,000 died, were injured or disappeared.

Reliable casualty figures are not easy to obtain for WWII. It is estimated that around three million Russians were killed in action. A further three million died as prisoners of war, while eight million people died in occupied Russia. Germany suffered three and three-quarter million military casualties, around six million total casualties, and lost a million prisoners of war. Japan suffered just over two million military casualties and just over a quarter of a million civilian deaths. France lost a total of half a million dead, and Britain and the Commonwealth just over 600,000. The USA suffered just over 300,000 casualties. In addition, it is believed that around six million Jews died in concentration camps such as Auschwitz, Bergen-Belsen and Dachau.

KOREAN WAR (1950–53) A war between Communist and non-Communists forces in Korea, which had been partitioned along the 38th parallel in 1945 after Japan's defeat in World War II. The leaders of both North and South Korea, Kim-Il Sung and Syngman Rhee, wished to unite the country by military force. The Communist North invaded the South in 1950 after a series of border clashes, and a UN force intervened, driving the invaders back to the Chinese frontier.

China then entered the war and, together with the North Koreans, occupied Seoul, the South Korean capital. American air commanders attempted to win the war by bombing the enemy into submission but the North Koreans' resolve exceeded the bombers' capacity for destruction. Nevertheless many civilians were killed or injured. Finally, the UN forces counter-attacked, and by 27 July 1953, when an armistice was signed, had retaken all territory south of the 38th parallel.

Though in effect the war had changed nothing it encouraged many powerful people in America to believe the USA could triumph in any war, given the overwhelming superiority of its resources.

VIETNAM WAR (1964–75) A war between Communist North Vietnam and non-Communist South Vietnam which broadened to include the USA. It was preceded by the Indo-China War (1946–54) between France and the Viet Minh, which ended with the defeat of the French at Dien Bien Phu. The Geneva Conference left North Vietnam under the rule of Ho Chi Minh, while the South was ruled first by the Emperor Bao Dai and then by Ngo Dinh Diem. Elections were planned to choose a single government for all of Vietnam, but when they failed to take place, fighting was renewed.

With President Kennedy in the White House, from 1961, in an attempt to stop the spread of Communism, the USA increased its aid to South Vietnam and the number of its so-called military advisers and backed to Ngo Dinh Diem to stave off the Communist threat. Diem, however, was ineffectual and in the autumn of 1963, Kennedy withdrew support for him. In November that same year Diem was assassinated and a succession of generals took control in Saigon.

By now there were around 1,600 American military 'advisers' in Vietnam helping to defend the pro-West Saigon government, and the first Americans had died as a result of combat. At the time of President Kennedy's death, on 21 November 1963, the US was being dragged into the morass of a land war in south-east Asia. 'The whole basis of the escalation,' wrote David Halberstam in *The Brightest and the Best*, 'was that it would be brief . . . All we had to do was show them some of our muscle and give them a sense of our determination. Just six months.'

In 1964, following a North Vietnamese attack on US ships, President Lyndon Johnson ordered retaliatory bombing of North Vietnam. Although the US Congress never declared war officially, it passed the Gulf of Tonkin Resolution which authorised US forces in south-east Asia to repel any armed attack and to prevent further aggression. US bombing of North Vietnam was continued, and in 1965 the USA stepped up its troop commitment substantially. By 1968 over 500,000 US soldiers were involved in the war.

As the conflict dragged on, victory against the elusive Communist guerrilla forces seemed unattainable. Opposition to the war within the USA badly divided the country, and pressure mounted to bring the conflict to an end. In 1968 peace negotiations were begun in Paris, and in 1973 a ceasefire agreement was signed. However hostilities did not end until two years later when North Vietnam's victory was completed with the capture of Saigon, which was later renamed Ho Chi Minh City. Over two million, mostly unsung Vietnamese, were killed in the war. The names of the 58,000 Americans who died in it are inscribed in black marble on the wall memorial in Washington, which has become a place of pilgrimage for Vietnam veterans and American families.

FALKLANDS WAR (April–June 1982) On 2 April 1982, Argentina invaded the Falklands Islands (Malvinas in Spanish), which since 1833 had been in British hands. However, the sovereignty of the islands had long been disputed by Argentina, which laid claim to them on the basis of previous Spanish occupation and geography. Britain had been in protracted negotiations with Argentina on sovereignty over the Falklands, involving either a leaseback arrangement or a joint administration. When these talks broke down, the government of General Galtieri issued a warning to the British. The British government announced the withdrawal of HMS *Endurance* from the South Atlantic, and on 19 March scrap merchants landed on South Georgia, ostensibly to demolish a whaling station, but they also raised the Argentine flag.

The full-scale invasion of the Falklands began on 2 April when the seventy Royal Marines on the islands were overwhelmed, and the Government was deported to Uruguay. Margaret Thatcher, the British prime minister, immediately ordered a task force to retake the islands, and the Foreign Office team, including Lord Carrington, resigned. The task force consisted of almost seventy ships, including some forty requisitioned merchantmen and well-known passenger vessels such as the *Queen Elizabeth II*. A 200-mile maritime exclusion zone was declared around the Falklands, and on 2 May the Argentine cruiser, *General Belgrano*, was sunk by the nuclear submarine, HMS *Conqueror*, with the loss of 368 lives.

This brought to an end peace initiatives conducted by the US Secretary of State, Alexander Haig, and the Peruvian government. On 25 April, South Georgia was retaken and on 4 May the destroyer HMS *Sheffield* was sunk by an Exocet missile. Five thousand British troops were landed at Port San Carlos on 21 May and more troops were subsequently landed at Bluff Cove, an operation attended by much loss of life when the Argentine air force attacked the *Sir Tristram* and *Sir Galahad*. The British forces took Darwin and Goose Green on 28 May, and after the recapture of the capital, Port Stanley, on 14 June the Argentinians surrendered.

The British war bill was £700 million; 254 British and well over 700 Argentine lives were lost. Some commentators claim that it did much to save the declining fortunes of the Thatcher government. It was a war that could have been prevented had Britain demonstrated more keenly its desire to hold on to the Falklands. The Argentinian military *junta* which ordered the invasion fell soon afterwards.

GULF WAR (1990–91) In the summer of 1990, Saddam Hussein, the Iraqi dictator, claimed that Kuwait had stolen oil from the Rumaila oilfield which straddles the Iraq–Kuwait border, and refused to pay back loans received from Kuwait to fund the recent Iran–Iraq War. The Iraqi army massed on the frontier and after being informed that the United States did not wish to become involved in the dispute Saddam ordered the invasion of Kuwait on 2 August.

This concentrated minds wonderfully and George Bush, the American president, worried that the Iraqis would advance into Saudi Arabia, which controlled half the world's oil reserves, demanded an immediate and unconditional withdrawal from Kuwait. When this was not forthcoming Operation Desert Storm was put into action, involving a US-led coalition, eventually comprising 700,000 troops from the United Kingdom, France, Egypt, Syria and Saudi Arabia, under the command of General Norman H. Schwarzkopf.

The war lasted a month and a half, during which time Baghdad was repeatedly bombed. Iraq responded by attacking Israel with a Scud missile, purportedly carrying a chemical warhead, which landed in Tel Aviv. Thereafter Patriot missiles were employed to find and destroy Scuds, the first use of anti-missiles in the history of war. Schwarzkopf soon had the Iraqis surrounded and by 24 February had begun direct attacks into Kuwait, launching rockets with more explosive power than the Hiroshima atomic bomb. Saddam, who was known to have chemical and biological weapons, chose not to reply in kind and on 25 February he ordered the withdrawal from Kuwait. The coalition showed no appetite to pursue him further, allowing him to remain as leader of Iraq and to wreak vengeance on the Kurds and Shiites who had been encouraged to rise against him. For the moment, the status quo pertained.

YUGOSLAVIA (1991–) In June 1991 Slovenia and Croatia moved towards independence from Yugoslavia. Serbia, led by Slobodan Milosevic, saw this as an attempt to break up Yugoslavia and declared that it would defend Serbs who would otherwise be forced to live under hated Croatian rule. There was immediately the prospect of bloody conflict between Yugoslav army units – manned mainly by Serbs – stationed in barracks in Slovenia and Croatia, and local militias. After intervention by the European Community, civil war was avoided in Slovenia but Croatia, which had a large Serbian population, was attacked by the Serbs, who captured the eastern region of the new country. In the spring of 1992, through the good offices of the EC and the United States, a truce was brokered and a United Nations peacekeeping force was sent to keep the two sides apart.

In March 1992 Bosnia-Herzegovina proclaimed its independence, heralding an even greater tragedy. With a mixed ethnic population – 44 per cent Muslim, 33 per cent Serb-Christian, 17 per cent Croat-Christian – the potential for violence was self-evident. Serbs, Croats and Muslims murdered minorities in their midst. The Croats refused to recognise borders of the republic of Bosnia-Herzegovina and captured regions in the north and east inhabited by a majority of 600,000 Croats. Serbs, meanwhile, engaged in 'ethnic cleansing', by driving the Muslim population out of Bosnia-Herzegovina, thus contributing to the lexicon of genocide. Many Muslims were killed or sent to concentration camps and Sarajevo, the capital of Bosnia-Herzegovina, was blitzed. No one was safe from the carnage and no distinction was made between civilians and combatants. While all sides committed atrocities, none behaved quite so appallingly as the Serbs.

Tens of thousands lost their lives, many of whom were buried in unmarked mass graves. More than two million people were reduced to refugees and compelled to seek succour wherever they could be admitted. Germany accepted the most. Switzerland took in 70,000 and Austria 57,000. While the killing continued, leaders in the West talked. Eventually, in February 1994, the UN acted and brokered a peace between Muslims and Croats. Following the Croatian conquest of Serb Krajina in August 1995, NATO planes destroyed the Bosnian Serbs' command and control. On 5 October there was a ceasefire.

That, however, was not that. An uneasy peace ended in 1998, when Milosevic began expelling Kosovar Albanians from a part of southern Serbia where they comprised 90 per cent of the population. This new wave of ethnic cleansing galvanised the rest of the world and Milosevic agreed to an international monitoring force. Soon, however, he reverted to type and the atrocities recommenced. NATO responded with air strikes and the Serbs took their revenge on the Muslims. In July 1999, the Serbs withdrew from Kosovo, allowing NATO to enter.

In September 2000 Milosevic called elections and was dramatically ousted from power and subsequently arrested and charged with war crimes. At the time of writing his trial at the Hague is ongoing.

CHECHEN WAR (1994–96) On 11 December 1994 Russian forces were despatched to Chechnya, formerly part of the USSR, to restore constitutional order after three years of tension. But what began as a skirmish turned into a major conflict, with the Chechens proving stubborn and resourceful adversaries. With victory elusive, Russia's generals and politicians had to answer to a new and enquiring media and a less biddable body politic. Nor was the public silent. A petition against the war attracted over a million signatures. Finally, in August 1996, after eighteen months of armed conflict and uneasy ceasefires, an agreement was reached between the Russian Federation and Chechnya's leaders. Federal troops were withdrawn and a five-year moratorium imposed on any discussion of the republic's disputed status. But in the summer of 1999, the new government, with Vladimir Putin as prime minister, decided to 'do the job properly'. Before all the bodies of those killed in the first campaign had been located or identified, thousands more were slaughtered in another round of fighting. Both sides were guilty of atrocities. In September, the Chechens were held responsible for the bombing of two apartment blocks in Moscow in which 200 people were killed as they slept. The following month Russian missiles killed dozens of Chechen civilians in a market in Grozny. To date, several thousand Russian soldiers and many more Chechens have died.

IRAQ WAR (March–April 2003) Following the attacks on 11 September 2001, when over 3,000 Americans were killed by members of the terrorist organisation Al Qaeda, the government of the United States, under the presidency of George W. Bush, promised to punish those responsible. On 7 October 2001, the US went to war with Afghanistan, where it was believed Osama bin Laden, Al Qaeda's leader, was based and from where he had planned 9/11. By mid-November, the Taliban regime had fallen, though bin Laden had not been caught or killed.

The focus in the White House now moved to Iraq which several sources previously close to President Bush later insisted had been the target from the outset. It was widely publicised that Saddam Hussein, the Iraqi leader, had weapons of mass destruction and was prepared to use them. None, however, had been found by United Nations weapons inspectors. Nor had any evidence been found which linked Saddam to Al Qaeda. That he was a dangerous and despotic ruler was not in dispute.

A coalition, whose members included the US, the United Kingdom, Italy, Spain and Turkey, launched an 'attack of opportunity' against specified targets in Iraq on 20 March 2003. The coalition forces were commanded by General Tommy Franks. In a matter of days, Basra was taken and Baghdad fell on 9

April. Tikrit, the home town of Saddam Husseim, and the last town not under coalition control, was taken by the Americans on 13 April. The war was declared effectively over two days later. Saddam was discovered hiding in a bunker by American soldiers on 13 December. The following day, President Bush said: 'In the history of Iraq, a dark and painful era is over. A hopeful day has arrived. All Iraqis can now come together and reject violence and build a new Iraq.'

Bibliography

Agate, James *The Selected Ego. The Diaries of James Agate*. Harrap, London, 1976.

Alanbrooke, Field Marshal Lord, *War Diaries 1939–1945*. Phoenix Press, London, 2002.

Allaire, Anthony in Lyman C. Draper *King's Mountains and its Heroes: History of the Battle of King's Mountain Oct 7 1780 and the events which led to it*. P.G. Thomson, Cincinatti, 1881.

American Diaries: An Annotated Bibliography of American Diaries Written Prior to the Year 1861 University of California Press, Berkeley, 1945.

American Diaries: An Annotated Bibliography of Published American Diaries and Journals Volume 1: Diaries written from 1492 to 1844. Gale Research Company, Detroit, 1983. *Volume 2: Diaries written from 1845 to 1980*. Gale Research Company, Detroit, 1987.

The American Revolution: Writings from the War of Independence. Selected by John Rhodehamel. The Library of America, New York, 2001.

And So To Bed: A Bibliography of Diaries Published in English. The Scarecrow Press, Metuchen, New Jersey, 1987.

Ardizzone, Edward, *Diary of a War Artist*. The Bodley Head, London, 1974.

Asquith, Lady Cynthia, *The Diaries of Lady Cynthia Asquith*. Century, London, 1968.

Auden, W.H. *Another Time*. Faber and Faber, London, 1940.

Barbellion, W.N.P. *The Journal of a Disappointed Man*. Penguin, Harmondsworth, England, 1948.

Beaton, Cecil *Self Portrait with Friends: The Selected Diaries of Cecil Beaton 1926–1974*. Weidenfeld and Nicolson, London, 1979.

— *The Years Between. Diaries 1939–44*. Weidenfeld and Nicolson, London, 1965.

Beevor, Anthony, *Berlin: The Downfall 1945*. Viking, London, 2002.

— *Stalingrad*. Viking, London, 1998.

— and Cooper, Artemis, *Paris After the Liberation: 1944–1949*. Penguin, Harmondsworth, England, 1995.

Benn, Tony, *The Benn Diaries*. Hutchinson, London, 1995.

Bennett, Alan, *Writing Home*. Faber and Faber, London, 1995.

— *The Journals of Arnold Bennett*. Penguin, Harmondsworth, England, 1954.

Berg, A. Scott *Lindbergh*. Macmillan, London, 1998.

Berenson, Bernard, *Rumour and Reflection*. Constable, London, 1952.

Berger, Josef and Dorothy, *Diary of America: The Intimate Story of Our Nation, Told By 100 Diarists*. Simon and Schuster, New York, 1957.

Biddle, George, *Artist at War*. The Viking Press, 1944.

Blunt, Wilfred Scawen, *My Diaries*. London, 1922.

Blythe, Ronald, *Each Returning Day: The Pleasure of Diaries*. Selected by Ronald Blythe. Viking, London, 1989.

Bonham Carter, Violet, *Champion Redoubtable. The Diaries and Letters of Violet Bonham Carter, 1914–1945*. Phoenix, London, 1999.

Bosworth, R.J.B., *Mussolini*. Arnold, London, 2002.

Brittain, Vera, *Chronicle of Youth: Vera Brittain's War Diary 1913–1917*. Book Club Associates, London, 1981.

— *Wartime Chronicle: Vera Brittain's Diary 1939–45*. Gollancz, London, 1989.

Bullock, Alan, *Hitler and Stalin: Parallel Lives*. HarperCollins, London, 1991.

Butts, Mary, *The Journals of Mary Butts*. Yale University Press, New Haven, 2002.

Byron, George Gordon, sixth baron, *'For Freedom's Battle': Byron's Letters and Journals, Volume II 1823–1824*. John Murray, London, 1981.

Cadogan, Sir Alexander, *The Diaries of Sir Alexander Cadogan 1938–1945*. Cassell, London, 1971.

Calder, Angus, *The People's War: Britain 1939–1945*. Jonathan Cape, London, 1969.

— ed., *Wars*. Penguin, Harmondsworth, England, 1999.

— and Sheridan, Dorothy, eds., *Speak for Yourself: A Mass-Observation Anthology, 1937–1949*. Oxford University Presss, Oxford, 1985.

Carlyle, Thomas, *The French Revolution*. Oxford University Press, 1989.

Chambers Dictionary of World History, Chambers Harrap, Edinburgh, 1993

Chambers, John Whiteclay II, ed., *The Oxford Companion to American Military History*. Oxford University Press, Oxford, 1999.

Channon, Chips, *Chips: The Diaries of Sir Henry Channon*. Edited by Robert Rhodes James. Penguin, Harmondsworth, England, 1984.

Churchill, Winston, *The Second World War*. Pimlico, London, 2002.

Ciano, Count Galeazzo, *Ciano's Diary 1937–1943*. Phoenix Press, London, 2002.

Clark, Alan, *Diaries: Into Politics. The Long-awaited Early Years*. Weidenfeld & Nicolson, London, 2000.

Clark, Reverend Andrew, *Echoes of the Great War: The Diaries of the Reverend Andrew Clark 1914–1919*. Edited by James Munsun. Oxford University Press, Oxford, 1985.

Clark, Ossie, *The Ossie Clark Diaries*. Bloomsbury, London, 1998.

Coleridge, Samuel Taylor, *Selected Poems*. Bloomsbury, London, 1993.

Colville, John, *The Fringes of Power. Downing Street Diaries. Volume One: 1939–October 1941*. Sceptre, London, 1986.

— *The Fringes of Power. Downing Street Diaries. Volume 2: 1941–April 1955*. Sceptre, London, 1987.

Connell, Evan S., *Son of the Morning Star: General Custer and the Battle of the Little Big Horn*. Pimlico, London, 1999.

Coppola, Eleanor, *Notes by Eleanor Coppola*. Limelight Editions, USA, 1979.

Couglin, Sean T., *Storming the Desert: A Marine Lieutenant's Day-by-Day Chronicle of the Persian Gulf War*. McFarland & Company Inc, Jefferson, North Carolina, 1996.

Coward, Noël, *The Noël Coward Diaries*. Papermac, London, 1983.

Crick, Bernard, *George Orwell: A Life*.

Penguin, Harmondsworth, England, 1982.

Curtis, Michael, *Verdict on Vichy: Power and Prejudice in the Vichy France Regime.* Weidenfeld and Nicolson, London, 2002.

Diary of America: The intimate story of our nation, told by 100 diarists — public figures and plain citizens, natives and visitors — over the five centuries from Columbus, the Pilgrims, the George Washington to Thomas Edison, Will Rogers, and our own time. Edited by Josef and Dorothy Berger. Simon and Schuster, New York, 1957.

A Diary of an Iraqi Soldier (anonymous), Center for Research and Studies on Kuwait, 1992.

Dallas, Gregor, *1918: War and Peace.* Pimlico, London, 2002.

Dudeney, Mrs Henry, *A Lewes Diary 1916–1944.* Tartarus Press, England, 1998.

Dunlop, E.E. *The War Diaries of Weary Dunlop: Java and the Burma–Thailand Railway 1942–1945.* Viking Books, Australia, 1989.

Dworkin, Deborah and Jan van Pelt, Robert, *Holocaust: A History.* John Murray, London, 2002.

Ellis, Edward Robb, *A Diary of the Century.* Kodansha America, New York, 1995.

Erickson, John, *The Road to Berlin.* Weidenfeld and Nicolson, London, 1983.

Evelyn, John, *The Diary of John Evelyn.* Oxford University Press, Oxford, 1985.

Fahey, James, J., *Pacific War Diary 1942–1945. The Secret Diary of an American Sailor.* Houghton Mifflin, Boston, 1963.

Farmborough, Florence, *Nurse at the Russian Front: A Diary 1914–18.*

Book Club Associates, by arrangement with Constable and Company Ltd, London, 1974.

Ferguson, Niall, *The Pity of War.* Allen Lane, Harmondsworth, England, 1998.

Ferro, Marc, *The Great War 1914–1918.* Routledge and Kegan Paul, London, 1973.

Fest, Joachim, *Inside Hitler's Bunker.* Macmillan, London, 2004.

Filipovic, Zlata, *Zlata's Diary. A Child's Life in Sarajevo.* Viking, London, 1994.

Foote, Shelby, *The Civil War: A Narrative.* 3 vols. The Bodley Head, London, 1991.

Frank, Anne, *The Diary of a Young Girl.* Puffin Books, London, 1997.

Gide, André, *Journals 1889–1949.* Penguin, Harmondsworth, England, 1967.

Gilbert, Martin, *First World War.* Weidenfeld and Nicolson, London, 1994.

— *The Righteous: The Unsung Heroes of the Holocaust.* Doubleday, London, 2002.

Gillam, DSO, Major John, *Gallipoli Diary.* The Strong Oak Press with Tim Donovan Publishing, PO Box 47, Stevenage, Herts, SE2 8UH.

Gillespie, Andrew, *Desert Fire: The Diary of a Gulf War Gunner.* Leo Cooper, Barnsley, 2001.

Glass, Fiona ed., *Articles of War: The Spectator Book of World War II.* Grafton Books, London, 1989.

Glenny, Misha, *The Balkans: 1804–1999.* Granta Books, London, 1999.

Goebbels, Josef, *The Goebbels Diaries 1939–41.* Hamish Hamilton, London, 1982.

Goncourt, Edmond and Jules de, *Pages from the Goncourt Journal.* Oxford University Press, Oxford, 1962.

Gordon, General (Charles George), *General Gordon's Khartoum Journal.* William Kimber and Co, Ltd, London, 1961.

Graves, Robert, *Goodbye To All That.* Jonathan Cape, London, 1929.

Grenfell, Joyce, *The Time of My Life: Entertaining the Troops – her Wartime Journals.* Sceptre, London, 1989.

Guevara, Ernesto 'Che', *Bolivian Diary.* Jonathan Cape/Lorrimer, London, 1968.

Halberstam, David, *The Brightest and the Best.* The Modern Library, New York, 2001.

Handley, C.S., *An Annotated Bibliography of Diaries Printed in English.* Hanover Press, Whitley Bay, England, 2002.

Hastings, Max, *Going to the Wars.* Macmillan, London, 2000.

Heller, Joseph, *Catch-22.* Simon and Schuster, New York, 1961.

Hernon, Ian, *Britain's Forgotten Wars: Colonial Campaigns of the 19th Century.* Sutton Publishing, Stroud, Gloucestershire, 2003.

Hersey, John, *Hiroshima.* Knopf, New York, 1946.

Herzberg, Abel J., *Between Two Streams: A Diary from Bergen-Belsen.* I.B. Tauris, London, 1997.

Hibbert, Christopher, *Arnhem.* The Windrush Press, Gloucestershire, 1998.

Hillesum, Etty, *Etty Hillesum: An Interrupted Life. The Diaries 1941–43 and Letters from Westerbork.* Henry Holt, New York, 1986.

Hoess, Rudolf, *Commandant of Auschwitz: The Autobiography of Rudolf Hoess.* Weidenfeld and Nicolson, London, 1959.

Holmes, Richard, *Riding the Retreat: Mons to Marne 1914 Revisited.* Jonathan Cape, London, 1995.

—Holmes, Richard ed., *The Oxford Companion to Military History.* Oxford University Press, Oxford, 2001.

Horne, Alistair, *How Far From Austerlitz? Napoleon 1805–1815.* Macmillan, London, 1966.

— *The Price of Glory: Verdun 1916.* Macmillan, London, 1962.

Howarth, David, *Waterloo: A Near Run Thing.* The Windrush Press, Gloucestershire, 1997.

Inber, Vera, *Leningrad Diary.* Hutchinson, London, 1971.

Isherwood, Christopher, *Diaries. Volume One: 1939–1960.* Methuen, London, 1996.

Jenkins, Roy, *Churchill.* Macmillan, London, 2001.

— *Roosevelt.* Macmillan, London, 2004.

Johnson, Alexandra, *The Hidden Writer: Diaries and the Creative Life.* Doubleday, New York, 1997.

—Johnson, Alexandra, *Leaving a Trace: On Keeping a Journal.* Little, Brown, New York, 2001.

Johnson, Lady Bird, *A White House Diary.* Weidenfeld and Nicolson, London, 1970.

Kafka, Franz, *The Diaries of Franz Kafka. Volume Two, 1914–1923.* Secker & Warburg, London, 1949.

Keegan, John, *The First World War: An Illustrated History.* Pimlico, London, 2002.

— *The Penguin Book of War: Great Military Writings.* Viking, Harmondsworth, England, 1999.

— *The Second World War.* Century Hutchinson, London, 1989.

— *War and Our World: The Reith Lectures 1998.* Hutchinson, London, 1998.

Kershaw, Ian, *Hitler, 1936–45: Nemesis.* Allen Lane, Harmondsworth, England, 2000.

Kessler, Count Harry, *The Diaries of a Cosmopolitan 1918–1937*. Weidenfeld and Nicolson, London, 1971.

Klemperer, Victor, *I Will Bear Witness: The Nazi Years 1933–1941*. Weidenfeld & Nicolson, London, 1998.

— *To the Bitter End: The Diaries of Victor Klemperer 1942–45*. Weidenfeld & Nicolson, London, 1999.

Knightley, Phillip, *The First Casualty: The War Correspondent as Hero and Myth-Maker from the Crimea to Kosovo*. Prion Books, London, 2000.

Lacouture, Jean, *De Gaulle: The Rebel, 1890–1944*. Harvill, London, 1993.

Lanning, Michael Lee, *The Only War We Had: A Platoon Leader's Journal of Vietnam*. Ivy Books, New York, 1987.

Lascelles, Sir Alan 'Tommy', *End of an Era: Letters and Journals of Sir Alan Lascelles*. Hamish Hamilton, London, 1986.

Last, Nella, *Nella Last's War: A Mother's Diary 1939–45*. Falling Wall Press, Bristol, 1981.

Leaves in a Storm: A Book of Diaries. Edited with a running commentary by Stefan Schimanski and Henry Treece. Lindsay Drummond Ltd, London, 1947.

Lee, Carol Ann, *The Hidden Life of Otto Frank*. Viking, Harmondsworth, England, 2002.

Lee, General Raymond E., *The London Observer. The Journal of General Raymond E. Lee 1940–1941*. Hutchison, London, 1972.

Lees-Milne, James, *Ancestral Voices*. Chatto & Windus, London, 1975.

Le Ruez, Nan, *Jersey Occupation Diary: Nan Le Ruez, Her Story of the German Occupation 1940–45*. Seaflower Books, St Helier, Jersey, 1994.

Levi, Primo, *If This Is a Man*. The Folio Society, London, 2000.

Lewis, Norman, *Naples '44: An Intelligence Officer in the Italian Labyrinth*. Eland, London, 1989.

Lindbergh, Anne Morrow, *War Within and Without: Diaries and Letters of Anne Morrow Lindbergh*. Harcourt Brace Janovich, New York, 1980.

MacDonald, Charles, *The Battle of the Bulge*. Weidenfeld and Nicolson, London, 1984.

Macdonald, Lyn, *Anthem for Doomed Youth: Poets of the Great War*. The Folio Society, London, 2000.

— *1914: The Days of Hope*. Michael Joseph, London, 1987.

— *1915: The Death of Innocence*. Hodder Headline, London, 1993.

Macnaughtan, Sarah Broom, *A Woman's Diary of the War*. Thomas Nelson, London, 1915.

MacNeice, Louis, *Autumn Journal*. Faber and Faber, London, 1939.

Malcolm, Noel, *Kosovo: A Short History*. Macmillan, London, 1998.

Mallon, Thomas, *A Book of One's Own: People and Their Diaries*. Pan, London, 1985.

The Mammoth Book of War Diaries and Letters: Life on the Battlefield in the Words of the Ordinary Soldier, 1775–1991. Edited by Jon E. Lewis. Carroll & Graf, New York, 1999.

Mann, Thomas, *Thomas Mann Diaries 1918–1939*. André Deutsch, 1983, London.

Mansel, Captain John, *The Mansel Diaries: The Diaries of Captain John Mansel Prisoner-of-War and Camp Forger in Germany 1940–1945*. Privately published, 1977.

Mansfield, Katherine. *The Journal of Katherine Mansfield 1904–1922*. Constable, London, 1954.

May, Henry John, *Music of the Guns.* Jarrolds, London, 1970.

Men Who March Away: Poems of the First World War. Edited by I.M. Parsons. Chatto & Windus, London, 1965.

Mencken, H.L., *The Diary of H.L. Mencken.* Knopf, New York, 1989.

Milburn, Clara, *Mrs Milburn's Diaries, An Englishwoman's Reflections 1939–45.* Harrap, London, 1979.

Mitchison, Naomi, *Among You Taking Notes: The Wartime Diary of Naomi Mitchison 1939–45.* Gollancz, London, 1985.

Muggeridge, Malcolm, *Like it Was. A Selection from the Diaries of Malcolm Muggeridge.* Collins, London, 1981.

Musto, Walter, *The War and Uncle Walter. The Diary of an Eccentric.* Doubleday, London, 2003.

The New Yorker Book of War Pieces: London 1939 to Hiroshima 1945. Bloomsbury, London, 1989.

Nicolson, Harold, *Diaries and Letters 1939–1945.* Collins, London, 1967.

Nin, Anaïs, *Nearer the Moon. The Unexpurgated Diary of Anaïs Nin 1937–1939.* Peter Owen, London, 1996.

Origo, Iris, *War in Val D'Orcia: An Italian War Diary 1943–1944.* David R. Godine, Boston, 1984.

Orwell, George, *The Collected Essays, Journalism and Letters of George Orwell Volume 2: My Country Right or Left 1940–1943.* Secker & Warburg, London, 1968.

Other Men's Flowers. An Anthology of Poetry. Compiled by A.P. Wavell. Jonathan Cape, London, 1944.

The Oxford Companion to the Second World War. General Editor I.C.B. Dear. Oxford University Press, Oxford, 1995.

The Oxford History of the American West. Edited by Clyde A. Milner II, Carol A. O'Connor and Martha A. Sandweiss. Oxford University Press, Oxford, 1994.

Pakenham, Thomas, *The Boer War.* Weidenfeld and Nicolson, London, 1997.

Parks, David, *GI Diary.* Howard University Press, Washington D.C., 1984.

Partridge, Frances, *A Pacifist's War. Diaries 1939–1945.* The Hogarth Press, London, 1978.

Pavese, Cesare, *This Business of Living: Diary 1935–50.* Peter Owen, London, 1961.

Pax, Salam, *The Baghdad Blog.* Atlantic Books, London, 2003.

Pepys, Samuel, *The Diary of Samuel Pepys. Vols VI, VII and VIII.* HarperCollins, London, 1995.

Politkovskaya, Anna, *A Dirty War: A Russian Reporter in Chechnya.* Harvill, London, 2001.

Ponsonby, Arthur, *English Diaries: A Review of English Diaries from the Sixteenth to the Twentieth Century.* George H. Doran, New York, 1922.

— *More English Diaries: Further Reviews of Diaries from the Sixteenth to the Nineteenth Century.* George H. Doran, New York, 1927.

— *Scottish and Irish Diaries from the Sixteenth to the Nineteenth Century.* George H. Doran, New York, 1927.

Powell, Anthony, *Journals 1982–1986.* Heinemann, London, 1995.

Powell, Dawn, *The Diaries of Dawn Powell, 1931–1935.* Steerforth Press, South Royalton, Vermont, 1995.

Pym, Barbara, *A Very Private Eye: The Diaries, Letters and Notebooks of Barbara Pym.* Macmillan, London, 1984.

Rabe, John, *The Good German of*

Nanking: The Diaries of John Rabe. Little, Brown & Co., London, 1999.

Ranfurly, Countess of, To War with Whitaker: The Wartime Diaries of the Countess of Ranfurly 1939–45. Mandarin, London, 1997.

Reith, Lord, The Reith Diaries. Collins, London, 1975.

Reuth, Ralf Georg, Goebbels. Constable, London, 1993.

Ritchie, Charles, The Siren Years: Undiplomatic Diaries 1937–45. Macmillan, London, 1974.

Roberts, John Stuart, Siegfried Sassoon. Richard Cohen Books, London, 1999.

Russell William Howard, My Diary North and South. Bradbury and Evans, London, 1863.

— My Indian Mutiny Diary. Cassell, London, 1957.

Saint-Exupery, Antoine de, Wartime Writings: 1939–1944. Harcourt Brace Jovanovich, New York, 1986.

Sartre, Jean Paul, War Diaries: Notebooks from a Phoney War, November 1939–March 1940. Verso Editions, London, 1984.

Sassoon, Siegfried Diaries 1915–1918. Faber and Faber, London, 1983.

Scott, Sir Walter, The Journal of Sir Walter Scott. Canongate, Edinburgh, 1998.

Scott-Ellis, Priscilla, The Chances of Death: A Diary of the Spanish Civil War. Michael Russell, Norwich, 1995.

Service, Robert, A History of Twentieth-Century Russia. Allen Lane, Harmondsworth, 1997.

Shehadeh, Raja, The Sealed Room: Selections from the Diary of a Palestinian living under Israel's occupation September 1990 – August 1991. Quartet Books, London, 1992.

Shirer, William L., Berlin Diary 1934-41, The Rise of the Third Reich. Promotional Reprint Company, London, 1997.

Simpson, John, The Wars Against Saddam: Taking the Hard Road to Baghdad. Macmillan, London, 2003.

Soutar, William Diaries of a Dying Man. Canongate, Edinburgh, 1991.

Spears, Edward, Liaison 1914. Eyre & Spottiswoode, London, 1930.

Spender, Stephen, Journals 1939–83. Faber and Faber, London, 1985.

Stahlenberg, Elisabeth von, Nazi Lady; The Diaries of Elisabeth von Stahlenberg: 1933–1948. Blond & Briggs, London, 1978.

Taylor, A.J.P., The Origins of the Second World War. Hamish Hamilton, London, 1961.

Terkel, Studs, 'The Good War': An Oral History of World War Two. Hamish Hamilton, London, 1985.

Thomas, Hugh, The Spanish Civil War. Eyre and Spottiswoode, London, 1961.

Tolstoy, Leo, Tolstoy's Diaries. Flamingo, London, 1994.

—War and Peace. Oxford University Press, Oxford, 1941.

Tomalin, Claire, Samuel Pepys: The Unequalled Self. Viking, London, 2002.

Tory, Avraham, Surviving the Holocaust. The Kovno Ghetto Diary. Pimlico, London, 1991.

Vassiltchikov, Marie, 'Missie' The Berlin Diaries. 1940–1945. Pimlico, London, 1999.

Vaughan, Keith, Journals 1939–1977. John Murray, London, 1989.

Velmans, Edith, Edith's Book. Viking, London, 1998.

Victoria, Queen, Queen Victoria in her Letters and Journals. Selected by

Christopher Hibbert, 1984. Penguin Books, London, 1985.

Vidal, Gore, *Lincoln*. The Modern Library, New York, 1998.

Von Hassell, Ulrich, *The Von Hassell Diaries 1938–1944*. Hamish Hamilton, London, 1948.

Ward, Geoffrey, with Burns, Ric and Burns, Ken, *The Civil War: An Illustrated History of the War Between the States*. The Bodley Head, London, 1991.

Waugh, Auberon, *The Diaries of Auberon Waugh: A Turbulent Decade*. Private Eye Productions Ltd, in association with André Deutsch Ltd, London, 1985.

Waugh, Evelyn, *The Diaries of Evelyn Waugh*. Weidenfeld and Nicolson, London, 1976.

— *Scoop*. Chapman and Hall, London, 1938.

Webb, Beatrice, *The Diaries of Beatrice Webb*. Virago, London, 2000.

Welch, Denton, *The Journals of Denton Welch*. Penguin, Harmondsworth, 1987.

West, Arthur Graeme, *The Diary of a Dead Officer: Being the Posthumous Papers of Arthur Graeme West*. Imperial War Museum, Dept of Printed Books, London, 1991.

Williams, Kenneth, *The Kenneth Williams Diaries*. Edited by Russell Davies. HarperCollins, London, 1993.

Windham, Lieut. General Sir Charles Ash, *The Crimean Diary and Letters of Lieut. General Sir Charles Ash Windham*. Kegan Paul, Trench, Tribune and Co., London, 1897.

Zapruder, Alexandra, *Salvaged Pages: Young Writers' Diaries of the Holocaust*. Yale University Press, New Haven and London, 2002.

Woolf, Virginia, *The Diary of Virginia Woolf. Vol. 1: 1915–1919. Vol. 5: 1936–1941*. The Hogarth Press, London, 1977.

Wyndham, Joan, *Love Lessons: A Wartime Diary*. Virago, London, 2001.

Zamoyski, Adam, *1812: Napoleon's Fatal March on Moscow*. HarperCollins, London, 2004.

Permissions Acknowledgements

Every effort has been made to contact copyright holders of the extracts used in this volume before going to press. However, the publisher will be happy to rectify any errors or omissions in future editions. Various publishers and estates have generously given permission to use extracts from the following works:

Extracts from *The Selected Ego* by James Agate, published by George Harrap & Co., Ltd. Copyright held by Chambers Harrap Publishers. Extracts from *War Diaries 1939–45* by Field Marshal Lord Alanbrooke, Phoenix Press 2002. Reprinted by permission of David Higham Associates Ltd. Extracts from *Diary of a War Artist* by Edward Ardizzone published by The Bodley Head. Used by permission of The Random House Group Ltd. Extracts from *The Diaries of Lady Cynthia Asquith* by Lady Cynthia Asquith published by Century. Used by permission of The Random House Group Ltd. Extracts from *The Years Between* and *Self Portrait With Friends* by Cecil Beaton published by Weidenfeld & Nicolson, a division of The Orion Publishing Group Ltd. Used by permission of The Literary Executors of the late Sir Cecil Beaton and Rupert Crew Ltd. Extracts from *The Benn Diaries* by Tony Benn published by The Random House Group Ltd. Used by permission of the author. Extracts from *Writing Home* by Alan Bennett published by Faber and Faber Ltd. Used by permission of Faber and Faber Ltd. Extracts from *The Journals of Arnold Bennett* by Arnold Bennett published by Penguin. Used by permission of A.P. Watt Ltd on behalf of Jacques Eldin. Extracts from *Rumour and Reflection* by Bernard Berenson published by Constable & Robinson Ltd. Extracts from *Each Returning Day: The Pleasure of Diaries* by Ronald Blythe published by Viking. Used by permission of Penguin Books Ltd. Extracts from Vera Brittain's *Chronicle of Youth* (Book Club Associates) and *Wartime Chronicle* (Victor Gollancz) are included by permission of Mark Bostridge and Rebecca Williams, her literary executors. Extracts from *For Freedom's Battle* by George Gordon Byron (Lord Byron) edited by Leslie March and published by John Murray (Publishers) Ltd. Extracts from *Champion Redoubtable* by Lady Violet Bonham Carter, edited by Mark Pottle published by Weidenfeld & Nicolson, a division of The Orion Publishing Group Ltd. Extracts from *The Diary of Landon Carter of Sabine Hall* edited by Jack P. Greene used by permission of University of Virginia Press. Extracts from *'Chips': The Diaries of Sir Henry Channon* by Sir Henry Channon published by Weidenfeld & Nicolson, a division of The Orion Publishing Group Ltd. Extracts from *Ciano's Diary 1937–43* by Count Galeazzo Ciano published by Weidenfeld & Nicolson, a division of The Orion Publishing Group Ltd. Extracts from *Diaries: Into Politics* by Alan Clark published by Weidenfeld & Nicolson, a division of The Orion Publishing Group Ltd. Extracts from *The Ossie Clark Diaries* by Ossie Clark published by Bloomsbury. Extracts from *Echoes of the Great War* by Reverend Andrew Clark published by Oxford University Press. Extracts from *The Fringes of Power* by John Colville published by Hodder and Stoughton. Extracts from *The Cormany Diaries: A Northern Family in the Civil War*, James C. Mohr, editor, by permission of the University of Pittsburgh Press. Copyright © 1982 by University of Pittsburgh Press. Extracts from *The Noël Coward Diaries* by Noël Coward published by Weidenfeld & Nicolson, a division of The Orion Publishing Group. Extracts from *A Lewes Diary 1916–44* by Mrs Henry Dudeney edited by Diana Crook published by Tartarus Press. Reproduced by kind permission of the Library of the Sussex Archaeological Society, Lewes. Extracts from *The War Diaries of Weary Dunlop* by E.E. Dunlop published by Penguin Group Australia Ltd. Extracts from *The Diary of John Evelyn* by John Evelyn published by Oxford University Press. Extracts from *Pacific War Diary, 1942–45* by James J. Fahey. Copyright © 1963, and renewed 1991 by James J. Fahey. Reprinted by permission of Houghton Mifflin Company. All rights reserved. Extracts from *A Nurse at the Russian Front* by Florence Farmborough published by Constable & Robinson Ltd. Extracts from *Zlata's Diary: A Child's Life in Sarajevo* by Zlata Filipovic, translated by Christina Pribichevich-Zoric published by Viking. First published in France as *Le Journal de Zlata* by Fixot et editions Robert Laffont. Extracts from the Philip Vickers Fithian journal in the Manuscripts Division, Department of Rare Books and Special Collections, Princeton University Library. Published with permission of the Princeton University Library. Extracts taken from *Desert Fire: The Diary of a Gulf War Gunner* by Andrew Gillespie, published by Leo Cooper/Pen & Sword Books Ltd. Extracts from *The Goebbels Diaries 1939–41* by Josef Goebbels, edited and translated by Fred Taylor published by Hamish Hamilton. Used by permission of Penguin Books Ltd. Extracts from *The Goncourt Journal* by Edmond and Jules de Goncourt edited by Robert Baldick published by Oxford University Press. Used by permission of David Higham Associates Ltd. Extracts from *Between Two Streams: A Diary From Bergen-Belsen* by Abel J. Herzberg published by I.B. Tauris 1997. Extracts from *An Interrupted Life: The Diaries 1941–1943* by Etty Hillesum. Translated from the Dutch by Arnold J. Pomerans. English translation copyright © 1983 by Jonathan Cape Ltd. Reprinted by permission of Henry Holt and Company, LLC. Extracts from *Leningrad Diary* by Vera Inber published by Hutchison. Used by permission of The Random House Group Ltd. Extracts from *Diaries, Volume 1: 1939–60* by Christopher Isherwood. Used by permission of The Random House Group Ltd. Extracts from *The Diaries of Franz Kafka* by Franz Kafka published by Secker & Warburg. Used by permission of The Random House Group Ltd. Extracts from *To The Bitter End* and *I Will Bear Witness* by Victor Klemperer published by Weidenfeld & Nicolson, a division of The Orion Publishing Group Ltd. Extracts from *The Diaries of a Cosmopolitan 1918–37* by Count Harry Kessler published by

Weidenfeld & Nicolson, a division of The Orion Publishing Group. Extracts
from *Ancestral Voices* by James Lees-Milne published by Chatto and Windus.
Used by permission of David Higham Associates Ltd. Extracts from *Jersey
Occupation Diary* by Nan Le Ruez. Copyright by Nan Du Feu 1994. Reprinted
by permission of Seaflower Books, St Helier, Jersey, on behalf of the author
Nan Le Ruez. Extracts from *Naples '44* by Norman Lewis published by Eland
Publishing Ltd. Extracts from *1914–18: Voices and Images of the Great War* by
Lyn MacDonald with research by Shirley Seaton published by Penguin Books.
Extracts from *Diary of Frederick Mackenzie, Volume 1*, edited by Allen French,
published by Harvard University Press © 1930, 1958 by the President and
Fellows of Harvard College. Extracts from John Mills' diaries, edited by Ian
Fletcher and published by Spellmount Ltd in *For King and Country*, 1995.
Extracts from *Among You Taking Notes* by Naomi Mitchison published by
Victor Gollancz. Reproduced with permission of Curtis Brown Group Ltd,
London, on behalf of the Trustees of the Mass-Observation Archive. Copyright
© Naomi Mitchison and the Trustees of the Mass-Observation Archive, 1985.
Extracts from *Like It Was* by Malcolm Muggeridge published by Collins, 1981.
Used by permission of David Higham Associates Ltd. Extracts from *Diaries
and Letters, 1939–45* by Harold Nicolson published by Collins, 1967. Reprinted
by permission of the Harold Nicolson Estate © Harold Nicolson, 1967.
Reprinted by permission of the Estate of Harold Nicolson and HarperCollins
Publishers Ltd. Extracts from *War in Val D'Orcia* by Iris Origo reprinted by
permission of David R. Godine, Publisher, Inc. Copyright © by Iris Origo.
Extracts from *GI Diary* by David Parks copyright © 1968 by David Parks
reprinted with the permission of Howard University Press. All rights reserved.
Extracts from *A Pacifist's War* by Frances Partridge published by Weidenfeld
& Nicolson, a division of The Orion Publishing Group. Extracts from *The
Baghdad Blog* by Salam Pax published by Atlantic Grove/Atlantic, Inc. Used
by permission of Grove/Atlantic Inc. Extracts from *Diary of Samuel Pepys*,
edited by Robert Latham and William Matthews. Reprinted by permission
of HarperCollins Publishers Ltd. Copyright © Robert Latham and William
Matthews, 1995. Extracts from *A Dirty War* by Anna Politkovskaya published
by The Harvill Press. Used by permission of The Random House Group Ltd.
Extracts from *Journals, 1982–86* by Anthony Powell published by Heinemann.
Used by permission of David Higham Associates Ltd. Extracts from *The Diaries
of Dawn Powell* by Dawn Powell published by Steerforth Press of Hanover,
New Hampshire. Copyright © 1995 by The Estate of Dawn Powell. Extracts
from *A Very Private Eye* by Barbara Pym, published by Pan MacMillan, used
by permission of Pan Macmillan. Extracts from *To War With Whitaker* by the
Countess of Ranfurly published by Arrow. Used by permission of The Random
House Group Ltd. Extracts reprinted from John B. Reeves, ed., 'Extracts from
the Letter-Book of Lieutenant Eno Reeves, of the Pennsylvania Line',
Pennsylvania Magazine of History and Biography 21 (1897): 72–80. Extracts from
The Reith Diaries by Lord Reith published by Collins, 1975. Used by permis-
sion of HarperCollins Publishers Ltd. Extracts from *The Siren Years* by Charles
Ritchie, published by Macmillan. Used by permission of Macmillan Publishers

Ltd. Extracts from *Diaries* by Siegfried Sassoon copyright © Siegfried Sassoon. Reproduced by kind permission of George Sassoon. Extract from *The Journal of Sir Walter Scott* published by Canongate Books Ltd. Used by permission of W.E.K. Anderson. Extracts from *The Diaries of a Dying Man* by William Soutar published by Canongate Books Ltd. Used by permission of the Trustees of the National Library of Scotland. Extracts from Gillian Freeman's fictional diary *Nazi Lady: The Confessions of Elisabeth Von S.* published by Futura in 1979 (originally published by Blond & Briggs, 1978). Copyright © 1978 Elisabeth von Stahlenberg, Thorpe Writers Ltd. Extracts from *Tolstoy's Diaries* by Leo Tolstoy, edited by R.F. Christian published by Flamingo, 1994. Used by permission of HarperCollins Publishers Ltd. Extracts from *Surviving the Holocaust: The Kovno Ghetto Diary* by Avraham Tory, edited by Martin Gilbert, translated by Jerzy Michalowicz, with textual and historical notes by Dina Porat, Cambridge, Mass., Harvard University Press, copyright © 1990 by the President and Fellows of Harvard College. Reprinted by permission of the Harvard University Press. Extract from *The Berlin Diaries 1940–45 by Marie Vassiltchikov* published by Pimlico. Reprinted by permission of PFD on behalf of The Estate of Marie Vassiltchikov. Extracts from *Journals 1939–77* by Keith Vaughan published by John Murray (Publishers) Ltd. Extracts from *Edith's Book* by Edith Velmans published by Penguin. Used by permission of Penguin Books Ltd. Extracts reprinted from 'Valley Forge,1777–1778: Diary of a Surgeon, Albigence Waldo, of the Connecticut Line', *Pennsylvania Magazine of History and Biography* 21 (1897): 299–323. Extracts from *The Diaries of Evelyn Waugh* by Evelyn Waugh, edited by Michael Davie published by Weidenfeld & Nicolson, a division of The Orion Publishing Group Ltd. Extracts from *The Diaries of Beatrice Webb* by Beatrice Webb published by Virago. Used by permission of Time Warner Books. Extracts from *The Journals of Denton Welch* by Denton Welch published by Penguin. Used by permission of David Higham Associates Ltd. Extracts from *The Kenneth Williams Diaries* by Kenneth Williams published by HarperCollins Publishers Ltd, 1993. Extracts from *The Crimean Diary and Letters of Lieutenant General Sir Charles Ash Windham* by Lieutenant General Sir Charles Ash Windham published by Taylor & Francis Books Ltd. Extracts from *German Student War Letters*, edited by Philip Witkopp (Adolf Sturmer and Helmut Zschuppe) published by University of Pennsylvania Press. Extracts from *The Diary of Virginia Woolf* published by Hogarth Press. Used by permission of the executors of the Virginia Woolf Estate and The Random House Group Ltd. Extracts from *Love Lessons* by Joan Wyndham published by Virago. Used by permission of Time Warner Books.

Index of Diarists

Agate, James, 10 Feb 1944, 27 May
1945, 28 May 1941, 3 June 1940,
28 July 1940, 6 Sept 1939, 8 Sept
1942, 30 Oct 1939, 21 Dec 1944,
28 Dec 1944

Alanbrooke, Field Marshal Lord, 24
Jan 1940, 21 Mar 1940, 31 Oct
1939, 4 Nov 1939, 11 Nov 1939,
23 Nov 1939

Allaire, Anthony, 14 Oct 1780, 17 Oct
1780, 18 Oct 1780

André, John, 3 Sept 1777

Anon, 8 Feb 1864

Anon Iraqi soldier, 21 Jan 1991, 1 Feb
1991, 4 Feb 1991, 8 Feb 1991, 14
Feb 1991

Ardizzone, Edward, 10 July 1943, 16
July 1943, 15 Sept 1943, 26 Sept
1943, 1 Oct 1943

Asquith, Lady Cynthia, 21 Jan 1917,
16 April 1915, 18 April 1915, 26
April 1915, 27 April 1915, 8 May
1915, 9 May 1918, 15 May 1918, 19
May 1916, 31 May 1915, 2 June
1915, 13 June 1918, 13 Oct 1915, 11
Nov 1915, 8 Dec 1915, 26 Dec 1916

Bangs, Isaac, 10 July 1776

Barbellion, W.N.P., 24 Mar 1915, 3
June 1916, 4 June 1916, 31 July 1916,
1 Aug 1914, 2 Aug 1914, 12 Aug
1914, 6 Oct 1917, 12 Oct 1914, 13
Oct 1915, 24 Oct 1914, 27 Nov
1915

Beaton, Cecil, 4 May 1945, 11 May
1940, 30 May 1942, 22 June 1942,
5 July 1942, 16 Aug 1940, 23 Aug

1944, 30 Aug 1940, 12 Oct 1940,
29 Oct 1944, 8 Nov 1944, 11 Nov
1944, 25 Dec 1943, 30 Dec 1940

Benn, Tony, 2 April 1982, 3 April
1982, 15 April 1982, 28 April 1982,
10 May 1982, 25 May 1982, 15 June
1982

Bennett, Alan, 4 June 1982, 15 June
1982, 16 June 1982, 20 June 1982

Bennett, Arnold, 4 Feb 1915, 20 Feb
1918, 19 April 1915, 3 June 1915,
8 June 1916, 9 June 1917, 24 June
1915, 25 July 1917, 6 Aug 1914,
9 Oct 1916, 4 Dec 1914

Berenson, Bernard, 5 Feb 1941, 20
April 1941, 6 Nov 1941

Biddle, George, 26 April 1943, 27
April 1943, 14 May 1943, 23 May
1943, 4 June 1943, 18 June 1943,
27 June 1943, 24 July 1943, 28 July
1943, 10 Aug 1943

Blunt, Wilfred Scawan, 30 June 1914

Bonham Carter, Violet, 23 April 1915,
3 May 1945, 21 May 1940, 11 June
1940, 26 Oct 1943

Brittain, Vera, 9 April 1942, 13 April
1945, 21 April 1915, 28 April 1943,
1 May 1945, 30 Sept 1915, 27 Dec
1915, 31 Dec 1915

Britten, Sergeant S.V., 22 April 1915,
23 April 1915

Bruckshaw, Pvt. Horace, 11 May 1915,
13 May 1915, 15 May 1915

Buerstatte, Pvt. Frederick C, 12 Feb
1864, 15 May 1864, 22 May 1864,
20 July 1864, 21 July 1864, 19 Dec
1864, 25 Dec 1864